A TEXT BOOK OF

THEORY OF STRUCTURE - II

SEMESTER – VI

THIRD YEAR DEGREE COURSE IN CIVIL ENGINEERING

As Per New Revised Syllabus of
North Maharashtra University, Jalgaon (2014)

Dr. SR PAREKAR

M. E. Ph. D (Structures)
Professor and Head
Civil Engineering Department,
AISSM's College of Engineering,
PUNE.

N 3342

THEORY OF STRUCTURE : (TE CIVIL SEM. VI NMU) ISBN : 978-93-5164-395-1
First Edition : January 2015
© : Author

The text of this publication, or any part thereof, should not be reproduced or transmitted in any form or stored in any computer storage system or device for distribution including photocopy, recording, taping or information retrieval system or reproduced on any disc, tape, perforated media or other information storage device etc., without the written permission of Author with whom the rights are reserved. Breach of this condition is liable for legal action.

Every effort has been made to avoid errors or omissions in this publication. In spite of this, errors may have crept in. Any mistake, error or discrepancy so noted and shall be brought to our notice shall be taken care of in the next edition. It is notified that neither the publisher nor the author or seller shall be responsible for any damage or loss of action to any one, of any kind, in any manner, therefrom.

Published By :
NIRALI PRAKASHAN
Abhyudaya Pragati, 1312, Shivaji Nagar,
Off J.M. Road
PUNE – 411005
Tel - (020) 25512336/37/39, Fax - (020) 25511379
Email : niralipune@pragationline.com

Printed By :
REPRO INDIA LTD,
Mumbai.

DISTRIBUTION CENTRES

PUNE
Nirali Prakashan
119, Budhwar Peth, Jogeshwari Mandir Lane
Pune 411002, Maharashtra
Tel : (020) 2445 2044, 66022708 Fax : (020) 2445 1538
Email : bookorder@pragationline.com

MUMBAI
Nirali Prakashan
385, S.V.P. Road, Rasdhara Co-op. Hsg. Society Ltd.,
Girgaum, Mumbai 400004, Maharashtra
Tel : (022) 2385 6339 / 2386 9976, Fax : (022) 2386 9976
Email : niralimumbai@pragationline.com

DISTRIBUTION BRANCHES

NAGPUR
Pratibha Book Distributors
Above Maratha Mandir, Shop No. 3, First Floor,
Rani Jhanshi Square, Sitabuldi, Nagpur 440012,
Maharashtra, Tel : (0712) 254 7129, Mob : 98222 01952

NASIK
Nirali Prakashan
741, Gaydhani Sankul, First Floor, Raviwar Karanja,
Nasik 422001, Maharashtra
Tel : (0253) 250 6438, Mob : 94222 53538

HYDERABAD
Nirali Book House
22, Shyam Enclave, 4-5-947, Badi Chowdi
Hyderabad 500095, Andhra Pradesh
Tel : (040) 6554 5313, Mob : 94400 30608
Email : niralibooks@yahoo.com

JALGAON
Nirali Prakashan
34, V. V. Golani Market, Navi Peth, Jalgaon 425001,
Maharashtra, Tel : (0257) 222 0395
Mob : 94234 91860

KOLHAPUR
Nirali Prakashan
New Mahadvar Road,
Kedar Plaza, 1st Floor Opp. ICICI Bank
Kolhapur 416 012, Maharashtra. Mob : 9855046155

BENGALURU
Pragati Book House
House No. 1,Sanjeevappa Lane, Avenue Road Cross,
Opp. Rice Church, Bangalore – 560002.
Tel : (080) 64513344, 64513355,
Mob : 9880582331, 9845021552
Email:bharatsavla@yahoo.com

CHENNAI
Pragati Books
9/1, Montieth Road, Behind Taas Mahal, Egmore, Chennai 600008 Tamil Nadu
Tel : (044) 6518 3535, Mob : 94440 01782 / 98450 21552 / 98805 82331
Email : bharatsavla@yahoo.com

RETAIL OUTLETS
PUNE

Pragati Book Centre
157, Budhwar Peth, Opp. Ratan Talkies,
Pune 411002, Maharashtra
Tel : (020) 2445 8887 / 6602 2707, Fax : (020) 2445 8887

Pragati Book Centre
152, Budhwar Peth, Pune 411002, Maharashtra
Tel : (020) 2445 2254 / 6609 2463

Pragati Book Centre
676/B, Budhwar Peth, Opp. Jogeshwari Mandir,
Pune 411002, Maharashtra
Tel : (020) 6601 7784 / 6602 0855

Pragati Book Centre
917/22, Sai Complex, F.C. Road, Opp. Hotel Roopali,
Shivajinagar, Pune 411004, Maharashtra
Tel : (020) 2566 3372 / 6602 2728

Pragati Book Centre
Amber Chamber, 28/A, Budhwar Peth, Appa Balwant Chowk,
Pune : 411002, Maharashtra, Tel : (020) 20240335 / 66281669
Email : pbcpune@pragationline.com

MUMBAI
Pragati Book Corner
Indira Niwas, 111 - A, Bhavani Shankar Road, Dadar (W), Mumbai 400028, Maharashtra
Tel : (022) 2422 3526 / 6662 5254
Email : pbcmumbai@pragationline.com

www.pragationline.com   info@pragationline.com

PREFACE ......

The book titled **"Theory of Structure - II"** is written according to the New revised syllabus of North Maharashtra University, Jalgoan. This book serves as a text book for the students of Third Year Degree Course in Civil Engineering, (2014 Pattern).

It consists of 5 units covering all of new revised syllabus. Each Unit gives fundamental and simple treatment to the subject with a clear and distinct presentation of theoretical concepts and well-graded examples.

I express our sincere thanks, to Prof. Awari (AISSPMS COE), Prof. Deulkar, Dr. Lad, Prof. Bajare SAE, Kondhwa, Pune.

I will be missing if I don't thank My Wife Mrs. Smita Parekar whose moral support and wishes have gone a long way in the making of this book.

I express my sincere thanks to Shri. Dineshbhai Furia, Jignesh Furia and M. P. Munde for publishing this book. I am also thankful to Mrs. Deepali Lachake (co-ordinator) and Mrs. Roshan Khan for their kind help.

We are also thankful to **Mr. Pruthviraj M. More,** Branch Manager, Jalgaon office for his valuable help and efforts for promotion of our books.

Suggestions for improvement and constructive criticism of this book are warmly welcomed and will be incorporated in next edition.

Pune   **Dr. S. R. Parekar**

SYLLABUS ......

Unit I   (08 Hours 16 Marks)

(a) **Basic Concepts of Structural Analysis :** Types of skeletal structures, static and kinematics indeterminacy, equilibrium and compatibility conditions, stress-strain relations, force-displacement relations, concept of linear/non-linear structures. Energy theorem, Miller Breslau principle, Concept of complementary energy, Fundamental concept of Force and the displacement method of analysis.

(b) **Slope Deflection Method :** Applied to continuous and rigid jointed frames, transverse and rotational yielding of supports.(up to three unknown).

UNIT – II   (08 Hours 16 marks)

(a) **Moment Distribution Method :** Applied to continuous beams and rigid jointed rectangular frames, transnational and rotational yielding of supports.

(b) **Approximate Analysis of Multistory Frames :** Vertical and lateral loads, substitute frame, portal frame and cantilever method.

UNIT – III   (08 Hours 16 marks)

Fundamental Concept of Flexibility : Method for structural analysis , flexibility coefficient, matrix formulation for flexibility methods, degree of freedom. Influence coefficients, physical significance, choice of basic determinate structure and redundant forces, compatibility equations, effect of settlement and rotation of supports, temperature and lack of fit, hand solution of simple problems on beams, pin jointed plane truss and rigid jointed frames (Involving not more than three unknown).

UNIT – IV   (07 Hours 16 marks)

Fundamental Concept of Stiffness : Method of structural analysis, stiffness coefficient, matrix formulation for stiffness methods, Degree of freedom. Influence coefficients, physical significance, effect of settlement and rotation of trusses and rigid jointed plane frames (involving less than three unknown).

UNIT – V   (08 Hours 16 marks)

Plastic Analysis of Steel Structures : Introduction, Shape factor, plastic hinge, collapse mechanism, upper bound and lower bound theories, application to continuous, fixed and single bay single storey rectangular frames.

CONTENTS ......

Unit I

1. Basic Concepts of Structural Analysis — 1.1 – 1.32
2. Slope-Deflection Method — 2.1-2.120

Unit II

3. Moment Distribution Method — 3.1-3.118
4. Approximate Analysis of Multistory Frames — 4.1-4.34

Unit III

5. Fundamental Concept of Flexibility — 5.1-5.106

Unit IV

6. Fundamental Concept of Stiffness — 6.1 – 6.84

Unit V

7. Plastic Theory — 7.1 – 7.26
8. Plastic Analysis — 8.1 – 8.66

UNIT - I

Chapter 1
BASIC CONCEPTS OF STRUCTURAL ANALYSIS

1.1 STRUCTURAL SYSTEMS

A structure is any construction built in a stable equilibrium configuration of a particular form or shape consisting of

- Members or elements
- Joints or nodes and
- Supports or constraints.

A structure has to resist the external forces or disturbances and transfer them safely to other points, joints and finally to supports of the structure so that there is no rigid body movement. According to the configuration, the structures are idealised as follows :

- **Discrete System :** It consists of one-dimensional elements also called *line elements* which are long in comparison to their cross-sectional dimensions, such as ties, struts, columns, beams, shafts, cables, arches etc. Skeletal structures or framed structures like continuous beams, portal frames, trusses are the examples of the discrete system.
- **Continuum System :** It consists of two-dimensional or three-dimensional elements.
  - Surface structures such as plates, slabs, shells etc. consist of two-dimensional plane or curved surface elements. Two dimensions of surface elements are large compared to third dimension i.e. thickness.
  - Volume structures like walls, deep beams, dams, massive foundations etc. consist of three dimensional elements. All dimensions of such elements are significant.
- **Combined System :** Hybrid structures made of line elements and surface or volume elements are considered as combined system. Stiffened plates, bridge decks, beam and slabs of buildings are the examples of hybrid structures.

The different structural systems are outlined in Fig. 1.1.

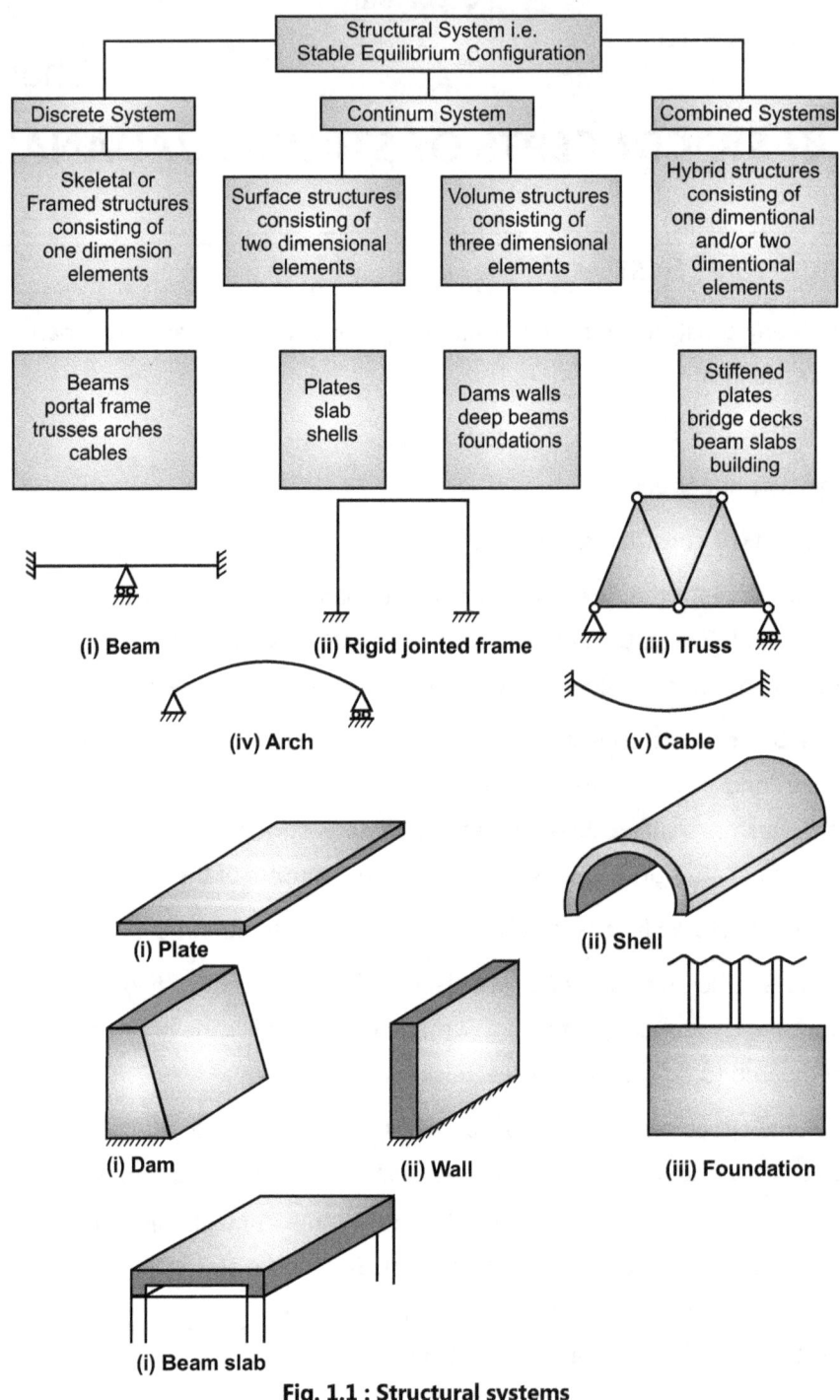

Fig. 1.1 : Structural systems

1.2 Types of Skeletal Structures

Skeletal structures are idealised as theoretical models with the assumption of one-dimensional behaviour of members and point specifications of joints. Skeletal structures are also termed as framed structures.

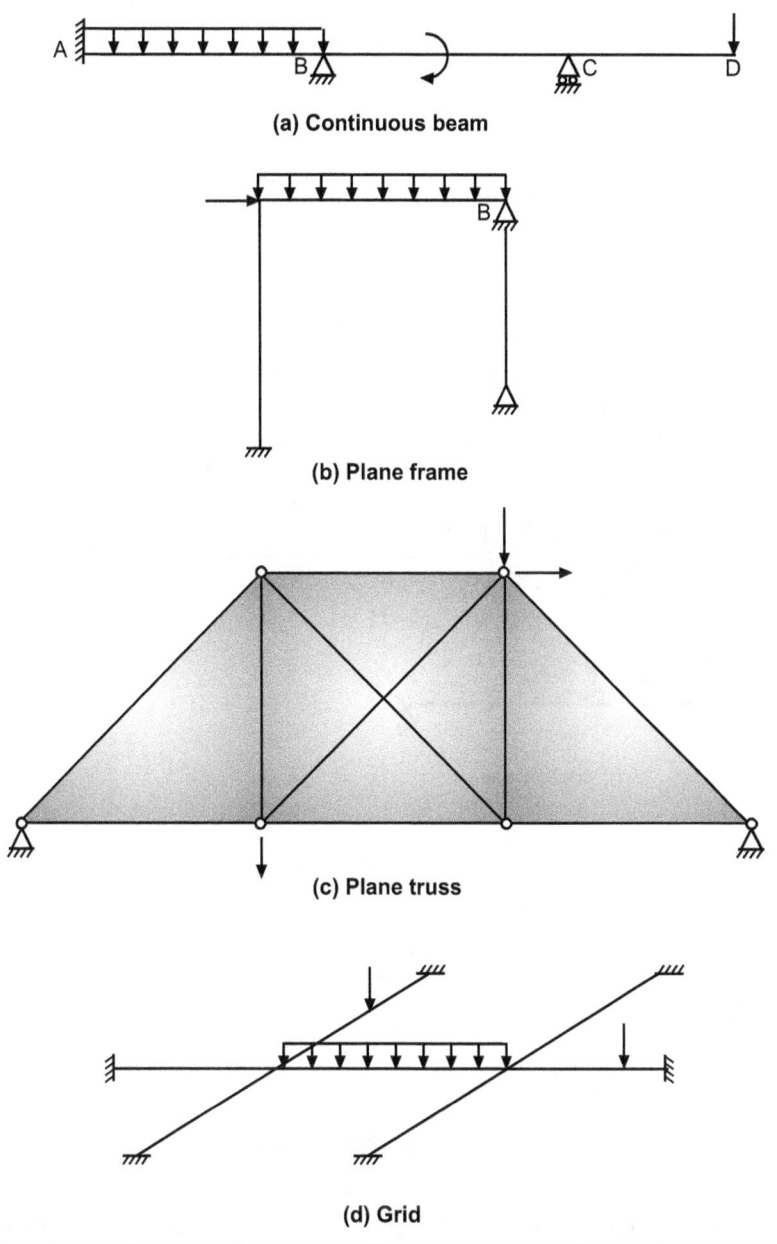

(a) Continuous beam

(b) Plane frame

(c) Plane truss

(d) Grid

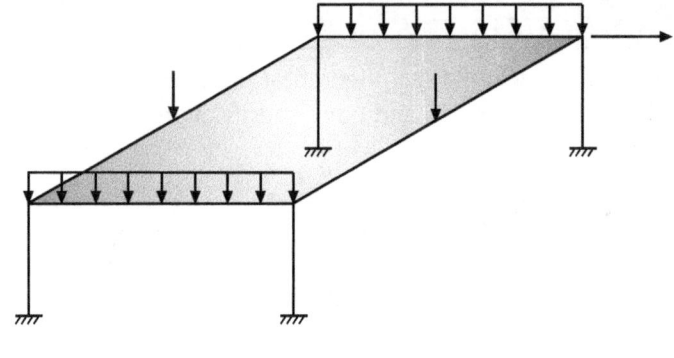

(e) Space frame

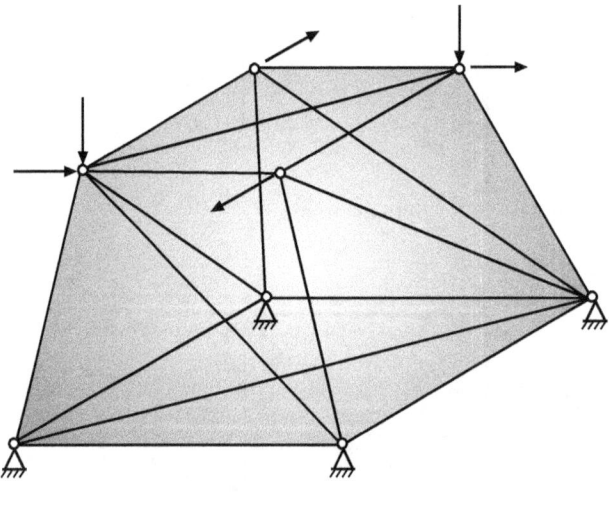

(f) Space truss

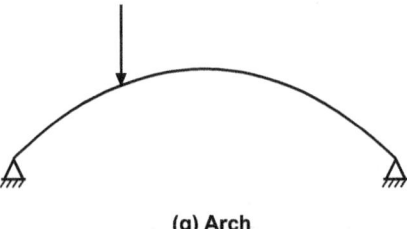

(g) Arch

Fig. 1.2 : Types of skeletal structures

A framed structure is considered as an assembly of prismatic members, joints and supports. Framed structure ≡ Members + Joints + Supports. The basic feature of a framed structure is that the individual members of the structure are treated as one-dimensional or line members. Therefore, framed structures are represented by lined diagrams. A straight member of uniform cross-section is termed as a prismatic member.

The joints of a framed structure are : (i) points of intersection of the prismatic members, (ii) points of supports and (iii) free ends of the members.

The joints may be (i) rigid or (ii) pinned.

The supports of a structure may be (i) fixed, (ii) hinged, (iii) roller. The loads on a structure may be (i) concentrated forces, (ii) distributed loads and (iii) couples applied directly or indirectly.

The types of framed structures are categorised by their geometrical form and by the method of connection of the individual members one to another, as given below.

- Continuous beam, shown in Fig. 1.2 (a), consists of members aligned in a common direction and supported at different points by different types of supports.

- Plane rigid jointed frame, shown in Fig. 1.2 (b), is an assembly of members rigidly connected to each other such that any rotation of the joint is common to all members meeting the joint. Such structure is also called as plane frame. All members of the plane frame lie in a single plane and all applied loads act in this plane. The plane frame can carry loads distributed along the lengths of the members as well as at the joints. The members of the frame are subjected to bending moments, shear forces and axial forces.

- Plane truss, shown in Fig. 1.2 (c), is a structure in which the joints are assumed as the frictionless pins so that all members are free to rotate individually at the joint. A structure and all applied loads lie in a single plane. Moreover, the loads are applied at the pin joints only and the members are assumed to carry only an axial force.

- Grid, shown in Fig. 1.2 (d), is a two-dimensional rigid jointed frame but is distinguished from the plane frame by the fact that loads applied to the grid, act normal to the plane of the grid rather than in the plane of the grid.

- Rigid jointed space frame, shown in Fig. 1.2 (e), is a structure of unrestricted geometrical form consisting of members, connected by rigid joints and supports in three dimensions. The members are subjected to axial and shearing forces, bending moments and twisting moments due to the application of a general type of loading.

- Space truss, shown in Fig. 1.2 (f), is a ball-jointed space frame of unrestricted geometrical form. The members of the space truss are assumed and carry only axial forces set up by the joint loads only.

Arch, shown in Fig. 1.2 (g), is the special type of skeletal structure consisting of curved line elements. Therefore, arches are considered separately and not included in framed structures.

Analysis of the following structures is only dealt within this text :

- Continuous beams,
- Plane frames
- Plane trusses
- Two hinged arches

1.3 STRUCTURAL BEHAVIOUR

The effects of the external forces or disturbances acting on a structure, can be listed as follows :

- Strains and stresses are developed in the material of the structure.
- The deformations of the members occur and the structure deforms.
- All points, except immovable points of supports, are displaced to new positions due to cumulative effects of deformation.
- Internal forces i.e. stress resultants exist at any cross-section of a member of a structure.
- Reactions are induced at the supports.

Thus, the behaviour of a structure is stated as if certain forces and/or displacements are imposed upon a structure at some points than at other points the forces and/or displacements are developed in the structure. This is called *response of a structure*. The calculation of these developed forces and displacements is the essential part of structural analysis. Forces and/or displacements are considered as the causes and the effects. Structural behaviour or analysis is interpreted as cause-effect phenomenon.

Structural behaviour ≡ Cause-Effect Phenomenon.

The behaviour of a structure is mathematically modelled by force-displacement equations using the concepts of equilibrium, compatibility, stress-strain laws and superposition.

Depending upon the nature of loading, the structure may respond in the different ways as follows :

- It may deform statically in stable elastic manner - static analysis.
- It may yield - Plastic analysis of structure.
- It may vibrate - Dynamic analysis.
- It may buckle - Stability analysis.

The purpose of structural analysis is to predict accurately the response of a given structure to a given loading. This text is mainly concerned with the static behaviour in the elastic range i.e. static analysis of linear elastic structure.

1.4 PRIMARY CONCEPTS

Mechanics is the soul of structural engineering. Mechanics is the study of forces and displacements. It may be mechanics of rigid bodies, mechanics of materials or mechanics of structures. The relationship between forces and displacements is the main theme of structural analysis. Therefore, it is worth to review the important concepts related to mechanics. The information of these concepts will help to pave the way of the subject.

1.4.1 Frame of Reference

The basic quantities involved in structural analysis such as forces and displacements, are specified with respect to cartesian co-ordinate system i.e. rectangular right hand system of mutually perpendicular axes OX, OY and OZ as shown in Fig. 1.3 (a). The plane structures are considered to lie in X - Y plane, in general.

The quantities are considered positive if they are in positive directions of axes of co-ordinate system.

1.4.2 Forces

A force is defined as the action of one body on the other, either through direct contact or otherwise. A force in general, has a tendency to cause a translation and/or a rotation of a body and hence a force means either a translational force or a rotational force i.e. moment, couple. A force is completely specified by the following information :

- **Magnitude :** Numerical value of the force with its unit.
- **Direction :**
    (a) Line of action of the force.
    (b) Angle of line of action of the force with respect to the reference axis.
    (c) Sense in which the force acts along the line of action represented by the arrow head.

- **Point of application of the force and the plane in which the force acts :**

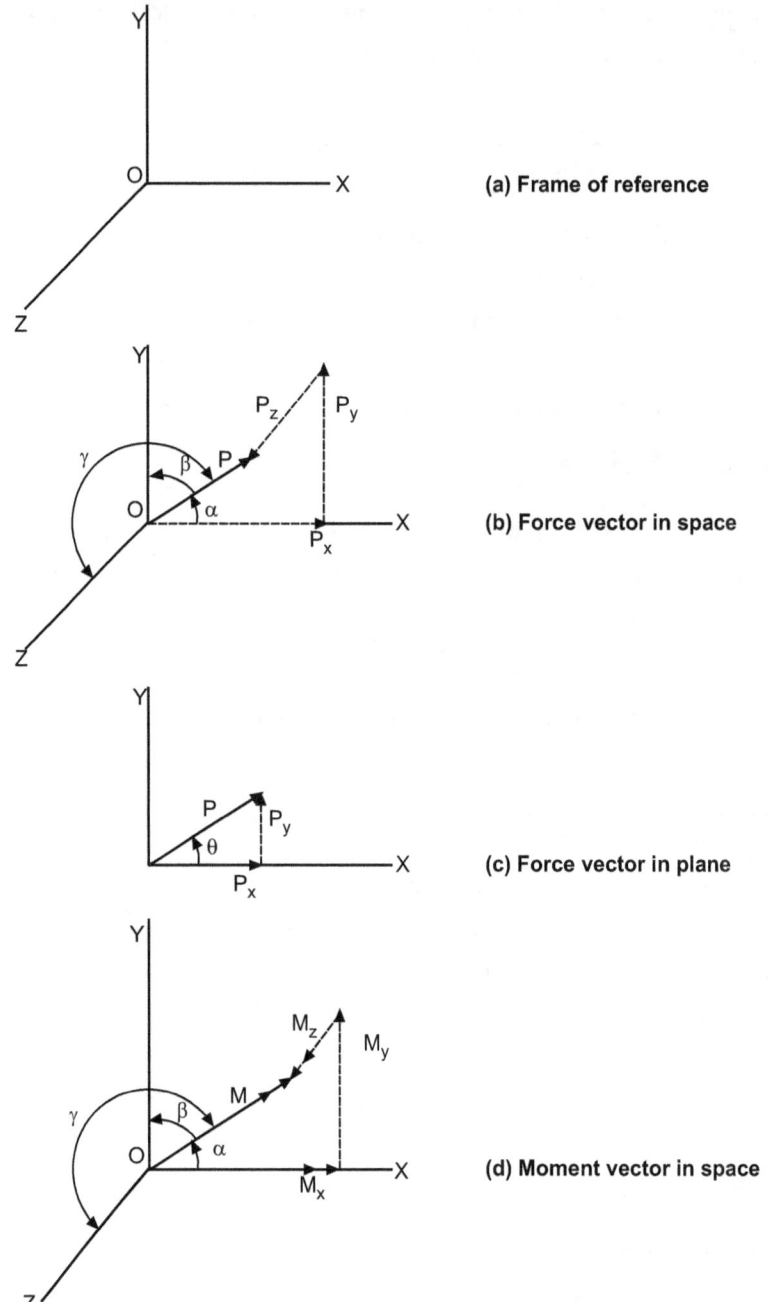

(a) Frame of reference

(b) Force vector in space

(c) Force vector in plane

(d) Moment vector in space

Fig. 1.3 : Reference system

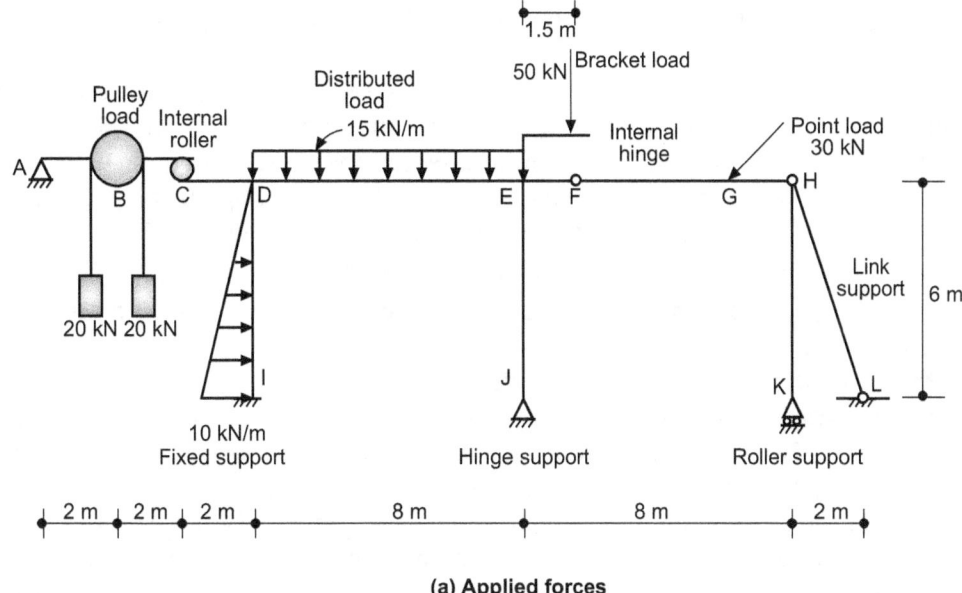

(a) Applied forces

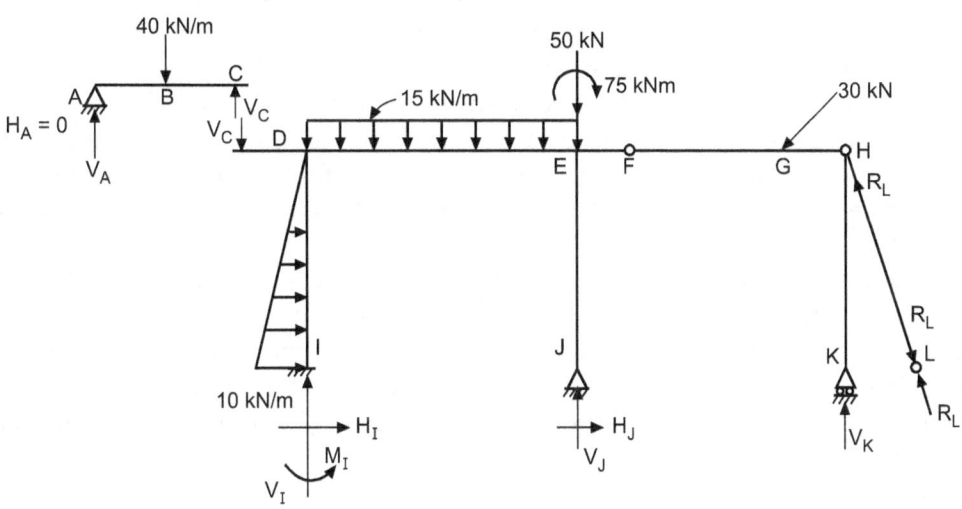

(b) Active and reactive forces

Fig. 1.4 : External forces

A translational force, generally called only force, P, is represented by a vector having magnitude and direction defined by the angles α, β, γ measured with respect to x, y, z axes of the co-ordinate system. A force is also specified by its orthogonal components in three co-ordinate axes directions as $P_x = P \cos \alpha$, $P_y = P \cos \beta$ and $P_z = P \cos \gamma$ as shown in Fig. 1.3 (b).

A force P in plane is generally represented by its components $P_x = P \cos \theta$ and $P_y = P \sin \theta$ as shown in Fig. 1.3 (c).

A rotational force, generally called moment M, is represented by a vector with double headed arrow, having magnitude and direction normal to the plane in which it acts. The direction of the arrow is that of the advancement of the right handed screw turned in the same sense as the moment. A moment is also specified by its components,

$M_x = M \cos \gamma$, $M_y = M \cos \beta$, $M_z = M \cos \gamma$ as shown in Fig. 1.3 (d).

The moment in the plane x - y is represented by $M_z = M$.

For static analysis of structure, all forces are considered as static forces and assumed to be gradually applied.

The forces acting on a structure are classified as follows :

- **External Forces :** The forces acting on a structure as a whole are considered as external forces. Body forces and surface forces are mainly considered as the external forces. They may be applied forces i.e. active forces and reactive forces.
    (a) Applied forces are also called *loads*. The loads may be concentrated load, distributed load and couple or moment acting directly or indirectly through the arrangements like bracket, pulley etc. The applied forces are shown in Fig. 1.4 (a).
    (b) Reactive forces are the actions of supports on a structure. According to the types of supports, the reactive forces may be forces and moments as shown in Fig. 1.4 (b).
- **Internal Forces :** The stresses are developed to resist the external forces and deformations of a structure. The stress resultant at the cut section of the member of a structure is considered as the internal force. Internal forces can also be interpreted as the actions of a part of structure on the adjacent part of the structure and in this sense the internal forces are also considered as the reaction forces. Thus, the member end forces are the internal forces.
- **Load Effects :** Load effects at a section of a member of a structure are the algebraic sum of the external forces or algebraic sum of the moments of the external forces acting on one side of the section. The load effects at a section are equal in magnitude but opposite in direction of the internal forces at that section. In this context, at a section, the load effects are actions and internal forces are reactions and may be of the following types in general as shown in Fig. 1.5.
    (a) Axial force, P_x
    (b) Shear forces, P_y and P_z
    (c) Twisting moment, M_x
    (d) Bending moments, M_y and M_z.

Three force components and three moment components i.e. six components may exist at a section as the actions.

Corresponding to these basic structural actions as shown in Fig. 1.5, the structural members are named as :

(a) Axial member i.e. tie, strut
(b) Shear member i.e. pin, rivet, bolt
(c) Bending member i.e. beam
(d) Twisting member i.e. shaft.

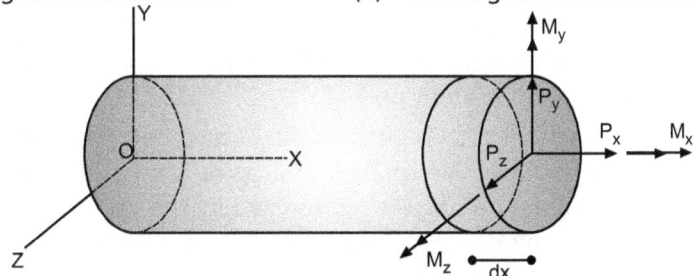

Fig. 1.5 : Basic structural actions

1.4.3 Deformation and Displacement

A structure deforms under the action of forces. The change in the shape is called *deformation*. Corresponding to the structural actions, deformations are basically of the following types, as shown in Fig. 1.6 : (a) Axial deformation, (b) Shearing deformation, (c) Bending or flexural deformation and (d) Twisting deformation. The displacement at a point of the structure is the cumulative effect of the deformations. All points, except immovable points of supports, will be displaced to new positions. The physical and material properties are required to obtain the displacements. The displacements are of two types : (i) translational displacement and (ii) rotational displacement.

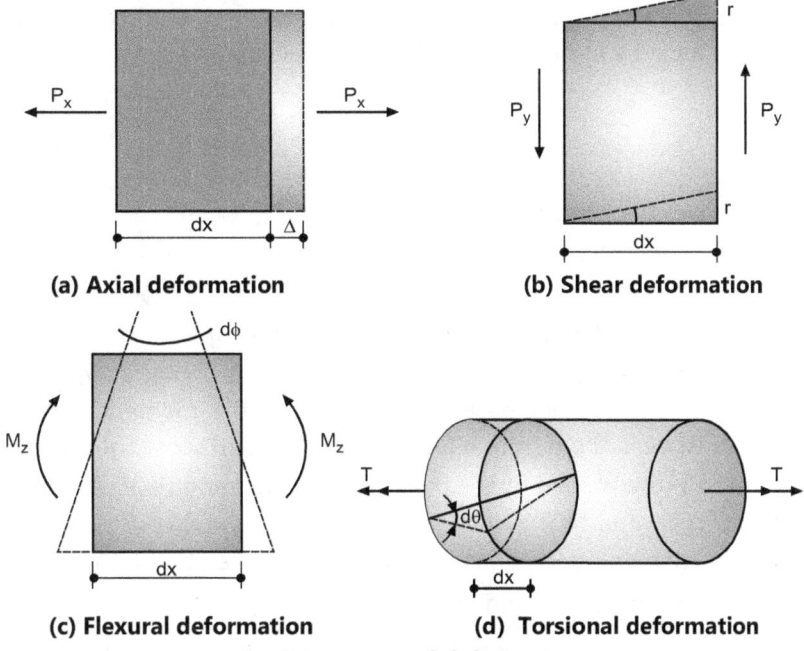

(a) Axial deformation

(b) Shear deformation

(c) Flexural deformation

(d) Torsional deformation

Fig. 1.6 : Structural deformation

A translation, generally called as *displacement*, means the distance moved by a point in the structure. A displacement at a point is represented by a vector having magnitude and direction. A displacement at a point is specified by its three independent components in three co-ordinate axes and denoted by u, v, w. For plane structures, a displacement is represented by two components, u and v only.

A rotation refers to the angle of rotation of the axis of member. The deformed axis of the member is called the *elastic curve*. The rotation at a point is considered as the cumulative effects of curvature. A rotation at a point is represented by the vector having magnitude in radians and direction shown by double headed arrow. A rotation at a point is specified in general by three components θ_x, θ_y and θ_z as rotations about co-ordinate axes. For plane structures in x-y plane, a rotation at a point is specified by only one component $\theta_z = \theta$.

Three translation-components and three rotation-components i.e. six components may exist as displacements at a point of a structure. These six components of the displacement at a point are also referred as the degrees of freedom (DOF).

1.4.4 Correspondence Between Force and Displacement

Force and displacement are corresponding when they are analogous and located at the same point on a structure without regard to the actual cause. This is known as one to one correspondence between force and displacement and stated as :

- Translation at a point is corresponding to the concentrated force acting at the same point. The translation is not necessarily caused by the force at that point. The translation must be in the direction (i.e. line of action and sense) of the force.

Fig. 1.7 : Co-ordinate numbering

- Rotation at a point is corresponding to the concentrated moment at the same point. The rotation is not necessarily caused by the moment at that point. The rotation must be in the direction (i.e. line of action and sense) of the moment.

This correspondence is established by the co-ordinate numbering i.e. i, j as shown in Fig. 1.7 where i, j may be particular numbers.

i represents vertical translation at B i.e. Δ_B and vertical force at B i.e. P_B.

j represents rotation at B i.e. θ_B and moment at B i.e. M_B.

This technique of co-ordinate numbering will be of great help to develop the concepts of stiffness and flexibility coefficients in matrix methods.

1.4.5 Equilibrium

A body, that is initially at rest and remains at rest when acted upon by a system of forces, is said to be in a state of static equilibrium. For a body to be in equilibrium, the resultant of the system of forces must be zero. Therefore, the independent equations of equilibrium, in general, are : $\sum F_x = 0, \sum F_y = 0, \sum F_z = 0, \sum M_x = 0, \sum M_y = 0, \sum M_z = 0$

Three force equilibrium equations and three moment equilibrium equations i.e. six equations are called as *conditions of equilibrium*.

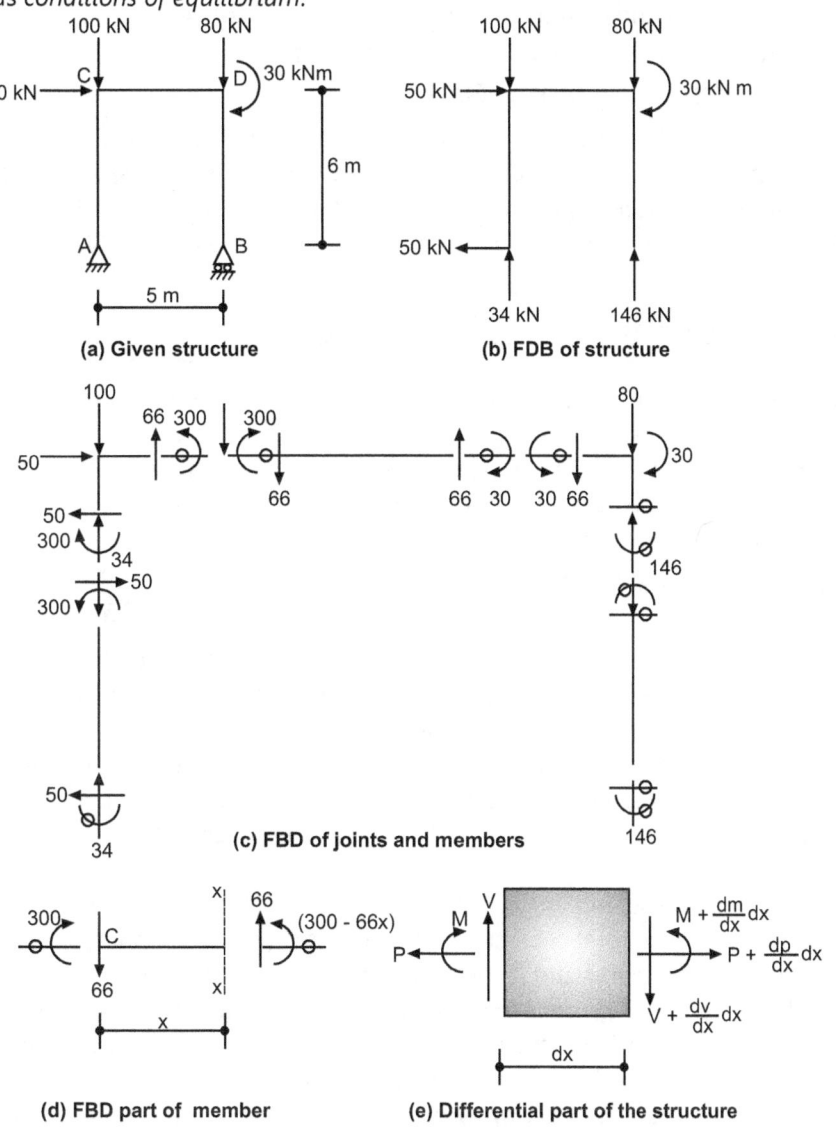

Fig. 1.8 : Free body diagrams

The fundamental concept of a structure is the static equilibrium. A structure as a whole must be in equilibrium under the external forces i.e. applied loads and reactions of the supports. If a structure is in equilibrium, then its part and parcel will be in equilibrium under external and internal forces. It implies that any part of the structure, each member, each joint, any point must be in equilibrium.

For plane structures, the conditions of equilibrium are $\sum F_x = 0$, $\sum F_y = 0$, $\sum M = 0$ i.e. two force equilibrium equations and one moment equilibrium equation. These three equations may be replaced by the independent moment equations, $\sum M_A = 0$, $\sum M_B = 0$ and $\sum M_C = 0$ where A, B, C are the points which do not lie in a straight line.

1.4.6 Free Body Diagram (FBD)

FBD is a diagram showing (i) the body isolated from its surroundings and (ii) all the forces acting on the body. FBD is the effective technique employed extensively in considering the equilibrium of (i) a structure, (ii) a part of the structure, (iii) a member of the structure, (iv) a part of the member, (v) a joint, (vi) a differential part of the member, as shown in Fig. 1.8 (a) to (e).

1.4.7 Compatibility

The displacements of any point of a structure must be compatible with the overall deformation of the whole structure corresponding to the types of joints and types of the supports. The geometrical condition of displacements, consistent with the constraints, is called *compatibility*. This is the physical requirement of a structure for the continuity. The conditions of deformations along with the force conditions are explained subsequently as per types of supports and joints.

1.4.8 Types of Supports

A structure must be constrained by the supports so that there is no rigid body movement of the structure upon the application of any type of loads. The restrictions on rigid body motion of a structure are called the restraints. Such restraints are provided by the supports which connect the structure to stationary body.

The forces exerted by the supports, to prevent the movements, are called the reactions.

The supports may be classified as (i) position restraint, (ii) direction restraint. Accordingly the following types of the supports are commonly used for plane structures to provide the particular restraint.

- Roller support, represented in Fig. 1.9 (a), provides (a) the complete restraint against the translation perpendicular to the plane of the support, (b) no restraint to the translation along the plane of the support and (c) no restraint to the rotation.

Therefore, the force condition at a point of roller support specifies that roller support 'A' provides a reactive force which is acting at known point and acts in a known direction of perpendicular to the plane of the support but the magnitude of which is unknown. The sense of the reaction may be either away or to the structure. There cannot be moment as a reaction. Thus, one unknown reaction component is considered at a roller support.

Displacement condition at a point of roller support, in general, is stated as there is the translation along the plane of roller and the rotation i.e. two DOF.

The compatibility condition at a point of roller support is specified by zero translation perpendicular to the plane of support.

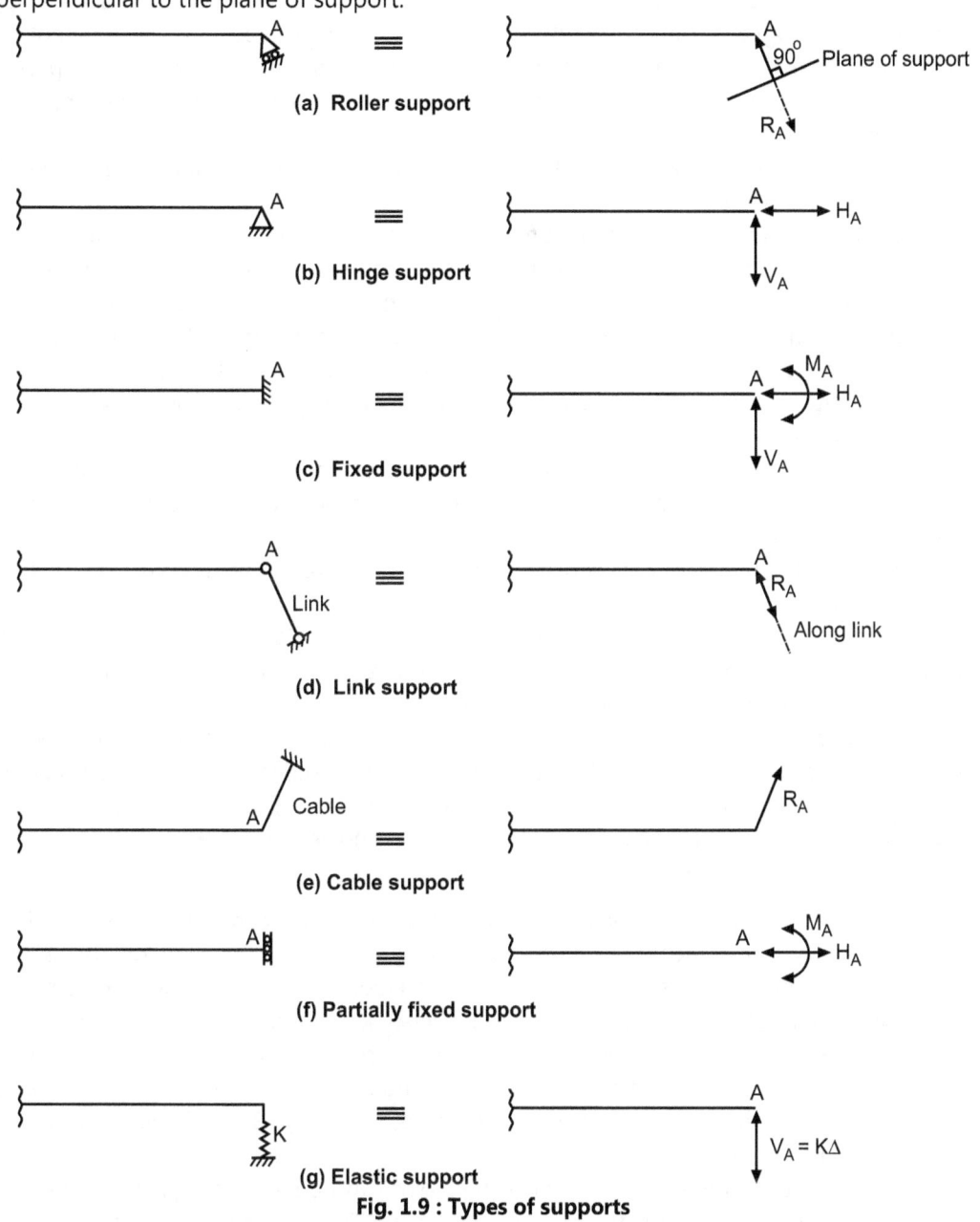

Fig. 1.9 : Types of supports

- Hinge support, shown in Fig. 1.9 (b), provides (a) the full restraint against translation in any direction and (b) no restraint against rotation. Therefore, the force condition at a point of the hinge support is that there is the reaction of known point of application but unknown magnitude and unknown direction i.e. line of action. The same condition is interpreted as two unknown orthogonal components of the reaction in x and y directions. There cannot be a moment as a reaction. Thus, two reaction components are considered at a hinge support.

The displacement condition at a point of hinge support is that translation is zero but the rotation exists i.e. one DOF.

The compatibility condition at a point of hinge support is given by zero translations in x and y directions i.e. $u = v = 0$.

- Fixed support, shown in Fig. 1.9 (c), provides the complete restraint against translations and rotations. Therefore, the force condition at a point of fixed support is that there is a unknown reactive moment and two unknown force components of the reactions in x and y directions. Thus, three unknown reaction components are considered at a fixed support.

All displacement components at a point of fixed support are zero, thus the dof is zero.

The compatibility condition at fixed support is therefore given by the equations $u = 0$, $v = 0$ and $\theta = 0$.

- Link support is analogous to the roller support. It provides the reaction force of known direction along the link, as shown in Fig. 1.9 (d), and known point of application but of unknown magnitude.

(v) Cable support offers only reaction force of tensile nature i.e. tension in the cable as shown in Fig. 1.9 (e).

- Partially fixed support or fixed guide support shown in Fig. 1.9 (f) provides the full restraint against rotation but may not provide complete restraint against translations. One of the component of translations is free and other is restrained.

(vii) Elastic support : According to the elastic property of the support, it provides partial restraint to the corresponding translation or rotation. The reactive force is proportional to the stiffness of the elastic support and therefore reactive force is given by the product of the stiffness and displacement at the point of the support as shown in Fig. 1.9 (g).

1.4.9 Types of Joints

A structure is formed by inter-connection of members. The inter-connections are called as *joints*. The joints are idealised as pinned or rigid. The types of joints play the key role in the behaviour of structures. Analysis of a structure is characterized by the joint displacements.

Following information of types of joints will be very useful for further work :

- **Pinned Joint :** A joint shown in Fig. 1.10 (a) which provides no restraint to rotation is considered as pinned joint. Therefore, the force condition at a point of pinned joint is that it can resist and transfer forces only and it cannot resist moments. A pinned joint is the non-moment resisting joint.

The displacement conditions at a point of pinned joint can be stated as : (a) There may be translations in x and y directions for plane structures. (b) There is relative rotation between the connected members. It means that there are different rotations at ends of the members meeting at the joint; causing discontinuity.

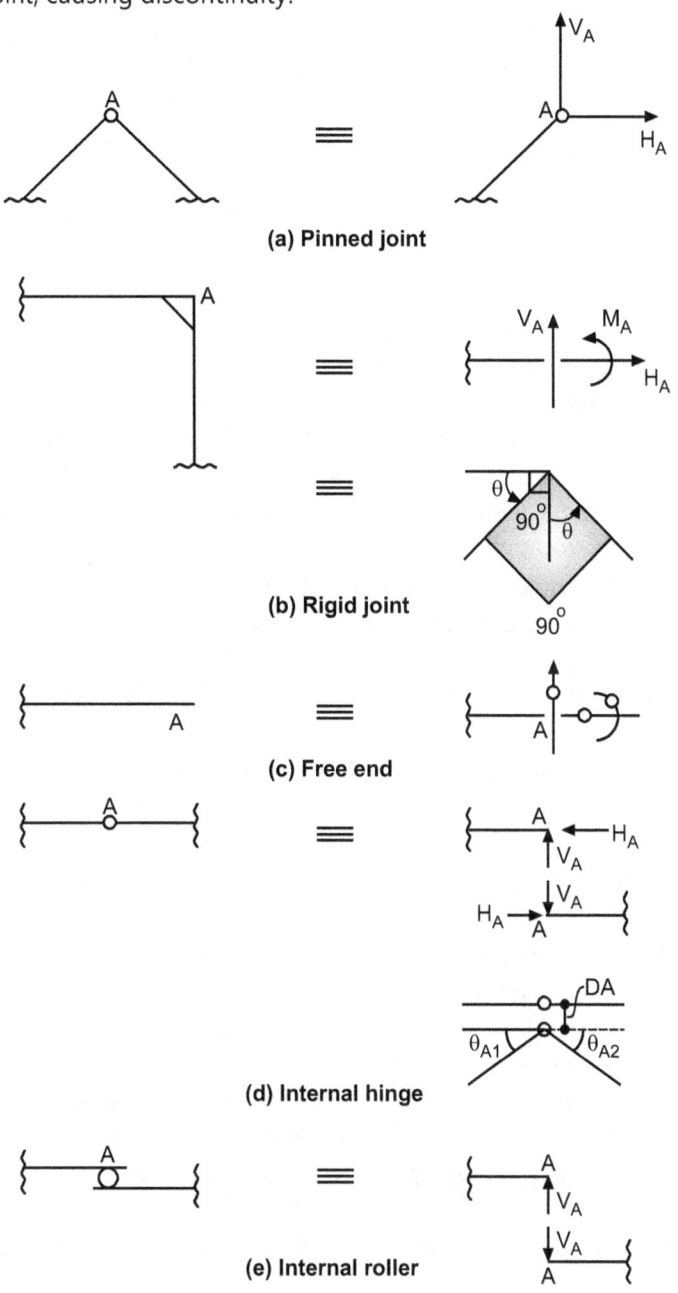

Fig. 1.10 : Types of joints

The compatibility condition at a point of pinned joint is that there is no continuity of deformation.

- **Rigid Joint :** A joint, shown in Fig. 1.10 (b), which rotates as a whole is called as *rigid joint*. The force condition at a point of rigid joint is that it can resist and transfer forces as well as moments. Therefore, a rigid joint is the moment-resisting joint.

The displacement condition at a point of rigid joint of a plane structure in x - y plane is considered as follows : (a) There may be translations in x and y directions. (b) There is no relative rotation, but a single rotation of joint as a whole maintaining the continuity of a structure.

The compatibility condition at a point of rigid joint is specified as follows :

The rotations at ends of the members meeting at the joint are the same in magnitude and direction. It implies that the angle between the members remains constant even on loading. The number of DOF at a rigid joint is three.

- **Free End :** Free end of a structure, shown in Fig. 1.10 (c), is also considered as the joint, if necessary. There are no forces and moment at unloaded free end. However, there may be displacements and therefore the number of DOF at free end of a plane structure is three i.e. two translations and one rotation.

- **Internal Hinge :** If a hinge, as shown in Fig. 1.10 (d), is inserted in a continuous beam or a plane frame, then it is considered as a joint and additional conditions of forces and displacements are to be considered carefully. Displacement conditions are the same that of hinge joint having discontinuity with respect to rotation. Force conditions are stated as follows :

    (a) If two members are connecting at a hinge, then one additional equation of equilibrium of zero moment at the point of hinge is taken into account in addition to the conventional equations of equilibrium.

    (b) If three members are meeting at a hinge, then two additional equations of equilibrium are considered.

- **Internal Roller :** If a roller, shown in Fig. 1.10 (e), is inserted in a continuous beam or a plane frame to transfer the load from one member to another, then it is considered as joint. Displacement conditions are that there may be two translations and one rotation unlike rigid joint. Force condition specifies that the force along the plane of the roller is zero and moment at the point of roller is also zero. Therefore, two additional equations are available at the point of internal roller, in addition to the conventional equations of equilibrium.

1.4.10 Shear and Bending Moment Diagrams

The relation between load w, shear v and bending moment m, are $\dfrac{dv}{dx} = w$ and $\dfrac{dm}{dx} = v$.

Accordingly the load diagrams, shear force diagrams and bending moment diagrams for beams subjected to transverse loads are drawn by using the following principles :

- The slope of the shear force diagram at any point is equal to the intensity of the distributed load at that point.
- Sudden changes in the ordinates of the shear diagram occur at points of application of concentrated loads.
- The slope of the bending moment diagram at any point is equal to the ordinate of the shear force diagram at that point.
- At points of concentrated loads, there are sudden changes in the ordinates of the shear force diagram and abrupt changes in the slopes of the bending moment diagram.
- It is usually necessary to compute the numerical values of the ordinates of the shear force diagram and bending moment diagrams only at points where the shapes of the diagrams change or points where the maximum or minimum values occur.
- The difference in the ordinates of the shear force diagram between any two points is equal to the total load applied to the beam between these two points.
- The difference in the ordinates of the bending moment diagram between any two points is equal to the area under shear force diagram between these two points.
- The shear force diagram is one degree higher curve than the load diagram.
- The bending moment diagram is one degree higher curve than the shear force diagram.

1.4.11 Stability

Stability of a structure essentially means the stability of its equilibrium configuration. Equilibrium is a kinematic state of body. In the context of stability, three types of equilibrium i.e. (a) stable, (b) unstable and (c) neutral, are considered as shown in Fig. 1.3 (a). In a mathematical sense, stability is interpreted to mean that infinitesimal disturbances will cause only infinitesimal displacements of the structure. Loss of structural stability is termed as structural instability. Although there are different types of instability, the present study of this text is mainly concerned with the stable equilibrium and corresponding stability. Structural stability corresponding to stable state of equilibrium is defined as the ability of structure to remain in position when subjected to any system of forces.

- External stability is related to the support system of a structure. A structure should be supported adequately so that there is no rigid body motion. A structure is externally stable if the supports are capable of providing the required number of independent reaction components for static equilibrium of the structure.

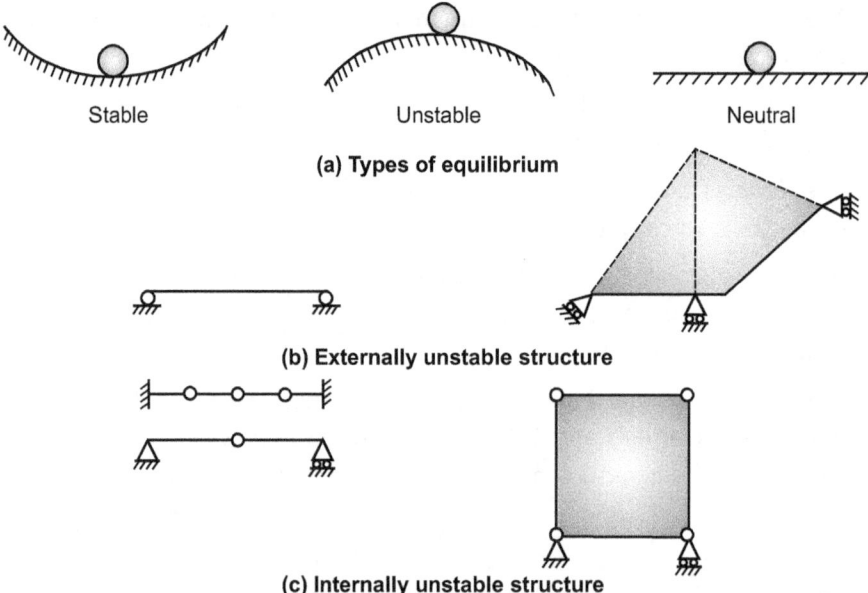

Fig. 1.11 : Stability of structure

For stability of a plane structure, according to three conditions of equilibrium, the support system should provide non-trivial reaction forces along any two orthogonal axes in the plane of structure and a non-trivial reaction couple about any point in this plane. It means that for stability, the three reactive forces should be (i) non-parallel and (ii) non-concurrent. It may be noted that the structures having support systems shown in Fig. 1.11 (b) are not stable.

- Internal stability depends on the types and arrangements of the joints and members of the structure. The arrangement should be such that the geometry of the structure or part of the structure should not change under any system of forces. A structure is internally stable, if internal forces are developed in the members of a structure as a result of even small deformation i.e. changes in the geometry. This means that a structure should resist the deformation by developing the internal forces. If the changes in the geometry do not cause the internal forces, then it is known as a mechanism and not a structure. The structures, shown in Fig. 1.11 (c), are not stable internally.

Therefore, a structure must be stable externally as well as internally.

1.4.12 Linearity and Elasticity

The deformation of a structure is assumed to be linear (reversible) and elastic. Linearity implies that the magnitudes of the displacements and internal forces of the structure are directly proportional to the magnitude of the external loading. The property of regaining original size and shape of the body after removal of force is known as *elasticity*. It means that the internal forces and displacements are recovered completely on removal of external forces and there should be no permanent deformation of a structure. In this context it is said that a structure behaves like a spring and cause-effect relationship is linear. The assumption that structural behaviour is linear elastic leads to considerable simplification in analysis and is justified in practice since most real structures respond approximately linearly to loads within their working range.

1.4.13 Statically Determinate Structures

If all reactions and internal forces in a structure can be found using the equilibrium conditions alone, then the structure is statically determinate. Statically determinate structures are also named as *determinate structures*. Internal forces in the determinate structure are independent of the physical and material properties of the structure. Displacements of determinate structure can be obtained separately from internal forces by using the concepts of elasticity and compatibility.

1.4.14 Statically Indeterminate Structures

If the reactions and internal forces in a structure cannot be found using the conditions of equilibrium, then the structure is statically indeterminate or hyperstatic or redundant. It is necessary to use directly three concepts of elasticity, equilibrium and compatibility so as to obtain the forces and displacements in the structure.

As the forces and displacements of an indeterminate structure are related to the physical and material properties of the structure, it needs prior knowledge of cross-sectional properties and material properties of the structure.

1.4.15 Static Indeterminacy

The reactive forces and the internal forces of a structure are considered as unknown forces in general. Available equations of equilibrium and unknown forces are compared to decide the static stability, determinacy and indeterminacy.

If the unknown forces are less than that the available equations of equilibrium, then the structure is not stable.

If the unknown forces are equal to the available equations of equilibrium, then the structure is statically determinate and can be analysed by statics only.

If the unknown forces are more than the available equations of equilibrium, then the structure is statically indeterminate and cannot be solved by statics only.

A statically indeterminate structure is said to have a degree of static indeterminacy or degree of redundancy. A degree of static indeterminacy is defined as the number of unknown reaction and internal force components in excess of the number of available equations of static equilibrium. A degree of static indeterminacy is denoted by the symbol (D_{si}) and given by

(D_{si}) = (Number of unknown reaction and internal force components)
– (Available equations of static equilibrium)

The most fundamental approach to determine the degree of static indeterminacy is to remove supports and/or to cut members until the structure has been reduced to a statically determinate and stable structure.

(D_{si}) = The number of restraints removed to reduce the given structure to determinate.

Alternatively the degree of static indeterminacy may be investigated as follows :

The degree of static indeterminacy is considered in the following two parts :

1. **Degree of External Indeterminacy :** It is denoted by the symbol $(D_{si})_e$ and it is related to the reaction components of the supports of a structure. $(D_{si})_e$ is defined as the number of unknown reaction components in excess of number of equations of static equilibrium of a structure as a whole. The number of reaction components, denoted by r, depends on the types of supports of a structure. For plane structures, the number of equations of equilibrium is three in general. Therefore, $(D_{si})_e$ is given by the equation

$$(D_{si})_e = r - 3 \qquad \ldots (1.1) \text{ (a)}$$

If r < 3, then it means that the structure is not adequately supported and the structure is not stable. Therefore, r should not be less than three.

If r = 3, then the structure is determinate externally and the reaction components can be obtained by the equations of equilibrium alone.

If r > 3, the structure is statically indeterminate externally and the reaction components can only be obtained by all conditions of structure i.e. equilibrium, compatibility and elasticity.

2. **Degree of Internal Indeterminacy :** It is related to the internal forces i.e. member forces. Member forces depend on the type of structure. After knowing the reaction components of the structure, if member forces can be found using conditions of equilibrium alone, then the structure is said to be internally determinate. If not, the structure is internally indeterminate, and degree of internal indeterminacy denoted by $(D_{si})_i$ needs additional considerations of type of the structure and the number and arrangement of members in the structure, as explained below.

(a) **Continuous Beams :** The internal forces of a member of a continuous beam are generally axial force, shear force and bending moment i.e. three components of internal forces for a member. Once the reaction components are known, these internal forces can be obtained by statics. Therefore, continuous beams are internally determinate.

i.e. $(D_{si})_i = 0.$ ... (1.1) (b)

(b) **Plane Frames :** A plane frame is statically determinate internally if it has open configuration i.e. no loops. The member forces of a plane frame are specified by the axial force, shear and bending moment i.e. three components of internal forces for a member. An internally indeterminate plane frame may be converted into a statically determinate by making sufficient number of cuts 'C', to have open configuration of the frame. At each cut, three components of internal forces are released. Therefore, the degree of internal indeterminacy is given by the equation

$$(D_{si})_i = 3C \qquad \ldots (1.1)\,(c)$$

(c) **Plane Trusses :** The internal force in a member of a truss is the axial force in the member i.e. one component. A plane truss is statically determinate internally if the truss has number of members, m, equals to (2j − 3) where j is the number of joints of the truss. If m is less than (2j − 3), then the truss is not stable and if m is greater than (2j − 3), then the truss is internally indeterminate and the degree of internal indeterminacy is given by the equation

$$(D_{si})_i = m - (2j - 3) \qquad \ldots (1.1)\,(d)$$

For the cantilever trusses :

$$(D_{si})_i = m - 2j \qquad \ldots (1.1)\,(e)$$

where j is number of joints except support joints, m is number of members excluding support plane.

3. Combined Degree of Static Indeterminacy :

(A) First Approach : The combined degree of static indeterminacy of a structure (D_{si}) is obtained as the sum of $(D_{si})_e$ and $(D_{si})_i$.

i.e. $\qquad (D_{si}) = (D_{si})_e + (D_{si})_i$

Accordingly, for different plane structures, the (D_{si}) may be obtained as follows :

(a) Continuous beams

$$(D_{si}) = (D_{si})_e + (D_{si})_i$$
$$\therefore \quad (D_{si}) = (r - 3) + 0$$
$$\therefore \quad (D_{si}) = (r - 3) \qquad \ldots (1.2)\,(a)$$

(b) Plane frames

$$(D_{si}) = (D_{si})_e + (D_{si})_i \qquad \ldots (1.2)\,(b)$$
$$\therefore \quad (D_{si}) = (r - 3) + 3C$$

(c) Plane trusses

$$(D_{si}) = (D_{si})_e + (D_{si})_i$$
$$\therefore \quad (D_{si}) = (r - 3) + [m - (2j - 3)]$$
$$\therefore \quad (D_{si}) = r - 3 + m - 2j + 3$$
$$\therefore \quad (D_{si}) = (m + r - 2j) \qquad \ldots (1.2)\,(c)$$

Cantilever trusses

$$D_{si} = (m - 2j) \qquad \ldots (1.2)\,(d)$$

(B) Second Approach : The combined degree of static indeterminacy is directly obtained by this general approach from the basic concept of

(D_{si}) = (Number of unknown reaction components and internal forces)
− (Available equations of equilibrium)

Unknown reaction components are counted according to the type of supports of the structure as follows : One reaction component for each roller support, two reaction components for each hinged support, three reaction components for each fixed support. Unknown internal forces are counted according to the type of structure as follows : One internal force component for each member of a truss, three internal force components for each member of a continuous beam or a frame. Available equations of equilibrium are counted according the joint of a type of structure as follows : Two equations for each joint of a truss including support, three equations for each joint of a beam or a frame including support. Additional available equations of equilibrium are counted for the insertion of a hinge in a beam or a frame, as follows :

(number of members meeting at the internal pin -1) equation for each internal pin. The number of additional equations is represented by 'h'.

Additional available equations of equilibrium are counted for the insertion of roller in a continuous beam structure. Two equations for each roller inserted in a beam structure. The number of additional equations is represented by 'ro'.

As per above rules, the criteria of stability and determinacy for the different plane structures can be generalised as follows :

(a) Continuous Beams

If $(3m + r) < (3j + h + ro)$, the continuous beam is unstable.

If $(3m + r) = (3j + h + ro)$, the continuous beam is statically determinate.

If $(3m + r) > (3j + h + ro)$, the continuous beam is statically indeterminate.

$$\therefore \quad (D_{si}) = (3m + r) - (3j + h + ro) \quad \ldots (1.3)\ (a)$$

(b) Plane Frames

If $(3m + r) < (3j + h)$, the frame is unstable

If $(3m + r) = (3j + h)$, the frame is statically determinate

If $(3m + r) > (3j + h)$, the frame is statically indeterminate

$$\therefore \quad (D_{si}) = (3m + r) - (3j + h) \quad \ldots (1.3)\ (b)$$

(c) Plane Trusses

If $(m + r) < (2j)$, the truss is unstable

If $(m + r) = (2j)$, the truss is statically determinate

If $(m + r) > (2j)$, the truss is statically indeterminate

$$\therefore \quad (D_{si}) = (m + r) - (2j) \quad \ldots (1.3)\ (c)$$

In this approach, $(D_{si})_e$ and $(D_{si})_i$ cannot be identified separately. Using this approach, static stability, determinacy and indeterminacy of different structures are investigated as given in Tables 1.1, 1.2 and 1.3.

Table 1.1 : Stability and Indeterminacy of Beams

Sr. No.	Structure	m	r	j	h	ro	(3m+r)	3j+h+ro	D_{si} (3m+r) − (3j+h−ro)	D_{ki}	Remarks
1.		1	2	2	−	−	5	6	−1	2	Unsable
2.		2	3	3	−	−	9	9	0	3	Statically determinate
3.		1	6	2	1	−	9	7	2	3	Indeterminate to second degree
4.		1	6	2	−	2	9	8	1	2	Indeterminate to first degree
5.		2	4	3	−	2	10	11	−1	5	Unstable
6.		2	3	3	−	−	9	9	0*	3	* Rule fails, unstable as three links intersect at the point
7.		2	8	3	−	−	14	9	5	1	Indeterminate to fifth degree
8.		3	6	4	1	−	15	13	2*	6	* Indeterminate to first degree
9.		1	6	2	2	−	9	8	1&	6	* Rule fails. The structure is determinate
10.		1	4	2	1	−	7	7	0*	5	* Rule fails. The structure in unstable.

Table 1.2 : Stability and Indeterminacy of Frames

Sr. No.	Structure	m	r	(3m+r)	j	h	(3j + h)	D_{si} (3m+r) − (3j+h)	D_{ki}	Remarks
1.		2	3	9	3	–	9	0	3	Determinate
2.		2	3	9	9	–	9	0*	3	* Rule fails unstable as reactions are concurrent
3.		3	3	12	4	–	12	0	6	Determinate
4.		5	9	24	6	–	18	6	4	Indeterminate sixth degree
5.		3	6	15	4	–	12	3	3	Indeterminate third degree
6.		3	6	15	4	1	13	2	4	Indeterminate second degree
7.		5	9	24	6	2	20	4	8	Indeterminate fourth degree
8.		3	6	15	4	3	15	0*	–	Rule fails, unstable.

Table 1.3 : Stability and Indeterminacy of Trusses

Sr. No.	Structure	m	r	(m+r)	j	(2j)	D_{si} (m+r)−(2j)	D_{ki}	Remarks
1.		13	3	16	8	16	0	−	*Rule fails, unstable
2.		2	4	6	3	6	0	2	Determinate
3.		5	4	9	4	8	1	4	Indeterminate, first degree
4.		5	4	9	4	8	1	4	Indeterminate, first degree
5.		6	4	10	4	8	2	4	Indeterminate, second degree
6.		5	4	9	4	8	1	4	Indeterminate, first degree

1.4.16 Kinematic Indeterminacy

Any structure, determinate or indeterminate, is said to have a certain degree of freedom. The degree of freedom is also called as degree of *kinematic indeterminacy* of a structure and denoted by (D_{ki}). In structural analysis, the overall behaviour of a structure is characterised by the displacements at the joints of the structure. The degree of kinematic indeterminacy of a structure is defined as the number of non-zero joint displacements of the structure. It may be noted again that the points of supports are also considered as the joints.

As per frame of reference, non-zero displacement components of all joints are counted, taking into account the compatibility conditions according to types of joints and types of supports and types of structures. For a plane structure, the general rules to count the non-zero joint displacements are given below as per the type of structure.

- **Continuous Beams :** At a point of a continuous beam, there are in general three degrees of freedom i.e. two translations in the direction of x and y axes and one rotation about z-axis. The axial deformation of the members of this structure is generally assumed to be neglected, being insignificant. Therefore, the horizontal translation in x-axis i.e. beam axis is not considered and hence the degree of freedom at a point is reduced to two. The points of supports and free ends are taken as the joints. Accordingly, to determine the degree of kinematic indeterminacy, the non-zero displacements are counted as follows :

    Two displacement components for each roller support in the inclined plane.

    One displacement component for each roller support in the horizontal plane.

    One displacement component for each hinge support.

    Two displacement components for each free end.

    One displacement component for each fixed vertical guides support.

    Three displacement components for each insertion of a hinge in a structure.

    Two displacement components for each insertion of a roller in a structure.

- **Rectangular Plane Frames :** At a point of a plane frame also there are three DOF unlike continuous beams. As the axial deformations of the members are generally neglected, the vertical translations at the joints of a rectangular frame are considered as zero and the horizontal translations at the joints at a beam level are assumed to be the same. This is known as sway. The concept of a rigid joint specifies a single rotation at the joint. Therefore, non-zero displacements are counted as per the following rules :

    One displacement component for each rigid joint.

    One displacement component for each pair of rigid joints at the same level.

    Two displacement components for each roller support in the horizontal plane.

    One displacement component for each roller support in the vertical plane.

    One displacement component for each hinge support.

    One displacement component for each fixed vertical guide support.

    Three displacement components for each insertion of a hinge in a member.

- **Plane Trusses :** At a point of plane truss, there are in general two translations along x and y axes. There is no rotation as joints are pinned. Therefore, the counts of non-zero displacements are as follows :

    Two displacement components for each joint. One displacement component for each roller support in horizontal plane, two displacement components for each roller support in inclined plane. Using above methods, kinematic indeterminacy of different structures is investigated as given in Tables 1.1, 1.2 and 1.3.

1.5 ENERGY THEOREMS

1.5.1 General

Energy concepts in addition to the principles of equilibrium, compatibility and superposition are also useful in structural analysis. Energy methods play a vital role in structural theory, especially for the analysis of continuum. A structure, when subjected to the gradually applied external forces, deforms and internal stresses are induced. The work is done by external forces while undergoing the displacements. This work is stored in the structure in the form of strain energy. Strain energy is potential energy of internal forces i.e. elastic forces.

For linear structure the external work done W, by force P or moment M is given by

$$W = \frac{1}{2} P \cdot \Delta$$

Or,
$$W = \frac{1}{2} M \cdot \theta \qquad \ldots(1.4)$$

The work done is represented by the area between the force-displacement curve and displacement axis as shown in Fig.

The strain energy 'U', is defined as the internal work of stresses acting through incremental strains, integrated over the total strains and over the volume. The general expression of strain energy for a structure is given by,

$$U = \int_V \left[\int_0^{\varepsilon_1} \sigma \, d\varepsilon \right] dv$$

and for a linear structure it is expressed as :

$$U = \frac{1}{2} \int_V \sigma_I \cdot \varepsilon_I \, dv \qquad \ldots(1.5)$$

and it is represented by the area between stress-strain curve and strain axis as shown in Fig. 1.1.5.

Complementary strain energy U* is defined as the internal work of strains multiplied by incremental stresses integrated over the total stresses and over the volume. The general expression for U* is,

$$U^* = \int_V \left[\int_0^{\sigma_1} \sigma \, d\varepsilon \right] dv \qquad \ldots(1.6)$$

For linear elastic structure the strain energy is equal to the complementary strain energy.

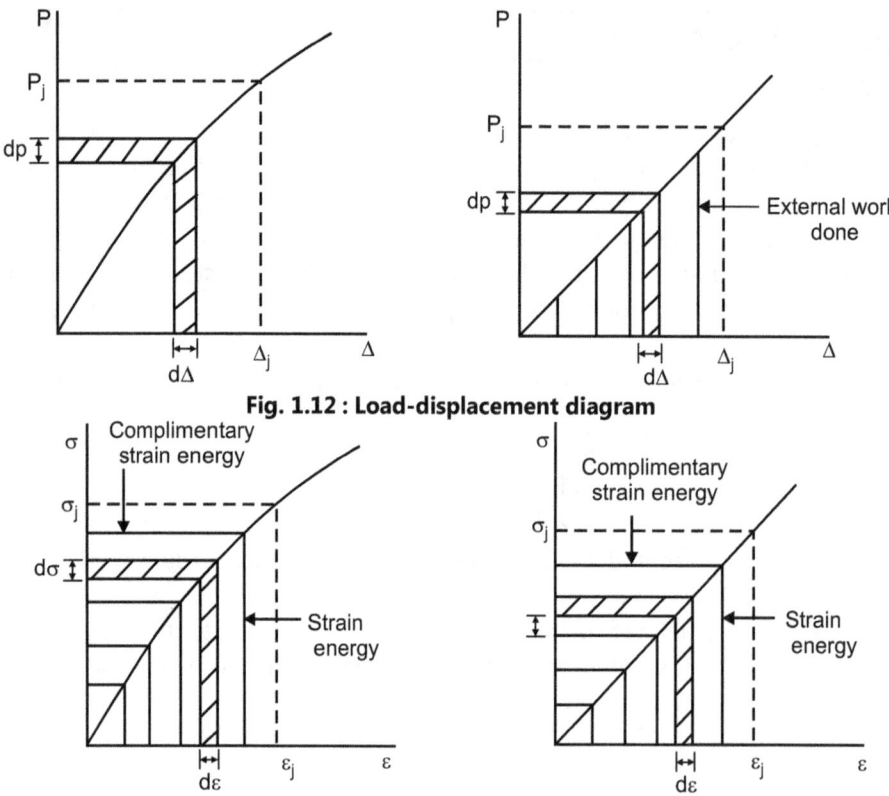

Fig. 1.12 : Load-displacement diagram

Fig. 1.13 : Stress-strain diagram

1.6 LINEAR AND NON-LINEAR STRUCTURES

If the displacements and the internal forces of a structure are directly proportional to the applied loads then the structure is called the linear structure. Elasticity is implied in the linear structure. This is also considered as linear response of the structure. Thus the cause-effect phenomenon is linear.

The response of the structure is linear under the following general assumptions :

- The structure is in stable static equilibrium.
- The displacements of the structure caused by the monotonic applied loads are small in comparison with the structure.
- The equilibrium equations are referred to the unloaded configuration of the structure rather than to the loaded configuration.
- The material of the structure is continuous, homogenous, isotropic, elastic and follows Hooke's law i.e. stress is directly proportional to strain. The mechanical properties of the material are same in tension and compression.

- There is no self-straining.
- Supports are unyielding.
- Transverse displacements due to transverse loads and axial displacements due to axial loads are independent.

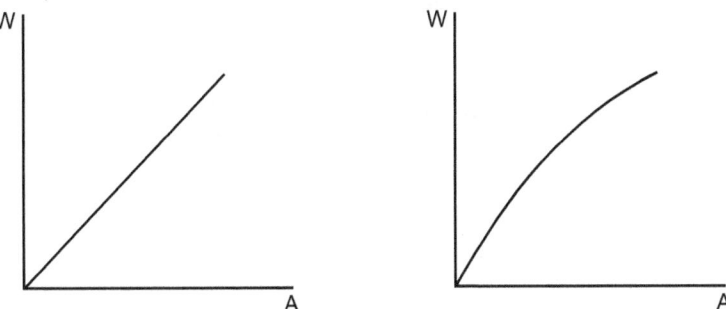

Fig. 1.14 : Linear and non-linear structures

Although most structures respond linearly within the working range of loads there are exceptions to this linear-behaviour. Such structures are treaded as non-linear structures. It may be noted that this non-linearity is not because of material behaviour. Behaviour of the beam-column is the example of non-linear structure. Wherein the deformation cannot be considered to be small and the effects of deformation must be taken into account.

If the internal forces due to self straining of structures i.e. effects of thermal changes, fabrication errors, prestress yielding of supports etc., are appreciable, the response of the structure to external forces is non-linear.

If deflections alter the structural geometry in a significant way then load and deflection are not linearly related. Linear and non-linear structural behaviour is represented in Fig. Only linear structures are dealt-with in this text.

1.7 Force-Displacement Relations and Stiffness and Flexibility of Prismatic Members

Using the basic principles of Mechanics it is possible to develop the exact relationships between the translational forces and rotational forces i.e. moments at ends of a particular prismatic member and corresponding end translations and rotations. In general, the end displacements and end forces (internal) of a prismatic member of a skeletal structure are uniquely related.

The important force-displacement relations are derived here for the particular prismatic members which are of prime importance to formulae the methods of analysis of different types of skeletal structures.

Stiffness is defined as the force required to produce unit displacement. Flexibility is the displacement caused by the unit force. It will be seen that the stiffness and flexibility are the reciprocal of each other and their product is equal to unity. The relationship between force and displacement is expressed either by a displacement equation.

$$\text{Displacement} = \text{Flexibility} \times \text{Force}$$

or by a force equation

$$\text{Force} = \text{Stiffness} \times \text{Displacement}$$

◈ ◈ ◈

Chapter 2
SLOPE-DEFLECTION METHOD

2.1 Preliminaries

Indeterminate rigid jointed plane framed structures are analysed by the slope-deflection method, denoted hereafter by SD method. Beams and plane frames or portals are considered as rigid jointed plane framed structures. Members, joints, supports, forces, deformations and displacements of the structure are in one plane i.e. the plane of structure which contains the axes of symmetry of cross-sections of all members of the structure. Such structures are diagrammatically represented by lines, as the axes of members, as in Figs. 2.1 and 2.2 showing (a) geometrical arrangement of members, joints and supports; called structural configuration; including dimensions, member properties and (b) applied loads including magnitude, direction and position.

Members are prismatic i.e. straight and of uniform cross-section. Members are mainly flexural members.

Joints are the (a) points of intersection of the prismatic members, (b) points of supports and (c) free ends of the members. The joints are mainly rigid. A rigid joint of a structure rotates as a whole and resists a moment as shown in Figs. 2.1 and 2.2.

At a rigid joint, the angles between the tangents to the elastic curves of the members meeting at the joint remain the same as those in the original undeformed members. In short, at a rigid joint, the angle between the members meeting the joint does not change. In general, joint of prismatic members in beams is considered as 180° rigid joint and a joint of prismatic members in rectangular frames is considered as 90° rigid joint as shown in Figs. 2.1 and 2.2.

Supports may be (a) roller support, (b) hinged support, and (c) fixed support.

Forces including moments are in the plane of structure. Moments have their vectors normal to the plane of a structure. Forces to be considered are as follows :

(1) Applied Loads :

(a) Member loads may be concentrated forces or moments and distributed loads, acting directly or indirectly through arrangements like brackets, pulleys, cables etc. as shown in Figs. 2.1 and 2.2.

(b) Joint loads are concentrated forces and moments acting at the point of joint directly or indirectly as shown in Figs. 2.1 and 2.2.

(2) Reactive Forces :

Actions of supports on a structure are the reactive forces or reactions and may be force and/or moment acting at the point of support according to the type of constraint as shown in Figs. 2.1 and 2.2.

(3) Internal Forces :

Forces at a cut-section are the internal forces, considered as either stress resultants or actions of the cut-part of a structure. Member-end forces are the internal forces as the actions of the joints. Member-end forces may be (a) axial force, (b) shear force, and (c) bending moment as shown in Figs. 2.1 and 2.2. It may be noted that there is no twisting moment because of special characteristics of rigid-jointed plane structure and loading condition. The internal forces at a point in a structure are self-equilibrated forces as actions and reactions.

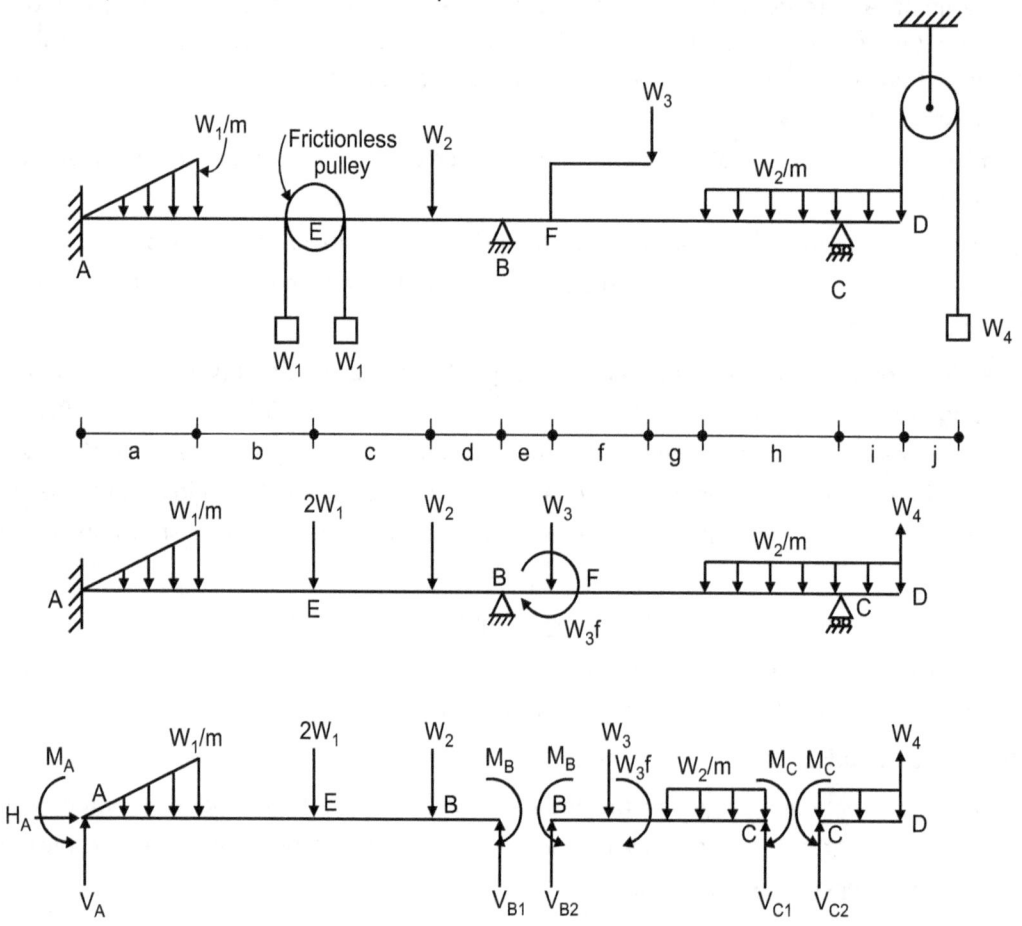

Fig. 2.1 : Beam showing members, joints, supports, structural configuration, loads, and internal forces

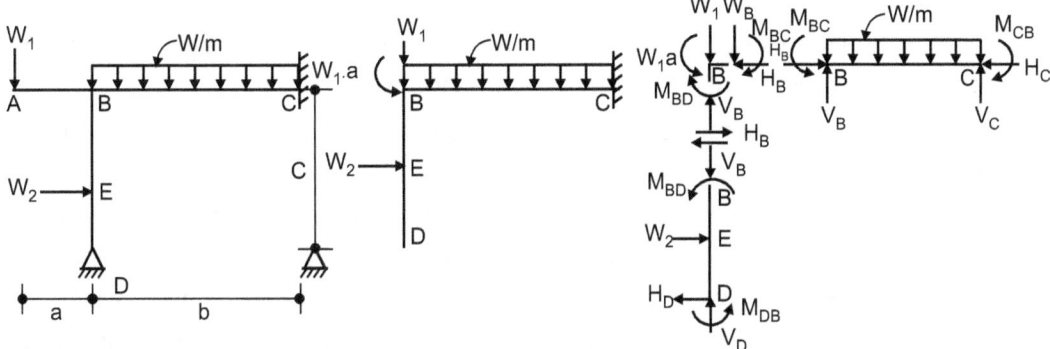

Fig. 2.2 : Frame showing types of members, joints, supports, loads, and internal forces

Structural deformations are due to the stresses and strains developed in the structure when it is subjected to the forces or other disturbances. Deformations are compatible with respect to the joints and the supports of a structure. Only flexural deformation is considered. Axial deformation and shear deformation are neglected. The deformed shape of a member/structure is called as the elastic curve as shown in Figs. 2.1 and 2.2.

Displacements are the cumulative effects of deformations. Displacement at a point in the plane structure may be (a) translation i.e. linear displacement in horizontal and vertical directions and (b) rotation i.e. angle between the tangent to the elastic curve at the point and the line of original member. Displacements are as shown in Figs. 2.1 and 2.2 in the plane of a structure. Rotations have their vectors normal to the plane of a structure.

Rotation of a joint is called slope. Deflection is the translation perpendicular to the axis of member. The translation along the axis of member is not considered in SD method. It may be noted that there cannot be rigid body displacements in a stable structure. Slope and deflections are important in SD method of structural analysis.

In general sense, a force means a force or a moment at a point and displacement means a translation or a rotation at a point. A force at a point is associated with the translation at the same point and in the same direction of the force, and a moment at a point is associated with the rotation at the same point and in the same direction of the moment. This is called one to one correspondence between force and displacement and plays important role in structural analysis.

2.2 INTRODUCTION OF SLOPE-DEFLECTION METHOD

SD method is basically a displacement method i.e. stiffness method (i.e. equilibrium method). Unlike other methods, SD method is based on (a) compatibility of joint displacements including support points, (b) moment - equilibrium of joints and force - equilibrium of a structure also called shear-equilibrium and (c) relations between member-end moments and member-end displacements. The method mainly involves slopes and deflections of the member at its joints and hence it is named as SD method.

SD method begins with the compatible joint displacements and it ends with the equilibrium equations called simultaneous equations. Therefore, SD method is the method of simultaneous solution of equations. The basic unknowns in SD method are the non-zero joint displacements of a structure. The number of such non-zero joint displacements is the degree of kinematic indeterminacy of a structure or degree of freedom. Therefore, kinematically indeterminate structures are analysed by SD method. Rigidity of a joint implies one single rotation at the joint. Selecting the appropriate unknown joint displacements, the compatibility is indirectly satisfied.

Member end displacements are the same as its joint displacements and called as slope and deflection. For every member of a structure, member-end moments are related to (a) member-end slopes and deflections, and (b) loading on the member by slope-deflection equations of the member, to be denoted hereafter by SD equations.

Using SD equations of all members of a structure, moment-equilibrium equations for the joints and shear-equilibrium equations for the structure are formulated in terms of unknown joint displacements. It should be noted that number of equilibrium equations must be same as the number of unknown joint displacements. The equilibrium equations are solved to obtain unknown joint displacements.

Knowing the joint displacements, member-end moments are found from SD equations of the members and rest of the analysis is completed by laws of statics.

Thus the SD method is pivoted on the SD equations and it is the member approach.

2.3 REFERENCE SYSTEM AND SIGN CONVENTIONS

Member and its two end joints are the basic components of SD method. To represent a member with its two ends, following reference system is suitable. One of the ends is taken as the origin. Member axis is considered as the x-axis. The y-axis, perpendicular to the member, is so chosen that the right hand system of Cartesian coordinates is formed as shown in Fig. 2.3. Accordingly for horizontal member, left end of the member as the origin, x-axis along the member and y-axis normal to the member will be the reference system. For vertical member, bottom end of the member as the origin x-axis along the member and y-axis normal to the member become the reference system.

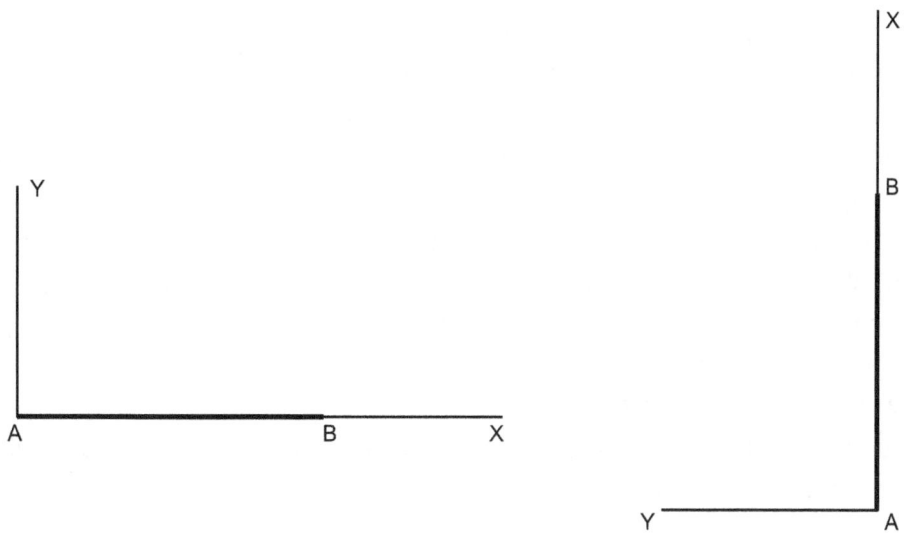

Fig. 2.3 : Frame of reference

Basic quantities of SD method are (a) member-end moment, (b) member-end slope or joint rotation, (c) member-end deflection or joint translation. Consistent with the reference system, following sign conventions are adopted for the basic quantities as shown in Fig. 2.4.

A member-end moment in anticlockwise direction is considered as positive. It is negative if clockwise.

A member end slope or a joint rotation in anticlockwise direction is considered as positive. It is taken negative if clockwise. A member-end deflection or a joint translation is considered positive if it is in positive y direction. It is taken negative in negative y direction.

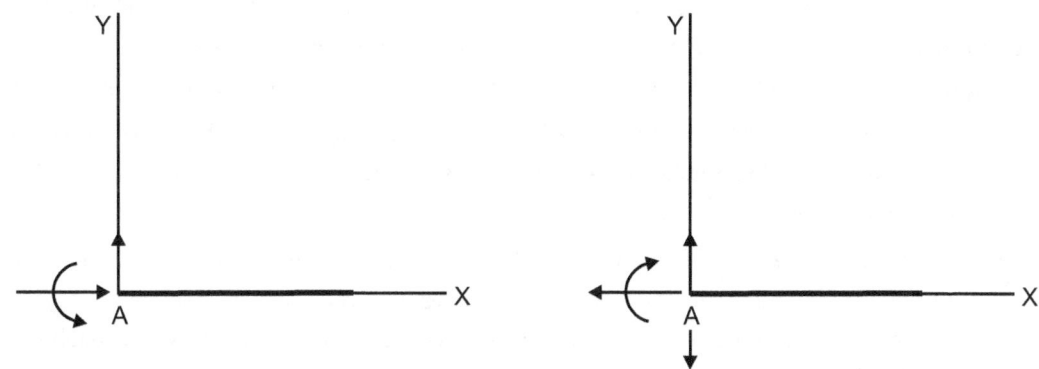

+ve member-end forces and displacements   −ve member-end forces and displacements

Fig. 2.4 : Sign convention for member-end moments and forces

Other member-end forces i.e. axial force and shear force are considered positive if they are in positive direction of x and y axes and negative in negative direction of axes.

Sign conventions for bending moment (BM), shear force (SF) and axial force (AF) at a section of a member of a structure are different and should not be mixed with that of member-end moments and forces.

Sagging bending moment is considered as positive and hogging bending moment is negative. When member-end moment is considered as a bending moment, the sign convention of bending moment is applicable. Shear force to the left of the section, in positive y-axis of a member is considered as positive. Shear force to the left of the section, in negative axis of a member is taken as negative.

Pull i.e. tensile axial force is treated as positive and push or thrust i.e. compressive axial force is taken as negative.

2.4 SD Equations

A member of a structure is bounded by two rigid joints at its ends. When a structure is loaded, member deforms, joints are displaced and internal forces are developed. The member-end moments can be expressed in terms of (a) the fixed-end moments of the member due to transverse loads on the member, (b) the member end-slopes or the joint rotations and (c) the member-end deflections or the joint translations. These expressions are called SD equations of the member.

There are two SD equations for a member of a structure, corresponding to the member-end moment at two ends i.e. joints. SD equations are the primary requirements of SD method. SD equations for a rigid jointed prismatic member are derived systematically from the superposition of the member-end moments caused by the following sequential operations.

- Restraining the member-end displacements i.e. locking the member-end joints and considering the fixed member-end moments due to the applied transverse loading on the member.
- Releasing the restrained member for its end joint displacements one at a time and obtaining the member-end moments due to the released displacement, such a operation is carried out sequentially for all the four displacements, two at each end i.e. slope and deflection.

During these operations, to obtain member-end moment separately due to each cause, the following fundamental principles of analysis are applied.

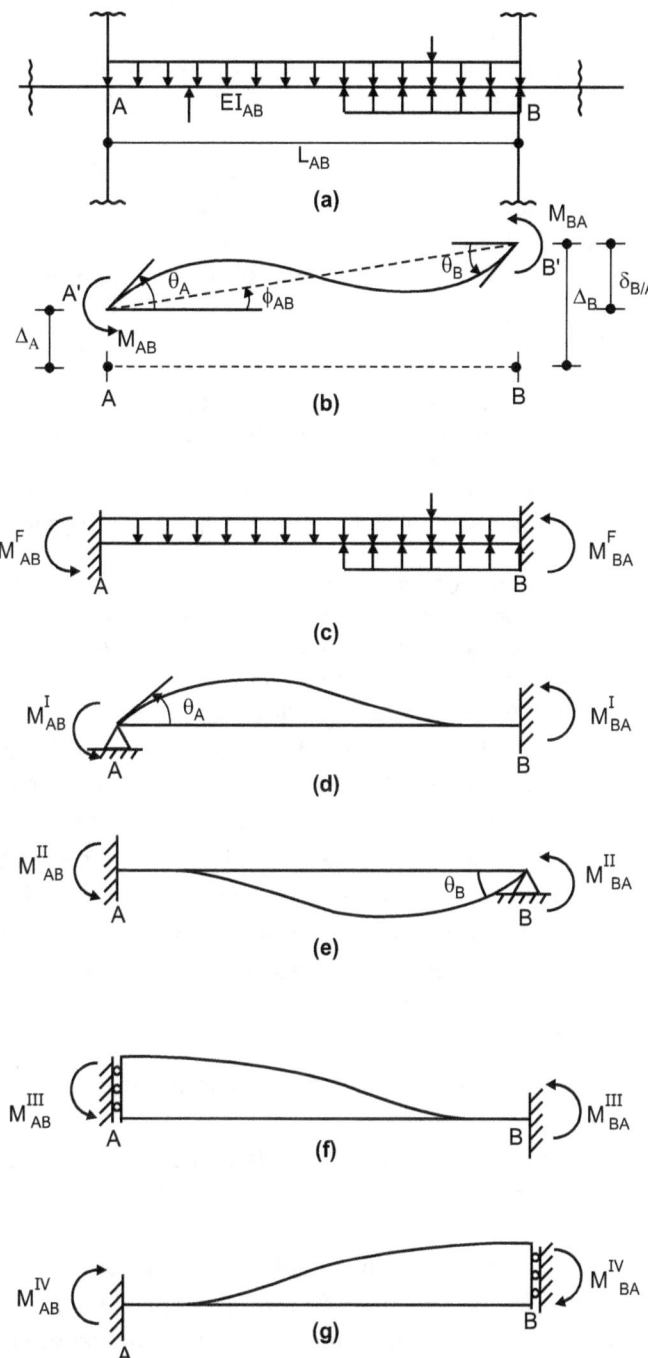

Fig. 2.5 : Development of SD equations by superposition

- Compatibility of member-end displacements.
- Equilibrium of member loads and / or member-end forces.
- Force-displacement relations in terms of flexural rotational and translational stiffnesses of the member.

This superposition technique is illustrated in Fig. 2.5 and SD equations are developed using some standard results of the member-end moments due to its joint displacements. These results are already derived earlier.

Before recapitulation of the results for the superposition, following points are worth to be noted with reference to Fig. 2.5.

- All primary quantities of SD equations are treated positive as per sign conventions, although the resisting forces are opposite to the deformations.
- As SD equations involve only member-end moments, only member-end moments are shown in Fig. 2.5, although other member-end forces exist for the equilibrium.
- Fig. 2.5 (a) shows a prismatic member AB of a structure, connected to the rigid joints A and B. The length of the member is L_{AB} and its flexural rigidity is denoted by EI_{AB}. The applied loads on the member AB, whatever may be, are also shown symbolically in Fig. 2.5 (a).
- The general deformed shape of the member AB, due to the loads on the structure, is sketched in Fig. 2.5 (b). Basic displacements of joints A and B are shown in Fig. 2.5 (b); and considered to establish general SD equations of the member. The translation along the member is of no interest and hence not shown.

  The joint displacements are represented by following symbols :

  θ_A = Member-end slope at A or the rotation of the joint A
  θ_B = Member-end slope at B or the rotation of the joint B
  Δ_A = Member-end deflection at A or the translation of joint A
  Δ_B = Member-end deflection at B or the translation of joint B
  $\Delta_{B/A}$ = Relative translation of joint B with respect to joint A
  ϕ_{AB} = Angle between the undeformed member and the line joining the deflected joints. Relative rotation as a rigid body.

  $$\phi_{AB} \cong \tan \phi_{AB} = \frac{\Delta_{B/A}}{L_{AB}}$$

  Δ_B is assumed to be more than Δ_A, so that $\Delta_{B/A}$ is positive and consequently ϕ_{AB} is anticlockwise i.e. positive.

- The member-end moments developed due to the loads on the structure are shown in Fig. 2.5 (b) and are termed as,

  M_{AB} = Moment at A for the member AB
  M_{BA} = Moment at B for the member AB.

- Fig. 2.5 (c) shows the restrained member AB with the applied loads on the member. This is the fixed beam action. Fixed member-end moments to be denoted hereafter by FEM, due to the transverse loads on AB are shown in the figure and expressed as :

M_{AB}^F = Fixed-end moment at A for the member AB

M_{BA}^F = Fixed-end moment at B for the member AB

- The unloaded restrained beam AB is released for θ_A only as shown in Fig. 2.5 (d). According to the flexural rotational stiffness of the member, the member-end moment required at the end A and the member-end moment developed at the end B to cause θ_A are given by,

$$M_{AB}^I = \left(\frac{4 EI_{AB}}{L_{AB}}\right) \times \theta_A$$

$$M_{BA}^I = \left(\frac{2 EI_{AB}}{L_{AB}}\right) \times \theta_A$$

These member-end moments are shown in Fig. 2.5 (d).

- The restrained beam AB is then released for θ_B only and member-end moments, as shown in Fig. 2.5 (e) are obtained by similar concepts of stiffnesses. They are written as

$$M_{AB}^{II} = \left(\frac{2 EI_{AB}}{L_{AB}}\right) \times \theta_B$$

$$M_{BA}^{II} = \left(\frac{4 EI_{AB}}{L_{AB}}\right) \times \theta_B$$

- The restrained beam AB is now released for Δ_A only.

This is the case of flexural translational stiffness. The member-end moments are of interest as shown in Fig. 2.5 (f). Using standard results, these moments are taken as

$$M_{AB}^{III} = \left(\frac{6 EI_{AB}}{L_{AB}^2}\right) \times \Delta_A$$

$$M_{BA}^{III} = \left(\frac{6 EI_{AB}}{L_{AB}^2}\right) \times \Delta_A$$

- Similarly, when the restrained beam AB is released for Δ_B only, member-end moments, as shown in Fig. 2.5 (g), are given by

$$M_{AB}^{IV} = -\left(\frac{6 EI_{AB}}{L_{AB}^2}\right) \times \Delta_B$$

$$M_{BA}^{IV} = -\left(\frac{6 EI_{AB}}{L_{AB}^2}\right) \times \Delta_B$$

It may be noted that M_{AB}^{IV} and M_{BA}^{IV} are negative for the positive Δ_B.

- Joint displacements along the member do not cause any member end moments.

Superposing the moments obtained due to all causes, the equations for the resulting member-end moments are simplified as follows:

$$M_{AB} = M_{AB}^F + M_{AB}^I + M_{AB}^{II} + M_{AB}^{III} + M_{AB}^{IV}$$

$$= M^F_{AB} + \frac{4EI_{AB}}{L_{AB}}(\theta_A) + \frac{2EI_{AB}}{L_{AB}}(\theta_B) + \frac{6EI_{AB}}{L^2_{AB}}(\Delta_A) - \frac{6EI_{AB}}{L^2_{AB}}(\Delta_B)$$

$$= M^F_{AB} + \frac{4EI_{AB}}{L_{AB}}(\theta_A) + \frac{2EI_{AB}}{L_{AB}}(\theta_B) - \frac{6EI_{AB}}{L^2}(\Delta_{B/A}) \quad \ldots (2.1\ a)$$

If $\Delta_{B/A}$ is known to be negative as in the case of sinking of support or assumed to be negative as in the case of sway frames; the SD equation of M_{AB} will be,

$$M_{AB} = M^F_{AB} + \frac{4EI_{AB}}{L_{AB}}(\theta_A) + \frac{2EI_{AB}}{L_{AB}}(\theta_B) + \frac{6EI_{AB}}{L^2_{AB}}(\Delta_{B/A})$$

and

$$M_{BA} = M^F_{BA} + M^I_{BA} + M^{II}_{BA} + M^{III}_{BA} + M^{IV}_{BA}$$

$$= M^F_{BA} + 2\frac{EI_{AB}}{L_{AB}}(\theta_A) + \frac{4EI_{AB}}{L_{AB}}(\theta_B) + \frac{6EI_{AB}}{L^2_{AB}}(\Delta_A) - \frac{6EI_{AB}}{L^2_{AB}}(\Delta_B)$$

$$= M^F_{BA} + \frac{2EI_{AB}}{L_{AB}}(\theta_A) + \frac{4EI_{AB}}{L_{AB}}(\theta_B) - \frac{6EI_{AB}}{L^2_{AB}}(\Delta_{B/A}) \quad \ldots (2.1\ b)$$

If $\Delta_{B/A}$ is known to be negative as in the case of sinking of supports, or assumed to be negative as in the case of sway frames, the SD equation of M_{BA} will be

$$M_{BA} = M^F_{BA} + \frac{2EI_{AB}}{L_{AB}}(\theta_A) + \frac{4EI_{AB}}{L_{AB}}(\theta_B) + \frac{6EI_{AB}}{L^2_{AB}}(\Delta_{B/A})$$

The member end moment equations 2.1 (a) and 2.1 (b) expressed in terms of joint displacements and the applied loading are termed as the general SD equations for a member. The SD equations are applicable irrespective of the orientation of the member.

It is interesting to note the different terms in SD equation of a member and its interpretation. Each term in SD equation represents the moment contribution due to the different causes. The member end of interest is called the near-end and other end is termed as the far-end. Accordingly, in the expression of M_{AB}, the moments at the end A are of interest, therefore A is the near-end and B is the far-end and different moment-contributions are as follows :

- M^F_{AB} is FEM contribution due to the applied loads on AB, at A.
- $\left[\frac{4EI_{AB}}{L_{AB}}(\theta_A)\right]$ is the near-end rotation contribution at A.
- $\left[\frac{2EI_{AB}}{L_{AB}}(\theta_B)\right]$ is the far-end rotation contribution at A.
- $\left[\frac{6EI_{AB}}{L^2_{aB}}(\Delta_{B/A})\right]$ is the relative translation contribution at A.

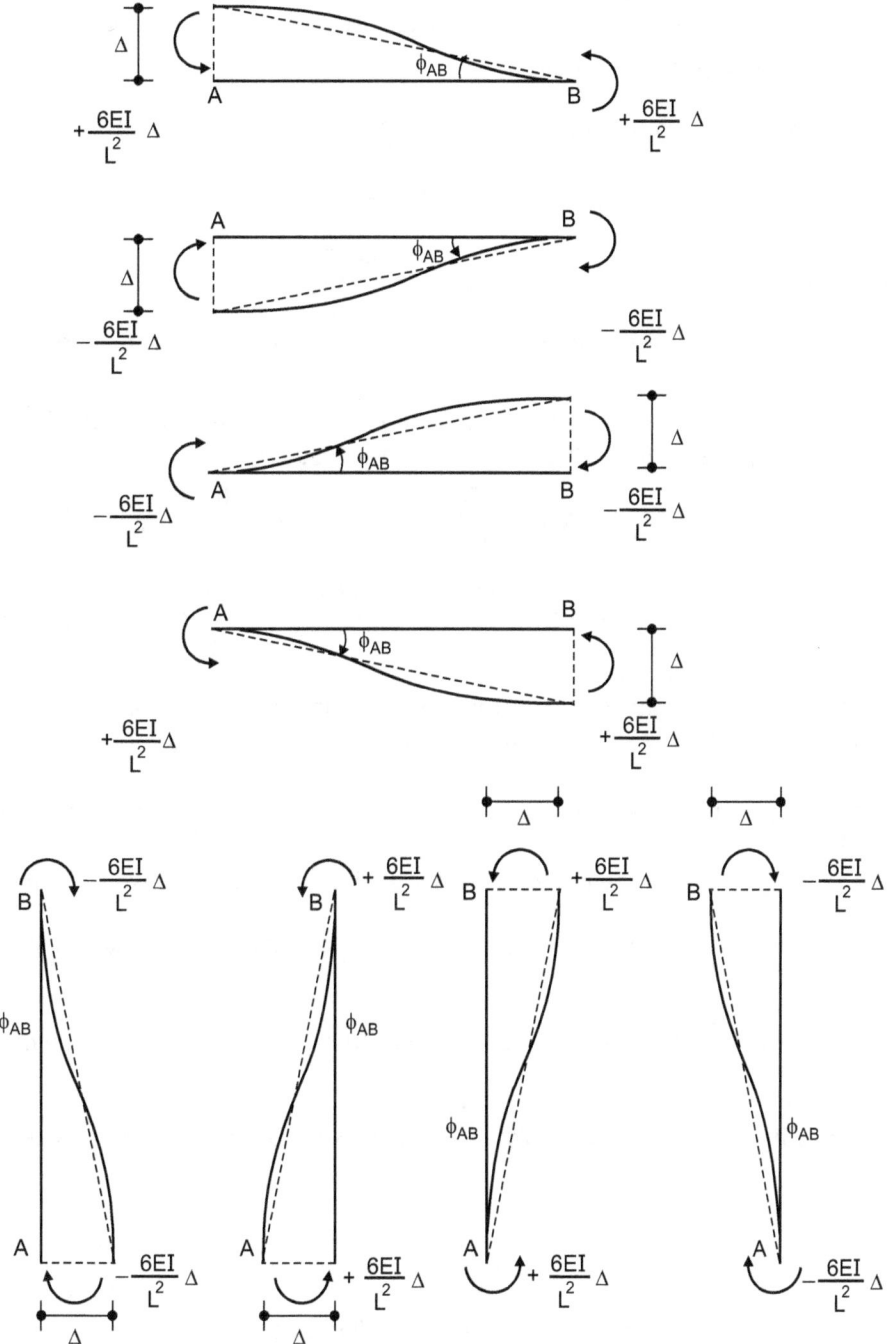

Fig. 2.6 : Relative translation contribution

Similarly for the end B, the contributions in the expression of M_{BA} can be stated.

In general, it can be remembered that:

- The near-end rotation contribution is always $\left[\dfrac{4EI}{L}\theta\right]$.
- The far-end rotation contribution is always $\left[\dfrac{2EI}{L}\theta\right]$.
- The relative translation contribution is always $\left[\dfrac{6EI}{L^2}\Delta\right]$.

Again it is emphasised to take care of the direction of the relative translation contribution in SD equations.

For the solution of problems of analysis of structures, the SD equations for any K^{th} member having joints i and j, are written in the following generalized form:

$$\left. \begin{array}{l} M_{ij} = M_{ij}^{F} + \dfrac{4EI_{ij}}{L_{ij}}(\theta_i) + \dfrac{2EI_{ij}}{L_{ij}}(\theta_j) \pm \dfrac{6EI_{ij}}{L_{ij}^{2}}(\Delta_{j/i}) \\[2ex] M_{ji} = M_{ji}^{F} + \dfrac{2EI_{ij}}{L_{ij}}(\theta_i) + \dfrac{4EI_{ij}}{L_{ij}}(\theta_j) \pm \dfrac{6EI_{ij}}{L_{ij}^{2}}(\Delta_{j/i}) \end{array} \right\} \quad \ldots (2.2)$$

It may be noted that for positive $\Delta_{j/i}$, the angle between the undeformed i.e. original member and the line joining the deflected joints, ϕ_{ij} is anticlockwise as shown in Fig. 2.6 and the quantity $\dfrac{6EI_{ij}}{L_{ij}^2}\Delta_{j/i}$ is negative. And for negative $\Delta_{j/i}$, the angle between the undeformed member and the line joining the deflected joints, ϕ_{ij} is clockwise as shown in figure and the quantity $\dfrac{6EI_{ij}}{L_{ij}^2}(\Delta_{j/i})$ is positive. Therefore, it is suggested that as per the direction of ϕ_{ij}, decide the sign for $\dfrac{6EI_{ij}}{L_{ij}^2}(\Delta_{j/i})$ and do not give sign to $\Delta_{j/i}$ i.e. use absolute value of $\Delta_{j/i}$. The general rule is, if ϕ_{ij} is anticlockwise take $\dfrac{6EI_{ij}}{L_{ij}^2}(\Delta_{j/i})$ as negative and if ϕ_{ij} is clockwise take $\dfrac{6EI_{ij}}{L_{ij}^2}(\Delta_{j/i})$ as positive.

If there are no joint translations, i.e. member end deflections, the SD equations are reduced to the following simple form:

$$M_{ij} = M_{ij}^F + \frac{4EI_{ij}}{L_{ij}}(\theta_i) + \frac{2EI_{ij}}{L_{ij}}(\theta_j)$$

$$M_{ji} = M_{ji}^F + \frac{2EI_{ij}}{L_{ij}}(\theta_i) + \frac{4EI_{ij}}{L_{ij}}(\theta_j) \quad \ldots (2.3)$$

The joint translations are absent in the following special situations :
- Beams consisting of prismatic members in between the supports which are non-yielding.
- Non-sway rectangular frames i.e. symmetrical rectangular frames.

2.5 FEM

Fixed end moments (FEM) are the pre-requisites of the SD method. FEM at two ends of a fixed beam, prismatic along its length, due to standard transverse loads on the beam are listed in Table 2.5. These results of FEM can be directly used in SD equations without its derivation from the first principles. If a member of a structure carries the combination of the standard loads, the FEM are computed by the superposition technique. For a member supporting distributed loads partly on the span, FEM are obtained by integrating the effects of infinitesimal elements and special tricks of compensations. The directions of FEM should be carefully accounted for considering as member end moment and not as BM. Generally for horizontal member ij with vertical downward transverse loads, the FEM are hogging bending moments, but with respect to sign conventions of member end moments, M_{ij}^F is positive as it is anticlockwise and M_{ji}^F is negative being clockwise. Special attention should be given to the direction of FEM due to the couple as a member load.

2.6 Equilibrium Equations of SD Method

Equilibrium equations of SD method are expressed initially in terms of the member end moments of the structure. When a structure is in equilibrium, its part and parcel must be in equilibrium i.e. every member, each joint, every point, any part of the structure should be in equilibrium. FBD is the best tool for equilibrium. The forces in FBD, in a plane must satisfy three equations of equilibrium,

(i) $\sum F_x = 0$,   (ii) $\sum F_y = 0$,   (iii) $\sum M = 0$.

Moment equilibrium of a joint and shear equilibrium of a structure are the key considerations of SD method.

(A) Moment Equilibrium of a Joint :

Member-end moments act on the connecting joints in the reversed direction as a action of a member on the joint. Moment equilibrium of a rigid joint therefore involves (a) the member-end moments in reversed direction of the members connected to the joint, and (b) the applied joint moment if any. Moment equilibrium of a joint requires that sum of all moments must be zero. To illustrate this, consider a rigid jointed structure loaded with the moment, M_A at A as shown in Fig. 2.7 (a). The FBD of the joint A is shown in Fig. 2.7 (b), indicating only moments for convenience.

Assuming member-end moments, M_{AB} and M_{AC} as anticlockwise and also applied moment M_A as anticlockwise, the moment equilibrium for the joint A leads to

$$\Sigma M_A = 0$$

i.e. $\quad M_A - M_{AB} - M_{AC} = 0$

i.e. $\quad M_A - [M_{AB} + M_{AC}] = 0$

i.e. $\quad M_A = M_{AB} + M_{AC}$

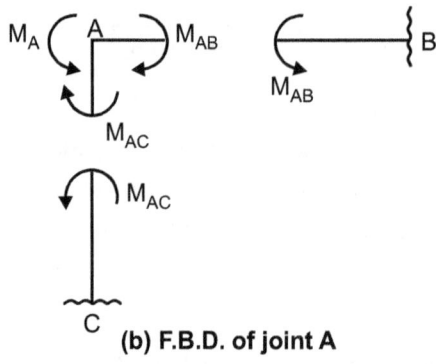

(a) Frame with moment at joint A

(b) F.B.D. of joint A

Fig. 2.7 : Moment equilibrium of joint

i.e. Applied moment at joint A = Sum of the member-end moments for the members meeting at the joint. As the applied joint moment and member-end moment are written on opposite side of the equation, it is concluded that the same sign conventions can be used for the applied joint moment and the member-end moment. This may be noted for further treatment of SD method. Therefore, general rule of moment equilibrium of joint is to equate the sum of the member end moments, meeting at the joint to the applied moment at the joint. This can be expressed, in general, at i^{th} joint as

$$\sum M_{ij} = M_i \qquad \qquad \text{... (2.4 a)}$$

It is also interesting to note that if there is no applied moment at a joint, the sum of the end moments of the members meeting at the joint must be zero to satisfy the condition of equilibrium.

i.e.
$$\sum M_{ij} = 0 \qquad \qquad \text{... (2.4 b)}$$

This is the common situation as the joints are seldom loaded with the moment.

Joint equilibrium conditions are adequate if unknowns are only joint rotations and joint translations are zero. This also indicates association of rotation with moment and one to one correspondence of force and displacement.

(B) Shear Equilibrium of Structure :

Joint equilibrium equations are inadequate if the unknown joint displacements are translations in addition to rotations.

According to one to one correspondence of force and displacement, the unknown translations need force equilibrium conditions of the structure in addition to moment equilibrium of joints.

Force equilibrium condition is called shear equilibrium with reference to SD method.

The shear equilibrium involves the members connected to the supports of the structure. Considering FBD of member, the end shear force at the support joint of the member is related to the member end moments and the applied member loads. This relationship is established by taking moments about the joint other than support joint. The end shears of the members connected to the supports also correspond to the reaction components of the supports of the structure. For equilibrium of the structure, the algebraic sum of (a) the end shears of the members at the support points of the structure and (b) the applied forces on the structure in the direction of shears, must be zero.

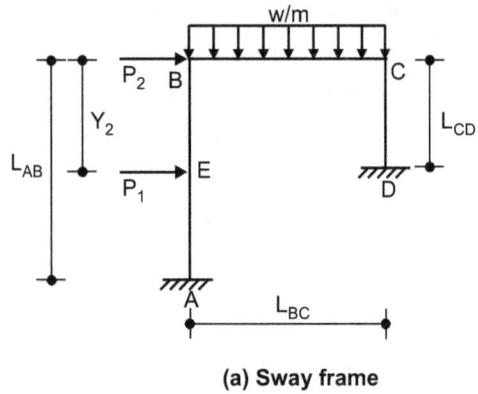

(a) Sway frame

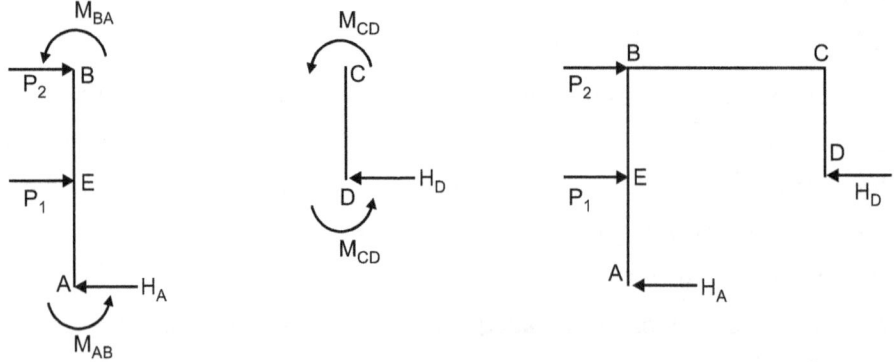

(b) F.B.D. of columns   (c) Shear equilibrium

Fig. 2.8 : Shear Equilibrium of frame

The concept of shear equilibrium is illustrated with the rectangular frame as shown in Fig. 2.8 (a). The FBD of the members AB and DC connected to the supports are shown in Fig. 2.8 (b). It may be noted that only member end moments, member end shears at the supports and applied member loads are shown in FBD. Member-end moments are considered positive for formulation of shear equilibrium. From FBD of the member AB and taking moments about B, the equilibrium equation $\sum M_B = 0$ is written as

$$H_A \times L_{AB} - M_{AB} - M_{BA} - P_1 \times Y_1 = 0$$

From this, the shear of AB at A is given by,

$$\therefore \quad H_A = \frac{(M_{AB} + M_{BA} + P_1 Y_1)}{L_{AB}}$$

Similarly from FBD of the member DC and taking moments about C, the equilibrium equation $\sum M_C = 0$ gives end shear H_D of DC, as

$$H_D = \frac{(M_{DC} + M_{CD})}{L_{CD}}$$

Fig. 2.8 (c) shows the structure consisting of only forces in the direction of shears. The force equilibrium, $\sum F_x = 0$, establishes the necessary shear equilibrium as :

$$P_1 + P_2 - H_A - H_D = 0$$

i.e. $\quad H_A + H_D = P_1 + P_2$

In general, shear equilibrium can be stated as :

Sum of the end shears of the members connected to the supports = Sum of the applied forces on the structure, in the direction of shears with due care of signs.

2.7 Procedure of SD Method

The SD method is very systematic. The important steps of procedure of SD method to analyse rigid jointed structure are given below :

(A) Data :
1. Configuration of the structure - line diagram showing the arrangement of joints and members and support conditions including dimensions.
2. Applied loads on members and joints of the structure showing position, direction and magnitude.
3. Sectional properties of members moment of inertia (relative values).
4. Properties of materials - modulus of elasticity.
5. Yielding of supports (translational and rotational) stiffness of elastic supports, if any.

(B) Objectives :
1. Joint displacements - translations and rotations (i.e. slopes and deflections).
2. Member-end moments.
3. Member-end forces - axial force and shear force - FBD of members.
4. FBD of joints.
5. Reactions at supports - FBD of structure.
6. Variation of shear force and bending moment along the length of members SFD and BMD.
7. Elastic curve

(C) Equations and Concepts :
1. SD equations.
2. Moment-equilibrium equations of joints.

3. Shear-equilibrium equations for structure.
4. Equilibrium of member - FBD.
5. Equilibrium of structure - FBD.

(D) Procedure :
1. Unknown joint displacement - Degree of kinematic indeterminacy.
2. FEM of members.
3. SD equations of members.
4. Formulation of equilibrium equations in terms of member-end moments.
   (a) Moment equilibrium of joint
   (b) Shear equilibrium of structure.
5. Verification of number of unknown displacements is equal to number of equilibrium equations.
6. Formulation of a problem by substituting SD equations in equilibrium equations.
7. Formation of simultaneous equations for unknown joint displacements.
8. Verification of diagonal symmetry of the simultaneous equations.
9. Solution of simultaneous equations to obtain unknown joint displacements.
10. Member-end moments by substituting joint displacements in SD equations of members.
11. Member-end forces-axial and shear from equilibrium of FBD of members.
12. FBD of members.
13. FBD of joints.
14. FBD of structure-reactions of supports.
15. SFD
16. BMD
17. Elastic curve (qualitative).

2.8 SD Method Applied to Beams

Statically indeterminate beams having more than two supports of any type i.e. continuous beams are analysed by SD method by hand calculations if unknown displacements are few, say three. If unknowns are more, the method becomes tedious as it involves large number of simultaneous equations which demand the use of computer. The general procedure given in the previous article is applied to analyse the continuous beams with the necessary simplifications wherever possible. Following situations are common in the analysis of beams.

2.8.1 Beams Without Joint Translations

The necessary and sufficient conditions for no joint translations in a continuous beam are as follows :

1. The members of the beam in between the supports are prismatic i.e. of uniform section. This means that the joints are only at support points.
2. All joints in the beam must remain in their original locations. This means that the supports are non-sinking and axial deformation is neglected.

The analysis of the beams without joint translations by SD method involves only (a) joint rotations and (b) moment equilibrium of joints.

2.8.2 Application of SD Method to Beams Without Joint Translations

Example 2.1 : *A beam BCD fixed at B and D and continuous over C. BC = 3 m and CD = 4m. BC is loaded with UDL of intensity 40 kN/m and CD is loaded with UDL of intensity 50 kN/m.*

Solution : (1) Data : The beam is supported and loaded as shown in Fig. 2.9.

(2) All supports are at same level.

Object : Structural analysis.

Equations : S. D. Equations.

Procedure : Step I : Degree of kinematic indeterminary.

Unknown Displacement : θ_C = D_{KP} = 1

Known Displacmenet : θ_B = θ_D = 0

Step II : Fixed End Moments :

$$\overline{M}_{BC} = -\overline{M}_{CB} = -\frac{wl^2}{12}$$

$$= \frac{-40 \times 3 \times 3}{12} = -30 \text{ kN-m}$$

$$\overline{M}_{CD} = -\overline{M}_{DC} = -\frac{wl^2}{12}$$

$$= -\frac{50 \times 4 \times 4}{12} = -66.67 \text{ kN-m}$$

Step III : Slope Deflection Equations :

$$\therefore \quad M_{BC} = -\overline{M}_{BC} + \frac{2EI}{l}\left(2\theta_B + \theta_c - \frac{3\delta}{l}\right)$$

$\delta = 0$, $\theta_B = 0$

∴
$$M_{BC} = -30 + \frac{2EI}{3}(\theta_C)$$

$$M_{CB} = \overline{M}_{CB} + \frac{2EI}{l}\left(2\theta_c + \theta_b - \frac{3\delta}{l}\right)$$

∴
$$M_{CB} = 30 + \frac{2EI}{3}(2\theta_C)$$

$$M_{CD} = -66.67 + \frac{2EI}{4}(2\theta_C)$$

$$M_{DC} = 66.67 + \frac{2EI}{4}(\theta_C)$$

Step IV : Equilibrium Equations :

∴ $\quad M_{CB} + M_{CD} = 0$

Step V : Formulation of Equilibrium Equations :

$$-36.67 + 4\,EI\theta_c\left(\frac{1}{3} + \frac{1}{4}\right) = 0$$

Step VI : Solution of Equations for Joint Displacements :

$$\theta_c = \left(\frac{15.71}{EI}\right)$$

Step VII : Member end Moments :

$$M_{BC} = -30 + \frac{2EI}{3}(\theta_c)$$
$$= -30 + \frac{2EI}{3}\left(\frac{15.71}{EI}\right)$$
$$= -19.52 \text{ kN-m}$$

$$M_{CB} = 30 + \frac{2EI}{3}(2\theta_c)$$
$$= 30 + \frac{2EI}{3}\left(2 \times \frac{15.71}{EI}\right)$$
$$= 50.95 \text{ kN-m}$$

$$M_{CD} = -66.67 + \frac{2EI}{4}(2\theta_c)$$
$$= -66.67 + \frac{2EI}{4}\left(\frac{2 \times 15.71}{EI}\right)$$

$$= -50.95 \text{ kN-m}$$

$$M_{DC} = 66.67 + \frac{2EI}{4}(\theta_c)$$

$$= 66.67 + \frac{2EI}{4}\left(\frac{15.71}{EI}\right)$$

$$= 74.525 \text{ kN-m}$$

Reaction at A = 60 − 10.48 = 49.52 kN

Reaction at B = 60 + 100 + 10.48 − 5.9 = 164.58 kN

Reaction at C = 100 + 5.9 − 105.9 kN

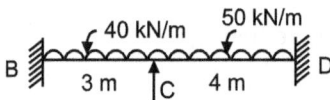

(a) Given structure

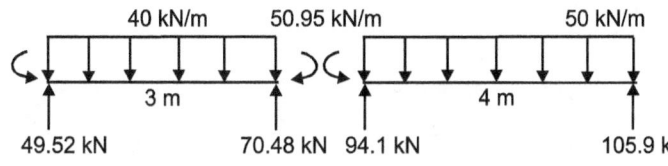

(b) FBD of members

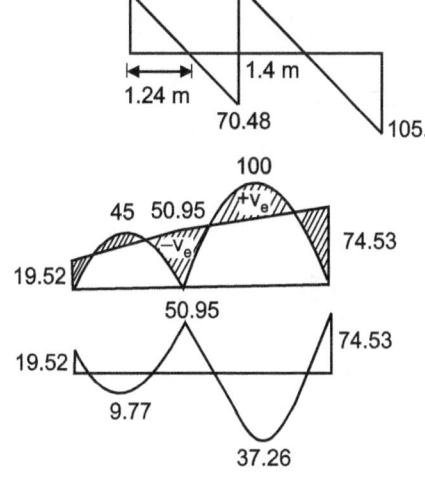

(c) S.F.D.

(d) BMD by superposition

(e) BMD on tension side

Fig. 2.9

Example 2.2: A two span continuous beam is fixed at A and simply supported at B and C. Given AB = BC = 6 m with $I_{AB} = 3I$ and $I_{BC} = 2I$.

The span AB carries a UDL of 40 kN/m, while a concentrated load of 100 kN acts at the centre of span BC. Using slope deflection method, analyze the beam and compute the support moments at A, B and C. Draw S. F. D and B.M.D.

Solution: (1) Data: The beam is supported and loaded as shown in Fig. 2.10.

(2) All supports are at same level.

Object: Structural analysis.

Equations: S. D. Equations.

Procedure: Step I: Degree of kinematic indeterminacy

$$= D_{ki} = 2$$

Unknown Displacement: θ_B, θ_C

Known Displacment: $\theta_A = 0$

Step II: Fixed end Moments:

$$\overline{M}_{AB} = -\frac{wl^2}{2} = -\frac{40 \times 6 \times 6}{12} = -120 \text{ kN-m}$$

$$\overline{M}_{BA} = \frac{wl^2}{12} = 120 \text{ kN-m}$$

$$\overline{M}_{BC} = -\frac{wl}{8} = -\frac{100 \times 6}{8} = -75 \text{ kN-m}$$

$$\overline{M}_{CB} = \frac{wl}{8} = 75 \text{ kN-m}$$

Step III: Slope Deflection Equations:

$$M_{AB} = \overline{M}_{AB} + \frac{2EI}{l}(2\theta_A + \theta_B) \qquad \theta_A = 0 \text{ as end A is fixed}$$

$$\therefore M_{AB} = -120 + \frac{2E(3I)}{6}(\theta_B)$$

$$= -120 + EI\theta_B$$

$$M_{BA} = \overline{M}_{BA} + \frac{2EI}{l}(2\theta_B + \theta_A)$$

$$= 120 + \frac{2E(3I)}{6}(2\theta_B)$$

TOS – II (TE CIVIL SEM. VI NMU)   SLOPE-DEFLECTION METHOD

$$= 120 + 2 EI\theta_B$$

$$M_{BC} = \overline{M}_{BC} + \frac{2EI}{l}(2\theta_B + \theta_C)$$

$$= -75 + 0.67EI(2\theta_B + \theta_C)$$

$$M_{CB} = \overline{M}_{CB} + \frac{2EI}{l}(2\theta_C + \theta_B)$$

$$= 75 + 0.67 EI(2\theta_C + \theta_B)$$

Step IV : Equilibrium Equations :

1. $M_{BA} + M_{BC} = 0$
2. $M_{CB} = 0$

Step V : Formulation of Equilibrium Equations :

1. $M_{BA} + M_{BC} = 0$

$$120 + 2 EI\theta_B - 75 + 1.34 EI\theta_B + 0.67 EI\theta_C = 0$$

$$3.34 EI\theta_B + 0.67 EI\theta_C = -45$$

2. $M_{CB} = 0$

$$75 + 0.67 EI\theta_B + 1.34 EI\theta_C = 0$$

$$0.67 EI\theta_B + 1.34 EI\theta_C = -75$$

Step VI : Solution of Equations of Joint Displacements :

$$EI\,\theta_B = -2.5$$

$$EI\,\theta_C = -54.7$$

Step VII : Member End Moments :

$$M_{AB} = -120 + EI\,\theta_B = -120 + (-2.5)$$

$$= -122.5 \text{ kN-m}$$

$$M_{BA} = 120 + 2 EI\,\theta_B = 120 + 2 \times (-2.5)$$

$$= 115 \text{ kN-m}$$

$$M_{BC} = -75 + 0.67 EI(2\theta_B + \theta_C)$$

$$= -75 + 0.67 EI(2 \times -2.5 - 54.7)$$

$$= -115 \text{ kN-m}$$

$$M_{CB} = 75 + 0.67 EI(2\theta_C + \theta_B)$$

$$= 75 + 0.67 EI(2 \times -54.7 - 2.5) = 0$$

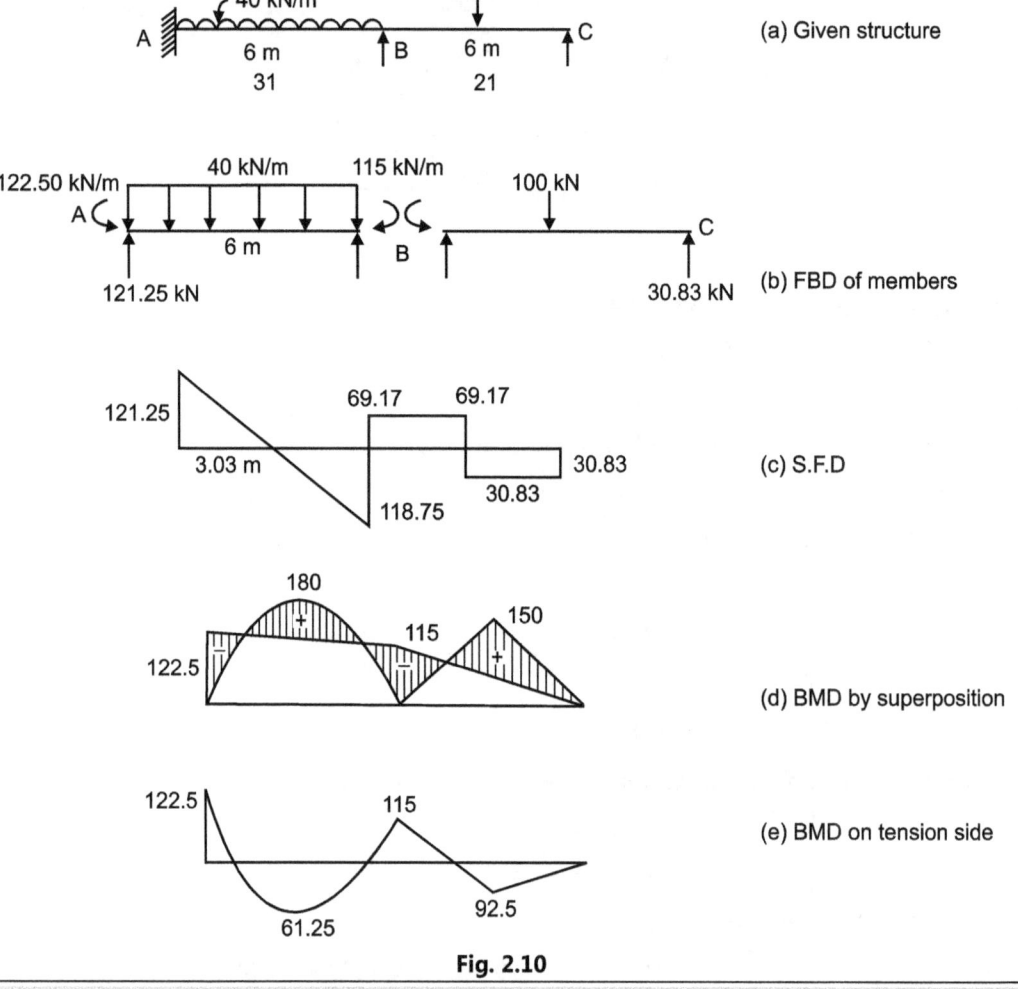

Fig. 2.10

Example 2.3 : Analyze the continuous beam by slope deflection method. Also draw shear force and bending moment diagrams.

Solution : (1) **Data :** The beam is supported and loaded as shown in Fig. 2.11.

(2) All supports are at same level.

Object : Structural analysis.

Equations : S. D. Equations.

Procedure : Step I : Degree of kinematic indeterminancy

$$= D_{ki} = 2$$

Unknown Displacements : θ_A, θ_B

Known Displacement : $\theta_C = 0$

Step II : Fixed End Moments :

$$\overline{M}_{AB} = -\overline{M}_{BA} = -\frac{wl}{8}$$

$$= \frac{-24 \times 3}{8}$$

$$= -9 \text{ kN-m}$$

$$\overline{M}_{BC} = \overline{M}_{CB} = \frac{M}{4} = -\frac{40}{4}$$

$$= -10 \text{ kN-m}$$

Step III : Slope Deflection Equations :

$$M_{AB} = \overline{M}_{AB} + \frac{2EI}{L}(2\theta_A + \theta_B)$$

$$= -9 + \frac{2EI}{3}(2\theta_A + \theta_B)$$

$$M_{BA} = 9 + \frac{2EI}{3}(2\theta_B + \theta_A)$$

$$M_{BC} = -10 + \frac{2EI}{3}(2\theta_B + \theta_C)$$

$$= -10 + \frac{2EI}{3}(2\theta_B)$$

Step IV : Equilibrium Equations :

$$M_{BA} + M_{BC} = 0, \quad M_{AB} = 0$$

Step V : Formulation of Equilibrium Equations :

$$9 + \frac{2E(1.5)}{3}(2\theta_B + \theta_A) - 10 + \frac{2EI}{3}(2\theta_B) = 0$$

$$2EI\,\theta_B + EI\,\theta_A + \frac{4EI\theta_B}{3} = 1$$

$$\frac{10\,EI}{3}\theta_B + EI\,\theta_A = 1 \qquad \qquad \ldots(1)$$

$$M_{AB} = 0$$

$$-9 + \frac{2E}{3}(1.5\,I)(2\theta_A + \theta_B) = 0$$

$$2EI\theta_A + EI\theta_B = 9 \qquad \qquad \ldots(2)$$

Step VI : Solution of Equations for Joint Displacements :

$$\theta_B = \frac{-1.23}{EI} \text{ and } \theta_A = \frac{5.11}{EI}$$

Step VII : Member End Moments :

$$M_{BA} = \overline{M}_{AB} + \frac{2EI}{l}(2\theta_B + \theta_A)$$

$$= 9 + \frac{2E(1.5\,I)}{3}(2 \times 5.11 - 1.234)$$

$$= 11.642 \text{ kN-m}$$

$$M_{BC} = -10 + \frac{2EI}{3}(2 \times -1.23)$$

$$= -11.642 \text{ kN-m}$$

$$M_{CB} = -10 + \frac{2EI}{3}(-1.23)$$

$$= -10.826 \text{ kN-m}$$

(a) Given structure

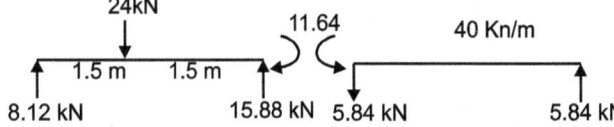
(b) F.B.D of members

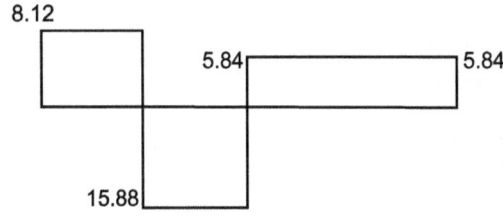
(c) S.F.D

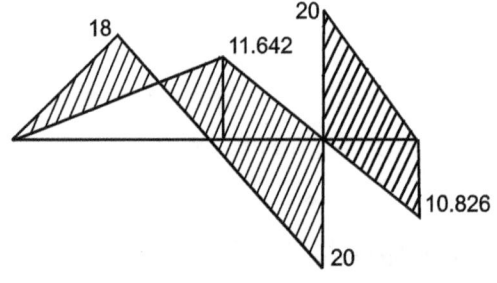
(d) BMD by superposition

Fig. 2.11

Example 2.4 : Find the moments at continuous support for beam ABC. AB = 5 m, BC = 6 m. A point load of 20 kN is acting on AB at 3 m from B and BC is loaded with UDL of 10 kN/m. EI is constant for the beam. Supports A and C are simple supports.

Solution : (1) **Data :** The beam is supported and loaded as shown in Fig. 2.12.

(2) All supports are at same level.

Object : Structural analysis.

Equations : S. D. Equation.

Procedure : Step I : Degree of kinematic indeterminacy = D_{ki} = 3

Unknown Displacements : $\theta_A, \theta_B, \theta_C$

Step II : Fixed End Moments :

$$\overline{M}_{AB} = -\frac{wab^2}{l^2} = -\frac{20 \times 2 \times 3^2}{5^2}$$

$$= -14.4 \text{ kN-m}$$

$$\overline{M}_{BA} = \frac{wa^2b}{l} = \frac{20 \times 2^2 \times 3}{5^2}$$

$$= 9.6 \text{ kN-m}$$

$$\overline{M}_{BC} = -\overline{M}_{CB} = -\frac{wl^2}{12} = -\frac{10 \times 6^2}{12}$$

$$= -30 \text{ kN-m}$$

Step III : Slope Deflection Equations :

Span AB :

$$M_{AB} = \overline{M}_{AB} + \frac{2EI}{l}\left(2\theta_A + \theta_B - \frac{3\delta}{l}\right)$$

$$\delta = 0$$

$$M_{AB} = -14.4 + \frac{2EI}{5}(2\theta_A + \theta_B)$$

$$M_{BA} = \overline{M}_{BA} + \frac{2EI}{l}(\theta_A + 2\theta_B)$$

$$= 9.6 + \frac{2EI}{5}(\theta_A + 2\theta_B)$$

Span BC :

$$M_{BC} = -30 + \frac{2EI}{6}(2\theta_B + \theta_C)$$

$$M_{CB} = 30 + \frac{2EI}{6}(\theta_B + 2\theta_C)$$

Ends A and C are simply supported.

Step IV : Equilibrium Equations:

$$M_{AB} = 0 \quad \text{(As simple support)}$$
$$M_{CB} = 0 \quad \text{(As simple support)}$$
$$M_{BA} + M_{BC} = 0$$

Step V : Formulation of Equilibrium Equations in Terms of Joint Displacements:

$$\therefore \quad M_{AB} = 0 = -14.4 + \frac{2EI}{5}(2\theta_A + \theta_B)$$

$$\therefore \quad 2\theta_A + \theta_B = \frac{36}{EI} \quad \ldots(1)$$

$$M_{CB} = 0 = 30 + \frac{2EI}{6}(2\theta_C + \theta_B)$$

$$\therefore \quad 2\theta_C + \theta_B = -\frac{90}{EI} \quad \ldots(2)$$

$$M_{BA} + M_{BC} = 0$$

$$9.6 + \frac{2EI}{5}(\theta_A + 2\theta_B) - 30 + \frac{2EI}{6}(2\theta_B + \theta_C) = 0$$

$$-20.4 + 0.4\theta_A + 0.8\theta_B + 0.667\theta_B + 0.33\theta_C = 0$$

$$-20.4 + 0.5\theta_A + 1.467\theta_B + 0.44\theta_C = 0 \quad \ldots(3)$$

Step VI : Solution of Equations for Joint Displacements :

Solving equations (1), (2) and (3),

$$\theta_A = 5.28/EI$$
$$\theta_B = 25.45/EI$$
$$\theta_C = -57.72/EI$$

Step VII : Member End Moments :

$$\therefore \quad M_{AB} = -14.4 + \frac{2EI}{5}(2\theta_A + \theta_B)$$

$$= -14.4 + \frac{2EI}{5}(2 \times 5.28 + 25.45)$$

$$= 0$$

$$M_{BA} = 9.6 + \frac{2EI}{5}(\theta_A + 2\theta_B) = 9.6 \frac{2EI}{5}(5.17 + 2 \times 25.67)$$

$$= 32.28$$

$$M_{BC} = -30 + \frac{2EI}{6}(2\theta_B + \theta_C)$$

$$= -30 + \frac{2EI}{6}(2 \times 25.67 - 57.84)$$

$$= -32.28$$

$$M_{CB} = 30 + \frac{2EI}{l}(2\theta_C + \theta_B)$$

$$= 30 + \frac{2EI}{6}(2 \times -57.84 + 25.67)$$

$$= 0.0$$

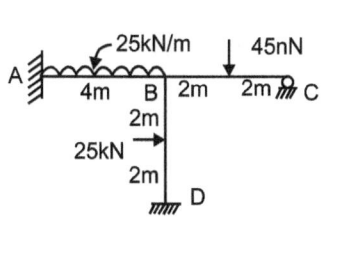

(a) Given structure

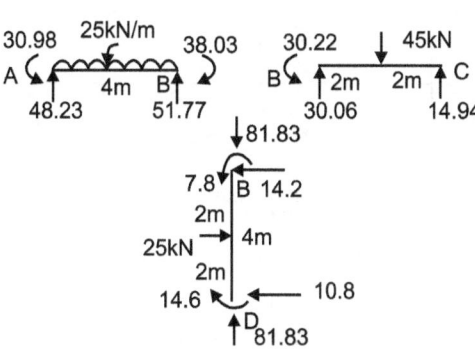

(b) FBD of members

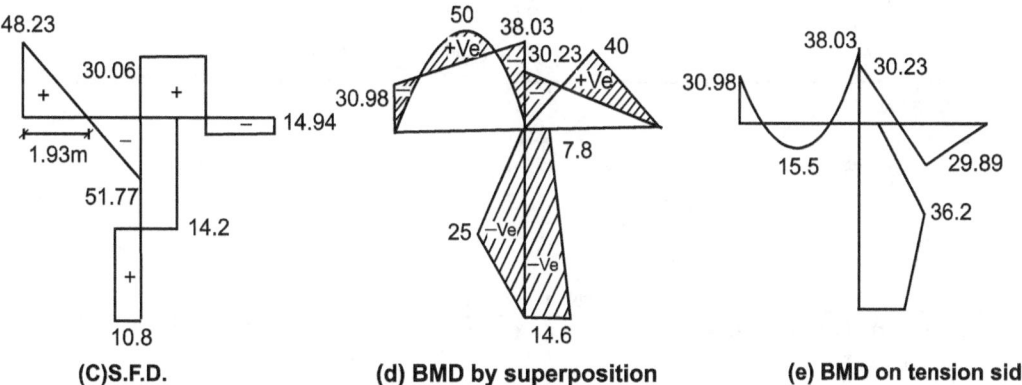

(C) S.F.D. (d) BMD by superposition (e) BMD on tension side

Fig. 2.12

Example 2.5 : Analyse the beam as shown in Fig. 2.9 (a) by slope-deflection method.

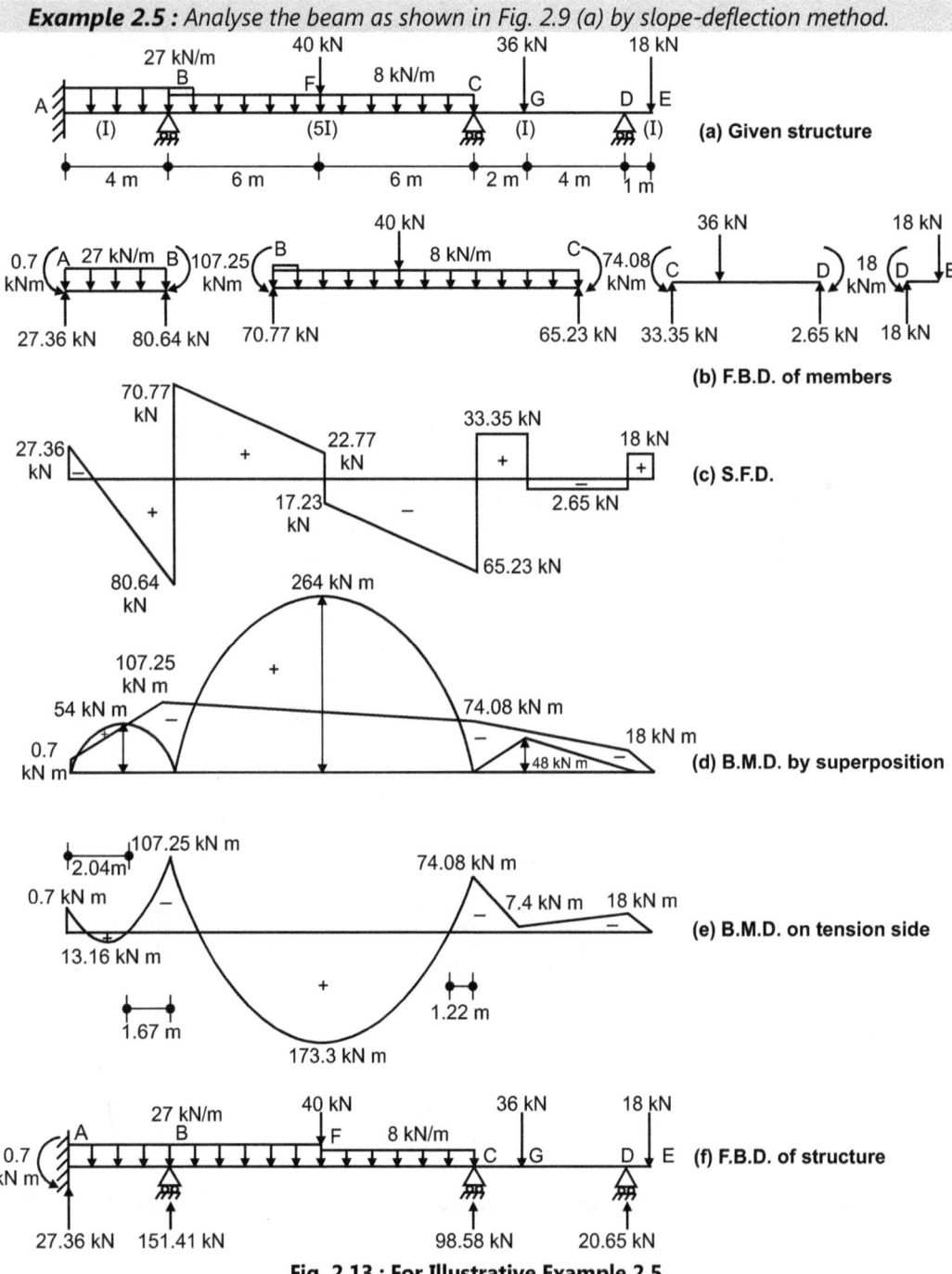

Fig. 2.13 : For Illustrative Example 2.5

TOS – II (TE CIVIL SEM. VI NMU)   SLOPE-DEFLECTION METHOD

Solution : (1) **Data :** The beam is supported and loaded as shown in Fig. 2.13 (b).

(2) All supports are at same levels.

Object : Structural analysis which includes;
1. Joint displacement;
2. Member-end moments;
3. Member-end forces – FBD of members;
4. Reactions at supports for structure – FBD of structure;
5. Variation of shear force and bending moment along the length of member – plotting SFD and BMD; and
6. Elastic curve – Deflected shape of structure.

Equations :

$$M_{ij} = \frac{4EI}{L}(\theta_i) + \frac{2EI}{L}(\theta_j) \pm \frac{6EI}{L^2}(\Delta) + M^F_{ij}$$

$$M_{ji} = \frac{4EI}{L}(\theta_j) + \frac{2EI}{L}(\theta_i) \pm \frac{6EI}{L}(\Delta) + M^F_{ji}$$

Procedure :

Step I : Degree of kinematic indeterminacy = D_{ki} = 5 (θ_B, θ_C, θ_D, θ_E, Δ_{VE}) for given structure.

Degree of kinematic indeterminacy = D_{ki} = 3 (θ_B, θ_C, θ_D) for modified structure.

Unknown Displacements = θ_B, θ_C, θ_D

Known Displacement = θ_A = 0

Step II : Fixed Moments :

$$M^F_{AB} = -M^F_{BA} = \frac{wl^2}{12} = \frac{27 \times 4^2}{12} = 36 \text{ kNm}$$

$$M^F_{BC} = -M^F_{CB} = \frac{wl^2}{12} + \frac{WL}{8} = \frac{8 \times 12^2}{12} + \frac{40 \times 12}{8} = 156 \text{ kNm}$$

$$M^F_{CD} = \frac{Wab^2}{L^2} = \frac{36 \times 2 \times (4)^2}{(6)^2} = 32 \text{ kNm}$$

$$M^F_{DC} = \frac{-Wa^2b}{L^2} = \frac{-36 \times (2)^2 \times 4}{(6)^2} = -16 \text{ kNm}$$

Step III : Slope-deflection equations :

Member AB : $M_{AB} = \frac{4EI}{L}(\theta_A) + \frac{2EI}{L}(\theta_B) \pm \frac{6EI}{L^2}(\Delta) + M^F_{AB}$

$\phantom{M_{AB}} = 0.5 \, EI \, (\theta_B) + 36$ ... (i)

$$M_{BA} = \frac{4EI}{L}(\theta_B) + \frac{2EI}{L}(\theta_A) \pm \frac{6EI}{L^2}(\Delta) + M_{BA}^F$$

$$= EI(\theta_B) - 36 \qquad \ldots \text{(ii)}$$

Member BC :
$$M_{BC} = \frac{4EI}{L}(\theta_B) + \frac{2EI}{L}(\theta_C) \pm \frac{6EI}{L^2}(\Delta) + M_{BC}^F$$

$$= \frac{4(5EI)}{12}(\theta_B) + \frac{2(5EI)}{12}(\theta_C) + 156$$

$$= 1.67\,EI(\theta_B) + 0.83\,EI(\theta_C) + 156 \qquad \ldots \text{(iii)}$$

$$M_{CB} = \frac{4EI}{L}(\theta_C) + \frac{2EI}{L}(\theta_B) \pm \frac{6EI}{L^2}(\Delta) + M_{CB}^F$$

$$= \frac{4(5EI)}{12}(\theta_C) + \frac{2(5EI)}{12}(\theta_B) - 156$$

$$= 1.67\,EI(\theta_C) + 0.83\,EI(\theta_B) - 156 \qquad \ldots \text{(iv)}$$

Member CD :
$$M_{CD} = \frac{4EI}{L}(\theta_C) + \frac{2EI}{L}(\theta_D) \pm \frac{6EI}{L^2}(\Delta) + M_{CD}^F$$

$$= \frac{4EI}{6}(\theta_C) + \frac{2EI}{6}(\theta_D) + 32$$

$$= 0.67\,EI(\theta_C) + 0.34\,EI(\theta_D) + 32 \qquad \ldots \text{(v)}$$

$$M_{DC} = \frac{4EI}{L}(\theta_D) + \frac{2EI}{L}(\theta_C) \pm \frac{6EI}{L^2}(\Delta) + M_{DC}^F$$

$$= \frac{4EI}{6}(\theta_D) + \frac{2EI}{6}(\theta_C) - 16$$

$$= 0.67\,EI(\theta_D) + 0.34\,EI(\theta_C) - 16 \qquad \ldots \text{(vi)}$$

Step IV : Moment equilibrium condition for joints :

At joint B ; $\quad M_{BA} + M_{BC} = 0 \qquad \ldots$ (A)

At joint C ; $\quad M_{CB} + M_{CD} = 0 \qquad \ldots$ (B)

At joint D ; $\quad M_{DC} = -18$ kNm $\qquad \ldots$ (C)

Step V : Formulation of equilibrium equations in terms of joint displacement :

Substituting equations (ii) and (iii) in equation (A), we get

$(EI\,\theta_B - 36) + (1.67\,EI\,\theta_B + 0.83\,EI\,\theta_C + 156) = 0$

$2.67\,EI\,\theta_B + 0.83\,EI\,\theta_C + 120 = 0 \qquad \ldots$ (A)

Substituting equations (iv) and (v) in equation (B), we get

$(1.67\,EI\,\theta_C + 0.83\,EI\,\theta_B - 156) + (0.67\,EI\,\theta_C + 0.33\,EI\,\theta_D + 32) = 0$

$0.83\,EI\,\theta_B + 2.34\,EI\,\theta_C + 0.33\,EI\,\theta_D - 124 = 0 \qquad \ldots$ (B)

Substituting equation (vi) in equation (C), we get

$0.67 \, EI \, \theta_D + 0.33 \, EI \, \theta_C - 16 = -18$

$0.67 \, EI \, \theta_D + 0.33 \, EI \, \theta_C + 2 = 0$ ... (C)

Step VI : Solution of equations for joint displacement :

$$\theta_B = \frac{-71.25}{EI}, \quad \theta_C = \frac{84.62}{EI}, \quad \theta_D = \frac{-44.66}{EI}$$

Step VII : Member-End Moments :

Substituting values of above displacements in slope-deflection equations, member-end moments are obtained as under :

$$M_{AB} = 0.5 \, EI \left(-\frac{71.25}{EI}\right) + 36 = 0.7 \text{ kNm}$$

$$M_{BA} = EI \left(-\frac{71.25}{EI}\right) - 36 = -107.25 \text{ kNm}$$

$$M_{BC} = 1.67 \, EI \left(-\frac{71.25}{EI}\right) + 0.83 \, EI \left(\frac{84.62}{EI}\right) + 156 = 107.25 \text{ kNm}$$

$$M_{CB} = 1.67 \, EI \left(\frac{84.62}{EI}\right) + 0.83 \, EI \left(-\frac{71.25}{EI}\right) - 156 = 14.08 \text{ kNm}$$

$$M_{CD} = 0.67 \, EI \left(\frac{84.62}{EI}\right) + 0.33 \, EI \left(-\frac{44.66}{EI}\right) + 32 = 74.08 \text{ kNm}$$

$$M_{DC} = 0.67 \, EI \left(-\frac{44.66}{EI}\right) + 0.33 \, EI \left(\frac{84.62}{EI}\right) - 16 = -18 \text{ kNm}$$

$$M_{DE} = 18 \text{ kNm}$$

Step VIII : FED of members : as shown in Fig. 2.13 (b).

Step IX : Shear force diagram : as shown in Fig. 2.13 (c).

Step X : Bending moment diagram :

BMD by superposition is shown in Fig. 2.13 (d).

BMD on tension side is shown in Fig. 2.13 (e).

Step XI : FBD of structure : as shown in Fig. 2.13 (f).

Example 2.6 : *A beam is fixed at A and D and continuous over supports B and C, AB = 9 m, BC = 6 m and CD = 8 m. The span AB carries UDL 20 kN/m, a concentrated load of 80 kN acts at the centre of BC and the span CD carries UDL of 15 kN/m. Analyse the beam using slope- deflection method. EI is given in Fig. 2.14 (a).*

Solution : (1) The beam is supported and loaded as shown in Fig. 2.14 (a).

(2) All supports are at same level.

Object : Structural analysis.

Equations : SD equations.

Procedure : Step I : Degree of kinematic indeterminacy = D_{ki} = 2.
Unknown Displacements : θ_B, θ_C.
Known Displacements : $\theta_A = \theta_D = 0$.
Step II : Fixed-end moments :

$$M_{AB}^F = -M_{AB}^F = \frac{WL^2}{12} = \frac{20 \times 9^2}{12} = 135 \text{ kN-m}$$

$$M_{BC}^F = -M_{CB}^F = \frac{WL}{8} = \frac{80 \times 6}{8} = 60 \text{ kN-m}$$

$$M_{CD}^F = -M_{DC}^F = \frac{WL^2}{12} = \frac{15 \times 8^2}{12} = 80 \text{ kN-m}$$

Step III : Slope-deflection equations :

Member AB :
$$M_{AB} = \frac{4EI}{L}(\theta_A) + \frac{2EI}{L}(\theta_B) \pm \frac{6EI\Delta}{L^2} + M_{AB}^F$$

$$= \frac{2E}{9}\left(\frac{4}{3}I\right)\theta_B + 135$$

$$= 0.29EI\,\theta_B + 135 \qquad \ldots \text{(i)}$$

$$M_{BA} = \frac{4EI}{L}(\theta_B) + \frac{2EI}{L}(\theta_A) \pm \frac{6EI\Delta}{L^2} + M_{BA}^F$$

$$= \frac{4E}{9}\left(\frac{4}{3}I\right)\theta_B - 135$$

$$= 0.59EI\,\theta_B - 135 \qquad \ldots \text{(ii)}$$

Member BC :
$$M_{BC} = \frac{4EI}{L}(\theta_B) + \frac{2EI}{L}(\theta_C) \pm \frac{6EI\Delta}{L^2} + M_{BC}^F$$

$$= \frac{4E}{6}\left(\frac{2}{3}I\right)\theta_B + \frac{2E}{6}\left(\frac{2}{3}I\right)\theta_C + 60$$

$$= 0.44EI\,\theta_B + 0.22EI\,\theta_C + 60 \qquad \ldots \text{(iii)}$$

$$M_{CB} = \frac{4EI}{L}(\theta_C) + \frac{2EI}{L}(\theta_B) \pm \frac{6EI\Delta}{L^2} + M_{CB}^F$$

$$= \frac{4E}{6}\left(\frac{2}{3}I\right)\theta_C + \frac{2E}{6}\left(\frac{2}{3}I\right)\theta_B - 60$$

$$= 0.44EI\,\theta_C + 0.22EI\,\theta_B - 60 \qquad \ldots \text{(iv)}$$

Member CD :
$$M_{CD} = \frac{4EI}{L}(\theta_C) + \frac{2EI}{L}(\theta_D) + \frac{6EI\Delta}{L^2} + M_{CD}^F$$

$$= \frac{4EI}{8}\theta_C + 80$$

$$= 0.5EI\,\theta_C + 80 \qquad \ldots \text{(v)}$$

$$M_{DC} = \frac{4EI}{L}(\theta_D) + \frac{2EI}{L}(\theta_C) \pm \frac{6EI\Delta}{L^2} + M^F_{DC}$$

$$= \frac{2EI}{8}(\theta_C) - 80$$

$$= 0.25EI\,\theta_C - 80 \qquad \ldots \text{(vi)}$$

Step IV : Moment equilibrium condition for joint :

At joint B : $\qquad M_{BA} + M_{BC} = 09 \qquad \ldots$ (A)

At joint C : $\qquad M_{CB} + M_{CD} = 0 \qquad \ldots$ (B)

Step V : Formulation of equilibrium equations in terms of joint displacement.

Substituting equations (ii) and (iii) in equation (A),

$$0.593EI\,\theta_B - 135 + 0.444EI\,\theta_B + 0.222EI\,\theta_C + 60 = 0$$

$$1.037EI\,\theta_B + 0.222EI\,\theta_C - 75 = 0 \qquad \ldots \text{(A)}$$

Substituting equations (iv) and (v) in equation (B),

$$0.444EI\,\theta_C + 0.222EI\,\theta_B - 60 + 0.5EI\,\theta_C + 80 = 0$$

$$0.222EI\,\theta_B + 0.944EI\,\theta_C + 20 = 0 \qquad \ldots \text{(B)}$$

Step VI : Solution of equations for joint displacement :

$$\theta_B = \frac{80.93}{EI},\; \theta_C = -\frac{40.22}{EI}$$

Step VII : Member-end moments :

$$M_{AB} = 0.296EI\left(\frac{80.93}{EI}\right) + 135 = 159.95 \text{ kN-m}$$

$$M_{BA} = 0.593EI\left(\frac{80.93}{EI}\right) - 135 = 87.01 \text{ kN-m}$$

$$M_{BC} = 0.444EI\left(\frac{81.43}{EI}\right) + 0.222EI\left(-\frac{40.33}{EI}\right) + 60 = 87.01 \text{ kN-m}$$

$$M_{CB} = 0.444EI\left(-\frac{40.22}{EI}\right) + 0.222EI\left(\frac{80.93}{EI}\right) - 60 = -59.89 \text{ kN-m}$$

$$M_{CD} = 0.5EI\left(-\frac{40.22}{EI}\right) + 80 = 59.89 \text{ kN-m}$$

$$M_{DC} = 0.25EI\left(-\frac{40.22}{EI}\right) - 80 = -90.06 \text{ kN-m}$$

Step VIII : FBD of members is as shown in Fig. 2.14 (b).

Step IX : Shear force diagram is as shown in Fig. 2.14 (c).

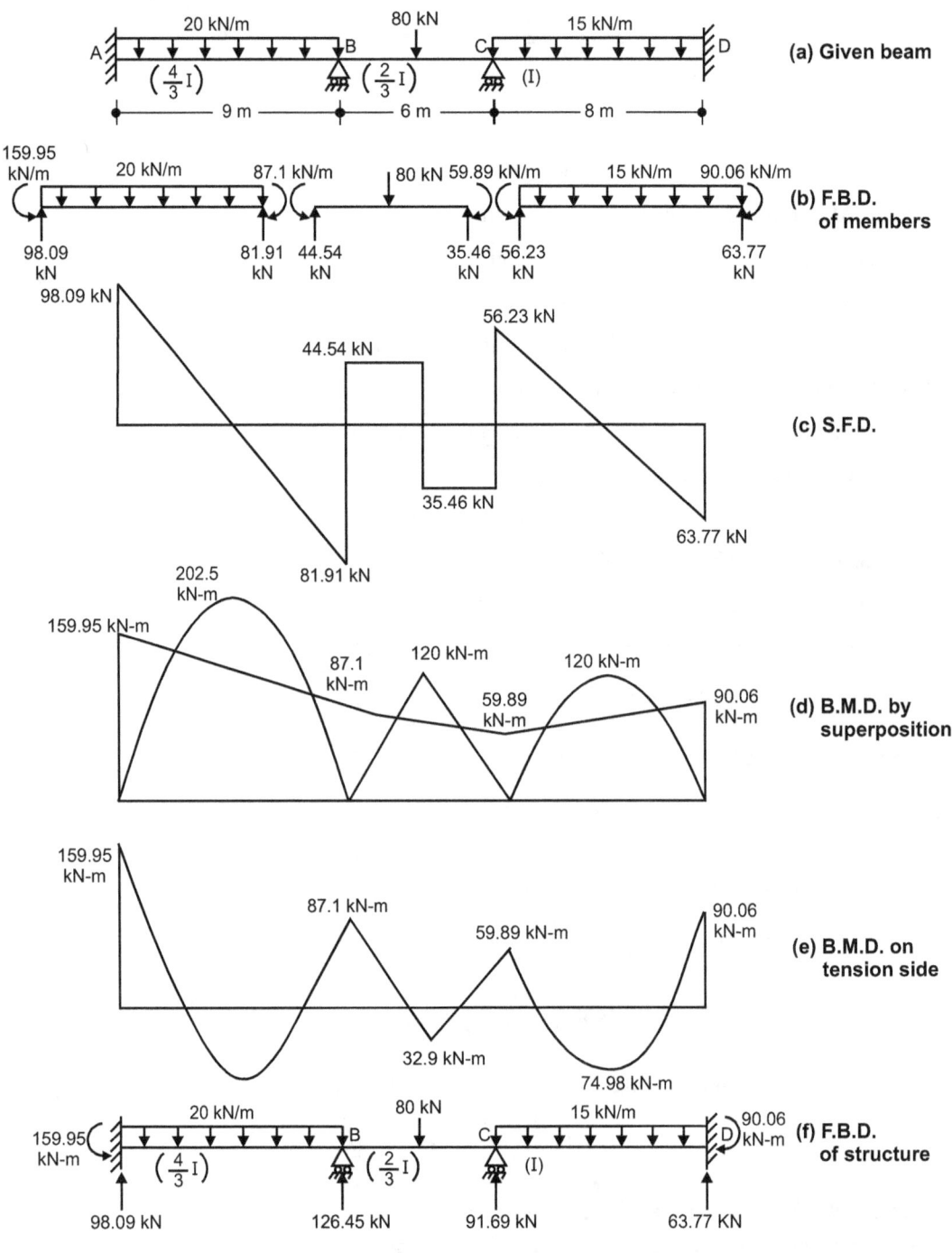

Fig. 2.14 : For Illustrative Example 2.6

Step X : Bending moment diagram.

BMD by superposition is as shown in Fig. 2.14 (d).

BMD on tension side is as shown in Fig. 2.14 (e).

Step XI : FBD of structure is as shown in Fig. 2.14 (f).

Example 2.7 : *A continuous beam ABCD is fixed at D and continuous over supports B and C and portion AB is overhanged. The beam is loaded as shown in Fig. 2.15 (a). Analyse the beam using slope-deflection deflection method. The support D sinks by 2 mm. Draw SFD and BMD. $E = 2 \times 10^5$ N/mm², $I = 10{,}000$ cm⁴.*

Solution : (1) **Data :** The beam is loaded and supported as shown in Fig. 2.15 (a).

(2) Supports B and C are at same level and support D sinks by 2 mm.

Object : Structural analysis.

Equations : SD equations.

Procedure : Step I : Degree of kinematic indeterminacy = D_{ki} = 2.

Unknown Displacements : θ_B, θ_C, θ_D.

Step II : Fixed-end moments.

$$M^F_{BA} = -10 \times 2 = -20 \text{ kN-m}$$

$$M^F_{BC} = -M^F_{CB} = \frac{WL^2}{12} = \frac{16 \times 6^2}{12} = 48 \text{ kN-m}$$

$$M^F_{CD} = -M^F_{DC} = \frac{WL}{8} = \frac{8 \times 4}{8} = 4 \text{ kN-m}$$

Step III : Slope-deflection equations.

$$EI = 2 \times 10^5 \times 10000 \times 10^4 = 2 \times 10^{13} \text{ N-mm}^2 = 2 \times 10^4 \text{ kN-m}^2$$

Member AB : $M_{BA} = M^F_{BA} = -20$ kN-m ... (i)

Memebr BC :
$$M_{BC} = \frac{4EI}{L}(\theta_B) + \frac{2EI}{L}(\theta_C) + \frac{6EI\Delta}{L^2} + M^F_{BC}$$

$$= \frac{4EI}{6}(\theta_B) + \frac{2EI}{6}(\theta_C) + 48$$

$$= 0.67\,EI\,\theta_B + 0.33\,EI\,\theta_C + 48 \quad \text{... (ii)}$$

$$M_{CB} = \frac{4EI}{L}(\theta_C) + \frac{2EI}{L}(\theta_B) \pm \frac{6EI\Delta}{L^2} - 48$$

$$= \frac{4EI}{6}(\theta_C) + \frac{2EI}{6}(\theta_B) - 48$$

$$= 0.67\,EI\,\theta_C + 0.33\,EI\,\theta_B - 48 \quad \text{... (iii)}$$

Member CD :
$$M_{CD} = \frac{4EI}{L}(\theta_C) + \frac{2EI}{L}(\theta_D) \pm \frac{6EI\Delta}{L^2} + M^F_{CD}$$

$$= \frac{4EI}{4}\left(\theta_C + \frac{2EI}{4}\theta_D\right) + \frac{6 \times 2 \times 10^4 \times 2 \times 10^{-3}}{4^2} + 4$$

$$= EI\,\theta_C + 0.5\,EI\,\theta_D + 15 + 4$$

$$= EI\,\theta_C + 0.5\,EI\,\theta_D + 19 \qquad \ldots \text{(iv)}$$

$$M_{DC} = \frac{4\,EI}{L}(\theta_D) + \frac{2\,EI}{L}(\theta_C) + \frac{6\,EI\Delta}{L^2} + M_{DC}^F$$

$$= \frac{4\,EI}{4}(\theta_D) + \frac{2\,EI}{4}(\theta_C) + \frac{6 \times 2 \times 10^4 \times 2 \times 10^{-3}}{4^2} - 4$$

$$= EI\,\theta_D + 0.5\,EI\,\theta_C + 15 - 4$$

$$= EI\,\theta_D + 0.5\,EI\,\theta_C + 11 \qquad \ldots \text{(v)}$$

Step IV : Moment equilibrium conditions for joint.

At joint B : $\quad M_{BA} + M_{BC} = 0 \qquad \ldots$ (A)
At joint C : $\quad M_{CB} + M_{CD} = 0 \qquad \ldots$ (B)
At joint D : $\quad M_{DC} = 0 \qquad \ldots$ (C)

Step V : Formulation of equilibrium equations in terms of joint displacement.

Substituting equations (i) and (ii) equation (A),

$$-20 + 0.667\,EI\,\theta_B + 0.333\,EI\,\theta_C + 48 = 0$$

$$0.667\,EI\,\theta_B + 0.333\,EI\,\theta_C + 28 = 0 \qquad \ldots \text{(I)}$$

Substituting equations (iii) and (iv) in equation (B),

$$0.667\,EI\,\theta_C + 0.33\,EI\,\theta_B - 48 + EI\,\theta_C + 0.5\,EI\,\theta_D + 19 = 0$$

$$1.667\,EI\,\theta_C + 0.33\,EI\,\theta_B + 0.5\,EI\,\theta_D - 29 = 0 \qquad \ldots \text{(II)}$$

Substituting equation (v) in equation (C),

$$EI\,\theta_D + 0.5\,EI\,\theta_C + 11 = 0 \qquad \ldots \text{(III)}$$

Step VI : Solution of equation for joint displacement.

$$\theta_B = -\frac{61.33}{EI},\quad \theta_C = \frac{38.76}{EI},\quad \theta_D = -\frac{30.38}{EI}$$

Step VII : Member-end moments :

$$M_{BA} = -20 \text{ kN-m}$$

$$M_{BC} = 0.67\,EI\left(-\frac{61.33}{EI}\right) + 0.333\,EI\left(\frac{38.76}{EI}\right) + 48 = 20 \text{ kN-m}$$

$$M_{CB} = 0.67\,EI\left(\frac{38.76}{EI}\right) + 0.33\,EI\left(-\frac{61.33}{EI}\right) - 48 = -42.6 \text{ kN-m}$$

$$M_{CD} = EI\left(\frac{38.76}{EI}\right) + 0.5\,EI\left(-\frac{30.38}{EI}\right) + 19 = 42.6 \text{ kN-m}$$

$$M_{DC} = EI\left(\frac{-30.38}{EI}\right) + 0.5\,EI\left(\frac{38.76}{EI}\right) + 11 = 0$$

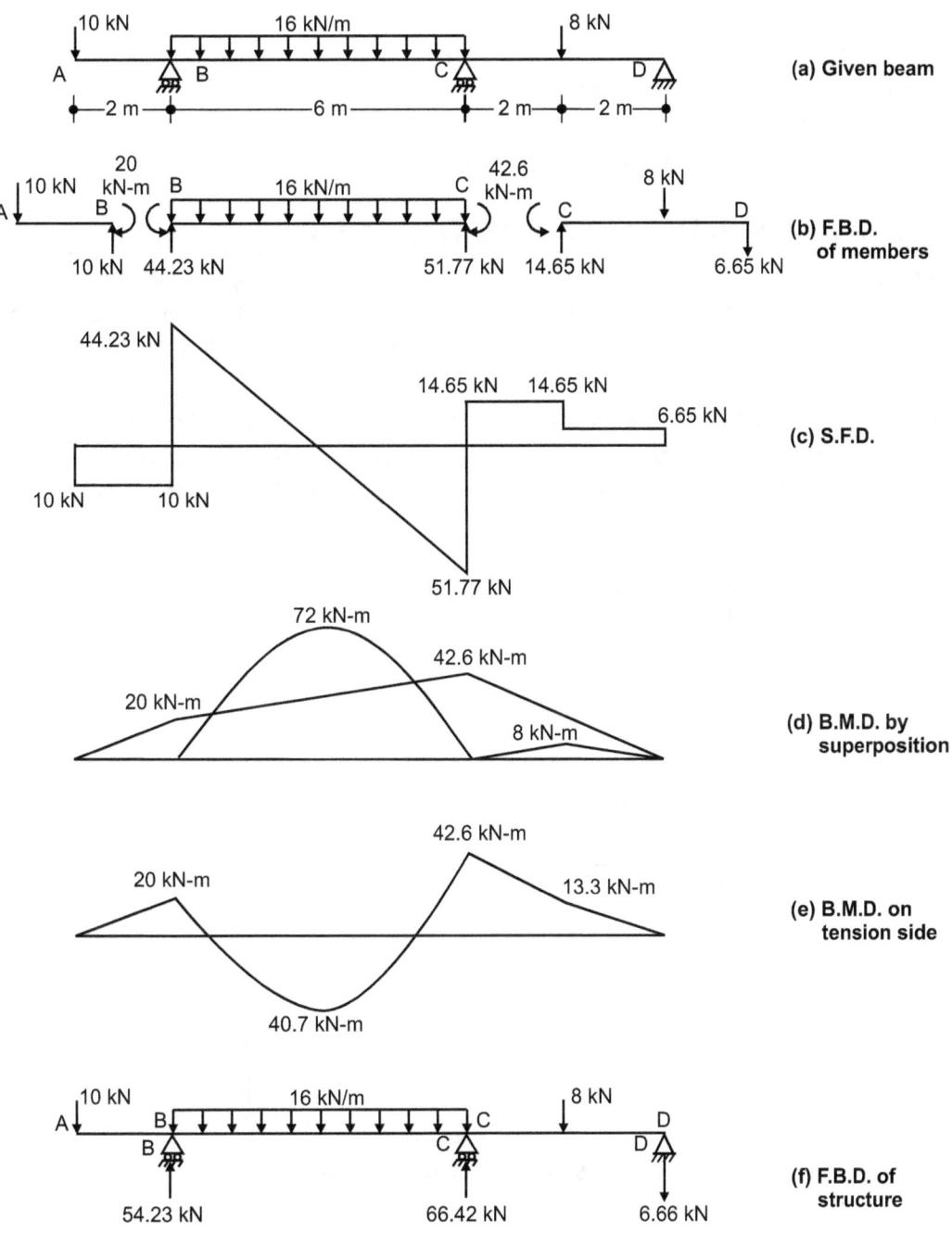

Fig. 2.15 : For Illustrative Example 2.7

Step VIII : FBD of members is as shown in Fig. 2.15 (b).
Step IX : Shear force diagram is as shown in Fig. 2.15 (c).
Step X : Bending moment diagram.
BMD by superposition is as shown in Fig. 2.15 (d).
BMD on tension side is as shown in Fig. 2.15 (e).
Step XI : FBD of structure is as shown in Fig. 2.15 (f).

2.8.3 Beams with Unknown Joint Translations

When a beam consists of non-prismatic member between the supports, additional joint is considered at the point where moment of inertia changes. At this point, both translation and rotation exist. Therefore, shear equilibrium exists and the general procedure of SD method is used.

The shear equilibrium for such a case is illustrated in Fig. 2.16 and developed as follows :

In FBD of the members connected to supports, only positive member-end moments and member-end shears at supports are shown in Fig. 2.16 (b). For FBD of AB and applying $\Sigma M_B = 0$, V_A is obtained as follows :

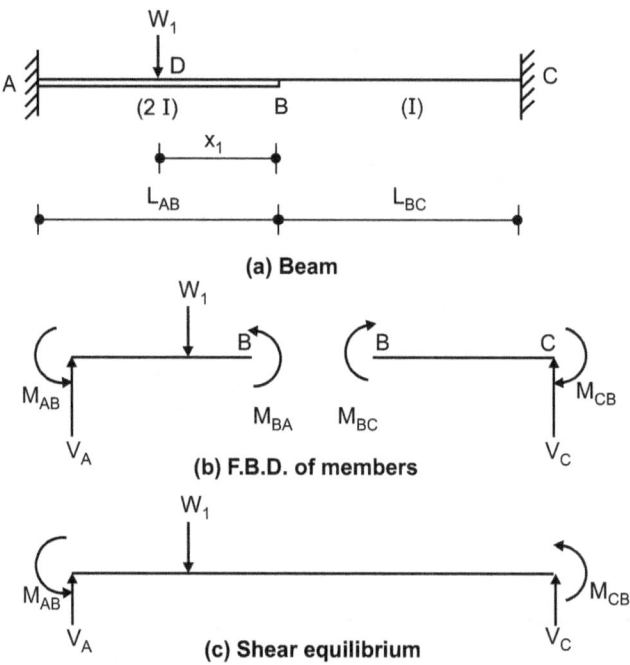

(a) Beam

(b) F.B.D. of members

(c) Shear equilibrium

Fig. 2.16 : Shear equilibrium of beam

$$V_A \times L_{AB} - W_1 \times x_1 - M_{AB} - M_{BA} = 0$$

i.e. $$V_A = \frac{M_{AB} + M_{BA} + W_1 x_1}{L_{AB}}$$

For FBD of BC, $\sum M_B = 0$ will lead to
$$V_C \times L_{BC} - M_{BC} - M_{CB} = 0$$
i.e. $$V_C = \frac{M_{BC} + M_{CB}}{L_{BC}}$$

Considering only forces shown in FBD of structure, shear equilibrium equation is given by,
$$V_A - V_C = W_1$$
i.e. $$\left(\frac{M_{AB} + M_{BA} + W_1 x_1}{L_{AB}}\right) - \left(\frac{M_{BC} + M_{CB}}{L_{BC}}\right) = W_1 \qquad \ldots (2.5)$$

2.8.4 Application of SD Method to Beams with Unknown Joint Translations

Example 2.8 : *Analyse the beam shown in Fig. 2.17 (a) by slope-defection method. Draw SFD, BMD and elastic curve.*

Solution : (1) Data : The beam is supported and loaded as shown in Fig. 2.17 (a).
(2) All supports are at same level.
(3) **Object :** Structural analysis.

Equations : SD equations.

Procedure :

Step I : Degree of kinematic indeterminacy D_{ki} = 2. (Considering point B as node).
Unknown Displacements = θ_B; Δ_B
Known Displacements = $\theta_A = \theta_C = 0$

Step II : Fixed-end moments :
$$M_{AB}^F = -M_{BA}^F = \frac{WL}{8} = \frac{100 \times 2}{8} = 25 \text{ kNm}$$
$$M_{BC}^F = M_{CB}^F = 0$$

Step III : SD equations : (Assuming Δ_B upwards i.e. positive).

Member AB :
$$M_{AB} = \frac{4EI}{L}(\theta_A) + \frac{2EI}{L}(\theta_B) \pm \frac{6EI}{L^2}(\Delta_B) + M_{AB}^F$$
$$= \frac{2(2EI)}{2}(\theta_B) - \frac{6(2EI)}{2^2}(\Delta_B) + 25$$
$$= 2EI(\theta_B) - 3EI(\Delta_B) + 25 \qquad \ldots (i)$$

$$M_{BA} = \frac{4EI}{L}(\theta_B) + \frac{2EI}{L}(\theta_A) + \frac{6EI}{L^2}(\Delta_B) + M_{BA}^F$$
$$= \frac{4(2EI)}{2}(\theta_B) - \frac{6(2EI)}{2^2}(\Delta_B) - 25$$
$$= 4EI(\theta_B) - 3EI(\Delta_B) - 25 \qquad \ldots (ii)$$

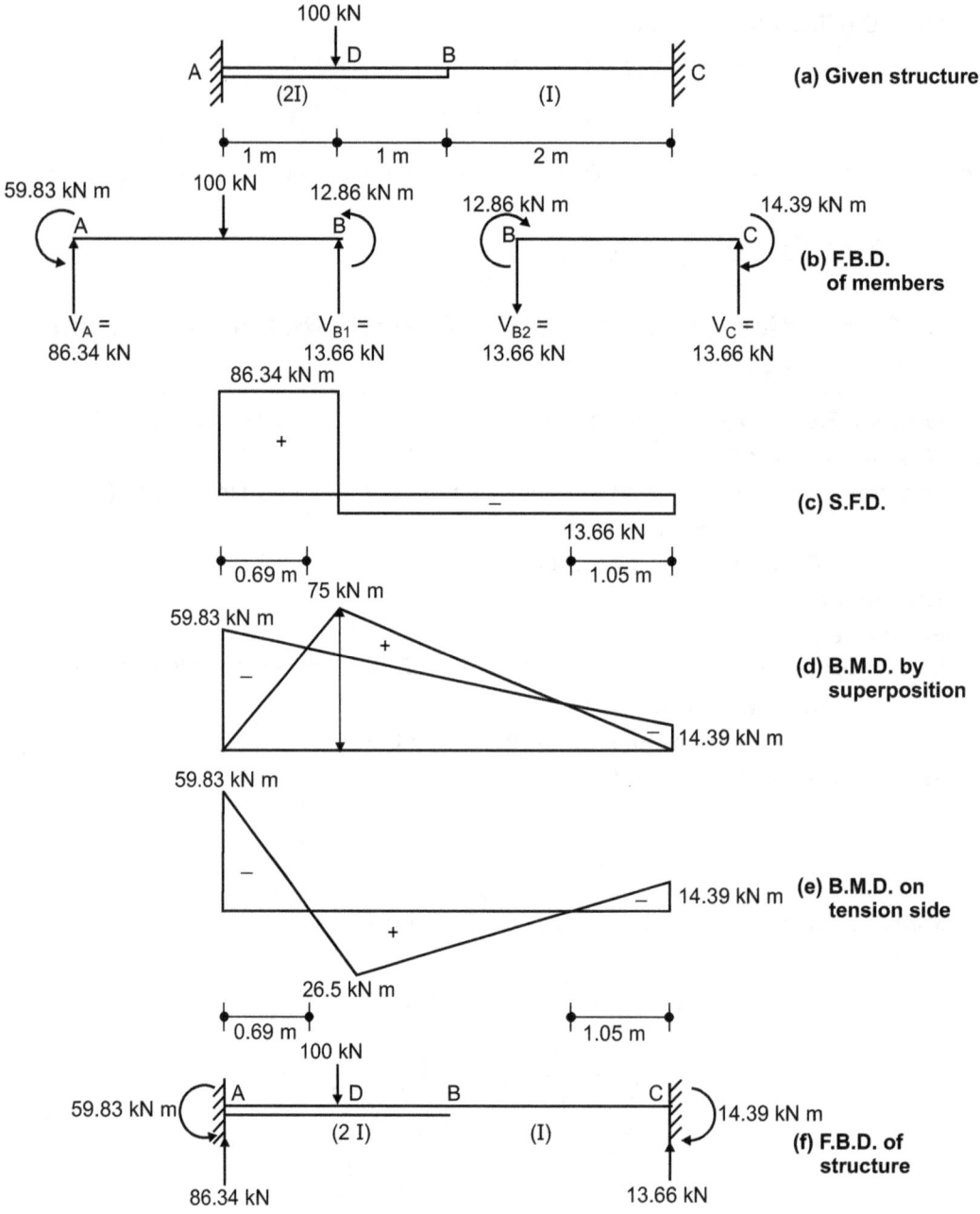

Fig. 2.17 : For Illustrative Example 2.8

Member BC : $\quad M_{BC} = \dfrac{4\,EI}{L}(\theta_B) + \dfrac{2\,EI}{L}(\theta_C) \pm \dfrac{6\,EI}{L^2}(\Delta_B) + M^F_{BC}$

$$= \frac{4EI}{2}(\theta_B) + \frac{6EI}{2^2}(\Delta_B) = 2EI(\theta_B) + 1.5EI(\Delta_B) \quad \ldots \text{(iii)}$$

$$M_{CB} = \frac{4EI}{L}(\theta_C) + \frac{2EI}{L}(\theta_B) \pm \frac{6EI}{L^2}(\Delta_B) + M_{CB}^F$$

$$= \frac{2EI}{2}(\theta_B) + \frac{6EI}{2^2}(\Delta_B) = EI(\theta_B) + 1.5EI(\Delta_B) \quad \ldots \text{(iv)}$$

Step IV : Equilibrium Conditions for Joints :
Moment equilibrium at joint B; $\quad M_{AB} + M_{BC} = 0 \quad \ldots$ (A)
Shear equilibrium for structure, $\quad V_A - V_C - 100 = 0 \quad \ldots$ (B)
where, $\quad V_A = \dfrac{M_{AB} + M_{BA}}{2} + 50 \;\text{ and }\; V_C = \dfrac{M_{BC} + M_{CB}}{2}$

equation (B) becomes,
$$\left(\frac{M_{AB} + M_{BA}}{2} + 50\right) - \left(\frac{M_{BC} + M_{CB}}{2}\right) - 100 = 0$$
$$M_{AB} + M_{BA} + 100 - M_{BC} - M_{CB} - 200 = 0$$
i.e. $\quad M_{AB} + M_{BA} - M_{BC} - M_{CB} = 100 \quad \ldots$ (B)

Step V : Formulation of equilibrium equations in terms of joint displacements.
Substituting equations (ii) and (iii) in equation (A), we get
$$[4EI(\theta_B) - 3EI(\Delta_B) - 25] + [2EI(\theta_B) + 1.5EI(\Delta_B)] = 0$$
$$6EI(\theta_B) - 1.5EI(\Delta_B) - 25] \quad \ldots \text{(A)}$$

Substituting equations (i), (ii), (iii) and (iv) in equation (B), we get
$$[2EI(\theta_B) - 3EI(\Delta_B) + 25] + [4EI(\theta_B) - 3EI(\Delta_B) - 25] -$$
$$[2EI(\theta_B) + 1.5EI(\Delta_B)] - [EI(\theta_B) + 1.5EI(\Delta_B)] = 100$$
$$3EI(\theta_B) - 9EI(\Delta_B) = 100 \quad \ldots \text{(B)}$$

Step VI : Solution of equations for joint displacements : Solving equations (A) and (B), we get,

$$\boxed{\theta_B = \frac{1.515}{EI} \text{ and } \Delta_B = -\frac{10.60}{EI}}$$

Step VII : Member-End Moments : Substituting the values of above displacements in SD equations, member-end moments are obtained as under :

$$M_{AB} = 2EI\left(\frac{1.515}{EI}\right) - 3EI\left(-\frac{10.60}{EI}\right) + 25 = 59.83 \text{ kNm}$$

$$M_{BA} = 4EI\left(\frac{1.515}{EI}\right) - 3EI\left(\frac{-10.60}{EI}\right) - 25 = 12.86 \text{ kNm}$$

$$M_{BC} = 2EI\left(\frac{1.515}{EI}\right) + 1.5EI\left(-\frac{10.60}{EI}\right) = -12.86 \text{ kNm}$$

$$M_{CB} = EI\left(\frac{1.515}{EI}\right) + 1.5EI\left(-\frac{10.60}{EI}\right) = -14.385 \text{ kNm}$$

Step VIII : FBD of members is as shown in Fig. 2.14 (b). Support reactions :
$\sum M_B = 0_{(AB)}$, $59.83 + 12.86 + 100 \times 1 - V_A \times 2 = 0 \Rightarrow V_A = 86.345$ kN (↑)
$\sum F_y = 0$; $V_A + V_C = 100$ $V_C = 13.655$ (↑)

Step IX : Shear force diagram is as shown in Fig. 2.17 (c).
Step X : Bending moment diagram :
BMD by superposition is shown in Fig. 2.17 (d).
BMD on tension side is shown in Fig. 2.17 (e).
Step XI : FBD of structure is as shown in Fig. 2.17 (f).

Example 2.9 : *Analyse the beam shown in Fig. 2.18 (a) by slope-deflection method. Draw SFD and BMD.*

Solution : (1) Data : The beam is supported and loaded as shown in Fig. 2.18 (a).
        (2) All supports are at same level.
Object : Structural analysis.
Equations : SD equations.
Procedure :
Step I : Degree of kinematic indeterminacy = D_{ki} = 3.
Unknown Displacements : $\theta_{BA}, \theta_{BC}, \Delta_B$.
Known Displacements : $\theta_A = \theta_C = 0$.
Step II : Fixed-End Moments :

$$M_{AB}^F = -M_{BA}^F = \frac{wl^2}{12} = \frac{60 \times 1^2}{12} = 5 \text{ kNm}$$

$$M_{BC}^F = -M_{CB}^F = \frac{wl^2}{12} = \frac{60 \times 2^2}{12} = 20 \text{ kNm}$$

Step III : SD equations : (Assuming Δ_B upwards i.e. positive).

Member AB : $M_{AB} = \frac{4EI}{L}(\theta_A) + \frac{2EI}{L}(\theta_{BA}) \pm \frac{6EI}{L^2}(\Delta) + M_{AB}^F$

        $= 2EI(\theta_{BA}) - 6EI(\Delta) + 5$ ... (i)

    $M_{BA} = \frac{4EI}{L}(\theta_{BA}) + \frac{2EI}{L}(\theta_A) \pm \frac{6EI}{L^2}(\Delta) + M_{BA}^F$

        $= 4EI(\theta_{BA}) - 6EI(\Delta) - 5$ ... (ii)

Member BC : $M_{BC} = \frac{4EI}{L}(\theta_{BC}) + \frac{2EI}{L}(\theta_C) \pm \frac{6EI}{L^2}(\Delta) + M_{BC}^F$

        $= \frac{4EI}{2}(\theta_{BC}) + \frac{6EI}{2^2}(\Delta) + 20$

        $= 2EI(\theta_{BC}) + 1.5EI(\Delta) + 20$ ... (iii)

    $M_{CB} = \frac{4EI}{L}(\theta_C) + \frac{2EI}{L}(\theta_{BC}) \pm \frac{6EI}{L^2}(\Delta) + M_{CB}^F$

$$= \frac{2EI}{2}(\theta_{BC}) + \frac{6EI}{2^2}(\Delta) - 20$$
$$= EI(\theta_{BC}) + 1.5\,EI(\Delta) - 20 \qquad \ldots \text{(iv)}$$

Step IV : Equilibrium conditions for joint. Moment equilibrium at joint B,

$$M_{BA} = 0 \qquad \ldots \text{(A)}$$
and $$M_{BC} = 0 \qquad \ldots \text{(B)}$$

Shear equilibrium of structure,
$$V_A - V_C - 60 \times 3 = 0 \qquad \ldots \text{(C)}$$

where,
$$V_A = M_{AB} + M_{BA} + 60 \times 1 \times \frac{1}{2} = M_{AB} + M_{BA} + 30$$
$$V_C = \frac{M_{CB} + M_{BC}}{2} - 60$$

Equation (C) becomes,
$$[M_{AB} + M_{BA} + 30] - \left[\frac{M_{CB} + M_{BC}}{2} - 60\right] - 180 = 0$$
$$M_{AB} + M_{BA} - \left[\frac{M_{CB} + M_{BC}}{2}\right] - 90 = 0 \qquad \ldots \text{(C)}$$

Step V : Formulation of equilibrium equations in terms of displacements :
Substituting equation (ii) in equation (A), we get
$$4\,EI(\theta_{BA}) - 6\,EI(\Delta) - 5 = 0 \qquad \ldots \text{(I)}$$
Substituting equation (iii) in equation (A), we get
$$2\,EI(\theta_{BC}) + 1.5\,EI(\Delta) + 20 = 0 \qquad \ldots \text{(II)}$$
Substituting equations (i), (ii), (iii) and (iv) in equation (C), we get
$$[2\,EI(\theta_{BA}) - 6\,EI(\Delta) + 5 + 4\,EI(\theta_{BA}) - 6\,EI(\Delta) - 5]$$
$$-\frac{1}{2}[2\,EI(\theta_{BC}) + 1.5\,EI(\Delta) + 20 + EI(\theta_{BC}) + 1.5\,EI(\Delta) - 20] - 90 = 0$$
$$6\,EI(\theta_{BA}) - 1.5\,EI(\theta_{BC}) - 13.5\,EI(\Delta) - 90 = 0 \qquad \ldots \text{(III)}$$

Step VI : Solution of equations for joint displacements :
Solving equations (I), (II) and (III), we get

$$\boxed{\theta_{BA} = -\frac{28.75}{EI};\ \theta_{BC} = \frac{5}{EI};\ \Delta = \frac{-20}{EI}}$$

Step VII : Member-End Moments : Substituting the values of above joint displacements in SD equations, member-end moments are obtained as under :

$$M_{AB} = 2\,EI\left(-\frac{28.75}{EI}\right) - 6\,EI\left(-\frac{20}{EI}\right) + 5 = 67.5\ \text{kNm}$$
$$M_{BA} = 4\,EI\left(-\frac{28.75}{EI}\right) - 6\,EI\left(-\frac{20}{EI}\right) - 5 = 0$$

$$M_{BC} = 2\,EI\left(\frac{5}{EI}\right) + 1.5\,EI\left(-\frac{20}{EI}\right) + 20 = 0$$

$$M_{CB} = EI\left(\frac{5}{EI}\right) + 1.5\,EI\left(-\frac{20}{EI}\right) - 20 = -45\text{ kNm}$$

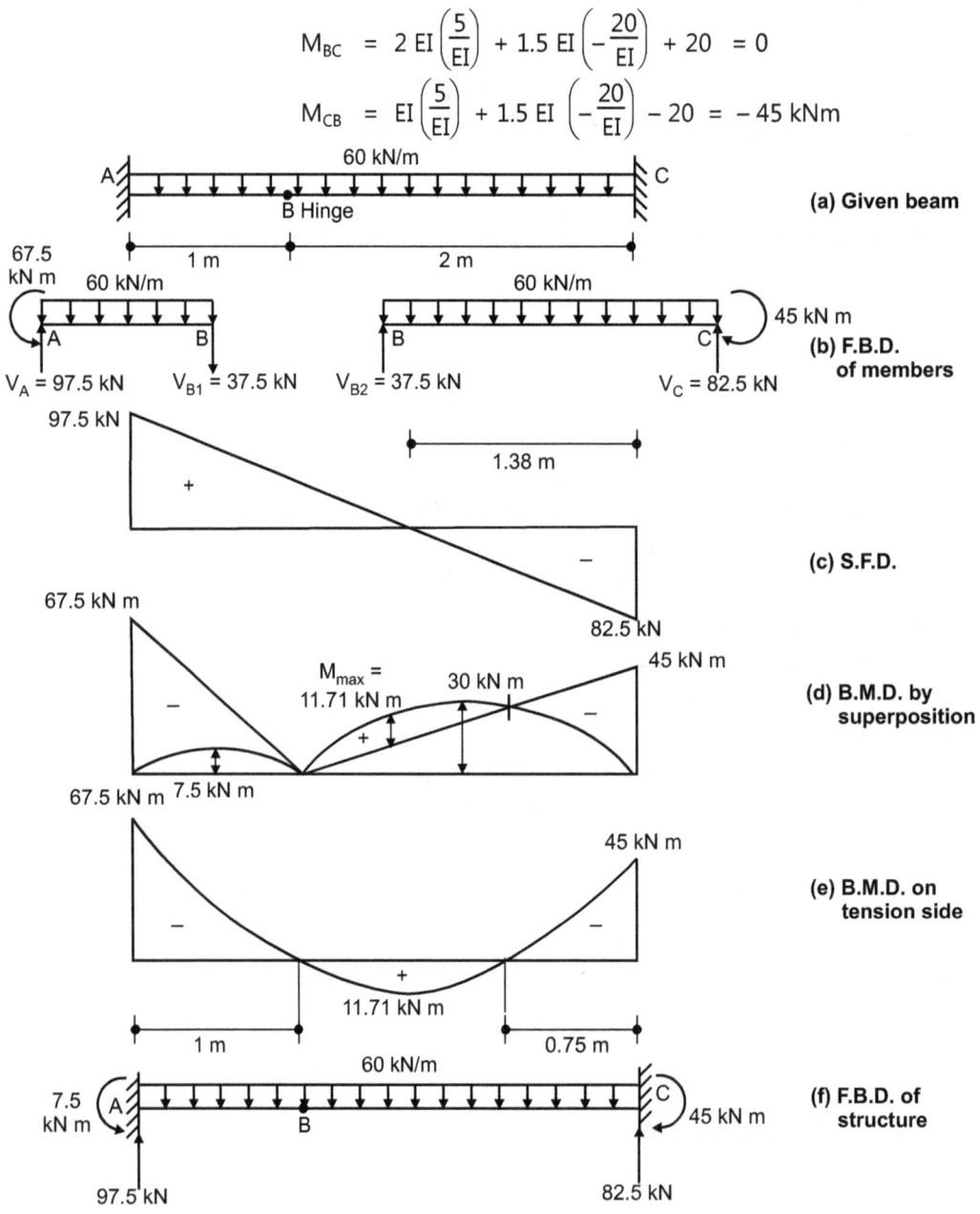

Fig. 2.18 : For Illustrative Example 2.9

Step VIII : FBD of members is as shown in Fig. 2.18 (b). Considering equilibrium of each member and of complete structure, all support reaction components are found out as shown in figure.

Step IX : Shear force diagram is as shown in Fig. 2.18 (c).
Step X : Bending moment diagram is BMD by superposition is shown in Fig. 2.18 (d). BMD on tension side is shown in Fig. 2.18 (e).
Step XI : FBD of structure is as shown in Fig. 2.18 (f).

2.9 SD Method Applied to Rectangular Frames

A structure, consisting of horizontal and vertical members connected by rigid joints is called a *rectangular frame*. Though the members are basically flexural members, the vertical members are called columns and horizontal members are beams. A large multibay, multi-storeyed frames are difficult to analyse by hand calculations of SD method because of large number of unknown displacements. Therefore, small frames like bent, single bay single storey frame, etc. are considered for analysis by SD method. The axial deformation is neglected. Therefore vertical translation is not possible if there is no uneven settlements of supports. The horizontal translation at a joint is called side sway or only sway. Axial forces are present as the shear of one member has effect of axial force on orthogonal member. Following cases of frames are involved in analysis by SD method.

2.9.1 Frames Without Sway or Non-Sway Frames

The basic requirement in such a frame is that all joints should not change the position during deformation. This may be possible because of constraints or configuration and loading condition. Symmetrical frames are non-sway frames. There should be symmetry in all respects i.e. configuration, supports, sectional properties, loads etc. Only joint rotations are unknown in a non- sway frame. A rigid joint implies one rotation. Moment equilibrium of joints formulates the analysis completely by SD method.

2.9.2 Application of SD Method to Non-Sway Frames

Example 2.10 : Analyse the portal frame shown in Fig. 2.19 (a) by slope-deflection method. Draw SFD and BMD.

Solution : (1) **Data :** The frame is supported and loaded as shown in Fig. 2.19 (a).
(2) Frame type : Non-sway frame.
(3) Structural analysis.

Equations : SD equations.

Procedure : Step I : Degree of kinematic indeterminacy = D_{ki} = 2

Unknown Displacements : θ_B; θ_C.

Known Displacements : $\theta_A = \theta_D = \theta_E = 0$. And horizontal sway = $\Delta = 0$.

Step II : Fixed-end moments :

$$M^F_{AB} = -M^F_{BA} = \frac{wl^2}{12} = \frac{40 \times 4^2}{12} = 53.33 \text{ kNm}$$

$$M^F_{BC} = -M^F_{CB} = \left[\frac{50 \times 1 \times 2^2}{3^2} + \frac{50 \times 2 \times 1^2}{3^2}\right] = 33.33 \text{ kNm}$$

$$M^F_{DB} = M^F_{BD} = M^F_{EC} = M^F_{CE} = 0$$

Step III : SD equations :

Member AB :
$$M_{AB} = \frac{4EI}{L}(\theta_A) + \frac{2EI}{L}(\theta_B) \pm \frac{6EI}{L^2}(\Delta) + M^F_{AB}$$
$$= \frac{2(3EI)}{4}(\theta_B) + 53.33 = 1.5\,EI\,(\theta_B) + 53.33 \qquad \ldots (i)$$

$$M_{BA} = \frac{4EI}{L}(\theta_B) + \frac{2EI}{L}(\theta_A) \pm \frac{6EI}{L^2} + M^F_{BA}$$
$$= \frac{4(3EI)}{4}(\theta_B) - 53.33 = 3\,EI\,(\theta_B) - 53.33 \qquad \ldots (ii)$$

Member BC :
$$M_{BC} = \frac{4EI}{L}(\theta_B) + \frac{2EI}{L}(\theta_C) \pm \frac{6EI}{L^2}(\Delta) + M^F_{BC}$$
$$= \frac{4(2EI)}{3}(\theta_B) + \frac{2(2EI)}{3}(\theta_C) + 33.33$$
$$= 2.67\,EI\,(\theta_B) + 1.33\,EI\,(\theta_C) + 33.33 \qquad \ldots (iii)$$

$$M_{CB} = \frac{4EI}{L}(\theta_C) + \frac{2EI}{L}(\theta_B) \pm \frac{6EI}{L^2}(\theta_B) + M^F_{CB}$$
$$= \frac{4(2EI)}{3}(\theta_C) + \frac{2(2EI)}{3}(\theta_B) - 33.33$$
$$= 2.67\,EI\,(\theta_C) + 1.33\,EI\,(\theta_B) - 33.33 \qquad \ldots (iv)$$

Member DB :
$$M_{DB} = \frac{4EI}{L}(\theta_D) + \frac{2EI}{L}(\theta_B) \pm \frac{6EI}{L^2}(\Delta) + M^F_{DB}$$
$$= \frac{2EI}{3}(\theta_B) \qquad \ldots (v)$$

$$M_{BD} = \frac{4EI}{L}(\theta_B) + \frac{2EI}{L}(\theta_D) \pm \frac{6EI}{L^2}(\Delta) + M^F_{BD}$$
$$= \frac{4EI}{3}(\theta_B) \qquad \ldots (vi)$$

Member EC :
$$M_{EC} = \frac{4EI}{L}(\theta_E) + \frac{2EI}{L}(\theta_C) \pm \frac{6EI}{L^2}(\Delta) + M^F_{EC}$$
$$= \frac{2EI}{3}(\theta_C) \qquad \ldots (vii)$$

$$M_{CE} = \frac{4EI}{L}(\theta_C) + \frac{2EI}{L}(\theta_E) \pm \frac{6EI}{L^2}(\Delta) + M^F_{CE}$$
$$= \frac{4EI}{3}(\theta_C) \qquad \ldots (viii)$$

Step IV : Moment equilibrium condition for joint :
At joint B; $M_{BA} + M_{BC} + M_{BD} = 0$ \qquad ... (A)

At joint C; $\quad M_{CB} + M_{CE} = 0$ ... (B)

Step V : Formulation of equilibrium equations in terms of joint displacements :
Substituting equations (ii), (iii) and (vi) in equation (A), we get,

$$[3\ EI\ (\theta_B) - 53.33] + [2.67\ EI\ (\theta_B) + 1.33\ EI\ (\theta_C) + 33.33] + \left[\frac{4\ EI}{3}(\theta_B)\right] = 0$$

$7\ EI\ (\theta_B) + 1.33\ EI\ (\theta_C) - 20 = 0.$ ... (I)

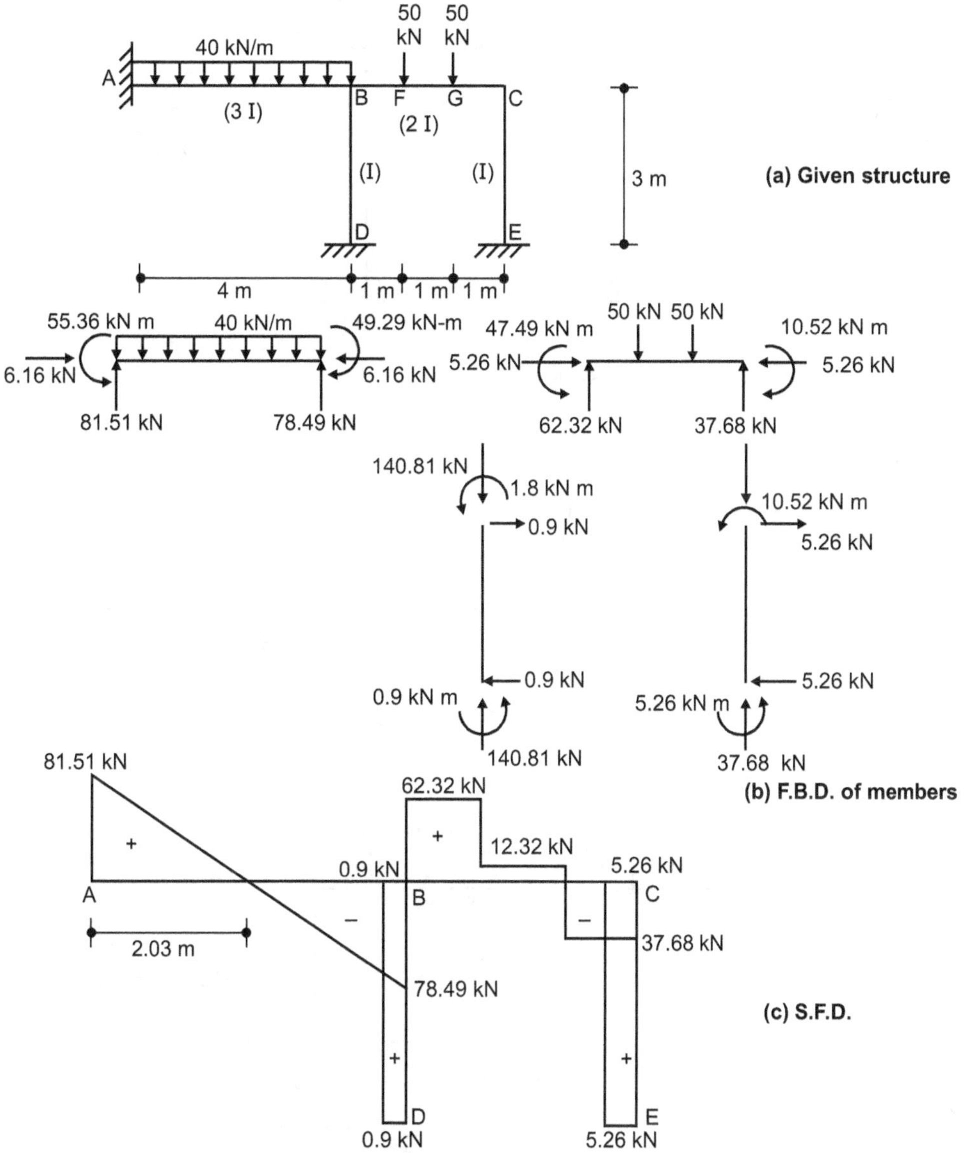

Fig. 2.19 (Contd.)

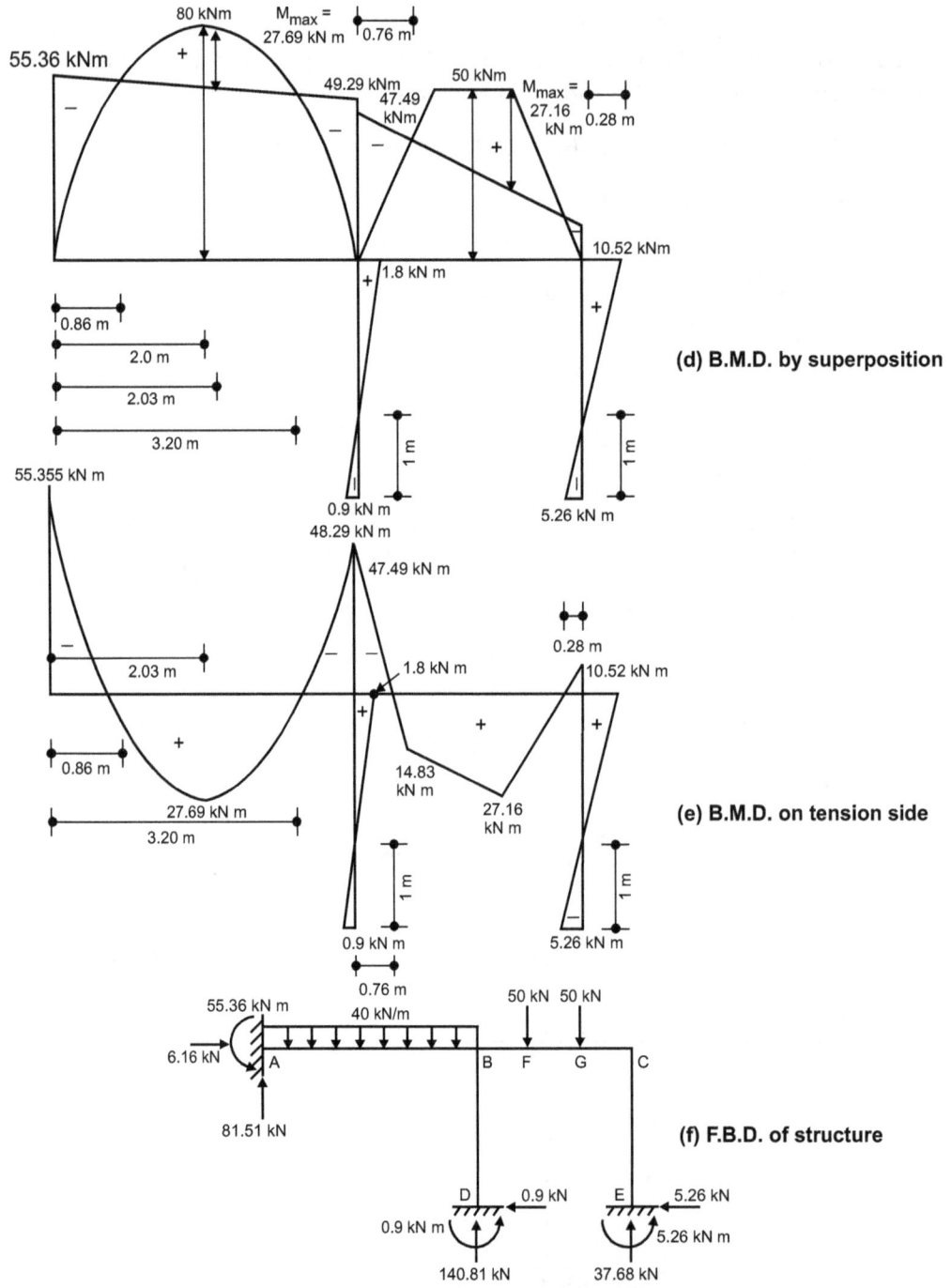

Fig. 2.19 : For Illustrative Example 2.10

Substituting equations (iv) and (viii) in equation (B), we get

$[2.67\ EI\ (\theta_C) + 1.33\ EI\ (\theta_B) - 33.33] + \left[\dfrac{4\ EI}{3}(\theta_C)\right] = 0$

$4\ EI\ (\theta_C) + 1.33\ EI\ (\theta_B) - 33.33 = 0$ ... (II)

Step VI : Solution of equations for joint displacements : Solving equations (I) and (II), we get

$$\boxed{\theta_B = \dfrac{1.35}{EI} \quad \text{and} \quad \theta_C = \dfrac{7.89}{EI}}$$

Step VII : Member-End Moments :

Substituting the values of above joint displacements in SD equations, member-end moments are obtained as under :

$M_{AB} = 1.5\ EI \left(\dfrac{1.35}{EI}\right) + 53.33 = 55.36\ kNm$

$M_{BA} = 3\ EI \left(\dfrac{1.35}{EI}\right) - 53.33 = -49.29\ kNm$

$M_{BC} = 2.67\ EI \left(\dfrac{1.35}{EI}\right) + 1.33\ EI \left(\dfrac{7.89}{EI}\right) + 33.33 = 47.49\ kNm$

$M_{CB} = 2.67\ EI \left(\dfrac{7.89}{EI}\right) + 1.33\ EI \left(\dfrac{1.35}{EI}\right) - 33.33 = -10.52\ kNm$

$M_{DB} = \dfrac{2\ EI}{3} \left(\dfrac{1.35}{EI}\right) = 0.9\ kNm$

$M_{BD} = \dfrac{4\ EI}{3} \left(\dfrac{1.35}{EI}\right) = 1.8\ kNm$

$M_{EC} = \dfrac{2\ EI}{3} \left(\dfrac{7.89}{EI}\right) = 5.26\ kNm$

$M_{CE} = \dfrac{4\ EI}{3} \left(\dfrac{7.89}{EI}\right) = 10.52\ kNm$

Step VIII : FBD of members is as shown in Fig. 2.19 (b). Considering equilibrium of each member and of complete structure, all reaction components are found out as shown in figure.

Step IX : Axial and shear force diagram is as shown in Fig. 2.19 (c).

Step X : Bending moment diagram.

BMD by superposition is shown in Fig. 2.19 (d). BMD by tension side is shown in Fig. 2.19 (e).

Step XI : FBD of structure is as shown in Fig. 2.19 (f).

Example 2.11 : *Analyse the frame as shown in Fig. 2.20 (a) by slope-deflection method.*

Solution : (1) Data : The beam is loaded and supported as shown in Fig. 2.20 (a).

(2) Frame type : Non-sway frame.

Object : Structural analysis.

Equations : SD equations.

Procedure : Step I : Degree of kinematic indeterminacy = D_{ki} = 2.

Unknown Displacements : θ_B, θ_C.

Known Displacements : $\theta_A = \theta_D = 0$ and horizontal sway = $\Delta = 0$.

Step II : Fixed-End Moments :

$$M_{AB}^F = -M_{BA}^F = 0$$

$$M_{BC}^F = -M_{CB}^F = \frac{WL}{8} = \frac{60 \times 4}{8} = 30 \text{ kN-m}$$

$$M_{CD}^F = -M_{CD}^F = 0$$

Step III : Slope-deflection equations :

Member AB :
$$M_{AB} = \frac{4EI}{L}(\theta_A) + \frac{2EI}{L}(\theta_B) \pm \frac{6EI\Delta}{L^2} + M_{AB}^F$$

$$= \frac{2E\left(\frac{4}{3}I\right)}{4} = 0.667 \, EI \, \theta_B \quad \ldots \text{(i)}$$

$$M_{BA} = \frac{4EI}{L}(\theta_B) + \frac{2EI}{L}(\theta_A) \pm \frac{6EI\Delta}{L^2} + M_{BA}^F$$

$$= \frac{4EI\left(\frac{4}{3}I\right)}{4} \theta_B = 1.33 \, EI \, \theta_B \quad \ldots \text{(ii)}$$

Member BC :
$$M_{BC} = \frac{4EI}{L}(\theta_B) + \frac{2EI}{L}(\theta_C) \pm \frac{6EI\Delta}{L^2} + M_{BC}^F$$

$$= \frac{4EI}{4}(\theta_B) + \frac{2EI}{4}(\theta_C) + 30$$

$$= EI \, \theta_B + 0.5 \, EI \, \theta_C + 30 \quad \ldots \text{(iii)}$$

$$M_{CB} = \frac{4EI}{L}(\theta_C) + \frac{2EI}{L}(\theta_B) \pm \frac{6EI\Delta}{L^2} + M_{CB}^F$$

$$= \frac{4EI}{4}(\theta_C) + \frac{2EI}{4}(\theta_B) - 30$$

$$= EI \, \theta_C + 0.5 \, EI \, \theta_B - 30 \quad \ldots \text{(iv)}$$

Member CD :

$$M_{CD} = \frac{4EI}{L}(\theta_C) + \frac{2EI}{L}(\theta_D) \pm \frac{6EI\Delta}{L^2} + M_{CD}^F$$

$$= \frac{4E\left(\frac{4}{3}I\right)}{4}\theta_C = 1.33\, EI\, \theta_C \qquad \ldots (v)$$

$$M_{DC} = \frac{4EI}{L}(\theta_D) + \frac{2EI}{L}(\theta_C) \pm \frac{6EI\Delta}{L^2} + M_{DC}^F$$

$$= \frac{2E\left(\frac{4}{3}I\right)}{4}\theta_C = 0.666\, EI\, \theta_C \qquad \ldots (vi)$$

Step IV : Moment equilibrium conditions for joint.

At joint B : $\quad M_{BA} + M_{BC} = 0 \qquad \ldots$ (A)

At joint C : $\quad M_{CB} + M_{CD} = 0 \qquad \ldots$ (B)

Step V : Formulation of equilibrium equations in terms of joint displacements. Substituting equations (ii) and (iii) in equation (A),

$1.33\, EI\, \theta_B + EI\, \theta_B + 0.5\, EI\, \theta_C + 30 = 0$

$2.33\, EI\, \theta_B + 0.5\, EI\, \theta_C + 30 = 0 \qquad \ldots$ (I)

Substituting equations (iv) and (v) in equation (B),

$EI\, \theta_C + 0.5\, EI\, \theta_B - 30 + 1.33\, EI\, \theta_C = 0$

$2.33\, EI\, \theta_C + 0.5\, EI\, \theta_B - 30 = 0 \qquad \ldots$ (II)

Step VI : Solution of equations for joint displacements : Solving equations (I) and (II), we get

$$\theta_B = \frac{-16.39}{EI}, \quad \theta_C = \frac{16.39}{EI}$$

Step VII : Member-end moments :

$$M_{AB} = 0.667\, EI\left(\frac{-16.39}{EI}\right) = -10.9 \text{ kN-m}$$

$$M_{BA} = 1.33\, EI\left(\frac{-16.39}{EI}\right) = -21.79 \text{ kN-m}$$

$$M_{BC} = EI\left(\frac{-16.39}{EI}\right) + 0.5\, EI\left(\frac{16.39}{EI}\right) + 30 = 21.79 \text{ kN-m}$$

$$M_{CB} = EI\left(\frac{16.39}{EI}\right) + 0.5\, EI\left(\frac{-16.39}{EI}\right) - 30 = -21.79 \text{ kN-m}$$

$$M_{CD} = 1.33\, EI\left(\frac{16.39}{EI}\right) = 21.79 \text{ kN-m}$$

$$M_{DC} = 0.666 \, EI \left(\frac{-16.39}{EI} \right) = 10.9 \text{ kN-m}$$

Step VIII : FBD of members is as shown in Fig. 2.20 (b).

Step IX : Shear force diagram is as shown in Fig. 2.20 (c).

Step X : Bending moment diagram.

BMD by superposition is as shown in Fig. 2.20 (d).

BMD on tension side is as shown in Fig. 2.20 (e).

Step XI : FBD of structure is as shown in Fig. 2.20 (f).

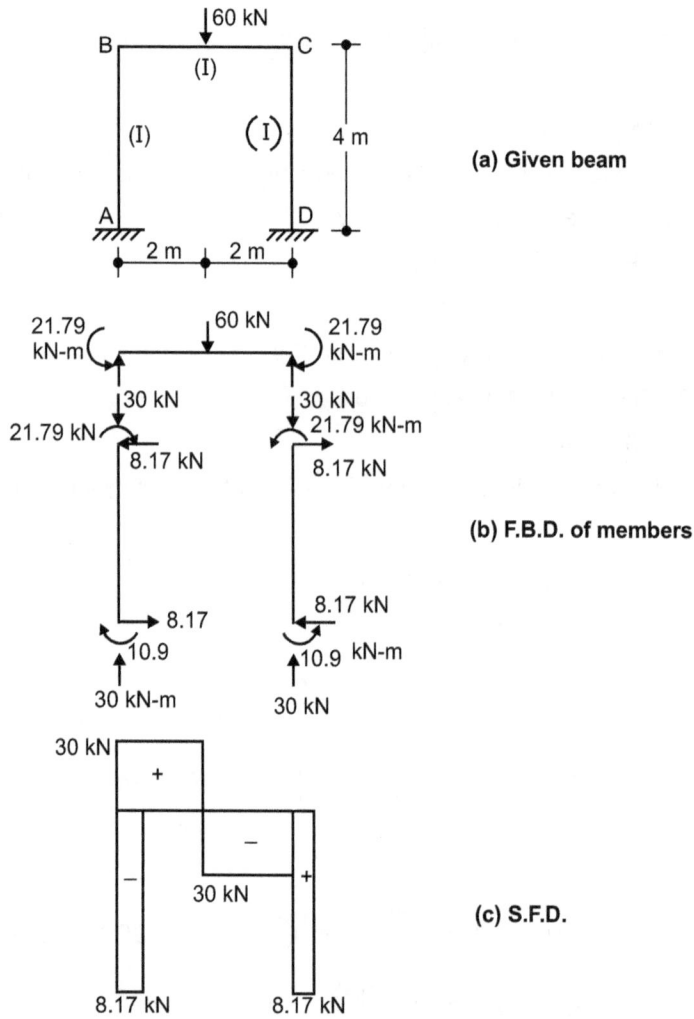

(a) Given beam

(b) F.B.D. of members

(c) S.F.D.

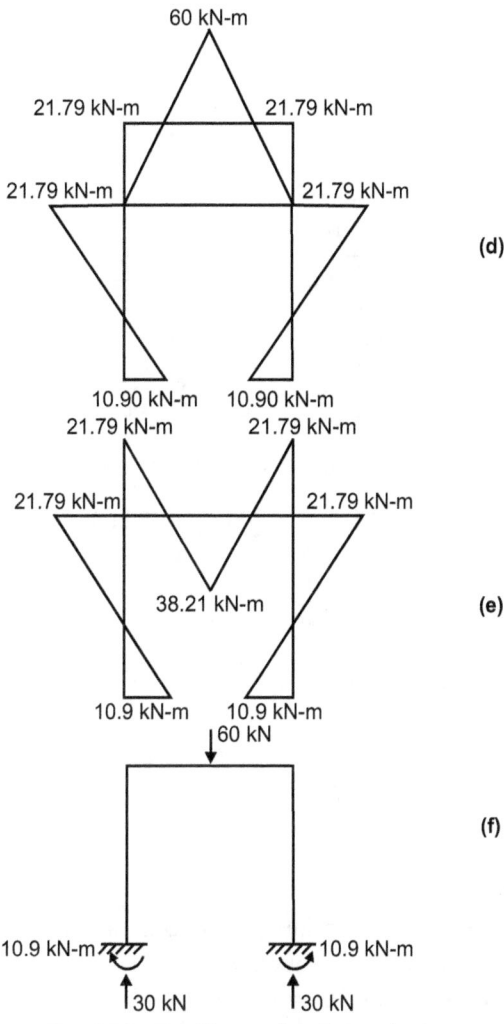

Fig. 2.20 : For Illustrative Example 2.11

Example 2.12 : Using the slope-deflection method, analyse the rigid jointed plane frame supported and loaded as shown in Fig. 2.21 (a). Assume uniform flexural rigidity EI for all the members.

Solution :

(1) **Data :** The frame is loaded and supported as shown in Fig. 2.21 (a).
Object : Structural analysis.
Equation : SD equations.
Procedure : Step I : Degree of kinematic indeterminacy = D_{ki} = 1.
Unknown Displacement : θ_B.
Known Displacements : $\theta_A = \theta_C = 0$ and horizontal sway = $\Delta = 0$.

Step II : Fixed-End Moments.

$$M_{AB}^F = M_{BA}^F = 0$$

$$M_{BC}^F = -M_{CB}^F = \frac{10 \times 5^2}{12} = 20.83 \text{ kN-m}$$

$$M_{BD}^F = -25 \times 2 = -50 \text{ kN-m}$$

Step III : Slope-deflection equations.

Member AB :

$$M_{AB} = \frac{4EI}{L}(\theta_A) + \frac{2EI}{L}(\theta_B) \pm \frac{6EI\Delta}{L^2} + M_{AB}^F = \frac{2EI(\theta_B)}{5}$$

$$= 0.4 EI \,\theta_B \quad \ldots \text{(i)}$$

$$M_{BA} = \frac{4EI}{L}(\theta_B) + \frac{2EI}{L}(\theta_A) \pm \frac{6EI\Delta}{L^2} + M_{BA}^F$$

$$= \frac{4EI}{5}\theta_B = 0.8 EI \,\theta_B \quad \ldots \text{(ii)}$$

Memebr BC :

$$M_{BC} = \frac{4EI}{L}(\theta_B) + \frac{2EI}{L}(\theta_C) \pm \frac{6EI\Delta}{L^2} + M_{BC}^F$$

$$= \frac{4EI}{5}(\theta_B) + 20.83 = 0.8 EI \,\theta_B + 20.83 \quad \ldots \text{(iii)}$$

$$M_{CB} = \frac{4EI}{L}(\theta_C) + \frac{2EI}{L}(\theta_B) \pm \frac{6EI\Delta}{L^2} + M_{CB}^F$$

$$= \frac{2EI}{5}(\theta_B) - 20.83 = 0.4 EI \,\theta_B - 20.83 \quad \ldots \text{(iv)}$$

Member BD : $\quad M_{BD} = -M_{BD}^F = -50 \quad \ldots \text{(v)}$

Step IV : Moment equilibrium condition for joint.

At joint B : $M_{BA} + M_{BC} + M_{BD} = 0 \quad \ldots \text{(A)}$

Step V : Formulation of equilibrium equations in terms of joint displacement. Substituting equations (ii), (iii) and (v) in equation (A),

$$0.8 EI \,\theta_B + 0.8 EI \,\theta_B + 20.83 - 50 = 0$$

$$1.6 EI \,\theta_B - 29.17 = 0 \quad \ldots \text{(I)}$$

Step VI : Solution of equations for joint displacement.

$$\theta_B = \frac{18.23}{EI}$$

Step VII : Member-End Moments :

$$M_{AB} = 0.4 EI \left(\frac{18.23}{EI}\right) = 7.29 \text{ kN-m}$$

$$M_{BA} = 0.8 EI \left(\frac{18.23}{EI}\right) = 14.58 \text{ kN-m}$$

$$M_{BC} = 0.8 EI \left(\frac{18.23}{EI}\right) + 20.83 = 35.42 \text{ kN-m}$$

$$M_{CB} = 0.4\,EI\left(\frac{18.23}{EI}\right) - 20.83 = -13.54 \text{ kN-m}$$
$$M_{BD} = -50 \text{ kN-m}$$

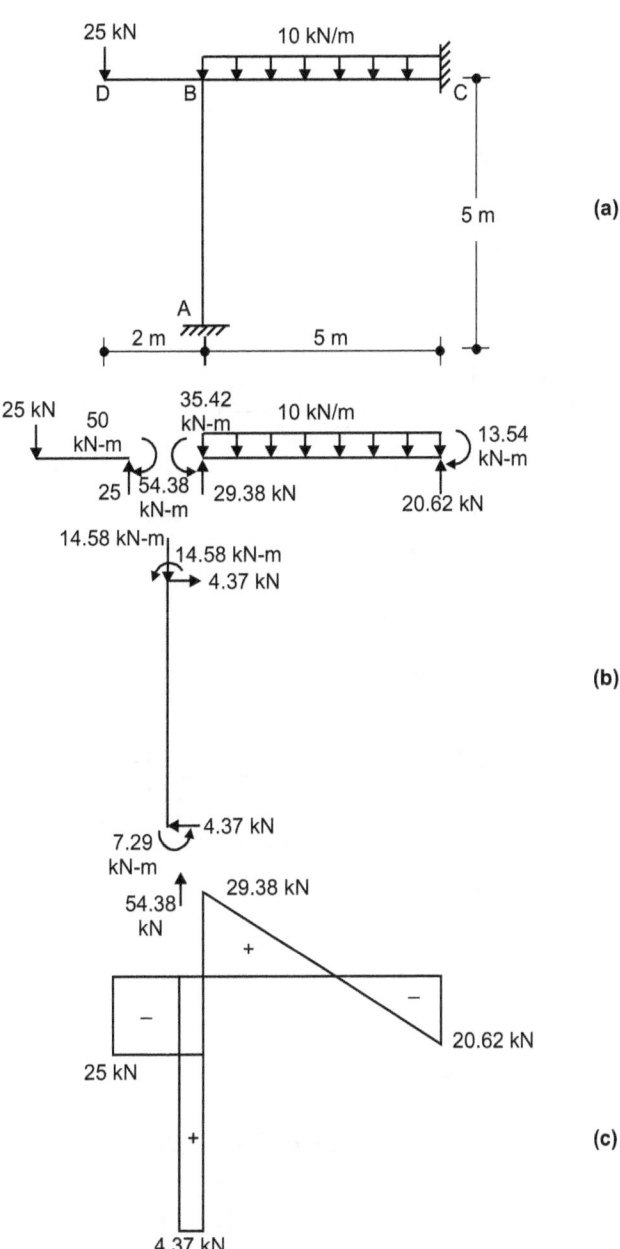

TOS – II (TE CIVIL SEM. VI NMU)   SLOPE-DEFLECTION METHOD

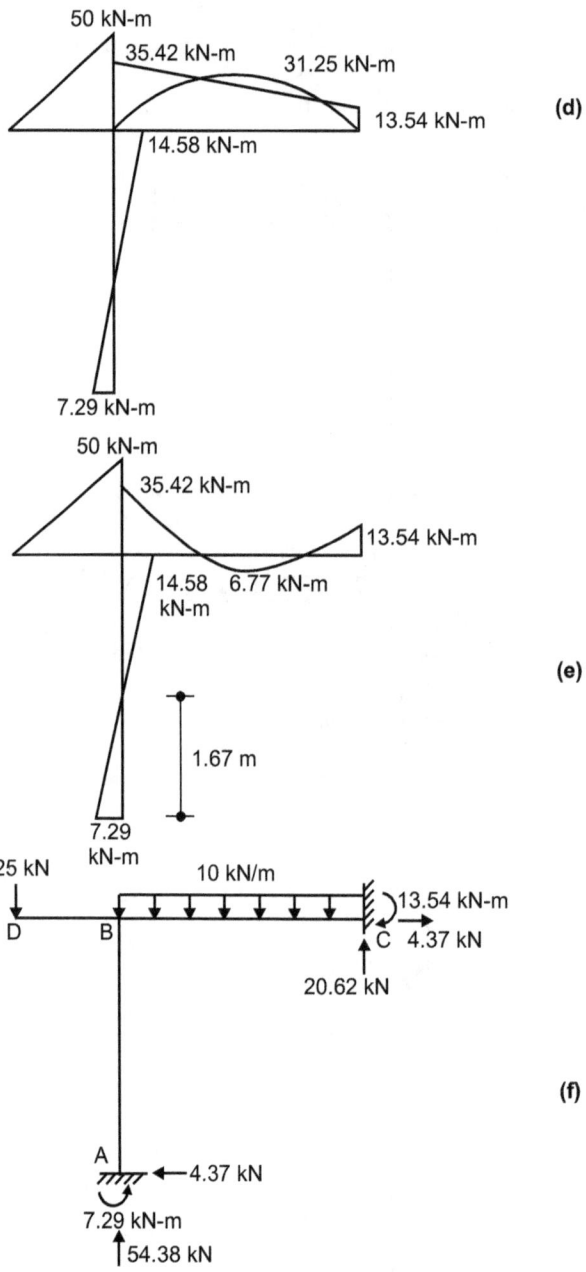

Fig. 2.21 : For Illustrative Example 2.12

Step VIII : FBD of member is as shown in Fig. 2.21 (a).
Step IX : Shear force diagram is as shown in Fig. 2.21 (c).
Step X : Bending moment diagram.

BMD by superposition is as shown in Fig. 2.21 (d)
BMD on tension side is as shown in Fig. 2.21 (e).
Step XI : FBD of structure is as shown in Fig. 2.21 (f).

Example 2.13 : *Find the end moments of the frame shown in Fig. 2.22 (a) by slope deflection method. EI = constant.*

Solution : (1) **Data :** The frame is supported and loaded as shown in Fig. 2.22.
(2) **Frame type :** Non-sway.
Object : Structural analysis.
Equations : S.D. equations.
Procedure : Step I : Degree of kinematic indeterminacy

$$D_{ki} = 2$$
$$\text{Unknown Displacement} = \theta_B, \theta_C$$
$$\text{Known Displacement} = \theta_A = \theta_D = 0$$

Step II : Fixed End Moments :

$$\overline{M}_{AB} = -\overline{M}_{BA} = -\frac{wl^2}{12} = -\frac{25 \times 4^2}{12} = -33.33 \text{ kN-m}$$

$$\overline{M}_{BC} = -\overline{M}_{CB} = -\frac{wl}{8} = -\frac{45 \times 4}{8} = -22.5 \text{ kN-m}$$

$$\overline{M}_{BD} = -\overline{M}_{DB} = -\frac{wl}{8} = -\frac{25 \times 4}{8} = -12.5 \text{ kN-m}$$

Step III : Slope Deflection Equations :

$$M_{AB} = -33.33 + \frac{2EI}{l}(2\theta_a + \theta_b)$$

$$M_{AB} = -33.33 + \frac{2EI}{4}(\theta_b)$$

$$M_{BA} = 33.33 + \frac{2EI}{4}(2\theta_b)$$

Span BC :
$$M_{BC} = -22.5 + \frac{2EI}{4}(2\theta_b + \theta_c)$$

$$M_{CB} = 22.5 + \frac{2EI}{4}(2\theta_c + \theta_b)$$

Span BD :
$$M_{BD} = -12.5 + \frac{2EI}{4}(2\theta_b)$$

$$M_{DB} = 12.5 + \frac{2EI}{4}(\theta_b)$$

Step IV : Equilibrium Equations :
$$M_{BA} + M_{BC} + M_{BD} = 0$$

Step V : Formulation of equilibrium equations in terms of joint displacements.
$$33.33 + EI\theta_b - 22.5 + EI\theta_b + 0.5\,EI\theta_c - 12.5 + EI\theta_b = 0$$

$3 EI\theta_b + 0.5 EI\theta_c = 1.67$ ...(1)

$M_{CB} = 0$ as simple supported end.

$22.5 + EI\theta_c + 0.5 EI\theta_b = 0$ ...(2)

Step VI : Solution of Equations for Joint Displacements :

$EI\theta_b = 4.7$

$EI\theta_c = -24.85$

Step VII : Member End Moments :

$M_{AB} = -30.98$ kN-m

$M_{BA} = 38.03$ kN-m

$M_{BC} = -30.225$ kN-m

$M_{BD} = -7.8$ kN-m

$M_{DB} = 14.6$ kN-m

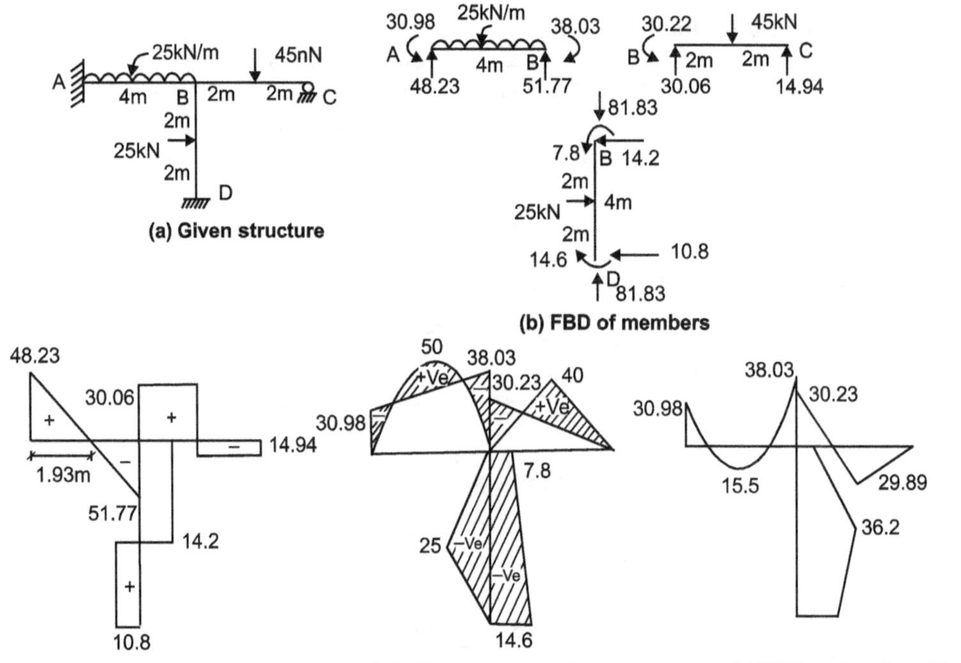

(a) Given structure

(b) FBD of members

(C) S.F.D.

(d) BMD by superposition

(e) BMD on tension side

Fig. 2.22

2.9.3 Sway Frames

The sway i.e. horizontal translation must be considered in unsymmetrical rectangular frames. The sway is same at the horizontal level joints as the axial deformation is neglected. As the sway is horizontal translation, it has effects only on columns i.e. vertical members in SD formulation. There is no effect of sway in horizontal member i.e. beam. The sway, Δ, at the joints at same level is unknown displacement, additional to joint rotations in SD method. The quantity $\frac{6EI}{L^2}(\Delta)$ in SD equation is called the sway moment. The SD equations for vertical members must contain the quantity $\frac{6EI}{L^2}(\Delta)$ in terms of unknown Δ, EI and L of the member. The positive quantity of sway moment means sway to the right. As no effect of sway in horizontal members, the term $\frac{6EI}{L^2}(\Delta)$ is absent in SD equation of the horizontal members. Shear equilibrium is must in sway frame in addition to the joint equilibrium, to formulate the SD method.

2.9.4 Application of SD Method to Frames With Side Sway

Example 2.14 : *Analyse the portal frame shown in Fig. 2.23 (a) by slope-deflection method. Draw SFD, BMD and elastic curve.*

Solution : (1) **Data :** The frame is supported and loaded as shown in Fig. 2.23 (a).
(2) Frame type : Sway frame.
Object : Structural analysis.
Equations : SD equations.
Procedure :
Step I : Degree of kinematic indeterminacy = D_{ki} = 3.
Unknown Displacements : θ_B, θ_C and horizontal sway = Δ
Known Displacements : $\theta_A = \theta_D = 0$.
Step II : Fixed-End Moments :
$$M^F_{AB} = M^F_{BA} = M^F_{BC} = M^F_{CB} = M^F_{CD} = M^F_{DC} = 0$$
Step III : SD equations : (Assuming horizontal sway = Δ towards right)

Member AB :
$$M_{AB} = \frac{4EI}{L}(\theta_A) + \frac{2EI}{L}(\theta_B) + \frac{6EI}{L^2}(\Delta) + M^F_{AB}$$
$$= \frac{2EI}{4}(\theta_B) + \frac{6EI}{4^2}(\Delta) = 0.5\,EI\,(\theta_B) + 0.375\,EI\,(\Delta) \quad \text{... (i)}$$

$$M_{BA} = \frac{4EI}{L}(\theta_B) + \frac{2EI}{L}(\theta_A) + \frac{6EI}{L^2}(\Delta) + M^F_{BA}$$
$$= \frac{4EI}{4}(\theta_B) + \frac{6EI}{4^2}(\Delta) = EI\,(\theta_B) + 0.375\,EI\,(\Delta) \quad \text{... (ii)}$$

Member BC :
$$M_{BC} = \frac{4EI}{L}(\theta_B) + \frac{2EI}{L}(\theta_C) \pm \frac{6EI}{L^2}(\Delta) + M^F_{BC}$$
$$= \frac{4(2EI)}{4}(\theta_B) + \frac{2(2EI)}{4}(\theta_C) = 2\,EI\,(\theta_B) + EI\,(\theta_C) \quad \text{... (iii)}$$

$$M_{CB} = \frac{4EI}{L}(\theta_C) + \frac{2EI}{L}(\theta_B) \pm \frac{6EI}{L^2}(\Delta) + M^F_{CB}$$

$$= \frac{4(2EI)}{4}(\theta_C) + \frac{2(2EI)}{4}(\theta_B) = 2EI(\theta_C) + EI(\theta_B) \quad ...(iv)$$

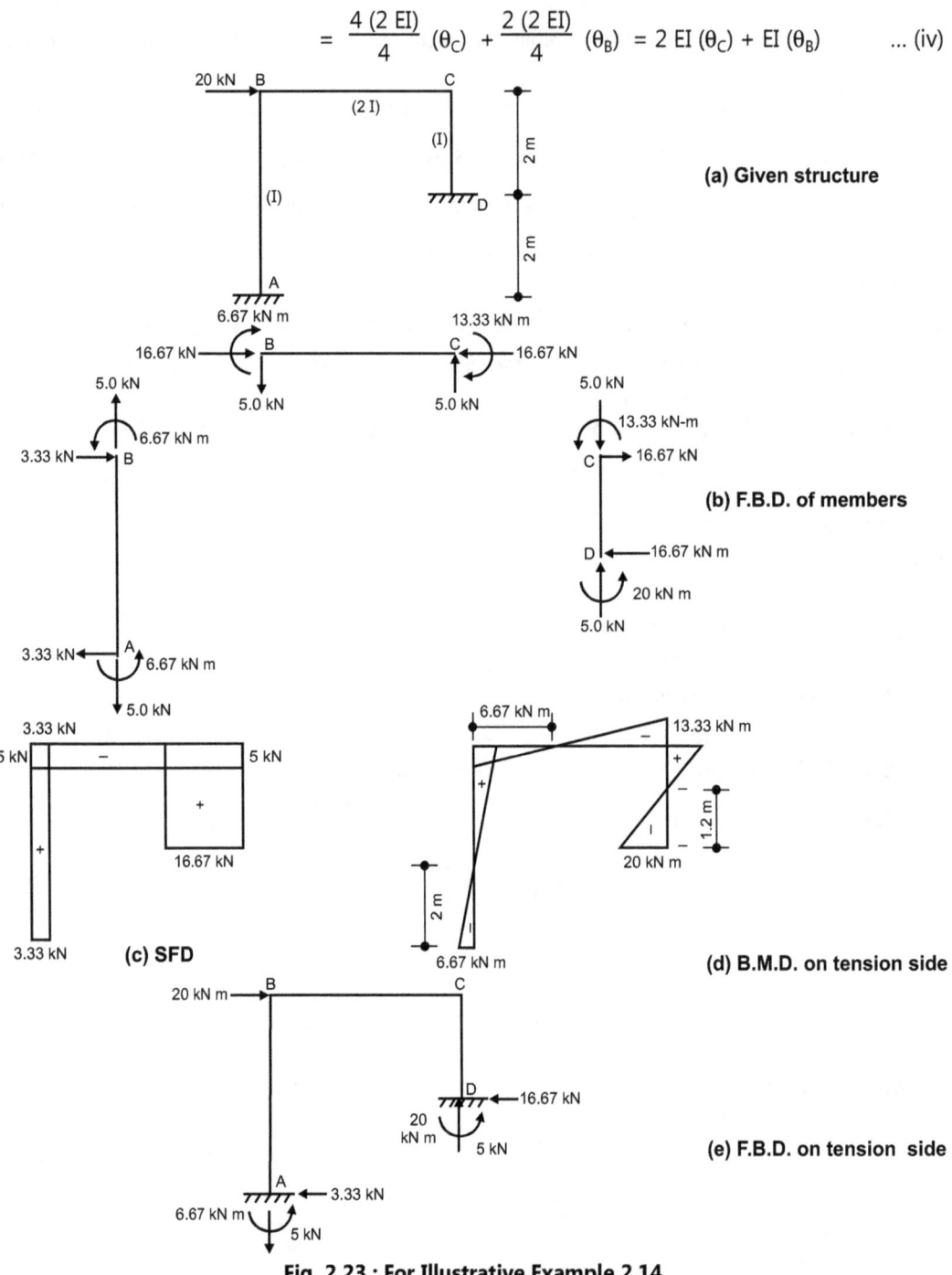

Fig. 2.23 : For Illustrative Example 2.14

SLOPE-DEFLECTION METHOD

Member CD :

$$M_{CD} = \frac{4EI}{L}(\theta_C) + \frac{2EI}{L}(\theta_D) + \frac{6EI}{L^2}(\Delta) + M^F_{CD}$$

$$= \frac{4EI}{2}(\theta_C) + \frac{6EI}{2^2}(\Delta) = 2EI(\theta_C) + 1.5EI(\Delta) \quad \text{... (v)}$$

$$M_{DC} = \frac{4EI}{L}(\theta_D) + \frac{2EI}{L}(\theta_C) + \frac{6EI}{L^2}(\Delta) + M^F_{DC}$$

$$= \frac{2EI}{2}(\theta_C) + \frac{6EI}{2^2}(\Delta) = EI(\theta_C) + 1.5EI(\Delta) \quad \text{... (vi)}$$

Step IV : Equilibrium conditions for joints :
Moment equilibrium of joint B; $M_{BA} + M_{BC} = 0$ ... (A)
Moment equilibrium of joint C; $M_{CB} + M_{CD} = 0$ ... (B)
Horizontal shear equilibrium of structure; $H_A + H_D - 20 = 0$

where, $H_A = \dfrac{M_{AB} + M_{BA}}{4}$ and $H_D = \dfrac{M_{DC} + M_{CD}}{2}$

$\therefore \quad \dfrac{M_{AB} + M_{BA}}{4} + \dfrac{M_{DC} + M_{CD}}{2} = 20$

$M_{AB} + M_{BA} + 2(M_{DC} + M_{CD}) = 80$ ... (C)

Step V : Formulation of equilibrium equations in terms of joint displacements :
Substituting equations (ii) and (iii) in equation (A), we get

$[EI(\theta_B) + 0.375 + EI(\Delta)][2EI(\theta_B) + EI(\theta_C)] = 0$

$3EI(\theta_B) + EI(\theta_C) + 0.375 EI(\Delta) = 0$ ... (I)

Substituting equations (iv) and (v) in equation (B), we get

$[2EI(\theta_C) + EI(\theta_B)] + [2EI(\theta_C) + 1.5EI(\Delta)] = 0$

$4EI(\theta_C) + EI(\theta_B) + 1.5EI(\Delta) = 0$ ... (II)

Substituting equations (i), (ii), (v) and (vi) in equation (C), we get

$[0.4 EI(\theta_B) + 0.375 EI(\Delta)] + [EI(\theta_B) + 0.375 EI(\Delta)]$

$+ 2[2EI(\theta_C) + 1.5EI(\Delta) + EI(\theta_C) + 1.5EI(\Delta)] = 80$

$1.5 EI(\theta_B) + 6 EI(\theta_C) + 6.75 EI(\Delta) = 80$ ... (III)

Step VI : Solution of equations for joint displacements :
Solving equations (I), (II) and (III), we get

$$\boxed{\theta_B = 0; \quad \theta_C = \frac{-6.67}{EI}; \quad \Delta = \frac{17.77}{EI}}$$

positive sign for Δ indicates that; sway is towards right.

Step VII : Member-End Moments : Substituting values of above joint displacements in SD equations; member-end moments are obtained as under :

$$M_{AB} = 0.5 EI(0) + 0.375 EI \left(\frac{17.77}{EI}\right)$$

$$= 6.67 \text{ kNm}$$

$$M_{BA} = EI(0) + 0.375\left(\frac{17.77}{EI}\right)$$
$$= 6.67 \text{ kNm}$$

$$M_{BC} = 2EI(0) + EI\left(-\frac{6.67}{EI}\right)$$
$$= -6.67 \text{ kNm}$$

$$M_{CB} = 2EI\left(-\frac{6.67}{EI}\right) + 0$$
$$= -13.33 \text{ kNm}$$

$$M_{CD} = 2EI\left(-\frac{6.67}{EI}\right) + 1.5EI\left(\frac{17.77}{EI}\right)$$
$$= 13.33 \text{ kNm}$$

$$M_{DC} = EI\left(-\frac{6.67}{EI}\right) + 1.5EI\left(\frac{17.77}{EI}\right)$$
$$= 20 \text{ kNm}$$

Step VIII : FBD of members is as shown in Fig. 2.23 (b). Considering equilibrium of each member and of complete structure; all reaction components are found out as shown in the figure.

Step IX : Shear force diagram is as shown in Fig. 2.23 (c).

Step X : Bending moment diagram : BMD on tension side is shown in Fig. 2.23 (d).

Step XI : FBD of structure is as shown in Fig. 2.23 (e).

Example 2.15 : *Analyse the portal frame shown in Fig. 2.24 (a) by slope-deflection method. Draw SFD and BMD.*

Solution : (1) Data : The frame is supported and loaded as shown in Fig. 2.24 (a).
(2) Frame type : Sway frame.

Object : Structural analysis.

Equations : SD equations.

Procedure : Step I : Degree of kinematic indeterminacy for a given structure =
$$D_{ki} = 5 \ (\theta_B, \theta_C, \theta_E, \Delta_{VE} \text{ and horizontal sway } \Delta)$$

Degree of kinematic indeterminacy for modified structure
$$= D_{ki} = 3 \text{ (See Fig. 2.25 b)}.$$

Unknown Displacements : θ_B, θ_C and horizontal sway $= \Delta$
Known Displacements : $\theta_A = \theta_D = 0$

Step II : Fixed-End Moments :
$$M_{AB}^F = M_{BA}^F = M_{DC}^F = M_{CD}^F = 0$$
$$M_{BC}^F = -M_{CB}^F = \frac{wl^2}{12} = \frac{20 \times 8^2}{12}$$
$$= 106.67 \text{ kNm}$$

Step III : SD equations : (Assuming horizontal sway = Δ towards right)

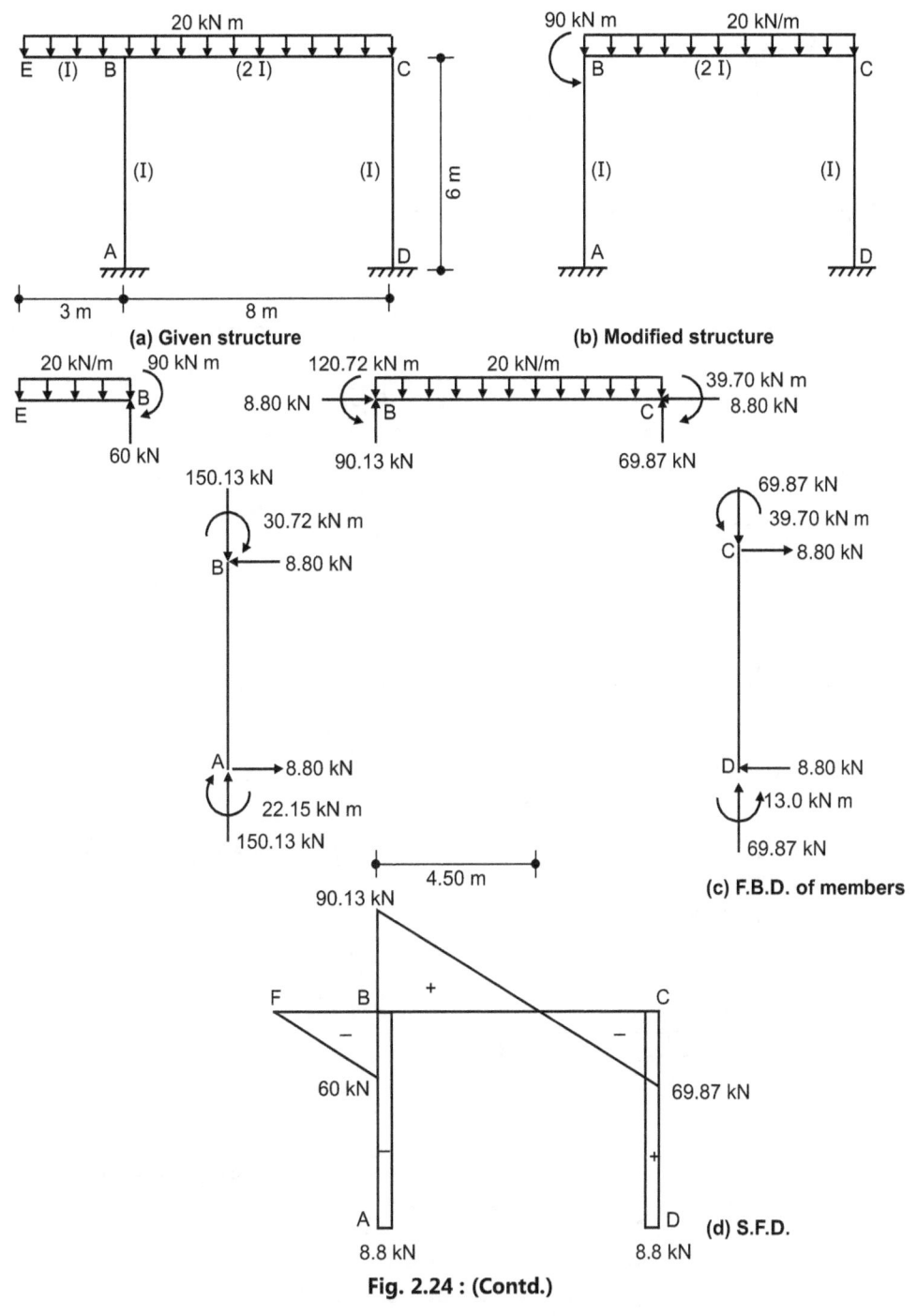

Fig. 2.24 : (Contd.)

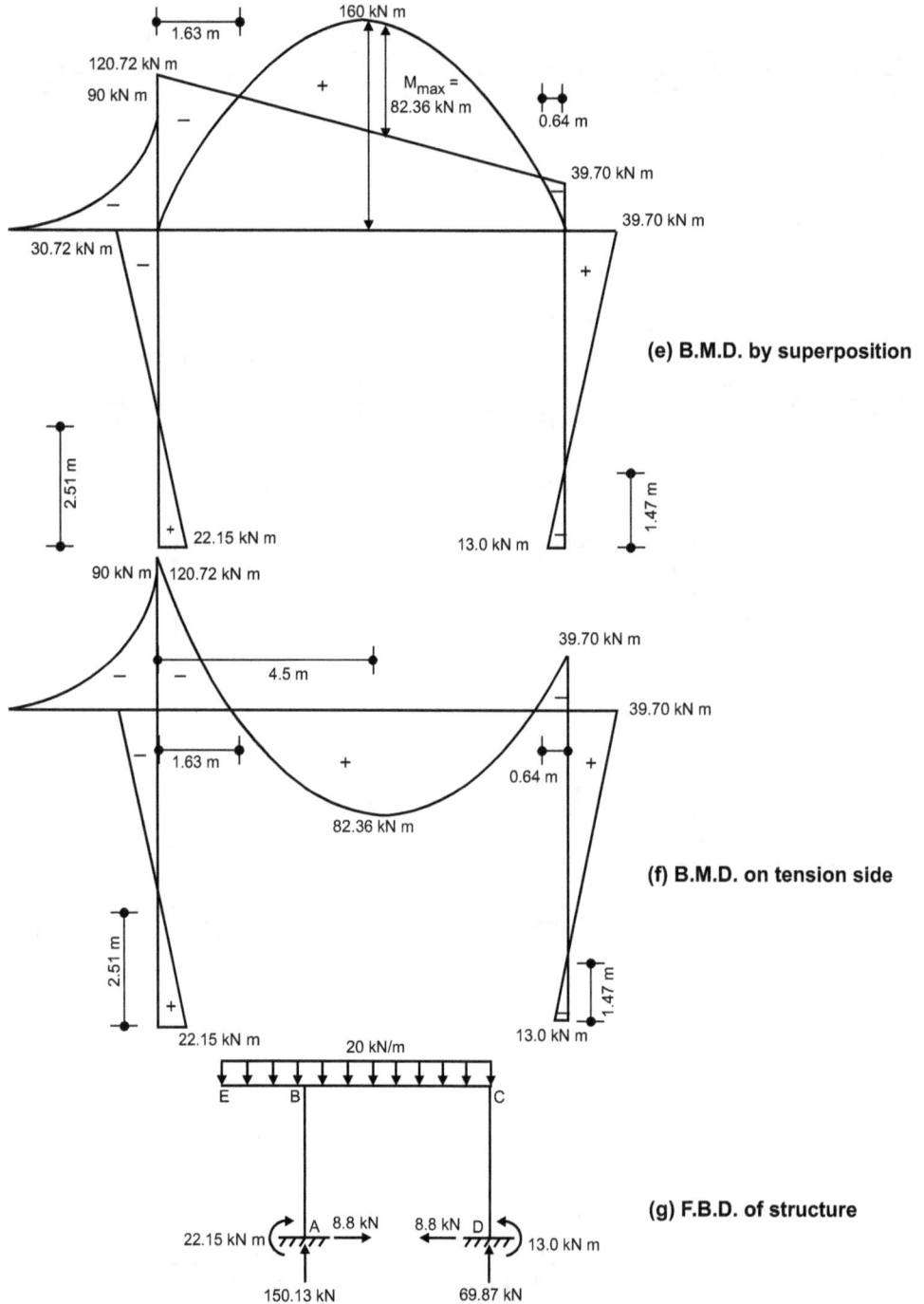

Fig. 2.24 : For Illustrative Example 2.15

Member AB :

$$M_{AB} = \frac{4EI}{L}(\theta_A) + \frac{2EI}{L}(\theta_B) + \frac{6EI}{L^2}(\Delta) + M_{AB}^F$$

$$= \frac{2EI}{6}(\theta_B) + \frac{6EI}{6^2}(\Delta) = \frac{EI}{3}(\theta_B) + \frac{EI}{6}(\Delta) \quad \ldots \text{(i)}$$

$$M_{BA} = \frac{4EI}{L}(\theta_B) + \frac{2EI}{L}(\theta_A) + \frac{6EI}{L^2}(\Delta) + M_{BA}^F$$

$$= \frac{4EI}{6}(\theta_B) + \frac{6EI}{6^2}(\Delta) = \frac{2EI}{3}(\theta_B) + \frac{EI}{6}(\Delta) \quad \ldots \text{(ii)}$$

Member BC :

$$M_{BC} = \frac{4EI}{L}(\theta_B) + \frac{2EI}{L}(\theta_C) \pm \frac{6EI}{L^2}(\Delta) + M_{BC}^F$$

$$= \frac{4(2EI)}{8}(\theta_B) + \frac{2(2EI)}{8}(\theta_C) + 106.67$$

$$= EI(\theta_B) + 0.5\,EI(\theta_C) + 106.67 \quad \ldots \text{(iii)}$$

$$M_{CB} = \frac{4EI}{L}(\theta_C) + \frac{2EI}{L}(\theta_B) \pm \frac{6EI}{L^2}(\Delta) + M_{CB}^F$$

$$= \frac{4(2EI)}{8}(\theta_C) + \frac{2(2EI)}{8}(\theta_B) - 106.67$$

$$= EI(\theta_C) + 0.5\,EI(\theta_B) - 106.67 \quad \ldots \text{(iv)}$$

Member DC :

$$M_{DC} = \frac{4EI}{L}(\theta_D) + \frac{2EI}{L}(\theta_C) + \frac{6EI}{L^2}(\Delta) + M_{DC}^F$$

$$= \frac{2EI}{6}(\theta_C) + \frac{6EI}{6^2}(\Delta) = \frac{EI}{3}(\theta_C) + \frac{EI}{6}\Delta \quad \ldots \text{(v)}$$

$$M_{CD} = \frac{4EI}{L}(\theta_C) + \frac{2EI}{L}(\theta_D) + \frac{6EI}{L^2}(\Delta) + M_{CD}^F$$

$$= \frac{4EI}{6}(\theta_C) + \frac{6EI}{6^2}(\Delta) = \frac{2EI}{3}(\theta_C) + \frac{EI}{6}(\Delta) \quad \ldots \text{(vi)}$$

Step IV : Equilibrium conditions for joints :

Moment equilibrium of joint B : $M_{BA} + M_{BC} = 90$ ... (A)

Moment equilibrium of joint C : $M_{CB} + M_{CD} = 0$ ... (B)

Horizontal shear equilibrium of structure :

$$H_A + H_D = 0, \quad \text{where}$$

$$H_A = \frac{M_{AB} + M_{BA}}{6} \quad \text{and} \quad H_D = \frac{M_{CD} + M_{DC}}{6}$$

Substituting :

$$M_{AB} + M_{BA} + M_{CD} + M_{DC} = 0 \quad \ldots \text{(C)}$$

Step V : Formulation of equilibrium equations in terms of joint displacements.
Substituting equations (ii) and (iii) in equation (A), we get

$$\left[\frac{2EI}{3}(\theta_B) + \frac{EI}{6}(\Delta)\right] + [EI(\theta_B) + 0.5 EI(\theta_C) + 106.67] = 90$$

$$1.67 EI(\theta_B) + 0.5 EI(\theta_C) + 0.167 EI(\Delta) + 16.67 = 0 \quad \ldots \text{(I)}$$

Substituting equations (iv) and (vi) in equation (B), we get

$$[EI(\theta_C) + 0.5 EI(\theta_B) - 106.67] + \left[\frac{2EI}{3}(\theta_C) + \frac{EI}{6}(\Delta)\right] = 0$$

$$1.67 EI(\theta_C) + 0.5 EI(\theta_B) + 0.167 EI(\Delta) - 106.67 = 0 \quad \ldots \text{(II)}$$

Substituting equations (i), (ii), (v) and (vi) in equation (C), we get

$$\left[\frac{EI}{3}(\theta_B) + \frac{EI}{6}(\Delta)\right] + \left[\frac{2EI}{3}(\theta_B) + \frac{EI}{6}(\Delta)\right] + \left[\frac{EI}{3}(\theta_C) + \frac{EI}{6}(\Delta)\right] + \left[\frac{2EI}{3}(\theta_C) + \frac{EI}{6}(\Delta)\right] = 0$$

$$EI(\theta_B) + EI(\theta_C) + 0.67 EI(\Delta) = 0 \quad \ldots \text{(III)}$$

Step VI : Solution of equations for displacements. Solving equations (I), (II) and (III), we get

$$\boxed{\theta_B = -\frac{25.7}{EI} \; ; \; \theta_C = \frac{79.74}{EI} \; ; \; \text{and} \; \Delta = -\frac{81.52}{EI}}$$

negative sign for Δ indicates that sway is towards left.

Step VII : Member-End Moments : Substituting the values of above joint displacements in SD equations, member-end moments are obtained as under :

$$M_{AB} = \frac{EI}{3}\left(-\frac{25.7}{EI}\right) + \frac{EI}{6}\left(-\frac{81.52}{EI}\right)$$

$$= -22.15 \text{ kNm}$$

$$M_{BA} = \frac{2EI}{3}\left(-\frac{25.7}{EI}\right) + \frac{EI}{6}\left(-\frac{81.52}{EI}\right)$$

$$= -30.72 \text{ kNm}$$

$$M_{BC} = EI\left(-\frac{25.7}{EI}\right) + 0.5 EI\left(\frac{79.74}{EI}\right) + 106.67$$

$$= 120.72 \text{ kNm}$$

$$M_{CB} = EI\left(\frac{79.74}{EI}\right) + 0.5 EI\left(-\frac{25.7}{EI}\right) - 106.67$$

$$= -39.70 \text{ kNm}$$

$$M_{CD} = \frac{2}{3}EI\left(\frac{79.74}{EI}\right) + \frac{EI}{6}\left(-\frac{81.52}{EI}\right)$$

= 39.70 kNm

$$M_{DC} = \frac{EI}{3}\left(\frac{79.74}{EI}\right) + \frac{EI}{6}\left(-\frac{81.52}{EI}\right)$$

= 13.0 kNm

Step VIII : FBD of members is as shown in Fig. 2.24 (c). Considering equilibrium of each member and of complete structure; all reaction components are found out as shown in figure.

Step IX : Shear force diagram is as shown in Fig. 2.24 (d).

Step X : Bending moment diagram : BMD by superposition is as shown in Fig. 2.24 (e).

BMD on tension side is as shown in Fig. 2.24 (f).

Step XI : FBD of structure is as shown in Fig. 2.24 (g).

Example 2.16 : *Analyse the portal frame shown in Fig. 2.25 (a) by slope-deflection method. Take EI = constant. Draw SFD and BMD.*

Solution : Data : (1) The frame is supported and loaded as shown in Fig. 2.25 (a).

(2) Frame type : Sway frame.

Object : Structural analysis.

Equations : SD equations.

Procedure :

Step I : Degree of kinematic indeterminacy = D_{ki} = 4.

Unknown Displacements : θ_B, θ_C, θ_D and horizontal sway = Δ.

Known Displacement : $\theta_A = 0$.

Step II : Fixed-End Moments :

$$M_{AB}^F = -M_{BA}^F = \frac{WL}{8} = \frac{160 \times 4}{8}$$

= 80 kNm

$$M_{BC}^F = -M_{CB}^F = \frac{wl^2}{12} = \frac{20 \times 4^2}{12}$$

= 26.67 kNm

$$-M_{DC}^F = M_{CD}^F = \frac{wl^2}{12} = \frac{20 \times 3^2}{12}$$

= 15 kNm

Step III : SD equations : (Assuming horizontal sway = Δ towards right)

Member AB : $\quad M_{AB} = \dfrac{4\,EI}{L}(\theta_A) + \dfrac{2\,EI}{L}(\theta_B) + \dfrac{6\,EI}{L^2}(\Delta) + M_{AB}^F$

$$= \frac{2(2EI)}{4}(\theta_B) + \frac{6(2EI)}{4^2}(\Delta) + 80$$

$$= EI(\theta_B) + 0.75\, EI(\Delta) + 80 \qquad \ldots \text{(i)}$$

$$M_{BA} = \frac{4EI}{L}(\theta_B) + \frac{2EI}{L}(\theta_A) + \frac{6EI}{L^2}(\Delta) + M^F_{BA}$$

$$= \frac{4(2EI)}{4}(\theta_B) + \frac{6(2EI)}{4^2}(\Delta) - 80$$

$$= 2\, EI(\theta_B) + 0.75\, EI(\Delta) - 80 \qquad \ldots \text{(ii)}$$

Member BC :

$$M_{BC} = \frac{4EI}{L}(\theta_B) + \frac{2EI}{L}(\theta_C) \pm \frac{6EI}{L^2}(\Delta) + M^F_{BC}$$

$$= \frac{4EI}{4}(\theta_B) + \frac{2EI}{4}(\theta_C) + 26.67$$

$$= EI(\theta_B) + 0.5\, EI(\theta_C) + 26.67 \qquad \ldots \text{(iii)}$$

$$M_{CB} = \frac{4EI}{L}(\theta_C) + \frac{2EI}{L}(\theta_B) \pm \frac{6EI}{L^2}(\Delta) + M^F_{CB}$$

$$= \frac{4EI}{4}(\theta_C) + \frac{2EI}{4}(\theta_B) - 26.67$$

$$= EI(\theta_C) + 0.5\, EI(\theta_B) - 26.67 \qquad \ldots \text{(iv)}$$

Member DC :

$$M_{DC} = \frac{4EI}{L}(\theta_D) + \frac{2EI}{L}(\theta_C) + \frac{6EI}{L^2}(\Delta) + M^F_{DC}$$

$$= \frac{4EI}{3}(\theta_D) + \frac{2EI}{3}(\theta_C) + \frac{6EI}{3^2}(\Delta) - 15$$

$$= 1.33\, EI(\theta_D) + 0.67\, EI(\theta_C) + 0.67\, EI(\Delta) - 15 \qquad \ldots \text{(v)}$$

$$M_{CD} = \frac{4EI}{L}(\theta_C) + \frac{2EI}{L}(\theta_D) + \frac{6EI}{L^2}(\Delta) + M^F_{CD}$$

$$= \frac{4EI}{3}(\theta_C) + \frac{2EI}{3}(\theta_D) + \frac{6EI}{3^2}(\Delta) + 15$$

$$= 1.33\, EI(\theta_C) + 0.67\, EI(\theta_D) + 0.67\, EI(\Delta) + 15 \qquad \ldots \text{(vi)}$$

Step IV : Equilibrium conditions for joints :

Moment equilibrium of joint B : $M_{BA} + M_{BC} = 0$ ... (A)

Moment equilibrium of joint C : $M_{CB} + M_{CD} = 0$ ... (B)

Moment equilibrium of joint D : $M_{DC} = 0$ ... (C)

Horizontal shear equilibrium of structure :

$$H_A + H_D - 160 + 20 \times 3 = 0$$

i.e. $H_A + H_D - 100 = 0$ ... (D)

SLOPE-DEFLECTION METHOD

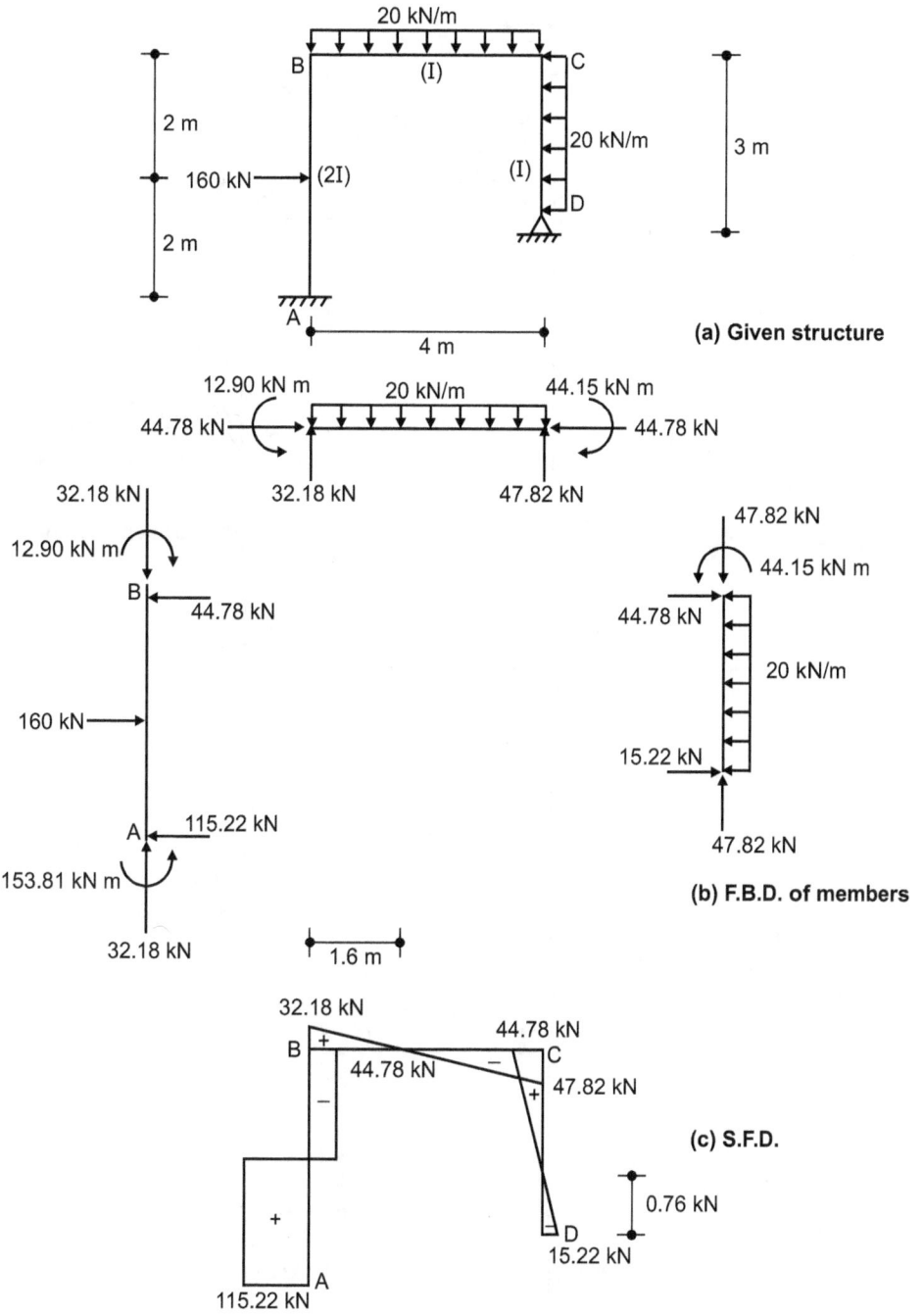

Fig. 2.25 : (Contd.)

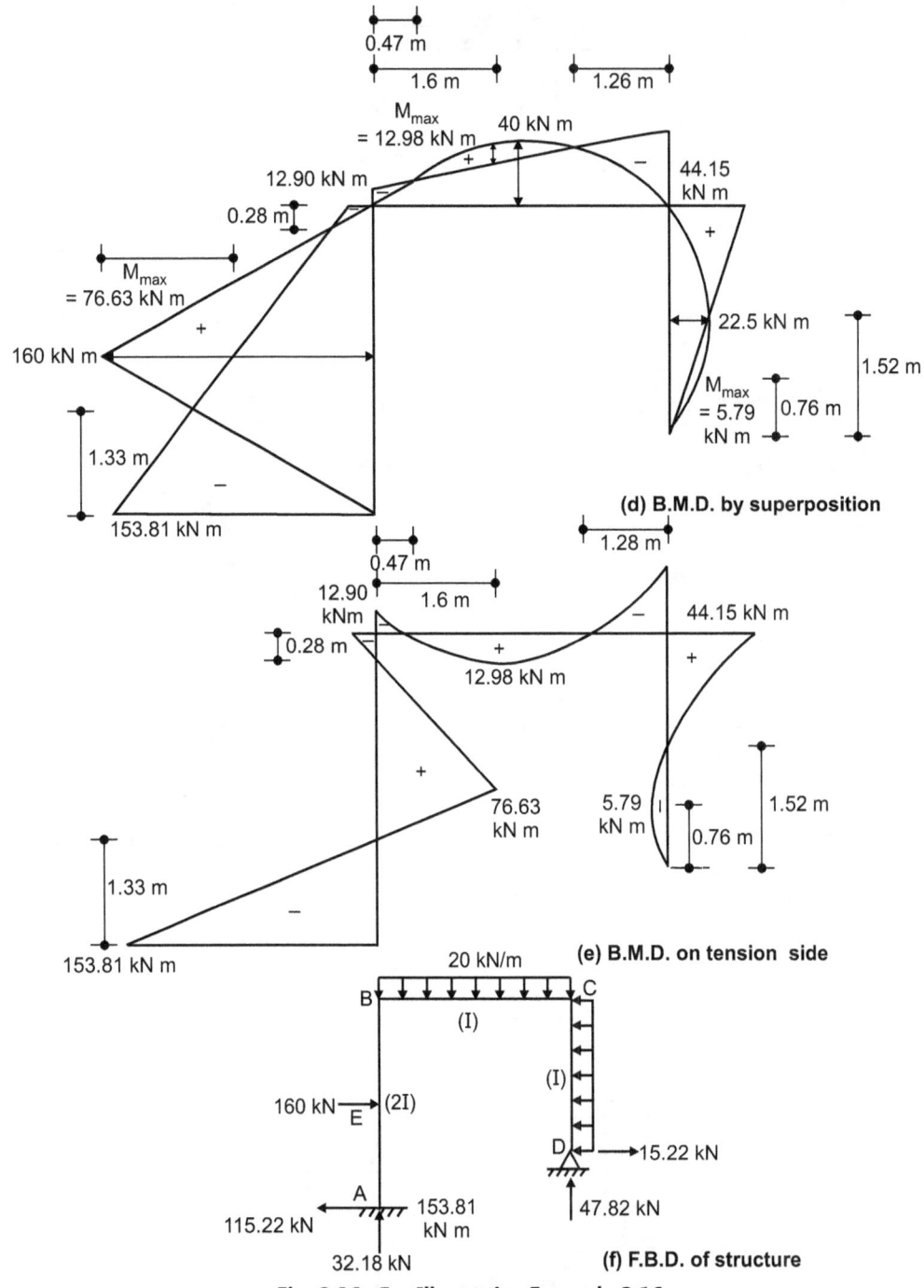

Fig. 2.26 : For Illustrative Example 2.16

where,
$$H_A = \frac{M_{AB} + M_{BA}}{4} + 80 \text{ and;}$$

$$H_D = \frac{M_{DC}}{3} - 30, \text{ equation (D) becomes,}$$

$$\frac{M_{AB} + M_{BA}}{4} + 80 + \frac{M_{CD}}{3} - 30 - 100 = 0$$

$$3(M_{AB} + M_{BA}) + 4 M_{CD} - 600 = 0 \qquad \ldots \text{(D)}$$

Step V : Formulation of equilibrium equations in terms of joint displacements :
Substituting equations (ii) and (iii) in equation (A), we get
$$[2 EI (\theta_B) + 0.75 EI (\Delta) - 80] [EI (\theta_B) + 0.5 EI (\theta_C) + 26.67] = 0$$
$$3 EI (\theta_B) + 0.5 EI (\theta_C) + 0.75 EI (\Delta) - 53.33 = 0 \qquad \ldots \text{(I)}$$

Substituting equations (iv) and (vi) in equation (B), we get
$$[EI (\theta_C) + 0.5 EI (\theta_B) - 26.67] [1.33 EI (\theta_C) + 0.67 EI (\theta_D) + 0.67 EI (\Delta) + 15] = 0$$
$$2.33 EI (\theta_C) + 0.5 EI (\theta_B) + 0.67 EI (\theta_D) + 0.67 EI (\Delta) - 11.67 = 0 \qquad \ldots \text{(II)}$$

Substituting equation (v) in equation (C), we get
$$1.33 EI (\theta_D) + 0.67 EI (\theta_C) + 0.67 EI (\Delta) - 15 = 0 \qquad \ldots \text{(III)}$$

Substituting equations (i), (ii) and (vi) in equation (D), we get
$$3 [EI (\theta_B) + 0.75 EI (\Delta) + 80 + 2 EI (\theta_B) + 0.75 EI (\Delta) - 80]$$
$$+ 4 [1.33 EI (\theta_C) + 0.67 EI (\theta_D) + 0.67 EI (\Delta) + 15] - 600 = 0$$
$$9 EI (\theta_B) + 5.33 EI (\theta_C) + 2.67 EI (\theta_D) + 7.18 EI (\Delta) - 540 = 0 \qquad \ldots \text{(IV)}$$

Step VI : Solution of equations for joint displacements :
Solving equations (I), (II), (III) and (IV), we get

$$\boxed{\theta_B = \frac{-6.70}{EI}, \quad \theta_C = \frac{-14.128}{EI}, \quad \theta_D = \frac{-35.37}{EI}, \quad \Delta = \frac{107.35}{EI}}$$

positive sign for Δ indicates that, sway is towards right.

Step VII : Member-End Moments : Substituting the values of above joint displacements in SD equations, member-end moments are obtained as under :

$$M_{AB} = EI \left(\frac{-6.70}{EI}\right) + 0.75 EI \left(\frac{107.35}{EI}\right) + 80 = 153.81 \text{ kNm}$$

$$M_{BA} = 2 EI \left(\frac{-6.70}{EI}\right) + 0.75 EI \left(\frac{107.35}{EI}\right) - 80 = -12.90 \text{ kNm}$$

$$M_{BC} = EI \left(\frac{-6.70}{EI}\right) + 0.5 EI \left(-\frac{14.128}{EI}\right) + 26.67 = 12.90 \text{ kNm}$$

$$M_{CB} = EI \left(-\frac{14.128}{EI}\right) + 0.5 EI \left(-\frac{6.70}{EI}\right) - 26.67 = -44.15 \text{ kNm}$$

$$M_{DC} = 1.33\,EI\left(-\frac{35.37}{EI}\right) + 0.67\,EI\left(-\frac{14.128}{EI}\right) + 0.67\,EI\left(\frac{107.35}{EI}\right) - 15 = 0$$

$$M_{CD} = 1.33\,EI\left(-\frac{14.128}{EI}\right) + 0.67\,EI\left(-\frac{35.37}{EI}\right) + 0.67\,EI\left(\frac{107.35}{EI}\right) + 15$$

$$= 44.15 \text{ kNm}$$

Step VIII : FBD of members is as shown in Fig. 2.25 (b). Considering equilibrium of each member and of complete structure, all reaction components are found out as shown in the figure.

Step IX : Shear force diagram is as shown in Fig. 2.25 (c).

Step X : Bending moment diagram :

BMD by superposition is shown in Fig. 2.25 (d).

BMD on tension side is shown in Fig. 2.25 (e).

Step XI : FBD of structure is as shown in Fig. 2.25 (f).

Example 2.17 : *Analyse the portal frame shown in Fig. 2.26 (a) by slope-deflection method. Draw SFD, BMD and elastic curve.*

Solution : Data : (1) The frame is loaded as shown in Fig. 2.26 (a).

(2) Frame type : Sway frame.

Object : Structural analysis.

Equations : SD equations.

Procedure :

Step I : Degree of kinematic indeterminacy = D_{ki} = 4.

Unknown Displacements : θ_B, θ_{CB}, θ_{CD}, horizontal sway = Δ.

Known Displacements : $\theta_A = \theta_D = 0$.

Step II : Fixed-End Moments :

$$M^F_{AB} = M^F_{BA} = M^F_{DC} = M^F_{CD} = 0$$

$$M^F_{BC} = -M^F_{CD} = \frac{WL}{8} = \frac{50 \times 4}{8} = 25 \text{ kNm}$$

Step III : SD equations : (Assuming horizontal sway = Δ towards right)

Member AB :

$$M_{AB} = \frac{4\,EI}{L}(\theta_A) + \frac{2\,EI}{L}(\theta_B) + \frac{6\,EI}{L^2}(\Delta) + M^F_{AB}$$

$$= \frac{2\,EI}{4}(\theta_B) + \frac{6\,EI}{4^2}(\Delta) = 0.5\,EI\,(\theta_B) + 0.375\,EI\,(\Delta) \quad \ldots \text{(i)}$$

$$M_{BA} = \frac{4\,EI}{L}(\theta_B) + \frac{2\,EI}{L}(\theta_A) + \frac{6\,EI}{L^2}(\Delta) + M^F_{BA}$$

$$= \frac{4\,EI}{4}(\theta_B) + \frac{6\,EI}{4^2}(\Delta)$$

$$= EI\,(\theta_B) + 0.375\,EI\,(\Delta) \quad \ldots \text{(ii)}$$

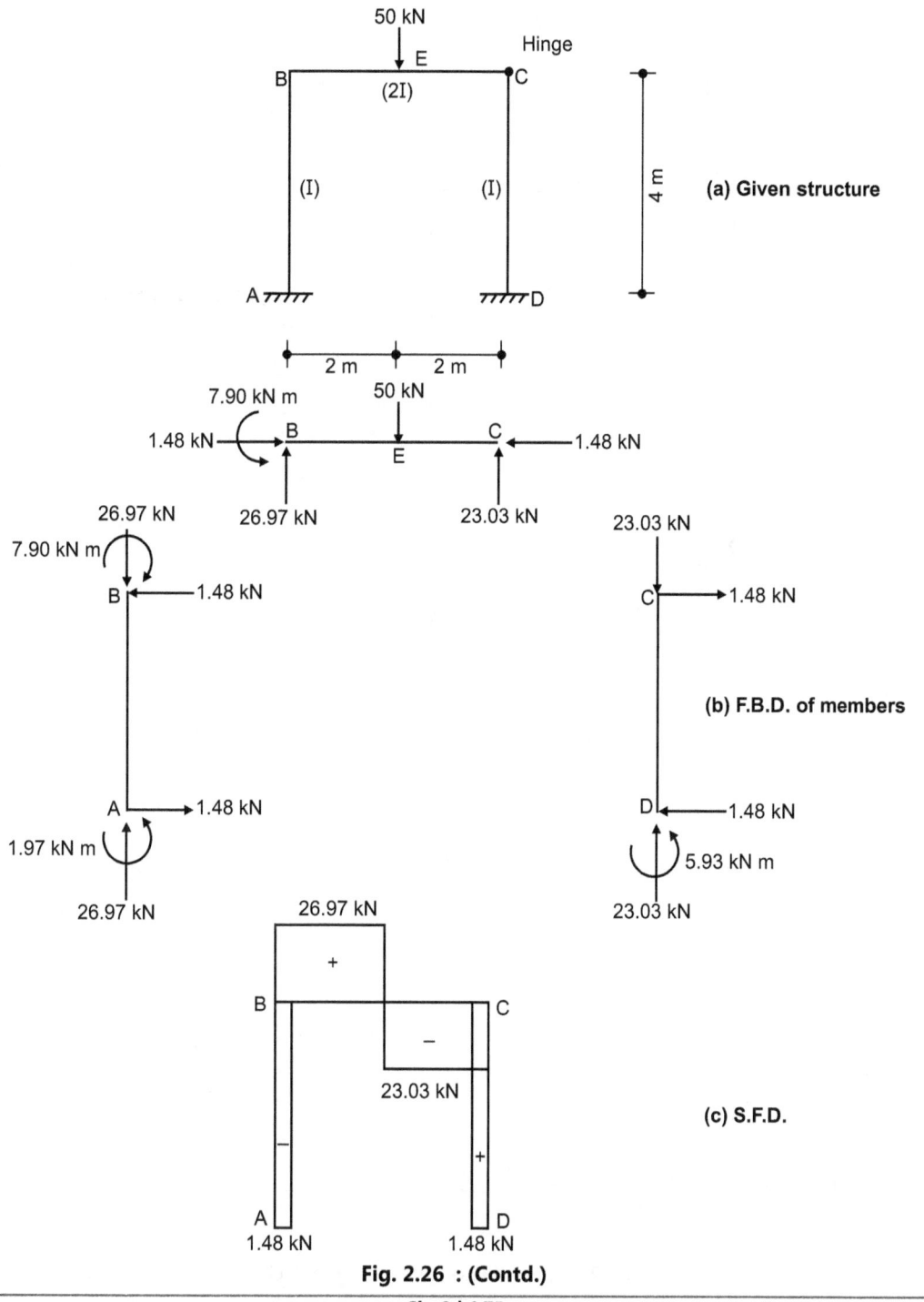

Fig. 2.26 : (Contd.)

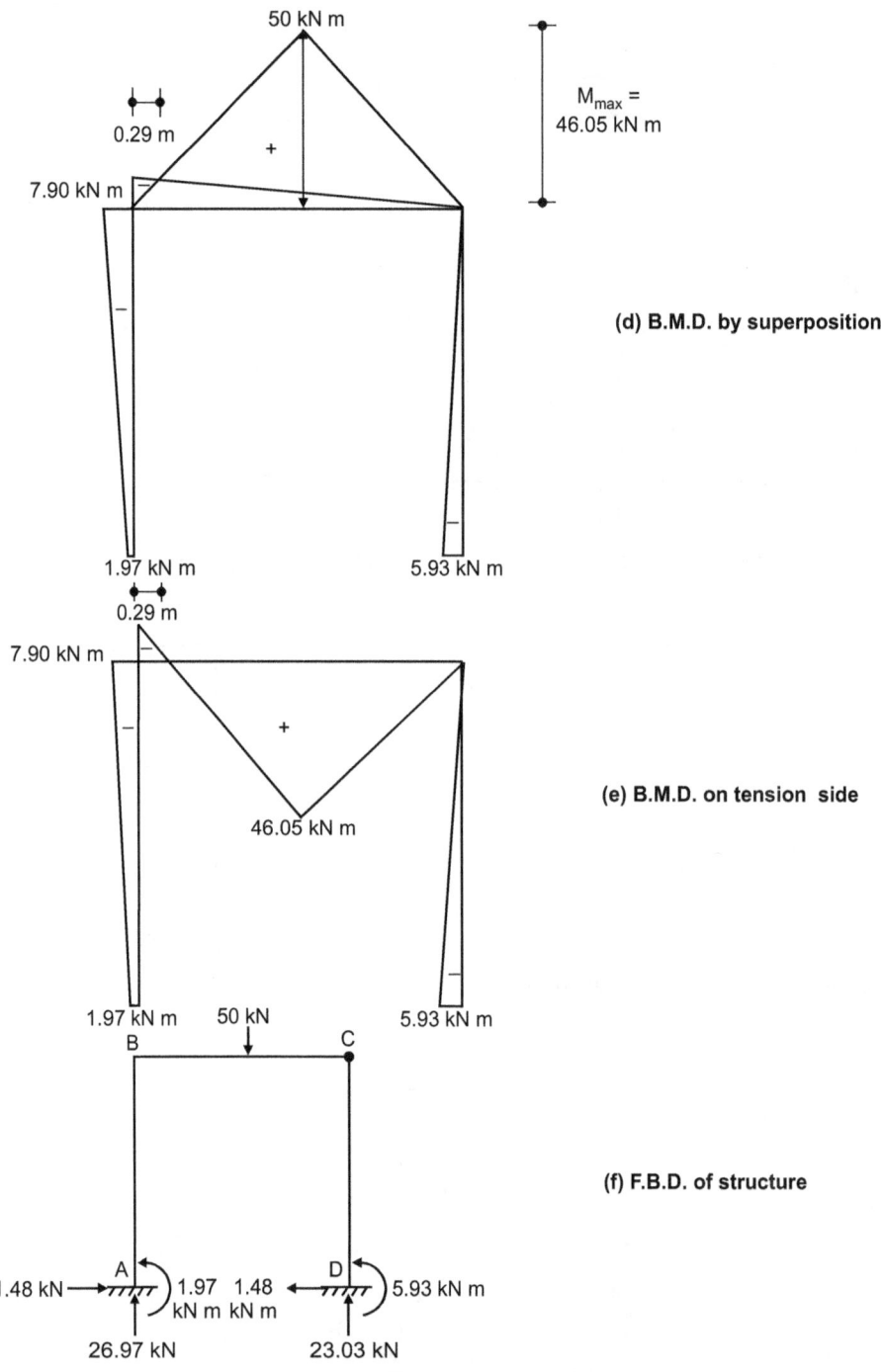

Fig. 2.26 : For Illustrative Example 2.17

Member BC :

$$M_{BC} = \frac{4EI}{L}(\theta_B) + \frac{2EI}{L}(\theta_{CB}) \pm \frac{6EI}{L^2}(\Delta) + M^F_{BC}$$

$$= \frac{4(2EI)}{4}(\theta_B) + \frac{2(2EI)}{4}(\theta_{CB}) + 25$$

$$= 2EI(\theta_B) + EI(\theta_{CB}) + 25 \qquad \ldots \text{(iii)}$$

$$M_{CB} = \frac{4EI}{L}(\theta_{CB}) + \frac{2EI}{L}(\theta_B) \pm \frac{6EI}{L^2}(\Delta) + M^F_{CB}$$

$$= \frac{4(2EI)}{4}(\theta_{CB}) + \frac{2(2EI)}{4}(\theta_B) - 25$$

$$= 2EI(\theta_{CB}) + EI(\theta_B) - 25 \qquad \ldots \text{(iv)}$$

Member DC :

$$M_{DC} = \frac{4EI}{L}(\theta_D) + \frac{2EI}{L}(\theta_{CD}) + \frac{6EI}{L^2}(\Delta) + M^F_{DC}$$

$$= \frac{2EI}{4}(\theta_{CD}) + \frac{6EI}{4^2}(\Delta) = 0.5\,EI(\theta_{CD}) + 0.375\,EI(\Delta) \qquad \ldots \text{(v)}$$

$$M_{CD} = \frac{4EI}{L}(\theta_{CD}) + \frac{2EI}{L}(\theta_D) + \frac{6EI}{L^2}(\Delta) + M^F_{CD}$$

$$= \frac{4EI}{L}(\theta_{CD}) + \frac{6EI}{4^2}(\Delta) = EI(\theta_{CD}) + 0.375\,EI(\Delta) \qquad \ldots \text{(vi)}$$

Step IV : Equilibrium conditions for joints :

Moment equilibrium of joint B : $M_{BA} + M_{BC} = 0$ ... (A)

Moment equilibrium of joint C : $M_{CB} = 0$ ... (B)

and $M_{CD} = 0$ ... (C)

Horizontal shear equilibrium of structure,

$$H_A + H_D = 0 \qquad \ldots \text{(D)}$$

where $H_A = \dfrac{M_{AB} + M_{BA}}{4}$ and $H_D = \dfrac{M_{DC}}{4}$;   equation (D) becomes

$$M_{AB} + M_{BA} + M_{DC} = 0 \qquad \ldots \text{(D)}$$

Step V : Formulation of equilibrium equations in terms of joint displacements :

Substituting equations (ii) and (iii) in equation (A), we get

$$[EI(\theta_B) + 0.375\,EI(\Delta)] + [2EI(\theta_B) + EI(\theta_{CB}) + 25] = 0$$

$$3EI + (\theta_B) + EI(\theta_{CB}) + 0.375\,EI(\Delta) + 25 = 0 \qquad \ldots \text{(I)}$$

Substituting equation (iv) in equation (B), we get

$$2EI(\theta_{CB}) + EI(\theta_B) - 25 = 0 \qquad \ldots \text{(II)}$$

Substituting equation (vi) in equation (C), we get

$$EI(\theta_{CD}) + 0.375\,EI(\Delta) = 0 \qquad \ldots \text{(III)}$$

Substituting equations (i), (ii) and (v) in equation (D), we get

$$[0.5\,EI(\theta_B) + 0.375\,EI(\Delta)] + [EI(\theta_B) + 0.375\,EI(\Delta)] + [0.5\,EI(\theta_{CD}) + 0.375\,EI(\Delta)] = 0$$

$$1.5\,EI(\theta_B) + 0.5\,EI(\theta_{CD}) + 1.125\,EI(\Delta) = 0 \qquad \ldots \text{(IV)}$$

Step VI : Solution of equations for displacements :
Solving equations (I), (II), (III) and (IV), we get

$$\theta_B = \frac{-19.73}{EI}, \quad \theta_{CB} = \frac{22.36}{EI}, \quad \theta_{CD} = \frac{-11.83}{EI} \quad \text{and} \quad \Delta = \frac{31.57}{EI}$$

positive sign for Δ indicates that; sway is towards right.

Step VII : Member-End Moments : Substituting the values of above joint displacements in SD equations, member-end moments are obtained as under :

$$M_{AB} = 0.5\,EI\left(-\frac{19.73}{EI}\right) + 0.375\,EI\left(\frac{31.57}{EI}\right) = 1.973 \text{ kNm}$$

$$M_{BA} = EI\left(-\frac{19.73}{EI}\right) + 0.375\,EI\left(\frac{31.57}{EI}\right) + 25 = -7.9 \text{ kNm}$$

$$M_{BC} = 2\,EI\left(-\frac{19.73}{EI}\right) + EI\left(\frac{22.36}{EI}\right) + 25 = 7.90 \text{ kNm}$$

$$M_{CB} = 2\,EI\left(\frac{22.36}{EI}\right) + EI\left(-\frac{19.73}{EI}\right) - 25 = 0$$

$$M_{DC} = 0.5\,EI\left(-\frac{11.83}{EI}\right) + 0.375\,EI\left(\frac{31.57}{EI}\right) = 5.93 \text{ kNm}$$

$$M_{CD} = EI\left(-\frac{11.83}{EI}\right) + 0.375\,EI\left(\frac{31.57}{EI}\right) = 0.$$

Step VIII : FBD of members is as shown in Fig. 2.26 (b). Considering equilibrium of each member and of complete structure, all reaction components are found out as shown in the figure.

Step IX : Shear force diagram is as shown in Fig. 2.26 (c).

Step X : Bending moment diagram :
BMD by superposition is shown in Fig. 2.26 (d).
BMD on tension side is shown in Fig. 2.26 (e).

Step XI : FBD of structure is as shown in Fig. 2.268 (f).

2.9.5 Frames Having Known Yielding of Supports

The yielding of support, in general, includes rotational yielding of the fixed support θ and translational yielding i.e. settlement of any type of support Δ. Numerical values of yielding of supports i.e. θ and Δ including direction are known.

2.9.6 Application of SD Method to Frames Having Known Yielding of Supports

Numerical values of EI are essential to calculate the moment contributions of $\frac{4EI}{L}(\theta)$ and $\frac{6EI}{L^2}(\Delta)$ in SD equations of the corresponding members. The moment contributions must be taken in correct direction according to the given direction of yielding of support. Rules of sign convention should be strictly observed. Rest of the analysis can be completed as per the procedure of SD method.

The general hints given for beam analysis are also applicable to frame analysis.

Example 2.18 : *Analyse the portal frame shown in Fig. 2.27 (a) by slope-deflection method, if support A sinks by 5 mm and support D is subjected to anticlockwise rotation of 0.002 radians. Take EI = 3000 kNm².*

Solution : Data : (1) The frame is supported and loaded as shown in Fig. 2.27 (a).
(2) EI = 3000 kNm2
(3) Frame type : Sway frame.

Object : Structural analysis.

Equations : SD equations.

Procedure :

Step I : Degree of kinematic indeterminacy = D_{ki} = 3.

Unknown Displacements : θ_B, θ_C and horizontal sway = Δ.

Known Displacements : $\theta_A = 0$, $\Delta_A = 5$ mm ($\downarrow$) $= \Delta_B$
$\theta_D = 0.002$ (Anticlockwise, hence positive)
$\Delta_D = \Delta_C = 0$

Step II : Fixed-End Moments :

$$M_{AB}^F = M_{BA}^F = M_{BC}^F = M_{CB}^F = M_{CD}^F = M_{DC}^F = 0$$

Step III : SD equations : (Assuming horizontal sway = Δ towards right).

Member AB :
$$M_{AB} = \frac{4EI}{L}(\theta_A) + \frac{2EI}{L}(\theta_B) + \frac{6EI}{L^2}(\Delta) + M_{AB}^F$$

$$= \frac{2EI}{4}(\theta_B) + \frac{6EI}{4^2}(\Delta) = 0.5\,EI\,(\theta_B) + 0.375\,EI\,(\Delta) \quad \ldots \text{(i)}$$

$$M_{BA} = \frac{4EI}{L}(\theta_B) + \frac{2EI}{L}(\theta_A) + \frac{6EI}{L^2}(\Delta) + M_{BA}^F$$

$$= \frac{4EI}{4}(\theta_B) + \frac{6EI}{4^2}(\Delta) = EI\,(\theta_B) + 0.375\,EI\,(\Delta) \quad \ldots \text{(ii)}$$

Note that sinking of support A (also of B by same amount as we shall be neglecting axial deformations of members) does not produce any moment in member AB.

Member BC :
$$M_{BC} = \frac{4EI}{L}(\theta_B) + \frac{2EI}{L}(\theta_C) \pm \frac{6EI}{L^2}(\Delta) + M_{BC}^F$$

$$= \frac{4(2EI)}{5}(\theta_B) + \frac{2(2EI)}{5}(\theta_C) - \frac{6(2 \times 3000)}{5^2}\left(\frac{5}{1000}\right)$$

$$= 1.6\,EI\,(\theta_B) + 0.8\,EI\,(\theta_C) - 7.2 \quad \ldots \text{(iii)}$$

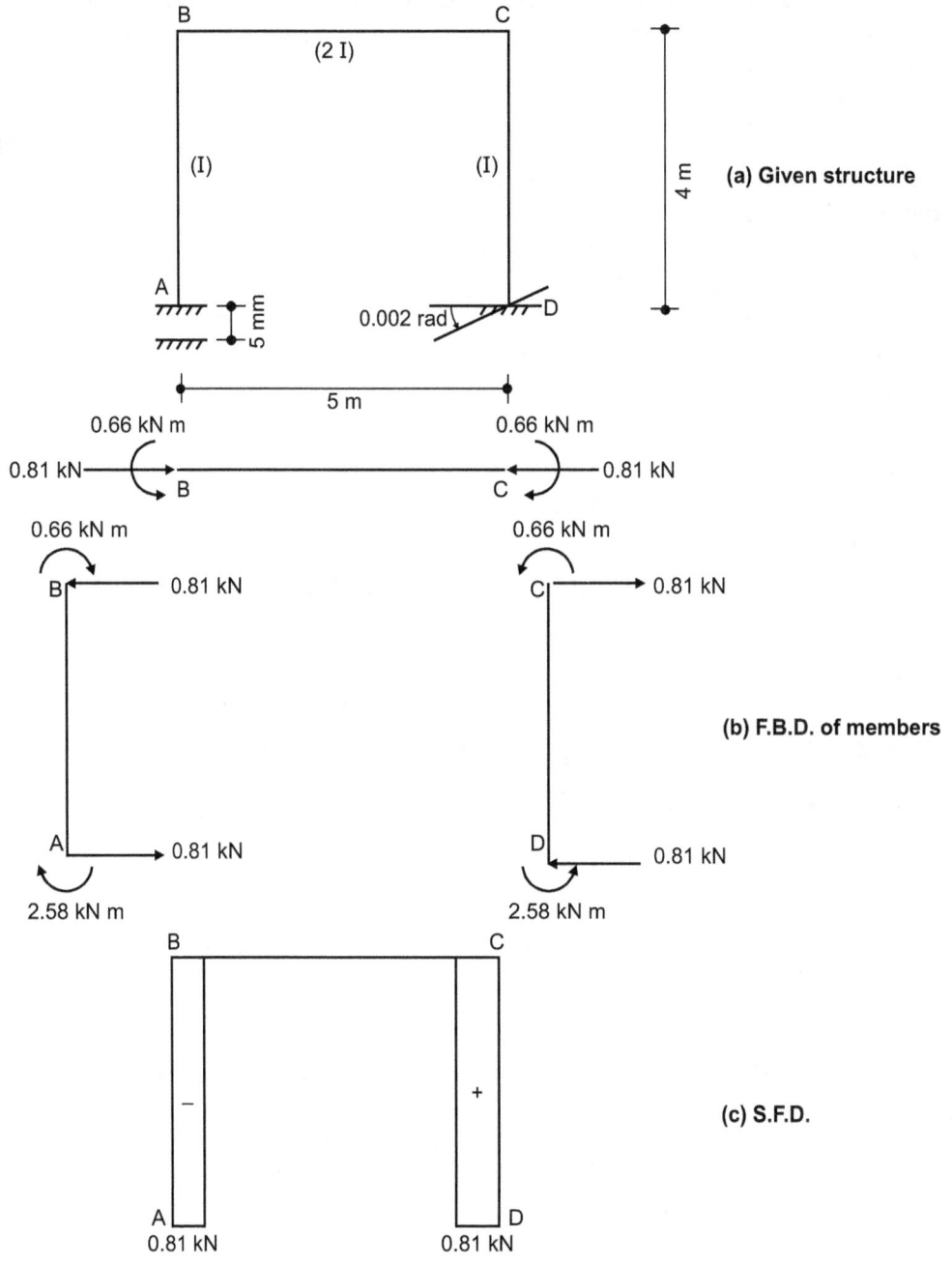

Fig. 2.27 : (Contd.)

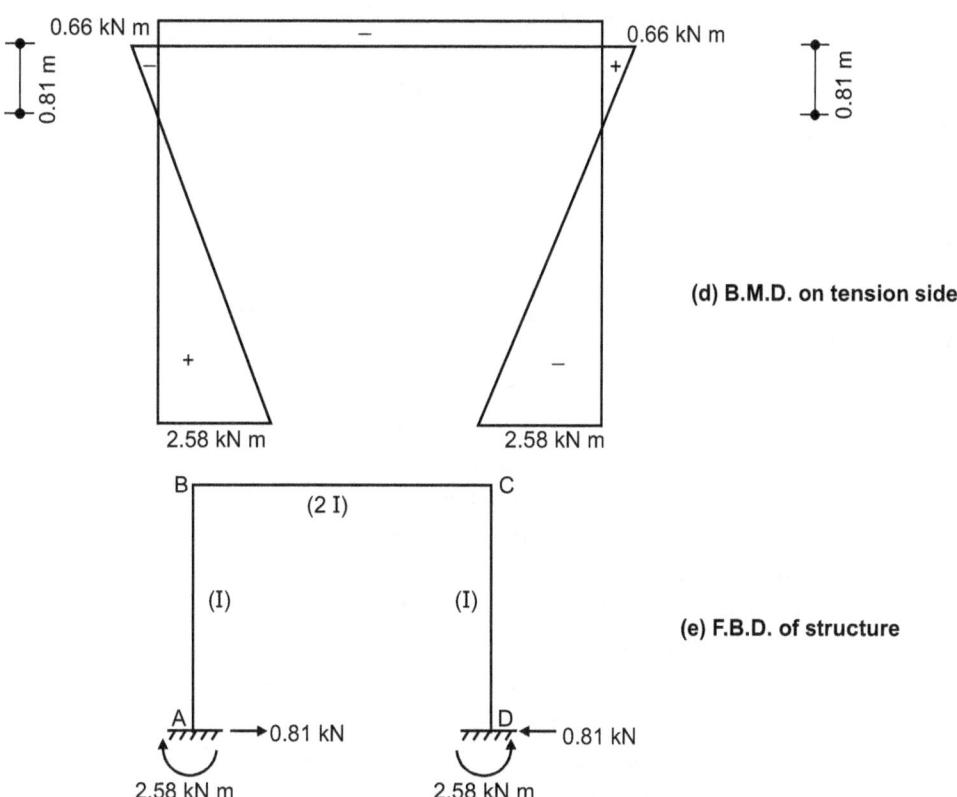

Fig. 2.27 : For Illustrative Example 2.18

$$M_{CB} = \frac{4EI}{L}(\theta_C) + \frac{2EI}{L}(\theta_B) \pm \frac{6EI}{L^2}(\Delta) + M^F_{CB}$$

$$= \frac{4(2EI)}{5}(\theta_C) + \frac{2(2EI)}{5}(\theta_B) - \frac{6 \times 2 \times 3000}{5^2}\left(\frac{5}{1000}\right)$$

$$= 1.6\,EI(\theta_C) + 0.8\,EI(\theta_B) - 7.2 \qquad \ldots \text{(iv)}$$

Note that, sinking of support A (i.e. of B) produces clockwise moments, hence negative for member BC.

Member CD :

$$M_{CD} = \frac{4EI}{L}(\theta_C) + \frac{2EI}{L}(\theta_D) + \frac{6EI}{L^2}(\Delta) + M^F_{CD}$$

$$= \frac{4EI}{4}(\theta_C) + \frac{2 \times 3000}{4}(0.002) + \frac{6EI}{4^2}(\Delta)$$

$$= EI(\theta_C) + 0.375\,EI(\Delta) + 3 \qquad \ldots \text{(v)}$$

$$M_{DC} = \frac{4EI}{L}(\theta_D) + \frac{2EI}{L}(\theta_C) + \frac{6EI}{L^2}(\Delta) + M^F_{DC}$$

$$= \frac{4 \times 3000}{4}(0.002) + \frac{2EI}{4}(\theta_C) + \frac{6EI}{4^2}(\Delta)$$

$$= 0.5\,EI\,(\theta_C) + 0.375\,EI\,(\Delta) + 6 \quad \ldots \text{(vi)}$$

Step IV : Equilibrium conditions for joints :

Moment equilibrium for joint B : $\quad M_{BA} + M_{BC} = 0 \quad \ldots$ (A)

Moment equilibrium for joint C : $\quad M_{CB} + M_{CD} = 0 \quad \ldots$ (B)

Horizontal shear equilibrium for structure,

$$H_A + H_D = 0$$

where, $\quad H_A = \dfrac{M_{AB} + M_{BA}}{4} \quad$ and $\quad H_D = \dfrac{M_{DC} + M_{CD}}{4}$

Above equation becomes $M_{AB} + M_{BA} + M_{DC} + M_{CD} = 0 \quad \ldots$ (C)

Step V : Formulation of equilibrium equations in terms of joint displacements :

Substituting equations (ii) and (iii) in equation (A), we get

$[EI\,(\theta_B) + 0.375\,EI\,(\Delta)] + [1.6\,EI\,(\theta_B) + 0.8\,EI\,(\theta_C) - 7.2] = 0$

$2.6\,EI\,(\theta_B) + 0.8\,EI\,(\theta_C) + 0.375\,EI\,(\Delta) - 7.2 = 0 \quad \ldots$ (I)

Substituting equations (iv) and (v) in equation (B), we get

$[1.6\,EI\,(\theta_C) + 0.8\,EI\,(\theta_B) - 7.2] + [EI\,(\theta_C) + 0.375\,EI\,(\Delta) + 3] = 0$

$2.6\,EI\,(\theta_C) + 0.8\,EI\,(\theta_B) + 0.375\,EI\,(\Delta) - 4.2 = 0 \quad \ldots$ (II)

Substituting equations (i), (ii), (v) and (vi) in equation (C), we get

$[0.5\,EI\,(\theta_B) + 0.375\,EI\,(\Delta)] + [EI\,(\theta_B) + 0.375\,EI\,(\Delta)] +$

$[EI\,(\theta_C) + 0.375\,EI\,(\Delta) + 3]\,[0.5\,EI\,(\theta_C) + 0.375\,EI\,(\Delta) + 6] = 0$

$1.5\,EI\,(\theta_B) + 1.5\,EI\,(\theta_C) + 1.5\,EI\,(\Delta) + 9 = 0 \quad \ldots$ (III)

Step VI : Solution of equations for joint displacements :

Solving equations (I), (II) and (III), we get,

$$\boxed{\theta_B = \frac{3.834}{EI}, \quad \theta_C = \frac{2.163}{EI}, \quad \Delta = -\frac{12}{EI}}$$

negative sign for Δ indicates that, sway is towards left.

Step VII : Member-End Moments :

Substituting the values of above displacements in SD equations, member-end moments are obtained as under :

$$M_{AB} = 0.5\,EI\left(\frac{3.834}{EI}\right) + 0.375\,EI\left(-\frac{12}{EI}\right) = -2.58 \text{ kNm}$$

$$M_{BA} = EI\left(\frac{3.834}{EI}\right) + 0.375\,EI\left(-\frac{12}{EI}\right) = -0.66 \text{ kNm}$$

$$M_{BC} = 1.6\,EI\left(\frac{3.834}{EI}\right) + 0.8\,EI\left(\frac{2.163}{EI}\right) - 7.2 = 0.66 \text{ kNm}$$

$$M_{CB} = 1.6\,EI\left(\frac{2.163}{EI}\right) + 0.8\,EI\left(\frac{3.834}{EI}\right) - 7.2 = -0.66 \text{ kNm}$$

TOS – II (TE CIVIL SEM. VI NMU) SLOPE-DEFLECTION METHOD

$$M_{CD} = EI\left(\frac{2.163}{EI}\right) + 0.375\ EI\left(-\frac{12}{EI}\right) + 3 = 0.66\ kNm$$

$$M_{DC} = 0.5\ EI\left(\frac{2.163}{EI}\right) + 0.375\ EI\left(-\frac{12}{EI}\right) + 6 = 2.58\ kNm$$

Step VIII : FBD of members is as shown in Fig. 2.27 (b). Considering equilibrium of each member and of complete structure, all reaction components are found out as shown in the figure.

Step IX : Shear force diagram is as shown in Fig. 2.27 (c).

Step X : Bending moment diagram :
BMD on tension side is shown in Fig. 2.27 (d).

Step XI : FBD of structure is as shown in Fig. 2.27 (e).

Example 2.19 : *Analyse the rigid frame shown in Fig. 2.28 using slope-deflection method. Draw BMD.*

Solution : **(1) Data :** The frame is supported and loaded as shown in Fig. 2.30.

  (2) Frame type : Sway frame.

Object : Structural analysis.

Equations : SD equations.

Procedure :

Step I : Degree of kinematic indeterminacy = D_{ki} = 3.

  Unknown Displacements : θ_B, θ_C and horizontal sway = Δ

  Known Displacements : $\theta_A = \theta_D = 0$

Step II : Fixed-end moments :

$$M^F_{AB} = M^F_{BA} = M^F_{CD} = M^F_{DC} = 0$$

$$M^F_{BC} = -M^F_{CB} = \frac{30 \times 3^2}{12} = 22.5\ kN\text{-}m$$

Step III : SD equations :

  (Assuming sway = Δ towards right)

Member AB :

$$M_{AB} = \frac{4\ EI}{L}\theta_A + \frac{2\ EI}{L}\theta_B + \frac{6\ EI\ \Delta}{L^2} + M^F_{AB}$$

$$= \frac{2\ EI}{4}\theta_B + \frac{6\ EI\ \Delta}{4^2} + 0 = 0.5\ EI\ \theta_B + 0.375\ EI\ \Delta \qquad \ldots (i)$$

$$M_{BA} = \frac{4\ EI}{L}\theta_B + \frac{2\ EI}{L}\theta_A + \frac{6\ EI\ \Delta}{L^2} + M^F_{BA}$$

$$= \frac{4\ EI}{4}\theta_B + \frac{6\ EI\ \Delta}{4^2} = EI\ \theta_B + 0.375\ EI\ \Delta \qquad \ldots (ii)$$

Member BC :

$$M_{BC} = \frac{4E(2I)}{L}\theta_B + \frac{2E(2I)}{L}\theta_C + \frac{6EI\Delta}{L^2} + M^F_{BC}$$

$$= \frac{8EI}{3}\theta_B + \frac{4EI}{3}\theta_C + 22.5$$

$$= 2.67\ EI\ \theta_B + 1.33\ EI\ \theta_C + 22.5 \quad \ldots \text{(iii)}$$

$$M_{CB} = \frac{4E(2I)}{L}\theta_C + \frac{2E(2I)}{L}\theta_B + \frac{6EI\Delta}{L^2} + M^F_{CB}$$

$$= \frac{8EI}{3}\theta_C + \frac{4EI}{3}\theta_B - 22.5$$

$$= 2.67\ EI\ \theta_C + 1.33\ EI\ \theta_B - 22.5 \quad \ldots \text{(iv)}$$

Member CD :

$$M_{CD} = \frac{4EI}{L}\theta_C + \frac{2EI}{L}\theta_D - \frac{6EI\Delta}{L^2} + M^F_{CD}$$

$$= \frac{4EI}{4}\theta_C + \frac{2EI}{4}\theta_D - \frac{6EI\Delta}{4^2} + 0$$

$$M_{CD} = EI\ \theta_C - 0.375\ EI\ \Delta \quad \ldots \text{(v)}$$

$$M_{DC} = \frac{4EI}{L}\theta_D + \frac{2EI}{L}\theta_C - \frac{6EI\Delta}{L^2} + M^F_{DC}$$

$$= \frac{4EI}{4}\theta_D + \frac{2EI}{4}\theta_C - \frac{6EI\Delta}{4^2} + 0$$

$$= 0.5\ EI\ \theta_C - 0.375\ EI\ \Delta \quad \ldots \text{(vi)}$$

Step IV : Equilibrium conditions for joints :
Moment of equilibrium of joint B
$$M_{BA} + M_{BC} = 0 \quad \ldots \text{(A)}$$
Moment of equilibrium of joint C
$$M_{CB} + M_{CD} = 0 \quad \ldots \text{(B)}$$
Horizontal shear equilibrium of structure
$$H_A + H_D = 0$$

where,
$$H_A = \frac{M_{AB} + M_{BA}}{4} \quad \text{and} \quad H_D = \frac{M_{DC} + M_{CD}}{4}$$

$$\frac{M_{AB} + M_{BA}}{4} - \frac{M_{DC} + M_{CD}}{4} = 0$$

$$M_{AB} + M_{BA} + M_{DC} + M_{CD} = 0 \quad \ldots \text{(C)}$$

Step V : Formulation of equilibrium equations in terms of joint displacements :
Substituting equations (ii) and (iii) in equation (A), we get
$$EI\ \theta_B + 0.375\ EI\ \Delta + 2.67\ EI\ \theta_B + 1.33\ EI\ \theta_C + 22.5 = 0$$
$$3.67\ EI\ \theta_B + 1.33\ EI\ \theta_C + 0.375\ EI\ \Delta = -22.5 \quad \ldots \text{(D)}$$
Substituting equations (iv) and (v) in equation (B), we get
$$2.67\ EI\ \theta_C + 1.33\ EI\ \theta_B - 22.5 + EI\ \theta_C - 0.375\ EI\ \Delta = 0$$

$1.33 \, EI \, \theta_B + 3.67 \, EI \, \theta_C - 0.375 \, EI \, \Delta = 22.5$ ... (E)

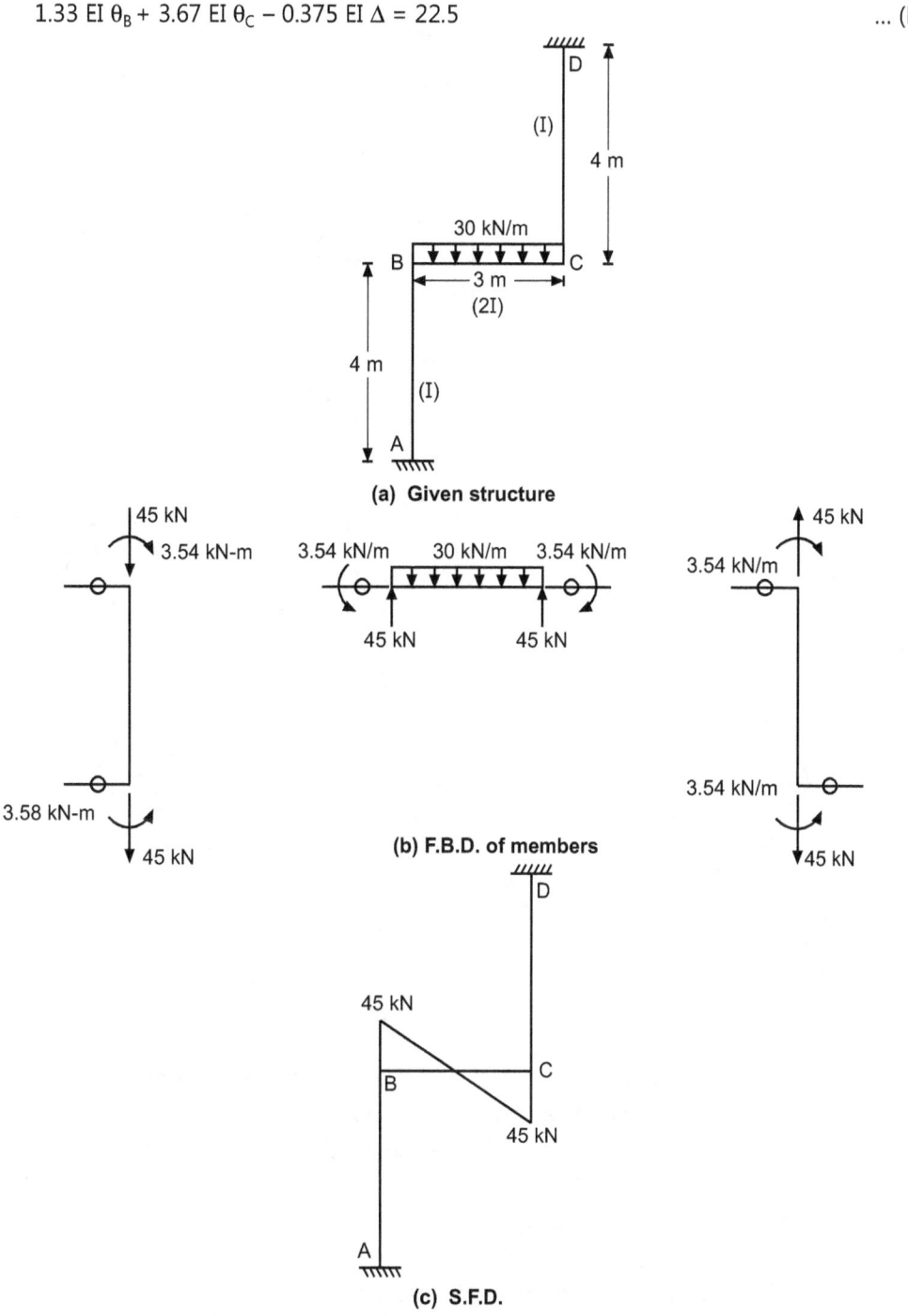

(a) Given structure

(b) F.B.D. of members

(c) S.F.D.

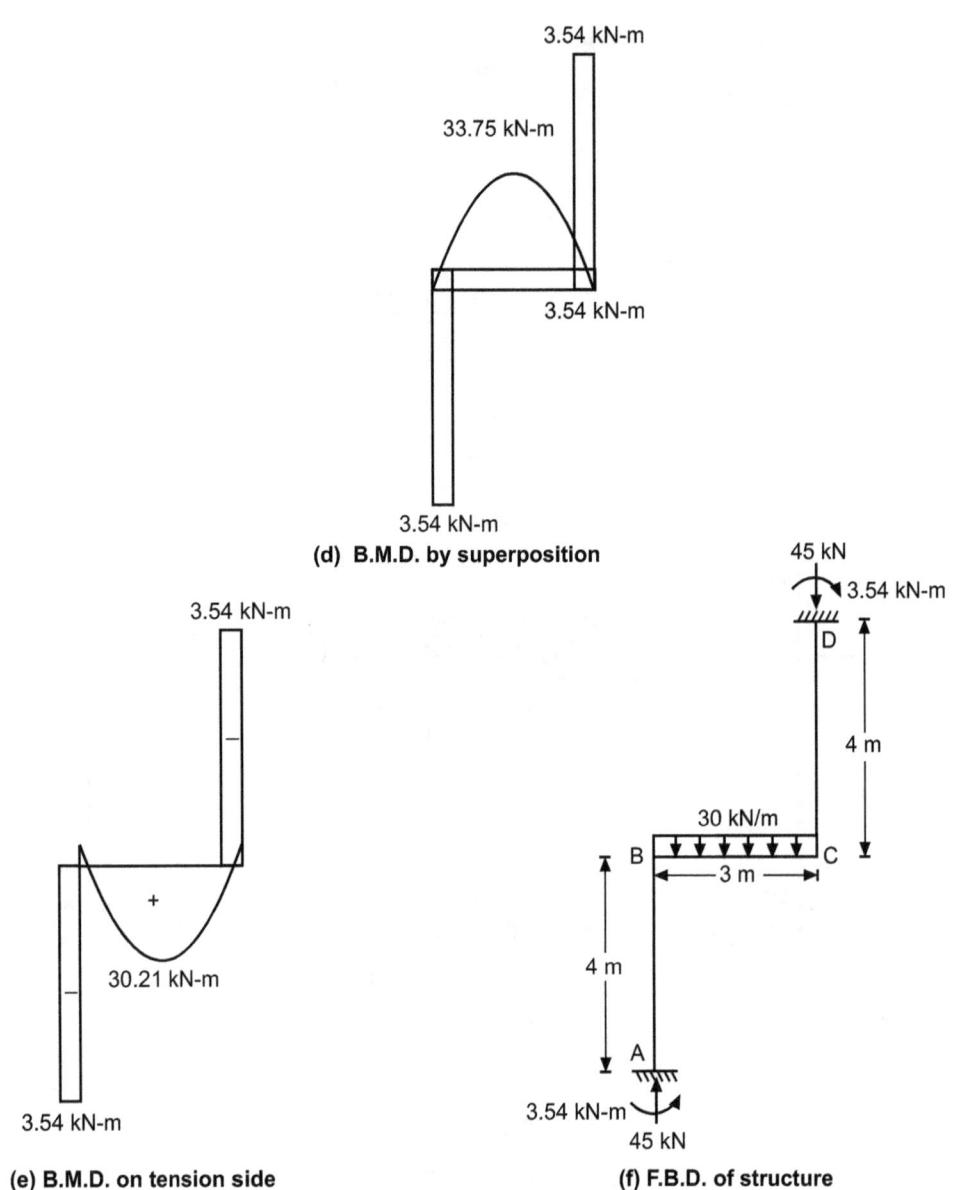

(d) B.M.D. by superposition

(e) B.M.D. on tension side

(f) F.B.D. of structure

Fig. 2.28 : For Illustrative Example 2.19

Substituting equations (i), (ii), (v) and (vi) in equation (C),

$0.5 \, EI \, \theta_B + 0.375 \, EI \, \Delta + EI \, \theta_B + 0.375 \, EI \, \Delta$
$- EI \, \theta_C + 0.375 \, EI \, \Delta - 0.5 \, EI \, \theta_C + 0.375 \, EI \, \Delta = 0$
$1.5 \, EI \, \theta_B - 1.5 \, EI \, \theta_C + 1.5 \, EI \, \Delta = 0$ ... (F)

Step VI : Solving equations (D), (E) and (F), we get

$$\boxed{\theta_B = -\frac{14.18}{EI}, \quad \theta_C = \frac{14.18}{EI}, \quad \Delta = \frac{28.36}{EI}}$$

$\Delta \rightarrow$ +ve indicates sway is towards right.

Step VII : Member-end moments

M_{AB} = 3.54 kN-m
M_{BA} = − 3.54 kN-m
M_{BC} = 3.54 kN-m
M_{CB} = − 3.54 kN-m
M_{CD} = 3.54 kN-m

Step VIII : FBD of members is as shown in Fig. 2.28 (b). Considering equilibrium of each member and of complete structure; all reaction components are found out as shown in figure.

Step IX : Shear force diagram is as shown in Fig. 2.28 (c).

Step X : Bending moment diagram : BMD by superposition is shown in Fig. 2.28 (d). BMD on tension side is shown in Fig. 2.28 (e).

Step XI : F.B.D. of structure is as shown in Fig. 2.28 (f).

Example 2.20 : *Using slope-deflection method, determine the final-end moments for the plane rigid frame shown in Fig. 2.29 (a). Construct BMD.*

Solution : Data : (1) The frame is loaded and supported as shown in Fig. 2.29.
(2) Frame type : Sway frame.

Object : Structural analysis.

Equations : SD equations.

Procedure :

Step I : Degree of kinematic indeterminacy.
Unknown Displacements : θ_A, θ_B, θ_C, θ_D and Δ.

Step II : Fixed-end moments :

$$M^F_{AB} = M^F_{BA} = 0$$

$$M^F_{BC} = -M^F_{CB} = \frac{2.5 \times 4^2}{12} = 3.33 \text{ kN-m}$$

$$M^F_{CD} = \frac{wab^2}{l^2} = \frac{5 \times 1.5 \times 3.5^2}{5^2} = 3.675 \text{ kN-m}$$

$$M^F_{DC} = -\frac{wa^2b}{l^2} = -\frac{5 \times 1.5^2 \times 3.5}{5^2} = -1.575 \text{ kN-m}$$

Step III : SD equations (Assuming horizontal sway = Δ towards right).

Member AB : Modified slope-deflection method :

$$M_{AB} = \frac{3EI}{L}\theta_B + \frac{3EI}{L^2}\Delta + M^F_{BA}$$

$$= \frac{3EI}{4} \theta_B + \frac{3EI}{16} \Delta + 0$$
$$= 0.75 \, EI \, \theta_B + 0.1875 \, EI \, \Delta \quad \ldots \text{(I)}$$

Member BC :
$$M_{BC} = \frac{4EI}{L} \theta_B + \frac{2EI}{L} \theta_C + M_{BC}^F$$
$$= \frac{4E(2I)}{4} \theta_B + \frac{2E(2I)}{4} \theta_C + 3.33$$
$$= 2 \, EI \, \theta_B + EI \, \theta_C + 3.33 \quad \ldots \text{(II)}$$

$$M_{CB} = \frac{4EI}{L} \theta_C + \frac{2EI}{L} \theta_B + M_{CB}^F$$
$$= \frac{4E(2I)}{4} \theta_C + \frac{2E(2I)}{4} \theta_B - 3.33$$
$$= 2 \, EI \, \theta_C + EI \, \theta_B - 3.33 \quad \ldots \text{(III)}$$

Member CD : Using modified slope-deflection method,
$$M_{CD} = M_{CD}^F - \left(\frac{M_{DC}^F}{2}\right) + \frac{3EI}{L} \theta_C + \frac{3EI \, \Delta}{L^2}$$
$$= 3.675 - \left(-\frac{1.575}{2}\right) + \frac{3E(1.25I)}{5} \theta_C + \frac{3E(1.25I) \, \Delta}{5^2}$$
$$= 4.4625 + 0.75 \, EI \, \Delta + 0.15 \, EI \, \Delta \quad \ldots \text{(IV)}$$

Step IV : Equilibrium conditions for joints and formulation of equilibrium equations :
Moment equilibrium of joint B
$$M_{BA} + M_{BC} = 0$$
$$0.75 \, EI \, \theta_B + 0.1875 \, EI \, \Delta + 2 \, EI \, \theta_B + EI \, \theta_C + 3.33 = 0$$
$$2.75 \, EI \, \theta_B + EI \, \theta_C + 0.1875 \, EI \, \Delta = -3.33 \quad \ldots \text{(A)}$$
Moment equilibrium of joint C
$$M_{CB} + M_{CD} = 0$$

(a)

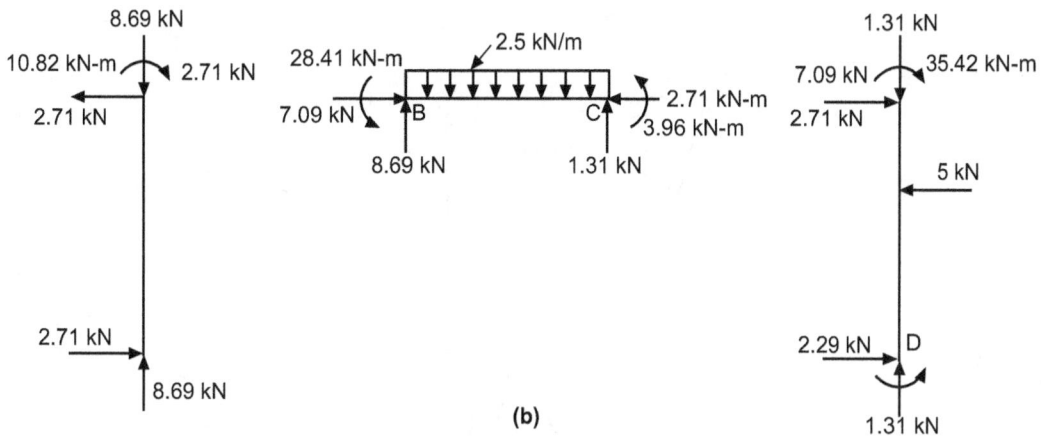

(b)

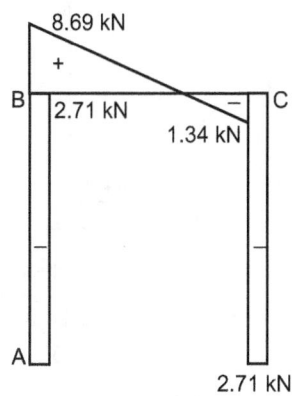

(c)

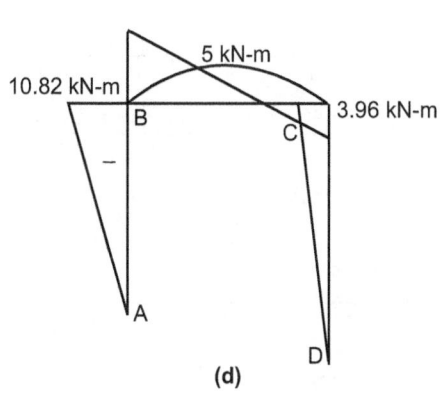

(d)

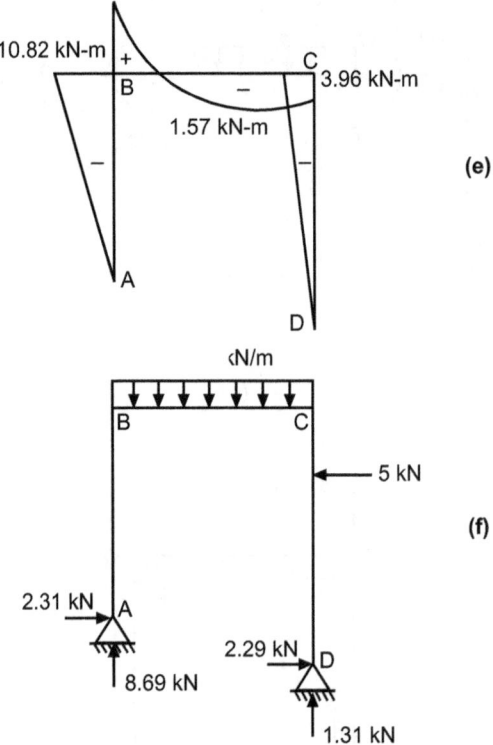

Fig. 2.28 : For Illustrative Example 2.20

$2\,EI\,\theta_C + EI\,\theta_B - 3.33 + 4.4625 + 0.75\,EI\,\Delta + 0.15\,EI\,\Delta = 0$

$EI\,\theta_B + 2.75\,EI\,\theta_C + 0.15\,EI\,\Delta = -1.132$ ... (B)

Horizontal shear equilibrium of structure,

$\qquad H_A + H_D + 5 = 0$

$$H_A = \frac{M_{AB} + M_{BA}}{4}, \quad H_D = \frac{M_{CD} + M_{DC} - 5 \times 1.5}{5}$$

$\therefore \dfrac{0.75\,EI\,\theta_B + 0.1875\,EI\,\Delta}{4} + \dfrac{4.4625 + 0.75\,EI\,\theta_C + 0.15\,EI\,\Delta - 7.5}{5} = -5$

$3.75\,EI\,\theta_B + 3\,EI\,\theta_C + 1.5375\,EI\,\Delta - 30 = -100$

$3.75\,EI\,\theta_B + 3\,EI\,\theta_C + 1.5375\,EI\,\Delta = -87.85$ ... (C)

Step V : Solving equations (A), (B) and (C),

$$\boxed{\theta_B = \frac{2.57}{EI}, \quad \theta_C = \frac{2.36}{EI}, \quad \Delta = -\frac{68.01}{EI}}$$

Step VI : Member-End Moments :

M_{AB} = 0
M_{BA} = − 10.82 kN-m
M_{BC} = 10.82 kN-m
M_{CB} = 3.96 kN-m
M_{CD} = − 3.96 kN-m
M_{DC} = 0

Step VII : FBD of members is as shown in Fig. 2.29 (b). Considering equilibrium of each member and of complete structure; all reaction components are found out as shown in figure.

Step VIII : Shear force diagram is as shown in Fig. 2.29 (c).

Step IX : Bending moment diagram : BMD by superposition is shown in Fig. 2.29 (d). BMD on tension side is shown in Fig. 2.29 (e).

Step X : FBD of structure is as shown in Fig. 2.29 (f).

2.10 INTRODUCTION

The analysis of structure by SD method is carried out conventionally by using the general SD equations and the required equilibrium equations. However, the minimization of the number of unknown joint displacements is very much desirable for easy and speedy working of SD method. This is possible in certain cases by simple modifications in the formulation as per fundamental concepts of structural analysis. In this context, some of the tricks are suggested here for its effective use in the specific problems of analysis.

2.10.1 Structure with the Overhanging Part

The unknown joint displacements i.e. translation and rotation at the end of the overhanging part of a structure, can be conveniently eliminated by removing the overhanging part and replacing the same by the statically equivalent loads on the corresponding joint. The equivalent load generally includes the joint force and the joint moment.

2.10.2 Symmetrical Structure

The joint translations are absent in perfectly symmetrical structure (i.e. symmetry with all respects) and there is specific relationship between the joint rotations. The general rules of symmetry with respect to the joint rotations are as follows :

- The joint rotations on the opposite sides of the axis of symmetry are equal but opposite in direction as shown in Fig. 2.30.
- The joint rotations on the axis of symmetry are zero as shown in Fig. 2.30.

The information of joint rotations because of symmetry are taken help of reducing the unknown displacements of the structure and further simplifying the SD method for analysis of structure. This is illustrated in the following example.

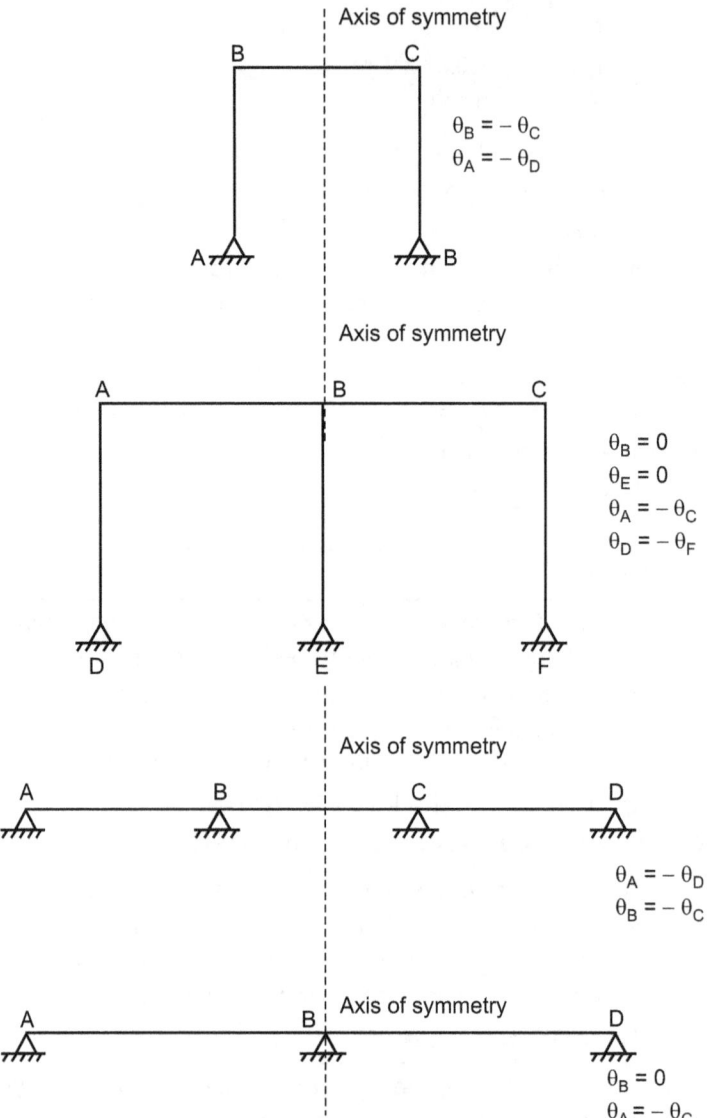

Fig. 2.30 : Symmetrical structures

Example 2.21 : Analyse the frame shown in Fig. 2.31 (a) by slope-deflection method. Take EI = constant.

Solution : Data : (1) The frame is supported and loaded as shown in Fig. 2.31 (a).

(2) EI = constant.

(3) Frame type : Non-sway frame (symmetrical).

Object : Structural analysis.

Equations : SD equations.

Procedure :

Step I : Degree of kinematic indeterminacy for given structure = $D_{ki} = 2$.

But, by symmetry, $\theta_B = -\theta_C$.

$\therefore$ Degree of kinematic indeterminacy = $D_{ki} = 1$.

Unknown Displacement : θ_B.

Known Displacements : $\theta_A = \theta_D = 0$.

Step II : Fixed-End Moments :

$$M_{AB}^F = M_{BA}^F = M_{CD}^F$$
$$= M_{DC}^F = 0$$
$$M_{BC}^F = -M_{CB}^F = \frac{wL^2}{12}$$

Step III : SD equations :

Member AB :
$$M_{AB} = \frac{4EI}{L}(\theta_A) + \frac{2EI}{L}(\theta_B) \pm \frac{6EI}{L^2}(\Delta) + M_{AB}^F$$
$$= \frac{2EI}{L}(\theta_B) \qquad \ldots (i)$$

$$M_{BA} = \frac{4EI}{L}(\theta_B) + \frac{2EI}{L}(\theta_A) \pm \frac{6EI}{L^2}(\Delta) + M_{BA}^F$$
$$= \frac{4EI}{L}(\theta_B) \qquad \ldots (ii)$$

Member BC :
$$M_{BC} = \frac{4EI}{L}(\theta_B) + \frac{2EI}{L}(\theta_C) \pm \frac{6EI}{L^2}(\Delta) + M_{BC}^F$$
$$= \frac{4EI}{L}(\theta_B) + \frac{2EI}{L}(-\theta_B) + \frac{wL^2}{12} = \frac{2EI}{L}(\theta_B) + \frac{wL^2}{12} \qquad \ldots (iii)$$

$$M_{CB} = \frac{4EI}{L}(\theta_C) + \frac{2EI}{L}(\theta_B) \pm \frac{6EI}{L^2}(\Delta) + M_{CB}^F$$
$$= \frac{4EI}{L}(-\theta_B) + \frac{2EI}{L}(\theta_B) - \frac{wL^2}{12}$$
$$= -\frac{2EI}{L}(\theta_B) - \frac{wL^2}{12} \qquad \ldots (iv)$$

Member CD :
$$M_{CD} = \frac{4EI}{L}(\theta_C) + \frac{2EI}{L}(\theta_D) \pm \frac{6EI}{L^2}(\Delta) + M_{CD}^F$$
$$= -\frac{4EI}{L}(\theta_B) \qquad \ldots (v)$$

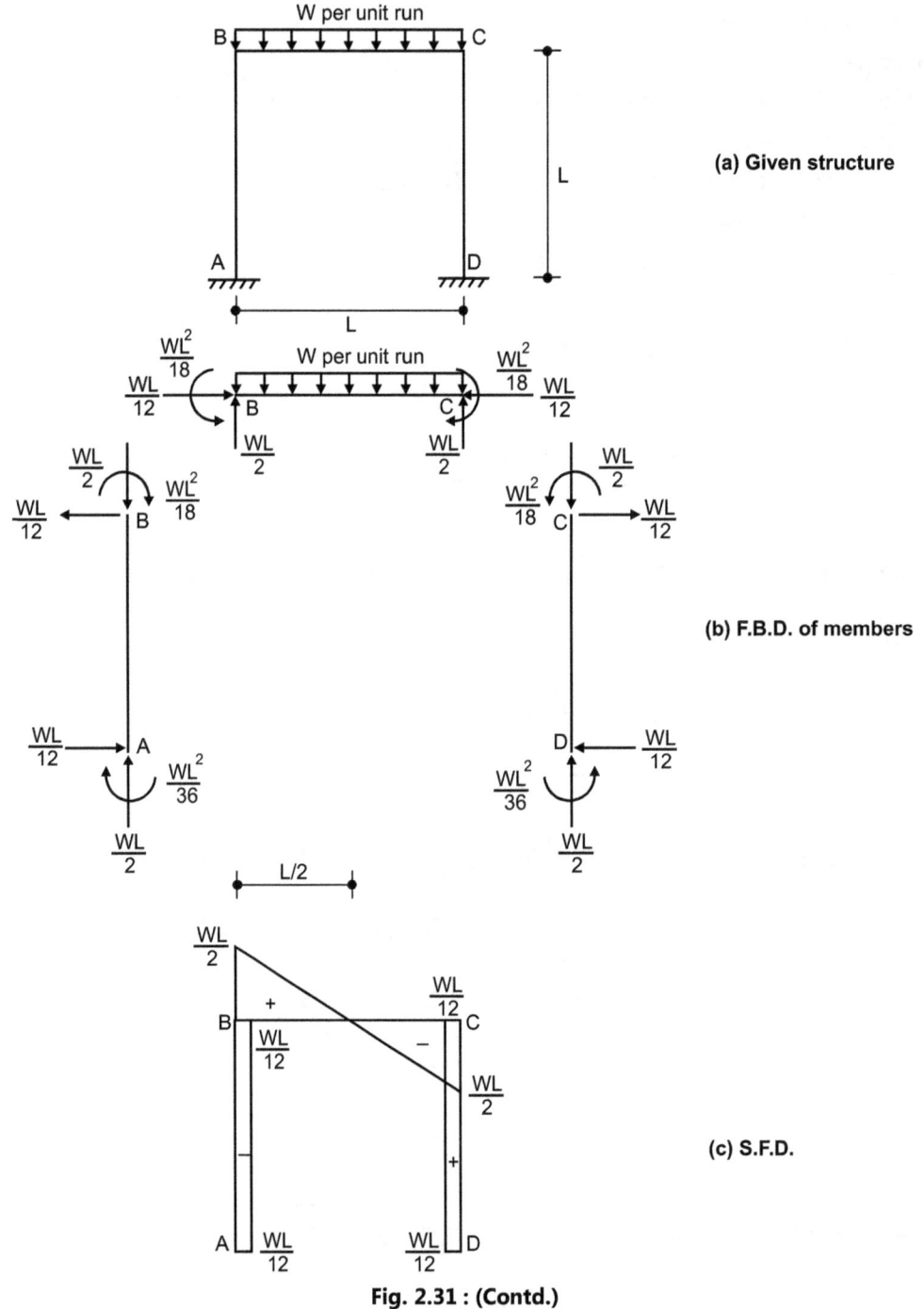

Fig. 2.31 : (Contd.)

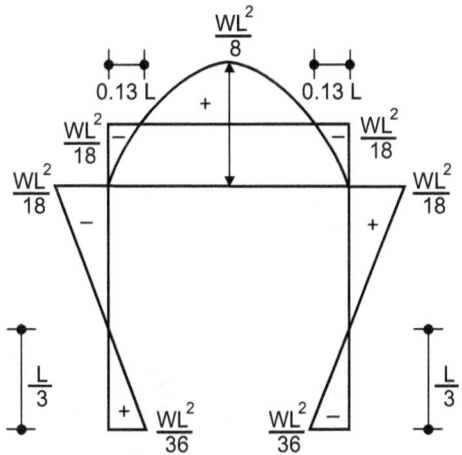

(d) B.M.D. by superposition

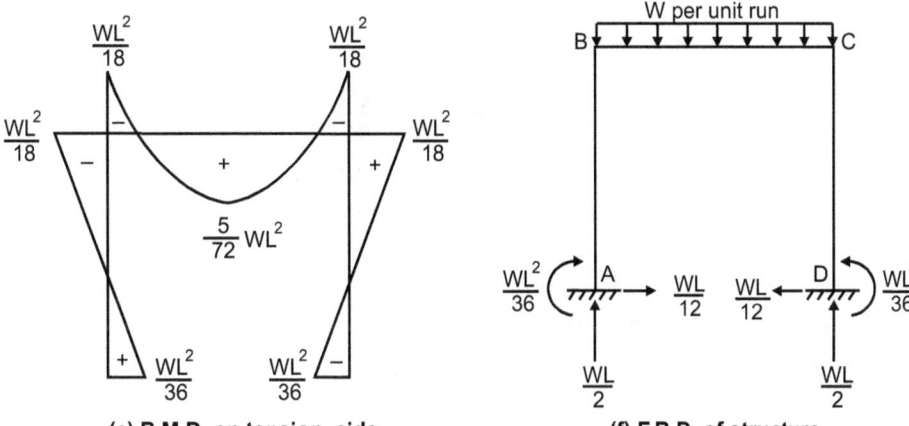

(e) B.M.D. on tension side (f) F.B.D. of structure

Fig. 2.31 : For Illustrative Example 2.21

$$M_{DC} = \frac{4EI}{L}(\theta_D) + \frac{2EI}{L}(\theta_C) \pm \frac{6EI}{L^2}(\Delta) + M_{DC}^F$$

$$= -\frac{2EI}{L}(\theta_B) \qquad \ldots \text{(vi)}$$

Step IV : Equilibrium conditions for joints :

Moment equilibrium of joint B : $M_{BA} + M_{BC} = 0$ ... (A)

Step V : Formulation of equilibrium equations in terms of joint displacements :

Substituting equations (ii) and (iii) in equation (A), we get

$$\frac{4EI}{L}(\theta_B) + \frac{2EI}{L}(\theta_B) + \frac{wL^2}{12} = 0 \quad \text{i.e.} \quad \frac{6EI}{L}(\theta_B) + \frac{wL^2}{12} = 0 \qquad \ldots \text{(A)}$$

Step VI : Solution of equations for displacements :

Solving equation (A), we get

$$\boxed{\theta_B = -\frac{wL^3}{72\,EI}}$$

Step VII : Member-end moments : Substituting the values of above displacements in SD equations; member-end moments are obtained as under :

$$M_{AB} = \frac{2\,EI}{L}\left(-\frac{wL^3}{72\,EI}\right) = -\frac{wL^2}{36}$$

$$M_{BA} = \frac{4\,EI}{L}\left(-\frac{wL^3}{72\,EI}\right) = -\frac{wL^2}{18}$$

$$M_{BC} = \frac{2\,EI}{L}\left(-\frac{wL^3}{72\,EI}\right) + \frac{wL^2}{12} = \frac{wL^2}{18}$$

$$M_{CB} = -\frac{2\,EI}{L}\left(-\frac{wL^3}{72\,EI}\right) - \frac{wL^2}{12} = -\frac{wL^2}{18}$$

$$M_{CD} = -\frac{4\,EI}{L}\left(-\frac{wL^3}{72\,EI}\right) = \frac{wL^2}{18}$$

$$M_{DC} = -\frac{2\,EI}{L}\left(-\frac{wL^3}{72\,EI}\right) = \frac{wL^2}{36}$$

Step VIII : FBD of members is as shown in Fig. 2.31 (b). Considering equilibrium of each member and of complete structure, all reaction components are found out as shown in the figure.

Step IX : Shear force diagram is as shown in Fig. 2.31 (c).

Step X : Bending moment diagram :
   BMD by superposition is shown in Fig. 2.31 (d).
   BMD on tension side is shown in Fig. 2.31 (e).

Step XI : FBD of structure is as shown in Fig. 2.31 (f).

2.10.3 Structure Without Joint Translation and With Hinge or Roller Support At Ends

2.10.3.1 Unloaded Hinge or Roller Support

The unknown rotations at the unloaded hinged/roller supports can be eliminated if desired so. To achieve this, the SD equation of the member connected to the hinged/roller support is modified and expressed in terms of the near-end rotation only. This modification is based on the following concepts :

- The final member-end moment at the hinged/roller support is zero.
- The flexural rotational stiffness of the member having the far end hinged is $\frac{3\,EI}{L}$.

The SD equation of such member is developed by the superposition technique as illustrated in Fig. 2.32.

- Fig. 2.32 (a) shows the member AB connected to the rigid joint at A and the non-yielding hinged support at B. The member loads are also shown.
- The final deformed shape, rotation of joints and member-end moments are shown in Fig. 2.32 (b). It may be noted that MBA should be zero.
- FEM due to member loads in the restrained beam are shown in Fig. 2.32 (c).

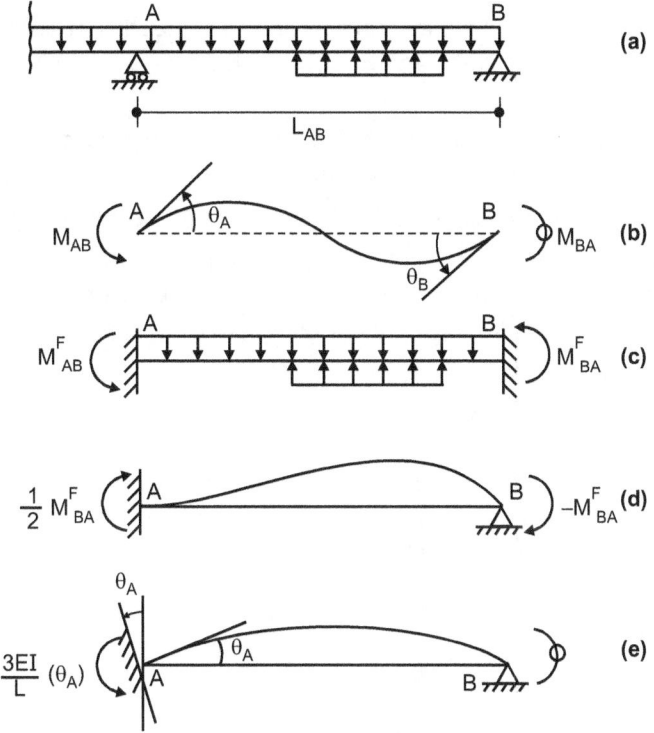

Fig. 2.32 : Development of modified SD equation

- As the condition of hinged support indicates that there should be no moment, the M_{BA}^F in reversed direction is applied at B as shown in Fig. 2.32 (d). The effect of this moment at A is $-\dfrac{1}{2} M_{BA}^F$ as the carry-over moment.
- The joint A is released for θ_A as shown in Fig. 2.32 (e). Keeping the joint B as hinged. The member-end moment in this case is $\dfrac{3\, EI_{AB}}{L_{AB}} (\theta_B)$ according to the rotational stiffness of member when the far end is hinged.

Superposing all the member-end moments at A, the modified SD equation of the member is obtained as

$$M_{AB} = M_{AB}^F - \frac{1}{2} M_{BA}^F + \frac{3 EI_{AB}}{L_{AB}} (\theta_A)$$

It is clear from Fig. 2.32 that $M_{BA} = 0$, even after superposition. In generalized form, SD equation becomes

$$M_{ij} = M_{ij}^F - \frac{1}{2} M_{ji}^F + \frac{3 EI_{ij}}{L_{ij}} (\theta_i) \quad \ldots (2.6)$$

Using the modified equation for the member having the hinged support at either of its ends, the SD method greatly simplifies the analysis of the structure. This is illustrated for two-span uniform beam ABC in example (2.20).

2.10.3.2 Application of modified SD equations to structures without joint translations and with unloaded hinged or roller support at the end

Example 2.22 : *Analyse the beam shown in Fig. 2.33 (a) by using modified SD equations.*

Solution : Step I : Basically the unknown joint displacements are θ_A, θ_B and θ_C. These three unknowns can be reduced to only one i.e. θ_B if the trick of modified SD equation is used in SD method. Following important steps complete the solution easily and quickly.

Unknown Displacement : θ_B.

Step II : Fixed-End Moments :

$$M_{AB}^F = +\frac{wL^2}{12}$$

$$M_{BA}^F = -\frac{wL^2}{12}$$

$$M_{BC}^F = +\frac{wL^2}{12}$$

$$M_{CB}^F = -\frac{wL^2}{12}$$

Step III : Modified SD equations : Modified SD equations are applicable to the members AB and BC as both the members are connected to the hinged or roller support.

$$M_{BA} = M_{BA}^F - \frac{1}{2} M_{AB}^F + \frac{3 EI_{AB}}{L_{AB}} (\theta_B)$$

i.e.
$$M_{BA} = -\frac{wL^2}{12} - \frac{1}{2}\left(+\frac{wL^2}{12}\right) + \frac{3 EI}{L} (\theta_B)$$

and
$$M_{BC} = M_{BC}^F - \frac{1}{2} M_{CB}^F + \frac{3 EI_{BC}}{L_{BC}} (\theta_B)$$

i.e.
$$M_{BC} = +\frac{wL^2}{12} - \frac{1}{2}\left(-\frac{wL^2}{12}\right) + \frac{3 EI}{L} (\theta_B)$$

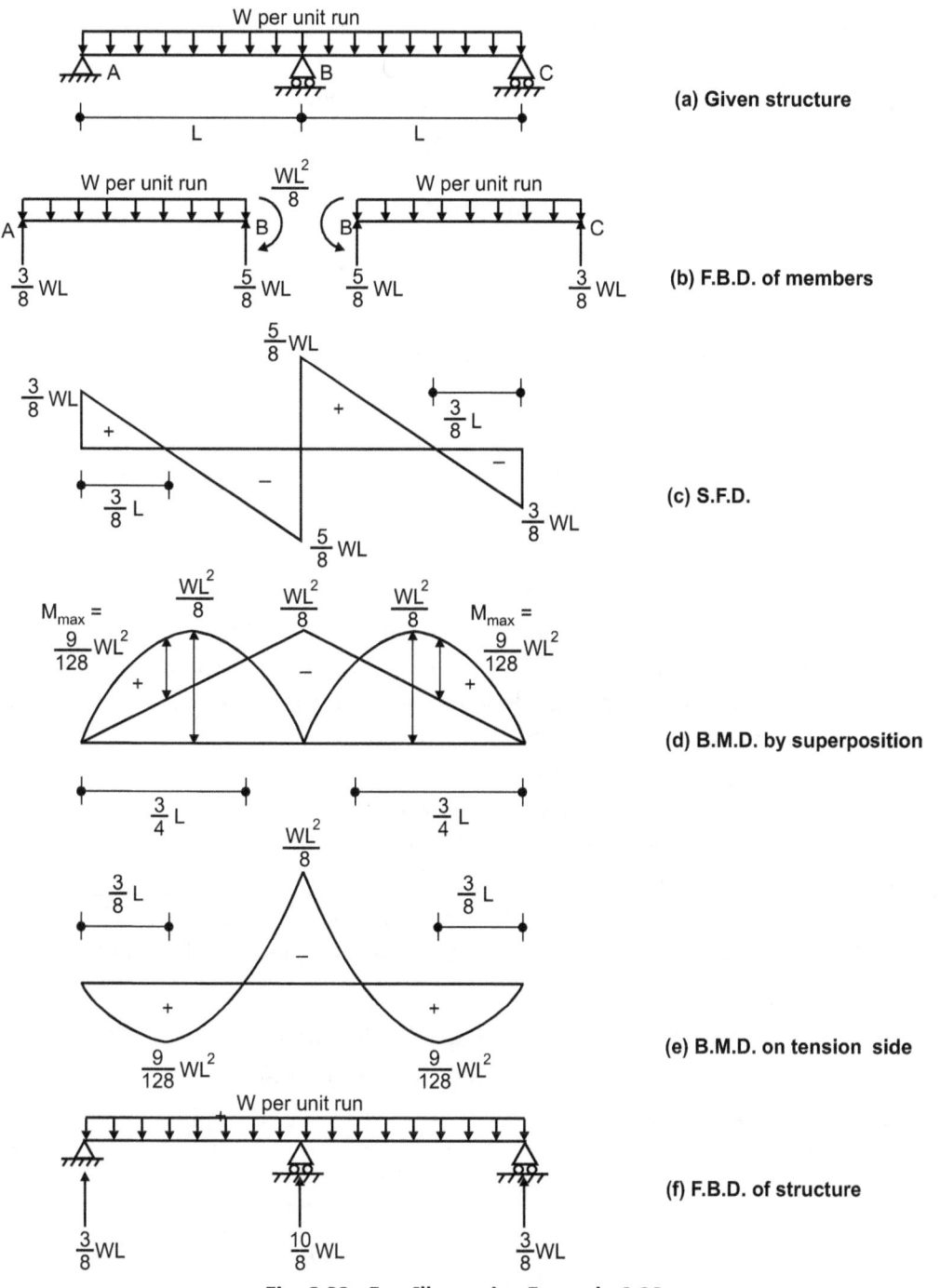

Fig. 2.33 : For Illustrative Example 2.22

Step IV : Equilibrium equation :
For joint B : $M_{BA} + M_{BC} = 0$

Step V : Substituting SD equations in equilibrium equation :

$$\left[-\frac{wL^2}{12} - \frac{wL^2}{24} + 3\frac{EI}{L}\theta_B\right] + \left[\frac{wL^2}{12} + \frac{wL^2}{24} + 3\frac{EI}{L}\theta_B\right] = 0$$

Step VI : Formation of equation for unknown :

$$\frac{6EI}{L}\theta_B = 0$$

$$\therefore \quad \theta_B = 0$$

The result of θ_B verifies the result tallies zero θ_B because of symmetry.

Step VII : Member-end moments :

$$M_{AB} = 0 = M_{CB}$$

$$M_{BA} = -\frac{wL^2}{12} - \frac{wL^2}{24} + \frac{3EI}{L}(0)$$

$$= -\frac{wL^2}{8}$$

$$M_{BC} = +\frac{wL^2}{8}$$

Step VIII : FBD of members is as shown in Fig. 2.33 (b). Considering equilibrium of each member, other reaction components are found out as shown in the figure.

Step IX : Shear force diagram is as shown in Fig. 2.33 (c).

Step X : Bending moment diagram :
BMD by superposition is shown in Fig. 2.33 (d).
BMD on tension side is shown in Fig. 2.33 (e).

Step XI : FBD of structure is as shown in Fig. 2.33 (f).

Example 2.23 : *Analyse the beam shown in Fig. 2.34 (a) using modified SD equations.*

Solution : Step I : $D_{ki} = 3$, Unknown displacements : θ_A, θ_B and θ_C. [Modified $D_{ki} = 1$ (θ_B)].

Step II : Fixed-End Moments :

$M_{AB}^F = 18.33$ kNm, $M_{BA}^F = -8.33$ kNm

$M_{BC}^F = 13.06$ kNm, $M_{CB}^F = -26.93$ kNm

Step III : Modified SD equations :

$$M_{BA} = \frac{3EI}{L}(\theta_B) + M_{BA}^F - \frac{M_{AB}^F}{2}$$

$$= \frac{3EI}{4}(\theta_B) - 8.33 - \frac{1}{2}(18.33) = \frac{3EI}{4}(\theta_B) - 17.5 \quad \ldots (i)$$

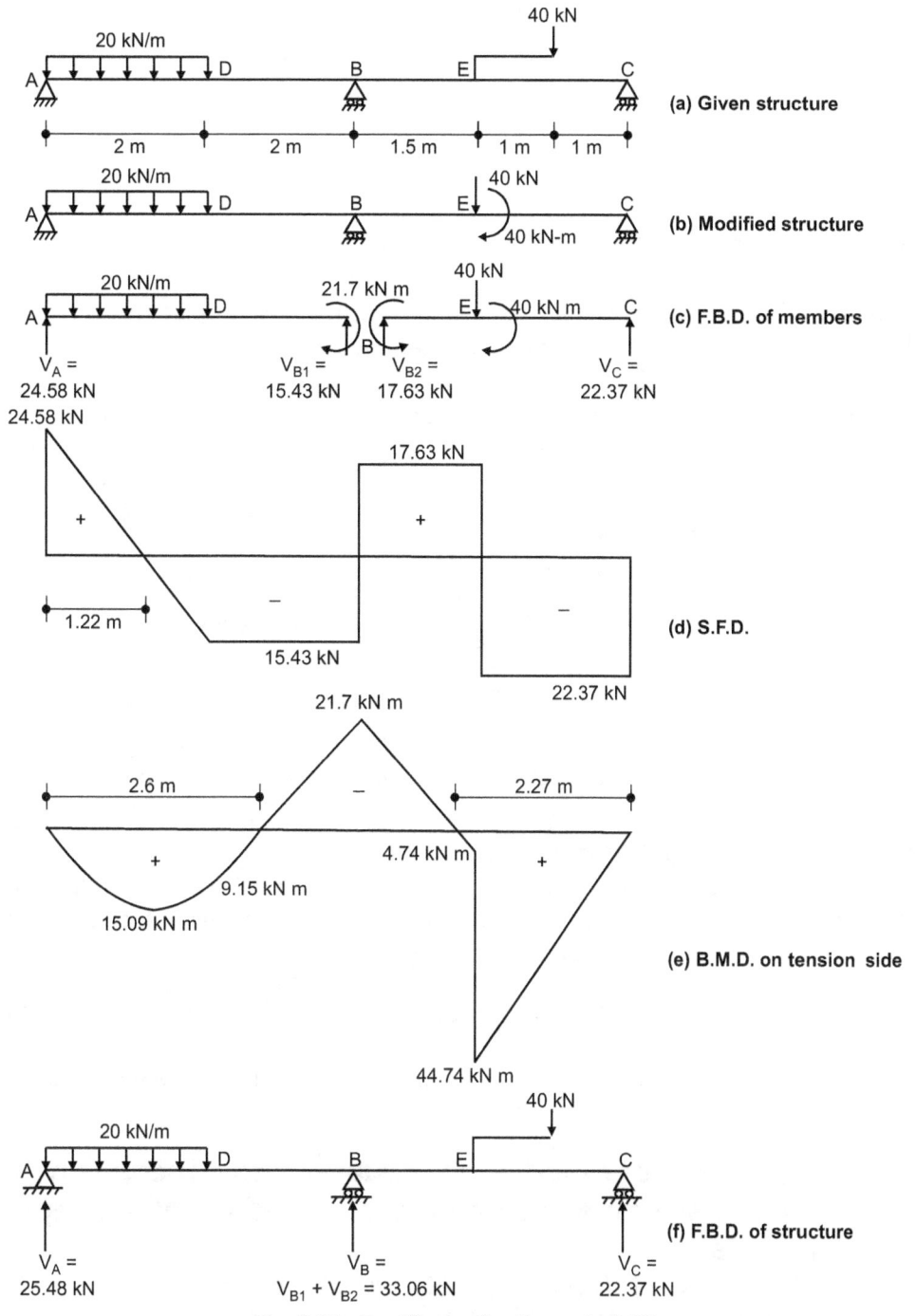

Fig. 2.34 : For Illustrative Example 2.23

$$M_{BC} = \frac{3\,EI}{L}(\theta_B) + M_{BC}^F - \frac{M_{CB}^F}{2}$$

$$= \frac{3\,EI}{3.5}(\theta_B) + 13.06 - \frac{1}{2}(-26.93)$$

$$= \frac{3\,EI}{3.5}(\theta_B) + 26.525 \qquad \ldots \text{(ii)}$$

Step IV : Moment equilibrium condition for joints :
At joint B : $\quad M_{BA} + M_{BC} = 0 \qquad \ldots$ (A)

Step V : Formulation of equilibrium equations in terms of joint displacements :
Substituting equations (i) and (ii) in equation (A), we get
$\quad (1.607)\,EI\,(\theta_B) + 9.025 = 0 \qquad \ldots$ (B)

Step VI : Solution of equations for joint displacements : Solving equation (B), we get

$$\boxed{\theta_B = -\frac{5.62}{EI}}$$

Step VII : Member-End Moments :

$$M_{AB} = 0 = M_{CB}$$

$$M_{BA} = \frac{3}{4}EI\left(-\frac{5.62}{EI}\right) - 17.5 = -21.7 \text{ kNm}$$

$$M_{BC} = \frac{3\,EI}{3.5}\left(-\frac{5.62}{EI}\right) + 26.525 = 21.7 \text{ kNm}$$

Rest of the analysis is the same as explained earlier.

It should be noted that, by using modified SD equations, the three unknown problems are reduced to only one unknown problem.

2.10.3.3 Loaded Hinged or Roller Support

Even if the end hinged/roller support is loaded, may be due to the equivalent loads of the overhanging part, the SD method could be tailored accordingly. Under such situation, the modified SD equation for the member having the hinged support is given by,

$$M_{AB} = M_{AB}^F - \frac{1}{2}M_{BA}^F + \frac{1}{2}M_{BA} + \frac{3\,EI_{AB}}{L_{AB}}(\theta_A) \qquad \ldots (2.7)$$

The additional term $\frac{1}{2}M_{BA}$ in the equation is the known applied moment at the hinged support, say M_B.

2.10.3.4 Application of modified SD equations to structures without joint translation and with loaded hinged or roller support at the ends

Example 2.24 : *Analyse the beam shown in Fig. 2.35 (a) using modified SD equation.*

Solution : Step I : $D_{ki} = 2$ for modified structure.

Unknown displacements : θ_B, θ_C. [Modified $D_{ki} = 1\ (\theta_B)$]

Step II : Fixed-End Moments :

$$M_{AB}^F = -M_{BA}^F = \frac{WL^2}{12} = \frac{6 \times 5^2}{12} = 12.5 \text{ kNm}$$

$$M_{BC}^F = -M_{CB}^F = \frac{WL^2}{12} = \frac{10 \times 4^2}{12} = 13.33 \text{ kNm}$$

Step III : Modified SD equations :

Span AB : $\quad M_{AB} = \dfrac{2EI}{5}(\theta_B) + 12.5$ ... (i)

$\quad\quad\quad\quad M_{BA} = \dfrac{4EI}{5}(\theta_B) - 12.5$ ... (ii)

Span BC : $\quad M_{BC} = \dfrac{3EI}{L}(\theta_B) + M_{BC}^F - \dfrac{1}{2}M_{CB}^F + \dfrac{1}{2}M_{CB}$

$\quad\quad\quad\quad\quad = \dfrac{3EI}{4}(\theta_B) + 13.33 - \dfrac{1}{2}(-13.33) - \dfrac{1}{2}(20)$

$\quad\quad\quad\quad\quad = 0.75\ EI\ (\theta_B) + 10$ ... (iii)

Step IV : Moment equilibrium condition for joints :

At joint B : $M_{BA} + M_{BC} = 0$ ... (A)

Step V : Formulation of equilibrium equations in terms of joint displacements :

Substituting equations (ii) and (iii) in equation (A), we get

$\quad 1.5\ EI\ (\theta_B) - 2.5 = 0$ ... (B)

Step VI : Solution of equations for joint displacements : Solving equation (B), we get

$$\boxed{\theta_B = \frac{1.61}{EI}}$$

Step VII : Member-End Moments :

$$M_{AB} = \frac{2EI}{5}\left(\frac{1.61}{EI}\right) + 12.5 = 13.14 \text{ kNm}$$

$$M_{BA} = \frac{4EI}{5}\left(\frac{1.61}{EI}\right) - 12.5 = -11.21 \text{ kNm}$$

$$M_{BC} = 0.75\ EI\left(\frac{1.61}{EI}\right) + 10 = 11.21 \text{ kNm}$$

$$M_{CB} = 0$$

Rest of the analysis is the same as explained earlier. It should be noted that two unknown problems reduced to one unknown problem by using modified SD equations.

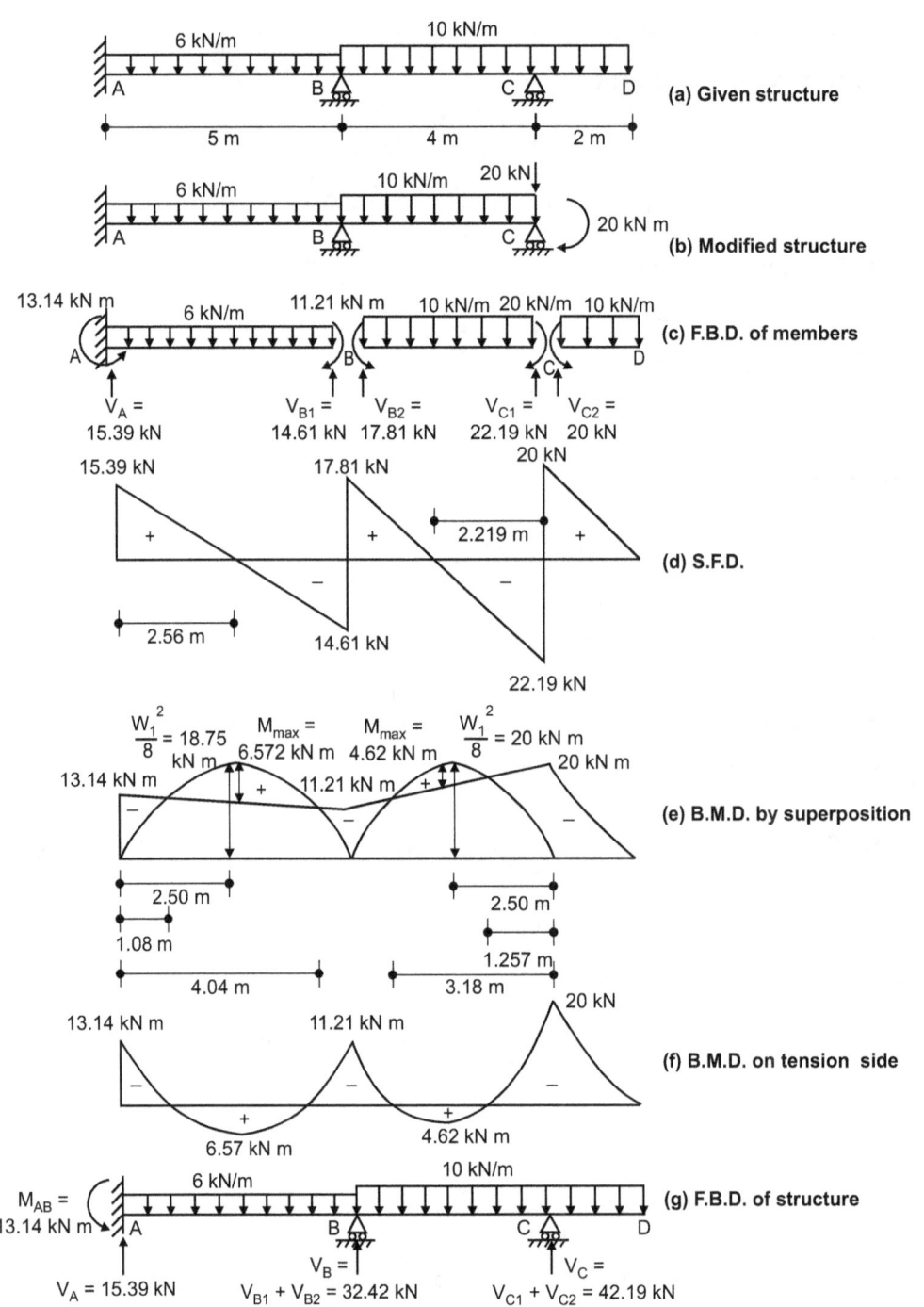

Fig. 2.35 : For Illustrative Example 2.24

2.10.4 Structure with Joint Translation and with Hinged or Roller Support at the End

Analogous tricks may be used to develop the SD equation for the member having joint translations and hinged/roller support to reduce the unknown displacements and simplify the SD method. This is very much useful especially in sway frames supported by hinged/roller support.

The modified SD equation for the member with joint translations can be derived on the same principles of superposition as shown in Fig. 2.36 and expressed as

$$M_{AB} = M^F_{AB} - \frac{1}{2} M^F_{BA} + \frac{1}{2} M_B + 3 \frac{EI_{AB}}{L_{AB}} (\theta_A) - 3 \frac{EI_{AB}}{L^2_{AB}} (\Delta)_{B/A} \quad \ldots (2.8)$$

where M_B is known applied joint moment if any and $\Delta_{B/A}$ is the relative joint translation, and $\frac{3EI}{L^2}$ is the translational stiffness of the member when the far end is hinged.

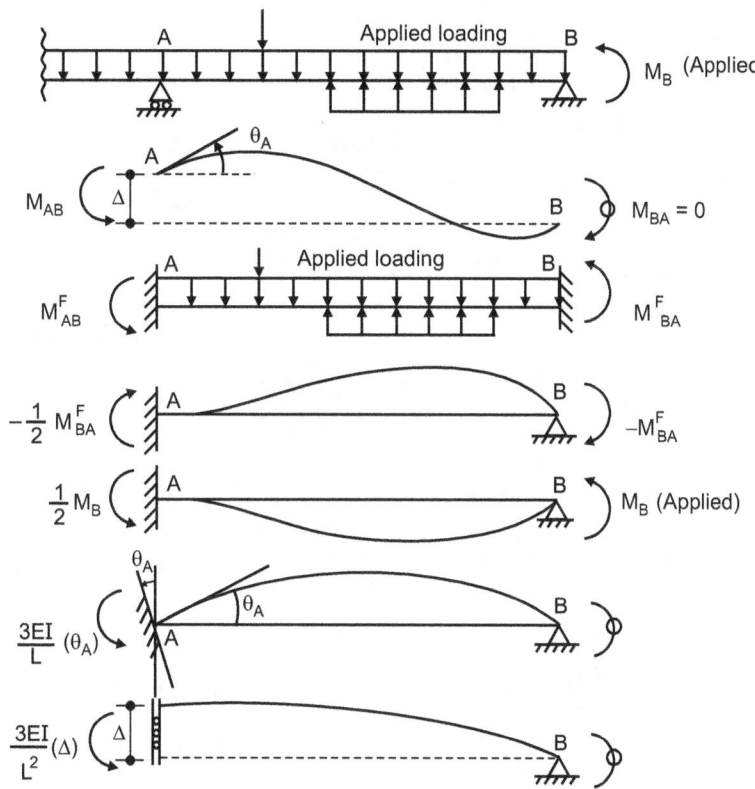

Fig. 2.36 : Development of modified SD equation considering translation

2.10.5 Application of Modified SD Equations to Structures with Joint Translations and with Hinged or Roller Support at the Ends

Example 2.25 : Analyse the beam shown in Fig. 2.37 (a) using modified SD equation.

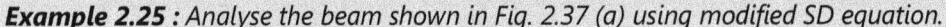

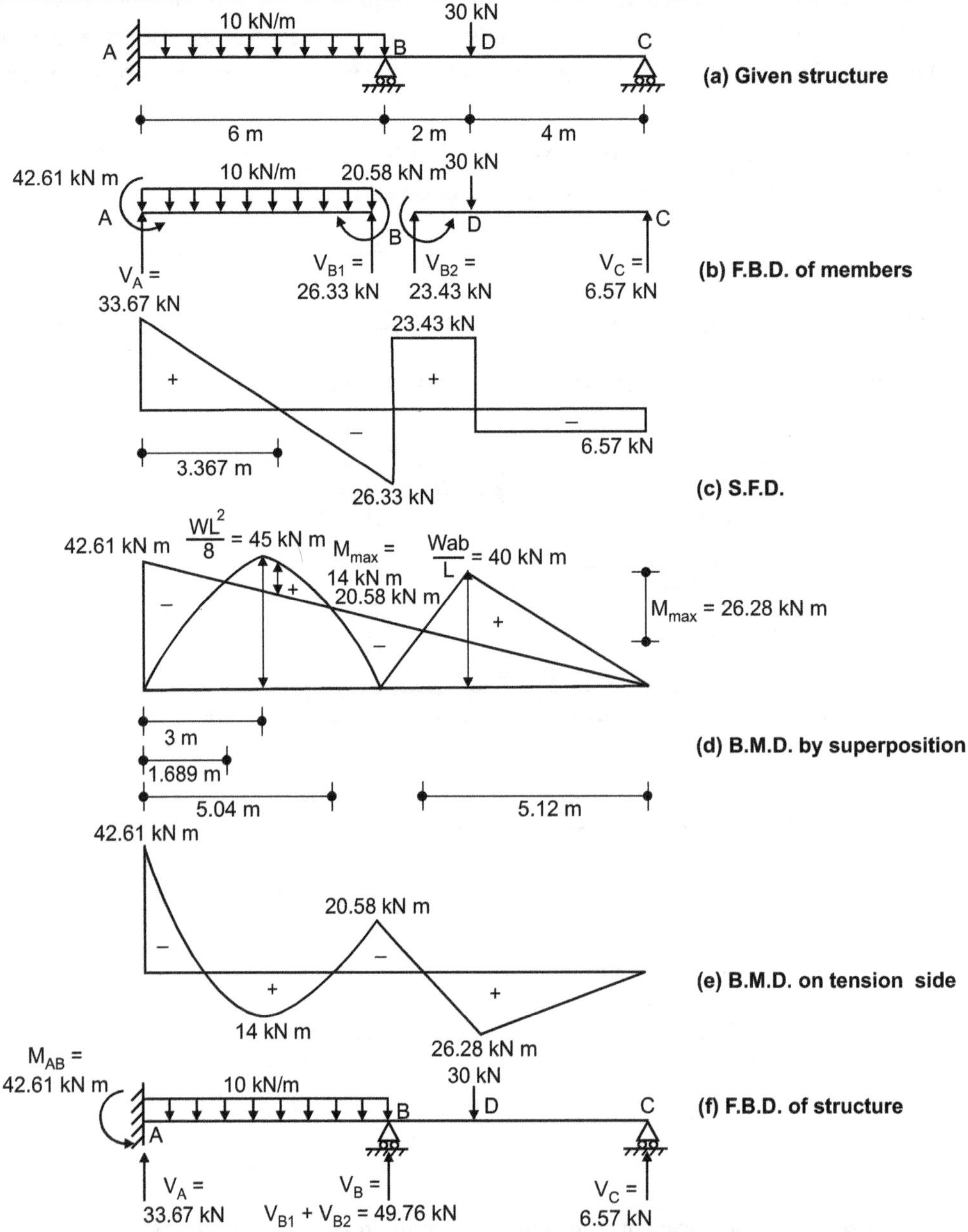

Fig. 2.37 : For Illustrative Example 2.25

Solution : Step I : $D_{ki} = 2$, Unknown displacements : θ_B, θ_C. [Modified $D_{ki} = 1\ (\theta_B)$].

Step II : Fixed-End Moments :
$$M^F_{AB} = -M^F_{BA} = 30 \text{ kNm}$$
$$M^F_{BC} = 26.67 \text{ kNm}$$
$$M^F_{CB} = -13.33 \text{ kNm}$$

Step III : Modified SD equations :

Span AB :
$$M_{AB} = \frac{EI}{3}(\theta_B) + 45.83 \quad \text{... (i)}$$
$$M_{BA} = \frac{2EI}{3}(\theta_B) - 14.16 \quad \text{... (ii)}$$

Span BC :
$$M_{BC} = \frac{3EI}{L}(\theta_B) + M^F_{BC} - \frac{1}{2}M^F_{CB} - \frac{3EI}{L^2}(\Delta)$$
$$= \frac{3EI}{6}(\theta_B) + 26.67 - \frac{1}{2}(-13.33) - \frac{3 \times 3800}{6^2}\left(\frac{25}{1000}\right)$$
$$= 0.5\ EI(\theta_B) + 25.41 \quad \text{... (iii)}$$

Step IV : Moment equilibrium condition for joint :
At joint B, $M_{BA} + M_{BC} = 0$ ... (A)

Step V : Substituting equations (ii) and (iii) in equation (A), we get
$$1.167\ EI(\theta_B) + 11.25 = 0 \quad \text{... (B)}$$

Step VI : Solution of equations for joint displacements :
Solving equation (A), we get
$$\boxed{\theta_B = -\frac{9.64}{EI}}$$

Step VII : Member-End Moments :
$$M_{AB} = \frac{EI}{3}\left(-\frac{9.64}{EI}\right) + 45.83 = 42.61 \text{ kNm}$$
$$M_{BA} = \frac{2EI}{3}\left(-\frac{9.64}{EI}\right) - 14.16 = -20.58 \text{ kNm}$$
$$M_{BC} = 0.5\ EI\left(-\frac{9.64}{EI}\right) + 25.41 = 20.58 \text{ kNm}$$
$$M_{CB} = 0$$

Rest of the analysis is the same as explained earlier. It should be noted that; two unknown problems are reduced to one unknown problem by using modified SD equations.

Example 2.26 : Analyse the beam shown in Fig. 2.38 using modified slope deflection method.

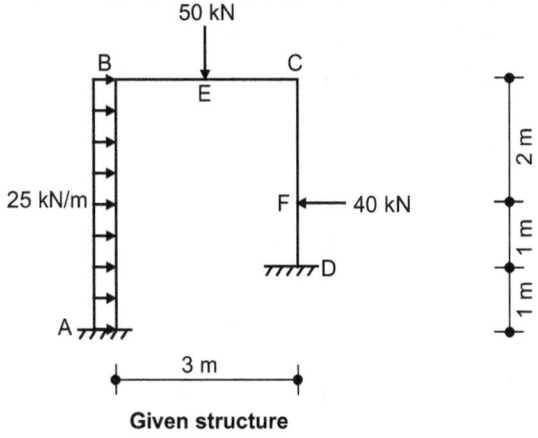

Given structure
Fig. 2.38

Solution : Step I : $D_{ki} = 4$, Unknown displacements : $\theta_B, \theta_C, \theta_D$ and horizontal sway = Δ.
Modified $D_{ki} = 3$ (θ_B, θ_C and Δ). Known displacement : $\theta_A = 0$.

Step II : Fixed-End Moments :

$$M_{AB}^F = -M_{BA}^F$$
$$= 80 \text{ kNm}$$
$$M_{BC}^F = -M_{CB}^F$$
$$= 26.67 \text{ kNm}$$
$$-M_{DC}^F = M_{CD}^F$$
$$= 15 \text{ kNm}$$

Step III : Modified SD equations : (Assuming horizontal sway = Δ towards right).

Member AB : $M_{AB} = EI(\theta_B) + 0.75 EI(\Delta) + 80$ ... (i)
$M_{BA} = 2 EI(\theta_B) + 0.75 EI(\Delta) - 80$ ... (ii)

Member BC : $M_{BC} = EI(\theta_B) + 0.5 EI(\theta_C) + 26.67$ ... (iii)
$M_{CB} = EI(\theta_C) + 0.5 EI(\theta_B) - 26.67$ ... (iv)

Member CD : $M_{CD} = \dfrac{3 EI}{L}(\theta_C) + \dfrac{3 EI}{L^2}(\Delta) + M_{CD}^F - \dfrac{1}{2} M_{DC}^F$

$= \dfrac{3 EI}{3}(\theta_C) + \dfrac{3 EI}{3^2}(\Delta) + 15 - \dfrac{1}{2}(-15)$

$= EI(\theta_C) + \dfrac{EI}{3}(\Delta) + 22.5$ ... (v)

Step IV : Equilibrium conditions for joints :
Moment equilibrium of joint B : $M_{BA} + M_{BC} = 0$ ... (A)
Moment equilibrium of joint C : $M_{CB} + M_{CD} = 0$ ... (B)
Horizontal shear equilibrium of structure,
$$H_A + H_D - 100 = 0$$
i.e. $\quad 3(M_{AB} + M_{BA}) + 4 M_{CD} - 600 = 0$ ... (C)

Step V : Formulation of equilibrium equations in terms of joint displacements :
Substituting equations (ii) and (iii) in equation (A), we get
$$3 \, EI \, (\theta_B) + 0.5 \, EI \, (\theta_C) + 0.75 \, EI \, (\Delta) - 52.33 = 0 \quad ... (A)$$
Substituting equations (iv) and (v) in equation (B), we get,
$$0.5 \, EI \, (\theta_B) + 2 \, EI \, (\theta_C) + \frac{EI}{3} (\Delta) - 4.17 = 0 \quad ... (B)$$
Substituting equations (i), (ii) and (v) in equation (C), we get
$$3 \, [EI \, (\theta_B) + 0.75 \, EI \, (\Delta) + 80 + 2 \, EI \, (\theta_B) + 0.75 \, EI \, (\Delta) - 80] +$$
$$4 \left[EI \, (\theta_C) + \frac{EI}{3} (\Delta) + 22.5 \right] - 600 = 0$$
i.e. $\quad 9 \, EI \, (\theta_B) + 4 \, EI \, (\theta_C) + 5.83 \, EI \, (\Delta) - 510 = 0 \quad ... (C)$

Step VI : Solution of equations for joint displacements : Solving equations (A), (B) and (C), we get

$$\boxed{\theta_B = -\frac{6.7}{EI}, \quad \theta_C = -\frac{14.128}{EI}, \quad \Delta = \frac{107.35}{EI}}$$

Step VII : Member-End Moments : Substituting the values of above joint displacements in modified SD equations, member-end moments are obtained as under :

$$M_{AB} = EI \left(-\frac{6.7}{EI}\right) + 0.75 \, EI \left(\frac{107.35}{EI}\right) + 80$$
$$= 153.81 \text{ kNm (Hogging)}$$

$$M_{BA} = 2 \, EI \left(-\frac{6.7}{EI}\right) + 0.75 \, EI \left(\frac{107.35}{EI}\right) - 80$$
$$= -12.9 \text{ kNm}$$
$$= 12.9 \text{ kNm (Hogging)}$$

$$M_{BC} = EI \left(-\frac{6.7}{EI}\right) + 0.5 \, EI \left(-\frac{14.128}{EI}\right) + 26.67$$
$$= 12.9 \text{ kNm (Hogging)}$$

$$M_{CB} = EI\left(-\frac{14.128}{EI}\right) + 0.5\,EI\left(-\frac{6.70}{EI}\right) - 26.67$$
$$= -44.15 \text{ kNm}$$
$$= 44.15 \text{ kNm (Hogging)}$$
$$M_{DC} = 0$$
$$M_{CD} = EI\left(-\frac{14.128}{EI}\right) + \frac{EI}{3}\left(\frac{107.35}{EI}\right) + 22.5$$
$$= 44.15 \text{ kNm (Sagging)}$$

Rest of the analysis is the same as explained earlier. It should be noted that, by using modified SD equations, four unknown problems reduced to three unknown problems.

EXERCISE

1. A 2 m long cantilever made of steel tube 150 mm external diameter and 10 mm thickness is loaded as shown in Fig. 2.118. Determine the maximum deflection. Assume E = 200 GPa.   (13.98 mm (↓))

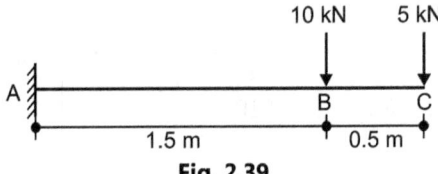

Fig. 2.39

2. A 2 m long cantilever is of rectangular section 100 mm wide and 200 mm deep. It is loaded as shown in Fig. 2.119. Find deflection at free end assuming E = 10 GPa.   (19.39 mm (↓))

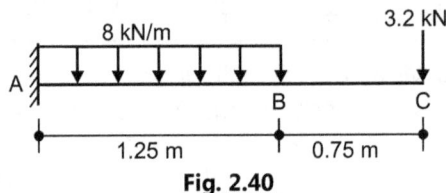

Fig. 2.40

3. A horizontal cantilever of uniform section and span 'L' is loaded as shown in Fig. 2.120. Find the deflection at free end. $\left(\frac{26.76}{EI}\,(\uparrow)\right)$

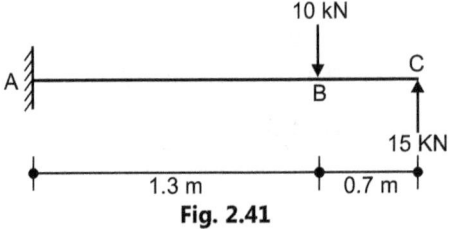

Fig. 2.41

4. A cantilever of uniform section is loaded as shown in Fig. 2.121. Find the deflection at B. If the cantilever is propped at B, find the reaction at prop assuming there is no deflection at B. $\left(y_B = \dfrac{33.75}{EI} (\downarrow);\ V_B = 30\ \text{kN} (\uparrow)\right)$

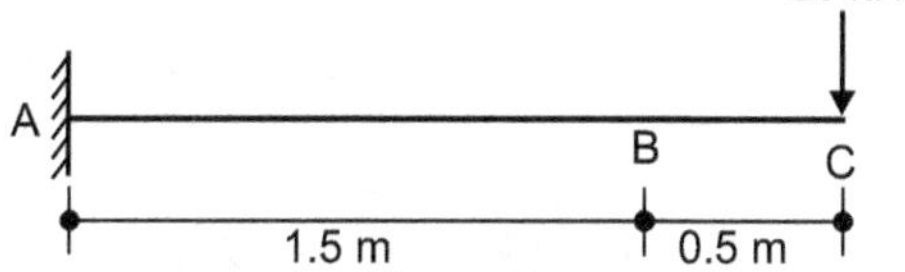

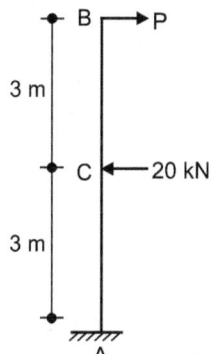

Fig. 2.42

5. A vertical post AB of constant flexural rigidity 4000 kNm² is fixed at the base A and subjected to a horizontal load of 20 kN at C as shown in Fig. 2.122. Determine the necessary force in horizontal tie at B such that the deflection at B is limited to 20 mm to the left. (5.13 kN)

Fig. 2.43

6. Two equal steel beams are built in at one end and connected by a steel rod as shown in Fig. 2.123. Show that the pull in the rod is

$$P = \dfrac{5\ WL^3}{32\left(\dfrac{6\ aI}{\pi d^2} + L^3\right)}$$

where ; d = diameter of the rod and
I = M.I. of each beam

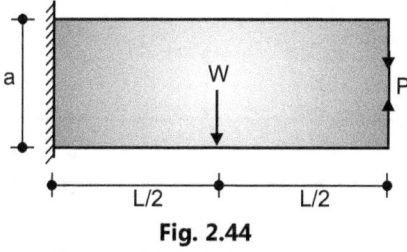

Fig. 2.44

7. For the beam shown in Fig. 2.124, show that the deflection under load is $\frac{W}{3.2 \text{ EI}}$.

W
A
B
C
D
E
1.5 m
0.5 m
0.5 m
0.5 m

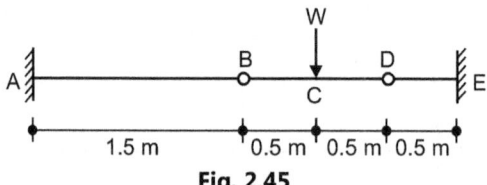

Fig. 2.45

8. A timber beam carries a UDL of 10 kN/m over a span of 6 m. The ends of the beam are simply supported. Determine the section of the beam if the central deflection is limited to 15 mm and the maximum bending stress to 10 MPa. Take E = 12 GPa.

(b = 154 mm, d = 417 mm)

9. The beam is supported and loaded as shown in Fig. 2.125. Find (i) the deflection under the load, (ii) the position and amount of maximum deflection.

Assume E = 200 GPa and $I = 50 \times 10^6$ mm^4

(y_C = 6 mm (↓); y_{max} = 6.53 mm (↓) at 2.45 m from A)

40 kN
A
B
C
3 m
1.5 m

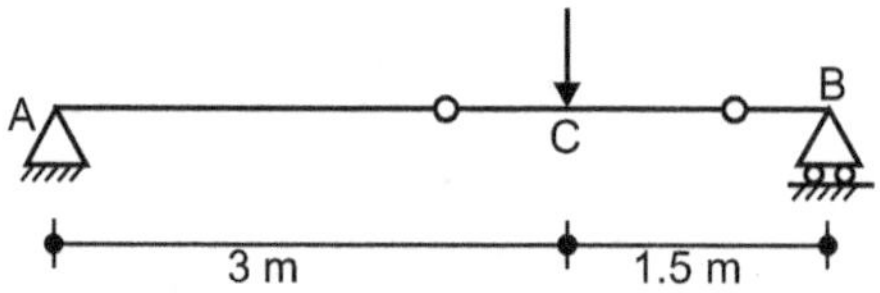

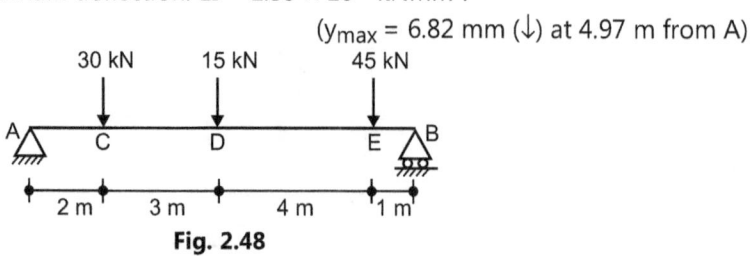

Fig. 2.46

10. The beam is supported and loaded as shown in Fig. 2.126. Find (i) the deflection under loads, (ii) the maximum deflection. Assume E = 200 GPa, $I = 70 \times 10^8$ mm^4.

(y_C = 2.34 mm (↓) ; y_D = 2.98 mm (↓) ; y_{max} = 3.54 mm (↓) at 6.87 m from A)

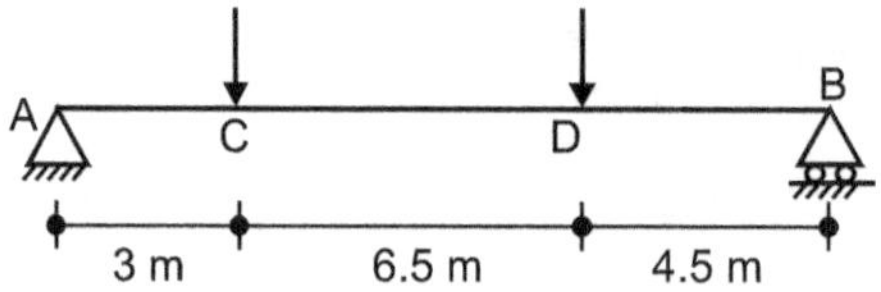

75 kN
50 kN
A
B
C
D
3 m
6.5 m
4.5 m

Fig. 2.47

11. The beam is supported and loaded as shown in Fig. 2.127. Determine the position and amount of maximum deflection. $EI = 1.39 \times 10^{11}$ kNmm^2.

(y_{max} = 6.82 mm (↓) at 4.97 m from A)

30 kN
15 kN
45 kN
A
B
C
D
E
2 m
3 m
4 m
1 m

Fig. 2.48

12. The beam is supported and loaded as shown in Fig. 2.128. Find deflection at C.

$$\left(y_C = \frac{3.75}{EI} (\downarrow)\right)$$

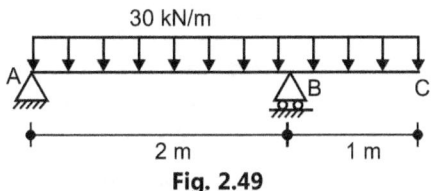

Fig. 2.49

13. The beam is supported and loaded as shown in Fig. 2.129. Assuming E = 200 GPa, I = 40 × 10⁶ mm⁴, find (i) the deflection at C; (ii) the maximum deflection, and (iii) slope at end A.

(y_C = 8.74 mm ($\downarrow$); y_{max} = 8.75 mm ($\downarrow$) at 1.958 m from A; θ_A = 0.417° ($\circlearrowright$))

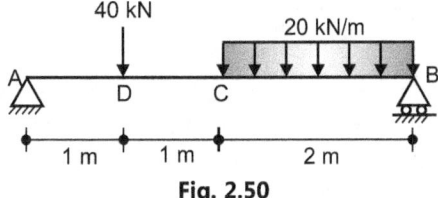

Fig. 2.50

14. The beam is supported and loaded as shown in Fig. 2.130. Calculate slope and deflection at point C.

$$\left(\theta_C = \frac{12.67}{EI} (\circlearrowright);\ y_C = \frac{20.85}{EI} (\downarrow)\right)$$

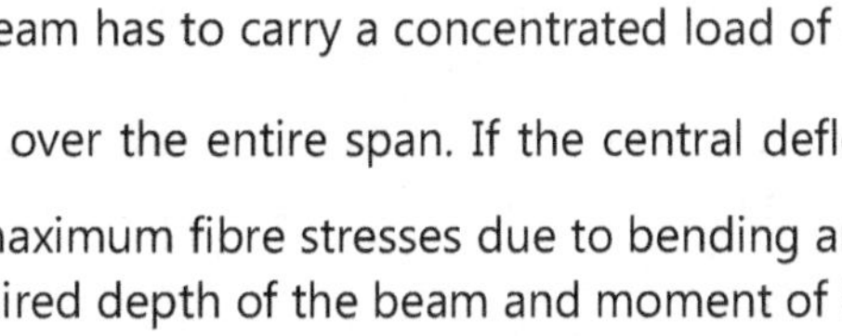

Fig. 2.51

15. A beam of constant section, symmetric about neutral axis is simply supported over a span of 8 m. The beam has to carry a concentrated load of 40 kN at the midspan and a UDL of 15 kN/m over the entire span. If the central deflection is limited to $\frac{1}{480}^{th}$ of the span and the maximum fibre stresses due to bending are not to exceed 118 MPa, determine the required depth of the beam and moment of inertia.

(d = 435 mm; I_{xx} = 3.686 × 10⁸ mm⁴)

16. The beam is supported and loaded as shown in Fig. 2.131. Determine the deflections at C and D and maximum deflection assuming EI = 3 × 10¹⁰ kNmm².

(y_C = 12.09 mm ($\downarrow$); y_D = 13.81 mm ($\downarrow$); y_{max} = 16.19 mm ($\downarrow$) at 3.55 m from A)

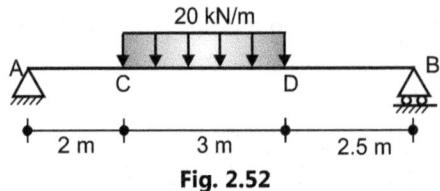

Fig. 2.52

17. Find slope and deflection at C and E for the beam supported and loaded as shown in Fig. 2.132. Assume E = 200 GPa, I = 2 × 10⁷ mm⁴.

$$(\theta_C = 0.0047° \ (\circlearrowright); \ y_C = 12.5 \text{ mm } (\downarrow); \ \theta_E = 0.568° \ (\circlearrowright); \ y_E = 9.916 \text{ mm } (\uparrow))$$

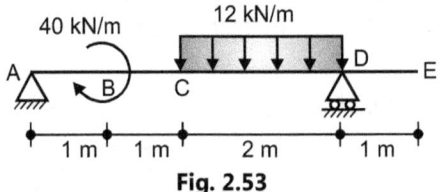

Fig. 2.53

18. A simply supported beam AB of length 'L' just touches a spring of midspan in unloaded condition. Find the stiffness k of the spring that will make the forces on the supports and on the spring equal for a uniformly distributed load. Assume EI = constant.

(54.857 EI/L³)

19. The beam is supported and loaded as shown in Fig. 2.133. Determine (i) the deflection at C and (ii) the maximum deflection between A and B. Assume EI = 2700 kNm².

$(y_C = 10.08 \text{ mm } (\downarrow); \ y_{max} \text{ in zone AB} = 11.4 \text{ mm } (\downarrow) \text{ at 2.46 m from A})$

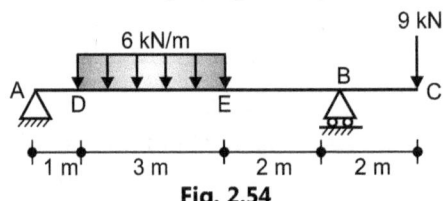

Fig. 2.54

20. Determine slope and deflection at free end of cantilever shown in Fig. 2.134. Assume uniform flexural rigidity. Take E = 2 × 10⁵ MPa; I = 8.5 × 10⁷ mm⁴.

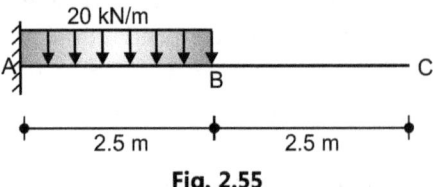

Fig. 2.55

$[\theta_C = 0.175° \ (\circlearrowright), \ y_C = 13.40 \text{ mm } (\downarrow)]$

21. Find slope and deflection at free end of cantilever shown in Fig. 2.135. Assume uniform flexural rigidity. Take $E = 2 \times 10^5$ MPa; $I = 2.5 \times 10^8$ mm^4.

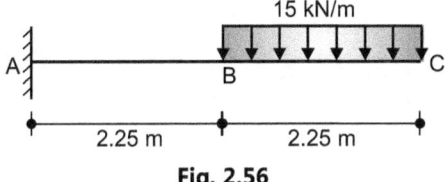

Fig. 2.56

$$\left[\theta_C = 0.228° \ (\circlearrowleft), \quad y_C = 13.13 \text{ mm} (\downarrow)\right]$$

22. Find midspan and maximum deflection for cantilever beam of uniform section shown in Fig. 2.136. Take $EI = 7560$ kNm^2.

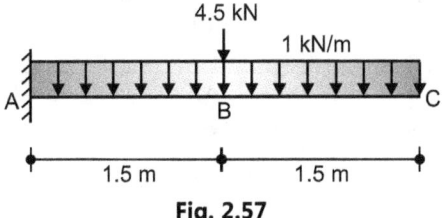

Fig. 2.57

$$\left[y_B = 11.44 \text{ mm} (\downarrow), y_{max} = 30.1 \text{ mm} (\downarrow)\right]$$

23. Find θ_B; θ_C; y_B; y_C for the cantilever beam shown in Fig. 2.137. Take $E = 2 \times 10^5$ MPa. $I = 5 \times 10^8$ mm^4.

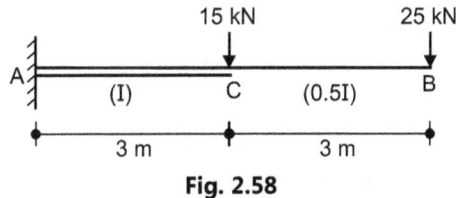

Fig. 2.58

$[\theta_B = 0.36° \ (\circlearrowleft); \ \theta_C = 0.23° \ (\circlearrowleft); \ y_B = 23.63 \text{ mm} (\downarrow); \ y_C = 6.98 \text{ mm} (\downarrow)]$

24. Find θ_B; θ_C; y_B; y_C for the cantilever beam shown in Fig. 2.138. Take $E = 2 \times 10^5$ MPa. $I = 5 \times 10^8$ mm^4.

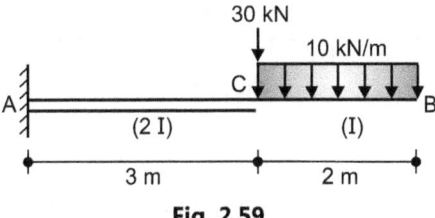

Fig. 2.59

$[\theta_B = 0.09° \ (\circlearrowleft); \ \theta_C = 0.08° \ (\circlearrowleft) \ y_B = 5.75 \text{ mm} (\downarrow); \ y_C = 2.7 \text{ mm} (\downarrow)]$

25. Find slope and deflection at free end of aluminium cantilever shown in Fig. 2.139. Take E = 70,000 MPa, $I_1 = 2 \times 10^6$ mm^4, $I_2 = 0.4 \times 10^6$ mm^4.

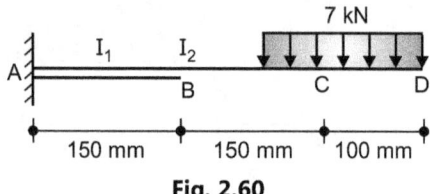

Fig. 2.60

$[\theta_D = 0.2575° \ (\circlearrowleft) \ ; \ y_D = 1.124 \text{ mm} \ (\downarrow)]$

26. A cantilever beam shown in Fig. 2.140 has a uniform rectangular cross section having d = 2b. Find the values of b, d if maximum deflection is not to exceed 15 mm.

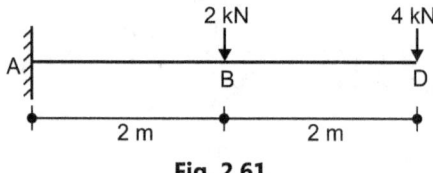

Fig. 2.61

[b = 217.5 mm; d = 435 mm]

27. Find the deflection at free end of cantilever shown in Fig. 2.141. Take E = 2×10^7 MPa, I = 4×10^6 mm^4. $[y_C = 8.33 \text{ mm} \ (\uparrow)]$

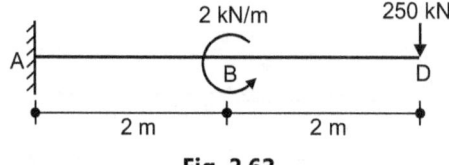

Fig. 2.62

28. Find the deflection at free end of cantilever shown in Fig. 2.142.

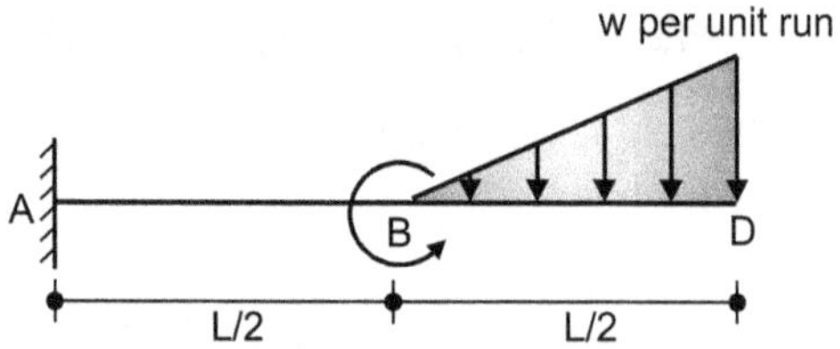

w per unit run

A ──── B ──── D
   L/2   L/2

Fig. 2.63

$\left[y = \dfrac{121}{1920} \left(\dfrac{wL^4}{EI} \right) \right]$

29. Find θ_B; θ_C; y_B and y_C for the cantilever beam shown in Fig. 2.143. Take E = 2×10^5 MPa; I = 6×10^8 mm^4.

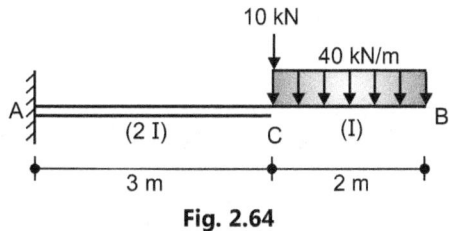

Fig. 2.64

[θ_B = 0.179° (↺); θ_C = 0.153° (↺); y_B = 10.916 mm (↓); y_C = 4.875 mm (↓)]

30. Find θ_B; θ_C; y_B and y_C for the cantilever beam shown in Fig. 2.144.

    Take $E = 2 \times 10^5$ MPa, $I = 5 \times 10^8$ mm^4.

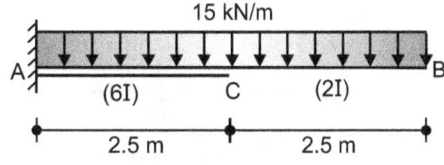

Fig. 2.65

[θ_B = 0.065° (↺); θ_C = 0.045° (↺); y_B = 4.4725 mm (↓); y_C = 1.435 mm (↓)]

31. Find θ_B; θ_C; y_B and y_C for the cantilever beam shown in Fig. 2.145.

    Take $E = 2 \times 10^5$ MPa; $I = 5 \times 10^8$ mm^4.

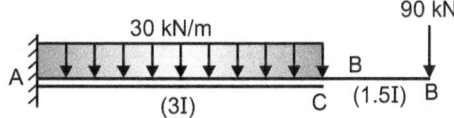

Fig. 2.66

[θ_B = 0.4° (↺); θ_C = 0.34° (↺), y_B = 27.73 (↓); y_C = 14.4 mm (↓)]

32. A beam of constant cross section 10 m long is simply supported at its ends and loaded with two concentrated loads of 6 kN each at a distance 3 m from either supports. Find the ratio of deflection at mid span to that under any one of the load.

    (1.22)

33. A simply supported beam of uniform section and span L is loaded with two equal loads w at point L/4 from each end. Show that the central deflection is $\dfrac{11}{384}\left[\dfrac{wL^3}{EI}\right]$.

34. A simply supported beam of uniform section has a span L and carries two equal loads w each at a distance L/3 from either ends. Show that the central deflection is $\dfrac{23}{648}\left[\dfrac{WL^3}{EI}\right]$.

35. Find the maximum deflection for simply supported beam shown in Fig. 2.146. Assume uniform flexural rigidity.

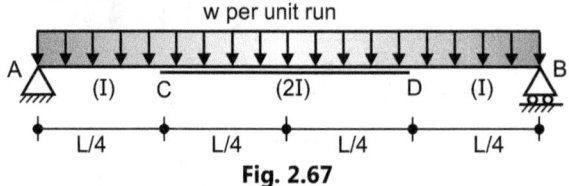

Fig. 2.67

$$\left[\frac{93}{12288}\left(\frac{wL^4}{EI}\right)\right].$$

36. Find θ_C and y_C from simply supported beam shown in Fig. 2.147. Take $E = 2 \times 10^5$ MPa; $I = 6 \times 10^8$ mm^4.

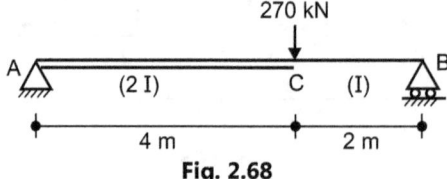

Fig. 2.68

[$\theta_C = 0.0225°$ (↶); $y_C = 3.2025$ mm (↓)]

37. Find θ_A; θ_C; θ_D; y_C and y_D and maximum deflection for the beam shown in Fig. 2.148. Take $E = 2 \times 10^5$ MPa; $I = 3 \times 10^8$ mm^4.

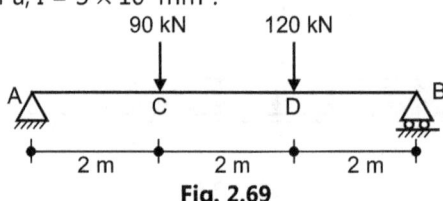

Fig. 2.69

[$\theta_A = 0.3945°$ (↶); $\theta_C = 0.204°$ (↶); $\theta_D = 0.198°$ (↶); $y_C = 11.55$ mm (↓); $y_D = 11.775$ mm (↓); $y_{max} = 13.425$ mm (↓) at 3.04 m from A]

38. Find θ_C and y_C for the beam shown in Fig. 2.149 using $E = 2 \times 10^5$ MPa; $I = 4 \times 10^8$ mm^4. Assume uniform flexural rigidity throughout.

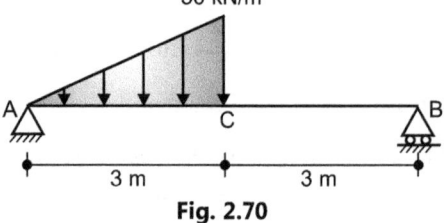

Fig. 2.70

[$\theta_C = 0.01°$ (↶); $y_C = 3.375$ mm (↓)]

39. Find θ_A; θ_B; y_C and y_D for the beam shown in Fig. 2.150. Take $E = 2 \times 10^5$ MPa; $I = 4.5 \times 10^8$ mm^4.

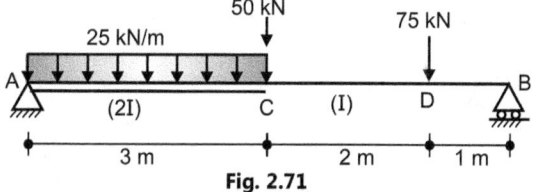

Fig. 2.71

$[\theta_A = 0.13° \,(\circlearrowleft); \; \theta_B = 0.175° \,(\circlearrowright); \; y_C = 5 \text{ mm} (\downarrow); \; y_D = 2.875 \text{ mm} (\downarrow)]$

40. Determine the maximum deflection of the beam carrying uniformly distributed load over the middle portion as shown in Fig. 2.151.

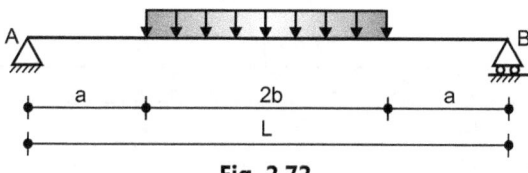

Fig. 2.72

$$\left[y_{max} = \frac{wb}{24 \, EI} (L^3 - 2Lb^2 + b^3) \right]$$

41. A beam of uniform section and length L is simply supported at its ends and carries a symmetrical triangular loading having intensity varying from zero at each end to w at centre. Find the slope at each end and the deflection at centre.

$$\left[\theta = \frac{5}{192} \frac{wL^3}{EI}, \; y = \frac{wL^4}{120 \, EI} (\downarrow) \right]$$

42. A beam 6 m long is subjected to couples as shown in Fig. 2.152. Find the deflections at the points of application of couple. Take $E = 2 \times 10^5$ MPa; $I = 3 \times 10^7$ mm^4.

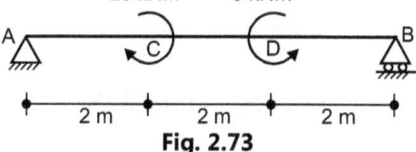

Fig. 2.73

$[y_C = 4.44 \text{ mm} (\downarrow); \; y_D = 4.88 \text{ mm} (\downarrow)]$

43. Find deflection at D for a beam shown in Fig. 2.153. Take $E = 2.1 \times 10^5$ MPa and $I = 3.7 \times 10^8$ mm^4.

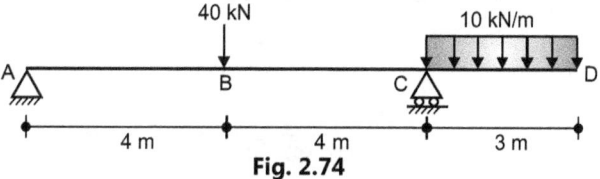

Fig. 2.74

$[0.242 \text{ mm} (\uparrow)]$

44. A uniform beam is supported and loaded as shown in Fig. 2.154. Find deflections under the loads and slopes at the supports. Take $E = 2 \times 10^5$ MPa; $I = 6 \times 10^8$ mm^4.

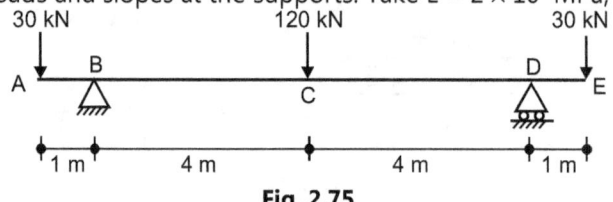

Fig. 2.75

[y_C = 8.67 mm (↓); y_A = y_E = 2.916 mm (↑); θ_B = θ_D = 0.171°]

45. Find out θ_C; θ_D; y_C and y_D for the beam shown in Fig. 2.156. Take $E = 2 \times 10^5$ MPa; $I = 4.5 \times 10^8$ mm^4.

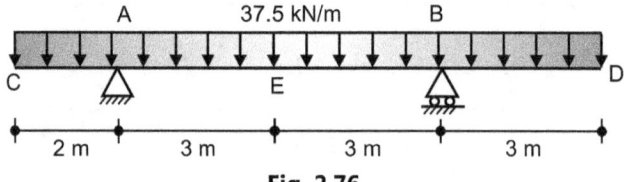

Fig. 2.76

[θ_C = 0.024° (↻), θ_D = 0.155° (↻), y_C = 0.416 mm (↓), y_D = 6.712 (↓)]

46. Determine the deflection at C for a beam shown in Fig. 2.156. Assume uniform flexural rigidity throughout.

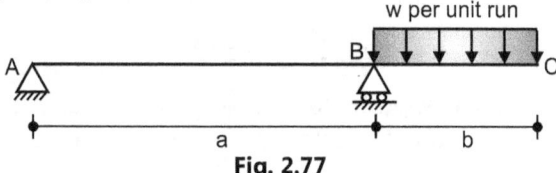

Fig. 2.77

$$\left[y_C = \frac{wb^3}{24\ EI}(4a + 3b) \right]$$

47. Find deflection at C for a beam shown in Fig. 2.157.

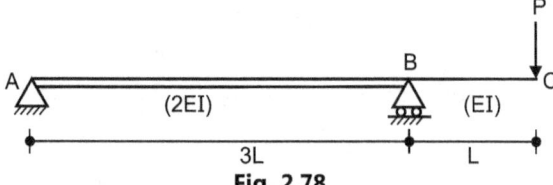

Fig. 2.78

$$\left[y_C = \frac{5\ PL^3}{16\ EI}(\downarrow) \right]$$

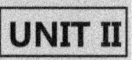

Chapter 3

MOMENT DISTRIBUTION METHOD

3.1 Stiffness and Carryover Factor

The moment distribution method is used to analyse the statically indeterminate rigid jointed structures. The method will be denoted hereafter as MD method. Unlike SD method, MD method is also the stiffness method or displacement method. However, the technique of MD method is quite different than SD method. Without calculating the values of unknown joint displacements, the member-end moments are obtained by successive approximations. The simultaneous equations need not to be formulated and solved. Restraining and releasing the joints of the member is the main characteristic of the stiffness method, may be SD method or MD method. In this context, following two basic cases as shown in Fig. 3.1 and Fig. 3.2 are very important and hence reviewed again to develop the technique of MD method.

Case I :

The prismatic member AB of length L and flexural rigidity EI is restrained against rotation at joints A and B as shown in Fig. 3.1 (a). One end i.e. near end A of AB is released when the far end B is fixed. To release the joint for rotation, the moment M_{AB} is to be applied at the joint A, to cause the rotation θ_A as shown in Fig. 3.1 (b). The moment M_{AB} is related to the rotation θ_A by the standard results of $M_{AB} = (4\,EI/L)\,\theta_A$. If θ_A is unity i.e. one radian, then $M_{AB} = (4\,EI/L)$ as shown in Fig. 3.1 (c). The quantity $4\,EI/L$ is called as flexural rotational stiffness of a member and defined as the moment required to be applied at A to cause an unit rotation at A when the far end B is fixed.

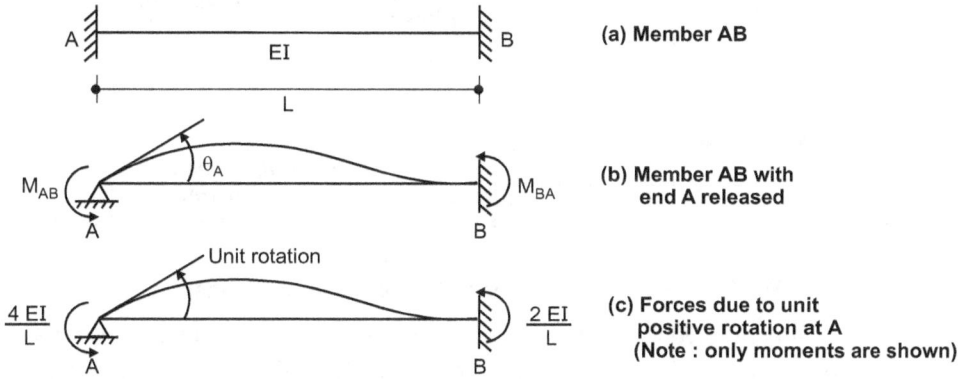

Fig. 3.1 : Releasing the near end when far end is fixed

When M_{AB} is applied at A to release the joint A, the moment M_{BA} is developed far or end B, being fixed as shown in Fig. 3.1 (b). M_{BA} is related to M_{AB} as $M_{BA} = \frac{1}{2} M_{AB}$. The direction of M_{BA} is same as M_{AB}.

$$\therefore \quad \frac{M_{BA}}{M_{AB}} = \frac{1}{2}$$

The moment M_{BA} is called carryover moment and it is defined as the moment developed at far end when the moment is applied at near end. The carryover moment is denoted by COM. The ratio of M_{BA} to M_{AB} is 1/2. This ratio is called carryover factor and defined as the ratio of moment developed at far end to the moment applied at near end. The carryover factor is denoted by COF.

Case II :

Fig. 3.2 (a) shows a prismatic member AB of length L and flexural rigidity EI, restrained at A and hinged at B. To release the joint A, the moment M_{AB} is applied at A to cause the rotation θ_A as shown in Fig. 3.2 (b). From the standard results already derived, M_{AB} is known to be $M_{AB} = (3 \text{ EI}/L) \theta_A$. If θ_A is unity then $M_{AB} = (3 \text{ EI}/L)$ as shown in Fig. 3.2 (c). The quantity (3 EI/L) is considered as the stiffness of a member and defined as the moment required to be applied at A to cause an unit rotation at A when the far end B is hinged.

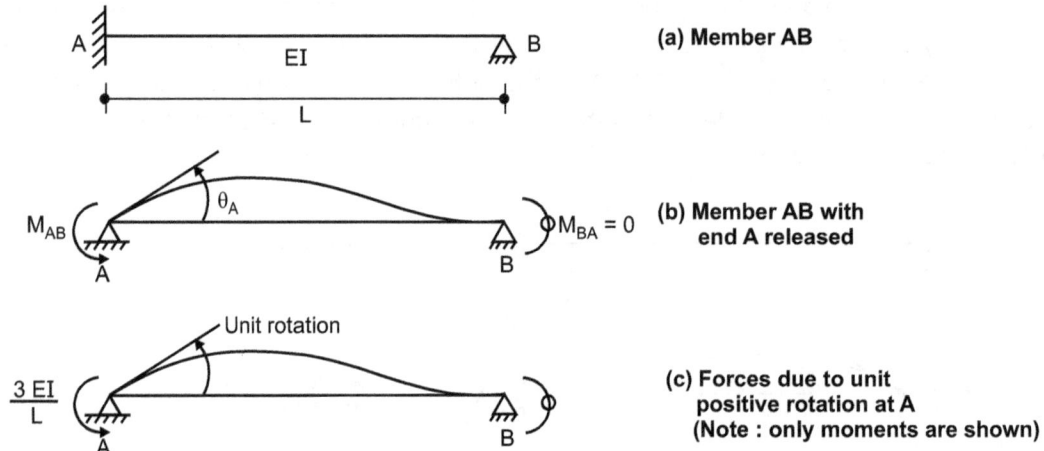

Fig. 3.2 : Releasing the near end when far end is hinged

As the joint B is already given as hinged support, the moment can not be developed at B and therefore there is no carryover moment at B and $M_{BA} = 0$. The ratio M_{BA}/M_{AB} is zero. Thus, carryover factor for this case is zero.

The comparison of these two cases reveals that (i) the stiffness of the member of second case is 3/4 of the stiffness of the member of first case.

For the analysis of structure by MD method, the flexural stiffnesses of members of same material are considered in terms of relative stiffness factor i.e. I/L of the members.

(ii) The carryover factor is 1/2 in first case and zero in second case. Therefore, COF is either 1/2 or 0.

It will be seen further that the carryover factor from one end to other end of the member and relative stiffness of the member play pivotal role in MD method. Therefore, following information will be very useful as prerequisite of MD method.

(1) COF

Type of the member end	COF
(a) Fixed support (FS or EFS)	$\frac{1}{2}$
(b) Intermediate support (IS or ISS)	$\frac{1}{2}$
(c) Rigid joint (RJ)	$\frac{1}{2}$
(d) Exterior simple, roller hinged support (ESS or ES or EHS)	0
(e) Internal pin	0

Thus, (a) fixed support, (b) interior support, (c) rigid joint are considered as carryover end of the member and COF is 1/3.

Exterior simple, or roller or hinged support (may be with overhanging part) is taken as non-carryover end of the member and COF is zero.

(2) Relative Stiffness I/L Factor

Type of member	Relative stiffness factor
(a) Member having both ends as carryover ends	(I/L)
(b) Member having one of the ends as non-carryover end.	(3/4) (I/L)
(c) Member having one of the ends as free.	0

It may be noted that the relative stiffness factor for the member having one of the ends as exterior simple or roller or hinged support, is required to be modified as (3/4) (I/L). This is called as modified relative stiffness factor. Further, the relative stiffness factors are normalized proportionately and are expressed in numbers by eliminating 1. Therefore, normalized relative stiffness factors of the members are taken in MD method for convenience. The normalized relative stiffness factor is denoted by K.

3.2 DISTRIBUTION FACTOR

The concept of distribution of load or moment at the joint, to the members meeting at the joint is the key consideration. The distribution of load or moment is very well formulated using the fundamental principles of (i) equilibrium, (ii) compatibility, and (iii) force-displacement relations in terms of stiffnesses of the members.

The forces acting on the structure are resisted by the members through the joints. The resistance of a member is proportional to its stiffness. The stiffness is the force required to cause unit displacement. The basic stiffness of a member is AE/L for axial deformation and 4 EI/L for flexural rotation. The stiffness of a member is related to :

(i) its cross-sectional and material properties, (ii) length of the member, and (iii) end conditions of the member. More the stiffness of a member, more will be its resistance i.e. contribution to load sharing.

The phenomenon of distribution of load or moment is illustrated as follows :

Case I :

The load W is supported by the structural system as shown in Fig. 3.3 (a). The information of the members is given as :

A_1 = Area of cross-section of member AB
A_2 = Area of cross-section of member CD
E_1 = Modulus of elasticity of material of member AB
E_2 = Modulus of elasticity of material of member CD
L_1 = Length of member AB
L_2 = Length of member CD

It is assumed that the connection of the members at the joint of the load is rigid, ensuring that the displacement at the joint is only vertical translation. The equilibrium of the joint as shown in Fig. 3.3 (b) gives the equation $W = W_1 + W_2$. The compatibility of the rigid joint stipulates the equation of deformation as $dL_1 = dL_2$. Force-displacement relations lead to

$$dL_1 = \frac{W_1 L_1}{A_1 E_1} \quad \text{and} \quad dL_2 = \frac{W_2 L_2}{A_2 E_2}$$

Therefore, we get,

$$\frac{W_1 L_1}{A_1 E_1} = \frac{W_2 L_2}{A_2 E_2} \quad \text{i.e.} \quad \frac{W_1}{\left(\frac{A_1 E_1}{L_1}\right)} = \frac{W}{\left(\frac{A_2 E_2}{L_2}\right)}$$

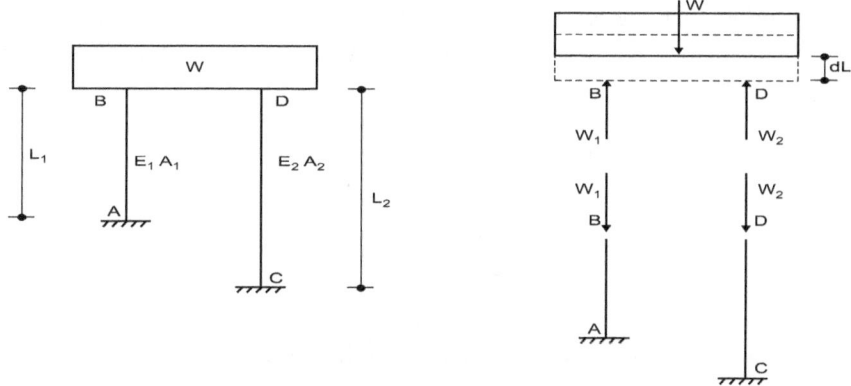

(a) Structural system   (b) Equilibrium of joints

Fig. 3.3 : Distribution of load

It is to be noted that load sharing is proportional to the stiffness. If the material for two bars is same and A/L is considered as relative stiffness, K then the above equation becomes

$$\frac{W_1}{K_1} = \frac{W_2}{K_2}$$

∴ $$W_2 = \frac{K_2}{K_1} W_1$$

Substituting this in equilibrium equation,

$$W = W_1 + \frac{K_2}{K_1} W_1 = \left(1 + \frac{K_2}{K_1}\right) W_1$$

$$W_1 = \left(\frac{K_1 + K_2}{K_1}\right) W_1$$

∴ $$W_1 = \left(\frac{K_1}{K_1 + K_2}\right) W$$

Similarly, $$W_2 = \left(\frac{K_2}{K_1 + K_2}\right) W$$

The term $\left(\dfrac{K_1}{K_1 + K_2}\right)$ is called the distribution factor DF_1 for the member 1 and $\left(\dfrac{K_2}{K_1 + K_2}\right)$ is DF_2 for the member 2.

∴ $$W_1 = (DF_1) W$$
∴ $$W_2 = (DF_2) W$$

Thus, it is concluded that the load is distributed according to the distribution factor which is function of the relative stiffnesses of the members. The distribution factor can also be expressed as

$$DF_1 = \left(\frac{K_1}{\sum K}\right)$$

$$DF_2 = \left(\frac{K_2}{\sum K}\right)$$

Case II :

The structure as shown in Fig. 3.4 (a) is subjected to the moment M_B applied at the rigid joint B. Other details are :

I_{AB} = Moment of inertia of cross-section of member AB about bending axis

I_{BC} = Moment of inertia of cross-section of member BC about bending axis

E_{AB} = Modulus of elasticity of material of member AB

E_{BC} = Modulus of elasticity of material of member BC

L_{AB} = Length of member AB

L_{BC} = Length of member BC

The member-end moment contributions are M_{BA} and M_{BC}.

From equilibrium of joint B as shown in Fig. 3.4 (b),

$$M_B = M_{BA} + M_{BC}$$

From compatibility of rigid joint,

$$\theta_{BA} = \theta_{BC}$$

From flexural rotational stiffness of the members,

$$M_{BA} = \frac{4 E_{AB} I_{AB}}{L_{AB}} \theta_{BA} \qquad \therefore \theta_{BA} = \frac{M_{BA} L_{AB}}{4 E_{AB} I_{AB}}$$

$$M_{BC} = \frac{4 E_{BC} I_{BC}}{L_{BC}} \theta_{BC} \qquad \therefore \theta_{BC} = \frac{M_{BC} L_{BC}}{4 E_{BC} I_{BC}}$$

$$\therefore \frac{M_{BA} L_{BA}}{4 E_{BA} I_{BA}} = \frac{M_{BC} L_{BC}}{4 E_{BC} I_{BC}}$$

$$\therefore \frac{M_{BA}}{\left(\dfrac{4 E_{BA} I_{BA}}{L_{BA}}\right)} = \frac{M_{BC}}{\left(\dfrac{4 E_{BC} I_{BC}}{L_{BC}}\right)}$$

Moment contributions of members are proportional to its stiffness 4 EI/L. If the material of members is same and I/L is taken as relative stiffness K of the member, then

$$\frac{M_{BA}}{K_{BA}} = \frac{M_{BC}}{K_{BC}}$$

$$\therefore M_{BC} = \left(\frac{K_{BC}}{K_{BA}}\right) M_{BA}$$

Putting M_{BC} in equilibrium equation,

$$M_B = M_{BA} + \left(\frac{K_{BC}}{K_{BA}}\right) M_{BA}$$

$$M_B = \left(1 + \frac{K_{BC}}{K_{BA}}\right) M_{BA} = \left(\frac{K_{BA} + K_{BC}}{K_{BA}}\right) M_{BA}$$

$$\therefore M_{BA} = \left(\frac{K_{BA}}{K_{BA} + K_{BC}}\right) M_B$$

$$M_{BC} = \left(\frac{K_{BC}}{K_{BA} + K_{BC}}\right) M_B$$

Again the distribution factors are expressed as

$$DF_{BA} = \frac{K_{BA}}{K_{BA} + K_{BC}} = \frac{K_{BA}}{\Sigma K}$$

$$DF_{BC} = \frac{K_{BC}}{K_{BA} + K_{BC}} = \frac{K_{BC}}{\Sigma K}$$

$$\therefore M_{BA} = (DF_{BA})(M_B)$$

$$M_{BC} = (DF_{BC})(M_B)$$

Case III : For the same structure of case II except the support condition at A as hinged is considered as shown in Fig. 3.4 (c). The distribution of moment at the joint B in this case is formulated on similar lines as follows :

$$M_B = M_{BA} + M_{BC} \text{ from equilibrium of joint B, as shown in Fig. 3.4 (d)}$$

$$\theta_{BA} = \theta_{BC} \text{ from compatibility of joint B}$$

$$\left. \begin{array}{l} \theta_{BA} = \dfrac{M_{BA} L_{AB}}{3 E_{AB} I_{AB}} \\[2mm] \theta_{BC} = \dfrac{M_{BC} L_{BC}}{4 E_{BC} I_{BC}} \end{array} \right\} \text{ from flexural rotational stiffness}$$

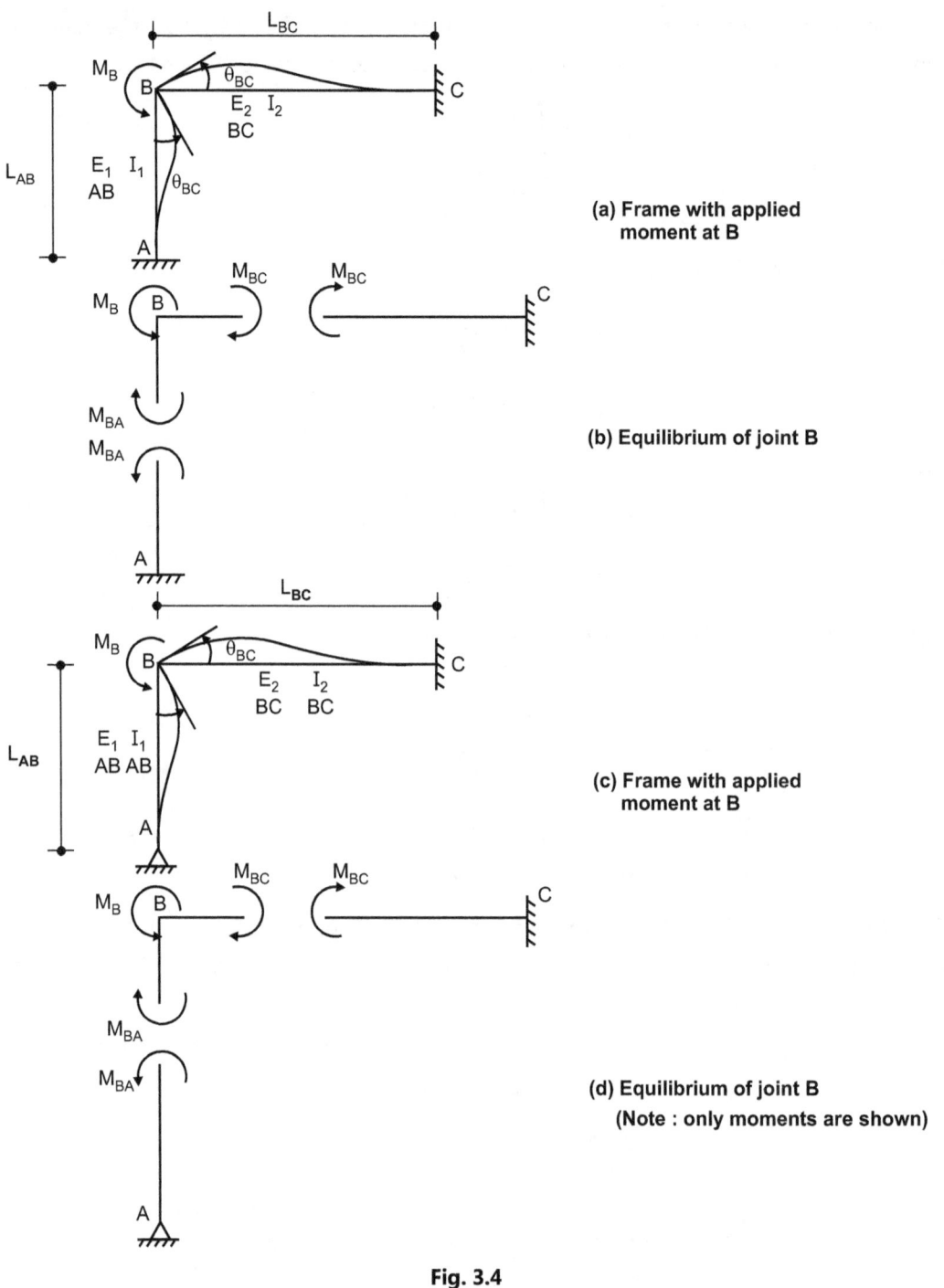

Fig. 3.4

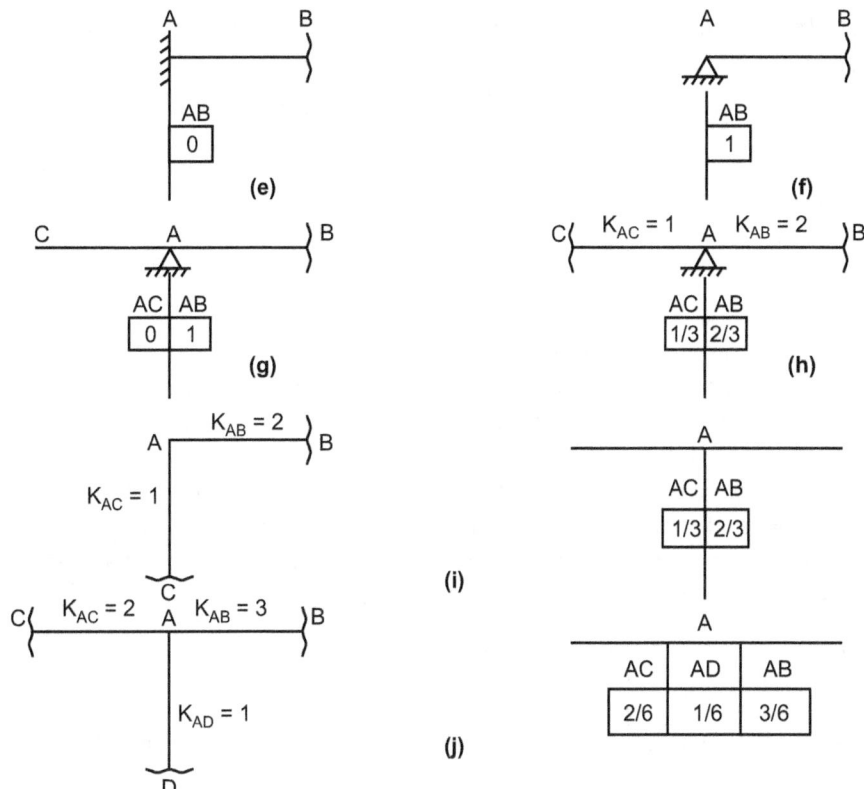

Fig. 3.4 : Distribution of moment

∴ $$\frac{M_{BA} L_{AB}}{3 E_{AB} I_{AB}} = \frac{M_{BC} L_{BC}}{4 E_{BC} I_{BC}}$$

∴ If $E_{AB} = E_{BC}$

$$\frac{M_{BA}}{K_{AB}} = \frac{M_{BC}}{K_{BC}}$$

Where K_{AB} is the modified relative stiffness i.e. (3/4) (I/L) for the member having hinged end.

∴ $M_{BA} = (DF_{BA})(M_B)$

∴ $M_{BC} = (DF_{BC})(M_B)$

Where $DF_{BA} = \dfrac{K_{BA}}{\Sigma K}$

$DF_{BC} = \dfrac{K_{BC}}{K}$

Thus, the moment at a rigid joint is distributed to the members meeting at the joint, in proportion to the distribution factors of the member at the joint. This is the basic phenomenon of moment distribution. The distribution factor plays vital role in moment distribution. The distribution factor is related to the relative stiffness of the member and sum of the relative stiffnesses of all members meeting at the joint.

The ratio $\dfrac{\text{Relative stiffness of the member}}{\text{Sum of relative stiffnesses of all the members meeting at the joint}}$ is called the distribution factor for the member end meeting at the joint. In general, the distribution factor is expressed as

$$DF_{ij} = \dfrac{K_{ij}}{\sum_i K_{ij}} \qquad \ldots (3.1)$$

Following hints will be useful in connection with DF :
- At fixed support, the distribution factor for the member end is zero.
- At end simple or roller or hinged support, the distribution factor for the member end is one.
- At exterior simple or roller or hinged support, the distribution factor for the member end is one for inside member end and zero for overhanging member end.
- At interior simple or roller or hinged support and at intermediate rigid joint, the distribution factor for the member end is less than one and to be obtained from

$$DF_{ij} = \dfrac{K_{ij}}{\sum_i K_{ij}}$$

- The sum of the distribution factors for the member ends meeting at the joint is one.

3.3 INTRODUCTION TO MD METHOD

The MD method mainly consists of successive operations of (i) restraining the joints, and (ii) releasing the joints. The effect of restraining the joints is fixed-end moments i.e. FEM in the first cycle and carryover moments i.e. COM in subsequent cycles. With FEM or COM, the joints may not satisfy the equilibrium conditions. Therefore, there is unbalanced moment at the joint. The balancing moment at the joint is equal and opposite to the unbalanced moment at the joint. The releasing of the joint means balancing the joints. In the operation of releasing the joint, the balancing moment is distributed to the members meeting at the joint. This is called as the distribution of moment in proportion to the normalized relative stiffness factors of the members meeting at the joint. In the first cycle, the FEM due to member loads, is the effect of restraining all the joints. The balancing of all joints means the distribution of moments. In subsequent cycles, the restraining of joints is equivalent to the carryover moments. Carryover and balancing operations are repeated in each cycles. Number of such cycles are performed till required degree of accuracy. Thus, MD method is iterative. The iterations of cycles should be discontinued only when the balancing moments are very small as compared to the initial FEM. The final member-end moments are obtained by adding all member-end moments of all cycles.

Initially, MD method is explained to analyse the indeterminate structures without joint transitions. In general, the MD method involves restraining of joints against rotation and releasing the joints for rotation. If the joint translations exist in the structure, the restraining of joints against translation will be additional concept, to be considered at the beginning of MD method, as dealt with at later stages.

MD method works with member-end moments as FEM, COM and DM (distributed moments). Compatibility and equilibrium of joints are indirectly taken care of in MD technique. MD method does not require the information of degree of static and kinematic indeterminacy of the structure. Kinematically determinate structures cannot be analysed by MD method.

3.3.1 Sign Conventions for Member-End Moments

Same sign conventions as used in SD method are used for MD method. This is restated as Anticlockwise member-end moment is positive and clockwise member-end moment is negative.

3.4 PROCEDURE OF MD METHOD

The primary information of FEM, COF, K, and DF, are initially obtained from data and then the cycles of restraining, releasing and balancing the joints, are systematically carried out in the tabular form. The moment distribution table will be denoted hereafter by MD table. The procedure of MD method is formulated in tabular form with reference to the following illustrated example 3.1.

Example 3.1 : *Analyse the beam shown in Fig. 3.5 (a) by MD method.*

Solution : Data : The structure is supported and loaded as shown in Fig. 3.5 (a). The data includes the following information.

(1) Structural configuration : Type of members; joints; supports; dimensions; cross-sectional properties and material properties of members.
(2) Applied loads: Magnitude, direction and position.
(3) Type of structure: Continuous beam without joint translations.

Object :

In general, the objective is the analysis of structure in all respects. However, the immediate objective i.e. target is to obtain member-end moments by MD method. Knowing the member-end moments, other results of analysis can be obtained easily using the equations of equilibrium.

Concepts and Equations :

MD technique based on normalized relative stiffness factors, carryover factors, and distribution factors.

Procedure :

The process of MD method consists of the following steps :

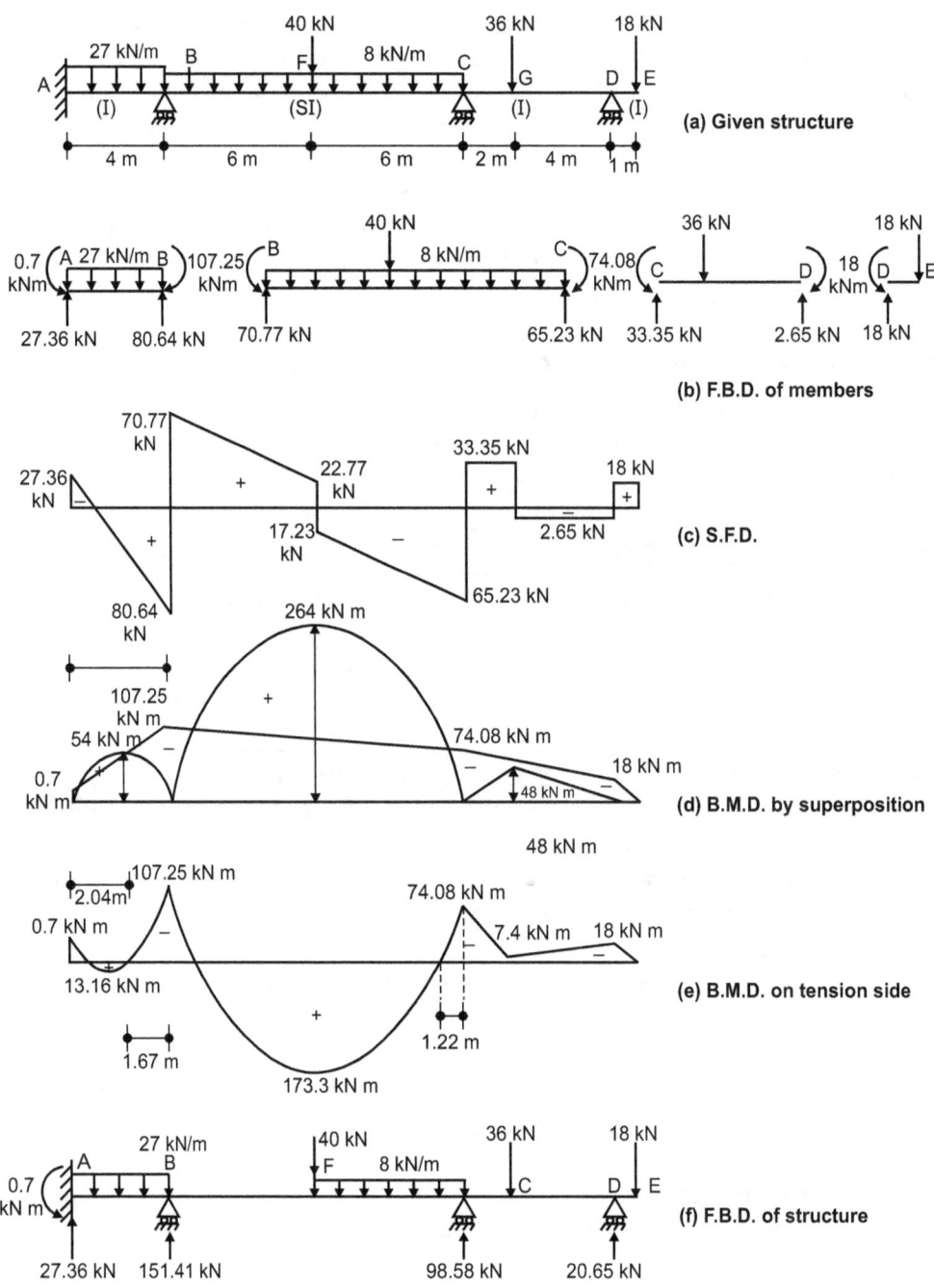

Fig. 3.5 : For Illustrative Example 3.1

Step I : FEM : The fixed-end moments for all members of the structure due to the transverse loads on the member are calculated using the standard results. If the member is not loaded, FEM will be zero. MD begins with the FEM, therefore correctness of FEM is important. For the given data, the FEM are calculated and presented in the following format.

Member	FEM with calculations
AB	$M_{AB}^F = +\left(\dfrac{27 \times 4 \times 4}{12}\right) = +36$ kNm $M_{BA}^F = -M_{AB}^F = -36$ kNm
BC	$M_{BC}^F = +\left(\dfrac{8 \times 12 \times 12}{12}\right) + \left(\dfrac{40 \times 12}{8}\right)$ $= +156$ kNm $M_{CB}^F = -M_{BC}^F = -156$ kNm
CD	$M_{CD}^F = +\left(\dfrac{36 \times 2 \times 4 \times 4}{6 \times 6}\right) = +32$ kNm $M_{DC}^F = -\left(\dfrac{36 \times 2 \times 2 \times 4}{6 \times 6}\right) = -16$ kNm
DE	$M_{DE}^F = +(18 \times 1) = +18$ kNm

Step II: Distribution Factors :

Joint	Member	K	ΣK	$DF = \dfrac{K}{\Sigma K}$
A	AB	–	–	0
B	BA	$\dfrac{4EI}{L} = 1$	2.67	0.375
	BC	$\dfrac{4EI}{L} = 1.67$		0.625
C	CB	$\dfrac{4EI}{L} = 1.67$	2.17	0.769
	CD	$\dfrac{3EI}{L} = 0.5$		0.231
D	DC	–	–	1
	DE	–	–	0

Step III : MD Table : The information of joints, type of joints, members meeting the joint, COF, K, DF are consolidated in concise manner in the beginning of cycles of moment distribution as shown in MD table.

The cycles of successive restraining and releasing and balancing the joints are then carried out and accordingly the distributed moments at ends of members are entered row-wise in every cycles of MD table. The operation of balancing of joints is represented by MD in MD table. The working procedure of MD table is explained below, noting that the method works with member-end moments, which are equal and opposite to the joint moments.

First Cycle :

(a) **Restraining All Joints Against Rotation :** The restraining moments are FEM due to member loads and are entered in first row of this cycle in respective column as shown in MD table.

(b) **Releasing and Balancing the Joints and Distributing the Moments :**

Joint A : It is the fixed support, the rotation at A is zero and hence it is not to be released. This is also clear from zero DF for the member AB at A.

Joint B : It is the interior support or rigid joint. This is to be released as there is rotation at B. At this joint, moments equal and opposite to member-end moments, M_{BA}^F and M_{BC}^F are acting as shown in Fig. 3.6 (a). Thus, there is unbalanced moment of 120 kNm clockwise as shown in Fig. 3.6 (b). For balancing the joint B, moment of – 120 kNm is distributed to the member ends of BA and BC in proportion to the distribution factors. The distributed member-end moments are calculated as follows :

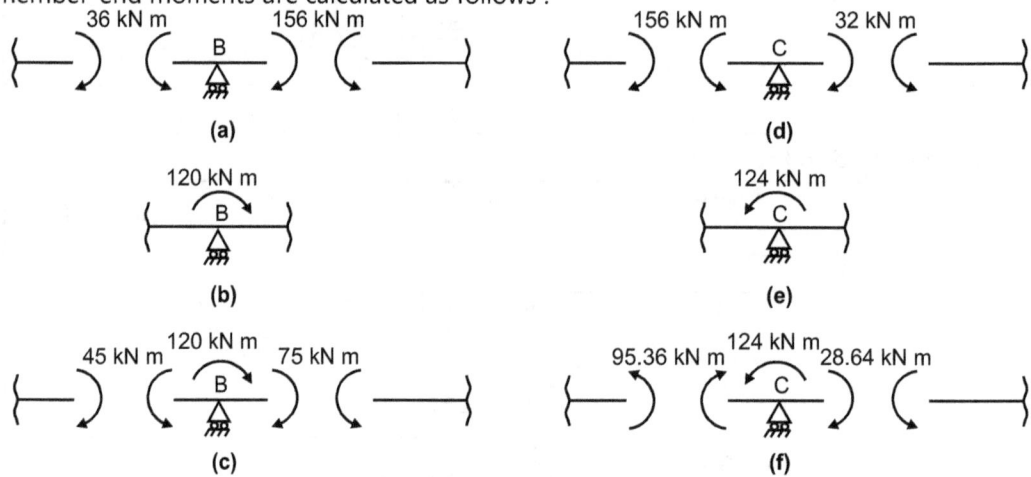

Fig. 3.6 : Balancing the joint

$$M_{BA}^D = (-120)(0.375) = -45 \text{ kNm}$$

$$M_{BC}^D = (-120)(0.625) = -75 \text{ kNm}$$

Balancing of the joint B is demonstrated in Fig. 3.6 (c). Alternatively the distribution of moments is mechanically done according to the following steps :

(1) Unbalanced member-end moment :

$$M_B^{ub} = -36 + 156 = +120 \text{ kNm}$$

(2) Change the sign of M^{ub} and obtain the balancing moment :

$$M_B^b = -120 \text{ kNm}$$

(3) Multiply by DF to obtain the distributed member-end moments :

$$M_{BA}^D = (-120) \times (0.375) = -45 \text{ kNm}$$
$$M_{BC}^D = (-120) \times (0.625) = -75 \text{ kNm}$$

Joint C : This is also to be released and balanced as demonstrated in Fig. 3.6 (d) as the physical phenomenon of distribution. However, the mechanical and mathematical procedure is given below :

(1) $M_C^{ub} = -156 + 32 = -124 \text{ kNm}$

(2) $M_C^b = -M_C^{ub} = +124 \text{ kNm}$

(3) $M_{CB}^D = M_C^b \times DF_{CB} = +124 \times 0.769 = +95.36 \text{ kNm}$

$M_{CD}^D = M_C^b \times DF_{CD} = +124 \times 0.231 = +28.64$

Joint D : This is exterior simple or hinged support and therefore it is to be released and balanced only once in the first cycle.

(1) $M_D^{ub} = -16 + 18 = +2 \text{ kNm}$

(2) $M_D^b = -M_D^{ub} = -2 \text{ kNm}$

(3) $M_{DC}^D = (-2)(1) = -2$

(4) $M_{DE}^D = (-2)(0) = 0$

All distributed moments obtained above by balancing all the joints are entered in second row of first cycle in the respective columns as shown in MD table. This completes the first cycle.

Second Cycle :

(a) Restraining the Joint : Restraining moments are carryover moments, COM of the distributed moments of first cycle. M^D at one end is carried over to the other end of the member.

$M^{COM} = M^D \times COF$ as shown by crossed arrows in MD table.

i.e.
$$M_{BA}^{COM} = (-45)\left(\frac{1}{2}\right) = -22.5 \text{ kNm}$$
$$M_{BC}^{COM} = (+95.36)\left(\frac{1}{2}\right) = +47.68 \text{ kNm}$$

and so on. It may be noted that there is no carryover to the exterior simple/hinged support D. It is balanced completely in first cycle itself and hence distribution at D is stopped at this stage.

Carryover moments are entered in first row of this cycle in the respective columns as shown in MD table.

(b) Releasing and Balancing the Joints and Distributing the Moments : Same procedure as in first cycle is followed. The balancing of one joint is illustrated again.

Joint B :

(1) $M_B^{ub} = 0 + 47.68 = +47.68$

(2) $M_B^b = -M^{ub} = -47.68$

(3) $M_{BA}^D = (-47.68) \times (0.375) = -17.88$ kNm

(4) $M_{BC}^D = (-47.65) \times (0.625) = -29.80$ kNm

Other Cycles :

The operations of carryover and balancing for further cycles are repeated till the desired degree of accuracy. In this sense, the iterations of MD table could be stopped at the end of any cycle so that the distributed moments are small compared to the initial FEM. Accuracy of the results will depend on the stage of terminating MD table. In the particular situations, MD table stops automatically as there may be no moments for distribution. The operations in MD table are represented by COM, DM.

Final Results of MD Tables :

Total member-end moments are obtained by adding the moments in the respective columns.

MD Table

Joint	A		B		C		D
Type of joint	EFS		ISS/RJ		ISS/RJ		ESS
Member	AB	BA	BC	CB	CD	DC	DE
COF	→1/2 1/2←		→1/2 1/2←		→0 1/2←		
DF	0	0.375	0.625	0.769	0.231	1	0
First cycle FEM	+ 36	− 36	+ 156	− 156	+ 32	− 16	+ 18
DM	−	− 45	− 75	+ 95.36	+ 28.64	− 2	−
Second cycle COM	− 22.5	−	+ 47.68	− 37.5	− 1.0	ST	OP
DM	−	− 17.88	− 29.80	+ 29.61	+ 8.89		
Third cycle COM	− 8.94	−	+ 14.80	− 14.90	−		
DM	−	− 5.55	− 9.25	+ 11.46	+ 3.44		
Fourth cycle COM	− 2.78	−	+ 5.73	− 4.62	−		
DM	−	− 2.15	− 3.58	+ 3.55	+ 1.07		
Fifth cycle COM	− 1.08	−	+ 1.78	− 1.79	−		
DM	−	− 0.67	− 1.11	+ 1.38	+ 0.41		
Total final moments	+ 0.7	− 107.25	+ 107.25	− 74.08	+ 74.08	− 18	+ 18

Step IV : FBD of members and member forces: Member-end moments are known from MD table. Member-end forces are obtained from equations of equilibrium applied to FBD of the member as shown in Fig. 3.6 (b).

Step V : SFD : With known values of member-end shears and member loads, the SFD is drawn as shown in Fig. 3.6 (c).

Step VI : BMD : Member-end moments are considered as bending moments at the supports. Span bending moments are obtained from member loads.

BMD by superposition and BMD on tension side is as shown in Fig. 3.6 (d) and Fig. 3.6 (e) respectively.

Step VII : FBD of Structure and Reactions : Member-end moments and forces at the support end of the member will correspond to the reactions of the supports.

For interior support, the reactions will be the sum of member-end forces meeting the support joint. FBD of structure is as shown in Fig. 3.6 (f).

Following rules of MD method are worth to be noted for further applications :

- The relative stiffness factor for members with one exterior simple or roller or hinged support is to be modified as (3/4) (I/L).
- The fixed support need not be released.
- The exterior simple or roller or hinged support need to be balanced only once in the first cycle.
- No carryover moments will ever be brought to the exterior simple or roller or hinged supports.

Example 3.2 : *A continuous beam ABCD with ends A and D is simply supported. A couple of 50 kN-m is acting at centre on AB having span 3m. BC is loaded with UDL of 15 kN/m and span 3.5m. A point load of 60 kN is acting on CD having span 4.5 m at 1 m from D. Draw S.F.D. and B.M.D.*

Solution : Data : The beam is loaded and supported as shown in Fig. 3.7.

Object : Structural analysis.

Concepts and Equations : MD technique based on normalized relative stiffness factors, carryover factors and distribution factors.

Procedure : Step I : Fixed End Moments :

$$\overline{M}_{AB} = +\frac{M}{4} = \frac{50}{4} = 12.5 \text{ kN-m}$$

$$\overline{M}_{BA} = +\frac{M}{4} = 12.5 \text{ kN-m}$$

$$\overline{M}_{BC} = -\frac{wl^2}{12} = -\frac{15 \times 3.5^2}{12} = -15.31 \text{ kN-m}$$

$$\overline{M}_{CB} = 15.31 \text{ kN-m}$$

$$\overline{M}_{CD} = -\frac{wab^2}{l^2} = -\frac{60 \times 3.5 \times 1^2}{4.5^2} = -10.37 \text{ kN-m}$$

$$\overline{M}_{DC} = \frac{wa^2b}{l^2} = \frac{60 \times 3.5^2 \times 1}{4.5^2} = 36.3 \text{ kN-m}$$

Step II : Distribution Factors :

Joint	Member	Type of Support	Carry over factor	K	ΣK	D.F.
A	AB	Simple support	A → B ½	-	-	-
B	BA	Continuous support	B → A 0	3/4 × I/3	11.5I/14	0.3
	BC		B → C ½	2I/3.5		0.7
C	CB	Continuous support	C → B ½	2I/3.5	4I.5I/42	0.58
	CD		C → D 0	3/4 × 2.5I/4.5		0.42
D	DC	Simple support	D → C ½	-	-	-

Step III : MD Table :

Joint	A	B		C		D
Member	AB	BA	BC	CB	CD	DC
D.F.	–	0.3	0.7	0.58	0.42	–
F.E.M.	12.5	12.5	–15.31	15.31	–10.37	36.3
Release Jt. A and D as S.S.	–12.5					–36.3
C.O.		–6.25			–18.15	
Total moments	0	6.25	–15.31	15.31	–28.52	0
Distribution		2.72	6.34	7.66	5.55	
C.O.			3.83	3.17		
Distribution		–1.15	–2.68	–1.84	–1.33	
C.O.			–0.92	–1.34		
	–	0.28	0.64	0.78	0.56	
Total moments	0	8.1	–8.1	23.74	–23.74	0

Step IV : FBD of members is an shown in Fig. Considering equilibrium of each member and of complete structure, all reaction components are found out as shown in Fig. 3.7.

Step V : Shear force diagram is as shown in Fig. 3.7.

Step VI : Bending moment diagrams are as shown in Fig. 3.7 (d) and (e).

Step VII : FBD of structure is as shown in Fig. 3.7.

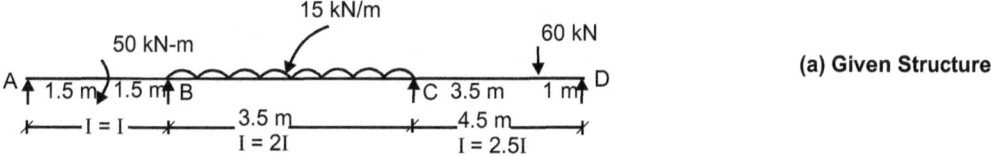
(a) Given Structure

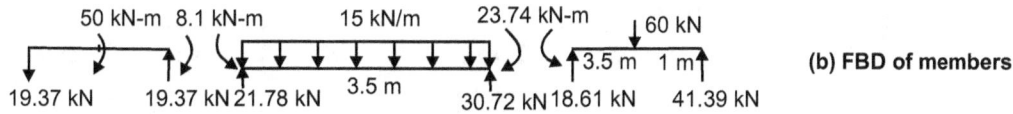
(b) FBD of members

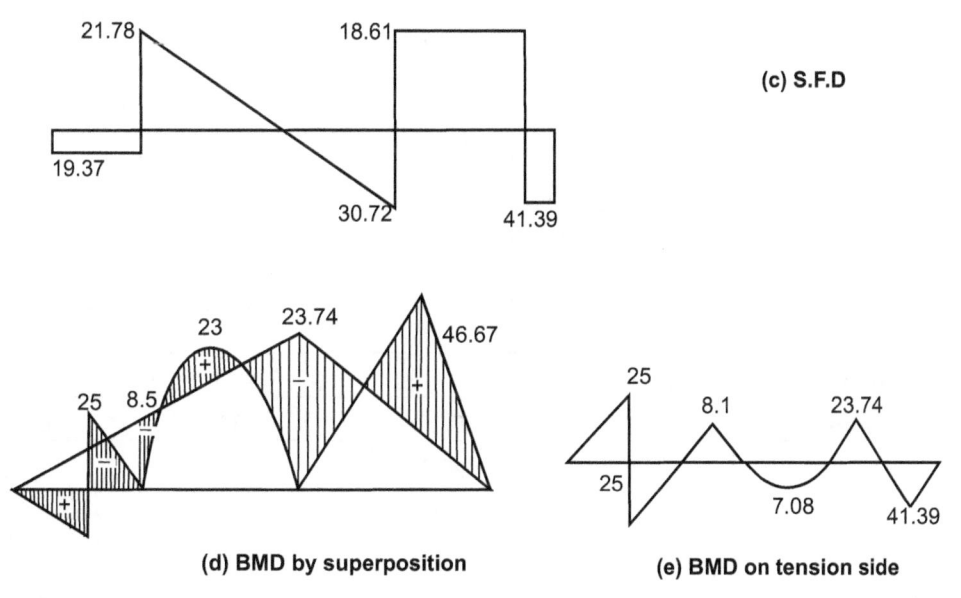
(c) S.F.D

(d) BMD by superposition

(e) BMD on tension side

Fig. 3.7

Example 3.3 : A continuous beam ABC is fixed at A and simply supported at B and C. The span AB is 6 m and carries UDL of 2 kN/m. The span BC is 4 m and carries UDL load of 3 kN/m. Determine the fixed end moments. (I is same throughout).

Solution : Data : The beam is loaded and supported as shown in Fig. 3.8

Object : Structural analysis:

Concepts and Equations : MD technique based on normlized relative stiffness factors, carry over factors and distribution factors.

Procedure : Step I : Fixed End Moments :

$$M_{AB} = -\frac{wl^2}{12} = -\frac{2 \times 6 \times 6}{12} = -6 \text{ kN-m}$$

$$M_{BA} = +6 \text{ kN-m}$$

$$M_{BC} = -\frac{wl^2}{2} = -\frac{3 \times 4 \times 4}{12} = -4 \text{ kN-m}$$

$$M_{CB} = +4 \text{ kN-m}$$

Step II : Distribution Factors :

Joint	Member	Type of support	Carryover factor	K	ΣK	D. F.
A	AB	Fixed	A → B 0	–	–	–
B	BA	Continuous	B → A 1/2	I/6	34I/96	0.471
	BC	Support	B → C 0	3/4 × I/4		0.529
C	CB	Simple	C → B 1/2	–	–	–

Step III : MD Table :

Joint	A	B		D
Member	AB	BA	BC	DC
D. F.	-	0.471	0.529	-
F.E.M.	–6	+6	–4	+4
Release moment at C				–4
C.O.			–2	
Total moments	–6	+6	–6	0

Step IV : FBD of members is an shown in Fig. 3.8 Considering equilibrium of each member and of complete structure, all reaction components are found out as shown in Fig. 3.8.

Step V : Shear force diagram is as shown in Fig. 3.8.

Step VI : Bending moment diagrams are as shown in Fig. 3.8.

Step VII : FBD of structure is as shown in Fig. 3.8.

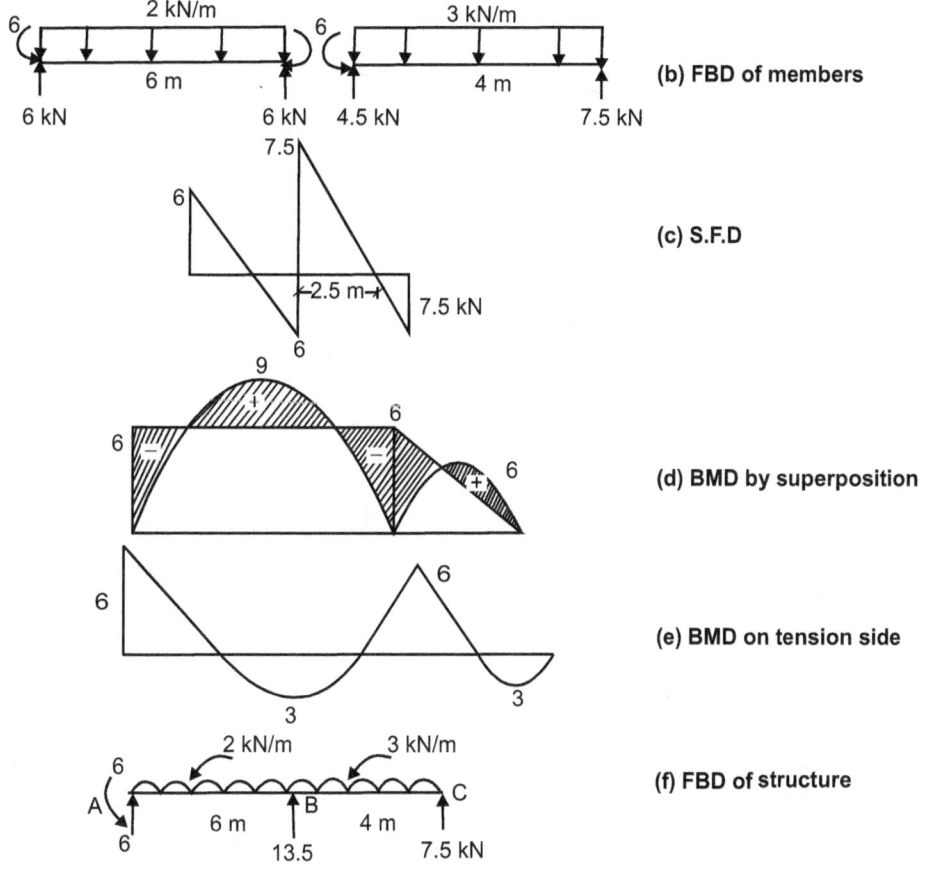

Fig. 3.8

Example 3.4 : *Find the reaction at the prop for the beam AB loaded with U.D.L. of intenstiy w/m run and span of AB is l metres.*

Solution : Data : The beam is loaded and supported as shown in Fig. 3.9.

Object : Structural analysis.

Concepts and Equations : MD technique based on normalized relative stiffness factors, carryover factors and distribution factors.

Procedure : Step I : Fixed End Moments :

$$M_A = -\frac{wl^2}{12}, \quad M_B = -\frac{wl^2}{12}$$

Step II : As no continuation at joint B and joint A is fixed, then there is no relative stiffness and there will not be any distribution factor.

Step III : MD Table :

Joint	A	B
F.E.M.	$-wl^2/12$	$+wl^2/12$
Released B		$-wl^2/12$
C.O.	$-wl^2/24$	
Final moments	$-wl^2/8$	0

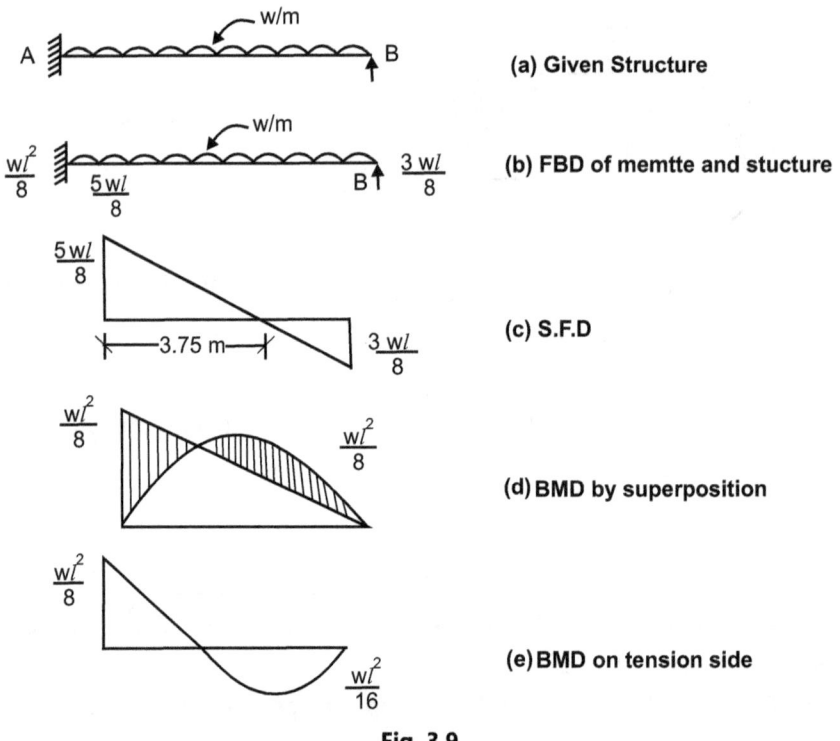

(a) Given Structure
(b) FBD of memtte and stucture
(c) S.F.D
(d) BMD by superposition
(e) BMD on tension side

Fig. 3.9

Step IV : FBD of members is as shown in Fig. 3.9 Considering equilibrium of each member and of complete structure, all reaction components are found out as shown in Fig.

Step V : Shear force diagram is as shown in Fig. 3.9

Step VI : Bending moment diagrams are as shown in Fig. 3.9

Step VII : FBD of structure is as shown in Fig. 3.9

Example 3.5 : *Analyse the beam shown in Fig. 3.10 (a) using moment distribution method.*

Solution : Data : The beam is supported and loaded as shown in Fig. 3.10 (a).

Object : Structural analysis.

Concepts and Equations : MD technique based on normalized relative stiffness factors, carryover factors and distribution factors.

Procedure: Step I : Fixed-End Moments :

Member	FEM with calculations
AB	$M_{AB}^F = \dfrac{WL^2}{12} = \dfrac{20 \times 9^2}{12} = 135$ kN-m $M_{BA}^F = \dfrac{-WL^2}{12} = -\dfrac{20 \times 9^2}{12} = -135$ kN-m
BC	$M_{BC}^F = \dfrac{WL}{8} = \dfrac{80 \times 6}{8} = 60$ kN-m $M_{CB}^F = -\dfrac{WL}{8} = -\dfrac{80 \times 6}{8} = -60$ kN-m
CD	$M_{CD}^F = \dfrac{WL^2}{12} = \dfrac{15 \times 8^2}{12} = 80$ kN-m $M_{DC}^F = \dfrac{-WL^2}{12} = -\dfrac{15 \times 8^2}{12} = -80$ kN-m

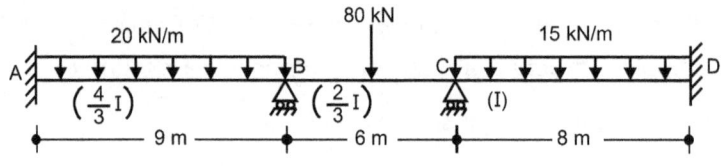

(a) Given structure

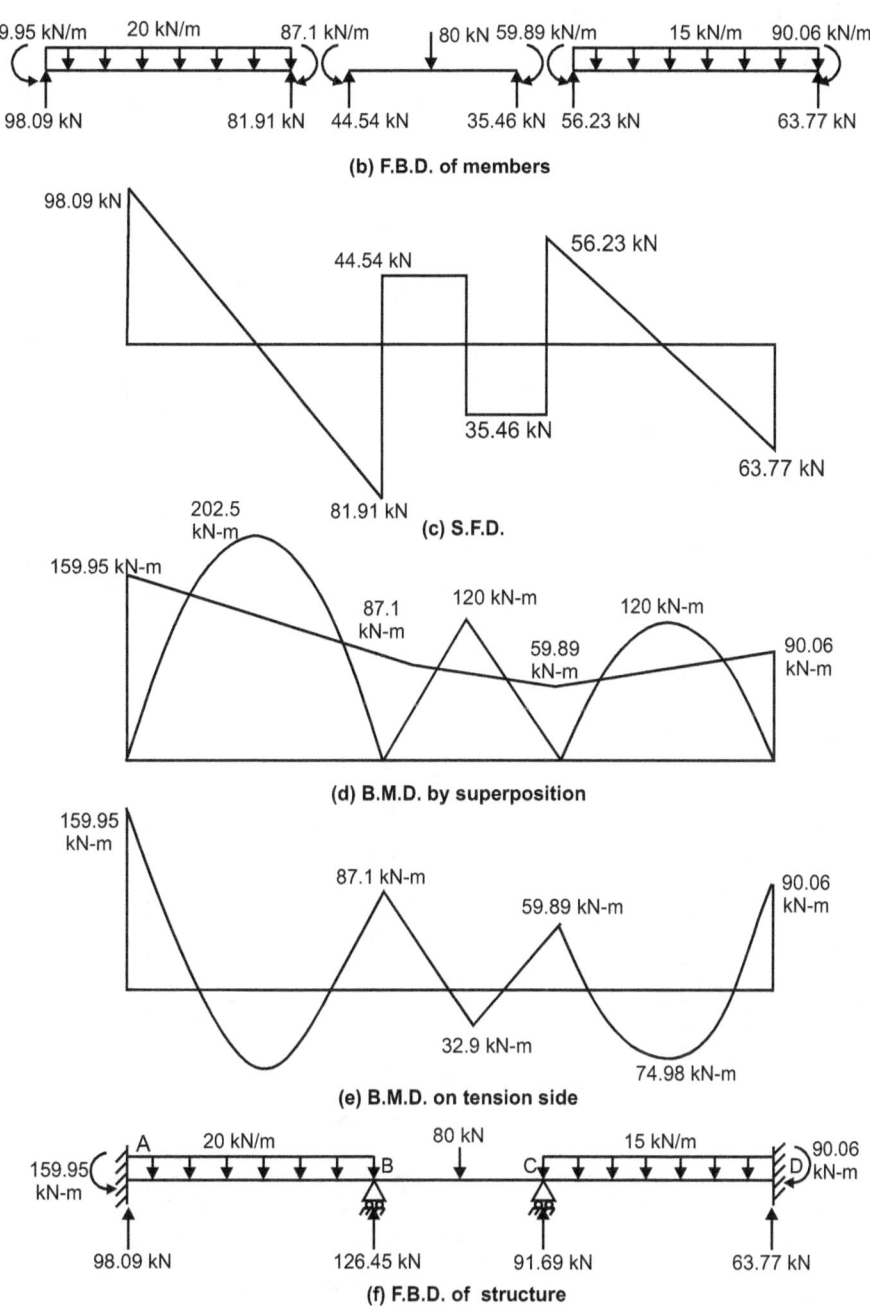

Fig. 3.10 : For Illustrative Example 3.5

Step II : Distribution Factors :

Joint	Member	K	ΣK	D.F.
A	AB	–	–	0
B	BA	$\frac{4EI}{L} = 0.59$	1.03	0.57
	BC	$\frac{4EI}{L} = 0.44$		0.43
C	CB	$\frac{4EI}{L} = 0.44$	0.94	0.47
	CD	$\frac{4EI}{L} = 0.5$		0.53
D	DC	–	–	0

Step III : MD Table :

Joint		A		B			C		D
Type of joint		EFS		RJ			RJ		EFS
Member		AB		BA	BC		CB	CD	DC
COF			→ 1/2		→ 1/2			→ 1/2	
DF			1/2 ←		1/2 →			1/2 →	
		0		0.57	0.43		0.47	0.53	0
First cycle	FEM	135		– 135	60		– 60	80	– 80
	DM	–		42.75	32.25		– 9.4	– 10.6	–
Second cycle	COM	21.38		–	– 4.7		16.12	–	– 5.3
	DM	–		2.69	2.02		– 7.58	– 8.54	–
Third cycle	COM	1.35		–	– 3.79		1.01	–	– 4.27
	DM	–		2.16	1.63		– 0.49	– 0.52	–
Fourth cycle	COM	1.08			– 0.24		0.81		– 0.26
	DM			0.14	0.10		– 0.38	– 0.43	
Fifth cycle	COM	0.07			– 0.19		0.05		– 0.21
	DM			0.11	0.08		– 0.024	– 0.026	
Sixth cycle	COM	0.060			– 0.012		0.04		– 0.013
	DM			0.007	0.005		– 0.019	– 0.021	
Seventh cycle	COM	0.004			– 0.009		0.002		– 0.010
	DM			0.005	0.004		– 0.001	– 0.001	
Total final moment		158.95		– 87.1	87.10		– 59.86	59.86	– 90.06

Step IV : FBD of members is as shown in Fig. 3.10 (b). Considering equilibrium of each member and of complete structure, all reaction components are found out as shown in Fig. 3.10 (d).

Step V : Shear force diagram is as shown in Fig. 3.10 (c).

Step VI : Bending moment diagrams are as shown in Fig. 3.10 (d) and Fig. 3.10 (e).

Step VII : FBD of structure is as shown in Fig. 3.10 (f).

Example 3.6 : *The beam is loaded and supported as shown in Fig. 3.11 (a). Analyse the beam using moment distribution method.*

Solution : Data : The beam is loaded and supported as shown in Fig. 3.11 (a).

Object : Structural analysis.

Concepts and Equations : MD technique based on normalized relative stiffness factors, carryover factors and distribution factors.

Procedure :

Step I : Fixed-End Moments :

Member	FEM with calculations		Total FEM
	FEM due to external loads	**FEM due to sinking of support D**	
AB	$M^F_{BA} = -10 \times 2 = -20$ kN-m	0	-20 kN-m
BC	$M^F_{BC} = \dfrac{WL^2}{12} = \dfrac{16 \times 6^2}{12}$ $= 48$ kN-m	0	48 kN-m
	$M^F_{CB} = -\dfrac{WL^2}{12} = -\dfrac{16 \times 6^2}{12}$ $= -48$ kN-m	0	-48 kN-m
CD	$M^F_{CD} = \dfrac{WL}{8} = \dfrac{8 \times 4}{8}$ $= 4$ kN-m $M^F_{DC} = -\dfrac{WL}{8} = -\dfrac{8 \times 4}{8}$ $= -4$ kN-m	$M^F_{CD} = \dfrac{6EI\delta}{L^2}$ $= \dfrac{6 \times 2 \times 10^4 \times 2 \times 10^{-3}}{4^2}$ $= 15$ kN-m $M^F_{DC} = \dfrac{6EI\delta}{L^2}$ $= \dfrac{6 \times 2 \times 10^4 \times 2 \times 10^{-3}}{4^2}$ $= 15$ kN-m	19 kN-m 11 kN-m

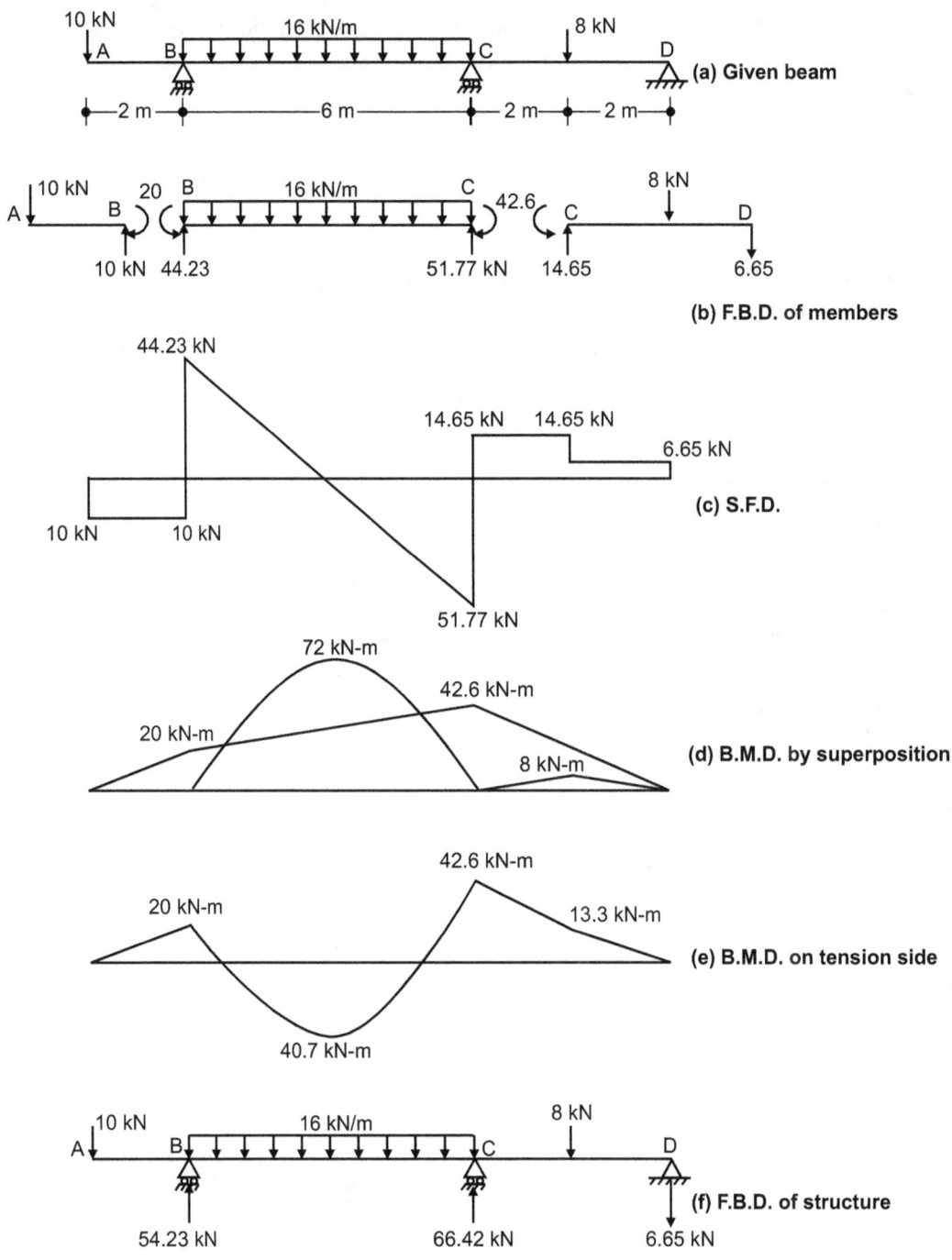

Fig. 3.11 : For Illustrative Example 3.6

Step II : Distribution Factors :

Joint	Member	K	ΣK	D.F.
B	BA	–	–	–
	BC	–	–	0
C	CB	$\frac{3EI}{L}$ = 0.5	1.25	0.40
	CD	$\frac{3EI}{L}$ = 0.75		0.60
D	DC	–	–	0

Step III : MD Table :

Joint		B			C		D
Type of joint		EFS			ISS/RJ		ESS
Member		BA	BC	CB	CD		DC
COF			→ 1/2		→ 0		
D.F.			0 ←		1/2 →		
		0	0.40	0.60		0
First cycle	FEM	– 20	48	– 48	19	11
	DM	–	– 28	11.6	17.4	– 11
Second cycle	COM			– 14	– 5.5	
	DM			7.8		
Total final moment		– 20	20	– 42.6	42.6	0

Step IV : FBD of members is as shown in Fig. 3.11 (b).

Step V : Shear force diagram is as shown in Fig. 3.11 (c).

Step VI : Bending moment diagrams are as shown in Fig. 3.11 (d) and Fig. 3.11 (e).

Step VII : FBD of structure is as shown in Fig. 3.11 (f).

Example 3.7 : A beam is loaded and supported as shown in Fig. 3.12 (a). The support B sinks by 25 mm. EI of the beam is 3800 kNm². Using moment distribution method, analyse the beam and draw SFD and BMD.

Solution : Data : The frame is supported and loaded as shown in Fig. 3.12 (a).

Object : Structural analysis.

Concepts and Equations : MD technique based on normalized relative stiffness factors, carryover factors and distribution factors.

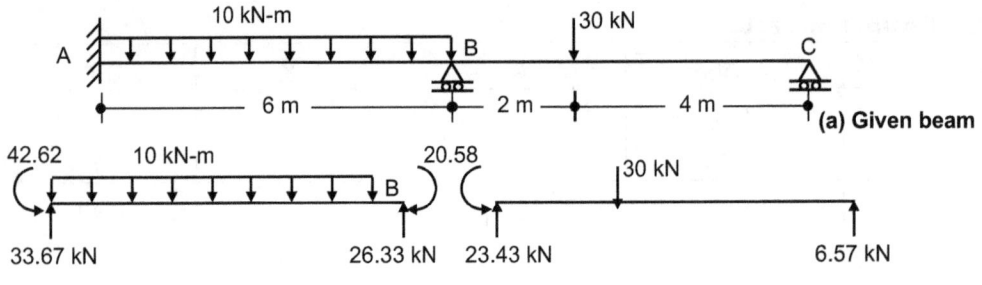

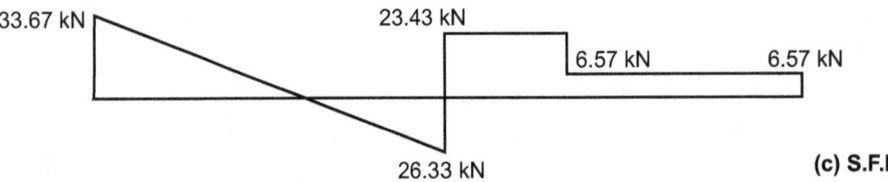

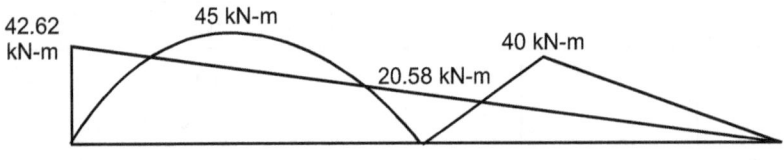

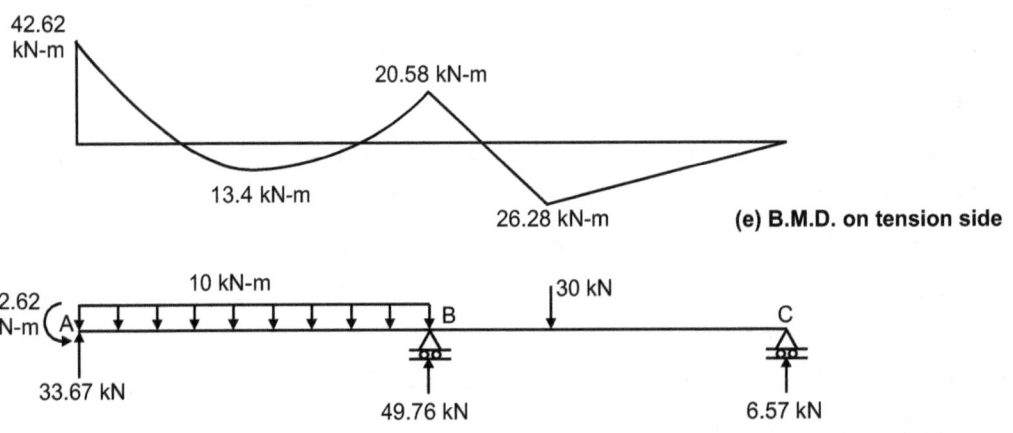

Fig. 3.12 : For Illustrative Example 3.7

Procedure :

Step I : Fixed-End Moments :

Member	FEM with calculations		Total
	FEM due to external loads	FEM due to sinking of support B	FEM
AB	$M_{AB}^F = \dfrac{WL^2}{12}$ $= \dfrac{10 \times 6^2}{12} = 30\text{kN-m}$	$M_{AB}^F = \dfrac{6EI\Delta}{L^2}$ $= \dfrac{6 \times 3800 \times 25 \times 10^{-3}}{6^2}$ $= 15.83 \text{ kN-m}$	$M_{AB}^F = 45.83 \text{ kN-m}$
	$M_{BA}^F = -\dfrac{WL^2}{12}$ $= -\dfrac{10 \times 6^2}{12}$ $= -30 \text{ kN-m}$	$M_{BA}^F = \dfrac{6\,EI\Delta}{L^2}$ $= \dfrac{6 \times 3800 \times 25 \times 10^{-3}}{6^2}$ $= 15.83 \text{ kN-m}$	$M_{BA}^F = -14.17 \text{ kN-m}$
BC	$M_{BC}^F = \dfrac{Wab^2}{L^2}$ $= \dfrac{30 \times 2 \times 4^2}{6^2}$ $= 26.67 \text{ kN-m}$	$M_{BC}^F = -\dfrac{6EI\Delta}{L^2}$ $= -\dfrac{6 \times 3800 \times 25 \times 10^{-3}}{6^2}$ $= -15.83 \text{ kN-m}$	$M_{BC}^F = 10.84 \text{ kN-m}$
	$M_{CB}^F = -\dfrac{Wa^2b}{L^2}$ $= -\dfrac{30 \times 2^2 \times 4}{6^2}$ $= -13.33 \text{ kN-m}$	$M_{CB}^F = -\dfrac{6EI\Delta}{L^2}$ $= -\dfrac{6 \times 3800 \times 25 \times 10^{-3}}{6^2}$ $= -15.83 \text{ kN-m}$	$M_{CB}^F = -29.16 \text{ kN-m}$

Step II : Distribution Factors :

Joint	Member	K	ΣK	D.F.
A	AB	–	0	0
B	BA	$\dfrac{4EI}{L} = 0.67$		0.57
	BC	$\dfrac{3EI}{L} = 0.50$	1.17	0.43
C	CB	–	–	0

Step III : MD Table :

Joint Type of joint	A EFS		B RS		C RS
Member	AB	BA	BC		CB
COF	→ 1/2 1/2 ←		→ 0 1/2 ←		
DF	0	0.57	0.43		0
First cycle FEM	45.83	− 14.17	10.84		− 29.16
DM	−	1.90	1.43		29.16
Second cycle COM	0.95	−	14.58		−
DM	−	− 8.31	− 6.27		
Third cycle COM	− 4.16	−	−		
Total final moments	42.62	− 20.58	20.58		0

Step IV : FBD of member is as shown in Fig. 3.12 (b).

Consider equilibrium of each member and of complete structure, all reaction components are found out as shown in Fig. 3.12 (b).

Step V : Shear force diagram is as shown in Fig. 3.12 (c).

Step VI : Bending moment diagrams are as shown in Fig. 3.12 (d) and Fig. 3.12 (e).

Step VII : FBD of structure is as shown in Fig. 3.12 (f).

3.5 Application of MD Method to Beams with Unknown Joint Translations

When flexural rigidity (EI) of the beam member suddenly changes, additional node (joint) is required to be assumed at such points, which is subjected to unknown translation in addition to rotation. Also in case, if the members of the beam are connected by unsupported internal hinge, this joint is subjected to translation in addition to rotation. The procedure to analyse such beams is similar to that of analysis of sway frames and is illustrated in following examples.

Example 3.8 : *Analyse the beam shown in Fig. 3.13 (a) by MD method.*

Solution : Data : The beam is supported and loaded as shown in Fig. 3.13 (a).

Object : Structural analysis.

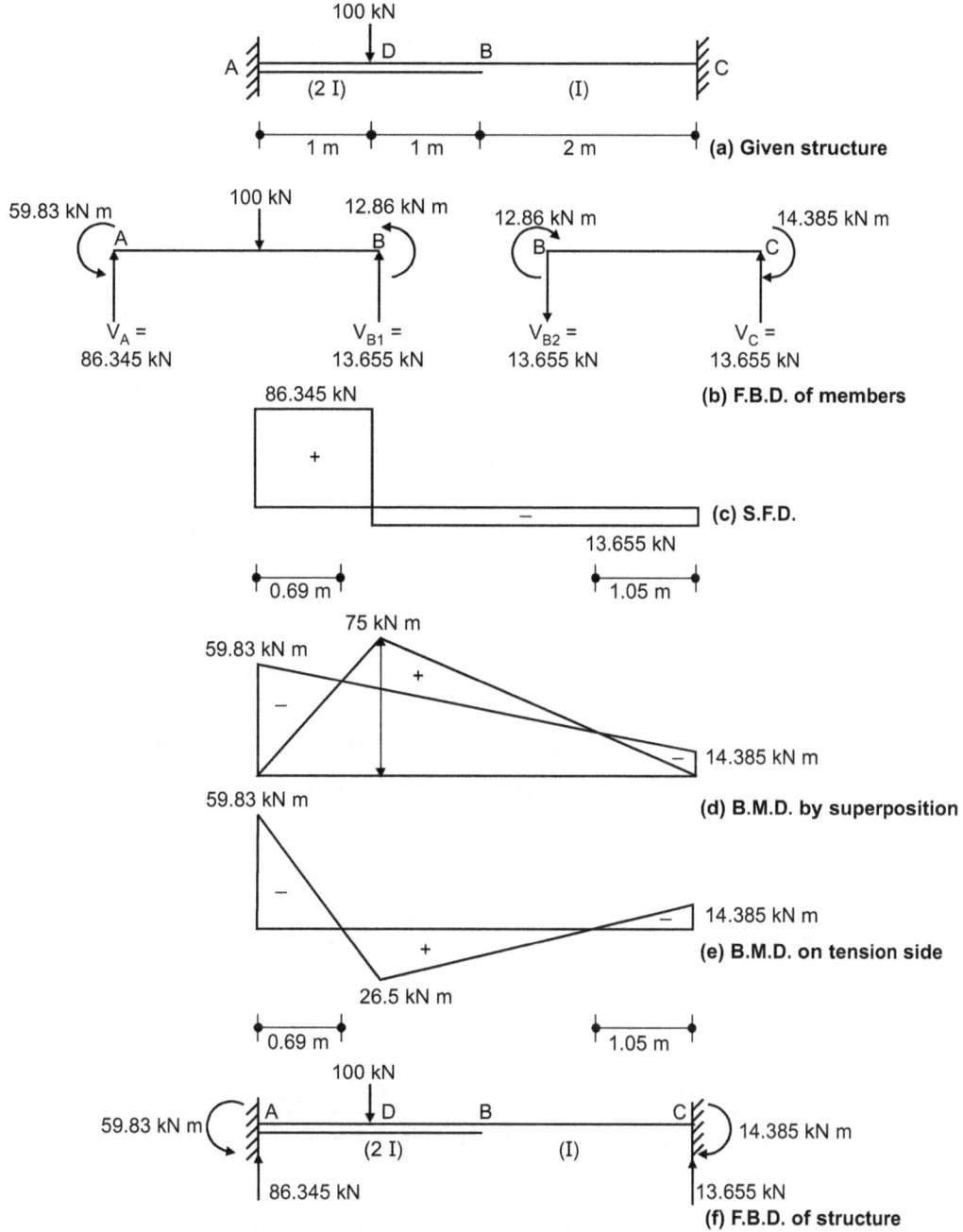

Fig. 3.13 : For Illustrative Example 3.8

Procedure :

Step I : Fixed-End Moments (considering additional node at B).

Member	FEM with calculations
AB	$M^F_{AB} = \dfrac{WL}{8} = \dfrac{100 \times 2}{8} = 25$ kNm $M^F_{BA} = -M^F_{AB} = -25$ kNm
BC	$M^F_{BC} = 0$ $M^F_{CB} = 0$

Step II : Distribution Factors :

Joint	Member	K	Σ K	DF = $\dfrac{K}{\Sigma K}$
A	AB	–	–	0
B	BA	$\dfrac{4EI}{L} = 4$	6	0.67
	BC	$\dfrac{4EI}{L} = 2$		0.33
C	CB	–	–	0

Step III : MD Table (I) for Moments without Joint Translation at B :

Joint		A	B			C
Type of Joint		EFS	RJ			EFS
Member		AB	BA	BC		CB
COF			$\rightarrow$ 1/2 1/2 $\leftarrow$		$\rightarrow$ 1/2 1/2 $\leftarrow$	
DF		0	0.67	0.33		0
First cycle	FEM	25	– 25	0		0
	DM	–	16.75	8.25		–
Second cycle	COM	8.38	–	–		4.13
	DM	–	–	–		–
First set of final moments		33.38	– 8.25	8.25		4.13

Step IV : MD for Moments Due to Joint Translation at B :

(a) The basic information of K, COF and DF remains the same.

(b) Normalized relative translational stiffness factors (K_S). Assuming negative joint translation at B i.e. downwards, which produces anticlockwise i.e. positive moments for member AB and clockwise i.e. negative moments for member BC.

Member	Relative translational stiffness factor	Normalized relative translational stiffness factor (K_s)
AB	$\dfrac{2I}{2^2} = \dfrac{I}{2}$	2
BC	$\dfrac{I}{2^2} = \dfrac{I}{4}$	1

(c) Moments Due to Translation at B :

Member	Arbitrary relative FEM due to translation
AB	$M_{AB}^{FS} = 200$ kNm $M_{BA}^{FS} = 200$ kNm
BC	$M_{BC}^{FS} = -100$ kNm $M_{CB}^{FS} = -100$ kNm

Step V : MD Table (II) for Moments Due to Translation :

Joint	A	B		C
Type of joint	EFS	RJ		EFS
Member	AB	BA	BC	CB
COF	$\to 1/2$ $1/2 \leftarrow$		$\to 1/2$ $1/2 \leftarrow$	
DF	0	0.67	0.33	0
First cycle FEM	200	200	– 100	– 100
DM	–	– 67	– 33	–
Second cycle COM	– 33.5	–	–	– 16.5
DM	–	–	–	–
Second set of final moments	166.5	133	– 133	– 116.5

Let, actual moments due to translation be 'C' times the above moments.

∴
$$M_{AB} = M_{AB}^{I} + C \cdot M_{AB}^{II} = 33.38 + C\,(166.5)$$
$$M_{BA} = M_{BA}^{I} + C \cdot M_{BA}^{II} = -8.25 + C\,(133)$$
$$M_{BC} = M_{BC}^{I} + C \cdot M_{BC}^{II} = 8.25 + C\,(-133)$$
$$M_{CB} = M_{CB}^{I} + C \cdot M_{CB}^{II} = 4.13 + C\,(-116.5)$$

where, C = Correction factor to be evaluated from the condition of shear equilibrium of the structure.

Step VI : Shear Equilibrium : Shear equilibrium of structure gives,

$$V_A - V_C - 100 = 0 \quad \ldots (A)$$

where, $\quad V_A = \dfrac{M_{AB} + M_{BA}}{2} + 50$

and $\quad V_C = \dfrac{M_{BC} + M_{CB}}{2}$

Substituting in equation (A), we get,

$$\left[\dfrac{M_{AB} + M_{BA}}{2} + 50\right] - \left[\dfrac{M_{BC} + M_{CB}}{2}\right] - 100 = 0$$

$$M_{AB} + M_{BA} - M_{BC} - M_{CB} - 100 = 0$$

Substituting the values of moments, we get,

$$33.38 + C\,(166.5) - 8.25 + C\,(133) - 8.25 - C\,(-133) - 4.13 - C\,(-116.5) - 100 = 0$$

$$\Rightarrow \boxed{C = 0.159}$$

Positive sign for 'C' indicates that translation at 'B' will be in the direction assumed i.e. downwards.

Step VII : Final Results :

Member	AB	BA	BC	CB
Corrected moments of second set	26.45	2.11	– 2.11	– 18.515
Moments of first set	33.38	– 8.25	8.25	4.13
Net final moments	59.83	12.86	– 12.86	14.385

Step VIII : FBD of members is as shown in Fig. 3.13 (b). Considering equilibrium of each member and of complete structure, all reaction components are found out as shown in figure.

Step IX : Shear force diagram is as shown in Fig. 3.13 (c).

Step X : Bending moment diagram is as shown in Fig. 3.13 (d) and Fig. 3.13 (e).

Step XI : FBD of structure is as shown in Fig. 3.13 (f).

Example 3.9 : *Analyse the beam shown in Fig. 3.14 (a) by MD method.*

Solution : Data : The beam is supported and located as shown in Fig. 3.14 (a).

Object : Structural analysis.

Procedure :

Step I : Fixed-End Moments :

Member	FEM with calculations
AB	$M^F_{AB} = \dfrac{wL^2}{12} = \dfrac{60 \times 1^2}{12} = 5$ kNm $M^F_{BA} = -M^F_{AB} = -5$ kNm
BC	$M^F_{BC} = \dfrac{60 \times 2^2}{12} = 20$ kNm $M^F_{CB} = -M^F_{BC} = -20$ kNm

Step II : Distribution Factors :

Joint	Member	K	ΣK	DF = $\dfrac{K}{\Sigma K}$
A	AB	–	–	0
B	BA	–	–	1
	BC	–	–	1
C	CB	–	–	0

Step III : MD Table (I) for Moments Without Joint Translation at B :

Joint		A	B		C
Type of joint		EFS	IH		EFS
Member		AB	BA	BC	CB
COF		→ 0 1/2 ←		→ 1/2 0 ←	
DF		0	1	1	0
First cycle	FEM	5	– 5	20	– 20
	DM	–	5	– 20	–
Second cycle	COM	2.5	–	–	– 10
	DM	–	–	–	–
First set of final moments		7.5	0	0	– 30

Step IV : MD for Moments Due to Joint Translation at B :

(a) The basic information of K, COF and DF remains the same.

(b) Normalized relative translational stiffness factors (K_s). Assuming negative joint translation at B i.e. downwards, which produces anticlockwise i.e. positive moments for member AB and clockwise i.e. negative moments for member BC.

Member	Relative translational stiffness factor	Normalized relative translational stiffness factor (K_s)
AB	$\dfrac{I}{1^2}$	4
BC	$\dfrac{I}{2^2}$	1

(c) Moments Due to Translation at B :

Member	Arbitrary relative FEM due to translation
AB	$M_{AB}^{FS} = 40$ kNm
	$M_{BA}^{FS} = 40$ kNm
BC	$M_{BC}^{FS} = -10$ kNm
	$M_{CB}^{FS} = -10$ kNm

Step V : MD Table (II) for Moments Due to Translation :

Joint		A	B		C
Type of joint		EFS	EHS		EFS
Member		AB	BA	BC	CB
COF			→ 0	→ 1/2	
			1/2 ←	0 ←	
K		6	6	3	3
DF		0	1	1	0
First cycle	FEM	40	40	− 10	− 10
	DM	−	− 40	10	−
Second cycle	COM	− 20	−	−	5
	DM	−	−	−	−
Second set of final moments		20	0	0	− 5

Let, actual moments due to translation be 'C' times the above moments.

$$M_{AB} = M_{AB}^{I} + C \cdot (M_{AB}^{II}) = 7.5 + C\,(20)$$

$$M_{BA} = M_{BA}^{I} + C \cdot (M_{BA}^{II}) = 0$$

$$M_{BC} = M_{BC}^{I} + C \cdot (M_{BC}^{II}) = 0$$

$$M_{CB} = M_{CB}^{I} + C \cdot (M_{CB}^{II}) = -30 + C\,(-5)$$

where, C = Correction factor to be evaluated from the condition of shear equilibrium of the structure.

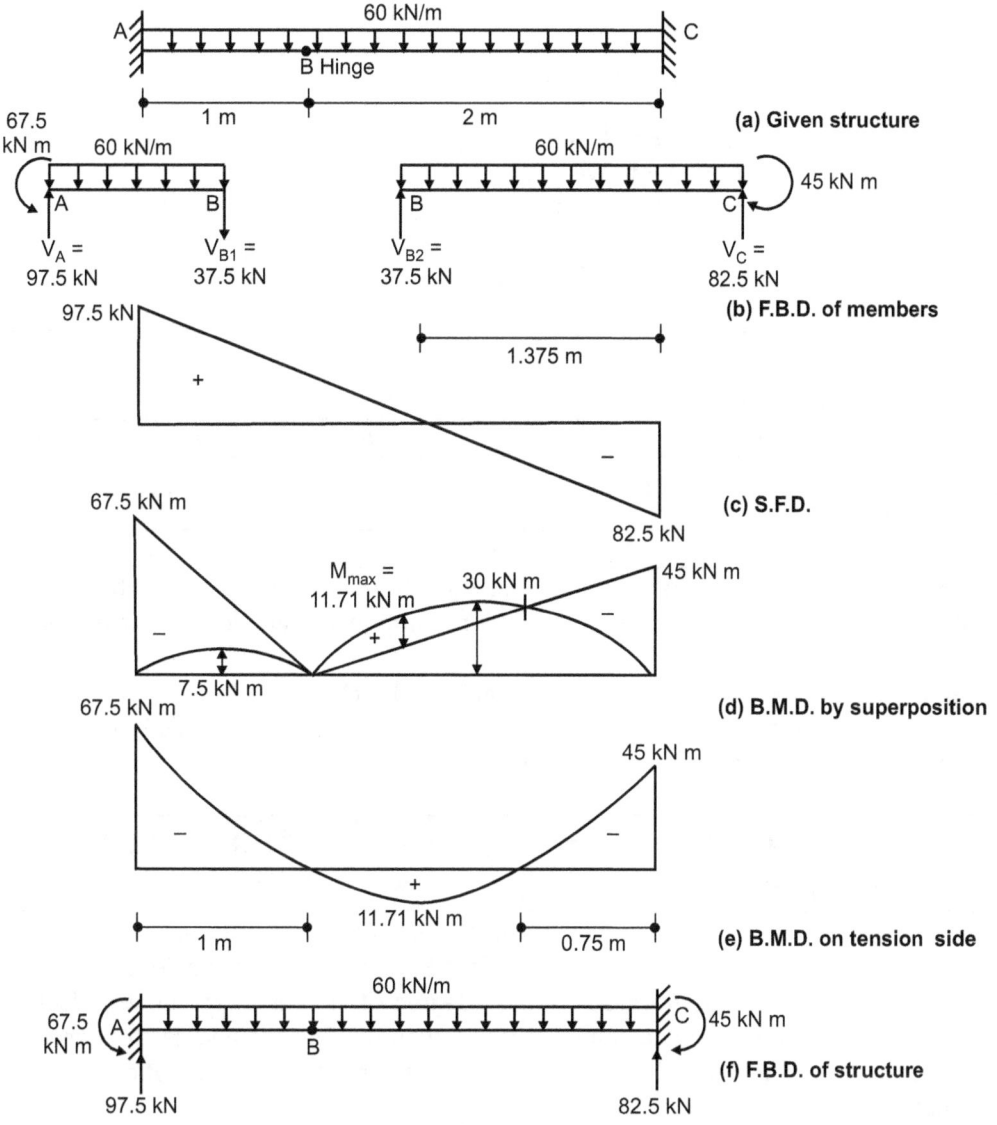

Fig. 3.14 : For Illustrative Example 3.9

Step VI : Shear Equilibrium : Shear equilibrium of structure gives,

$$V_A - V_C - 60 \times 3 = 0$$

i.e. $\qquad V_A - V_C - 180 = 0 \qquad \ldots (A)$

where, $\qquad V_A = M_{AB} + 60 \times 1 \times 0.5$

$$= M_{AB} + 30$$

and $\qquad V_C = \dfrac{M_{CB} - 60 \times 2 \times 1}{2} = \dfrac{M_{CB}}{2} - 60$

Substituting in equation (A), we get

$$M_{AB} + 30 - \frac{M_{CB}}{2} + 60 - 180 = 0$$

i.e. $\quad 2 M_{AB} - M_{CB} - 180 = 0$

Substituting the values of moments, we get

$2 (7.5 + C (20)) - (-30 + C (-5)) - 180 = 0$

$$45 (C) = 135$$
$$\boxed{C = 3}$$

Positive sign for 'C' indicates that translation at 'B' will be in the direction assumed i.e. downwards.

Step VII : Final Results :

Member	AB	BA	BC	CB
Corrected moments of second set	60	0	0	– 15
Moments of first set	7.5	0	0	– 30
Net final moments	67.5	0	0	– 45

Step VIII : FBD of members is as shown in Fig. 3.14 (b). Considering equilibrium of each member and of complete structure, all reaction components are found out as shown in figure.

Step IX : Shear force diagram is as shown in Fig. 3.14 (c).

Step X : Bending moment diagram is as shown in Fig. 3.14 (d) and Fig. 3.14 (e).

Step XI : FBD of structure is as shown in Fig. 3.14 (f).

3.6 APPLICATION OF MD METHOD TO FRAMES WITHOUT JOINT TRANSLATIONS

Rigid jointed indeterminate rectangular plane frames consisting of horizontal and vertical members are only covered in this text. MD method has been the convenient and powerful method to analyse the large frames with high degree of indeterminacy till introduction of computers and its application to matrix stiffness method. The rectangular frames without joint translations are common in the following situations with the assumption of the axial deformations are neglected.

1. The horizontal and vertical members of the rectangular frames are supported by the fixed or hinged support so that horizontal and vertical translations at supports are prevented.
2. The frames are symmetrical in all respects.

MD method applied to such frames is identical to beam problems except the configuration of the structure. The number of members meeting at a joint of frames may be more than two. Therefore, the MD table for frame analysis must be arranged to suit the requirements of (a) distribution factors of member ends meeting at the joint, (b) distribution of moments

TOS – II (TE CIVIL SEM. VI NMU) — MOMENT DISTRIBUTION METHOD

at the joint to the members meeting at the joint, and (c) carryover moments to be brought from one end to other end of the member. With the due attention to this, the process of MD method is tacitly used for the analysis of frames as illustrated in the following examples.

Example 3.10 : *Analyse the frame shown in Fig. 3.15 (a) by MD method.*

Solution : Data : The frame is supported and loaded as shown in Fig. 3.15 (a).

Object : Structural analysis.

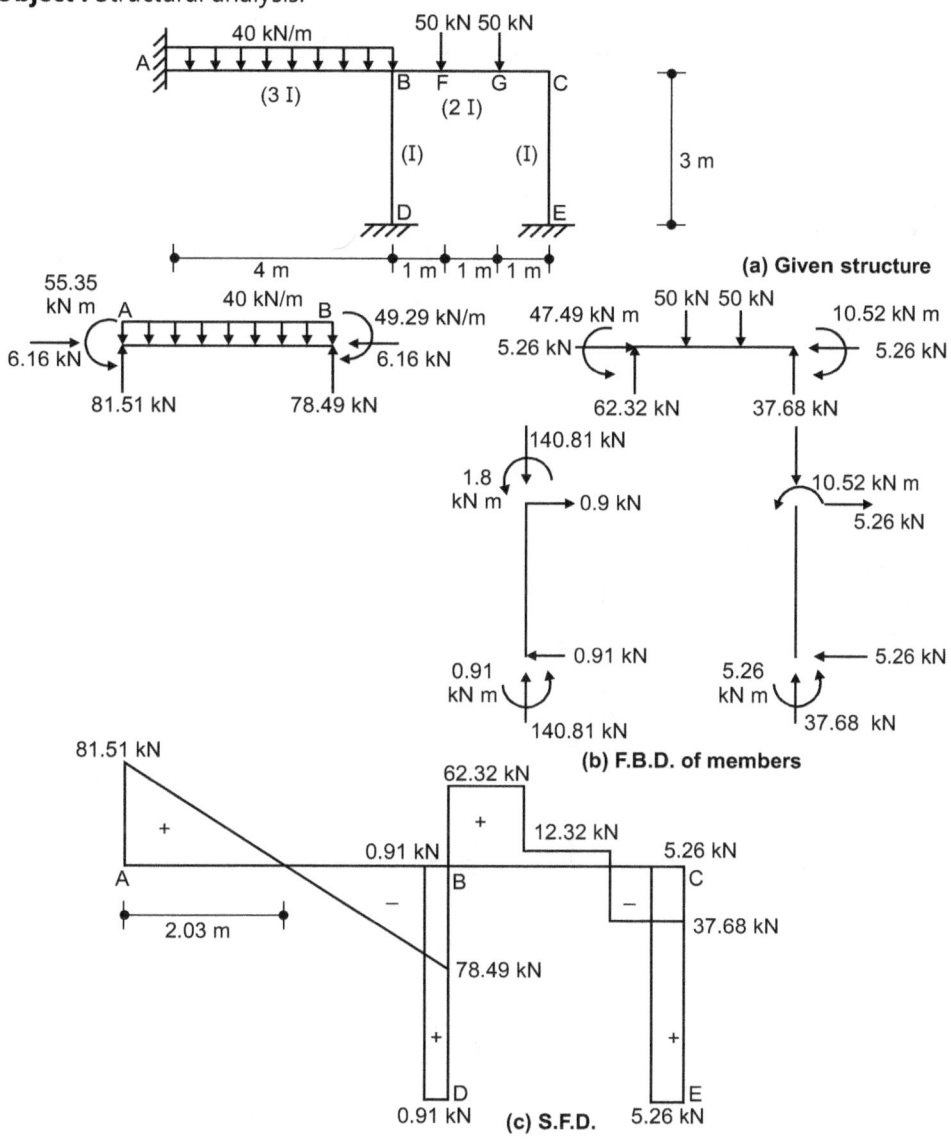

(a) Given structure

(b) F.B.D. of members

(c) S.F.D.

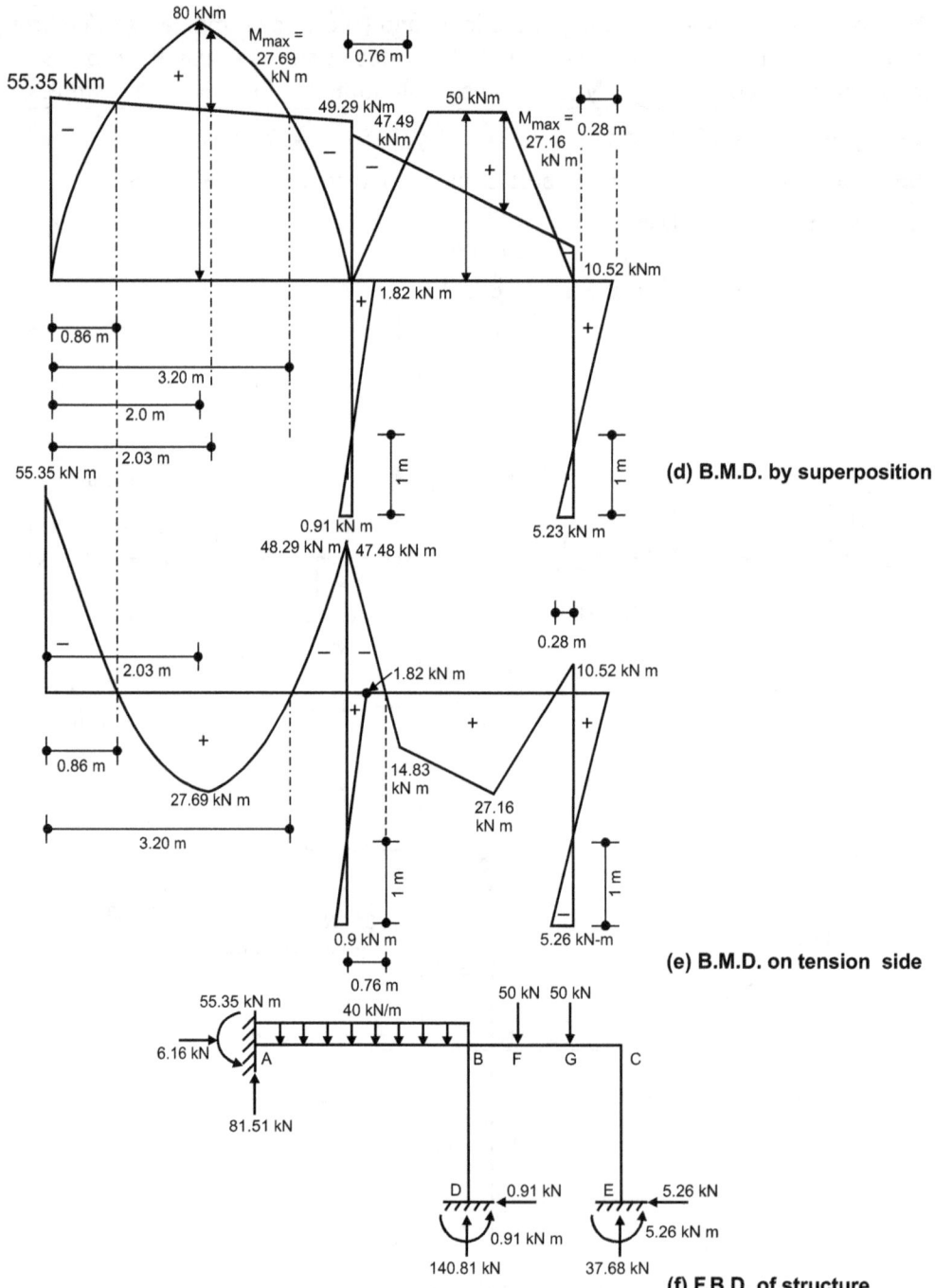

Fig. 3.15 : For Illustrative Example 3.10

Concepts and Equations : MD technique based on normalized relative stiffness factors and distribution factors.

Procedure :

Step I : Fixed-End Moments :

Member	FEM with calculations
AB	$M^F_{AB} = \dfrac{wL^2}{12} = \dfrac{40 \times 4^2}{12} = 53.33$ kNm
	$M^F_{BA} = -M^F_{AB} = -53.33$ kNm
BC	$M^F_{BC} = \dfrac{50 \times 1 \times 2^2}{3^2} + \dfrac{50 \times 2 \times 1^2}{3^2} = 33.33$ kNm
	$M^F_{CB} = -M^F_{BC} = -33.33$ kNm
DB	$M^F_{DB} = M^F_{BD} = 0$
EC	$M^F_{EC} = M^F_{CE} = 0$

Step II : Distribution Factors :

Joint	Member	K	ΣK	DF = $\dfrac{K}{\Sigma K}$
A	AB	–	–	0
B	BA	$\dfrac{4EI}{L} = 3$		0.43
	BD	$\dfrac{4EI}{L} = 1.34$	7.01	0.19
	BC	$\dfrac{4EI}{L} = 2.67$		0.38
C	CB	$\dfrac{4EI}{L} = 2.67$	4.01	0.67
	CE	$\dfrac{4EI}{L} = 1.34$		0.33
D	DB	–	–	0
E	EC	–	–	0

Step III : MD Table :

Joint	A		B		C		D	E
Type of joint	EFS		RJ		RJ		EFS	EFS
Member	AB	BA	BD	BC	CB	CE	DB	EC
COF		→1/2	→1/2		→1/2	→1/2	1/2←	1/2←
	1/2←		To D		1/2←	To E	To B	To C
DF	0	0.43	0.19	0.38	0.67	0.33	0	0
First cycle FEM	53.33	−53.33	0	33.33	−33.33	0	0	0
DM		−8.60	3.80	7.60	22.22	11.11		
Second cycle COM	4.30			11.11	3.80		1.90	5.55
DM		−4.77	−2.11	−4.23	−2.55	−1.25		
Third cycle COM	−2.39			−1.28	−2.11		−1.05	−0.63
DM		0.55	0.24	0.49	1.41	0.70		
Fourth cycle COM	0.27			0.70	0.25		0.12	−0.35
DM		−0.30	−0.13	−0.27	−0.17	−0.08		
Fifth cycle COM	−0.15			−0.09	−0.14		−0.06	−0.04
DM		0.04	0.02	0.03	0.09	0.05		
Total final moments	55.36	−49.21	1.82	47.39	−10.53	10.53	0.91	5.23

Step IV : FBD of members: as shown in Fig. 3.15 (b). Considering equilibrium of each member and of complete structure, all reaction components are found out as shown in figure.

Step V : Shear force diagram: as shown in Fig. 3.15 (c).

Step VI : Bending moment diagrams as shown in Fig. 3.15 (d) and Fig. 3.15 (e).

Step VII : FBD of structure: as shown in Fig. 3.15 (f).

Example 3.11 : Analyse the frame as shown in Fig. 3.16 (a) by moment distribution method.

Solution : Data : The frame is loaded and supported as shown in Fig. 3.16 (a).

Object : Structural analysis.

Concepts and Equations : MD technique based on normalized relative stiffness factors, carryover factors and distribution factors.

Procedure : Step I : Fixed-End Moments :

Member	FEM with Calculations
AB	$M^F_{AB} = 0$ $M^F_{BA} = 0$
BC	$M^F_{BC} = \dfrac{WL}{8} = \dfrac{60 \times 4}{8} = 30$ kN-m $M^F_{CB} = -\dfrac{WL}{8} = -\dfrac{60 \times 4}{8} = -30$ kN-m
CD	$M^F_{CD} = 0$ $M^F_{DC} = 0$

Step II : Distribution Factors :

Joint	Member	K	ΣK	D.F.
A	AB	–	–	0
B	BA	$\dfrac{4EI}{L} = 1.33$	2.33	0.57
	BC	$\dfrac{4EI}{L} = 1$		0.43
C	CB	$\dfrac{4EI}{L} = 1$	2.33	0.43
	CD	$\dfrac{4EI}{L} = 1.33$		0.57
D	DC	–	–	0

Step III : MD Table:

Joint		A	B			C		D
Type of joint		EFS	RJ			RJ		EFS
Member		AB	BA	BC		CB	CD	DC
COF		→ 1/2 1/2 ←		→ 1/2 1/2 ←			→ 1/2 1/2 →	
DF		0	0.57	0.43		0.43	0.57	0
First cycle FEM		0	0	30		– 30	0	0
DM			– 17.10	– 12.9		12.9	17.10	
Second cycle COM		– 8.55	6.45			– 6.45	–	8.55
DM			– 3.68	– 2.77		2.77	3.68	
Third cycle COM		– 1.84	1.39			– 1.39	–	1.84
DM			– 0.79	– 0.6		0.6	0.79	
Fourth cycle COM		– 0.40	0.3			– 0.3	–	0.40
DM			– 0.17	– 0.13		0.13	0.17	
Fifth cycle COM		– 0.09	0.065			– 0.065		
DM			– 0.04	– 0.025		0.025	0.04	0.02
Sixth cycle COM		– 0.02	0.013			– 0.013		0.02
DM			– 0.007	– 0.006		0.006	0.007	
Total final moment		–10.9	–21.79	21.79		– 21.79	21.79	10.9

Step IV : FBD of members is as shown in Fig. 3.16 (b).
Step V : Shear force diagram is as shown in Fig. 3.16 (c).
Step VI : Bending moment diagrams are as shown in Fig. 3.16 (d) and Fig. 3.16 (e).
Step VII : FBD of structure is as shown in Fig. 3.16 (f).

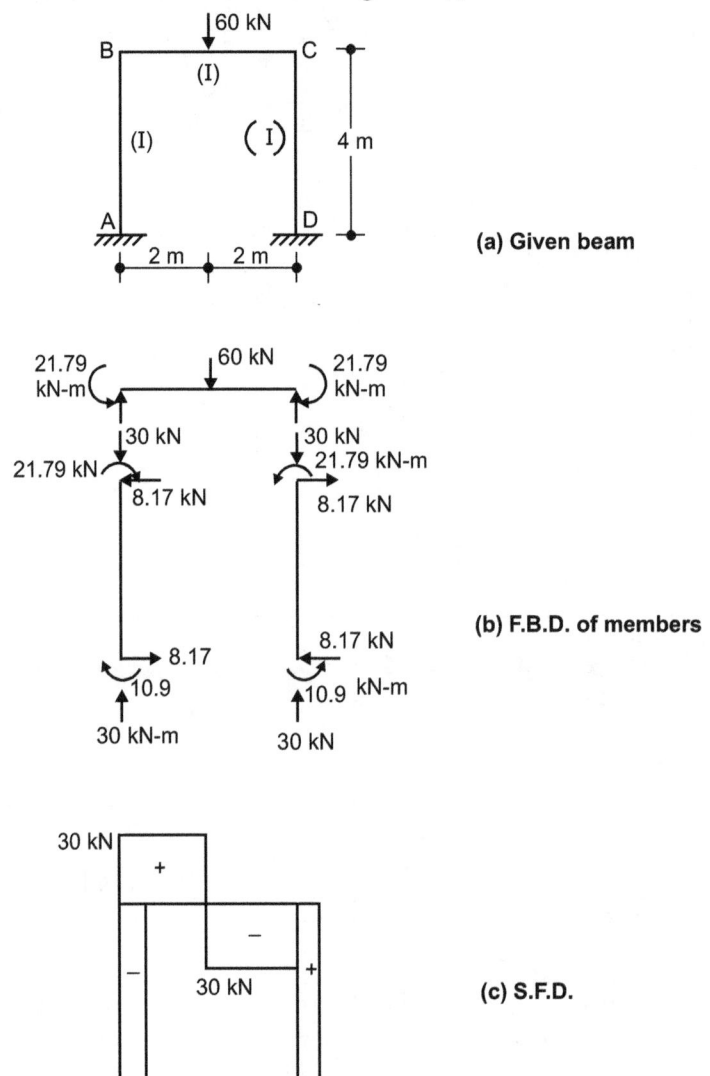

(a) Given beam

(b) F.B.D. of members

(c) S.F.D.

Fig. 3.16 (Cotd.)

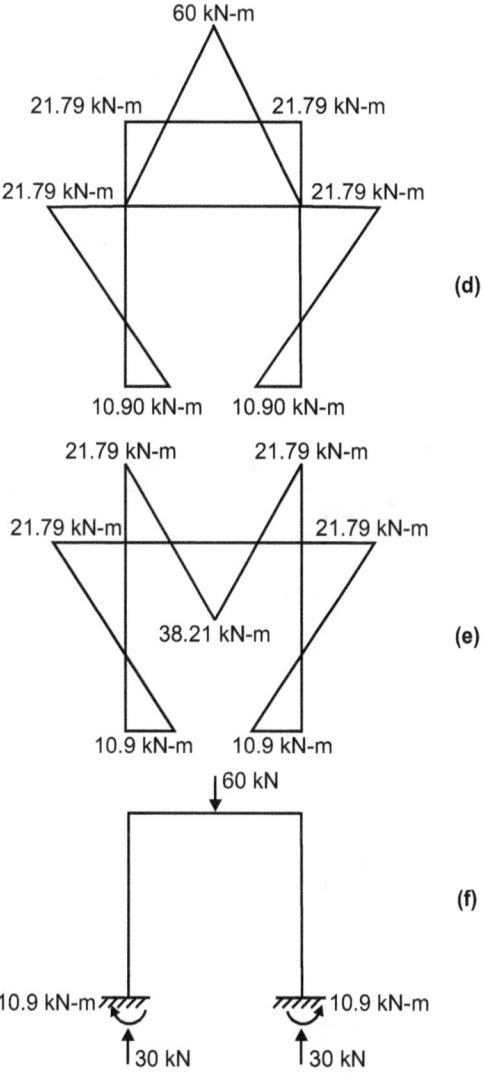

Fig. 3.16 : For Illustrative Example 3.11

Example 3.12 : *Using the slope-deflection method, analyse the rigid jointed plane frame supported and loaded as shown in Fig. 3.17 (a). Assume uniform flexural rigidity EI for all the members.*

Solution : Data : The frame is supported and loaded as shown in Fig. 3.17 (a).

Object : Structural analysis.

Concepts and Equations : MD technique based on normalized relative stiffness factors, carryover factors and distribution factors.

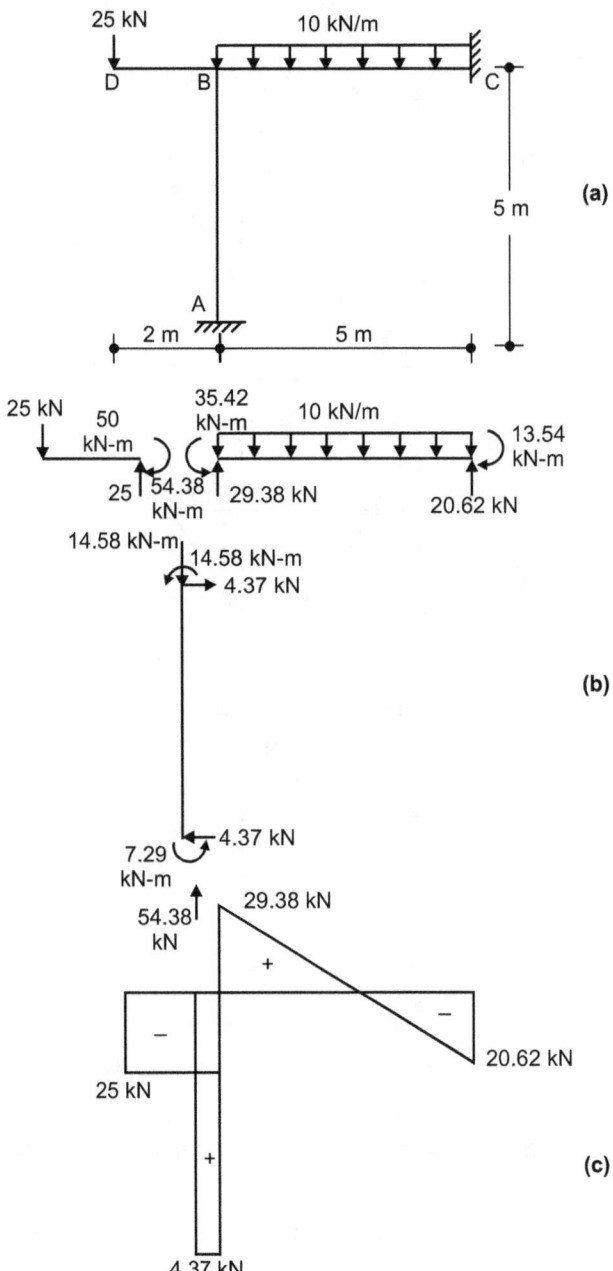

Fig. 3.17 (Contd.)

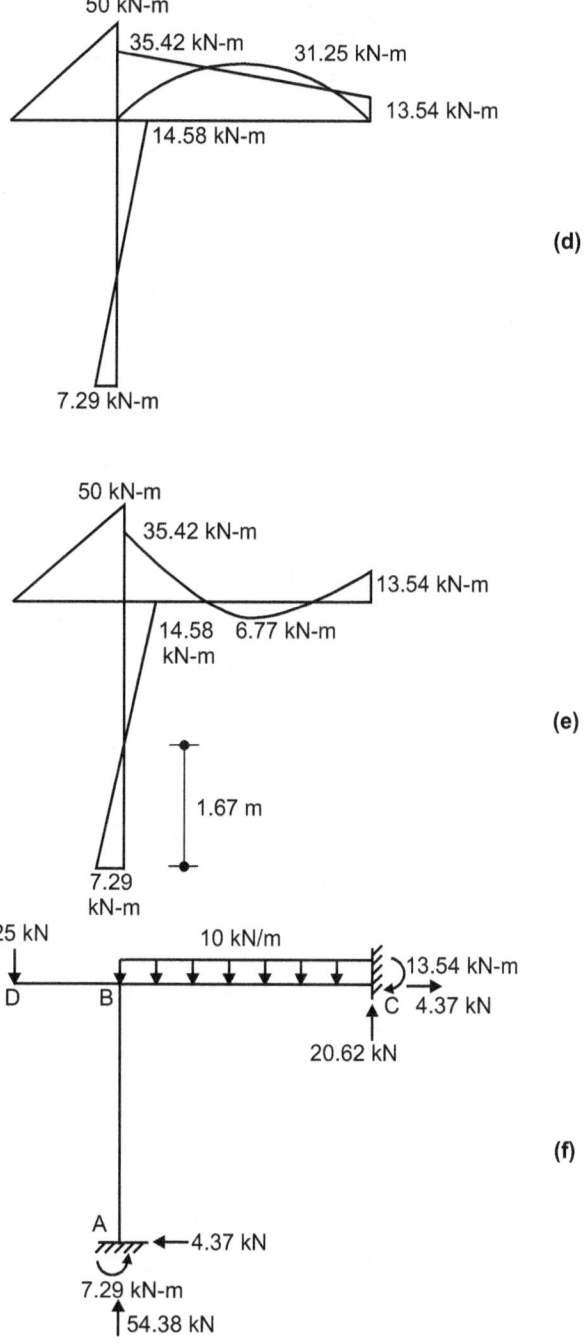

Fig. 3.17 : For Illustrative Example 3.12

Procedure : Step I : Fixed-End Moments :

Member	FEM with calculations
AB	$M_{AB}^F = 0$ $M_{BA}^F = 0$
BC	$M_{BC}^F = \dfrac{10 \times 5^2}{12} = 20.83$ kN-m $M_{CB}^F = -\dfrac{10 \times 5^2}{12} = -20.83$ kN-m
BD	$M_{BD}^F = -25 \times 2 = -50$ kN-m

Step II : Distribution Factors :

Joint	Member	K	ΣK	D.F.
A	AB	–	–	0
B	BA	$\dfrac{4EI}{L} = 0.8$	1.6	0.50
	BC	$\dfrac{4EI}{L} = 0.8$		0.50
	BD	–	–	0

Step III : MD Table :

Joint	A		B			C
Type of joint	EFS		RJ			EFS
Member	AB	BA		BD	BC	CB
COF	→1/2 1/2 ←				→1/2 1/2 ←	
D.F.	0	0.50		0	0.50	0
First cycle FEM	0	0		−50	20.83	−20.83
DM		14.58			14.59	
Second cycle COM	7.29					7.29
Total final moments	7.29	14.58		−50	35.42	−13.54

Step IV : FBD of members is as shown in Fig. 3.17 (b).

Step V : Shear force diagram is as shown in Fig. 3.17 (c).

Step VI : Bending moment diagrams are as shown in Fig. 3.17 (d) and Fig. 3.17 (e).

Step VII : FBD of structure is as shown in Fig. 3.17 (f).

Example 3.13 : Analyse the portal frame as shown in Fig. 3.18 by moment distribution method.

Solution : Data : The frame is supported and loaded as shown in Fig. 3.18.

Object : Structural Analysis.

Concepts and Equations : MD technique based on normalized relative stiffness factors and distribution factors.

Procedure : Step I :

$$\overline{M}_{AB} = -\frac{wab^2}{l^2} = -\frac{50 \times 1 \times 2 \times 2}{3^2} = -22.22 \text{ kN-m}$$

$$\overline{M}_{BA} = \frac{wa^2b}{l^2} = \frac{50 \times 1 \times 1 \times 2}{3^2} = 11.11 \text{ kN-m}$$

$$\overline{M}_{BC} = -\overline{M}_{CB} = -\frac{wl^2}{12} = -\frac{30 \times 4^2}{12} = -40 \text{ kN-m}$$

$$\overline{M}_{BD} = \overline{M}_{DB} = 0$$

Step II : Distribution Factors :

Joint	Member	Relative Stiffness	Total Stiffness	D. F.
B	BA	3/4 × 2I/3	5I/4	2/5
	BC	2I/4		2/5
	BD	I/4		1/5

Step III : MD Table :

Joint	A	B			C	D
Member	AB	BA	BD	BC	CB	DB
D.F.	-	2/5	1/5	2/5	-	-
F.E.M.	−22.22	11.11	0	−40	40	0
Release A	+ 11.11					
C.O.						
Total moments	0	22.22	0	−40	40	0
Distribution		7.11	3.56	7.11		
C.O.					3.55	1.78
Net moments	0	29.33	3.56	−32.89	43.55	1.78

Step IV : FBD of members as shown in Fig. 3.18(b) considering equilibrium of each member and of complete structure all reaction components are found out as shown in Fig. 3.18.

Step V : Shear force diagram is as shown in Fig. 3.18.

Step VI : Bending moment diagrams are as shown in Fig. 3.18 (d) and Fig. 3.18 (c).

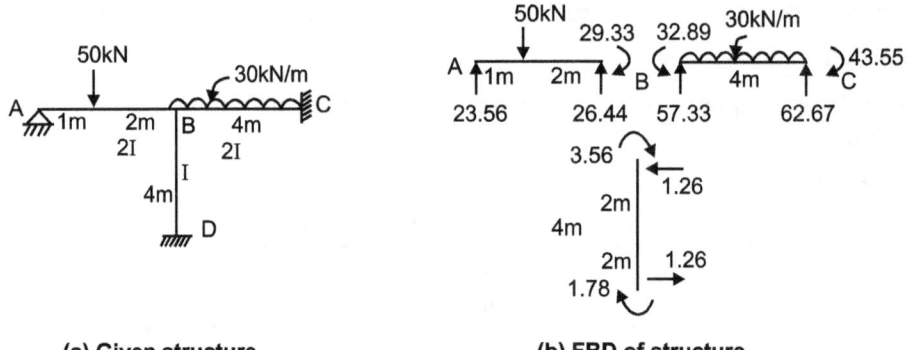

(a) Given structure

(b) FBD of structure

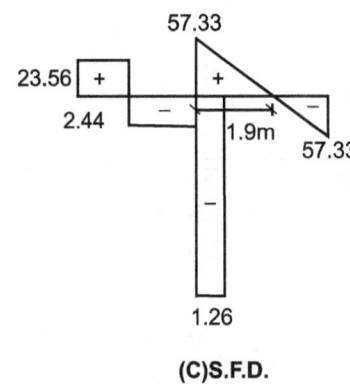

(C)S.F.D.

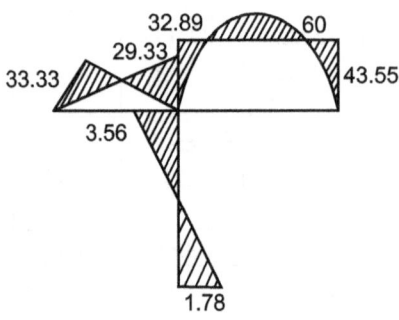

(d) BMD by superposition

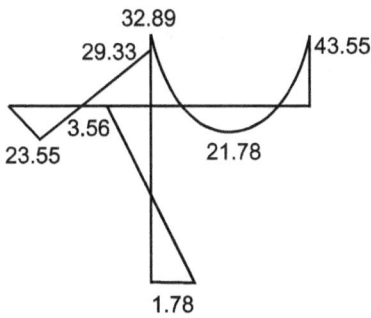

(e) BMD on tension side

Fig. 3.18 : Illustrative Example 3.13

Example 3.14 : *Analyse the non-sway frame as shown below in Fig. 3.19.*

$I_{ab} : I_{bc} : I_{cd} = 1 : 2 : 1$

Solution : Data : The frame is supported and coded as shown in Fig. 3.19.

Object : Structural Analysis:

Concepts and Equations : MD technique based on normalized relative stiffness factors and distribution factors.

Procedure : Step I : Fixed End Moments :

$$\overline{M}_{ab} = -\frac{wab^2}{l^2} = -\frac{6 \times 3 \times 1 \times 1}{4^2}$$

$$= 1.125 \text{ kN-m}$$

$$\overline{M}_{ba} = \frac{wa^2b}{l^2} = \frac{6 \times 3 \times 3 \times 1}{4^2}$$

$$= 3.375 \text{ klN-m}$$

$$\overline{M}_{bc} = -\overline{M}_{CB} = -\frac{wl^2}{12} = -\frac{20 \times 2 \times 2}{12}$$

$$= -6.67 \text{ kN-m}$$

$$\overline{M}_{cd} = -\frac{wab^2}{l^2} = -\frac{6 \times 1 \times 3 \times 3}{4^2}$$

$$= -3.375 \text{ kN-m}$$

$$\overline{M}_{dc} = \frac{wa^2b}{l^2} = \frac{6 \times 1 \times 1 \times 3}{4^2}$$

$$= 1.125 \text{ kN-m}$$

Step II : Distribution Factors :

Joint	Member	Relative Stiffness	Total Stiffness	D. F.
B	BA	(I/4)	5I/4	1/5
	BC	(2I/2)		4/5
C	CB	(2I/2)	5I/4	4/5
	CD	(I/4)		1/5

Step III : MD Table :

Joint	A	B		C		D
Member	AB	BA	BC	CB	CD	DC
D.F.	-	1/5	4/5	4/5	1/5	-
F.E.M.	−1.125	3.375	−6.67	6.67	−3.375	1.125
Distribution		0.629	2.636	−2.636	−0.659	
C.O.	0.33		−1.318	1.318		−0.33
Distribution		0.26	1.05	−1.05	−0.26	
C.O.	0.13		−0.53	0.53		−0.13
Distribution		0.106	0.424	−0.424	−0.106	
C.O.	0.053		−0.212	0.212		0.053
Distribution		0.042	−0.172	−0.172	−0.0424	
Net moments	−0.612	4.44	−4.44	4.44	−4.44	0.612

$$\text{Horizontals thrust (H) } (\rightarrow) = \frac{\text{(Fixed end moment + Moment due to external force)}}{\text{Length of column}}$$

$$= -\frac{0.612 + 4.44 - 6 \times 1}{4}$$

$$= -0.54 \text{ kN}$$

$$H = 0.54 \text{ kN } (\leftarrow)$$

Step IV : FBD of members as shown in figure, considering equilibrium of each member and of complete structure all reaction components are found out as shown in Fig. 3.19 (b).

Step V : Shear force diagram is as shown in Fig. 3.19 (c).

Step VI : Bending moment diagrams are as shown in Fig. 3.19 (d) and Fig. 3.19 (e).

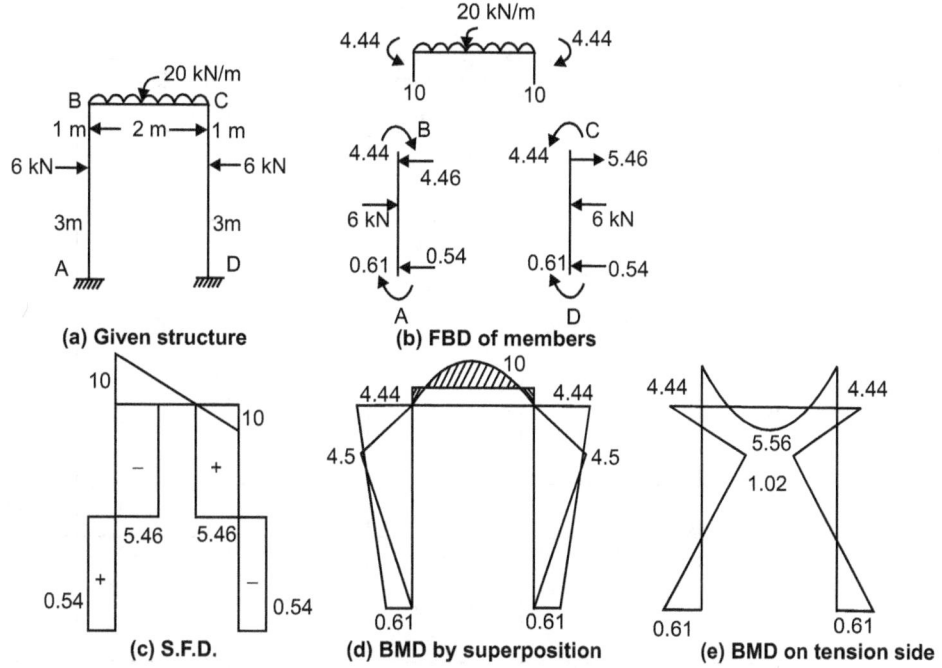

Fig. 3.19 : Illustrative Example 3.14

Example 3.15 : *Analyse the frame as shown in Fig. 3.20 (a) using moment distribution method.*

Solution : Data : The frame is supported and loaded as shown in Fig. 3.20 (a).
Object : Structural Analysis.
Concepts and Equations : MD technique based on normalized relative stiffness factors and distribution factors.
Procedure : Step I : Fixed End Moments :

$$\overline{M}_{AB} = -\frac{wl^2}{12} = -\frac{30 \times 4^2}{12} = -40 \text{ kN-m}$$

$$\overline{M}_{BA} = 40 \text{ kN-m}$$

$$\overline{M}_{BC} = -\frac{wab^2}{l^2} = -\frac{180 \times 1 \times 2^2}{3^2} = -80 \text{ kN-m}$$

Step II : Distribution Factors :

$$\overline{M}_{CB} = \frac{wa^2b}{l^2} = \frac{180 \times 1^2 \times 2}{3^2} = 40 \text{ kN-m}$$

$$\overline{M}_{BE} = \overline{M}_{EB} = 0$$

$$\overline{M}_{CD} = \overline{M}_{DC} = 0$$

Joint	Member	Type of support	Carryover factor	K	ΣK	D. F.
A	AB	Fixed	A → B 0	-	-	-
B	BA	Continuous	B → A 1/2	I/4	10I/12	0.3
	BC		B → C 1/2	I/3		0.4
	BE		B → E 0	3/4 × I/3		0.3
C	CB	Continuous	C → B 1/2	I/3	5I/6	0.4
	CD		C → D 1/2	I/2		0.6
D	DC	Fixed	D → C 0	-	-	-
E	EB	Simple	E → B 1/2	-	-	-

Step III : MD Table :

Joint	A	B			C		D	E
Mem.	AB	BA	BE	BC	CB	CD	CD	EB
D.F.	-	0.3	0.3	0.4	0.4	0.6	-	-
F.E.M.	− 40	40	0	− 80	40	0	0	0
Dist.		12	12	16	− 16	− 24	0	0
C.O.	6			− 8	8		− 12	
Dist.		+ 2.4	+ 2.4	+ 3.2	− 3.2	− 4.8		
C.O.	+ 1.2			− 1.6	+ 1.6		− 2.4	
Dist.		0.48	0.48	0.64	− 0.64	− 0.96		
C.O.	0.24			− 0.32	0.32		− 0.48	
Dist.		+ 0.096	+0.128	− 0.128	− 0.128	− 0.192		
Final	− 32.56	54.98	14.98	− 69.95	29.95	− 29.95	− 14.95	0

moments

Step IV : FBD of members as shown in figure, considering equilibrium of each member and of complete structure all reaction components are found out as shown in Fig. 3.20 (b).

Step V : Shear force diagram is as shown in figure. 3.20 (c).

Step VI : Bending moment diagrams are as shown in figure 3.20 (d) and figure. 3.20 (e).

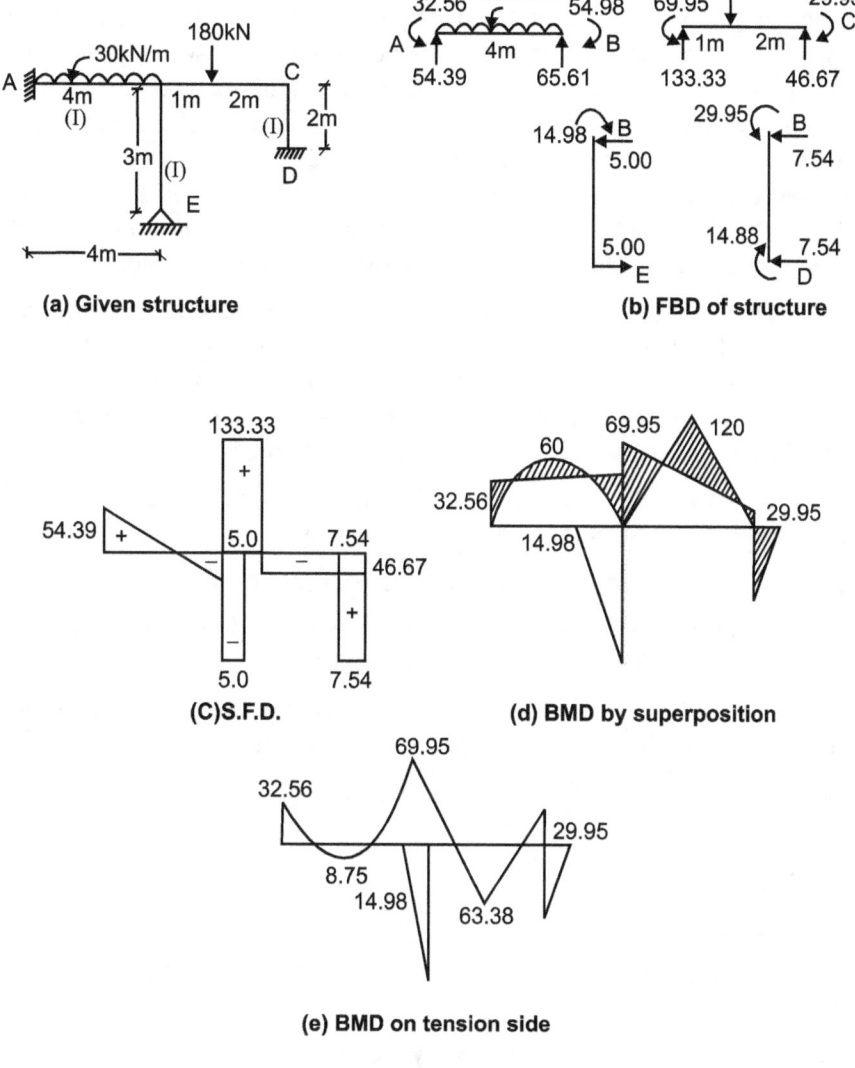

Fig. 3.20 : Illustrative Example 3.15

3.7 APPLICATION OF MD METHOD TO FRAMES WITH JOINT TRANSLATIONS

The MD method has been so far mainly dealt with the structures with joint rotations only. There may be joint translations in a structure in addition to joint rotations. This is the most general case of unsymmetrical frame. The joint translations along the members do not affect the MD method. But the joint translations perpendicular to the members are required to be considered and hence need special treatment in MD method.

In the rectangular frame, the horizontal translation of joints is termed as sway and the frame is called *sway frame*. In general, the unsymmetrical frames are sway frames. The sway of joints at the same level is assumed to be of same magnitude and direction because axial deformations are neglected. For the analysis of sway frames by MD method, the process of moment distribution is to be carried out twice. First MD is conventional starting with FEM due to member loads, as if no joint translations. First set of member-end moments are the results of first MD table. First MD is also called non-sway MD. In a particular case, if no loads are acting on the members of the structure, then first MD is null and void.

In second MD called as sway MD, arbitrary sway moments proportional to I/L^2 of members having sway, are distributed as per second MD table. The results of second set of arbitrary member-end moments are corrected by the correction factor obtained by shear equilibrium condition. This is the second set of corrected member-end moments. Final member-end moments are the sum of first set of moments and second set of corrected moments.

The procedure of analysis of sway frames by MD method is elaborated with the illustrated example 3.16, highlighting the special treatment, as follows :

Example 3.16 : *Analyse the frame shown in Fig. 3.21 (a) by MD method.*

Solution : Data : The rectangular frame is supported and loaded as shown in Fig. 3.21 (a). The data includes the following information:

(1) Structural configuration: Type of members, joints and supports, dimensions, cross-sectional properties and material properties of members.

(2) Applied loads: Magnitude, direction and position.

(3) Type of structure : Sway frame.

Object : Member-end moments.

Concepts and Equations :

(1) MD technique based on normalized stiffness factors, carryover factors and distribution factors.

(2) Normalized relative sway factors, sway moments.

(3) Shear equilibrium condition and correction factor.

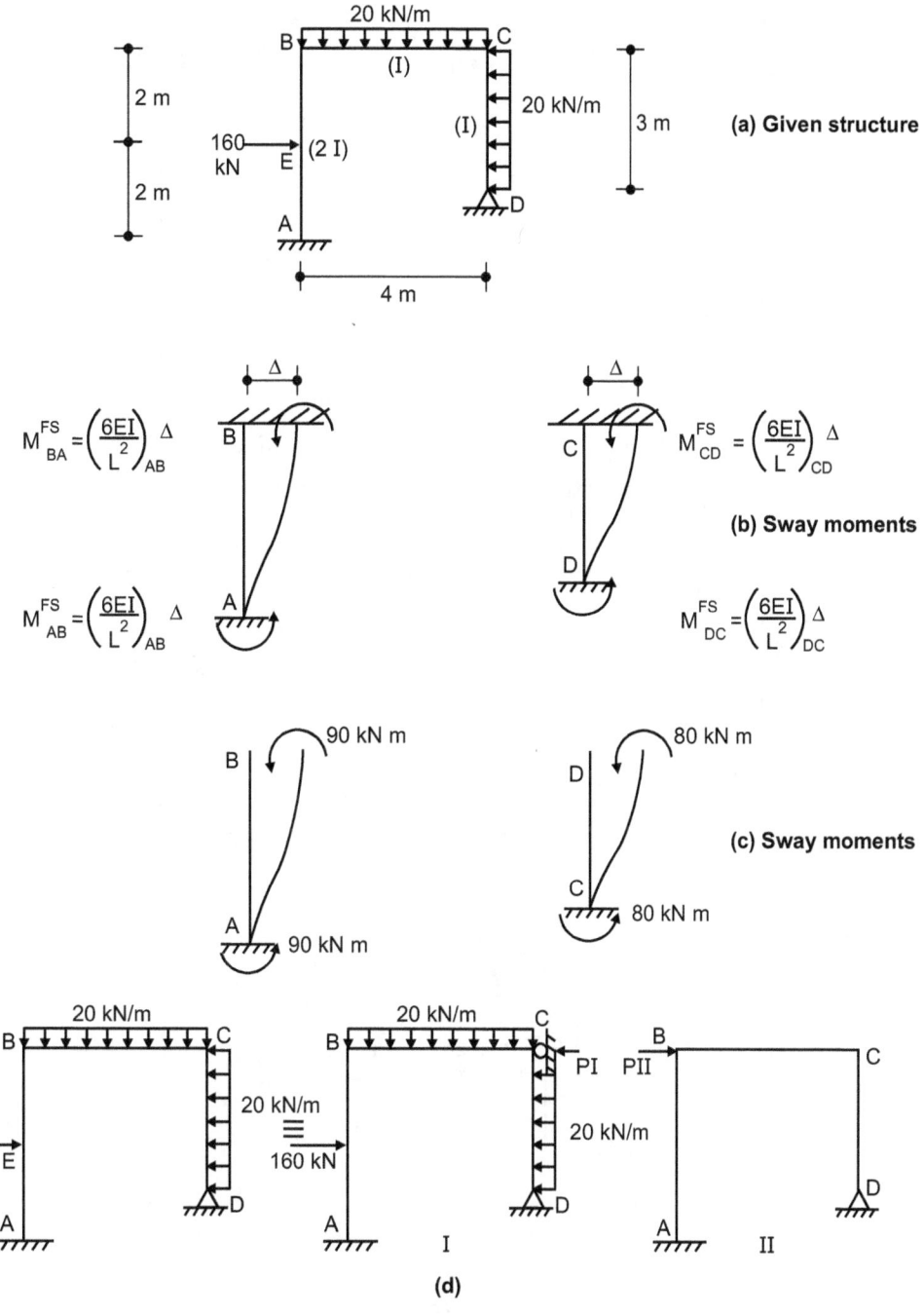

Fig. 3.21 (Contd.)

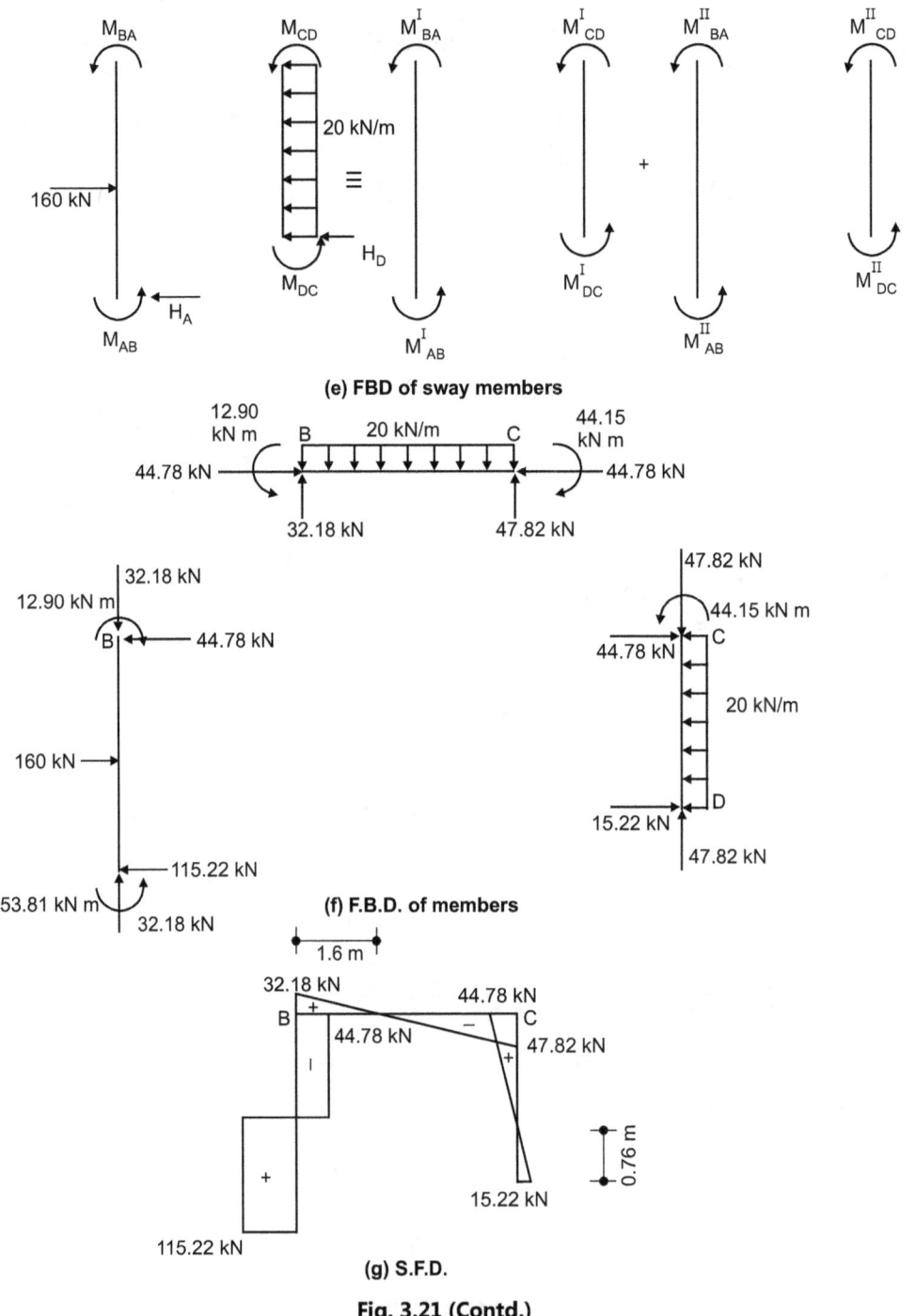

(e) FBD of sway members

(f) F.B.D. of members

(g) S.F.D.

Fig. 3.21 (Contd.)

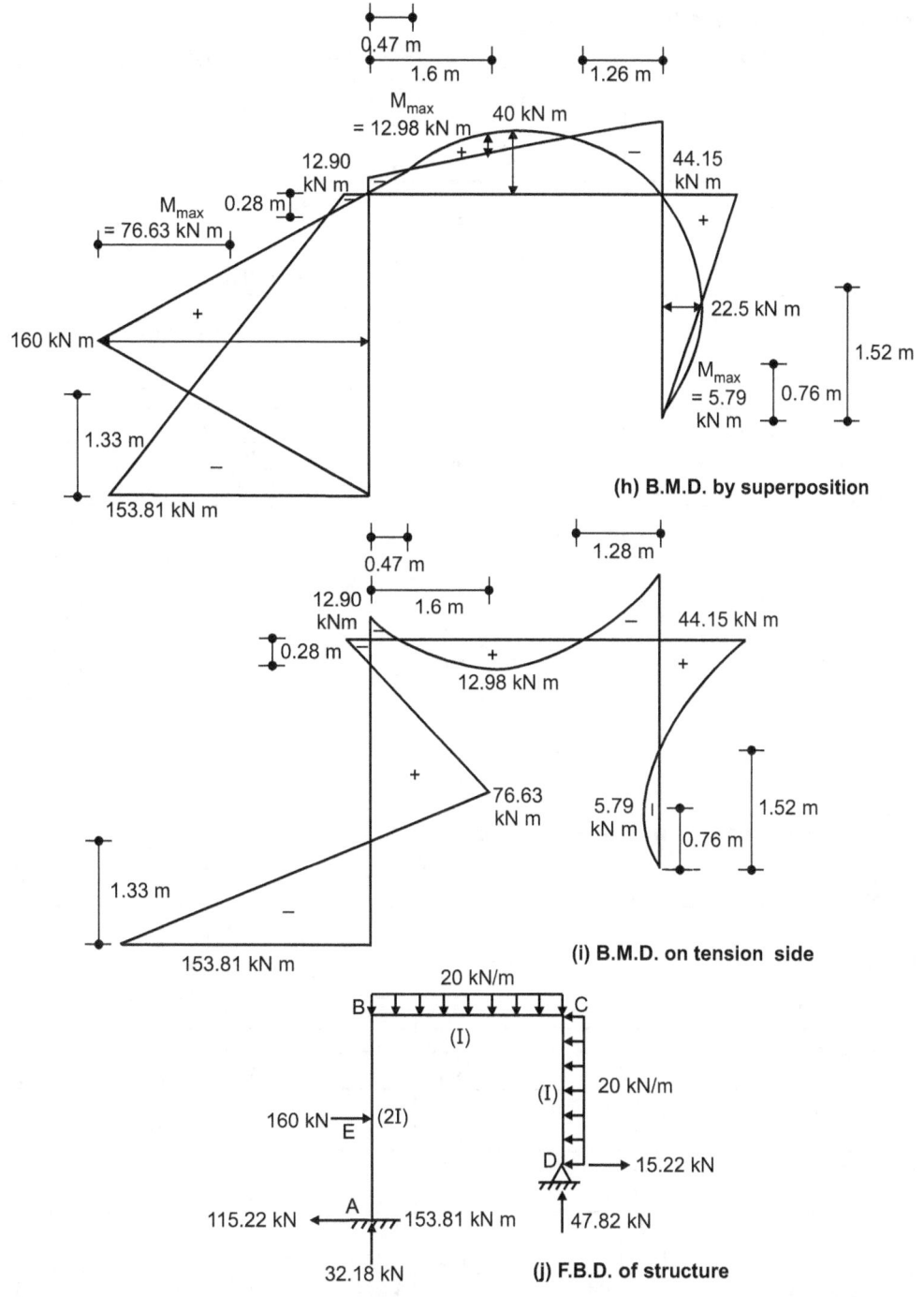

Fig. 3.21 : For Illustrative Example 3.16

Procedure : Step I : Fixed-End Moments :

Member	FEM with calculations
AB	$M^F_{AB} = \left(\dfrac{160 \times 4}{8}\right) = +80$ kNm $M^F_{BA} = -M^F_{AB} = -80$ kNm
BC	$M^F_{BC} = +\left(\dfrac{20 \times 4 \times 4}{12}\right) = +26.67$ kNm $M^F_{CB} = -M^F_{BC} = -26.67$ kNm
CD	$M^F_{CD} = +\left(\dfrac{20 \times 3 \times 3}{12}\right) = +15$ kNm $M^F_{DC} = -M^F_{CD} = -15$ kNm

Step II : Distribution Factors :

Joint	Member	K	ΣK	$DF = \dfrac{K}{\Sigma K}$
A	AB	–	–	0
B	BA	$\dfrac{4 EI}{L} = 2$	3	0.67
	BC	$\dfrac{4 EI}{L} = 1$		0.33
C	CB	$\dfrac{4 EI}{L} = 1$	2	0.5
	CD	$\dfrac{3 EI}{L} = 1$		0.5
D	DC	–	–	1

Step III : MD Table 1 for Non-Sway Moments :

Joint		A	B		C		D
Type of joint		EFS	RJ		RJ		EHS
Member		AB	BA	BC	CB	CD	DC
COF		→1/2 1/2←		→1/2 1/2←		→0 1/2←	
DF		0	0.67	0.33	0.5	0.5	0
First cycle	FEM	+80	–80	+26.67	–26.67	+15	–15
	DM	–	+35.33	18	5.84	5.84	+15
Second cycle	COM	+17.66	–	2.92	9	7.5	–
	DM	–	–1.94	–0.97	–8.25	–8.25	–
Third cycle	COM	–0.97	–	–4.13	–0.48	–	–
	DM	–	2.75	1.37	0.24	0.24	–
Fourth cycle	COM	1.38	–	0.12	0.68	–	–
	DM	–	–0.08	–0.04	–0.34	0.34	–
First set of final moments		98.07	–43.94	43.94	–19.98	19.98	0.0

Step IV : MD for Sway Moments :

(a) The basic information of K, COF and DF remains the same.

(b) **Sway :** There is equal sway Δ at joints B and C. The sway Δ is not known in magnitude and direction. The sway is also not required to be found in MD method.

(c) **Effect of Sway :** The sway moments of $\left(\dfrac{6\,EI}{L^2}\right) \times \Delta$ exist at both ends of the member having sway as shown in Fig. 3.21 (b). The arbitrary sway moments are considered for the members having sway. For the same sway and same material of the member, the sway moments are proportional to I/L^2. To decide the arbitrary sway moments, relative I/L^2 are obtained.

(d) **Relative Sway-Stiffness Factor :** The quantity I/L^2 of the member is defined as the relative sway-stiffness factor of the member. The relative sway-stiffness factors are expressed in the normalized form i.e. proportionate numerals eliminating I. The relative sway-stiffness factor of the member is considered as independent of the end conditions for the formulation of MD method. The end conditions of members are already accounted for in K.

Therefore, it is suggested that the relative sway-stiffness factors are taken as I/L^2 irrespective of end conditions of member. The sway moments are developed at ends of members AB and CD as shown in Fig. 3.21 (b). There is no effect of sway on the member BC. In rectangular frames with sway, the columns only are subjected to sway moments. Normalized relative sway-stiffness factors K_S are obtained as given in the following table.

Member	Relative sway-stiffness factor	Normalized relative sway-stiffness factor, K_S
AB	$\dfrac{2I}{4 \times 4} = \dfrac{I}{8}$	9
CD	$\dfrac{I}{3 \times 3} = \dfrac{I}{9}$	8

(e) **Sway Moments :** Corresponding to the normalized relative sway-stiffness factors of the members, the arbitrary but relative sway moments are considered at the ends of the members having sway as shown in Fig. 3.21 (c). These sway moments are treated as FEM to begin with second MD table and denoted as M_{ij}^{FS}. They are assumed as positive corresponding to Δ shown. M_{ij}^{FS} are given in the following table:

Member	Arbitrary relative FEM due to sway
AB	$M_{AB}^{FS} = +\ 90$ kNm $M_{BA}^{FS} = +\ 90$ kNm
CD	$M_{CD}^{FS} = +\ 80$ kNm $M_{DC}^{FS} = +\ 80$ kNm

Step V : MD Table for Sway Moments :

Joint	A		B			C		D
Type of joint	EFS		RJ			RJ		EHS
Member	AB		BA	BC		CB	CD	DC
COF		→1/2 1/2←			→1/2 1/2←		→0 1/2←	
DF	1	0	0.67	0.33		0.5	0.5	1
First cycle FEM	+90		+90	—		—	+80	+80
DM	—		−60	−30		−40	−40	−80
Second cycle COM	−30		—	−20		−15	−40	—
DM	—		+13.33	+6.67		+27.5	+27.5	—
Third cycle COM	+6.67		—	+13.25		3.33	—	—
DM	—		−8.83	−4.42		−1.67	−1.67	—
Fourth cycle COM	−4.42		—	−0.84		−2.21	—	—
DM	—		0.56	0.28		1.11	1.11	—
Second set of arbitrary final moments	+62.25		+35.06	−35.06		−26.94	26.94	0.0

$$P^I = C \times P^{II}$$
$$M_{AB} = M_{AB}^I + C \cdot M_{AB}^{II}$$
$$M_{BA} = M_{BA}^I + C \cdot M_{BA}^{II}$$
$$M_{CD} = M_{CD}^I + C \cdot M_{CD}^{II}$$
$$M_{DC} = M_{DC}^I + C \cdot M_{DC}^{II}$$

where C is the correction factor to be obtained from shear equilibrium equation developed as follows :

Step VI : Shear Equilibrium Condition

The arbitrary final moments obtained from second MD table are to be corrected to satisfy the shear equilibrium condition for the structure. The given structure is considered as the equivalent of the superposition of :

- Sway prevented structure.
- Sway structure with the correction factor C as shown in Fig. 3.21 (d).

The FBD of sway members are as shown in Fig. 3.21 (e) to formulate the shear equilibrium condition in terms of member-end moments and correction factor C. The formulation based on superposition equations, determines C, as follows :

FBD and shear equilibrium

FBD of AB

$$\sum M_B = 0$$
$$\therefore \quad M_{BA} + M_{AB} + 160 \times 2 + H_A \times 4 = 0$$

$$\therefore \quad H_A = \frac{M_{AB} + M_{BA} + 320}{4}$$

$$\therefore \quad H_A = \frac{(M_{AB}^I + CM_{AB}^{II}) + (M_{BA}^I + CM_{BA}^{II}) + 320}{4}$$

FBD of CD

$$\sum M_C = 0$$

$$\therefore \quad M_{CD} + M_{DC} - 20 \times 3 \times 1.5 - H_D \times 3 = 0$$

$$\therefore \quad H_D = \frac{M_{CD} + M_{DC} - 90}{3}$$

$$= \frac{(M_{CD}^I + CM_{CD}^{II}) + (M_{DC}^I + CM_{DC}^{II}) - 90}{3}$$

FBD of frame

$$\sum H = 0$$

$$+ 160 - 20 \times 3 - H_A - H_D = 0$$

$$\therefore \quad H_A + H_D = 100$$

The shear equilibrium equation is therefore expressed in terms of member-end moments

$$\frac{(M_{AB}^I + CM_{AB}^{II}) + (M_{BA}^I + CM_{BA}^{II}) + 320}{4} + \frac{(M_{CD}^I + CM_{CD}^{II}) + (M_{DC}^I + CM_{DC}^{II}) - 90}{3} = 100$$

Substituting the first set of moments and second set of moments obtained from first MD and second MD, in the expression

$$\frac{(+98.07 + C \times 62.25) + (-43.94 + C \times 35.06) + 320}{4} + \frac{(+19.98 + C \times 26.94) + (0 + C \times 0) - 90}{3} = 100$$

i.e. $\quad (33.30) \, C = 29.80$

$$\boxed{C = 0.894}$$

Step VII : Final Results : Corrected moments of second set will be obtained by multiplying by C and then added to first moments to get the net final moments:

	AB	BA	BC	CB	CD	DC
Second set of corrected moments	55.74	31.04	− 31.04	− 24.17	24.17	0
First set of moments	+ 98.07	− 43.94	+ 43.94	− 19.98	19.98	0
Net final moments	153.81	− 12.90	12.90	− 44.15	44.15	0

Step VIII : FBD of Members : as shown in Fig. 3.21 (f). Considering equilibrium of each member and of complete structure, all reaction components are found out as shown in Fig. 3.21.

Step IX : Shear force diagram is as shown in Fig. 3.21 (g).

Step X : Bending moment diagrams are as shown in Fig. 3.21 (h) and Fig. 3.21 (i).

Step XI : FBD of structure is as shown in Fig. 3.21 (j).

Example 3.17 : Analyse the frame shown in Fig. 3.22 (a) by MD method.

Solution : Data : (1) The frame is supported and loaded as shown in Fig. 3.22 (a).

(2) Type of frame: Sway frame.

Object : Structural analysis.

Concepts and Equations : (1) MD technique based on normalized relative-stiffness factors and distribution factors.

(2) Normalized relative sway factors.

(3) Shear equilibrium condition and correction factors.

Procedure :

Step I : Fixed End-Moments :

$$M^F_{AB} = M^F_{BA} = M^F_{BC} = M^F_{CB} = M^F_{CD} = M^F_{DC} = 0$$

Step II : Distribution Factors :

Joint	Member	K	ΣK	DF = $\frac{K}{\Sigma K}$
A	AB	–	–	0
B	BA	$\frac{4EI}{L} = 1$	3	0.33
	BC	$\frac{4EI}{L} = 2$		0.67
C	CB	$\frac{4EI}{L} = 2$	4	0.5
	CD	$\frac{4EI}{L} = 2$		0.5
D	DC	–	–	0

Step III : MD Table (I) for Non-Sway Moments : As member loads are absent, all FEMs are zero and hence MD for non-sway moments is not required.

Step IV : MD for sway moments :

(a) The basic information of K, COF and DF remains the same.

(b) Normalized relative-sway stiffness factors (K_S).

Member	Relative sway stiffness factor	Normalized relative-sway stiffness factor, K_S
AB	$\frac{I}{4^2}$	1
DC	$\frac{I}{2^2}$	4

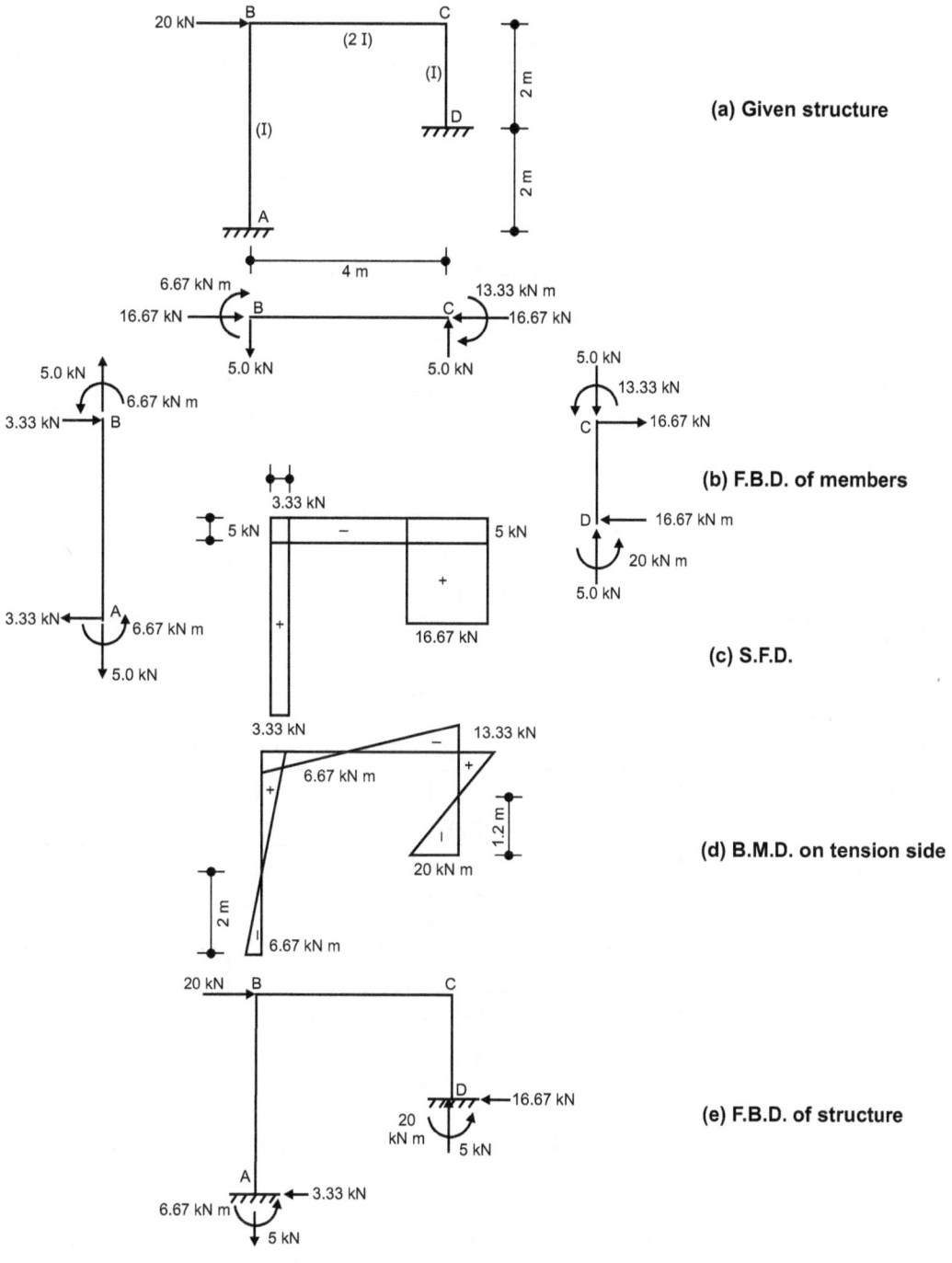

Fig. 3.22 : For Illustrative Example 3.17

(c) Sway Moments :

Member	Arbitrary relative FEM due to sway
AB	$M_{AB}^{FS} = 10$ kNm
	$M_{BA}^{FS} = 10$ kNm
DC	$M_{DC}^{FS} = 40$ kNm
	$M_{CD}^{FS} = 40$ kNm

Step V : MD Table (II) for Sway Moments :

Joint		A	B		C		D
Type of joint		EFS	RJ		RJ		EHS
Member		AB	BA	BC	CB	CD	DC
COF			→1/2	→1/2		→1/2	
			1/2←	1/2←		1/2←	
DF		0	0.33	0.67	0.5	0.5	0
First cycle	FEM	10	10		40		40
	DM	–	–3.33	–6.67	–20	–20	–
Second cycle	COM	–1.67	–	–10	–3.33	–	–10
	DM	–	3.33	6.67	1.67	1.67	–
Third cycle	COM	1.67	–	0.84	3.33	–	0.84
	DM	–	–0.28	–0.56	–1.67	–1.67	–
Fourth cycle	COM	–0.14	–	–0.84	–0.28	–	–0.84
	DM	–	0.28	–0.56	0.14	0.14	–
Fifth cycle	COM	0.14	–	0.07	0.28	–	0.08
	DM	–	–0.02	–0.05	–0.14	–0.14	–
Second set of final moments		10	9.98	–9.98	–20	20	30.08

Let, actual sway moments be 'C' times above sway moments.

$\therefore$
$$M_{AB} = M_{AB}^{I} + C \cdot M_{AB}^{II} = C(10)$$
$$M_{BA} = M_{BA}^{I} + C \cdot M_{BA}^{II} = C(9.98)$$
$$M_{DC} = M_{DC}^{I} + C \cdot M_{DC}^{II} = C(30.08)$$
$$M_{CD} = M_{CD}^{I} + C \cdot M_{CD}^{II} = C(20)$$

where, C = Correction factor to be evaluated from the condition of horizontal shear equilibrium for the structure.

Step VI : Horizontal Shear Equilibrium :

Horizontal shear equilibrium of structure gives,

$$H_A + H_D - 20 = 0 \quad \ldots (A)$$

where,

$$H_A = \frac{M_{AB} + M_{BA}}{4} \text{ and}$$

$$M_D = \frac{M_{DC} + M_{CD}}{2}$$

Substituting in equation (A), we get

$$\left(\frac{M_{AB} + M_{BA}}{4}\right) + \left(\frac{M_{DC} + M_{CD}}{2}\right) - 20 = 0$$

$$(M_{AB} + M_{BA}) + 2(M_{DC} + M_{CD}) - 80 = 0$$

Substituting values of moments, we get

$$[C(10) + C(9.98)] + 2[C(30.08) + C(20)] - 80 = 0$$

$$(120.14)C - 80 = 0 \quad \boxed{C = 0.667}$$

Step VII : Final result:

Member	AB	BA	BC	CB	CD	DC
Corrected moments of second set	6.67	6.67	− 6.67	− 13.33	13.33	20.0
Moments of first set	−	−	−	−	−	−
Net final moments	6.67	6.67	− 6.67	− 13.33	13.33	20.0

Step VIII : FBD of members is as shown in Fig. 3.22 (b). Considering equilibrium of each member and of complete structure, all reaction components are found out as shown in Fig. 3.22.

Step IX : Shear force diagram is as shown in Fig. 3.22 (c).

Step X : Bending moment diagrams are as shown in Fig. 3.16 (d) and Fig. 3.22 (e).

Step XI : FBD of structure is as shown in Fig. 3.22 (e).

Example 3.18 : *Analyse the frame shown in Fig. 3.23 (a) by MD method.*

Solution : Data : (1) The frame is supported and loaded as shown in Fig. 3.23 (a).

(2) Type of frame: Sway frame.

Object : Structural analysis.

Concepts and Equations :

(1) MD technique based on normalized relative stiffness factors and distribution factors.

(2) Normalized relative sway factors.

(3) Shear equilibrium condition and correction factor.

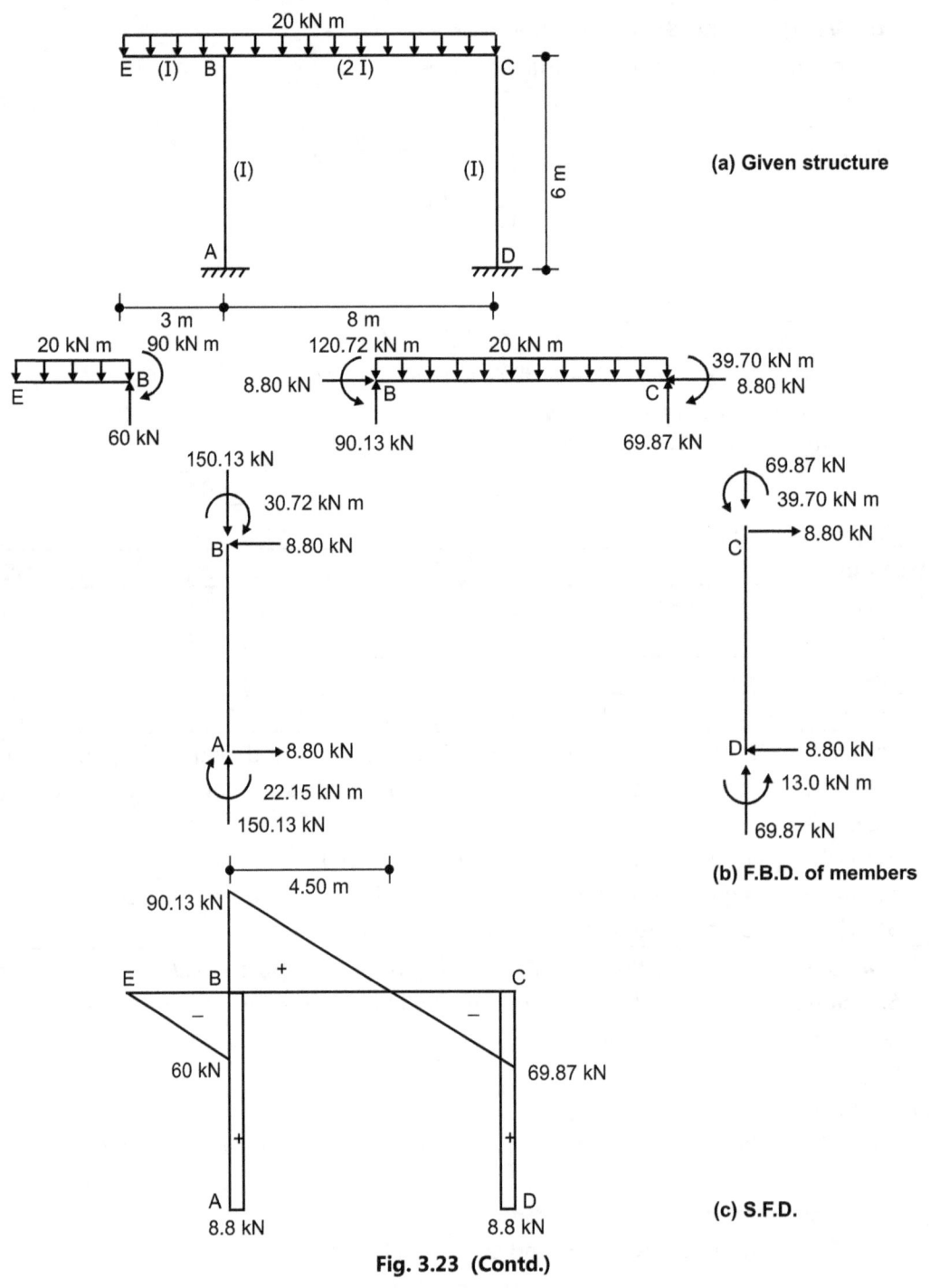

Fig. 3.23 (Contd.)

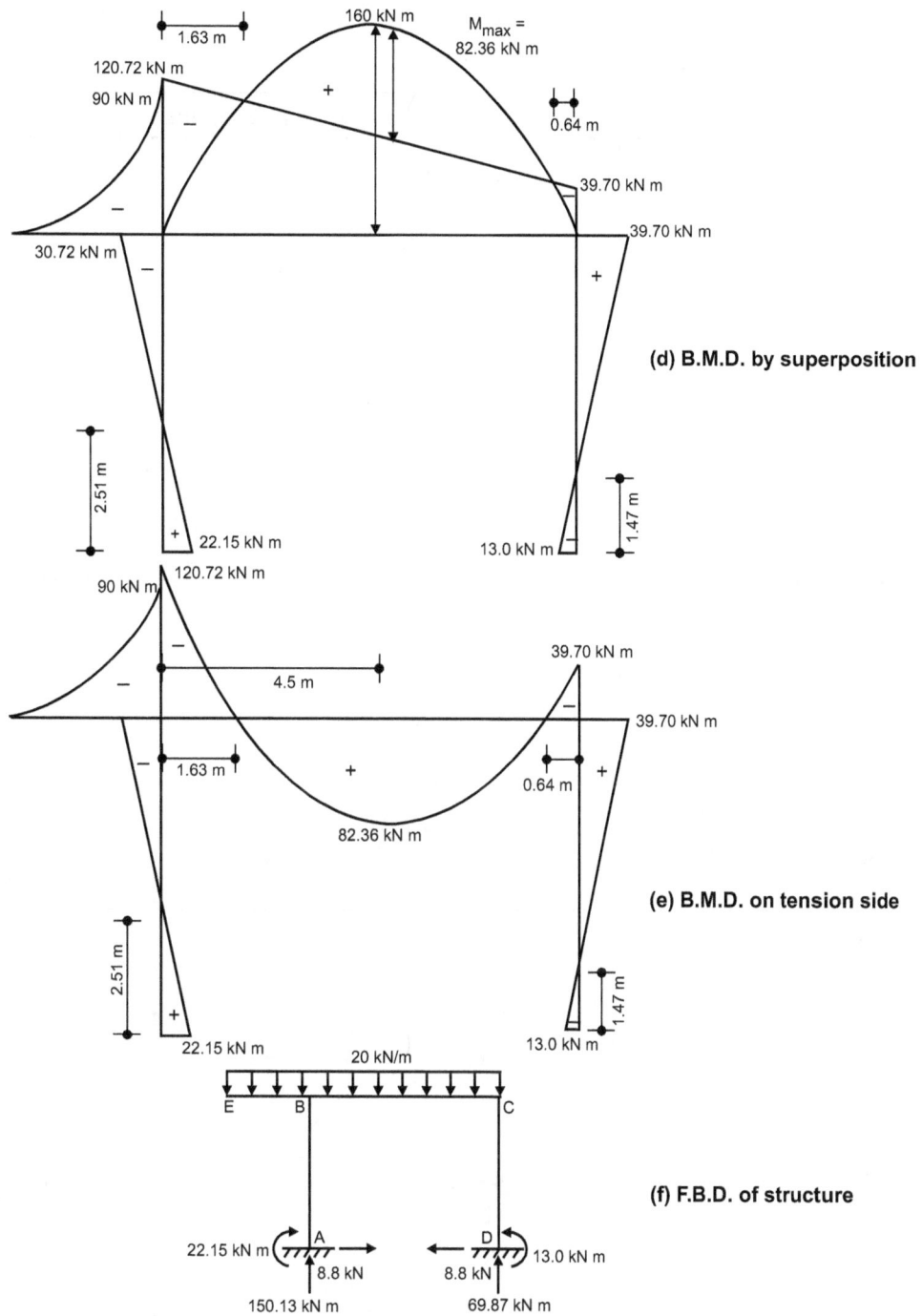

Fig. 3.23 : For Illustrative Example 3.18

Procedure:

Step I : Fixed-End Moments :

Member	FEM with calculations
AB	$M^F_{AB} = 0$ $M^F_{BA} = 0$
BC	$M^F_{BC} = \dfrac{wL^2}{12} = \dfrac{20 \times 8^2}{12}$ $= 106.67$ kNm $M^F_{CB} = -M^F_{BC}$ $= -106.67$
DC	$M^F_{DC} = 0$ $M^F_{CD} = 0$
BE	$M^F_{BE} = -\dfrac{wL^2}{2}$ $= \dfrac{-20 \times 3^2}{2}$ $= -90$ kNm

Step II : Distribution Factors :

Joint	Member	K	ΣK	DF = $\dfrac{K}{\Sigma K}$
A	AB	–	–	0
B	BA	$\dfrac{4EI}{L} = 0.67$	1.67	0.4
	BC	$\dfrac{4EI}{L} = 1$		0.6
	BE	–		0
C	CB	$\dfrac{4EI}{L} = 1$	1.67	0.6
	CD	$\dfrac{4EI}{L} = 0.67$		0.4
D	DC	–	–	0

MOMENT DISTRIBUTION METHOD

Step III : MD Table (I) for Non-Sway Moments :

Joint	A			B		C		D
Type of joint	EFS			RJ		RJ		EFS
Member	AB		BA	BE	BC	CB	CD	DC
COF		→ 1/2			→ 1/2		→ 1/2	
			1/2 ←			1/2 ←		1/2 ←
DF	0		0.4	0	0.6	0.6	0.4	0
First cycle FEM	0		0	− 90	106.67	− 106.67	0	0
DM	−		− 6.67		− 10.0	64	42.67	−
Second cycle COM	− 3.33				32	− 5.0		21.34
DM	−		− 12.8		− 19.2	3	2	−
Third cycle COM	− 6.4		−		1.5	− 9.6		1.0
DM	−		− 0.6		− 0.9	5.76	3.84	−
Fourth cycle COM	− 0.3				2.88	− 0.45		1.92
DM	−		− 1.15		− 1.73	0.27	0.18	−
Fifth cycle COM	− 0.56				0.14	− 0.87		0.09
DM	−		− 0.06		− 0.08	0.5	0.37	−
First set of final moments	− 10.59		− 21.28	− 90	111.28	− 49.06	49.06	24.35

Step IV : MD for Sway Moments :

(a) The basic information of K, COF and DF remains the same.

(b) Normalized relative sway stiffness factors (K_s).

Member	Relative sway stiffness factor	Normalized relative sway stiffness factor (K_s)
AB	$\dfrac{I}{6^2}$	1
DC	$\dfrac{I}{6^2}$	1

Ch. 3 | 3.73

(c) Sway Moments :

Member	Arbitrary relative FEM due to sway
AB	M_{AB}^{FS} = 100 kNm
	M_{BA}^{FS} = 100 kNm
DC	M_{DC}^{FS} = 100 kNm
	M_{CD}^{FS} = 100 kNm

Step V : MD Table (II) for Sway Moments :

Joint		A		B			C		D
Type of joint		EFS		RJ			RJ		EFS
Member		AB	BA	BE	BC		CB	CD	DC
COF			→ 1/2		→ 1/2			→ 1/2	
		1/2 →			1/2 →			1/2 →	
DF		0	0.4	0	0.6		0.6	0.4	0
First cycle	FEM	100	100	–	–		–	100	100
	DM	–	– 40		– 60		– 60	– 40	–
Second cycle	COM	– 20	–		– 30		– 30	–	– 20
	DM	–	12		18		18	12	–
Third cycle	COM	6	–		9		9	–	6
	DM	–	– 3.6		– 5.4		– 5.4	– 3.6	–
Fourth cycle	COM	– 1.8	–		– 2.7		– 2.7	–	– 1.8
	DM	–	1.08		1.62		1.62	1.08	–
Fifth cycle	COM	0.54	–		0.81		0.81	–	0.54
	DM	–	– 0.32		– 0.49		– 0.49	– 0.32	–
Sixth cycle	COM	– 0.16	–		– 0.25		– 0.25	–	– 0.16
	DM	–	0.10		0.15		0.15	0.10	–
Second set of final moments		84.58	69.26	0	– 69.26		– 69.26	69.26	84.58

Let the actual sway moments be 'C' times the above sway moments.

$\therefore$

$$M_{AB} = M_{AB}^{I} + C \cdot M_{AB}^{II} = -10.59 + C(84.58)$$

$$M_{BA} = M_{BA}^{I} + C \cdot M_{BA}^{II} = -21.28 + C(69.26)$$

$$M_{DC} = M_{DC}^{I} + C \cdot M_{DC}^{II} = 24.35 + C(84.58)$$

$$M_{CD} = M_{CD}^{I} + C \cdot M_{CD}^{II} = 49.08 + C(69.26)$$

where, C = Correction factor to be evaluated from the condition of horizontal shear equilibrium of the structure.

Step VI : Horizontal shear equilibrium: Horizontal shear equilibrium of structure gives,

$$H_A + H_D = 0 \quad \ldots (A)$$

where, $\quad H_A = \dfrac{M_{AB} + M_{BA}}{6}$

and $\quad H_D = \dfrac{M_{DC} + M_{CD}}{6}$

Substituting in equation (A), we get

$$M_{AB} + M_{BA} + M_{DC} + M_{CD} = 0$$

Substituting values of moments, we get

$$-10.59 + C(84.58) - 21.28 + C(69.26) + 24.35 + C(84.58) + 49.08 + C(69.26) = 0$$

$$\boxed{C = -0.135}$$

Step VII : Final Results :

Member	AB	BA	BE	BC	CB	CD	DC
Corrected moments of second set	− 11.56	− 9.44	0	9.44	9.36	− 9.36	− 11.35
Moments of first set	− 10.59	− 21.28	− 90	111.28	− 49.06	49.06	24.35
Net final moments	− 22.15	− 30.72	− 90	120.72	− 39.70	39.70	13.0

Step VIII : FBD of members is as shown in Fig. 3.23 (b). Considering equilibrium of each member and of complete structure, all reaction components are found out as shown in Fig. 3.23.

Step IX : Shear force diagram is as shown in Fig. 3.23 (c).

Step X : Bending moment diagrams are as shown in Fig. 3.23 (d) and Fig. 3.23 (e).

Step XI : FBD of structure is as shown in Fig. 3.23 (f).

Example 3.19 : *Analyse the frame shown in Fig. 3.24 (a) by MD method. Take EI = constant.*

Solution : Data : (1) The frame is supported and loaded as shown in Fig. 3.24 (a).

(2) Type of frame: Sway frame.

Object : Structural analysis.

Concepts and Equations :

(1) MD technique based on normalized relative stiffness factors and distribution factors.

(2) Normalized relative sway factors.

(3) Shear equilibrium condition and correction factor.

TOS – II (TE CIVIL SEM. VI NMU) — MOMENT DISTRIBUTION METHOD

Procedure :

Step I : Fixed-End Moments :

Member	FEM with calculations
AB	$M_{AB}^F = \dfrac{wL^2}{12} = \dfrac{25 \times 4^2}{12}$ $= 33.33$ kNm $M_{BA}^F = -M_{AB}^F$ $= -33.33$ kNm
BC	$M_{BC}^F = \dfrac{WL}{8} = \dfrac{50 \times 3}{8}$ $= 18.75$ kNm $M_{CB}^F = -M_{BC}^F$ $= -18.75$ kNm
DC	$M_{DC}^F = \dfrac{-Wab^2}{L^2} = \dfrac{-40 \times 1 \times 2^2}{3^2}$ $= -17.77$ kNm $M_{CD}^F = \dfrac{Wba^2}{L^2} = \dfrac{40 \times 2 \times 1^2}{3^2} = 8.88$ kNm

Step II : Distribution Factors :

Joint	Member	K	ΣK	DF = $\dfrac{K}{\Sigma K}$
A	AB	–	–	0
B	BA	$\dfrac{4EI}{L} = 1$	2.34	0.43
	BC	$\dfrac{4EI}{L} = 1.34$		0.57
C	CB	$\dfrac{4EI}{L} = 1.34$	2.68	0.5
	CD	$\dfrac{4EI}{L} = 1.34$		0.5
D	DC	–	–	0

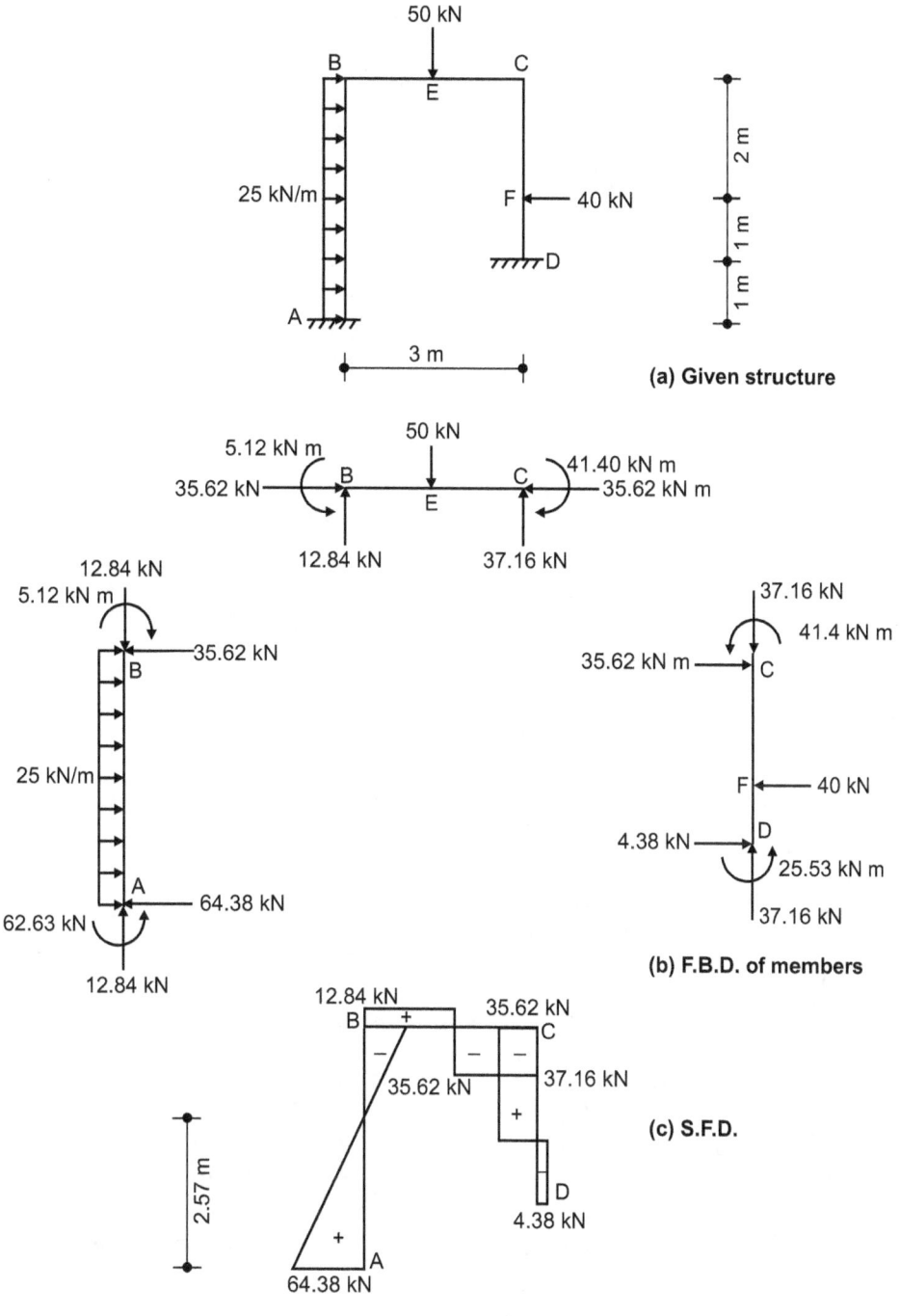

Fig. 3.24 (Contd.)

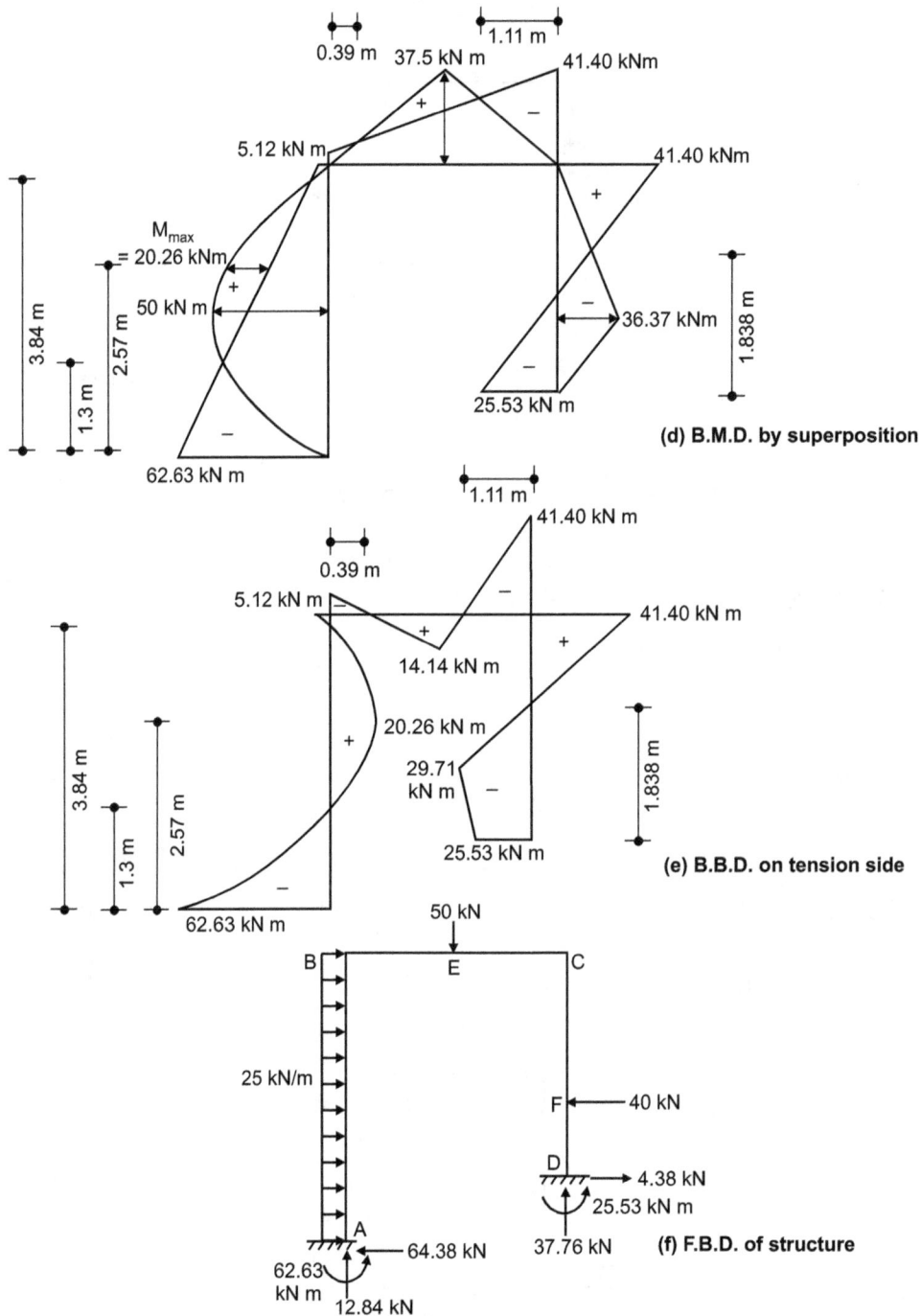

Fig. 3.24 : For Illustrative Example 3.19

Step III : MD Table (I) for Non-Sway Moments :

Joint		A	B		C		D
Type of joint		EFS	RJ		RJ		EFS
Member		AB	BA	BC	CB	CD	DC
COF			→ 1/2	→ 1/2		→ 0	
			1/2 ←	1/2 ←		1/2 ←	
DF		0	0.43	0.57	0.5	0.5	0
First cycle	FEM	33.33	− 33.33	18.75	− 18.75	8.88	− 17.77
	DM	−	6.27	8.31	4.94	4.94	−
Second cycle	COM	3.14	−	2.47	4.16	−	2.47
	DM	−	− 1.06	− 1.41	− 2.08	− 2.08	−
Third cycle	COM	− 0.53	−	− 1.04	− 0.70	−	− 1.04
	DM	−	0.45	0.59	0.35	0.35	−
Fourth cycle	COM	0.23	−	0.18	0.30	−	0.18
	DM	−	− 0.08	− 0.10	− 0.15	− 0.15	−
Fifth cycle	COM	− 0.04	−	− 0.08	− 0.05	−	− 0.08
	DM	−	0.03	0.05	0.03	0.03	−
First set of final moments		36.13	− 27.72	27.72	− 11.97	11.97	− 16.24

Step IV : MD for Sway Moments :

(a) The basic information of K, COF and DF remains the same.

(b) Normalized relative sway stiffness factors (K_S).

Member	Relative sway stiffness factor	Normalized relative sway stiffness factor (K_S)
AB	$\dfrac{I}{4^2}$	9
DC	$\dfrac{I}{3^2}$	16

(c) **Sway Moments :**

Member	Arbitrary relative FEM due to sway
AB	M_{AB}^{FS} = 90 kNm
	M_{BA}^{FS} = 90 kNm
DC	M_{DC}^{FS} = 160 kNm
	M_{CD}^{FS} = 160 kNm

Step V : MD Table (II) for Sway Moments :

Joint		A		B			C		D
Type of joint		EFS		RJ			RJ		EHS
Member		AB	BA	BC		CB	CD		DC
COF			→ 1/2		→ 1/2			→ 1/2	
			1/2 ←		1/2 ←			1/2 ←	
DF		0	0.43	0.57		0.5	0.5		0
First cycle	FEM	90		90	–	–	160		160
	DM	–	– 38.70	– 51.30		– 80	– 80		–
Second cycle	COM	– 19.35		– 40		– 25.65	–		– 40
	DM	–	17.20	– 3.66		12.83	12.83		–
Third cycle	COM	8.60		6.42		11.40	–		6.42
	DM	–	– 2.76	– 3.66		– 5.70	– 5.70		–
Fourth cycle	COM	– 1.38		– 2.85		– 1.83	–		– 2.85
	DM	–	1.23	1.62		0.92	0.92		–
Fifth cycle	COM	0.62		0.46		0.81	–		0.46
	DM	–	– 0.22	– 0.24		– 0.41	– 0.41		–
Second set of final moments		78.49	66.75	– 66.75		– 87.63	– 87.63		124.03

Let, the actual sway moments be 'C' times the above sway moments:

∴

$$M_{AB} = M^I_{AB} + C \cdot M^{II}_{AB} = 36.13 + C\,(78.49)$$

$$M_{BA} = M^I_{BA} + C \cdot M^I_{BA} = -27.72 + C\,(66.75)$$

$$M_{DC} = M^I_{DC} + C \cdot M^{II}_{DC} = -16.24 + C\,(124.03)$$

$$M_{CD} = M^I_{CD} + C \cdot M^{II}_{CD} = 11.97 + C\,(87.63)$$

where, C = Correction factor to be evaluated from the condition of horizontal shear equilibrium for the structure.

Step VI : Horizontal shear equilibrium,

Horizontal shear equilibrium of structure gives:

$$H_A + H_D - 25 \times 4 + 40 = 0$$

i.e. $\quad H_A + H_D - 60 = 0 \quad$ ... (A)

where, $\quad H_A = \dfrac{M_{AB} + M_{BA}}{4} + 50$

and $\quad H_D = \dfrac{M_{DC} + M_{CD}}{3} - 26.67$

Substituting in equation (A), we get

$$\left(\dfrac{M_{AB} + M_{BA}}{4} + 50\right) + \left(\dfrac{M_{DC} + M_{CD}}{3} - 26.67\right) - 60 = 0$$

i.e. $3 (M_{AB} + M_{BA}) + 4 (M_{DC} + M_{CD}) - 440 = 0$

Substituting values of moments, we get

$3 [36.13 + C (78.49) - 27.72 + C (66.75)]$

$\qquad\qquad + 4 [-16.24 + C (124.03) + 11.97 + C (87.63)] - 440 = 0$

$C (1282.36) - 431.85 = 0$

$\Rightarrow \boxed{C = 0.337}$

Step VII : Final Results : Corrected moments of second set will be obtained by multiplying these moments by C and when added to first set of moments gives net final moments.

Member	AB	BA	BC	CB	CD	DC
Corrected moments of second set	26.50	22.60	− 22.60	− 29.43	29.43	41.77
Moments of first set	36.13	− 27.72	27.72	− 11.97	11.97	− 16.24
Net final moments	62.63	− 5.12	5.12	− 41.40	41.40	25.53

Step VIII : FBD of members is as shown in Fig. 2.24 (b). Considering equilibrium of each member and of complete structure, all reaction components are found out as shown in Fig. 3.24.

Step IX : Shear force diagram is as shown in Fig. 3.24 (c).

Step X : Bending moment diagrams are as shown in Fig. 3.24 (d) and Fig. 3.24 (e).

Step XI : FBD of structure is as shown in Fig. 3.24 (f).

Example 3.20 : *Analyse the frame shown in Fig. 3.25 (a) by MD method.*

Solution : Data : (1) The frame is supported and loaded as shown in Fig. 3.25 (a).

(2) Type of frame: Sway frame.

Object : Structural analysis.

Concepts and Equations : (1) MD technique based on normalized relative stiffness factors and distribution factors.

(2)   Normalized relative sway factor.

(3)   Shear equilibrium condition and correction factor.

Procedure :

Step I : Fixed-End Moments :

Member	FEM with calculations
AB	$M^F_{AB} = 0$ $M^F_{BA} = 0$
BC	$M^F_{BC} = \dfrac{WL}{8} = \dfrac{50 \times 4}{8} = 25$ kNm $M^F_{CB} = -M^F_{BC} = -25$ kNm
DC	$M^F_{DC} = 0$ $M^F_{CD} = 0$

Step II : Distribution Factors :

Joint	Member	K	ΣK	DF = $\dfrac{K}{\Sigma K}$
A	AB	–	–	0
B	BA	$\dfrac{4EI}{L} = 1$	2.5	0.4
	BC	$\dfrac{3EI}{L} = 1.5$		0.6
C	CB	–	–	1
	CD	–	–	1
D	DC	–	–	0

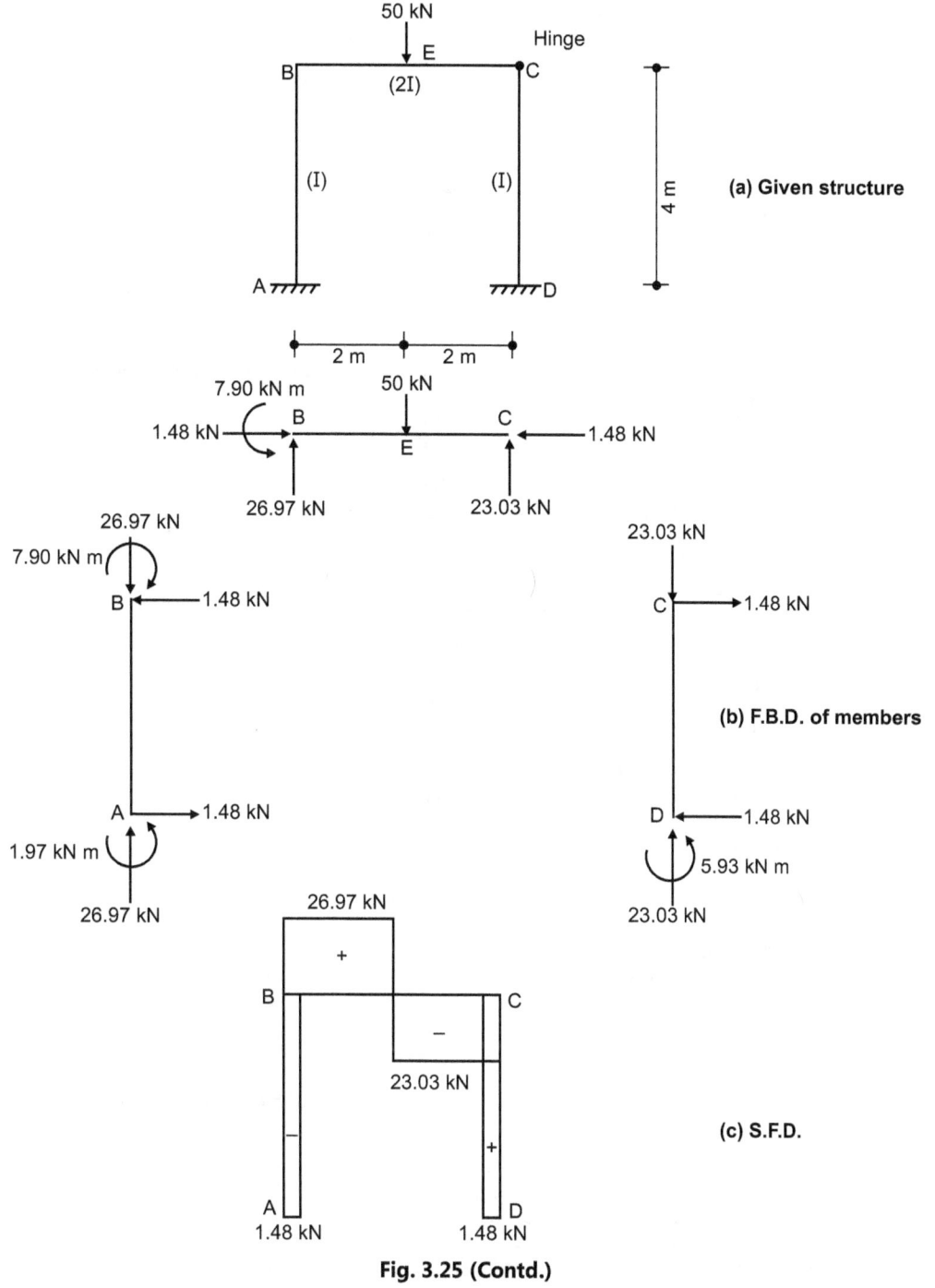

Fig. 3.25 (Contd.)

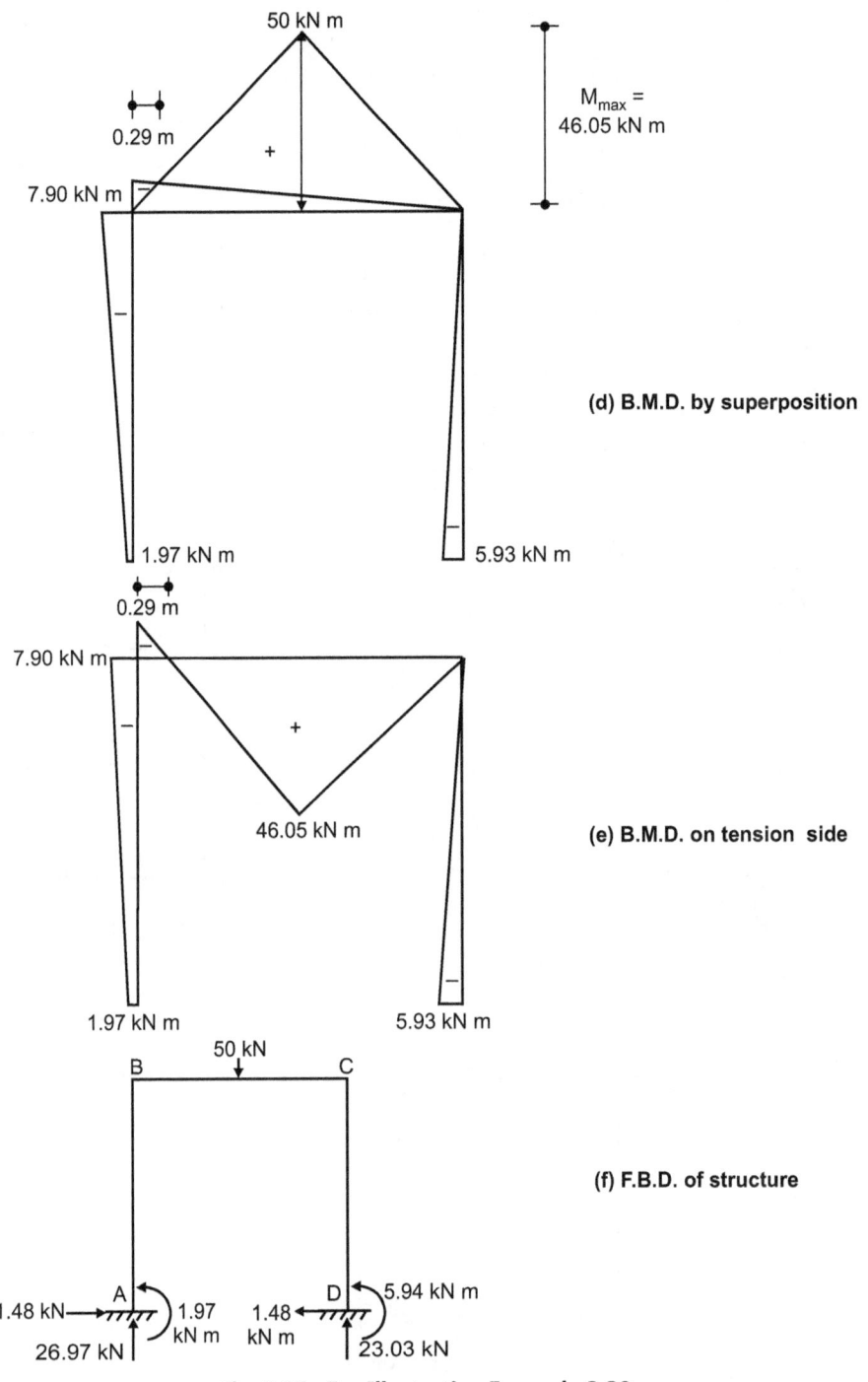

Fig. 3.25 : For Illustrative Example 3.20

Step III : MD Table (I) for non-sway moments :

Joint	A	B			C		D
Type of joint	EFS	RJ			IH		EFS
Member	AB	BA	BC		CB	CD	DC
COF		→ 1/2		→ 0		→ 1/2	
			1/2 ←		1/2 ←		0 ←
DF	0	0.4	0.6		1	1	0
First cycle FEM	0	0	25		− 25	0	0
DM	−	− 10	− 15		25		
Second cycle COM	− 5	−	12.5		−		
DM	−	− 5.0	− 7.50		−		
Third cycle COM	− 2.5	−	−		−		
DM	−	−	−		−		
First set of final moments	− 7.50	− 15.0	15.0		0	0	0

Step IV : MD for Sway Moments :

(a) The basic information of K, COF, and DF remains the same.

(b) Normalized relative sway stiffness factors (K_S).

Member	Relative sway stiffness factor	Normalized relative sway stiffness factor (K_S)
AB	$\dfrac{I}{4^2}$	1
DC	$\dfrac{I}{4^2}$	1

(c) **Sway Moments :**

Member	Arbitrary relative FEM due to sway
AB	M_{AB}^{FS} = 100 kNm
	M_{BA}^{FS} = 100 kNm
DC	M_{DC}^{FS} = 100 kNm
	M_{CD}^{FS} = 100 kNm

Step V : MD Table (II) for Sway Moments :

Joint	A	B		C		D
Type of joint	EFS	RJ		IH		EFS
Member	AB	BA	BC	CB	CD	DC
COF		→1/2	→0		→1/2	
		1/2←		1/2←		0←
DF	0	0.4	0.6	1	1	0
First cycle FEM	100	100	0	0	100	100
DM	–	– 40	– 60	–	– 100	–
Second cycle COM	– 20	–	–	–	–	– 50
DM	–	–	–	–	–	–
Second set of final moments	80	60	– 60	0	0	50

Let, the actual sway moments be 'C' times the above sway moments.

$\therefore \quad M_{AB} = M_{AB}^{I} + C \cdot M_{AB}^{II}$

$M_{BA} = M_{BA}^{I} + C \cdot M_{BA}^{II}$

$M_{DC} = M_{DC}^{I} + C \cdot M_{DC}^{II}$

where, C = Correction factor to be evaluated from the condition of horizontal shear equilibrium of the structure.

Step VI : Horizontal Shear Equilibrium :

Horizontal shear equilibrium of structure gives

$$H_A + H_D = 0 \qquad \ldots(A)$$

where, $\quad H_A = \dfrac{M_{AB} + M_{BA}}{4}$

and $\quad H_D = \dfrac{M_{DC}}{4}$

Substituting in equation (A), we get

$$\dfrac{M_{AB} + M_{BA}}{4} + \dfrac{M_{DC}}{4} = 0$$

i.e. $\quad M_{AB} + M_{BA} + M_{DC} = 0$

Substituting the values of moments, we get

$(-7.50) + C(80) - 15 + C(60) + C(50) = 0$

$$\boxed{C = 0.118}$$

Step VII : Final Results :

Member	AB	BA	BC	CB	CD	DC
Corrected moments of second set	9.47	7.10	– 7.10	0	0	5.93
Moments of first set	– 7.50	– 15.0	15.0	0	0	0
Net final moments	1.97	– 7.90	7.90	0	0	5.93

Step VIII : FBD of members is as shown in Fig. 3.25 (b).

Considering equilibrium of each member and of complete structure, all reaction components are found out as shown in Fig. 3.25.

Step IX : Shear force diagram is as shown in Fig. 3.25 (c).

Step X : Bending moment diagrams are as shown in Fig. 3.25 (d) and Fig. 3.25 (e).

Step XI : FBD of structure is as shown in Fig. 3.25 (f).

3.8 APPLICATION OF MD METHOD TO FRAMES WITH YIELDING OF SUPPORTS

Due to yielding of supports, the moments will be developed at the ends of the members having yielding supports:

$$M_{ij}^{FY} = \frac{4 E_{ij} \cdot I_{ij}}{L_{ij}} \theta_{iy} \text{ and } M_{ji}^{FY} = \frac{2 EI_{ij}}{L_{ij}} \theta_{iy} \text{ due to rotational yielding.}$$

$$M_{ij}^{FY} = \frac{6 E_{ij} I_{ij}}{L_{ij}^2} \Delta_{j/i} \text{ and } M_{ji}^{FY} = \frac{6 EI_{ij} I_{ij}}{L_{ij}^2} \Delta_{j/i} \text{ due to translational yielding.}$$

These moments are considered as the restraining moments i.e. FEM in the first cycle of MD and the distribution of moments is carried out as per the routine working of MD table. Thus, the effect of yielding of supports can be independently analysed by MD method.

Otherwise combined effect of loads and yielding of supports is obtained. For this FEM due to loads and FEM due to yielding of supports are added and MD table begins with the net FEM. Rest of the procedure of MD method is same. The following example illustrates the analysis of rectangular frames due to yielding of supports.

TOS – II (TE CIVIL SEM. VI NMU) — MOMENT DISTRIBUTION METHOD

Example 3.21 : *Analyse the frame shown in Fig. 3.26 (a) by MD method if support A sinks by 5 mm and support D undergoes anticlockwise rotation of 0.002 radians.*

Take $EI = 3 \times 10^3$ kN.m²

Solution : Data :

(1) The frame is supported and loaded as shown in Fig. 3.26 (a).

(2) $\Delta_A = 5$ mm ($\downarrow$) and $\theta_D = 0.002$ radian.

(3) $EI = 3 \times 10^3$ kNm²

(4) Type of frame: Sway frame.

Object : Structural analysis.

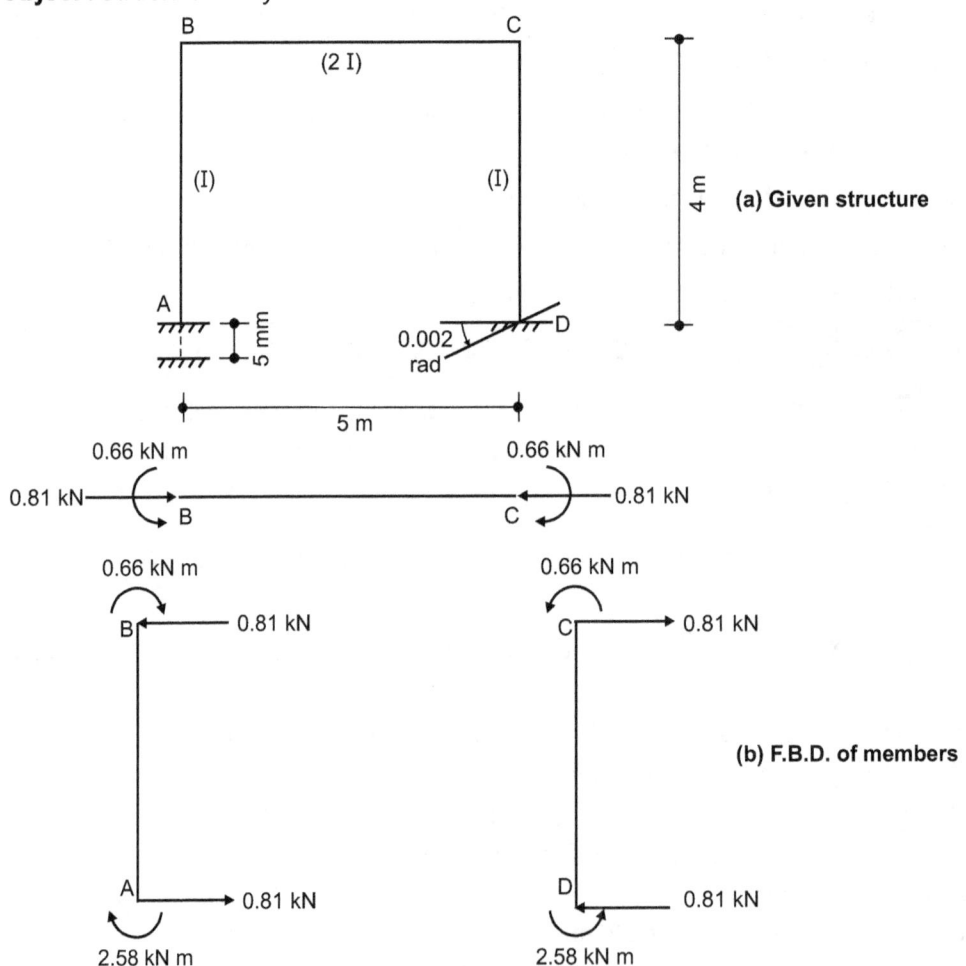

(a) Given structure

(b) F.B.D. of members

Fig. 3.26 (Contd.)

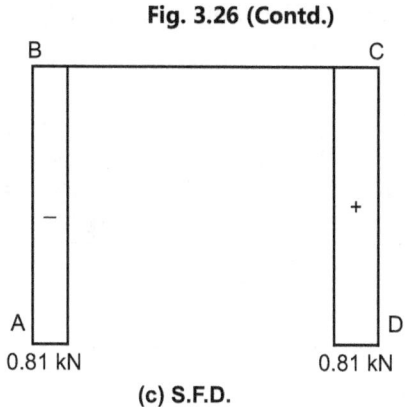

(c) S.F.D.

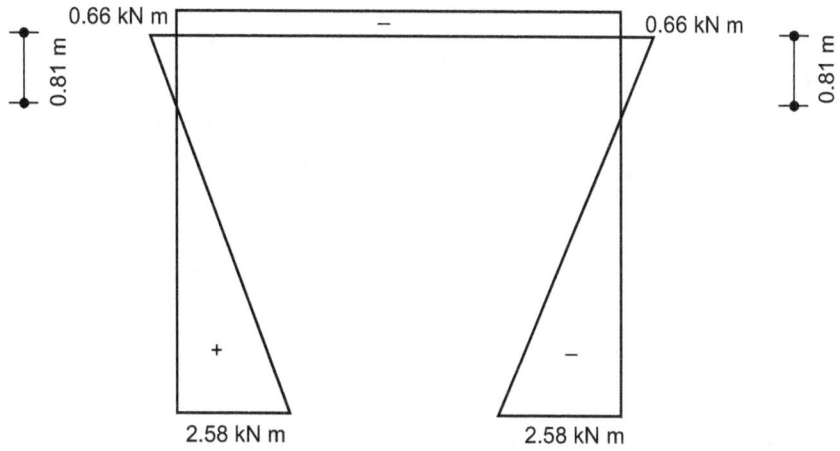

(d) B.M.D. on tension side

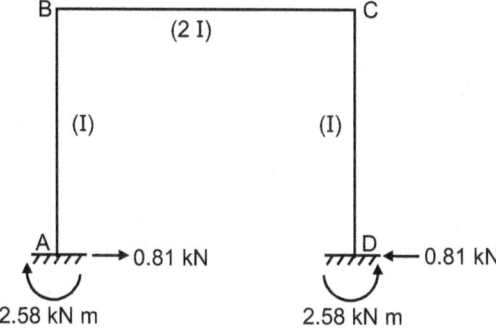

(e) F.B.D. of structure

Fig. 3.26 : For Illustrative Example 3.21

Procedure :

Step I : Fixed-End Moments :

Member	FEM with calculations		Total FEM
	FEM due to sinking of support A	FEM due to rotation of support D	
AB	$M^F_{AB} = 0$ $M^F_{BA} = 0$	$M^F_{AB} = 0$ $M^F_{BA} = 0$	$M^F_{AB} = 0$ $M^F_{BA} = 0$
BC	$M^F_{BC} = -6\,EI\,\Delta/L^2$ $= \dfrac{-6 \times 2 \times 3 \times 10^3 \times 0.005}{5^2}$ $= -7.2$ kNm $M^F_{CB} = M^F_{BC} = -7.2$ kNm	$M^F_{BC} = 0$ $M^F_{CB} = 0$	$M^F_{BC} = 7.2$ kNm $M^F_{CB} = -7.2$ kNm
DC	$M^F_{DC} = 0$ $M^F_{CD} = 0$	$M^F_{DC} = \dfrac{4\,EI\,\theta_D}{L}$ $= \dfrac{4 \times 3 \times 10^3 \times 0.002}{4}$ $= 6$ kNm $M^F_{CD} = \dfrac{2\,EI\theta_D}{L}$ $= 3$ kNm	$M^F_{DC} = 6$ kNm $M^F_{CD} = 3$ kNm

Step II : Distribution Factors :

Joint	Member	K	ΣK	DF = K/ΣK
A	AB	–	–	0
B	BA	$\dfrac{4EI}{L} = 1$	2.6	0.38
	BC	$\dfrac{4EI}{L} = 1.6$		0.62
C	CB	$\dfrac{4EI}{L} = 1.6$	2.6	0.62
	CD	$\dfrac{4EI}{L} = 1$		0.38
D	DC	–	–	0

Step III : MD Table (I) for Non-Sway Moments :

Joint		A	B			C		D
Type of joint		EFS	RJ			RJ		EHS
Member		AB	BA	BC		CB	CD	DC
COF			→ 1/2			→ 1/2		→ 1/2
			1/2 ←			1/2 ←		1/2 ←
DF		0	0.38	0.62		0.62	0.38	0
First cycle	FEM	0	0	− 7.2		− 7.2	3.0	6.0
	DM	−	2.74	4.46		2.60	1.60	−
Second cycle	COM	1.37	−	1.30		2.23	−	0.80
	DM	−	− 0.50	− 0.80		− 1.38	− 0.85	−
Third cycle	COM	− 0.25	−	− 0.69		− 0.40	−	− 0.43
	DM	−	0.26	0.43		0.25	0.15	−
Fourth cycle	COM	0.13	−	0.13		0.22	−	0.08
	DM	−	− 0.05	− 0.08		− 0.14	− 0.08	−
First set of final moments		1.25	2.45	− 2.45		− 3.82	3.82	6.45

Step IV : MD for Sway Moments :

(a) The basic information of K, COF and DF remains the same.

(b) Normalized relative sway stiffness factors (K_S).

Member	Relative sway stiffness factor	Normalized relative sway stiffness factor (K_S)
AB	$\dfrac{I}{4^2}$	1
DC	$\dfrac{I}{4^2}$	1

(c) Sway Moments :

Member	Arbitrary relative FEM due to sway
AB	$M_{AB}^{FS} = 100$ kNm
	$M_{BA}^{FS} = 100$ kNm

| | | DC | | | M^{FS}_{DC} = 100 kNm |
| | | | | | M^{FS}_{CD} = 100 kNm |

Step V : MD Table (II) for Sway Moments :

Joint		A	B		C		D
Type of joint		EFS	RJ		RJ		EFS
Member		AB	BA	BC	CB	CD	DC
COF		→1/2	1/2←	→1/2	1/2←	→1/2	1/2←
DF		0	0.38	0.62	0.62	0.38	0
First cycle	FEM	100	100	0	0	100	100
	DM	–	– 38	– 62	– 62	– 38	–
Second cycle	COM	– 19	–	– 31	– 31	–	– 19
	DM	–	11.78	19.22	19.22	11.78	–
Third cycle	COM	5.89	–	9.61	9.61	–	5.89
	DM	–	– 3.65	– 5.96	– 5.96	– 3.65	–
Fourth cycle	COM	– 1.83	–	– 2.98	– 2.98	–	– 1.83
	DM	–	1.13	1.85	1.85	1.13	–
Fifth cycle	COM	0.57	–	0.93	0.93	–	0.57
	DM	–	– 0.35	– 0.58	– 0.58	– 0.35	–
Sixth cycle	COM	– 0.18	–	– 0.29	– 0.29	–	– 0.18
	DM	–	0.11	0.18	0.18	0.11	–
Second set of final moments		85.45	71.02	– 71.02	– 71.02	71.02	85.45

Let, the actual sway moments be 'C' times the above sway moments.

∴

$$M_{AB} = M^{I}_{AB} + C \cdot M^{II}_{AB} = 1.25 + C\,(85.45)$$

$$M_{BA} = M^{I}_{BA} + C \cdot M^{II}_{BA} = 2.45 + C\,(71.02)$$

$$M_{DC} = M^{I}_{DC} + C \cdot M^{II}_{DC} = 6.45 + C\,(85.45)$$

$$M_{CD} = M_{CD}^{I} + C \cdot M_{CD}^{II} = 3.82 + C(71.02)$$

where, C = Correction factor to be evaluated from the condition of horizontal shear equilibrium of the structure.

Step VI : Horizontal Shear Equilibrium :

Horizontal shear equilibrium of structure gives,

$$H_A + H_D = 0 \quad \ldots (A)$$

where
$$H_A = \frac{M_{AB} + M_{BA}}{4}$$

and
$$H_D = \frac{M_{DC} + M_{CD}}{4}$$

Substituting in equation (A), we get

$$M_{AB} + M_{BA} + M_{DC} + M_{CD} = 0$$

Substituting the values of moments, we get

1.25 + C (85.45) + 2.45 + C (71.02) + 6.45 + C (85.45) + 3.82 + C (71.02) = 0

$$\boxed{C = -0.0448}$$

Step VII : Final Results :

Member	AB	BA	BC	CB	CD	DC
Corrected moments of second set	− 3.83	− 3.11	3.11	3.16	− 3.16	− 3.87
Moments of first set	1.25	2.45	− 2.45	− 3.82	3.82	6.45
Net final moments	− 2.58	− 0.66	0.66	− 0.66	0.66	2.58

Step VIII : FBD of members is as shown in Fig. 3.26 (b). Considering equilibrium of each member and of complete structure, all reaction components are found out as shown in Fig. 3.26.

Step IX : Shear force diagram is as shown in Fig. 3.26 (c).

Step X : Bending moment diagrams are as shown in Fig. 3.26 (d) and Fig. 3.26 (e).

Step XI : FBD of structure is as shown in Fig. 3.26 (f).

Example 3.22 : *Analyse the rigid frame shown in Fig. 3.27 (a) using moment distribution method.*

Solution : Data : (i) The frame is supported and loaded as shown in Fig. 3.27 (a).

(ii) Frame Type : Sway frame.

Object : Structural analysis.

Concepts and Equations :

(i) MD technique based on normalized relative stiffness factors and distribution factors.

(ii) Normalized relative sway factors.

(iii) Shear equilibrium condition and correction factors.

Procedure :

Step I : Fixed-End Moments.

Member	FEM with calculations
AB	$M^F_{AB} = 0$ $M^F_{BA} = 0$
BC	$M^F_{BC} = \dfrac{wl^2}{12} = \dfrac{30 \times 3^2}{12} = 22.5$ kN-m $M^F_{CB} = -M^F_{BC} = -22.5$ kN-m
DC	$M^F_{DC} = 0$ $M^F_{CD} = 0$

Step II : Distribution Factors :

Joint	Member	K	ΣK	$DF = \dfrac{K}{\Sigma K}$
A	AB	–	–	0
B	BA	$\dfrac{4EI}{L} = \dfrac{4EI}{4}$	$\dfrac{11 EI}{3}$	3/11
	BC	$\dfrac{4EI}{L} = \dfrac{4E(2I)}{3}$		8/11

C	CB	$\dfrac{4EI}{L} = \dfrac{4E(2I)}{3}$	$\dfrac{11EI}{3}$	8/11
	CD	$\dfrac{4EI}{L} = \dfrac{4EI}{4}$	$\dfrac{11EI}{3}$	3/11
D	DC	–	–	0

Step III : MD Table (I) for Non-Sway Moments :

Joint		A	B		C		D
Type of joint		EFS	RJ		RJ		EFS
Member		AB	BA	BC	CB	CD	DC
COF			→ 1/2 1/2 ←	→1/2 1/2 ←		→ 1/2 1/2 ←	
DF		0	3/11	8/11	8/11	3/11	
First cycle	FEM	0	0	22.5	–22.5	0	0
	DM		–6.14	–16.36	16.36	6.14	
Second cycle	COM	–3.07		8.18	–8.18		3.07
	DM		–2.23	–5.95	5.95	2.23	
Third cycle	COM	–1.12		2.98	–2.98		1.12
	DM		–0.81	–2.17	2.17	+0.81	
Fourth cycle	COM	–0.41		1.08	–1.08		+0.41
	DM		–0.29	–0.79	0.79	0.29	
Fifth cycle	COM	–0.14		0.395	–0.395		0.14
	DM		–0.11	–0.285	0.285	0.11	
First set of final moments		–4.74	–9.58	9.58	–9.58	9.58	4.74

Step IV : MD for Sway Moments :

(a) The basic information of K, COF and DF remains the same.

(b) Normalized relative sway stiffness factors [K_s].

Member	Relative sway stiffness factor	Normalized relative sway stiffness factor [K_s]
AB	$\dfrac{I}{4^2}$	1
DC	$\dfrac{I}{4^2}$	–1

(c) **Sway Moments :**

Member	Arbitrary relative FEM due to sway

AB	$M_{AB}^{FS} = 100$
	$M_{BA}^{FS} = 100$
DC	$M_{DC}^{FS} = -100$
	$M_{CD}^{FS} = -100$

Step V : MD Table II : For Sway Moments :

Joint		A	B			C	D
Type of joint		EFS	RJ			RJ	EHS
Member		AB	BA	BC	CB	CD	DC
COF			→ 1/2	→ 1/2		→ 1/2	
			1/2 ←	1/2 ←		1/2 ←	
DF			3/11	8/11	8/11	3/11	
First cycle	FEM	100	100	0	0	– 100	– 100
	DM		– 27.27	– 72.73	72.73	27.27	
Second cycle	COM	– 13.365		36.365	– 36.365		13.365
	DM		– 9.92	– 26.445	26.445	9.92	
Third cycle	COM	– 4.96		13.22	– 13.22		4.96
	DM		– 3.605	– 9.615	9.615	3.605	
Fourth cycle	COM	– 1.802		+ 4.808	– 4.808		–1.802
	DM		– 1.31	– 3.498	3.498	+ 1.31	
Fifth cycle	COM	– 0.655		1.749	– 1.749		0.655
	DM		– 0.477	– 1.272	1.272	0.477	
Second set of final moments		79.218	57.418	– 57.418	57.418	– 57.418	– 79.218

$$M_{AB} = M_{AB}^{I} + C\, M_{AB}^{II} = -4.74 + C \times 79.218$$
$$M_{BA} = M_{BA}^{I} + C\, M_{BA}^{II} = -9.58 + C \times 57.418$$
$$M_{CD} = M_{CD}^{I} + C\, M_{CD}^{II} = 9.58 - C \times 57.418$$
$$M_{DC} = M_{DC}^{I} + C\, M_{DC}^{II} = 4.74 - C \times 79.218$$

where C is a correction factor to be evaluated from the condition of horizontal shear equilibrium for structure.

Step VI : Horizontal shear equilibrium.

Horizontal shear equilibrium gives:

$$H_A - H_D = 0$$
$$H_A = \frac{M_{AB} + M_{BA}}{4}$$
$$H_D = \frac{M_{CD} + M_{DC}}{4}$$

$M_{AB} + M_{BA} - M_{CD} - M_{DC} = 0$

$-4.74 + C \times 79.218 - 9.58 + C \times 57.418$
$-9.58 + C \times 57.418 - 4.74 + C \times 79.218 = 0$

$$273.272C = 28.64$$

$\therefore \quad C = 0.105$

Step VII : Corrected moments of second set will be obtained by multiplying these moments by C and then added to first set of moments gives net final moments.

Member	AB	BA	BC	CB	CD	DC
Corrected moments of second set	8.32	6.03	− 6.03	6.03	− 6.03	− 8.32
Moments of first set	− 4.74	− 9.58	9.58	− 9.58	9.58	4.74
Net final moments	3.58	− 3.55	3.55	− 3.55	3.55	− 3.58

Step VIII : FBD of members is as shown in Fig. 2.27 (b). Considering equilibrium of each member and of complete structure all the reaction components are found out as shown in Fig. 3.27.

Step IX : Shear force diagram is as shown in Fig. 3.27 (c).

Step X : Bending moment diagrams are as shown in Fig. 3.27 (d) and Fig. 3.27 (e).

Step XI : FBD of structure is as shown in Fig. 3.27 (f).

MOMENT DISTRIBUTION METHOD

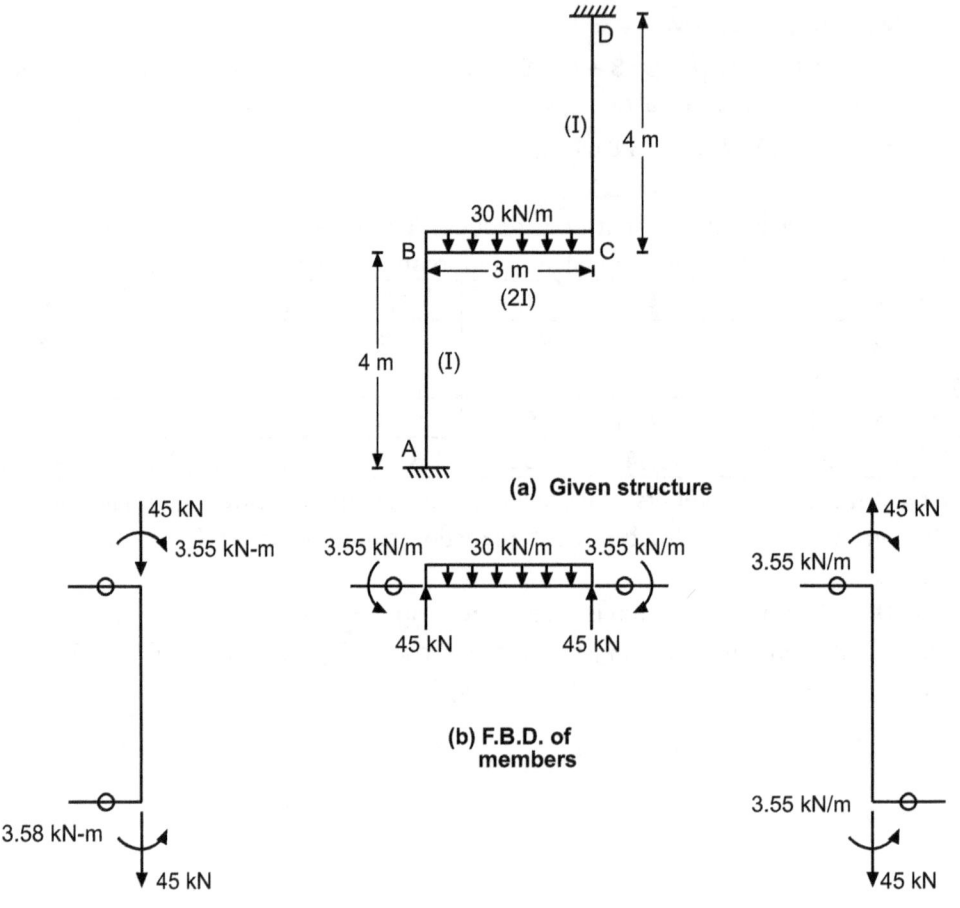

(a) Given structure

(b) F.B.D. of members

Ch. 3 | 3.98

TOS – II (TE CIVIL SEM. VI NMU)   MOMENT DISTRIBUTION METHOD

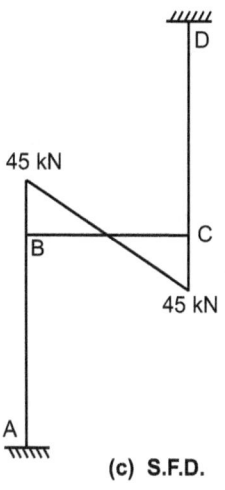

(c) S.F.D.

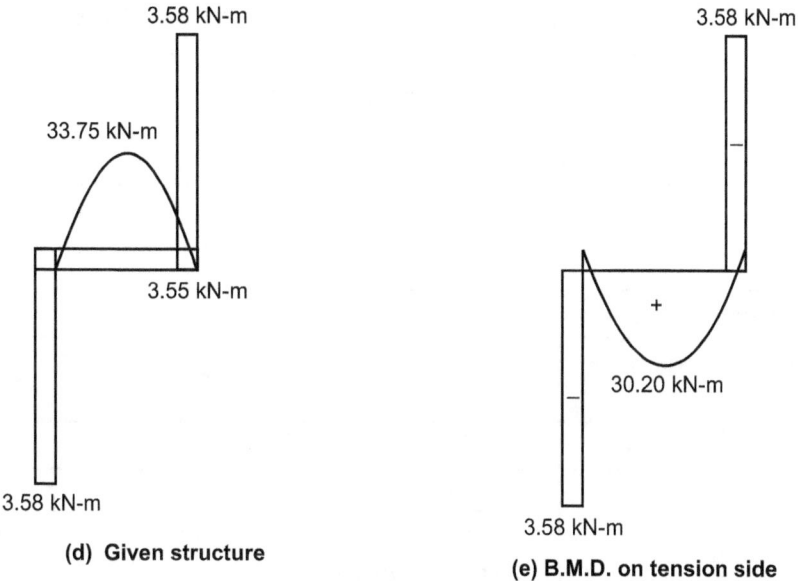

(d) Given structure   (e) B.M.D. on tension side

Fig. 3.27 : For Illustrative Example 3.22

Example 3.23 : A rectangular portal frame is hinged at support A and fixed at support D. AB = CD = 4 m and BC = 5 m. It carries UDL of 2.5 kN/m on horizontal member BC and a horizontal concentrated load of 50 kN on AB towards CD at 3 m from support A. If $I_{AB} = I_{CD} = 0.5\ I_{BC}$, find the moments at B, C and D and draw the BMD. Use moment distribution method only. Use five cycles of iteration for distribution of moments.

Solution : Data : (1) The frame is supported and loaded as shown in Fig. 3.28 (a).

(2) Type of frame : Sway frame.

Object : Structural analysis.

Concepts and Equations : (1) MD technique based on normalized relative stiffness factors and distribution factors.

(2) Normalized relative sway factors.

(3) Shear equilibrium condition and correction factors.

Procedure :

Step I : Fixed-End Moments :

Member	FEM with calculations
AB	$M^F_{AB} = \dfrac{wab^2}{l^2} = \dfrac{50 \times 3 \times 1^2}{4^2} = 9.375$ kN-m $M^F_{BA} = -\dfrac{wa^2b}{l^2} = -\dfrac{50 \times 3^2 \times 1}{4^2} = -28.125$ kN-m
BC	$M^F_{BC} = \dfrac{2.5 \times 5^2}{12} = 5.21$ kN-m $M^F_{CB} = -5.21$ kN-m
CD	$M^F_{CD} = 0$ $M^F_{DC} = 0$

Step II : Distribution Factors :

Joint	Member	K	ΣK	DF = $\dfrac{K}{\Sigma K}$
A	AB	–	–	0
B	BA	$\dfrac{3\,EI}{L} = \dfrac{3\,EI}{4}$	$\dfrac{23\,EI}{20}$	$\dfrac{15}{23}$
	BC	$\dfrac{4\,EI}{L} = \dfrac{4\,EI\,(0.5\,I)}{5}$		$\dfrac{8}{23}$
C	CB	$\dfrac{4\,EI}{L} = \dfrac{4\,E\,(0.5\,I)}{5}$	$\dfrac{7\,EI}{5}$	$\dfrac{2}{7}$
	CD	$\dfrac{4\,EI}{L} = \dfrac{4\,EI}{4}$		$\dfrac{5}{7}$
D	DC	–	–	0

Step III : MD Table (I) for Non-Sway Moments :

Joint		A	B		C		D
Type of joint		EHS	RJ		RJ		EFS
Member		AB	BA	BC	CB	CD	DC
COF			→ 1/2 0 ←	→ 1/2 1/2 ←		→ 1/2 1/2 ←	
DF		0	15/23	8/23	2/7	5/7	0
First cycle	FEM	9.375	− 28.125	5.21	− 5.21	0	0
	DM	− 9.375	14.94	7.97	1.49	3.72	
Second cycle	COM		− 4.69	0.75	3.99		1.86
	DM		2.57	1.37	− 1.14	− 2.85	
Third cycle	COM			− 0.57	0.69		− 1.43
	DM		0.37	0.20	− 0.20	− 0.49	
Fourth cycle	COM			− 0.1	0.1		− 0.25
	DM		0.065	0.035	− 0.029	− 0.071	
Fifth cycle	COM			− 0.015	0.017		− 0.035
	DM		0.009	0.005	− 0.005	0.012	
First set of final moments			− 14.86	14.86	− 0.30	0.30	0.14

Step IV : MD for Sway Moments :

(a) The basic information of K, COF and DF remains the same.

(b) Normalized relative sway stiffness factors (K_s).

Member	Relative sway stiffness factor	Normalized relative sway stiffness factor (K_s)
AB	$\dfrac{I}{4^2}$	1
DC	$\dfrac{I}{4^2}$	1

(c) Sway Moments :

Member	Arbitrary relative FEM due to sway
AB	M_{AB}^{FS} = 100 kN-m M_{BA}^{FS} = 100 kN-m
DC	M_{DC}^{FS} = 100 kN-m M_{CD}^{FS} = 100 kN-m

Step V : MD Table (II) for Sway Moments

Joint	A	B		C		D
Type of joint	EHS	RJ		RJ		EFS
Member	AB	BA	BC	CB	CD	DC
COF		→1/2		→1/2		→1/2
		0←		1/2←		1/2←
DF	0	15/23	8/23	2/7	5/7	
First cycle FEM	100	100	0	0	100	100
DM	−100	−65.22	−34.78	−28.57	−71.43	
Second cycle COM		−50	−14.28	−17.39		−35.72
DM		41.92	22.36	4.97	12.42	
Third cycle COM			2.49	11.18		6.21
DM		−1.63	−0.86	−3.19	−7.99	
Fourth cycle COM			−1.6	−0.43		−4.0
DM		1.04	0.56	0.12	0.31	
Fifth cycle COM			0.06	0.28		0.15
DM		−0.039	−0.021	−0.08	−0.2	
First set of final moments		26.07	−26.07	−33.11	33.11	66.64

$$M_{AB} = M^I_{AB} + C\,M^{II}_{AB} = 0$$

$$M_{BA} = M^I_{BA} + C\,M^{II}_{BA} = -14.86 + C \times 26.07$$

$$M_{CD} = M^I_{CD} + C\,M^{II}_{CD} = 0.30 + C \times 33.11$$

$$M_{DC} = M^I_{DC} + C\,M^{II}_{DC} = 0.18 + C \times 66.64$$

where C is a correction factor to be evaluated from the condition of horizontal shear equilibrium for structure.

Step VI : Horizontal shear equilibrium.

Horizontal shear equilibrium of structure gives:

$$H_A + H_D - 50 = 0$$

$$H_A = \frac{M_{AB} + M_{BA}}{4} + 50$$

$$H_D = \frac{M_{CD} + M_{DC}}{4}$$

$$\therefore\ M_{AB} + M_{BA} + 50 + M_{CD} + M_{DC} - 200 = 0$$

$$-14.86 + C \times 26.07 + 0.3 + C \times 33.11 + 0.18 + C \times 66.64 = 150$$

$$125.82\,C = 164.38$$

$$C = 1.31$$

Step VII : Corrected moments of second set will be obtained by multiplying these moments by C and then added to first set of moments gives net final moments.

Member	AB	BA	BC	CB	CD	DC
Corrected moments of second set	0	34.15	− 34.15	− 43.3	43.31	87.29
Moments of first set	0	− 14.86	14.86	− 0.30	0.30	− 0.14
Net final moments		19.29	− 19.29	− 43.60	43.67	87.15

Step VIII: FBD of members is as shown in Fig. 3.28 (b). Considering equilibrium of each member and of complete structure all the reaction components are found out as shown in Fig. 3.28.

Step IX : Shear force diagram is as shown in Fig. 3.28 (c).

Step X : Bending moment diagrams are as shown in Fig. 3.28 (d) and Fig. 3.28 (e).

Step XI : FBD of structure is as shown in Fig. 3.28 (f).

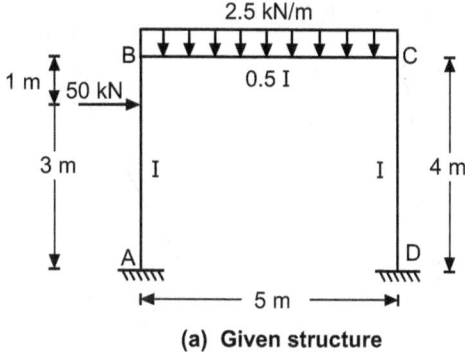

(a) Given structure

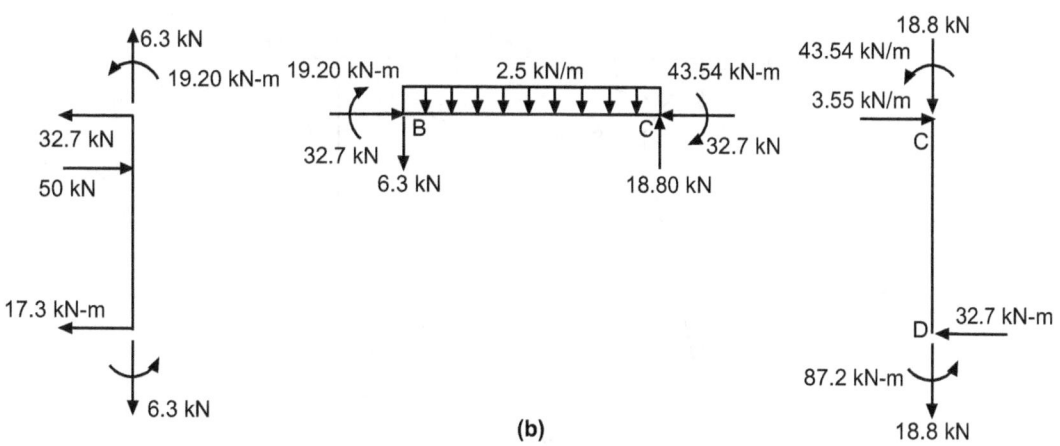

(b)

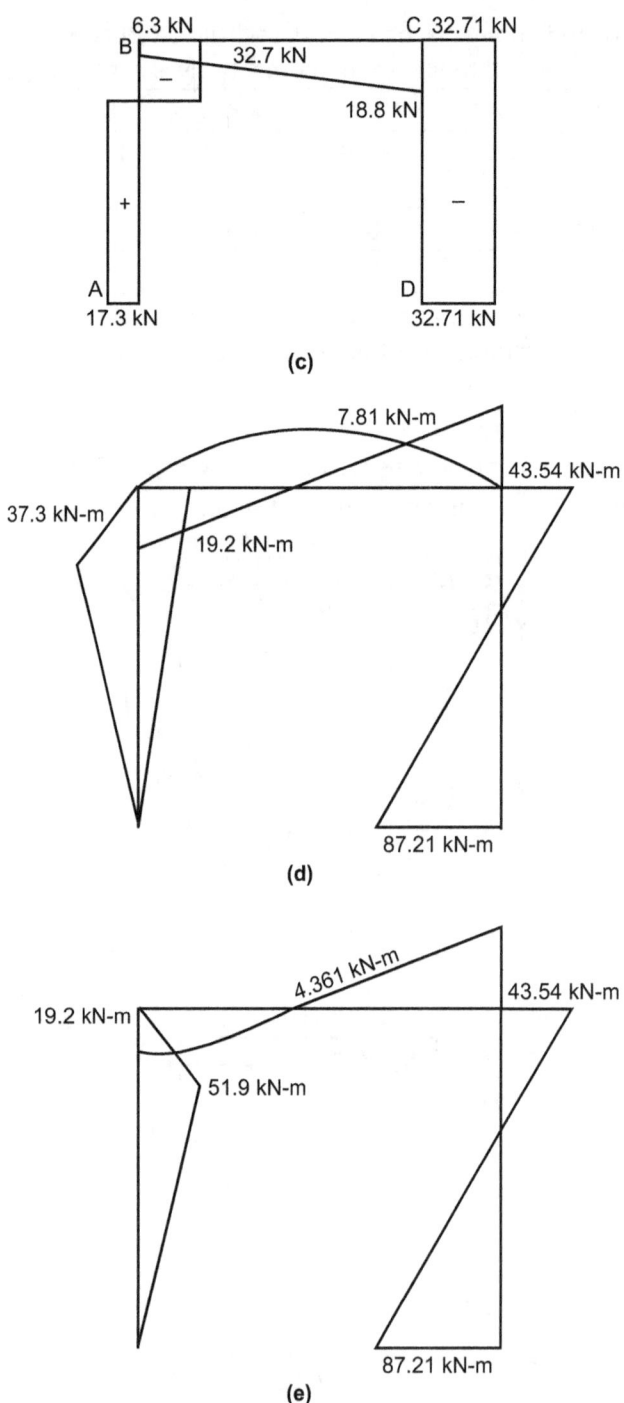

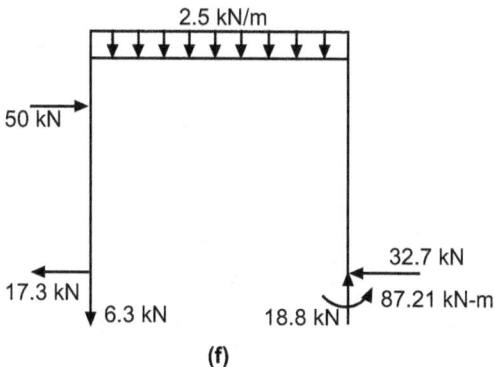

(f)

Fig. 3.28 : For Illustrative Example 3.23

Example 3.24 : *The frame loaded as shown in Fig. 3.29 (a) has members AB, BC and CD with flexural rigidities EI = 60×10^3 kN-m², 40×10^3 kN-m² and 90×10^3 kN-m² respectively. Analyse the frame by slope-deflection method.*

Data : The frame is supported and loaded as shown in Fig. 3.29 (a).

Type of Frame : Sway frame.

Object : Structural analysis.

Concepts and Equations : (1) M_D technique based on normalized relative stiffness factors and distribution factors,

(2) Normalized relative sway factors,

(3) Shear equilibrium condition and correction factors.

Procedure :

Step I : Fixed-End Moments :

Member	FEM with Calculations
AB	$M_{AB}^F = 0$
	$M_{BA}^F = 0$
BC	$M_{BC}^F = \dfrac{wab^2}{l^2} + \dfrac{w \times l^2}{12} = \dfrac{50 \times 1 \times 3^2}{4^2} + \dfrac{20 \times 4^2}{12} = 54.79$ kN-m
	$M_{CB}^F = -\dfrac{wa^2b}{l^2} - \dfrac{wl^2}{12} = -\dfrac{50 \times 1^2 \times 3}{4^2} - \dfrac{20 \times 4^2}{12} = -36.04$ kN-m
DC	$M_{DC}^F = 0$
	$M_{CD}^F = 0$

Step II : Distribution Factors :

Joint	Member	K	ΣK	DF = $\frac{K}{\Sigma K}$
A	AB	–	–	0
B	BA	$\frac{4\,EI}{L} = \frac{4\,E\,(1.5\,I)}{5}$	$\frac{44}{20}\,EI$	$\frac{6}{11}$
	BC	$\frac{4\,EI}{L} = \frac{4\,EI}{4}$		$\frac{5}{11}$
C	CB	$\frac{4\,EI}{L} = \frac{4\,EI}{4}$	$\frac{47}{20}\,EI$	$\frac{20}{47}$
	CD	$\frac{3\,EI}{L} = \frac{3\,E\,(2.25\,I)}{5}$		$\frac{27}{47}$
D	DC	–	–	

Step III : MD Table (I) for Non-Sway Moments :

Joint		A	B		C		D
Type of joint		EFS	RJ		RJ		EFS
Member		AB	BA	BC	CB	CD	DC
COF			→1/2 1/2←	→1/2 1/2←	→1/2 1/2←		
DF		0	6/11	5/11	20/47	27/47	
First cycle	FEM			54.79	–36.04		
	DM		–29.89	–24.9	15.34	20.70	
Second cycle	COM	–14.945	7.67		–12.45		
	DM		–4.18	–3.49	5.29	7.16	
Third cycle	COM	–2.09	2.645		–1.745		
	DM		–1.44	–1.205	0.74	1.005	
Fourth cycle	COM	–0.72	0.37		–0.602		
	DM		–0.20	–0.17	0.26	0.342	
Fifth cycle	COM	–0.10	0.13		–0.085		
	DM		–0.071	–0.059	0.036	0.049	
First set of final moments		–17.855	–35.781	35.781	–29.256	29.256	

Step IV : MD for Sway Moments.

(a) The basic information of K, COF and DF remains the same.

(b) Normalized relative sway stiffness factors (K_S).

Member	Relative sway stiffness factor	Normalized relative sway stiffness factor [K_S]
AB	$\dfrac{1.5\,I}{5^2}$	1.5
DC	$\dfrac{2.25\,I}{5^2}$	2.25

Step V : Sway Moments :

Member	Arbitrary relative FEM due to sway
AB	$M_{AB}^{FS} = 60$ kN-m $M_{BA}^{FS} = 60$ kN-m
DC	$M_{DC}^{FS} = 90$ kN-m $M_{CD}^{FS} = 90$ kN-m

Step VI : MD Table II for Sway Moments :

Joint		A	B		C		D
Type of joint		EFS	RJ		RJ		EFS
Member		AB	BA	BC	CB	CD	DC
COF			→ 1/2 1/2 ←	→ 1/2 1/2 ←		→ 1/2 1/2 ←	
DF		0	6/11	5/11	20/47	27/47	0
First cycle	FEM DM	60	60 − 32.72	0 − 27.28	0 − 38.29	90 − 51.71	90 − 90
Second cycle	COM DM	− 16.36	10.45	− 19.15 8.7	− 13.64 24.96	− 45 33.69	
Third cycle	COM DM	5.22	− 6.81	12.48 − 5.67	4.35 − 1.85	− 2.5	
Fourth cycle	COM DM	− 3.41	0.50	− 0.92 0.42	− 2.83 1.2	1.63	
Fifth cycle	COM DM	0.25	− 0.33	0.6 − 0.27	0.21 − 0.089	− 0.121	
Second set of final moments		45.7	31.09	− 31.09	− 25.99	25.99	0

$$M_{AB} = M_{AB}^{I} + C\,M_{AB}^{II}$$

$$M_{BA} = M_{BA}^{I} + C\,M_{BA}^{II}$$

$$M_{CD} = M_{CD}^{I} + C\,M_{CD}^{II}$$

$$M_{DC} = M_{DC}^{I} + C\,M_{DC}^{II}$$

where C is a correction factor to be obtained from shear equilibrium equations developed as follows.

Step VII : Shear Equilibrium Condition : Horizontal shear equilibrium gives:
$$H_A + H_D = 0$$
$$\frac{M_{AB} + M_{BA}}{5} + \frac{M_{CD} + M_{DC}}{5} = 0$$
$$M_{AB} + M_{BA} + M_{CD} + M_{DC} = 0$$
$$-17.855 + C \times 45.7 - 35.781 + C \times 31.09 + 29.256 + 25.99\,C = 0$$
$$102.78\,C = 24.38$$
$$C = 0.237$$

Step VIII : Corrected moments of second set will be obtained by multiplying these moments by C and then added to first set of moments gives net final moments.

Member	AB	BA	BC	CB	CD	DC
Corrected moments of second set	10.83	7.37	– 7.37	– 6.16	6.16	0
Moments of first set	– 17.855	– 35.781	35.781	– 29.256	29.256	0
Net final moments	– 7.02	– 28.41	28.41	– 35.416	35.416	0

Step IX : FBD of members is as shown in Fig. 3.29 (b). Considering equilibrium of each member and of complete structure all the reaction components are found out as shown in figure.

Step X : Shear force diagram is as shown in Fig. 3.29 (c).

Step XI : Bending moment diagrams are as shown in Fig. 3.29 (d) and Fig. 3.29 (e).

Step XII : FBD of structure is as shown in Fig. 3.29 (f).

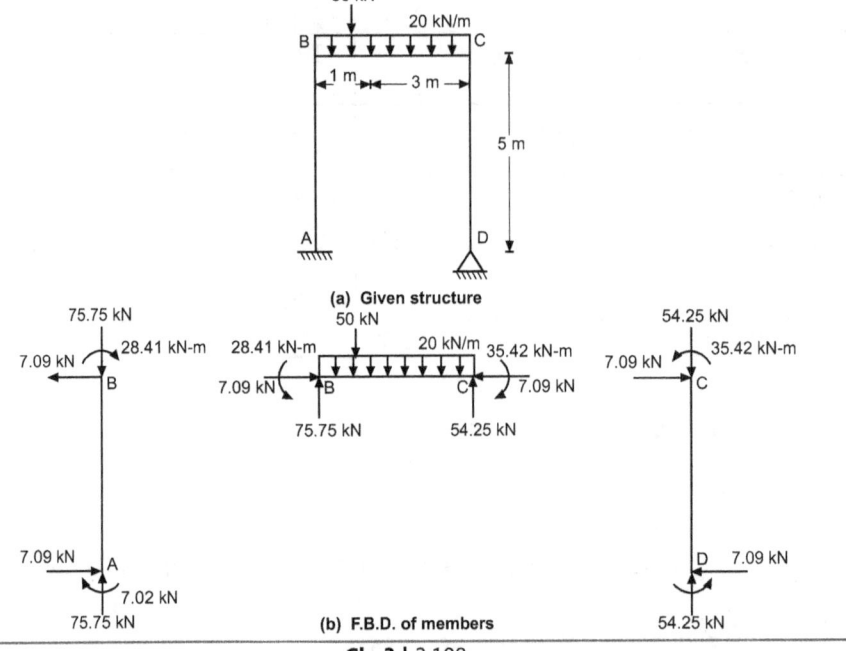

(a) Given structure

(b) F.B.D. of members

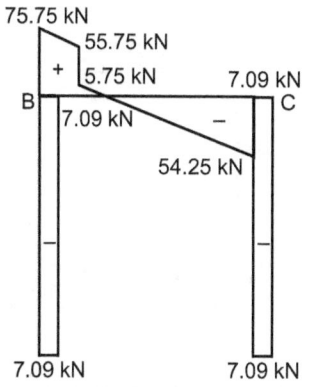

(c) S.F.D.

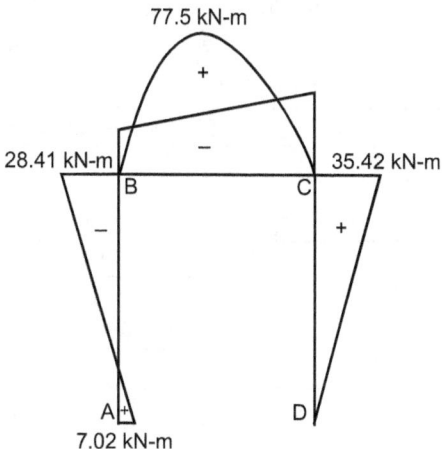

(d) B.M.D. by superposition

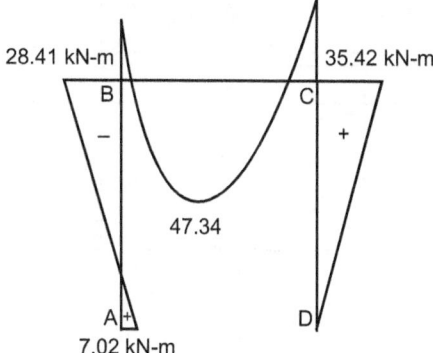

(e) B.M.D. on tension side

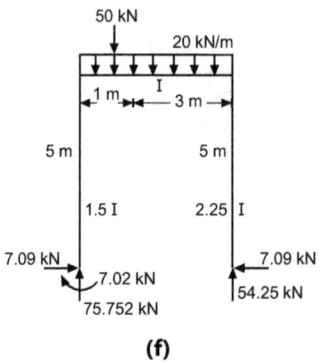

(f)

Fig. 3.29 : For Illustrative Example 3.24

Example 3.25 : *Analyse the portal frame shown in Fig. 3.30 (a). All members have the same flexural rigidities.*

Solution : Step I : Fixed-End Moments :

Member	FEM with calculations
AB	$M^F_{AB} = 0$ $M^F_{BA} = 0$
BC	$M^F_{BC} = \dfrac{wl^2}{12} = \dfrac{30 \times 4^2}{12} = 40$ kN-m $M^F_{CB} = -\dfrac{30 \times 4^2}{12} = -40$ kN-m
DC	$M^F_{DC} = 0$ $M^F_{CD} = 0$

Step II : Distribution Factors :

Joint	Member	K	ΣK	DF = $\dfrac{K}{\Sigma K}$
A	AB	–	–	0
B	BA	$\dfrac{3 EI}{L} = \dfrac{3 EI}{6} = \dfrac{EI}{2}$	$\dfrac{3}{2} I$	$\dfrac{1}{3}$
	BC	$\dfrac{4 EI}{L} = \dfrac{4 EI}{4} = EI$		$\dfrac{2}{3}$
C	CB	$\dfrac{4 EI}{L} = \dfrac{4 EI}{4} = EI$	2 EI	$\dfrac{1}{2}$
	CD	$\dfrac{3 EI}{L} = \dfrac{3 EI}{3} = EI^3$		$\dfrac{1}{2}$
D	DC	–	–	–

TOS – II (TE CIVIL SEM. VI NMU) — MOMENT DISTRIBUTION METHOD

Step III : MD Table (I) for Non-Sway Moments :

Joint		A	B		C		D
Type of joint		EFS	RJ		RJ		EFS
Member		AB	BA	BC	CB	CD	DC
COF			→ 1/2 1/2 ←		→ 1/2 1/2 ←		→ 1/2 1/2 ←
DF		0	1/3	2/3	1/2	1/2	
First cycle	FEM	0	0	40	– 40	0	0
	DM		– 13.33	– 26.67	20	20	
Second cycle	COM	–		10	– 13.33		–
	DM		– 3.33	– 6.67	6.67	6.67	
Third cycle	COM	–		3.33	– 3.33		–
	DM		– 1.11	– 2.22	+ 1.67	1.67	
Fourth cycle	COM	–		0.84	– 1.11		–
	DM		– 0.28	– 0.56	– 0.55	+ 0.55	
Fifth cycle	COM	–		0.27	– 0.28		–
	DM		– 0.09	– 0.18	0.14	0.14	
First set of final moments		0	– 18.14	18.14	– 29.02	29.02	0

Step IV : MD for Sway Moments :

(a) The basic information of K, COF and DF remains the same.

(b) Normalized relative sway stiffness factors [K_S].

Member	Relative sway stiffness factor	Normalized relative sway stiffness factor [K_S]
AB	$\dfrac{I}{6^2}$	9
DC	$\dfrac{I}{3^2}$	36

(c) **Sway Moments :**

Member	Arbitrary relative FEM due to sway
AB	$M_{AB}^{FC} = 9$ $M_{BA}^{FC} = 9$
DC	$M_{DC}^{FS} = 36$ $M_{CD}^{FS} = 36$

Step V : MD Table (II) for Sway Moments :

Joint		A		B			C		D
Type of joint		EFS		RJ			RJ		EHS
Member		AB	BA		BC	CB		CD	DC
COF			→1/2 1/2←		→1/2 1/2←			→1/2 1/2←	
DF				1/3	2/3	1/2		1/2	
First cycle	FEM	9	9		0	0		36	36
	DM	−9	−3		−6	−18		−18	−36
Second cycle	COM		−4.5		−9	−3		−18	
	DM		4.5		9	10.5		10.5	
Third cycle	COM				5.25	4.5			
	DM		−1.75		−3.5	−2.25		−2.25	
Fourth cycle	COM				−1.13	−1.75			
	DM		0.38		0.75	0.88		0.88	
Fifth cycle	COM				0.44	0.37			
	DM		−0.15		−0.29	−0.19		−0.19	
Second set of final moments			4.48		−4.48	−8.94		8.94	0

$$M_{AB} = M^I_{AB} + C\, M^{II}_{AB} = 0$$

$$M_{BA} = M^I_{BA} + C\, M^{II}_{BA} = -18.14 + C \times 4.48$$

$$M_{CD} = M^I_{CD} + C\, M^{II}_{CD} = 29.02 + C \times 8.94$$

$$M_{DC} = M^I_{DC} + C\, M^{II}_{DC} = 0$$

where C is a correction factor to be evaluated from the condition of horizontal shear equilibrium for structure.

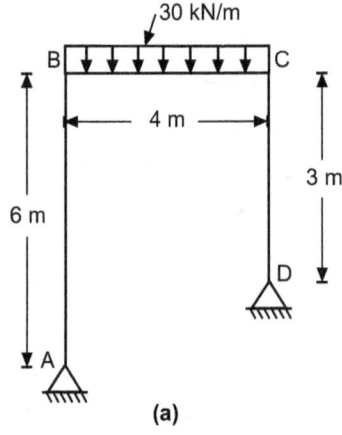

(a)

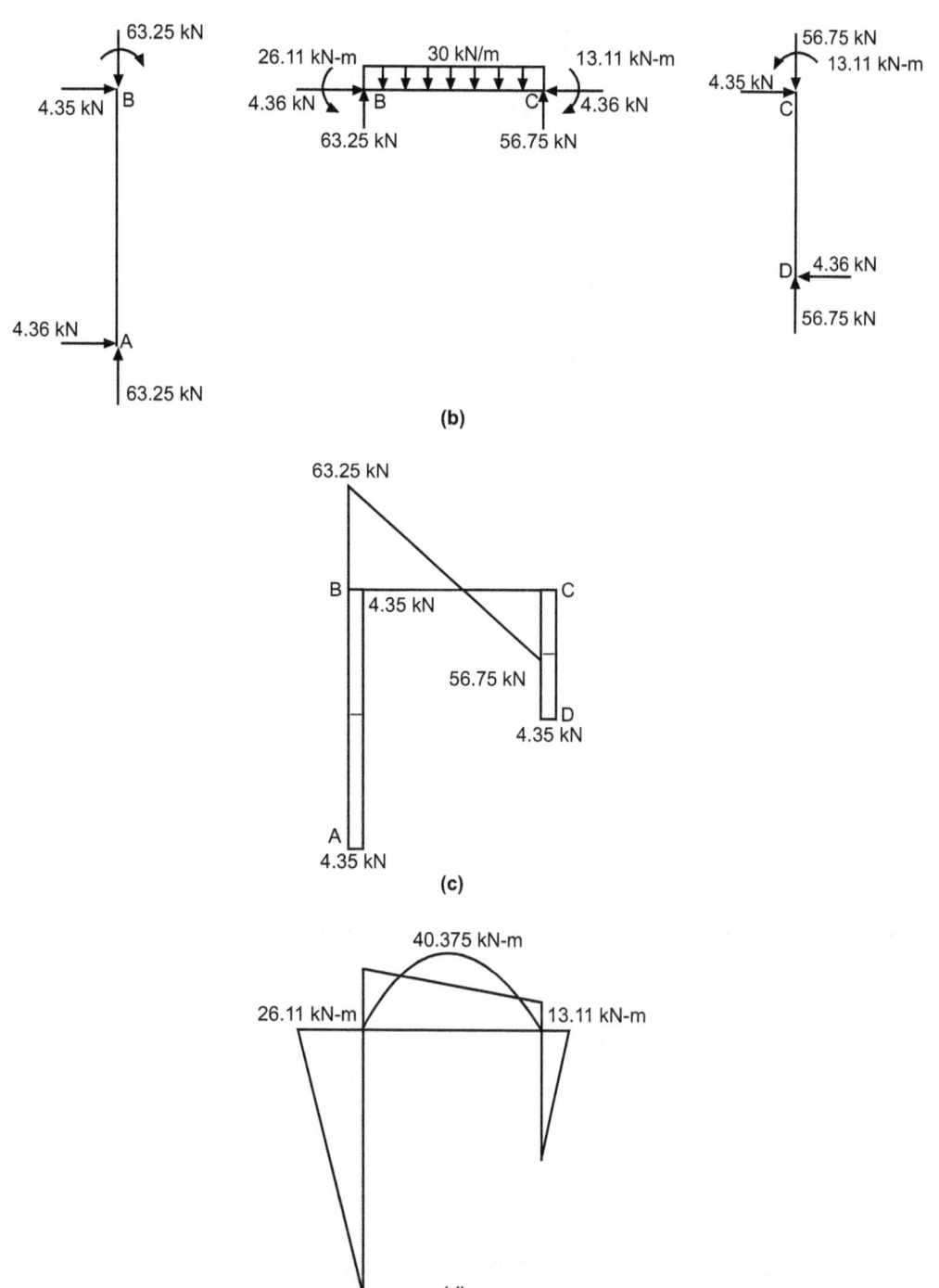

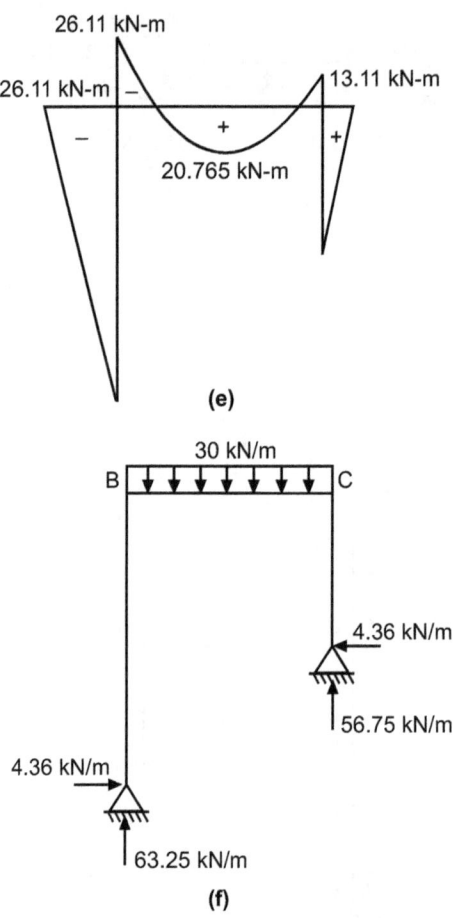

Fig. 3.30 : For Illustrative Example 3.25

Step VI : Horizontal shear equilibrium of structure gives :

$$-H_A + H_D = 0$$

$$\frac{M_{AB} + M_{BA}}{6} + \frac{M_{CD} + M_{DC}}{3} = 0$$

$$M_{BA} + 2 M_{CD} = 0$$

$$-18.14 + C \times 4.48 + (29.02 + 8.94\ C) \times 2 = 0$$

$$22.36\ C = -39.9$$

$$C = -1.784$$

Step VII : Corrected moments of second set will be obtained by multiplying these moments by C and then add to first set of moments gives net final moments.

Member	AB	BA	BC	CB	CD	DC
Corrected moments of second set		− 8.09	8.09	+ 15.94	− 15.94	
Moments of first set	0	− 18.14	18.14	− 29.02	29.02	
Net final moments		− 26.14	26.14	− 13.08	13.08	

Step VIII : FBD of members is as shown in Fig. 3.30 (b). Considering equilibrium of each member and of complete structure all the reaction components are found out as shown in Fig. 3.30.

Step IX : Shear force diagram is as shown in Fig. 3.30 (c).

Step X : Bending moment diagrams are as shown in Fig. 3.30 (d) and Fig. 3.30 (e).

Step XI : FBD of structure is as shown in Fig. 3.30 (f).

Example 3.26 : Analyse the frame shown in Fig. 3.31 (a).

Data : The frame is supported and loaded as shown in Fig. 3.31 (a).

Type of Frame : Sway frame.

Object : Structural analysis.

Concepts and Equations : (1) MD technique based on normalized relative stiffness factors and distribution factors, (2) Normalized relative sway factors, (3) Shear equilibrium condition and correction factor procedure.

Solution : Step I : Fixed-End Moments :

Member	FEM with calculations
AB	$M_{AB}^F = 0$ $M_{BA}^F = 0$
BC	$M_{BC}^F = \dfrac{2.5 \times 4^2}{12} = 3.33$ kN-m $M_{CB}^F = -\dfrac{2.5 \times 4^2}{12} = -3.33$ kN-m
DC	$M_{DC}^F = \dfrac{5 \times 1.5 \times 3.5^2}{5^2} = 3.675$ kN-m $M_{CD}^F = \dfrac{-5 \times 1.5^2 \times 3.5}{5^2} = -1.575$ kN-m

Step II : Distribution Factors :

Joint	Member	K	ΣK	$DF = \dfrac{K}{\Sigma K}$
A	AB	—	—	0
B	BA	$\dfrac{3}{4} \times \dfrac{I}{4} = \dfrac{3}{16} I$	$\left(\dfrac{11}{16} I\right)$	$\dfrac{3}{11} I$
	BC	$\dfrac{I}{4} = \dfrac{2I}{4} = \dfrac{I}{2}$		$\dfrac{8}{11} I$
C	CB	$\dfrac{I}{4} = \dfrac{2I}{4} = \dfrac{I}{2}$	$\left(\dfrac{11}{16} I\right)$	$\dfrac{8}{11} I$
	CD	$\dfrac{3}{4} \times \dfrac{I}{4} = \dfrac{3I}{16}$		$\dfrac{3}{11} I$
D	DC	—	—	0

Step III : MD Table (I) for Non-Sway Moments :

Joint		A	B		C		D
Type of joint		EFS	RJ		RJ		EFS
Member		AB	BA	BC	CB	CD	DC
COF			→ 1/2	→ 1/2		→ 1/2	
			1/2 ←	1/2 ←		1/2 ←	
DF		0	3/11	8/11	8/11	3/11	0
First cycle	FEM	0	0	3.33	− 3.33	3.675	− 1.575
	DM		− 0.91	− 2.42	− 0.25	− 0.09	+ 1.575
Second cycle	COM			− 0.12	− 1.21	0.78	
	DM		0.032	0.087	0.31	0.11	
Third cycle	COM			0.15	0.043		
	DM		− 0.04	− 0.11	− 0.031	− 0.011	
Fourth cycle	COM			− 0.015	− 0.05		
	DM		0.004	0.011	0.036	0.014	
Fifth cycle	COM			0.018	0.005		
	DM		− 0.005	− 0.013	− 0.0036	− 0.0014	
First set of final moments		0	− 0.92	0.92	− 4.48	4.48	0

Step IV : MD for Sway Moments :

(a) The basic information of K, COF and DF remains the same.

(b) Normalized relative sway stiffness factors $[K_S]$.

MOMENT DISTRIBUTION METHOD

Member	Relative sway stiffness factor	Normalized relative sway stiffness factor [K_S]
AB	$\dfrac{I}{4^2}$	1.25
DC	$\dfrac{1.25\,I}{5^2}$	1

(c) **Sway Moments :**

Member	Arbitrary relative FEM due to sway
AB	$M_{AB}^{FS} =$ $M_{BA}^{FS} =$
DC	$M_{DC}^{FS} =$ $M_{CD}^{FS} =$

Step V : MD Table II for sway Moments :

Joint		A	B		C		D
Type of joint		EFS	RJ		RJ		EHS
Member		AB	BA	BC	CB	CD	DC
COF			→ 1/2		→ 1/2		→ 1/2
			1/2 ←		1/2 ←		1/2 ←
DF		0	3/11	8/11	8/11	3/11	0
First cycle	FEM	20	20	0	0	16	16
	DM	−20	−5.96	−14.54	−11.64	−4.36	−16
Second cycle	COM		−10	−5.82	−7.27	−8	
	DM		4.31	11.51	11.11	4.16	
Third cycle	COM			5.55	5.75		
	DM		−1.51	−4.04	−4.18	−1.57	
Fourth cycle	COM			−2.09	−2.02	1	
	DM		0.57	1.52	1.47	0.55	
Fifth cycle	COM			0.73	0.76		
	DM		−0.2	−0.53	−0.55	−0.21	
Second set of final moments			−7.71	7.71	6.57	−6.57	

$$M_{AB} = M_{AB}^{I} + C\,M_{AB}^{II}$$

$$M_{BA} = M_{BA}^{I} + C\,M_{BA}^{II}$$

$$M_{CD} = M_{CD}^{I} + C\,M_{CD}^{II}$$

$$M_{DC} = M_{DC}^{I} + C\,M_{DC}^{II}$$

where C is a correction factor to be obtained from shear equilibrium equation developed as follows:

Step VI : Shear equilibrium condition :
Horizontal shear equilibrium gives

$$H_A + H_D = 0$$

$$\frac{M_{AB} + M_{BA}}{4} + \frac{M_{CD} + M_{DC}}{5} + 5 = 0$$

$$\frac{-0.92 - 7.71 C}{4} + \frac{4.48 - 6.57 C - 5 \times 1.5}{5} = -5$$

$$-0.23 - 1.93 C - 0.604 - 1.314 C = -5$$

$$-3.24 C = -4.16$$

$$C = 1.284$$

Step VII : Corrected moments of second set will be obtained by multiplying these moments by C and then added to first set of moments gives net final moments.

Member	AB	BA	BC	CB	CD	DC
Corrected moments of second set	0	− 9.90	9.90	8.44	− 8.44	0
Moments of first set	0	− 0.92	0.92	− 4.48	4.48	0
Net final moments	0	− 10.82	10.82	3.96	− 3.96	0

Step VIII : FBD of members is as shown in Fig. 3.31 (b).

Considering equilibrium of each member and of complete structure all the reaction components are found out as shown in Fig. 3.31.

Step IX : Shear force diagram is as shown in Fig. 3.31 (c).
Step X : Bending moment diagrams are as shown in Fig. 3.31 (d) and Fig. 3.31 (e).
Step XI : FBD of structure is as shown in Fig. 3.31 (f).

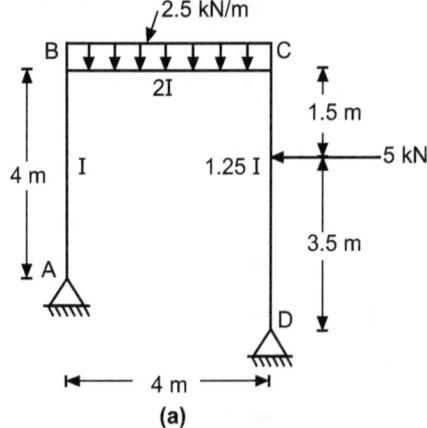

(a)

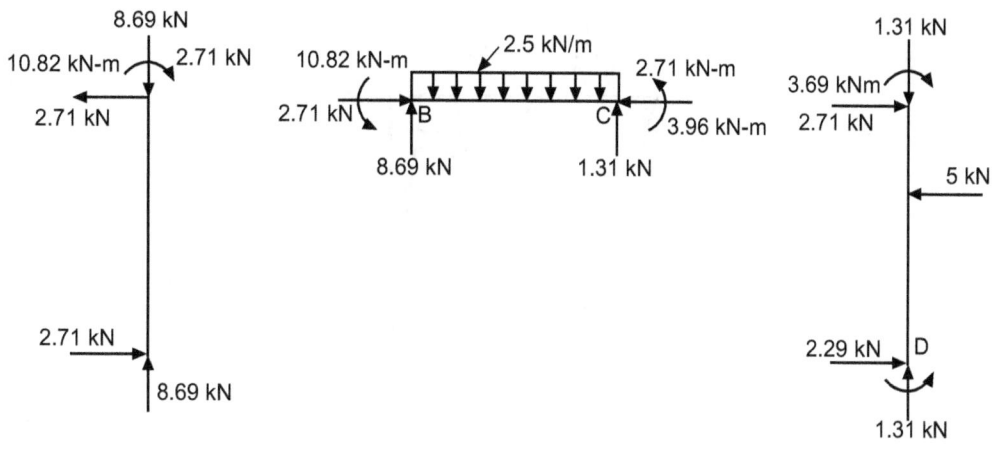

(b)

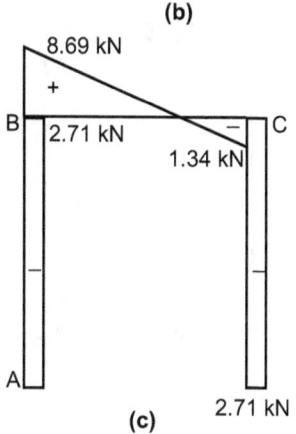

(c)

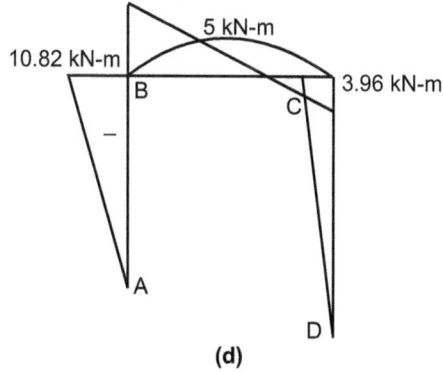

(d)

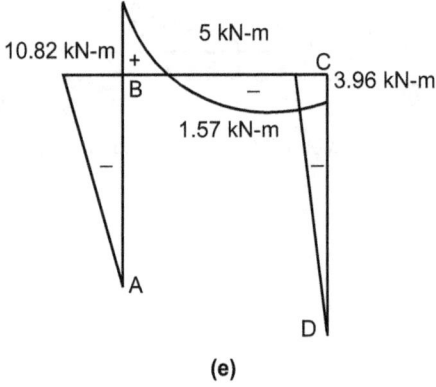

(e)

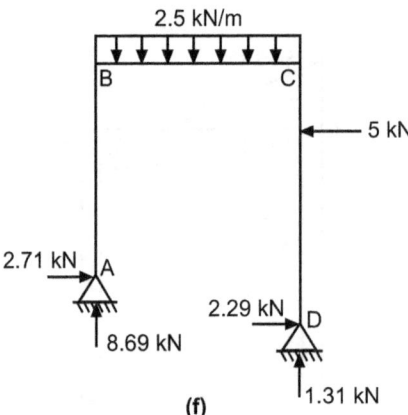

(f)

Fig. 3.31 : For Illustrative Example 3.26

Chapter 4
APPROXIMATE ANALYSIS OF MULTISTORY FRAMES

4.1 INTRODUCTION

Analysis of multistoreyed structures involves large number of unknowns, also geometric properties of cross-section of members and material properties are pre-requisites of exact analysis. Therefore, it becomes necessary to perform some approximate analysis to arrive at an estimate of member sizes. This type of analysis is also useful in checking the results obtained by computer program which uses more elaborate computations.

In approximate methods of analysis, statically indeterminate structure is converted to statically determinate structure by making appropriate assumptions and then analysed for member forces using laws of statics. This chapter deals with commonly used approximate methods of analysis for rigid jointed multistoreyed, multibay two-dimensional frames.

Following are approximate methods of analysis :

Substitute frame method for vertical loads.

Any one of the following methods for horizontal loads :

    (a) Portal method.

    (b) Cantilever method.

4.2 SUBSTITUTE FRAME METHOD

This method is used for the analysis of multistorey frames subjected to vertical (gravity) loads only. In this method, only a part of the frame is considered for the analysis. The part considered is called a **substitute frame**. Here, it is assumed that moments transferred from one floor to another floor are negligible and hence analysis can be made floor by floor. So, a substitute frame is consisting of floor beams and columns above and below it. Columns are considered as fixed at far ends.

To find moments and shears in the second floor of multistorey frame shown in Fig. 4.1, the substitute frame shown in Fig. 4.2 is considered.

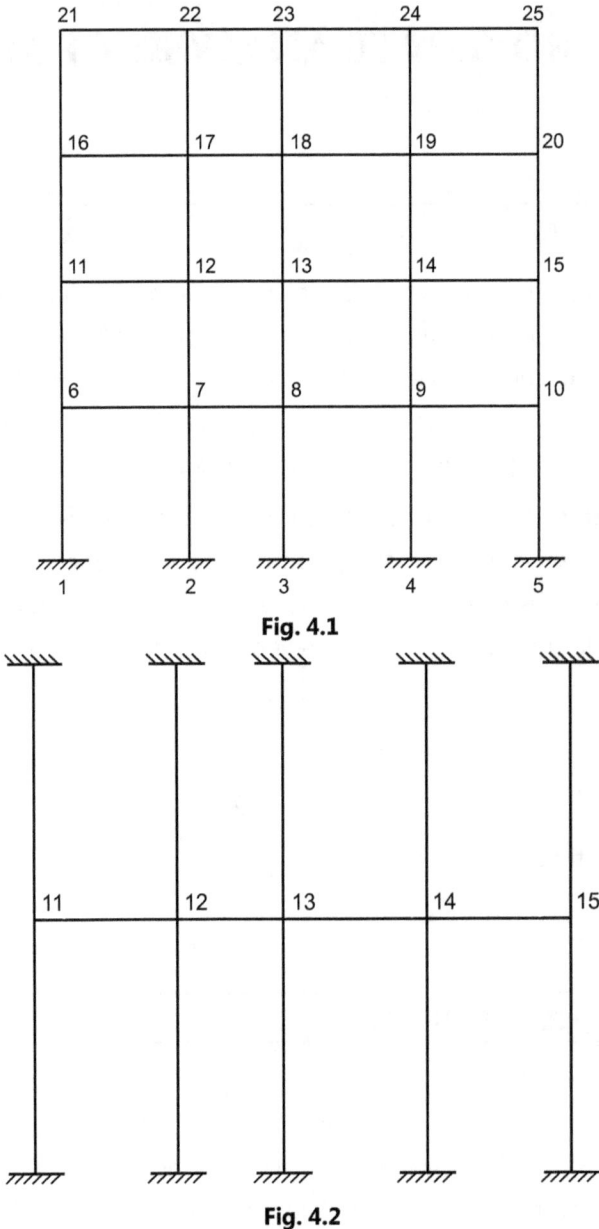

Fig. 4.1

Fig. 4.2

In the multistorey frame, both dead load and live load together constitute the vertical load. Dead load acts throughout the frame and at all times. Live load may act through out the frame or on a part of it at a particular time. Hence, for analysis, various combinations of live loads are to be considered.

Critical live load positions are shown in Fig. 4.3 to Fig. 4.5 to get various design moments in beams.

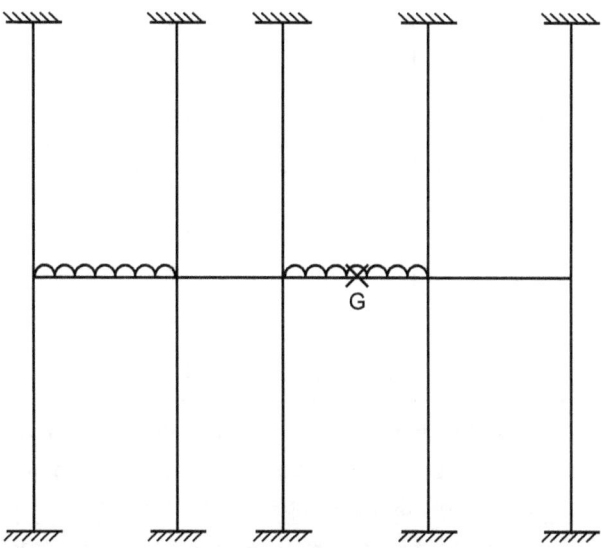

Fig. 4.3 : Live loading for maximum positive moment at G

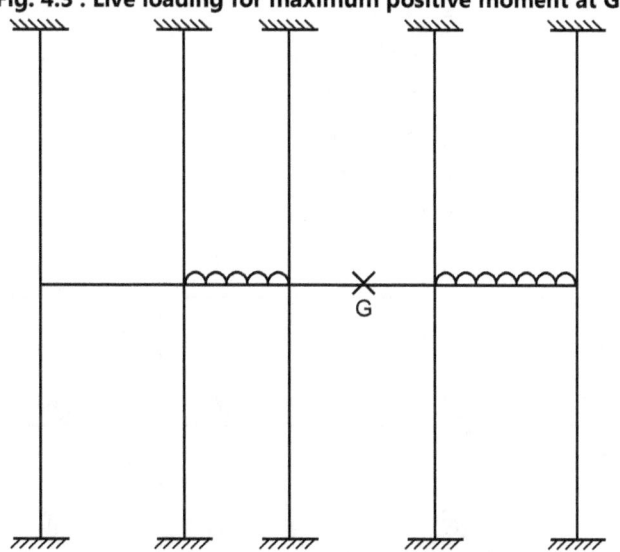

Fig. 4.4 : Live loading for maximum negative moment at G

The design moment in the column is obtained for any one series of alternate loading of spans.

Moment distribution is done for only two cycles and hence it is called the **two-cycle method**.

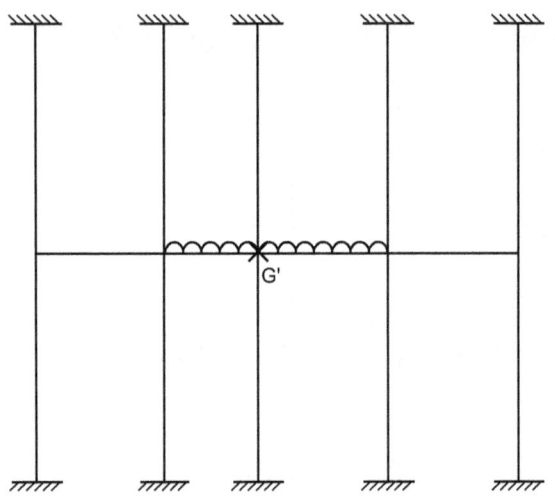

Fig. 4.5 : Live loading for maximum negative moment at G'

At any joint, moment is mainly due to the loadings on the two adjacent spans. Hence, to find the moment at a joint, only two adjacent spans are considered.

Example 4.1 : *Analyse the intermediate frame of a multistoreyed frame shown in Fig. 4.6.*

Given : Spacing of frame   = 4.0 m
         D.L. on floors   = 4 kN/m²
         L.L. on floors   = 3 kN/m²
         Self weight of beams = 5 kN/m for beams of span 9 m
                                = 4 kN/m for beams of span 6 m
                                = 3 kN/m for beams of span 3 m.

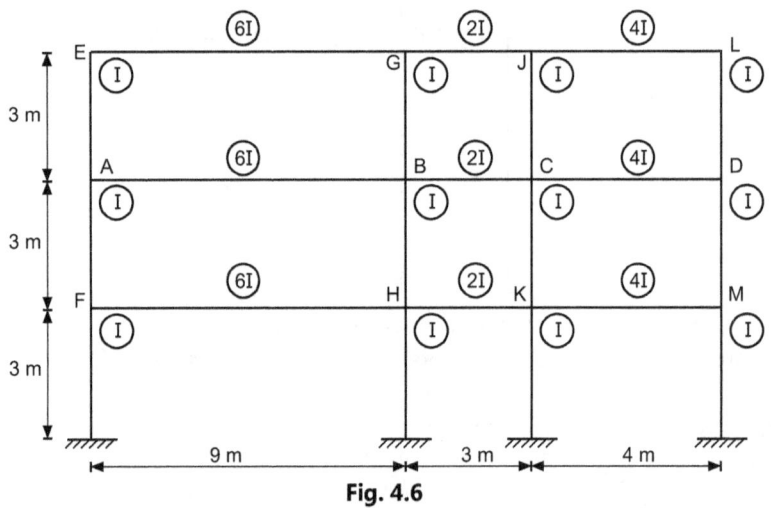

Fig. 4.6

Solution : The analysis for the second floor is given below. Similar analysis may be carried out to all the other floors to get the complete solution.

The substitute frame is as shown in Fig. 4.7.

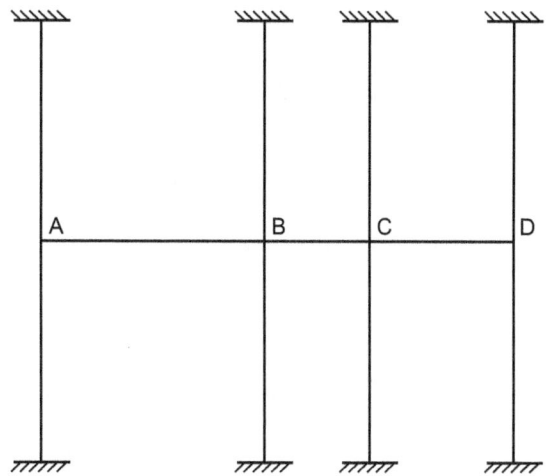

Fig. 4.7

The distribution factors are calculated in Table 4.1.

Table 4.1

Joint	Members	Relative stiffness	Sum	D.F.
	AE	$\dfrac{I}{3}$		$\dfrac{1}{4}$
A	AB	$\dfrac{6I}{9}$	$\dfrac{4I}{3}$	$\dfrac{1}{2}$
	AF	$\dfrac{I}{3}$		$\dfrac{1}{4}$
	BG	$\dfrac{I}{3}$		$\dfrac{1}{6}$
B	BA	$\dfrac{6I}{9}$	$\dfrac{6I}{3}$	$\dfrac{1}{3}$
	BC	$\dfrac{2I}{3}$		$\dfrac{1}{3}$
	BH	$\dfrac{I}{3}$		$\dfrac{1}{6}$

	CJ	$\frac{I}{3}$		$\frac{1}{6}$
C	CB	$\frac{2I}{3}$		$\frac{1}{3}$
	CD	$\frac{4I}{6}$	$\frac{6I}{3}$	$\frac{1}{3}$
	CK	$\frac{I}{3}$		$\frac{1}{6}$
D	DL	$\frac{I}{3}$		$\frac{1}{4}$
	DC	$\frac{4I}{6}$	$\frac{4I}{3}$	$\frac{1}{2}$
	DM	$\frac{I}{3}$		$\frac{1}{4}$

Loads :

Live load per meter run of girder = 3×4 = 12 kN/m

Dead load per meter run of girder = 4×4 = 16 kN/m

Dead load on 9 m beam = 16 + 5 = 21 kN/m

Dead load on 3 m beam = 16 + 3 = 19 kN/m

Dead load on 6 m beam = 16 + 4 = 20 kN/m

∴ Fixed-end moments due to dead load and total load are as shown in Table 4.2.

Table 4.2 : F.E.M. due to dead and total load

Span	F.M.E. due to DL	F.E.M. due to total load (DL + LL)
AB	141.75 kN-m	222.75 kN-m
BC	14.25 kN-m	23.25 kN-m
CD	60.0 kN-m	96.0 kN-m

Design Moments in Beams :

(1) To determine the maximum moments at mid-spans in AB and CD.

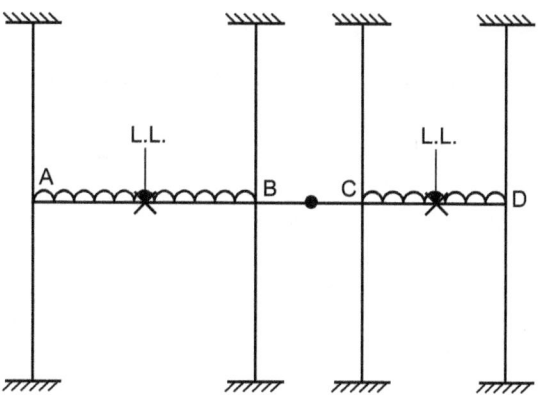

Fig. 4.8

Live load on AB and CD, dead load on ABCD.

D.F.	A $\frac{1}{2}$	$\frac{1}{3}$	B $\frac{1}{3}$	$\frac{1}{3}$	C $\frac{1}{3}$	D $\frac{1}{2}$
F.E.M.	− 222.75	+ 222.75	− 14.25	+ 14.25	− 96.0	+ 96.0
BAL	+ 111.38	− 69.5	− 69.5	+ 27.25	+ 27.25	− 48.0
COM	− 34.75	+ 55.69	+ 13.88	− 34.75	− 24.0	+ 13.88
BAL	+ 17.38	− 23.19	− 23.19	+ 19.58	+ 19.58	− 6.94
	− 128.74	+ 185.75	− 93.06	+ 26.33	− 73.17	+ 54.94
Free moment at centre of span = $\frac{wL^2}{8}$	334.12		21.38		144	
Mid-span moment	$334.12 - \frac{128.74 + 185.75}{2}$ = 176.88		$21.38 - \frac{93.06 + 26.33}{2}$ = −38.32		$144 - \frac{73.17 + 54.94}{2}$ = 79.95	

(2) To determine the maximum moment at mid-span in BC.

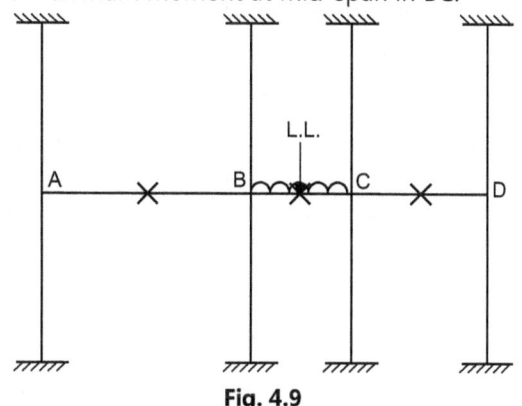

Fig. 4.9

Live load on BC, dead load on ABCD.

D.F.	A $\frac{1}{2}$	$\frac{1}{3}$	B $\frac{1}{3}$	$\frac{1}{3}$	C $\frac{1}{3}$	D $\frac{1}{2}$
F.E.M.	− 141.75	+ 141.75	− 23.25	+ 23.25	− 60.0	+ 60.0
BAL	+ 70.88	− 39.5	− 39.5	+ 12.25	+ 12.25	− 30.0
COM	− 19.75	+ 35.44	+ 6.13	− 19.75	− 15.0	+ 6.13
BAL	+ 9.88	− 13.86	− 13.86	+ 11.58	+ 11.58	− 3.06
	−80.74	+ 123.83	− 70.48	+ 27.33	− 51.17	+ 33.07
Free moment at mid-span $\left(=\frac{wl^2}{8}\right)$	212.63		34.88		90	
Final moment at mid-span	212.63 − $\frac{80.74 + 123.83}{2}$ = 110.35		34.88 − $\frac{70.48 + 27.33}{2}$ = −14.02		90 − $\frac{51.17 + 33.07}{2}$ = 47.88	

Design Moments in Columns :

For maximum moments in columns, alternate spans should be loaded with live load. In present case, there are two possibilities.

- Loading conditions are : Live load on AB and CD, while dead load on ABCD.
- Loading conditions are : Live load on BC, while dead load on ABCD.

Therefore, the possible cases for maximum moment in columns are the same as the two cases considered above. In the above moment distribution table, column moments are not noted down. At each cycle, distribution factor times unbalanced moment should have been noted as column moment. Column moments are not considered for distribution in beams. It can be determined after completing the moment distribution for the beam.

Column moment = Distribution factor of column × (−1) [FEMs + COMs]

These calculations are shown in tabular form below :

- Live load on AB and CD, dead load on ABCD.

	A		B		C	D
FEMs	− 222.75	+ 222.75	− 14.25	+ 14.25	− 96.0	+ 96.0
COMs	− 34.75	+ 55.69	+ 13.88	− 34.75	− 24.0	+ 13.88
FEMs + COMs	− 257.50	278.07		− 140.5		109.88
Column moment						
at top	64.38	− 46.34		+ 23.42		− 27.47
at bottom	64.38	− 46.34		+ 23.42		− 27.47

- Live load on BC only, dead load on ABCD.

	A	B		C		D
FEMs	− 141.75	+ 141.75	− 23.25	+ 23.25	− 60.0	+ 60.0
COMs	− 19.75	+ 35.44	+ 6.13	− 19.75	− 15.0	+ 6.13
FEMs + COMs	− 161.5	160.07		− 71.5		66.13
Column moment						
at top	40.38	− 26.68		+ 11.92		− 16.53
at bottom	40.38	− 26.68		+ 11.92		− 16.53

Design Moments in Columns :

	A	B	C	D
Design moment in columns				
at top	64.38	− 46.34	+ 23.42	− 27.47
at bottom	64.38	− 46.34	+ 23.42	− 27.47

Design Moments at Joints :

Moments at joints are negative (tension at top) moments and their maximum values occur only when adjoining panels are loaded with live loads.

For Maximum Moment at Joint A :

The condition of loading to obtain maximum moment at joint A is as,

Live load on AB only, while dead load on AB and BC.

The effect of dead load on other span is neglected.

	A	B		C		D
D.F.	$\frac{1}{2}$	$\frac{1}{3}$	$\frac{1}{3}$	$\frac{1}{3}$	$\frac{1}{3}$	$\frac{1}{2}$
F.E.M	− 222.75	+ 222.75	− 14.25	...	...	...
BAL	+ 111.38	− 69.5	− 69.5	...	...	...
COM	− 34.75	...	...	...	...	...
BAL	+ 17.38	...	...	...	...	...
Final	−128.74					

For Maximum Moment at Joint B :

Loading conditions are : Live load on AB and BC, while dead load on ABCD.

	A	B		C		D
D.F.	$\frac{1}{2}$	$\frac{1}{3}$	$\frac{1}{3}$	$\frac{1}{3}$	$\frac{1}{3}$	$\frac{1}{2}$
F.E.M.	− 222.75	+ 222.75	− 23.25	+ 23.25	− 60.0	+ 60.0
BAL	+ 111.38	− 66.50	− 66.50	+ 12.25	+ 12.25	...
COM	...	+ 55.69	+ 6.13	...	...	...
BAL	...	− 20.60	− 20.60	...	...	...
Final		+ 191.34	− 104.22			

For Maximum Moment at Joint C :

Loading conditions are : Live load on BC and CD, while dead load on AB.

	A	B		C		D
D.F.	$\frac{1}{2}$	$\frac{1}{3}$	$\frac{1}{3}$	$\frac{1}{3}$	$\frac{1}{3}$	$\frac{1}{2}$
F.E.M.	− 141.75	+ 141.75	− 23.25	+ 23.25	− 96.0	+ 96.0
BAL	...	− 39.5	− 39.5	+ 24.25	+ 24.25	− 48.0
COM	...	...	...	− 19.75	− 24.0	...
BAL	...	...	...	+ 14.58	+ 14.58	...
Final				+ 42.33	− 81.17	

For Mmaximum Moment at Joint D :

Loading conditions are : Live load on CD only, while dead load on BC and CD.
The effect of dead load on other spans is neglected.

	A	B		C		D
D.F.	$\frac{1}{2}$	$\frac{1}{3}$	$\frac{1}{3}$	$\frac{1}{3}$	$\frac{1}{3}$	$\frac{1}{2}$
F.E.M.	...	...	...	+ 14.25	− 96.0	+ 96.0
BAL	...	...	...	+ 27.25	+ 27.25	− 48.0
COM	...	...	...	...	...	+ 13.63
BAL	...	...	...	...	...	− 6.81
Final						+ 54.82

4.3 PORTAL METHOD

The Portal method is an approximate analysis used for analysing building frames subjected to lateral loading such as the one shown in Fig. 4.10 (a). This method is more appropriate for low rise (height is less than width) building frames. In the analysis, the following assumptions are made :

An inflection point is located at mid-height of each column,

An inflection point is located at centre of each beam, and

The horizontal shear is divided among all the columns on the basis that each interior column takes twice as much as the exterior columns.

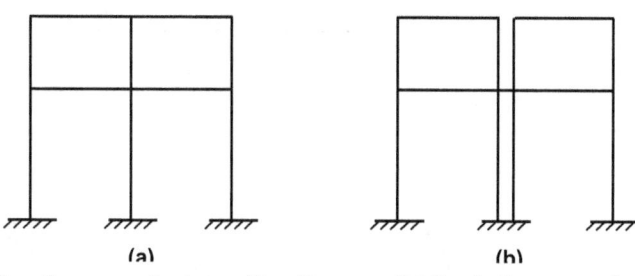

(a) Building frame under lateral loading   (b) Equivalent portals

Fig. 4.10

The basis of third assumption should be clear from Fig. 4.10 which indicates that interior column will resist the shear of two columns of individual portals.

Example 4.2 : Analyse the frame shown in Fig. 4.11 by portal method.

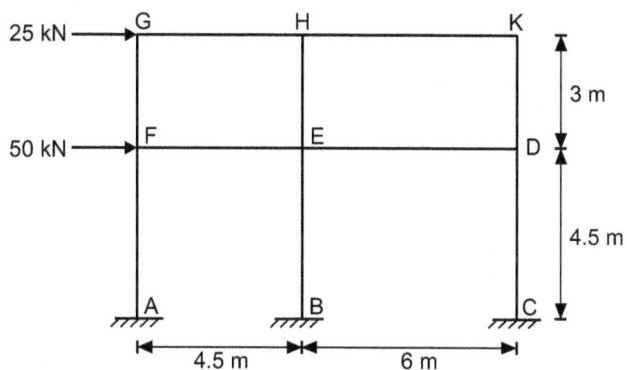

Fig. 4.11 : Given structure

Data : As shown in Fig. 4.11.

Required : BMD

Concept : Portal method.

Solution : Step 1 : Assuming points of contraflexure at mid-height of columns and considering FBD of upper storey as shown in Fig. 4.12 (a).

$\Sigma F_x = 0$,   25 = H + 2H + H

∴   H = 6.25 H

Points of contraflexure are also assumed at the centre of each beam and member forces are obtained by equilibrium for each part of the structure as shown in Fig. 4.12 (b).

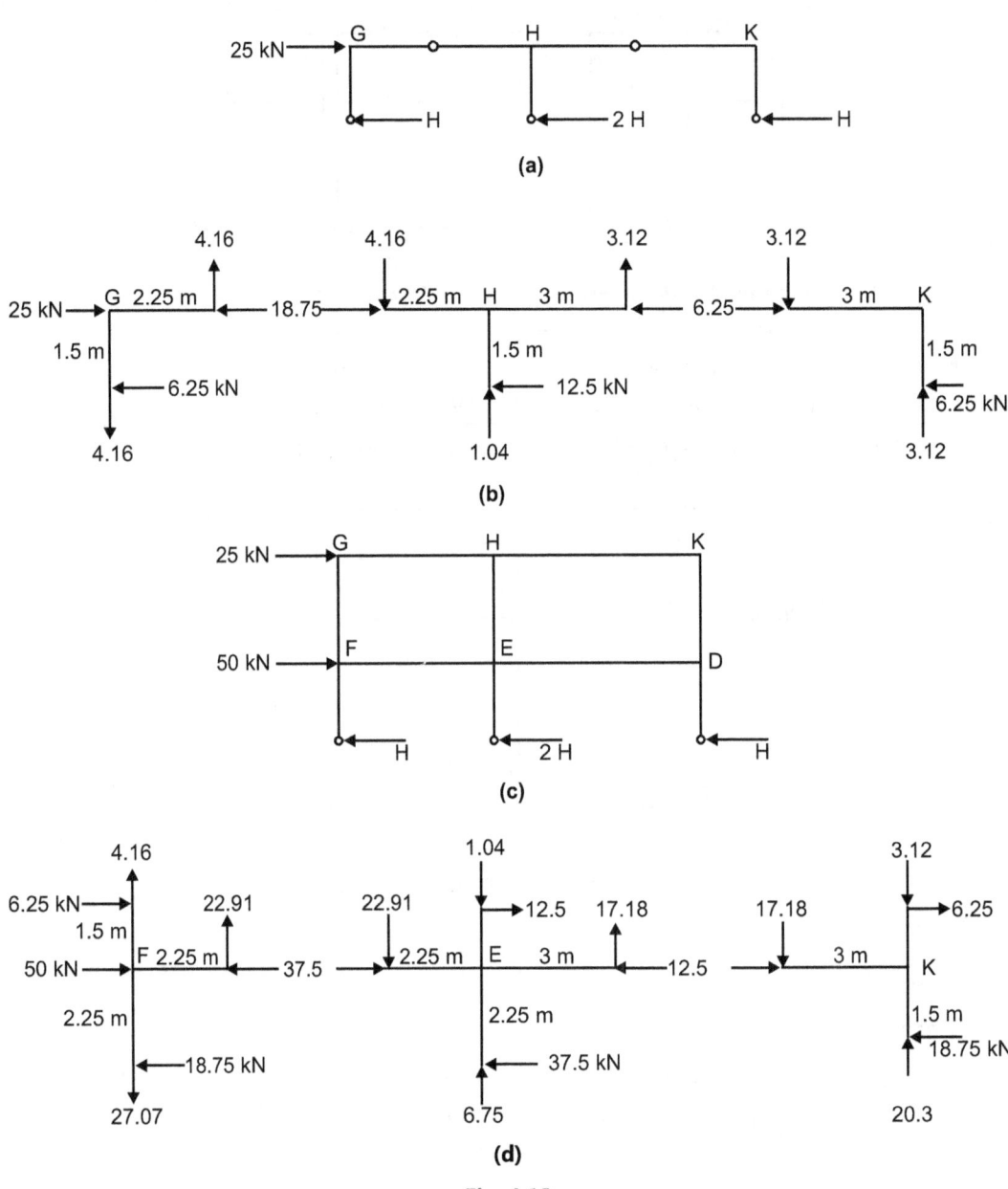

Fig. 4.12

Step II : Points of contraflexure are again assumed at mid-height of lower storey columns.

Thus, for lower storey,

$\Sigma F_x = 0$, $25 + 50 = H + 2H + H$

∴ $H = 18.75$ kN

The member forces for lower storey are obtained from FBD of part of structure as shown in Fig. 4.12 (d).

Step III : BMD : On tension side as shown in Fig. 4.13.

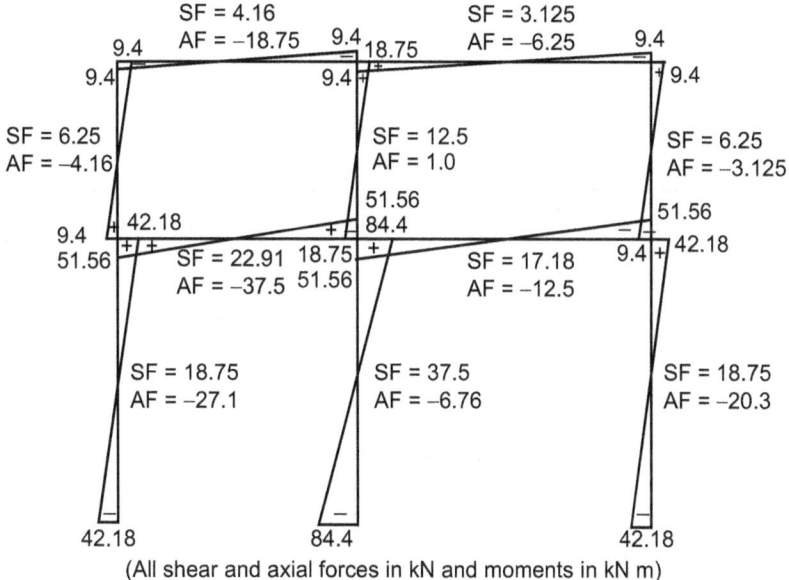

(All shear and axial forces in kN and moments in kN m)

Fig. 4.13

Example 4.3 : *Analyse the frame shown in Fig. 4.14 by portal method and draw BMD.*

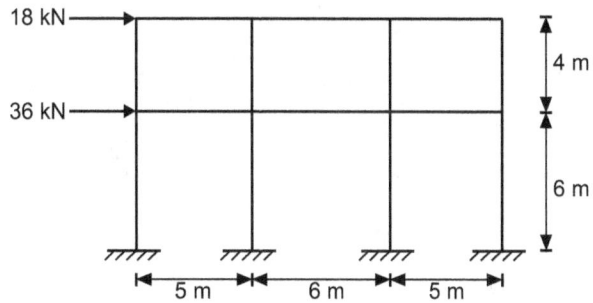

Fig. 4.14

Data : As shown in Fig. 4.15.

Required : BMD.

Concept : Portal method

Solution :

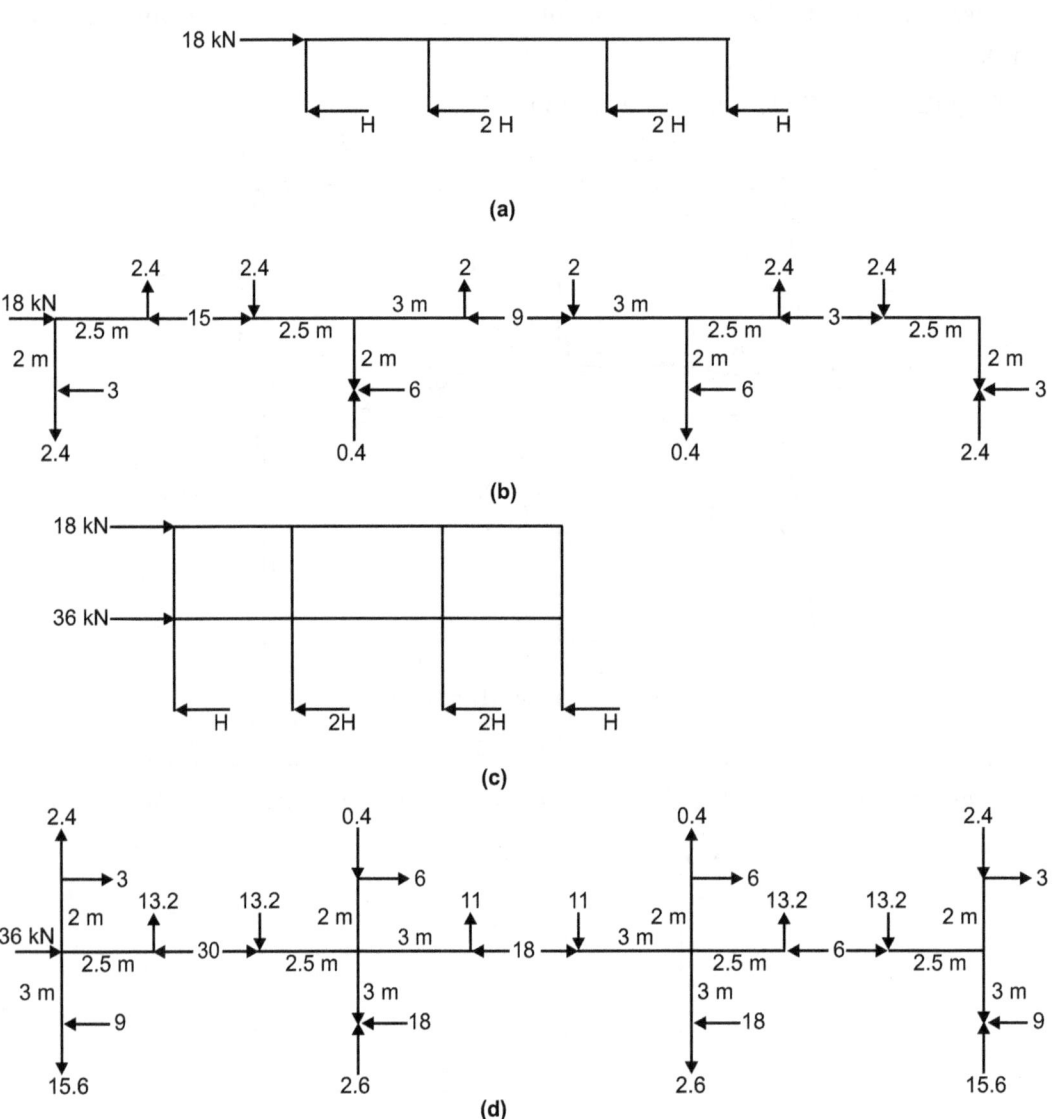

Fig. 4.15

BMD on tension side as shown in Fig. 4.16.

TOS – II (TE CIVIL SEM. VI NMU) APPROXIMATE ANALYSIS OF MULTISTORY FRAMES

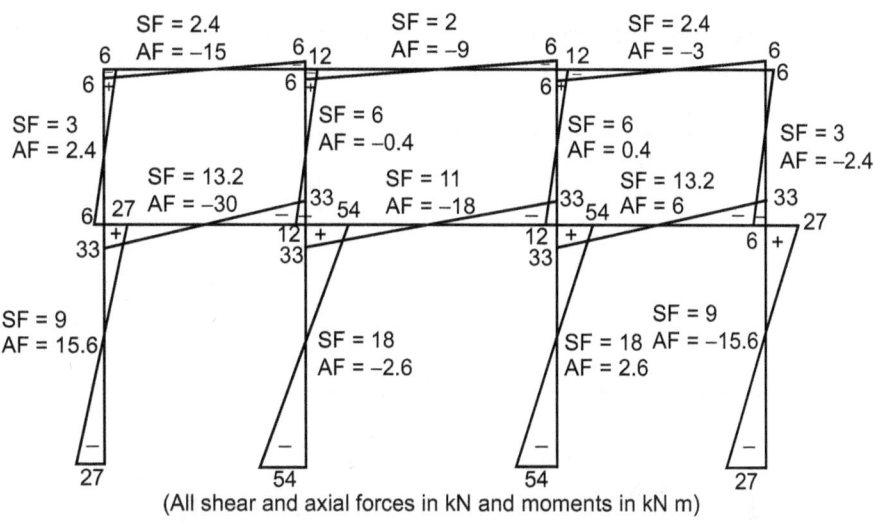

(All shear and axial forces in kN and moments in kN m)

Fig. 4.16

Example 4.4 : Analyse the portal frame shown in Fig. 4.17, under lateral loading by portal method.

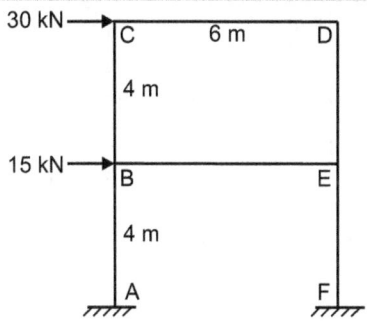

Fig. 4.17

Data : As shown in Fig. 4.17.

Required : BMD.

Concept : Portal method.

Solution : Step I : Assuming points of contraflexure at mid height of columns and considering FBD of upper storey as shown in Fig. 4.18 (a).

$$\Sigma F_x = 0$$
$$30 = H + H$$
$$\therefore H = 15 \text{ kN}$$

Points of contraflexure are also assumed at the centre of each beam and member forces are obtained by equilibrium for each part of the structure as shown in Fig. 4.18 (b).

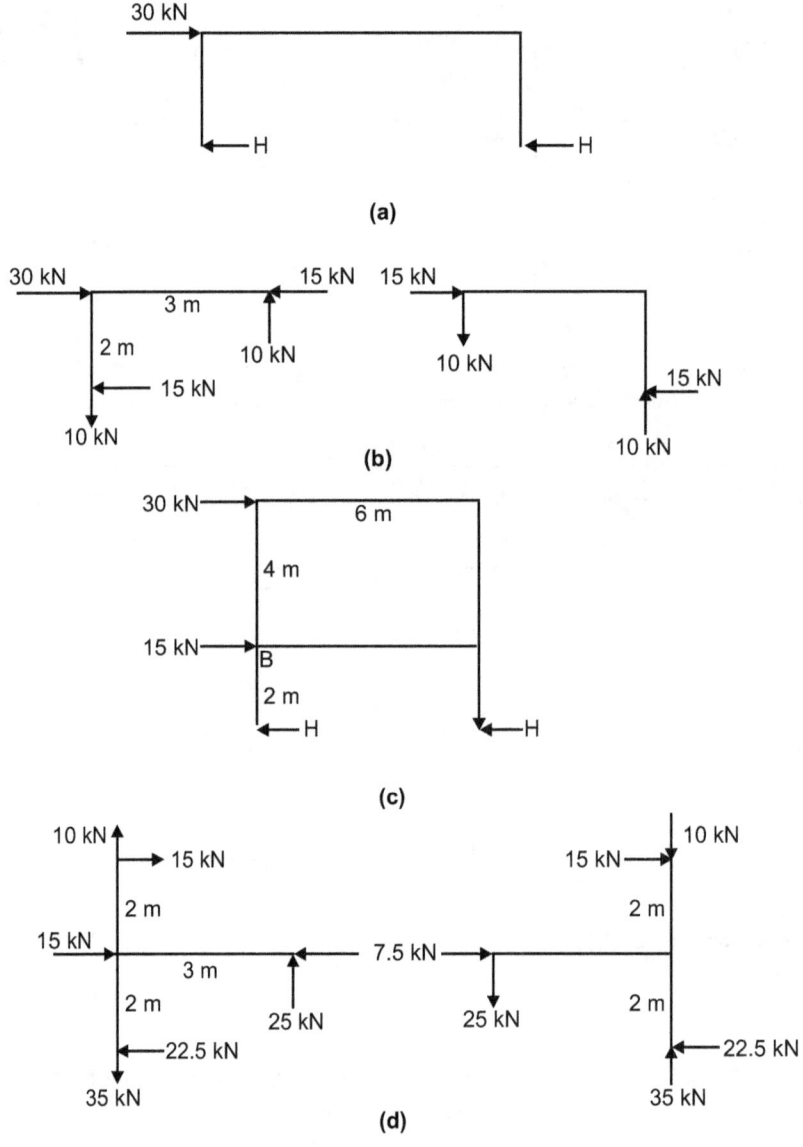

Fig. 4.18

Step II : Points of contraflexure are again assumed at mid-height of lower storey columns.

Thus for lower storey,

$$\Sigma f_x = 0$$
$$30 + 5 = H + H$$
$$\therefore H = 22.5 \text{ kN}$$

The member forces for lower storey are obtained from FBD of part of structure as shown in Fig. 4.18 (a).

Step III : BMD on tension side as shown in Fig. 4.19.

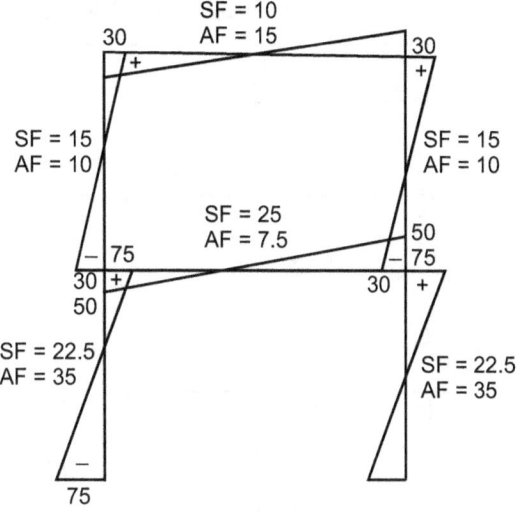

Fig. 4.19

Example 4.5 : *Determine the approximate value of moment, shear and axial force in each member of the frame loaded and supported as shown in Fig. 4.20. Use portal method for analysis.*

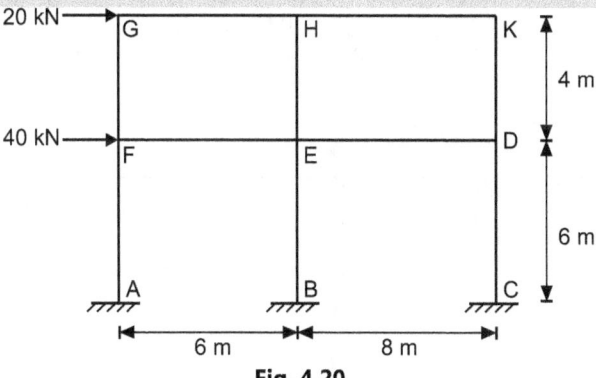

Fig. 4.20

Data : As shown in Fig. 4.20.
Required : BMD.

Concept : Portal method.

Solution : Step I : Assuming points of contraflexure at mid-height of columns and considering FBD of upper storey as shown in Fig. 4.21 (a).

$$\sum f_x = 0$$
$$20 = H + 2H + H$$
$$\therefore H = 5 \text{ kN}$$

Points of contraflexure are also assumed at the centre of each beam and member forces are obtained by equilibrium, for each part of the structure as shown in Fig. 4.21 (b).

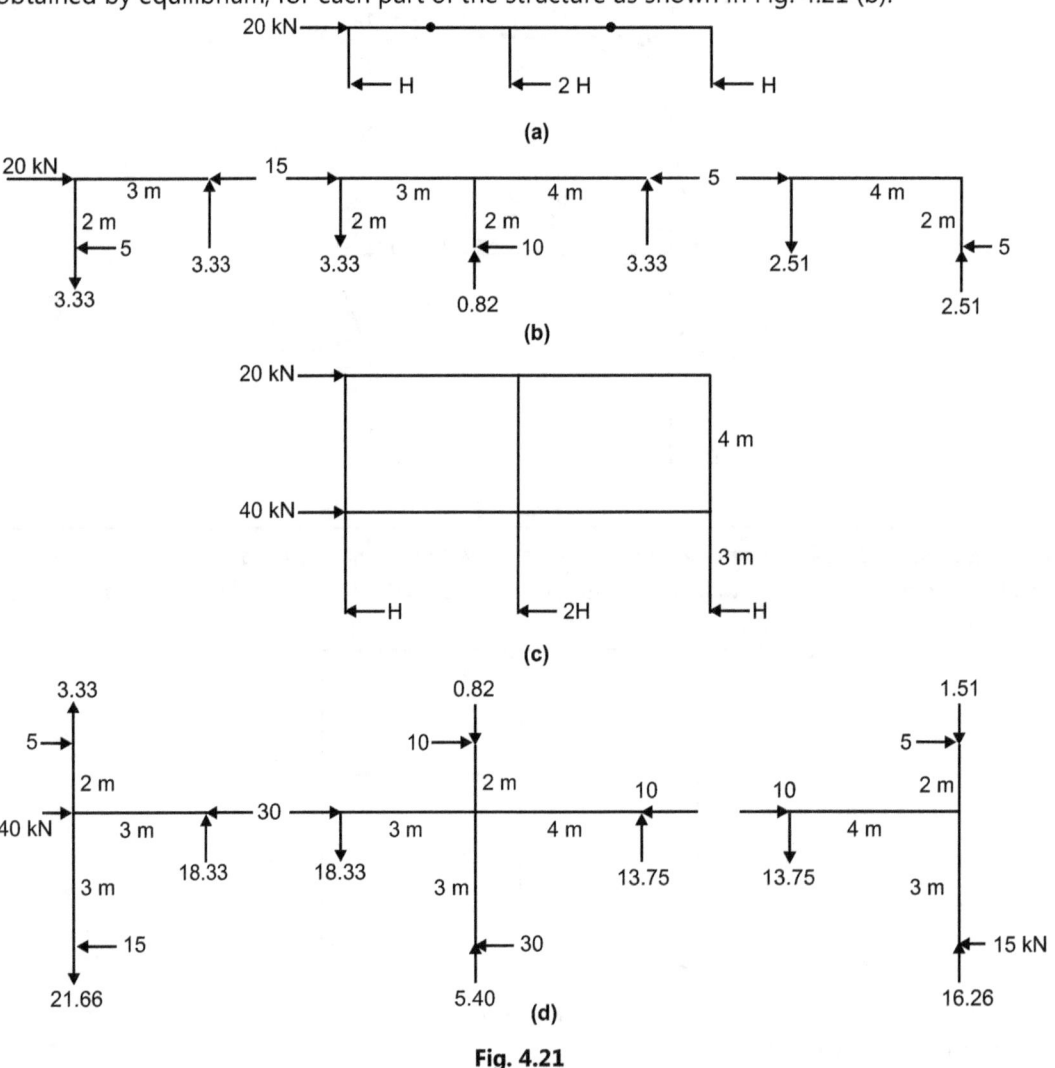

Fig. 4.21

Step II : Points of contraflexure are again assumed at mid-height of lower storey columns.

Thus for lower storey.

$$\Sigma f_x = 0$$
$$20 + 40 = H + 2H + H$$
$$\therefore H = 15 \text{ kN}$$

The member forces for lower storey are obtained from FBD of part of structure as shown in Fig. 4.21 (d).

Step III : BMD on tension side as shown in Fig. 4.22.

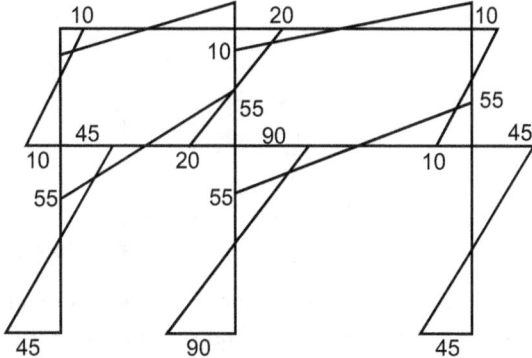

Fig. 4.22 : BMD on tension side

4.4 CANTILEVER METHOD

The cantilever method of analysis is more appropriate for all structures i.e. for a structure that has height greater than its width. This method is based on the assumption that the building frame acts like a cantilever beam with the columns as longitudinal fibres of the beam.

Consider the building frame loaded as shown in Fig. 4.23 (a). For such a tall building, the column strains resulting from the overall bending action are assumed to affect behaviour. We assume that the frame is a laterally loaded cantilever with a cross-section as indicated in Fig. 4.23 (b). The moment at a typical horizontal section AA is resisted by concentrated column forces as shown in Fig. 4.23 (c). The assumptions made in the analysis are :

1. An inflection point is located at the mid-height of the column in each storey;
2. An inflection point is located at the mid-point of each beam; and
3. Direct stresses in each column is proportional to its distance from the centroid of the areas of the column group at that level.

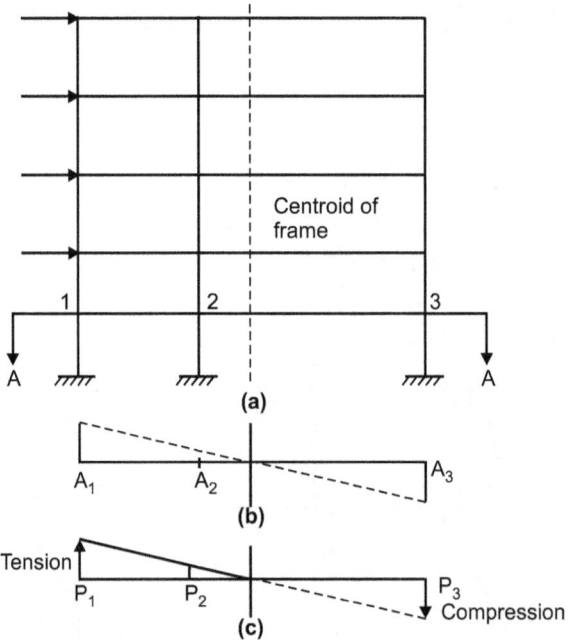

Fig. 4.23 : (a) Building frame, (b) Cross-section of frame, (c) Axial forces in columns

The first two assumptions are the same as in portal method. The third assumption gives the distribution of the axial forces in the columns instead of the distribution of the shear force among the columns as in the portal method. The last assumption enables one to include the effects of column having different cross-sectional areas.

Example 4.6 : *Analyse the frame as shown in Fig. 4.24 by cantilever method. Assume all columns to be of same cross-sectional area.*

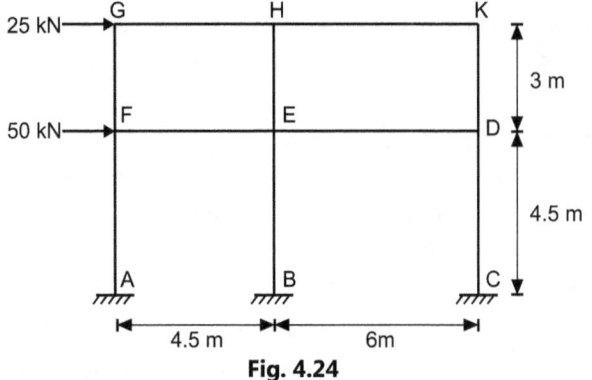

Fig. 4.24

Data : As shown in Fig. 4.24.
Required : BMD.
Concept : Cantilever method.

Solution : Step I : To locate CG of frame.
Taking moments of areas of column about the L.H.S. column,
$$\bar{x} = \frac{4.5 + 10.5}{3} = 5\text{ m}$$
Considering FBD of frame above the points of contraflexure in columns, as shown in Fig. 4.25 (a).

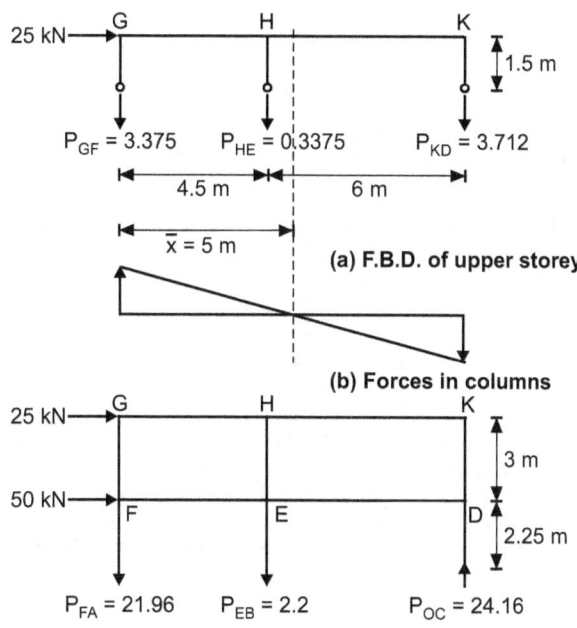

Fig. 4.25

From Fig. 4.25 (b),
$$\frac{P_{GF}}{5} = \frac{P_{HE}}{0.5} = \frac{P_{KD}}{5.5} \qquad ...(i)$$

Taking moments about points of contraflexure of right end column in Fig. 4.25 (a),
$$P_{GF} \times 10.5 + P_{HE} \times 6 - 25 \times 1.5 = 0 \qquad ...(ii)$$

Solving equations (i) and (ii), we get
$$P_{GF} = 3.375 \text{ kN} \quad \text{(Tension)}$$
$$P_{HE} = 0.3375 \text{ kN} \quad \text{(Tension)}$$
$$P_{KD} = 3.712 \text{ kN} \quad \text{(Compression)}$$

Axial forces in columns of lower storey are obtained in similar way and are shown in Fig. 4.25 (c).

Step II : Member Forces :

Having determined the axial forces for columns, the member forces are determined from the FBD as shown in Fig. 4.26.

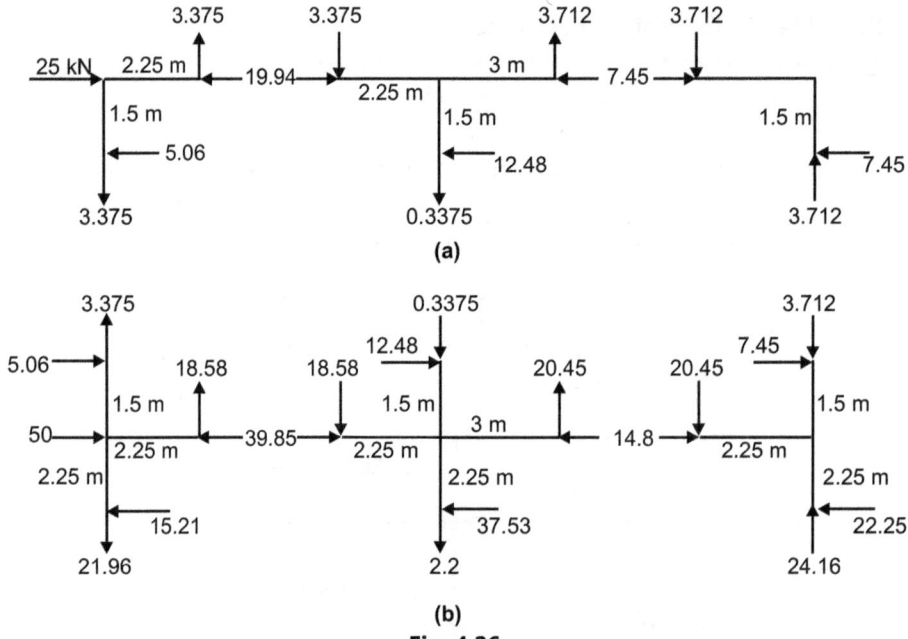

Fig. 4.26

Step III : BMD : As shown in Fig. 4.27.

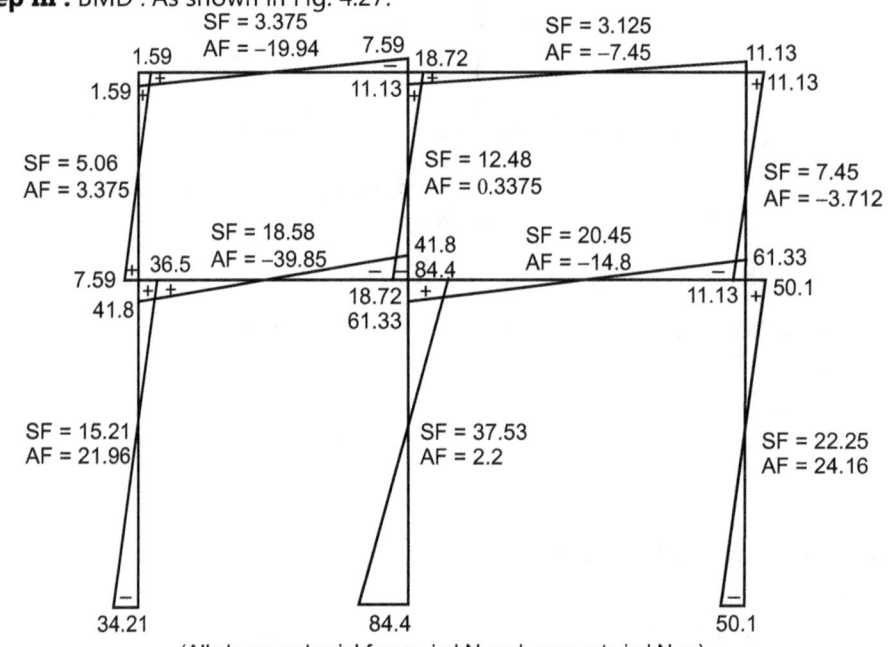

(All shear and axial forces in kN and moments in kN-m)

Fig. 4.27 : Forces in frame members

Example 4.7 : Analyse the frame shown in Fig. 4.28 by cantilever method assuming all columns to be of same cross-sectional area.

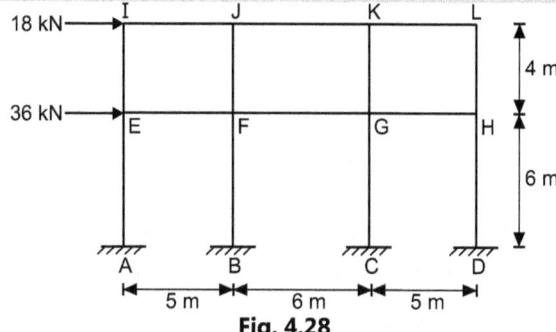

Fig. 4.28

Data : As shown in Fig. 4.28.
Required : BMD.
Concept : Cantilever method.
Solution :

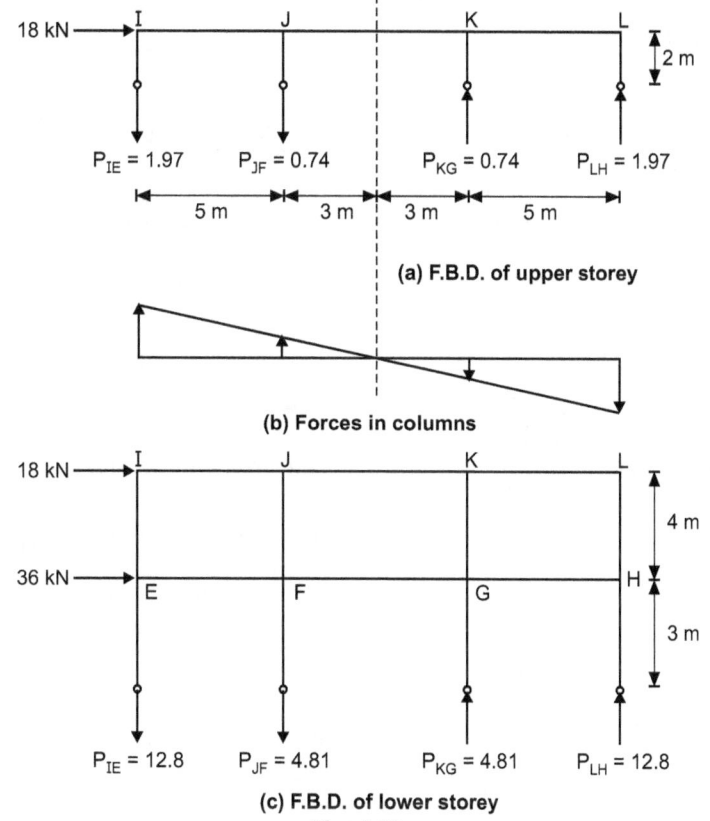

Fig. 4.29

Step I : By symmetry, CG of frame is as shown in Fig. 4.29.

From Fig. 4.29 (b),

$$P_{JF} = P_{KG} \quad \ldots (i)$$

$$P_{IE} = P_{LH} \quad \ldots (ii)$$

$$\frac{P_{IE}}{8} = \frac{P_{JF}}{3} \quad \ldots (iii)$$

Taking moments about point of contraflexure of right end column in Fig. 4.29 (a),

$$P_{IE}(16) + P_{JF}(11) - P_{KG}(5) - 18 \times 2 = 0$$

$$16\,P_{IE} + 6\,P_{JF} = 36 \quad \ldots (iv)$$

Solving equations (iii) and (i), we get

$$P_{JF} = P_{KG} = 0.74 \text{ kN}$$

$$P_{IE} = P_{LH} = 1.97 \text{ kN}$$

Step II : Member Forces :

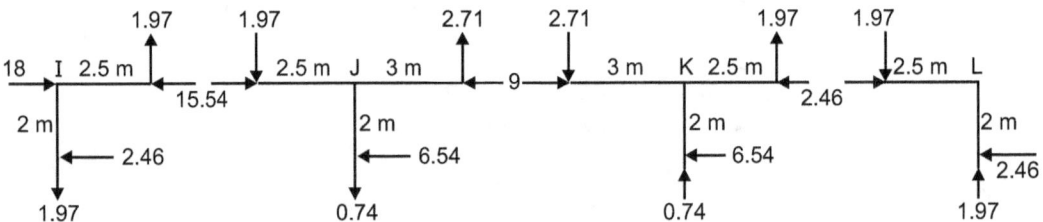

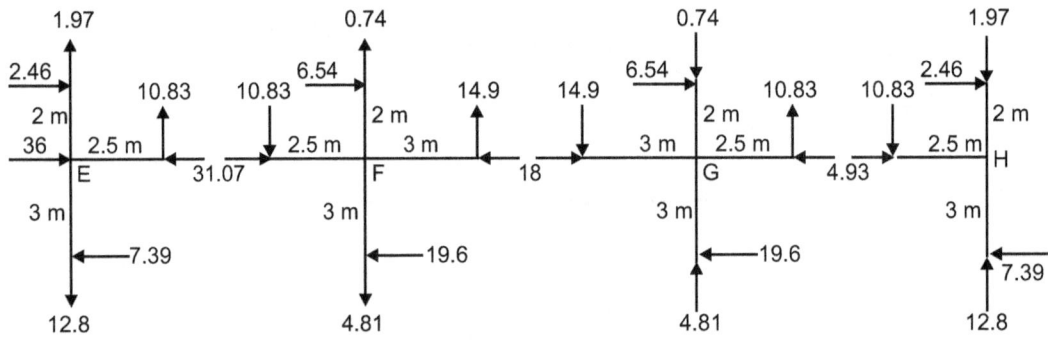

Fig. 4.30

Step III : BMD : As shown in Fig. 4.31.

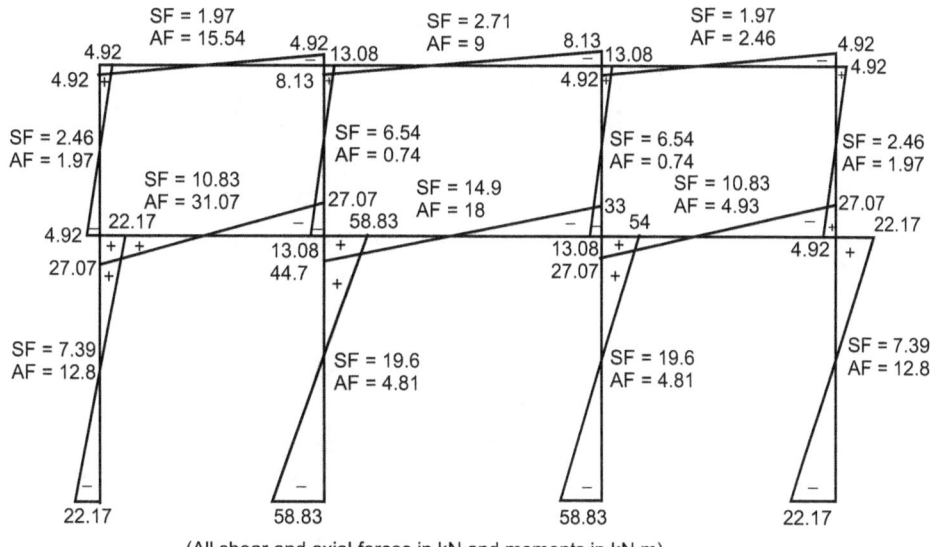

(All shear and axial forces in kN and moments in kN m)

Fig. 4.31 : Forces in frame members

Example 4.8 : *Analyse the portal frame under lateral loading by cantilever method. The columns are assumed to have equal cross-sectional areas.*

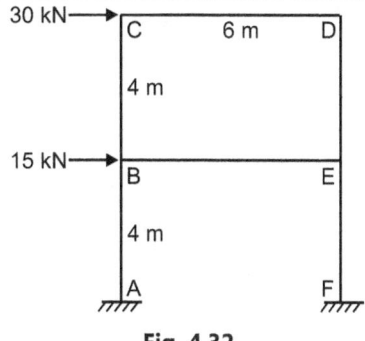

Fig. 4.32

Data : As shown in Fig. 4.32.
Required : BMD.
Concept : Cantilever method.
Solution : Step I : To locate C.G. of frame. Taking moment of areas of column about L.H.S. column.

$$\bar{x} = \frac{6}{2} = 3 \text{ m}$$

Considering F.B.D. of frame above the points of contraflexure in columns as shown in Fig. 4.33 (a).

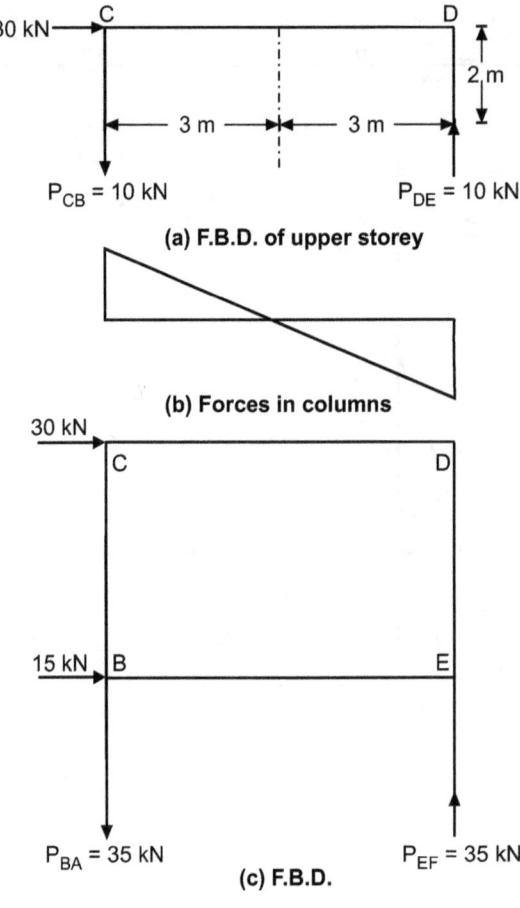

Fig. 4.33

$$\frac{P_{CB}}{3} = \frac{P_{DE}}{3} \qquad \ldots \text{(i)}$$

Taking moments about points of contraflexure of right end column in Fig. 4.33 (a).

$$P_{CB} \times 6 - 30 \times 2 = 0 \qquad \ldots \text{(ii)}$$

Solving equations (i) and (ii),

$$P_{CB} = 10 \text{ kN (Tension)}$$
$$P_{DE} = 10 \text{ kN (Compression)}$$

Axial forces in columns of lower storey are obtained in similar way and are shown in Fig. 4.33 (c).

Step II : Member forces.

Having determined the axial forces for column the member forces are determined from the FBD as shown in Fig. 4.34.

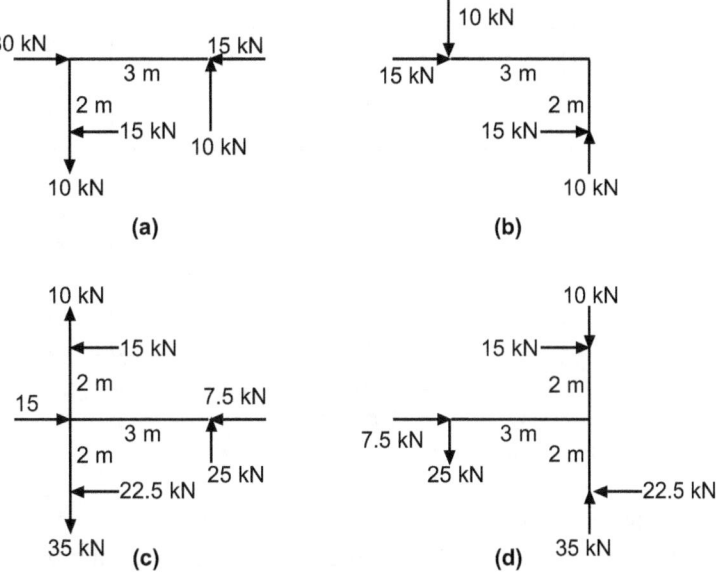

Fig. 4.34

Step III : BMD as shown in Fig. 4.35.

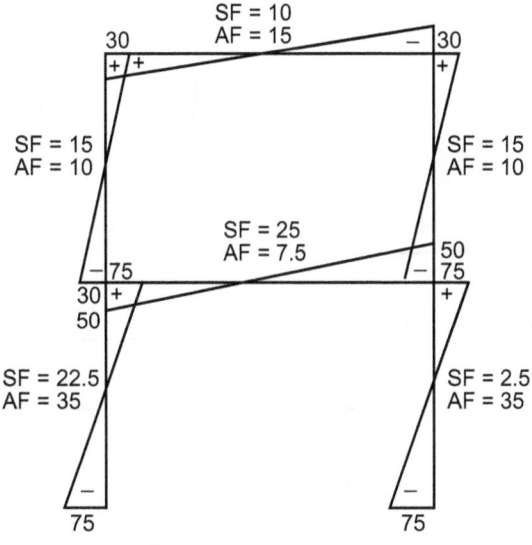

Fig. 4.35 : BMD on tension side

Example 4.9 : Determine the approximate values of moment, shear and axial force in each member of the frame loaded and supported as shown in Fig. 4.36 using cantilever method of analysis.

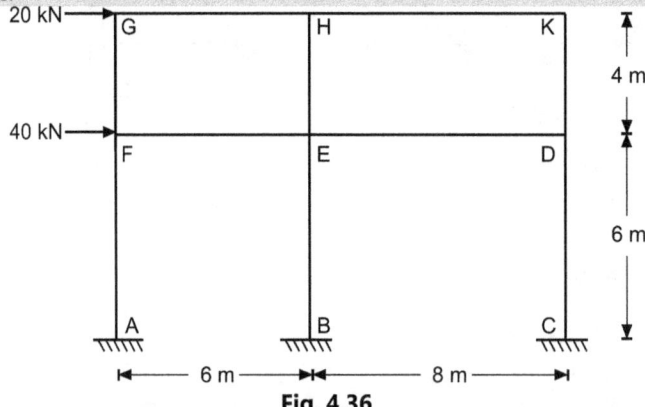

Fig. 4.36

Data : As shown in Fig. 4.36.
Required : BMD.
Concept : Cantilever method.
Solution : Step I : To locate C.G. of frame. Taking moments of areas of column about the L.H.S. column,

$$\bar{x} = \frac{14 + 6}{3} = \frac{20}{3} = 6.67 \text{ m}$$

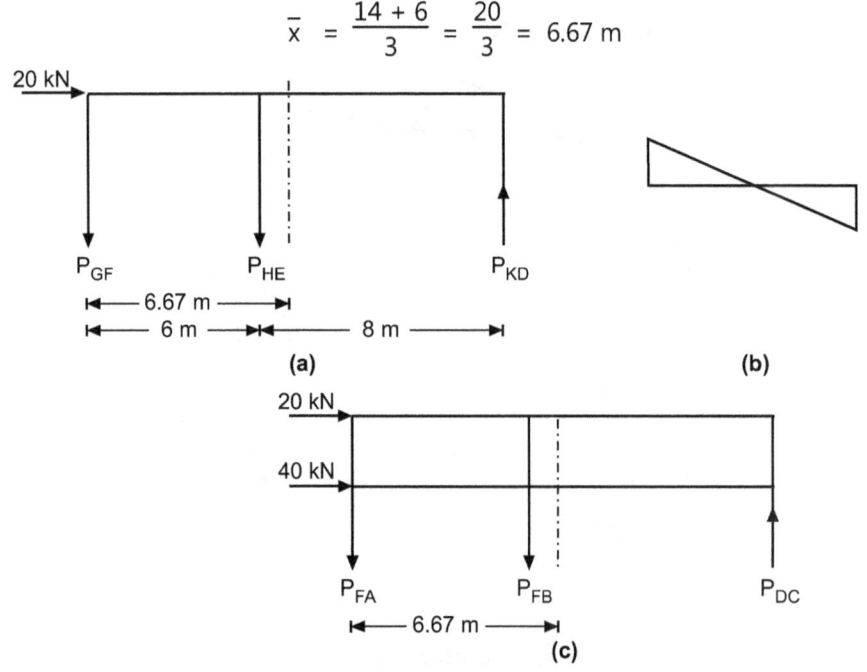

Fig. 4.37

Considering FBD of frame above the points of contraflexure, as shown in Fig. 4.37 (a).

$$\frac{P_{GF}}{6.67} = \frac{P_{He}}{0.67} = \frac{P_{KD}}{7.33} \qquad \ldots (i)$$

Taking moments about points of contraflexure of right end column in Fig. 4.37 (b).

$$P_{GF} \times 14 + P_{HE} \times 8 - 20 \times 2 = 0$$

$$14 P_{GF} + 8 P_{HE} = 40 \qquad \ldots (ii)$$

Solving equations (i) and (ii), we get,

$$P_{GF} = 2.7 \text{ kN (Tension)}$$

$$P_{HE} = 0.27 \text{ kN (Tension)}$$

$$P_{KD} = 2.97 \text{ kN (Compression)}$$

Axial forces in column of lower storey are obtained in similar way and are shown in Fig. 4.37 (c).

Step II : Member Forces : P_{FA} = 17.57 kN (Tension)

$$P_{EB} = 1.76 \text{ kN (Tension)}$$

$$P_{DC} = 19.33 \text{ kN (Compression)}$$

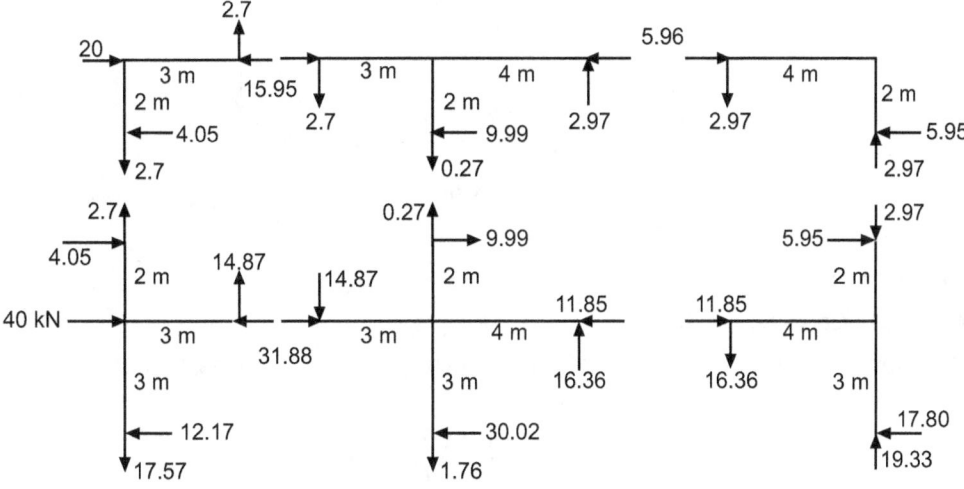

Fig. 4.38

Step III : BMD as shown in Fig. 4.39.

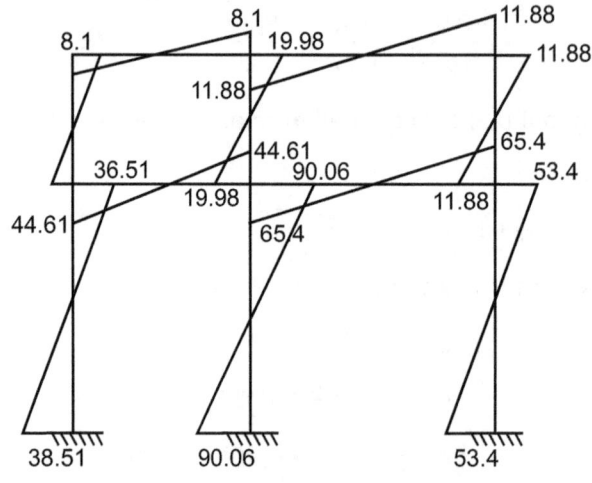

Fig. 4.39

Example 4.10 : Analyse the frame as shown in Fig. 4.40 by cantilever method. Area of each exterior column is one half of the area of the interior columns.

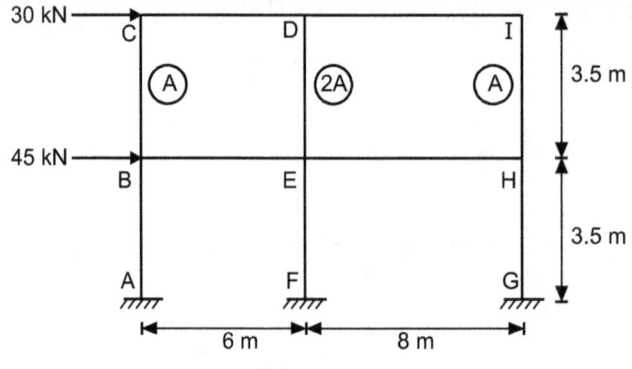

Fig. 4.40

Data : As shown in Fig. 4.40.

Required : BMD.

Concept : Cantilever method.

Solution : Step I : To locate C.G. of frame, taking moments of areas of column about the L.H.S. column.

$$\bar{x} = \frac{A \times 0 + 2A \times 6 + A \times 14}{4A}$$

$$= \frac{12 + 14}{4} = \frac{26}{4} = 6.5 \text{ m}$$

Considering FBD of frame above the points of contraflexure, as shown in Fig. 4.40. Direct stresses in the columns are proportional to the distances from the centroidal vertical axis of the frame. Let σ_{CB}, σ_{DE} and σ_{IH} be the stresses in columns CB, DE and IH respectively. The stresses in columns BA, EF and HG are σ_{BA}, σ_{EF} and σ_{HG} respectively.

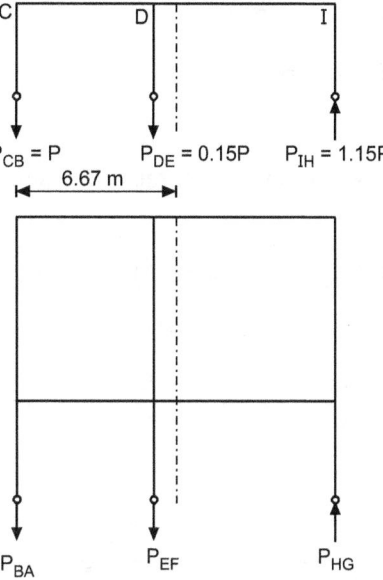

Fig. 4.41

$$\frac{\sigma_{CB}}{6.5} = \frac{\sigma_{DE}}{0.5} = \frac{\sigma_{IH}}{7.5}$$

∴ $\sigma_{DE} = 0.075\ \sigma_{CB}$

$\sigma_{IH} = 1.15\ \sigma_{CB}$

Force in column CB $= \sigma_{CB} \times A$

$= \dfrac{P}{A} \times A$

$= P$ kN (T)

Force in column DE $= \sigma_{DE} \times 2A$

$= 0.075 \dfrac{P}{A} \times 2A = 0.15\ P$ kN (T)

Force in column IH $= \sigma_{IH} \times A$

$= 1.15 \dfrac{P}{A} \times A = 1.15\ P$ kN (T)

Taking moments about the points of contraflexure of the right end column,

$$-30 \times 1.75 + P \times 14 + 0.15\,P \times 8 = 0$$

$$P = 3.45 \text{ kN}$$

∴ Force in column CB (P_{CB}) = 3.45 kN (T)

Force in column DE (P_{DE}) = 0.52 kN (T)

Force in column IH (P_{IH}) = 3.97 kN (C)

Axial forces in column of lower storey are obtained in similar way and are as shown in Fig. 4.42.

Force in column BA (P_{BA}) = 15.54 kN (T)

Force in column EF (P_{EF}) = 2.33 kN (T)

Force in column HG (P_{HG}) = 17.87 kN (C)

Step II : Member Forces :

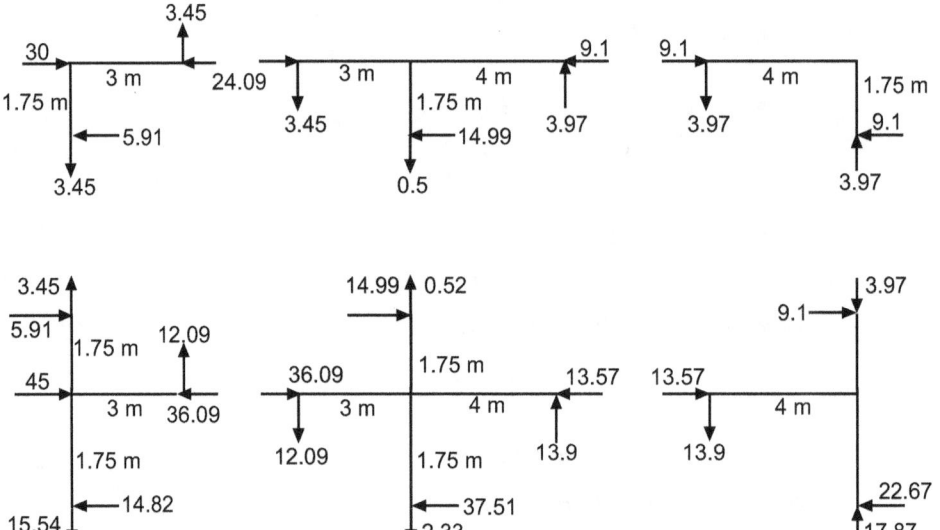

Fig. 4.42

Step III : BMD as shown in Fig. 4.42.

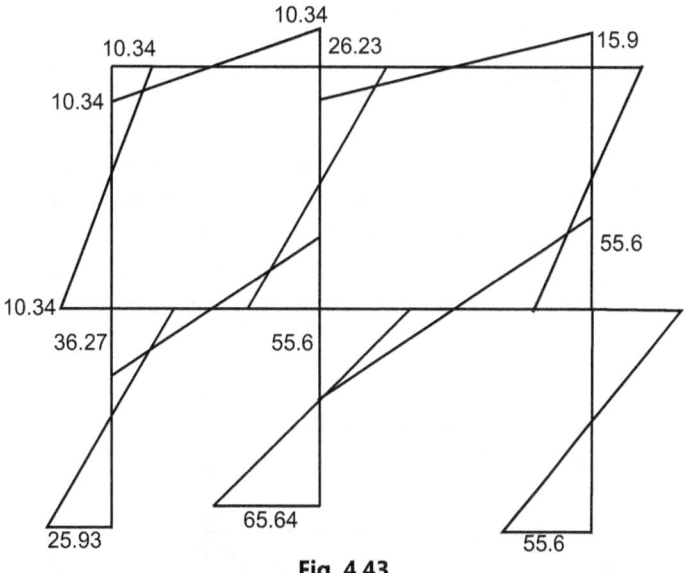

Fig. 4.43

EXERCISE

1. In a multistorey RC building, a central frame has the following data :
   Number of bays = 4, Number of storeys = 5.
   Floor to floor height = 4.50 m, Width of bays = 3.5 m.
   Live load = 15 kN/m.
   Dead load including self weight = 10 kN/m.
   Assume, stiffness of column 1.5 times the beam.
   Design a beam of lower storey for maximum bending moment at support and mid-span section.
   Seismic moments are induced in beam of lower storey of ± 50 kN-m.
   Use M 25 and Fe 415.
   Show the details of reinforcement.

2. A RC frame has following details.
   Number of bays = 3, Width of bay = 5 m.
   Number of storeys = 4 (total height = 14 m)
   Floor height = 3.5 m.
   $I_{beam} = I_{column}$.
   Horizontal load on each floor level = 30 kN.
   Analyse the frame by portal method and B.M., shear force and axial forces are marked in the free body diagram of the frame.
   Design a section of roof level beam at support if moment and shear force due to gravity load are 30 kN-m and 50 kN respectively.
   Use LSM and Fe 415, M 25.

Show details of reinforcement.

3. A rigid jointed R.C. plane frame is subjected to lateral loads as shown in Fig. 4.44. Analyse the frame using cantilever method, to get shear force and bending moments in beam ABC. All members have same EI. The beam ABC is subjected to ultimate dead load of intensity 10 kN/m and ultimate live load of intensity 20 kN/m. Analyse the beam ABC, using a proper substitute frame. Find the maximum span moments in AB and BC and the maximum support moment at B. Design the beam section for support moment at B, due to the combined effect of lateral loads and gravity loads for flexure only. Use M 20 concrete and Fe 415 steel.

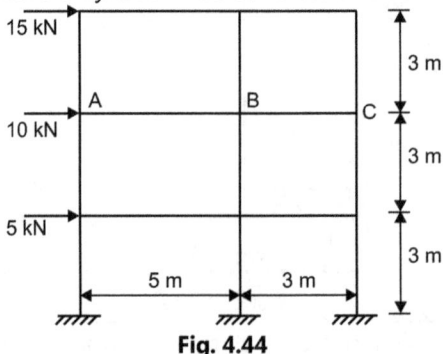

Fig. 4.44

4. A rigid jointed R.C. plane frame is subjected to lateral loads as shown in Fig. 4.45. Analyse the frame using portal method to get bending moments and shear forces in beam ABC. Assume same EI for all members. If the beam ABC is subjected to ultimate dead-load intensity of 12 kN/m and ultimate live load intensity of 22 kN/m, analyse the beam ABC using a proper substitute frame to get maximum span moment in AB and maximum support moment at B. Design the beam section for support moment at B due to combined effect of lateral loads and gravity loads for flexure only. Use M 20 concrete and Fe 415 steel.

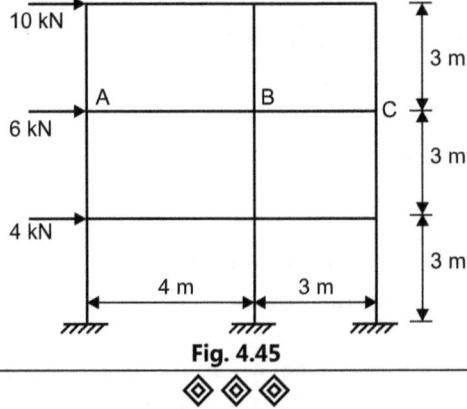

Fig. 4.45

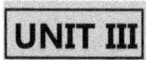

Chapter 5
FUNDAMENTAL CONCEPT OF FLEXIBILITY

5.1 Force Method or Flexibility Method

5.1.1 General

Force method since many years has been the most general and physical approach to analyse statically indeterminate structures. In recent years, it is being replaced by the displacement approach, being systematic and suitable for computers. All types of skeletal structures e.g. beams, plane frames, plane trusses, etc. are analysed by the force method. Redundant forces are considered as unknown in the method. Therefore, the method is called as **force method.** The number of redundant forces is equal to the degree of static indeterminacy. The force method is therefore convenient if the degree of static indeterminacy of the structure is small.

The technique of the method is briefly explained as follows :

- The unknown redundant forces are selected and the basic statically determinate structure is obtained by removing the constraints corresponding the selected redundant forces. The basic determinate structure is also called as the released structure and must be in stable equilibrium. Thus, the equilibrium is indirectly satisfied.

- The displacements of the basic determinate structure at points of and corresponding to redundant forces are computed :
    - Due to the given loads on the structure, and
    - Due to the unit force corresponding to the redundant forces. The displacement due to unit force is called as **flexibility.** The displacement due to the unknown redundant force is the product of the flexibility and the unknown force.

- The physical conditions of geometry at the points of redundants, also called as compatibility equations and also called as the superposition equations of displacements are formulated in terms of unknown redundant forces. There are always as many physical conditions of geometry as there are unknown redundant forces. The formulated equations are linear algebraic equations.

- Solution of the equations gives the unknown redundant forces.

- Once the redundant forces are known, the remaining analysis of the structure is completed by equations of statics.

The fundamental principle of the method is the physical requirements of the displacements of the basic determinate structure at the points of removed constraints due to the applied loading and unknown redundants. Basic requirements are listed as follows :

- If a roller support has been removed the translation at the support point in the direction perpendicular to the supporting surface must be zero.
- If a hinge support has been removed, the horizontal and vertical translations at the point must be zero.
- If a fixed support has been removed, the rotational, horizontal and vertical translations at the point must be zero.
- If an axially loaded member has been removed, the relative displacement along the member must be zero.

The force method starts with the equilibrium and ends with the compatibility of displacements, using the flexibility concepts. The force method is also named as :

- Method of consistent deformation as the displacement conditions should be consistent with the given constraints, or
- Compatibility method as the geometrical conditions of displacements are used for the formulation of the method, or
- Flexibility method as the displacement due to unit load corresponding to the redundant force, termed as the flexibility is used to obtain the displacement in terms of unknown redundant force.

5.1.2 Procedure of Force Method

The force method is mainly based on the displacement equation of compatibility. It therefore involves the determination of the following displacements of basic determinate structure corresponding to the redundant force, Q.

- The displacement at Q and corresponding to Q, due to the given loads (L). This is denoted by D_{QL}.
- The displacement at Q and corresponding to Q due to unit force. This is called the flexibility and denoted by F.
- The displacement at Q due to Q. This is denoted by D_{QQ} and is given by,

$$D_{QQ} = F \cdot Q$$

- The displacement at Q because of support condition of the structure. This is denoted by D_Q and D_Q is generally zero.

    With these displacements, the compatibility condition is formulated by superposition.

$$\therefore \quad D_Q = D_{QL} + D_{QQ} \quad \ldots (5.1)$$

$$\therefore \quad D_Q = D_{QL} + F \cdot Q$$
$$\therefore \quad 0 = D_{QL} + F \cdot Q$$

This is the basic equation of the force method. It is also interested to note that this equation is rearranged and expressed as the fundamental equation of the flexibility.

$$(D_Q - D_{QL}) = FQ$$

i.e. $\quad D = FQ$

The displacement at a point of determinate structure is generally obtained by the unit-load method. In particular cases, standard results of displacements and standard results of flexibilities may be used for convenience. Otherwise, the displacement analysis of determinate structure is itself an exercise. Moreover, the choice of redundant is not unique. Therefore, force method cannot be formulated specifically and hence not well suited to computer programming.

5.1.3 Flexibility Matrix

For multi-redundant structure, the redundant forces are considered as actions and identified by the co-ordinate numbering 1, 2, ... i, j, ... n, where n is the degree of static indeterminancy i.e. number of unknown redundant forces. Accordingly, the basic action-displacement equation $D = FQ = FA$ is formulated in the matrix form in the following manner.

The displacement at the co-ordinate i can be expressed as the sum of the displacements due to actions at different co-ordinates 1, 2, ... i, j, ... n acting separately, only one at a time.

The superposition equations of displacements are

$$D_1 = D_{11} + D_{12} + \ldots + D_{1i} + D_{1j} + \ldots + D_{1n}$$
$$D_2 = D_{21} + D_{22} + \ldots + D_{2i} + D_{2j} + \ldots + D_{2n}$$
$$\vdots$$
$$D_i = D_{i1} + D_{i2} + \ldots + D_{ii} + D_{ij} + \ldots + D_{in}$$
$$D_j = D_{ji} + D_{j2} + \ldots + D_{ji} + D_{jj} + \ldots + D_{jn}$$
$$\vdots$$
$$D_n = D_{n1} + D_{n2} + \ldots + D_{ni} + D_{nj} + \ldots + D_{nn}$$

in which D_{ij} is the displacement at co-ordinate i due to the action at the co-ordinate j. As per the concept of flexibility, D_{ij} is given by,

$$D_{ij} = F_{ij} A_j$$

Therefore, displacement equations can be written in terms of actions and flexibility coefficients.

$$D_1 = F_{11}A_1 + F_{12}A_2 + \ldots + F_{1i}A_i + F_{ij}A_j + \ldots + F_{1n}A_n$$
$$\vdots$$
$$D_i = F_{i1}A_1 + F_{i2}A_2 + \ldots + F_{ii}A_i + F_{ij}A_j + \ldots + F_{in}A_n$$
$$D_j = F_{j1}A_1 + F_{j2}A_2 + \ldots + F_{ji}A_i + F_{jj}A_j + \ldots + F_{jn}A_n$$
$$\vdots$$
$$D_n = F_{n1}A_1 + F_{n2}A_2 + \ldots + F_{ni}A_i + F_{nj}A_j + F_{nn}A_n$$

This set of equations represents the action-displacement relationship of a structure and may be expressed in the matrix form.

$$\begin{Bmatrix} D_1 \\ D_2 \\ \vdots \\ D_i \\ D_j \\ \vdots \\ D_n \end{Bmatrix} = \begin{bmatrix} F_{11} & F_{12} & F_{1i} & F_{ij} & F_{in} \\ F_{21} & F_{22} & F_{2i} & F_{2j} & F_{2n} \\ F_{i1} & F_{i2} & F_{ii} & F_{ij} & F_{in} \\ F_{j1} & F_{j2} & F_{ji} & F_{jj} & F_{jn} \\ F_{n1} & F_{n2} & F_{ni} & F_{nj} & F_{nn} \end{bmatrix} \begin{Bmatrix} A_1 \\ A_2 \\ \vdots \\ A_i \\ A_j \\ \vdots \\ A_n \end{Bmatrix} \quad \ldots (5.2)$$

i.e. $\{D\} = [F] \quad \{A\}$
$n \times 1 \quad n \times n \quad n \times 1$

where, $\{D\}$ = A column matrix of order $n \times 1$, known as displacement matrix.

$[F]$ = A square matrix of order $n \times n$, known as flexibility matrix.

$\{A\}$ = A column matrix of order $n \times 1$, known as action matrix

In flexibility concept, the cause is the unit positive force and effect is the displacement. For F_{ij}, i stands for effect and j for cause. If j is kept same and i varies then we get the effects i.e. displacements F_{1j}, F_{2j} … F_{ij} etc. due to the same cause. These coefficients represent the column coefficients of [F] matrix. Keeping same cause the effects are obtained and column of [F] is generated.

It may be noted that the elements of 'j'th column of the flexibility matrix are the displacements at co-ordinates 1, 2 … n due to a unit positive force at co-ordinate 'j'. Hence in order to generate the 'j'th column of the flexibility matrix, a unit positive force should be applied at co-ordinate 'j' and the displacements at all co-ordinates are determined. In order to develop the flexibility matrix [F], a unit positive force should be applied successively at co-ordinates 1, 2 …, n and displacements at all co-ordinates are computed.

Following properties of the flexibility matrix of a linear elastic structure in stable equilibrium will be observed subsequently.

- The flexibility matrix is a square matrix of order n × n where, n is the number of co-ordinates chosen for the example i.e. degree of static indeterminancy.
- The flexibility matrix is a symmetrical matrix i.e. $F_{ij} = F_{ji}$ in accordance with the reciprocal theorem.
- Each flexibility coefficient represents a displacement caused by a unit positive value of the action, while other actions are zero.
- In general, F_{ij} is the ith displacement due to unit value of jth action.
- The coefficient F_{ij} is taken as positive when it is in the positive direction of the ith action.
- F_{ij} that appear on the principal diagonal of [F] are called direct coefficients and represent displacements caused by unit values of the corresponding actions.
- The remaining coefficients are called cross coefficients.
- For direct flexibilities, i = j.
- For indirect flexibilities, i ≠ j.
- Direct flexibilities are always positive.
- Cross flexibilities may be positive or negative.
- For stable equilibrium structure, the flexibility matrix is non-singular, i.e. $|[F]| \neq 0$.
- If structure is unstable, the displacements are infinitely large. The flexibility matrix does not exist i.e. singular $|F| = 0$.

5.1.4 Procedure of Flexibility Matrix Method

The basic equation of the force method developed for one unknown is written in matrix form as $\{D_Q\} = \{D_{QL}\} + [F]\{Q\}$ for more number of unknown redundant forces. This is the key matrix equation of the method. Using this equation, the procedure of the flexibility matrix method is outlined as follows :

- The degree of static indeterminancy D_{si} (= n, say) is determined.
- The redundant i.e. actions are chosen and identified.
- The co-ordinate numbering 1, 2, ... n is assigned to redundants. Thus $Q_1, Q_2 ... Q_n$ are the redundant actions at co-ordinates 1, 2, ... n. This is the matrix $\{Q\}_{n \times 1}$ of unknown redundants. It is to be noted specifically that {Q} is not denoted by {A} because {Q} do not correspond to non-zero joint displacement of a structure. In fact, {Q} corresponds normally to zero displacements.

- The redundants are removed and a statically released structure i.e. determinate structure is obtained.
- The displacements at co-ordinates 1, 2, ... n in the released structure caused by applied loads 0 are calculated. This displacement analysis of determinate structure is carried out preferably using unit load method. These displacements are DQ_{L1}, DQ_{L2}, D_{Ln}. Thus the matrix $\{D_{QL}\}_{n \times 1}$ is obtained.
- The displacements at co-ordinates 1, 2, ... n in the released structure due to positive unit load corresponding to the redundants, applied successively at a time is calculated. These are the flexibility coefficients. The flexibility matrix $[F]_{n \times n}$ is generated column wise.
- The displacement equations are formulated using superposition equations.

  i.e.
  $$D_{Q1} = D_{QL1} + F_{11} Q_1 + F_{12} Q_2 + ... + F_{1n} Q_n$$
  $$D_{Q2} = D_{QL2} + F_{21} Q_1 + F_{22} Q_2 + ... + F_{2n} Q_n$$
  $$D_{Qn} = D_{QLn} + F_{n1} Q_1 + F_{n2} Q_2 + ... + F_{nn} Q_n$$

  i.e. in matrix $\{D_Q\}_{n \times 1} = \{D_{QL}\}_{n \times 1} + [F]_{n \times n} \{Q\}_{n \times 1}$.

- Compatibility conditions that apply to the geometry of the structure are used. If the net displacements at redundants are zero, $\{D_Q\}$ will be null matrix.

  $$\{D_Q\} = \{0\}_{n \times 1}$$

- Formulation of linear simulation equations for unknown redundants is ready at this stage.
- The redundants $Q_1, Q_2, ... Q_n$ are obtained from solution of equations

  $$\{D\}_{n \times 1} = \{D_{QL}\}_{n \times 1} + [F]_{n \times n} \{Q\}_{n \times 1}$$

  i.e.
  $$\{0\}_{n \times 1} = \{D_{Q1}\}_{n \times 1} + [F]_{n \times n} \{Q\}_{n \times 1}$$

- Knowing the redundants, the member-end forces i.e. stress resultants i.e. all other actions are obtained by using equations of statics.
- Variations of actions along the structure are plotted as SFD and BMD.
- When the actions throughout the structure have been found, the displacements at any point can also be found and deformed shape of a structure may be shown qualitatively from above information. Thus, the elastic curve is sketched.

In the nutshell, the flexibility matrix method requires the formation of following matrices with the help of elementary concepts of theory of structures.

1. $\{D_Q\}_{n \times 1}$.
2. $\{D_{QL}\}_{n \times 1}$.
5. $[F]_{n \times n}$.
4. $\{Q\}_{n \times 1}$ – unknown matrix to be obtained from basic equation of flexibility method.

$$\{D_Q\} = \{D_{QL}\} + [F]\{Q\}$$

5.2 INDETERMINATE TRUSEES

5.2.1 General

A plane truss is a skeletal structure consisting of number of prismatic members, all lying in one plane and hinged together at their ends in such a manner as to form a rigid i.e. stable configuration. The analysis of trusses is simplified by considering the truss as ideal with the following assumptions :

- The members are connected together at their ends by frictionless pin joints though the joints are riveted or welded.
- Loads and reactions are acting only at joints and in the plane of truss.
- The centroidal axis of each member is straight and coincides with the line connecting the centres of joints at each end of the member.
- The members are subjected to only axial forces, though there may be bending moment and shear force as secondary effects.
- The members remain straight even after the deformation.
- A member undergoes either elongation or contraction.
- The displacement of a joint of a truss is specified by the horizontal and vertical translations only.

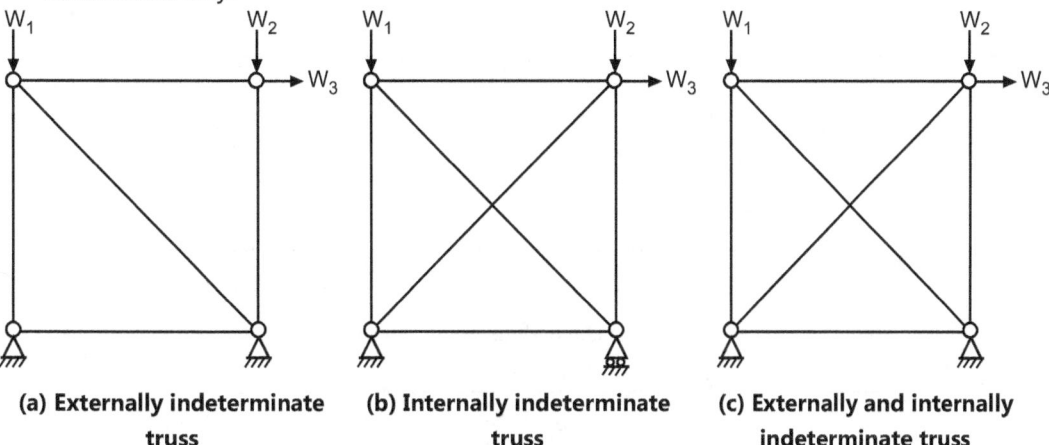

(a) Externally indeterminate truss (b) Internally indeterminate truss (c) Externally and internally indeterminate truss

Fig. 5.1 : Statically indeterminate trusses

The analysis of a truss mainly includes the determination of the axial forces in all members of the truss. Trusses may be statically indeterminate externally and/or internally. If the total number of reaction components is more than three, then the truss will be indeterminate externally as shown in Fig. 5.1 (a) and the degree of external indeterminacy is given by $(r - 3)$ where r is the number of reaction components. If the total number of members of a truss is more than that required for stable configuration, the truss will be indeterminate internally as shown in Fig. 5.1 (b) and the degree of internal indeterminacy is given by $[m - (2j - 3)]$ for a simply supported truss and [m − 2j] for a cantilever truss, where m is the number of members and j is the number of joints. Fig. 5.1 (c) shows a truss, indeterminate externally as well as internally. Statically indeterminate trusses are analysed by (i) force or flexibility method, (ii) displacement or stiffness method and (iii) energy method.

5.2.2 Force Method for Analysis of Indeterminate Trusses

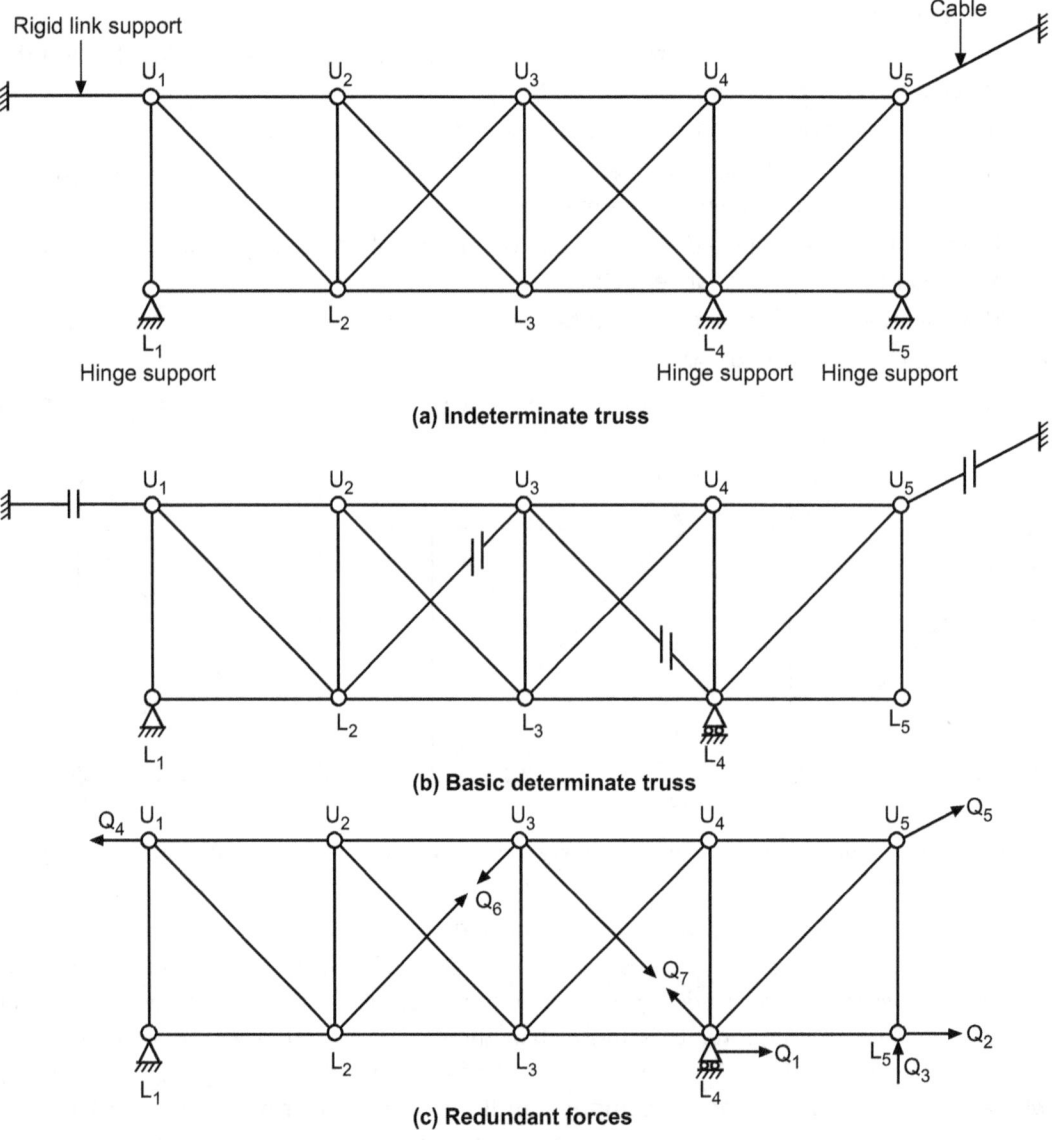

Fig. 5.2 : Released truss and redundant forces

Statically indeterminate trusses are generally analysed by the force method. The degree of kinematic indeterminacy of trusses is normally larger than the degree of static indeterminacy. Moreover, a truss consists of inclined members. Therefore displacement method is not convenient for the analysis of trusses by hand calculations.

Table 5.1

Sr. No.	Release	Release of the redundant	Redundant force	Geometrical condition of deformation
1.	One component of reaction at hinged support, at L_4.	Hinge support is replaced by the roller support as shown at L_4.	Force perpendicular to the plane of the roller support, Q_1 as shown at L_4.	The translation in the direction of Q_1 at L_4 is zero in the in-determinate truss.
2.	Hinge support at L_5.	Hinge support is removed as shown at L_5.	Two forces perpendicular to each other Q_2 and Q_3 as shown at L_5.	The translations in the direction of Q_2 and Q_3 at L_5 are zero in the indeterminate truss.
3.	Linked support assuming rigid.	The link is removed as shown at U_1.	Force along the link, Q_4 as shown at U_1.	The translation in the direction of the link at U_1 is zero in the indeterminate truss.
4.	Cable support assuming inextensible	The cable is removed as shown at U_5.	The tensile force in the cable Q_5 as shown at U_5.	The translation in the direction of the cable at U_5 is zero in the indeterminate truss.
5.	Member of the truss (a) Member $L_2 - U_3$ (b) Member $U_3 - L_4$	The member is cut with the gap in the member L_2U_3, in the member U_3L_4 at as shown in Fig. 5.2 (b).	Pair of tensile forces along the member. Q_6 forces acting at L_2 and U_3. Q_7 forces acting at U_3 and L_4.	There is no gap i.e. the relative translation along the member is zero in the in-determinate truss as the member is con-tinuous.
6.	Elastic support having flexibility Fes	The elastic support is removed.	The elastic force at the support say Q.	The translation at elastic support is equal to (Fes × Q).

The basic principle of consistent deformation is used to analyse the statically indeterminate trusses by the force method. The main aim of the method is to obtain redundant forces. The method consists of (i) choosing a basic determinate truss on which the applied loads and the redundant forces act and then (ii) applying the conditions of geometry i.e. compatibility requiring that the displacements in the direction of redundant forces must be zero. The redundant force may be the reaction component at the support and/or the axial force in the member. The basic determinate truss, also called released structure, is obtained from removing the selected redundants. In doing this, care must be taken that the released structure must be stable and determinate. This is particularly critical when the truss is internally indeterminate and a member is to be cut or removed to obtain the determinate truss.

The sign convention for axial force in the member of a truss is as follows :

Tensile force is considered as positive and compressive force as negative.

The selection of the redundants, obtaining the basic determinate i.e. released truss and applying the geometrical conditions of deformations are the primary considerations of the force method. This information, in general, is illustrated in Fig. 5.2 (a) and accordingly consolidated in the Table 5.1. The basic determinate truss after removing the redundant is shown in Fig. 5.2 (b) and the redundant forces are shown in Fig. 5.2 (c).

5.2.3 Basic Formulation of Force Method for Trusses

The superposition equation of the displacements, satisfying the requirement of the compatibility, is the basic equation of the force method as seen previously. This equation is restated in its simplest form of one unknown as

$$D_Q = D_{QL} + F \cdot Q \qquad \ldots (5.3)$$

where,

(i) Q is the unknown redundant force.

(ii) D_Q is the displacement in the given structure corresponding to the selected redundant force Q.

(iii) D_{QL} is the displacement corresponding to the redundant force in the basic determinate or released structure due to the applied loads.

(iv) F is the flexibility i.e. the displacement corresponding and due to unit positive redundant force in the basic determinate structure.

As D_Q is zero for the geometrical condition, the basic equation becomes,

$$0 = D_{QL} + FQ \qquad \ldots (5.4)$$

and therefore, $\quad Q = -\left(\dfrac{D_{QL}}{F}\right)$ gives the required redundant force.

Analysis of indeterminate trusses of one unknown is based on this equation and it consists of the following important phases.

(1) Basic Determinate Truss :

The selected redundant is removed and the given truss is considered as the equivalent to the superposition of (i) basic determinate truss under given loads and (ii) the basic determinate truss under redundant force 'Q' times unit positive redundant force, as shown in Fig. 5.3.

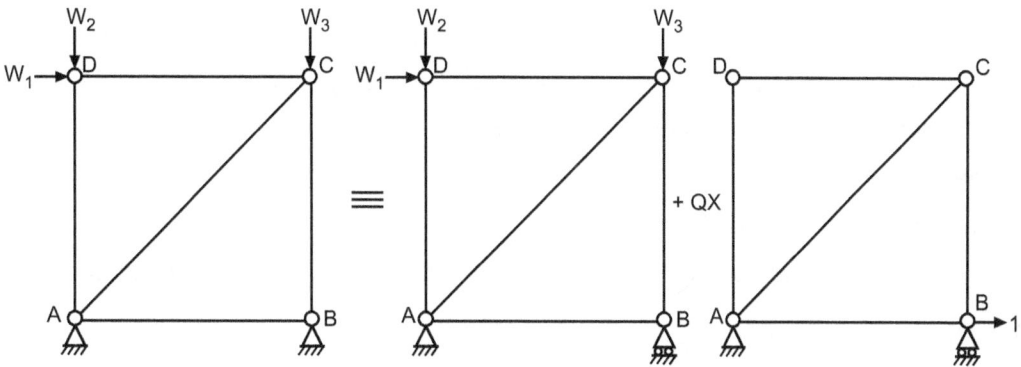

Fig. 5.3 : Superposition technique

(2) P-Analysis of Basic Determinate Truss :

Determination of forces in all members of the basic determinate truss due to the applied loads is called as P-analysis. This is the conventional force analysis of a simple determinate truss by laws of statics i.e. method of joints or method of sections. The technique of isolating a single joint with not more than two unknown forces and applying two conditions of static equilibrium, $\Sigma F_x = 0$ and $\Sigma F_y = 0$ for concurrent forces is called the method of joints to obtain the unknown forces. The technique of isolating a portion of a truss by a section and applying the three conditions of equilibrium, $\Sigma F_x = 0$, $\Sigma F_y = 0$ and $\Sigma M = 0$ for a non-concurrent system of forces including certain known applied loads and unknown member forces cut by the section is called the method of sections to obtain the three unknown forces.

(3) K-analysis :

Determination of forces in all the members including redundant members, which are cut, of the basic determinate truss due to only a unit positive force applied at the location and in the direction of the removed redundant is represented as K-analysis. For this also, method of joints or method of sections is used.

(4) Displacement Analysis of Basic Determinate Truss :

Using the results of P-analysis and K-analysis, the displacement D_{QL} at the location and in the direction of the redundant force due to applied loads is obtained. According to the unit load method, the displacement D_{QL} is given by the equation

$$D_{QL} = \sum_{\text{All members}} \left(\frac{PKL}{AE}\right) \quad \ldots (5.5)$$

where P is the force in a member of the basic determinate truss due to applied loads.

K is the force in the member of the basic determinate truss due to a unit positive force corresponding to the unknown redundant force.

L is the length of the member.

A is the area of cross-section of the member.

E is the modulus of elasticity of the material of the member. It may be noted that EA is called axial rigidity of a member and $\frac{L}{EA}$ is termed as the flexibility of a member.

(5) Flexibility of the Basic Determinate Truss :

The displacement of basic determinate truss at the location and in the direction of the redundant due to the unit positive force only applied at the location and in the direction of the redundant is called the flexibility 'F'. Thus, the flexibility F is the displacement (effect) due to the unit force (cause) and obtained by the following similar equation of the unit load method.

$$F = \sum_{\text{All members}} \left(\frac{KKL}{EA}\right) = \sum_{\text{All members}} \left(\frac{K^2 L}{EA}\right) \quad \ldots (5.6)$$

(6) Formulation of the Basic Equation of the Force Method :

Applying the condition of consistent deformation that $D_Q = 0$, the unknown redundant force 'Q' is calculated from the equation

$$D_Q = D_{QL} + F \cdot Q$$

∴ $\quad 0 = D_{QL} + F \cdot Q$

∴ $\quad Q = -\left(\dfrac{D_{QL}}{F}\right)$

$$\therefore \quad Q = -\frac{\sum_{i=1}^{n}\left(\frac{PKL}{EA}\right)_i}{\sum_{i=1}^{n}\left(\frac{K^2L}{EA}\right)_i} \quad \ldots (5.7)$$

This is the key equation of the analysis of indeterminate trusses by the force method to determine the redundant force. This equation is further modified if the information of E or A or L or EA or $\frac{L}{EA}$ of all members of the truss is same. Therefore the basic equation is expressed as

$$Q = -\frac{\sum_{i=1}^{n}\left(\frac{PKL}{EA}\right)_i}{\sum_{i=1}^{n}\left(\frac{K^2L}{EA}\right)_i} \quad \text{for general case}$$

$$= -\frac{\sum_{i=1}^{n}\left(\frac{PKL}{A}\right)_i}{\sum_{i=1}^{n}\left(\frac{K^2L}{A}\right)_i} \quad \text{if E is same for all members}$$

$$= -\frac{\sum_{i=1}^{n}(PKL)_i}{\sum_{i=1}^{n}(K^2L)_i} \quad \text{if EA i.e. axial rigidity is same for all members}$$

$$= -\frac{\sum_{i=1}^{n}(PK)_i}{\sum_{i=1}^{n}(K^2)_i} \quad \text{if } \frac{L}{EA} \text{ i.e. flexibility is same for all members}$$

(7) Forces in the Members of a Redundant Truss:

Using the concept of superposition, the final forces in the members are found from the general equation:

$$P_{fj} = P_i + Q \cdot K_j \qquad \ldots (5.8)$$

The above formulation is processed systematically in the tabular form to analyse the indeterminate trusses. The information of A, L and the results of P-analysis and K-analysis, and their products are presented in the tabular format as shown below:

Sr. No.	Member	Length L	Area A	E	P	K	$\dfrac{PKL}{EA}$	$\dfrac{K^2L}{EA}$	Q	KQ	$P_f = P + QK$
							$\Sigma =$				

This table should include all the members of the truss including redundant members though they are cut. This is to be noted that this is the general format. If the information of E or A is same for all members, the corresponding columns are not necessary. The algebraic sum of the quantities required are directly obtained from this table to find the redundant force and the final forces in all members as shown in the table.

The detailed procedure of the method is illustrated with the examples of trusses for the following cases.

Case I : External indeterminacy.
Case II : Internal indeterminacy.
Case III: Lack of fit or fabrication error.
Case IV : Temperature effects.
Case V : Yielding of supports.

Examples of only one unknown redundant force for each of the above cases are common in practice. Therefore, such examples of trusses with only one unknown are illustrated initially explaining the special features.

5.2.4 Externally Indeterminate Trusses

Example 5.1 : *Analyse the truss supported and loaded as shown in Fig. 5.4 (a).*
Take EA = constant.

Solution : Data :
(1) Truss is supported and loaded as shown in Fig. 5.4 (a).
(2) EA = constant.

Objects :

(1) Redundant force,

(2) Forces in all the members of truss and

(3) Reactions at supports.

Concepts and Equations :

(1) Principle of superposition,

(2) Analysis of determinate truss,

(3) Compatibility condition and

(4) $Q = -\left[\dfrac{\sum\limits_{i=1}^{n} \left(\dfrac{PKL}{EA}\right)_i}{\sum\limits_{i=1}^{n} \left(\dfrac{K^2L}{EA}\right)_i} \right]$

Procedure :

Step I : Degree of static indeterminacy (D_{si}) :

(a) Degree of external indeterminacy = $(D_{si})_e$ = $r - 3$ = $4 - 3$ = 1

(b) Degree of internal indeterminacy = $(D_{si})_i$ = $m - (2j - 3)$ = $9 - (2 \times 6 - 3)$ = 0

Total degree of static indeterminacy = D_{si} = $(D_{si})_e + (D_{si})_i$ = $1 + 0$ = 1

Step II : Selection of redundant force (Q) :

Let $\quad\quad\quad\quad Q = V_B (\uparrow)$

Step III : Basic determinate truss : Roller support at B is removed and determinate truss is obtained as shown in Fig. 5.4 (b).

Step IV : Superposition : The given indeterminate truss is considered as superposition of (a) basic determinate truss with given loads [Fig. 5.4 (b)] and (b) unknown redundant force Q times the basic determinate truss with unit positive redundant force [Fig. 5.4 (c)].

Step V : P-analysis of basic determinate truss due to applied loads : Considering static equilibrium of truss all the reaction components (R_p) are found out as shown in Fig. 5.4 (b). Also the forces (P) in all the members of truss are found out and shown in Fig. 5.4 (b).

Step VI : K-Analysis of Basic Determinate Truss : Unit positive force corresponding to Q is applied as shown in Fig. 5.4 (c). All the reaction components (R_K) and forces (K) in all the members of truss are found out and are shown in Fig. 5.4 (c).

Step VII : Table for numerical computations :

Sr. No.	Member	Length (m)	P (kN)	K	PKL	K²L	Q (kN)	QK (kN)	$P_f = P + QK$ (kN)
1.	AB	3	47.5	– 1/2	– 71.25	0.75		– 26.35	21.15
2.	BC	3	47.5	– 1/2	– 71.25	0.75		– 26.35	21.15
3.	CD	3	0	0	0	0		0	0
4.	DE	3	0	0	0	0		0	0
5.	EF	3	– 20	0	0	0	52.69	0	– 20
6.	FA	3	0	0	0	0		0	0
7.	EB	3	0	– 1	0	3		– 52.69	– 52.69
8.	AE	$3\sqrt{2}$	$-27.5\sqrt{2}$	$1/\sqrt{2}$	$-82.5\sqrt{2}$	$3/\sqrt{2}$		37.25	– 1.64
9.	CE	$3\sqrt{2}$	$-47.5\sqrt{2}$	$1/\sqrt{2}$	$-142.5\sqrt{2}$	$3/\sqrt{2}$		37.25	– 29.93
				Σ =	– 460.69	8.74			

Step VIII : Calculation of redundant force :

$$Q = -\left[\frac{\sum_{i=1}^{n}\left(\frac{PKL}{EA}\right)_i}{\sum_{i=1}^{n}\left(\frac{K^2L}{EA}\right)_i}\right] = -\left(\frac{\Sigma PKL}{\Sigma K^2L}\right) = -\left(\frac{-460.69}{8.74}\right)$$

$$= 52.69 \text{ kN } (\uparrow)$$

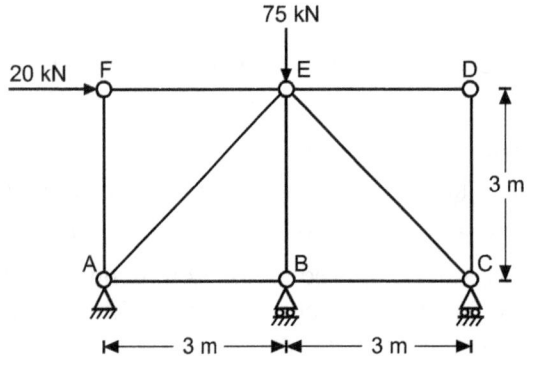

(a) Given truss

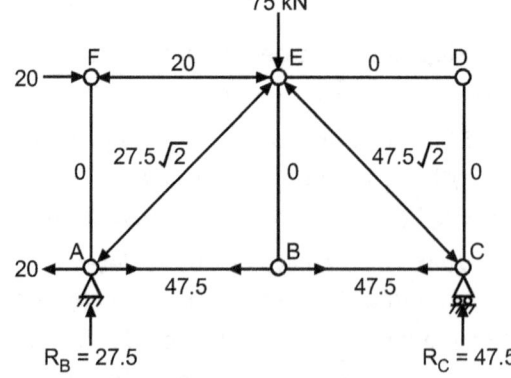

(b) Determinate truss with loads

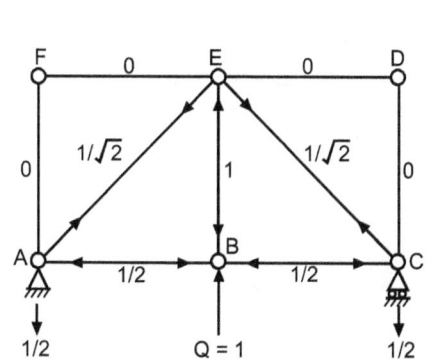
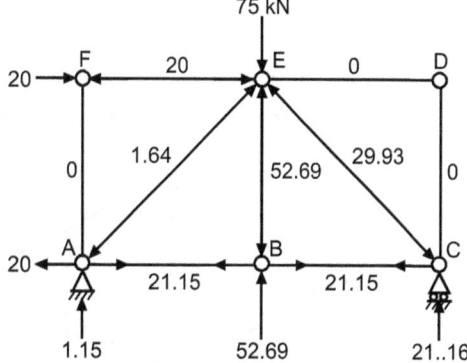

(c) Determinate truss with Q = 1   (d) Final member forces and reactions

Fig. 5.4 : Illustrative Example 5.1

Step IX : Final Forces in all the Members of Truss (P_f) :

Using the equation :

$$P_f = P + QK$$

final forces in all members of truss are computed and are as tabulated above and shown in Fig. 5.4 (d).

Step X : Final Reaction Components at Supports (R) :

Using the equation,

$$R = R_p + Q \cdot R_k$$

final reaction components at supports are computed and are as shown in Fig. 5.4 (d).

Example 5.2 : *Analyse the truss supported and loaded as shown in Fig. 5.5 (a). Cross-sectional area of each member in cm² is indicated in brackets. Take E = constant.*

Solution : Data :
(1) Truss is supported and loaded as shown in Fig. 5.5 (a).
(2) E = constant.

Objects :
(1) Redundant force,   (2) Forces in all the members of truss and
(3) Reactions at supports.

Concepts and Equations :
(1) Principle of superposition,   (2) Analysis of determinate truss,
(3) Compatibility condition and

(4) $Q = -\left[\dfrac{\sum_{i=1}^{n} \left(\dfrac{PKL}{EA}\right)_i}{\sum_{i=1}^{n} \left(\dfrac{K^2 L}{EA}\right)_i} \right]$

Ch. 5 | 5.17

Procedure : Step I : Degree of static indeterminacy (D_{si}) :
(a) Degree of external indeterminacy = $(D_{si})_e$ = r – 3 = 4 – 3 = 1
(b) Degree of internal indeterminacy = $(D_{si})_i$ = m – (2j – 3) = 5 – (2 × 4 – 3) = 0
  Total degree of static indeterminacy = D_{si} = $(D_{si})_e$ + $(D_{si})_i$ = 1 + 0 = 1

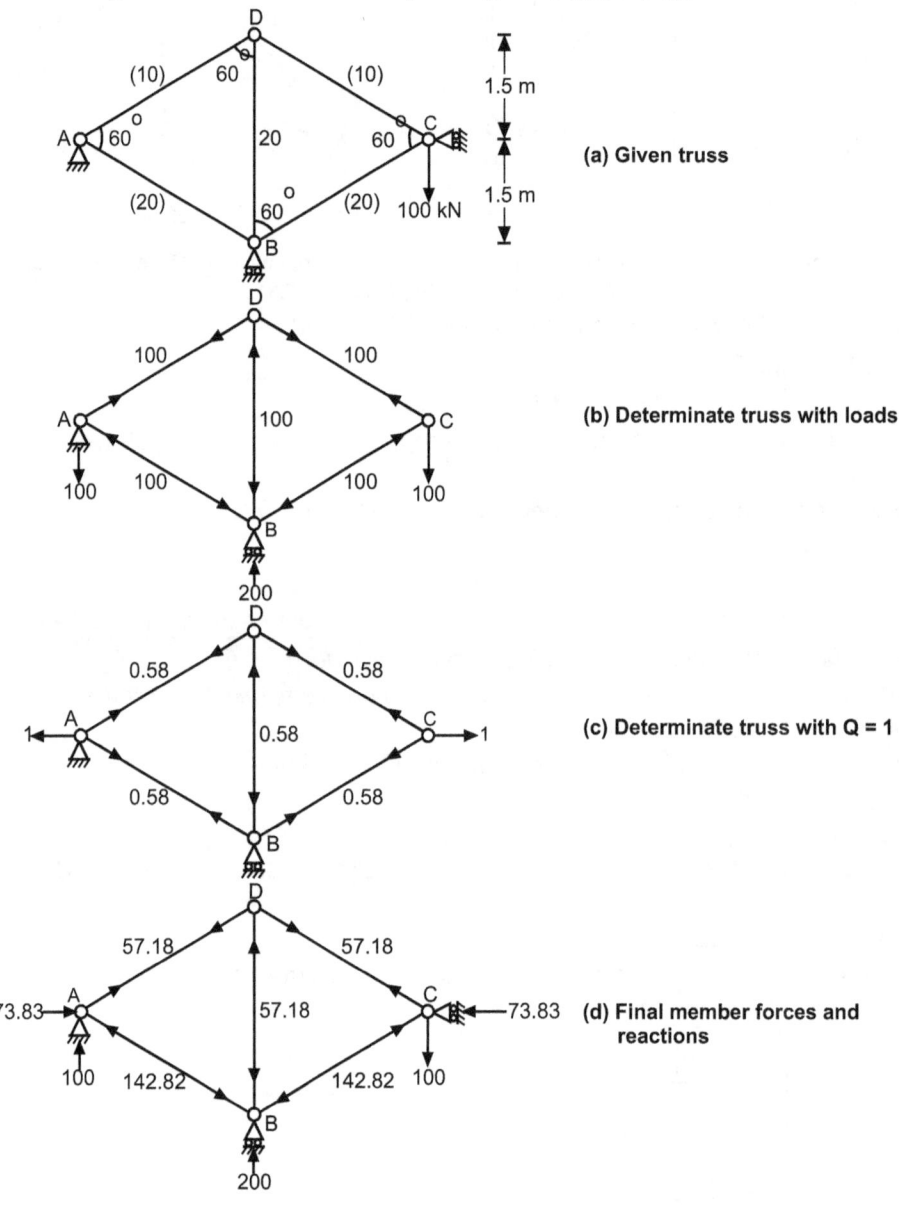

Fig. 5.5 : Illustrative Example 5.2

Step II : Selection of redundant force (Q) :

Let, $Q = H_c (\rightarrow)$

Step III : Basic determinate truss :

Roller support at C is removed and determinate truss is obtained as shown in Fig. 5.5 (b).

Step IV : Superposition : The given indeterminate truss is considered as superposition of (a) basic determinate truss with given loads [Fig. 5.5 (b)] and (b) unknown redundant force Q times the basic determinate truss with unit positive redundant force [Fig. 5.5 (c)].

Step V : P-analysis of basic determinate truss due to applied loads : Considering static equilibrium of truss all the reaction components (R_p) are found out as shown in Fig. 5.5 (b). Also the forces (P) in all the members of truss are found out and are shown in Fig. 5.5 (b).

Step VI : K-analysis of basic determinate truss : Unit positive force corresponding to Q is applied as shown in Fig. 5.5 (c). All the reaction components (R_k) and forces (K) in all the members of truss are found out and are shown in Fig. 5.5 (c).

Step VII : Table for numerical computations :

Sr. No.	Member	Length (mm)	Area (mm²)	P (kN)	K	$\frac{PKL}{A}$	$\frac{K^2L}{A}$	Q (kN)	QK (kN)	$P_f = P + QK$ (kN)
1.	AB	3000	2000	− 100	0.58	− 87	0.505		− 42.82	− 142.82
2.	BC	3000	2000	− 100	0.58	− 87	0.505		− 42.82	− 142.82
3.	CD	3000	1000	100	0.58	174	1.01	−73.83	− 42.82	57.18
4.	DA	3000	1000	100	0.58	174	1.01		− 42.82	57.18
5.	DB	3000	2000	− 100	− 0.58	87	0.505		42.82	− 57.18
						Σ = 261	3.535			

Step VIII : Calculation of redundant force :

$$Q = -\left[\frac{\sum_{i=1}^{n}\left(\frac{PKL}{EA}\right)_i}{\sum_{i=1}^{n}\left(\frac{K^2L}{EA}\right)_i}\right] = -\left[\frac{\sum\left(\frac{PKL}{A}\right)}{\sum\left(\frac{K^2L}{A}\right)}\right]$$

$$= -\left(\frac{261}{3.535}\right) = -73.83 \text{ kN} = 73.83 \text{ kN} (\rightarrow)$$

Step IX : Final forces in all the members of truss (P_f) :

Using the equation :

$$P_f = P + QK$$

final forces in all the members of truss are computed and are as tabulated above and shown in Fig. 5.5 (d).

Step X : Final reaction components at supports (R) :

Using the equation

$$R = R_p + Q \cdot R_k$$

final reaction components at supports are computed and are as shown in Fig. 5.5 (d).

Example 5.3 : *Analyse the truss supported and loaded as shown in Fig. 5.6 (a). Cross-sectional area of each member in cm² is indicated in brackets. Take E = constant.*

Solution : Data :

(1) Truss is supported and loaded as shown in Fig. 5.6 (a).

(2) E = constant

Objects :

(1) Redundant force,

(2) Forces in all the members of truss and

(3) Reactions at supports,

Concepts and Equations :

(1) Principle of superposition,

(2) Analysis of determinate truss,

(3) Compatibility condition and

(4) $Q = -\left[\dfrac{\sum\limits_{i=1}^{n} \left(\dfrac{PKL}{EA}\right)_i}{\sum\limits_{i=1}^{n} \left(\dfrac{K^2L}{EA}\right)_i} \right]$

Procedure :

Step I : Degree of static indeterminacy (D_{si}) :

(a) Degree of external indeterminacy = $(D_{si})_e$ = r − 3 = 4 − 3 = 1

(b) Degree of internal indeterminacy = $(D_{si})_i$ = m − (2j − 3) = 5 − (2 × 4 − 3) = 0

Total degree of static indeterminacy = D_{si} = $(D_{si})_e + (D_{si})_i$ = 1 + 0 = 1

Step II : Selection of redundant force (Q) :

Let, $Q = H_B (\rightarrow)$

Step III : Basic determinate truss :

Hinge support at B is replaced by roller support and determinate truss is obtained as shown in Fig. 5.6 (b).

Step IV : Superposition : The given indeterminate truss is considered as superposition of (a) basic determinate truss with given loads [Fig. 5.6 (b)] and (b) unknown redundant force Q times the basic determinate truss with unit positive redundant force [Fig. 5.6 (c)].

Step V : P-analysis of basic determinate truss due to applied loads : Considering static equilibrium of truss all the reaction components (R_p) are found out as shown in Fig. 5.6 (b). Also the forces (P) in all the members of truss are found out and are shown in Fig. 5.6 (b).

Step VI : K-analysis of basic determinate truss : Unit positive force corresponding to Q is applied as shown in Fig. 5.6 (c). All the reaction components (R_k) and forces (K) in all the members of truss are found out and are shown in Fig. 5.6 (c).

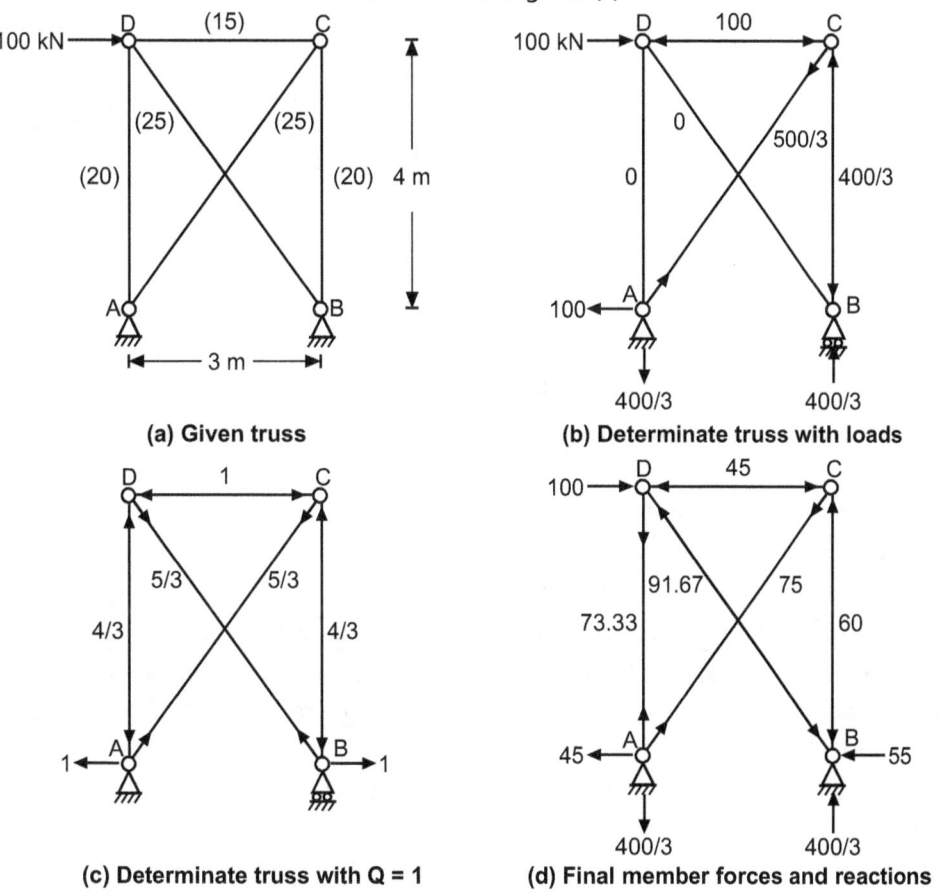

Fig. 5.6 : Illustrative Example 5.3

Step VII : Table for numerical computation :

Sr. No	Member	Length (mm)	Area (mm²)	P (kN)	K	PKL/A	K²L/A	Q (kN)	QK (kN)	Pf = P + QK (kN)
1.	BC	4000	2000	−400/3	−4/3	355.55	3.55		73.33	−60
2.	CD	3000	1500	−100	−1	200	2.0		55	−45
3.	DA	4000	2000	0	−4/3	0	3.55	−55	73.33	73.33
4.	AC	5000	2500	500/3	5/3	555.55	5.55		−91.67	75
5.	BD	5000	2500	0	5/3	0	5.55		−91.67	−91.67
						Σ = 1111.11	20.2			

Step VIII : Calculation of redundant force :

$$Q = -\left[\frac{\sum_{i=1}^{n}\left(\frac{PKL}{EA}\right)_i}{\sum_{i=1}^{n}\left(\frac{K^2L}{EA}\right)_i}\right] = -\left[\frac{\sum\left(\frac{PKL}{A}\right)}{\sum\left(\frac{K^2L}{A}\right)}\right] = -\left(\frac{1111.11}{20.2}\right)$$

$$= -55 \text{ kN} = 55 \text{ kN} (\leftarrow)$$

Step IX : Final forces in all the members of truss (P_f) :

Using the equation :

$$P_f = P + QK$$

final forces in all the members of truss are computed and are as tabulated above and shown in Fig. 5.6 (d).

Step X : Final reaction components at supports (R) :

Using the equation,

$$R = R_p + Q \cdot R_K$$

final reaction components at supports are computed and are as shown in Fig. 5.6 (d).

Example 5.4 : *Analyse the truss supported and loaded as shown in Fig. 5.7 (a). Cross-sectional area of each member in cm² is indicated in brackets. Take E = constant.*

Solution : Data :

(1) Truss is supported and loaded as shown in Fig. 5.7 (a).
(2) E = constant

Objects :

(1) Redundant force,
(2) Forces in all the members of truss and
(3) Reactions at supports.

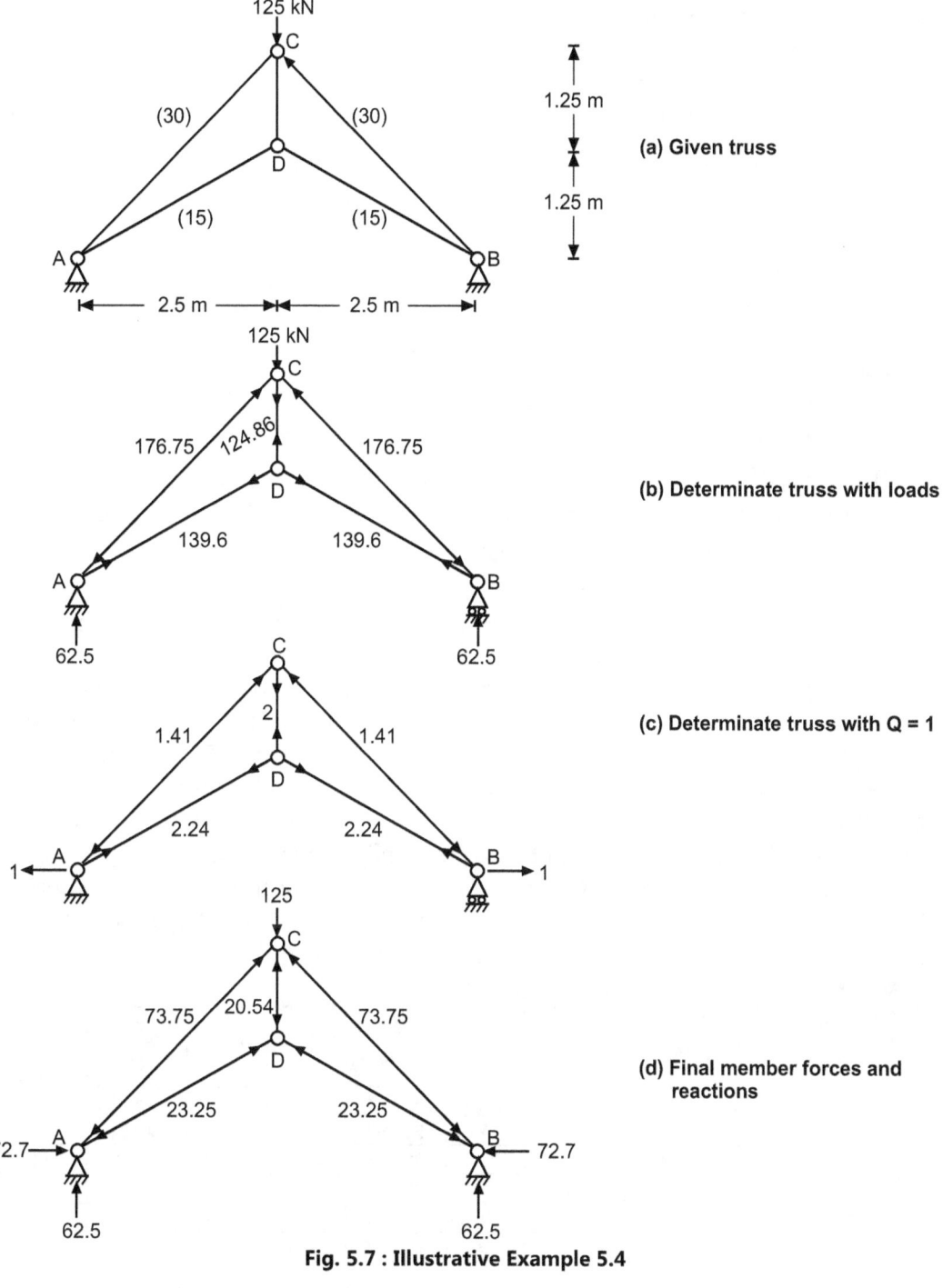

Fig. 5.7 : Illustrative Example 5.4

Concepts and Equations :
(1) Principle of superposition,
(2) Analysis of determinate truss,
(3) Compatibility condition and

(4) $Q = -\left[\dfrac{\sum_{i=1}^{n}\left(\dfrac{PKL}{EA}\right)_i}{\sum_{i=1}^{n}\left(\dfrac{K^2L}{EA}\right)_i} \right]$

Procedure :

Step I : Degree of static indeterminacy (D_{si}) :
(a) Degree of external indeterminacy = $(D_{si})_e$ = r – 3 = 4 – 3 = 1
(b) Degree of internal indeterminacy = $(D_{si})_i$ = m – (2j – 3) = 5 – (2 × 4 – 3) = 0
  Total degree of static indeterminacy = D_{si} = $(D_{si})_e$ + $(D_{si})_i$ = 1 + 0 = 1

Step II : Selection of redundant force (Q) :
Let, $\quad Q = H_B\ (\rightarrow)$

Step III : Basic determinate truss : Hinge support at B is replaced by roller support and determinate truss is obtained as shown in Fig. 5.7 (b).

Step IV : Superposition : The given indeterminate truss is considered as superposition of (a) basic determinate truss with given loads [Fig. 5.7 (b)] and (b) unknown redundant force 'Q' times the basic determinate truss with unit positive redundant force. [Fig. 5.7 (c)].

Step V : P-analysis of basic determinate truss due to applied loads : Considering static equilibrium of truss all the reaction components (R_p) are found out as shown in Fig. 5.7 (b). Also the forces (P) in all the members of truss are found out and are shown in Fig. 5.7 (b).

Step VI : K-analysis of Basic Determinate Truss : Unit positive force corresponding to 'Q' is applied as shown in Fig. 5.7 (c). All the reaction components (R_k) and forces (K) in all the members of truss are found out and are shown in Fig. 5.7 (c).

Step VII : Table for numerical computation :

Sr. No.	Member	Length (mm)	Area (mm^2)	P (kN)	K	$\dfrac{PKL}{A}$	$\dfrac{K^2L}{A}$	Q (kN)	QK (kN)	$P_f = P + QK$ (kN)
1.	AD	2795	1500	139.6	2.24	582.67	9.35		–18.21	–23.25
2.	BD	2795	1500	139.6	2.24	582.67	9.35		–18.21	–23.25
3.	AC	3535	3000	–176.25	–1.41	292.83	2.34	–72.7	– 76.92	–73.75
4.	BC	3535	3000	–176.25	–1.41	292.83	2.34		– 76.92	–73.75
5.	CD	1250	1000	124.86	2	312.15	5		–16.04	–20.54
					Σ =	2063.15	28.38			

Step VIII : Calculation of redundant force :

$$Q = -\left[\dfrac{\sum_{i=1}^{n}\left(\dfrac{PKL}{EA}\right)_i}{\sum_{i=1}^{n}\left(\dfrac{K^2L}{EA}\right)_i}\right] = -\left(\dfrac{\sum\dfrac{(PKL)}{A}}{(K^2L/A)}\right) = -\left(\dfrac{2063.15}{28.3}\right)$$

$$= -72.70 \text{ kN} = 72.70 \text{ kN } (\leftarrow)$$

Step IX : Final forces in all the members of truss (P_f) :
Using the equation,
$$P_f = P + QK$$
final forces in all the members of truss are computed and are as tabulated above and shown in Fig. 5.7 (d).

Step X : Final reaction components at supports (R) :
Using the equation,
$$R = R_p + Q \cdot R_k$$
final reaction components at supports are computed and are as shown in Fig. 5.7 (d).

5.2.5 Internally Indeterminate Trusses

Example 5.5 : *Analyse the truss supported and loaded as shown in Fig. 5.8 (a). Cross-sectional area of each member in cm^2 is indicated in brackets. Take E = constant.*

Solution : Data :
(1) Truss is supported and loaded as shown in Fig. 5.8 (a).

Objects :
(1) Redundant force (2) Forces in all the members of truss and
(3) Reactions at supports.

Concepts and Equations :
(1) Principle of superposition (2) Analysis of determinate truss,
(3) Compatibility condition and

$$(4)\ Q = -\left[\dfrac{\sum_{i=1}^{n}\left(\dfrac{PKL}{EA}\right)_i}{\sum_{i=1}^{n}\left(\dfrac{K^2L}{EA}\right)_i}\right]$$

Procedure :
Step I : Degree of static indeterminacy (D_{si}) :
(a) Degree of external indeterminacy = $(D_{si})_e$ = r − 3 = 3 − 3 = 0
(b) Degree of internal indeterminacy = $(D_{si})_i$ = m − 2j = 3 − 2 × 1 = 1
Total degree of static indeterminacy = D_{si} = $(D_{si})_e$ + $(D_{si})_i$ = 0 + 1 = 1

Step II : Selection of redundant force (Q) :

Step III : Basic determinate truss : Member CD is cut and determinate truss is obtained as shown in Fig. 5.8 (b).

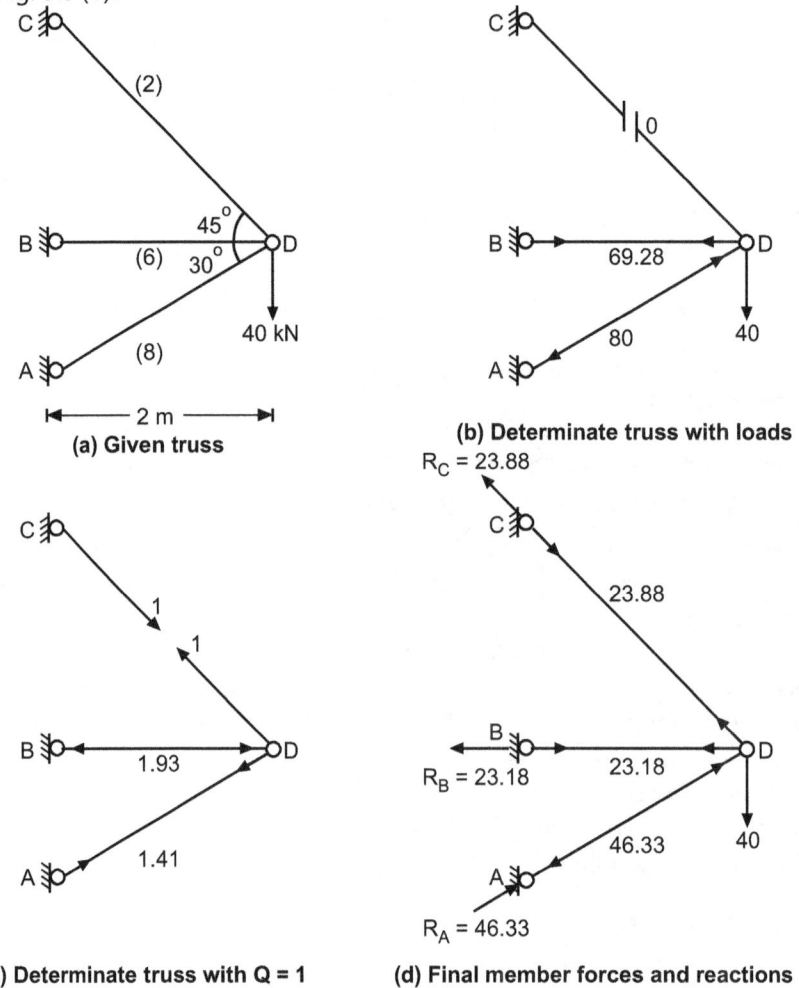

(a) Given truss

(b) Determinate truss with loads

(c) Determinate truss with Q = 1

(d) Final member forces and reactions

Fig. 5.8 : Illustrative Example 5.5

Step IV : Superposition : The given indeterminate truss is considered as superposition of (a) basic determinate truss with given loads [Fig. 5.8 (b)] and (b) unknown redundant force 'Q' times the basic determinate truss with unit positive redundant force. [Fig. 5.8 (c)].

Step V : P-analysis of basic determinate truss due to applied loads : The forces (P) in all the members of truss are found out and are shown in Fig. 5.8 (b).

Step VI : K-analysis of basic determinate truss : Unit positive force corresponding to 'Q' is applied as shown in Fig. 5.8 (c) forces (K) in all the members of truss are found out and are shown in Fig. 5.8 (c).

Step VII : Table for numerical computations :

Sr. No.	Member	Length (mm)	Area (mm²)	P (kN)	K	$\frac{PKL}{A}$	$\frac{K^2L}{A}$	Q (kN)	QK (kN)	$P_f = P + QK$ (kN)
1.	AD	2310	800	−80	1.41	−325.71	5.74		33.67	−46.33
2.	BD	2000	600	69.28	−1.93	−445.7	12.42	23.88	−46.10	23.18
3.	CD	2828	200	0	1	0	14.14		−23.88	−23.88
					Σ =	−771.41	32.3			

Step VIII : Calculation of redundant force :

$$Q = -\left[\frac{\sum_{i=1}^{n}\left(\frac{PKL}{EA}\right)_i}{\sum_{i=1}^{n}\left(\frac{K^2L}{EA}\right)_i}\right] = -\left[\frac{\sum\left(\frac{PKL}{A}\right)}{\sum\left(\frac{K^2L}{A}\right)}\right] = -\left(\frac{-771.41}{32.3}\right)$$

$$= 23.88 \text{ kN (Tensile)}$$

Step IX : Final force in all the members of truss (P_f) :
Using the equation,

$$P_f = P + QK$$

final forces in all the members of truss are computed and are as tabulated above and shown in Fig. 5.8 (d).

Step X : Final reaction components at supports (R) :
Using the equation,

$$R = R_p + Q \cdot R_k$$

final reaction components at supports are computed and are as shown in Fig. 5.8 (d).

Example 5.6 : *Analyse the truss supported and loaded as shown in Fig. 5.9 (a).*
Take EA = constant.

Solution : Data :
(1) Truss is supported and loaded as shown in Fig. 5.9 (a).
(2) EA = constant

Objects :
(1) Redundant force   (2) Forces in all the members of truss and
(3) Reactions at supports.

Concepts and Equations :
(1) Principle of superposition   (2) Analysis of determinate truss,
(3) Compatibility condition and

$$(4) \quad Q = -\left[\dfrac{\sum_{i=1}^{n} \left(\dfrac{PKL}{EA}\right)_i}{\sum_{i=1}^{n} \left(\dfrac{K^2L}{EA}\right)_i} \right]$$

Procedure :

Step I : Degree of static indeterminacy (D_{si}) :
(a) Degree of external indeterminacy = $(D_{si})_e$ = r − 3 = 3 − 3 = 0
(b) Degree of internal indeterminacy = $(D_{si})_i$ = m − (2j − 3) = 8 − (2 × 5 − 3) = 1
Total degree of static indeterminacy = D_{si} = $(D_{si})_e$ + $(D_{si})_i$ = 0 + 1 = 1

Step II : Selection of redundant force (Q) :
Let,   Q = Force in member BE (Tensile)

Step III : Basic determinate truss :
Member BE is cut and determinate truss is obtained as shown in Fig. 5.9 (b).

Step IV : Superposition : The given indeterminate truss is considered as superposition of (a) basic determinate truss with given loads [Fig. 5.9 (b)] and (b) unknown redundant force 'Q' times the basic determinate truss with unit positive redundant force (Fig. 5.9 (c)).

Step V : P-analysis of basic determinate truss due to applied loads : Considering static equilibrium of truss all the reaction components (R_p) are found out as shown in Fig. 5.9 (b). Also the forces (P) in all the members of truss are found out and are shown in [Fig. 5.9 (b)].

Step VI : K-analysis of basic determinate truss : Unit positive force corresponding to 'Q' is applied as shown in Fig. 5.9 (c).

Forces (K) in all the members of truss are found out and are shown in Fig. 5.9 (c). Reaction components (R_k) are zero for this analysis.

Step VII : Table for numerical computation :

Sr. No.	Member	Length (m)	P (kN)	K	PKL	K^2L	Q (kN)	QK (kN)	P_f = P + QK (kN)
1.	AB	2	25	$-1/\sqrt{2}$	−35.35	1		9.9	34.9
2.	BC	2	25	0	0	0		0	25
3.	CD	$2\sqrt{2}$	$-25\sqrt{2}$	0	0	0		0	$-25\sqrt{2}$
4.	DE	2	−50	$-1/\sqrt{2}$	70.71	1	−14.01	9.9	−40.1
5.	EA	2	0	$-1/\sqrt{2}$	0	1		9.9	9.9
6.	BD	2	0	$-1/\sqrt{2}$	0	1		9.9	9.9
7.	AD	$2\sqrt{2}$	$25\sqrt{2}$	1	100	$2\sqrt{2}$		−14.01	21.35
8.	BE	$2\sqrt{2}$	0	1	0	$2\sqrt{2}$		−14.01	−14.01
				Σ =	135.36	9.66			

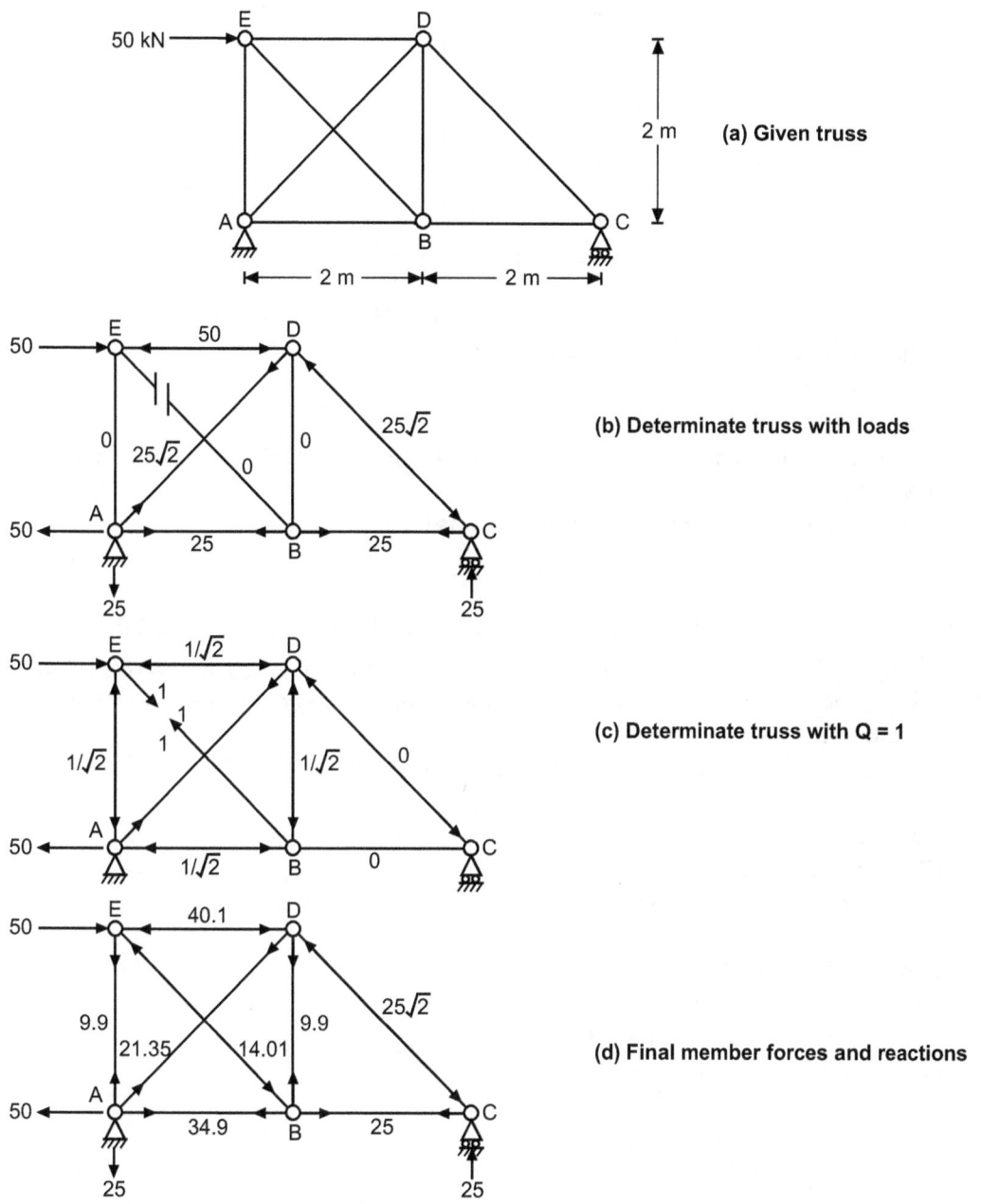

Fig. 5.9 : Illustrative Example 5.6

Step VIII : Calculation of redundant force :

$$Q = -\left[\dfrac{\sum\limits_{i=1}^{n}\left(\dfrac{PKL}{EA}\right)_i}{\sum\limits_{i=1}^{n}\left(\dfrac{K^2L}{EA}\right)_i}\right]$$

$$= -\left(\dfrac{\sum (PKL)}{\sum (K^2L)}\right) = -\left(\dfrac{135.36}{9.66}\right)$$

$$= -14.01 \text{ kN} = 14.01 \text{ kN (Compressive)}$$

Step IX : Final forces in all the members of truss (P_f) :

Using the equation,

$$P_f = P + QK$$

final forces in all the members of truss are computed and are as tabulated above and shown in Fig. 5.9 (d).

Step X : Final reaction components at supports (R) :

Using the relation,

$$R = R_p + Q \cdot R_k$$

final reaction components at supports are computed and are as shown in Fig. 5.9 (d).

Example 5.7 : *Analyse the truss supported and loaded as shown in Fig. 5.10 (a). Cross-sectional area of each member in cm^2 is indicated in brackets. Take E = constant.*

Solution : Data :
(1) Truss is supported and loaded as shown in Fig. 5.10 (a).
(2) E = constant

Objects :
(1) Redundant force,
(2) Forces in all the members of truss and
(3) Reactions at supports.

Concepts and Equations :
(1) Principle of superposition,
(2) Analysis of determinate truss,
(3) Compatibility condition and

(4) $Q = -\left[\dfrac{\sum\limits_{i=1}^{n}\left(\dfrac{PKL}{EA}\right)_i}{\sum\limits_{i=1}^{n}\left(\dfrac{K^2L}{EA}\right)_i}\right]$

Procedure :

Step I : Degree of static indeterminacy (D_{si}) :

(a) Degree of external indeterminacy = $(D_{si})_e$ = r − 3 = 3 − 3 = 0

(b) Degree of internal indeterminacy = $(D_{si})_i$ = m − (2j − 3) = 6 − (2 × 4 − 3) = 1

Total degree of static indeterminacy = D_{si} = $(D_{si})_e + (D_{si})_i$ = 0 + 1 = 1

Step II : Selection of redundant force (Q) :

Let,   Q = Force in member AB (Tensile)

Step III : Basic determinate truss :

Member AB is cut and determinate truss is obtained as shown in Fig. 5.10 (b).

Step IV : Superposition : The given indeterminate truss is considered as superposition of (a) basic determinate truss with given loads [Fig. 5.10 (b)] and (b) unknown redundant force 'Q' times the basic determinate truss with unit positive redundant force [Fig. 5.10 (c)].

Step V : P-analysis of basic determinate truss due to applied loads : Considering static equilibrium of truss all the reaction components (R_p) are found out as shown in Fig. 5.10 (b). Also the forces (P) in all the members of truss are found out and are shown in Fig. 5.10 (b).

Step VI : K-analysis of basic determinate truss : Unit positive force corresponding to 'Q' is applied as shown in Fig. 5.10 (c).

Forces (K) in all the members of truss are found out and are shown in Fig. 5.10 (c). Reaction components (R_k) are zero for this analysis.

Step VII : Table for numerical computation :

Sr. No.	Member	Length (mm)	Area (mm²)	P (kN)	K	$\frac{PKL}{A}$	$\frac{K^2L}{A}$	Q (kN)	QK (kN)	$P_f = P +$ QK (kN)
1.	BC	4000	2000	−400/3	4/3	−355.55	3.55		66.67	−66.67
2.	CD	3000	1500	−100	1	−20	2.0		50	−50
3.	DA	4000	2000	0	4/3	0	3.55	50	66.67	66.67
4.	AC	5000	2500	500/3	−5/3	−555.55	5.55		−83.33	83.33
5.	BD	5000	2500	0	−5/3	0	5.55		−83.33	−83.33
6.	AB	3000	1500	0	1	0	2.0		50	50
					Σ =	−1111.11	22.2			

Step VIII : Calculation of redundant force :

$$Q = -\left[\dfrac{\sum\limits_{i=1}^{n}\left(\dfrac{PKL}{EA}\right)_i}{\sum\limits_{i=1}^{n}\left(\dfrac{K^2L}{EA}\right)_i}\right]$$

$$= -\left[\dfrac{\sum\left(\dfrac{PKL}{A}\right)}{\sum\left(\dfrac{K^2L}{A}\right)}\right] = -\left(\dfrac{-1111.11}{22.22}\right) = 50 \text{ kN (Tensile)}$$

Step IX : Final forces in all the members of truss (P_f) :

Using the equation,
$$P_f = P + QK$$

final forces in all the members of truss are computed and are as tabulated above and shown in Fig. 5.10 (d).

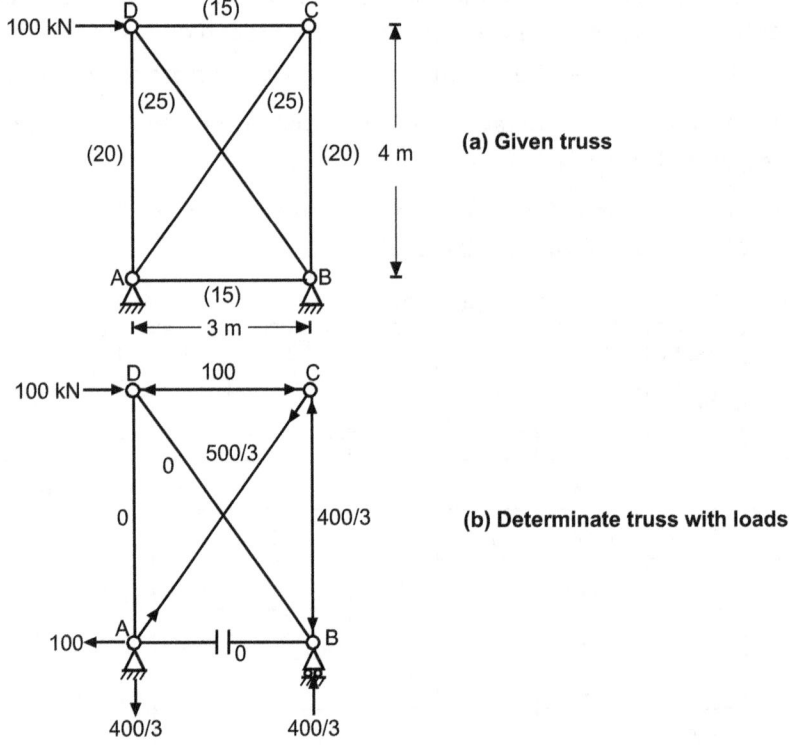

(a) Given truss

(b) Determinate truss with loads

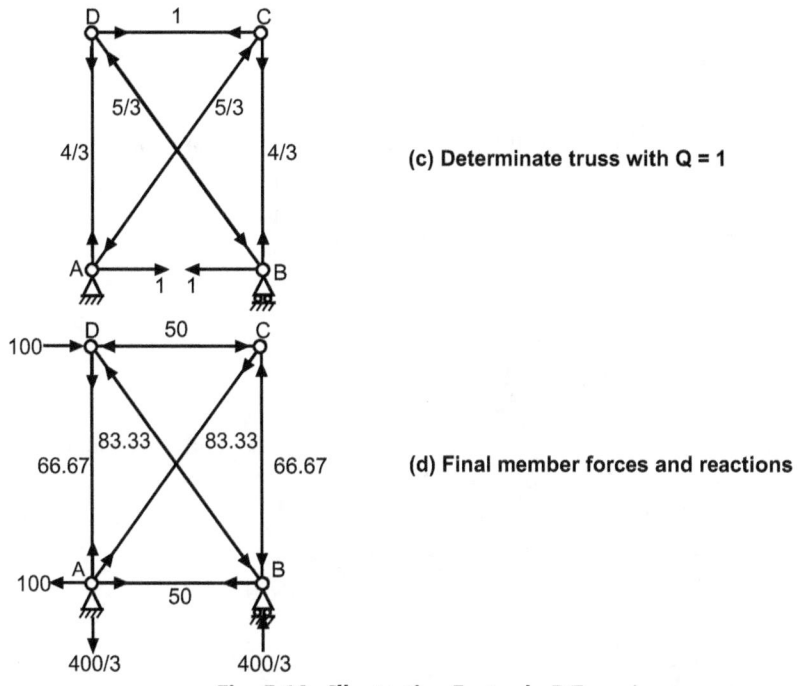

(c) Determinate truss with Q = 1

(d) Final member forces and reactions

Fig. 5.10 : Illustrative Example 5.7

Step X : Final reaction components at supports (R) :
Using the equation,
$$R = R_p + Q \cdot R_k$$
final reaction components at supports are computed and are as shown in Fig. 5.10 (d).

Example 5.8 : Analyse the truss supported and loaded as shown in Fig. 5.11 (a). Cross-sectional area of each member in cm² is indicated in brackets. Take E = constant.

Solution : Data :
(1) Truss is supported and loaded as shown in Fig. 5.11 (a). (2) E = constant.

Object :
(1) Redundant force (2) Forces in all the members of truss and
(3) Reactions at supports.

Concepts and Equations :
(1) Principle of superposition, (2) Analysis of determinate truss,
(3) Compatibility condition and

(4) $Q = -\left[\dfrac{\sum\limits_{i=1}^{n} \left(\dfrac{PKL}{EA}\right)_i}{\sum\limits_{i=1}^{n} \left(\dfrac{K^2 L}{EA}\right)_i} \right]$

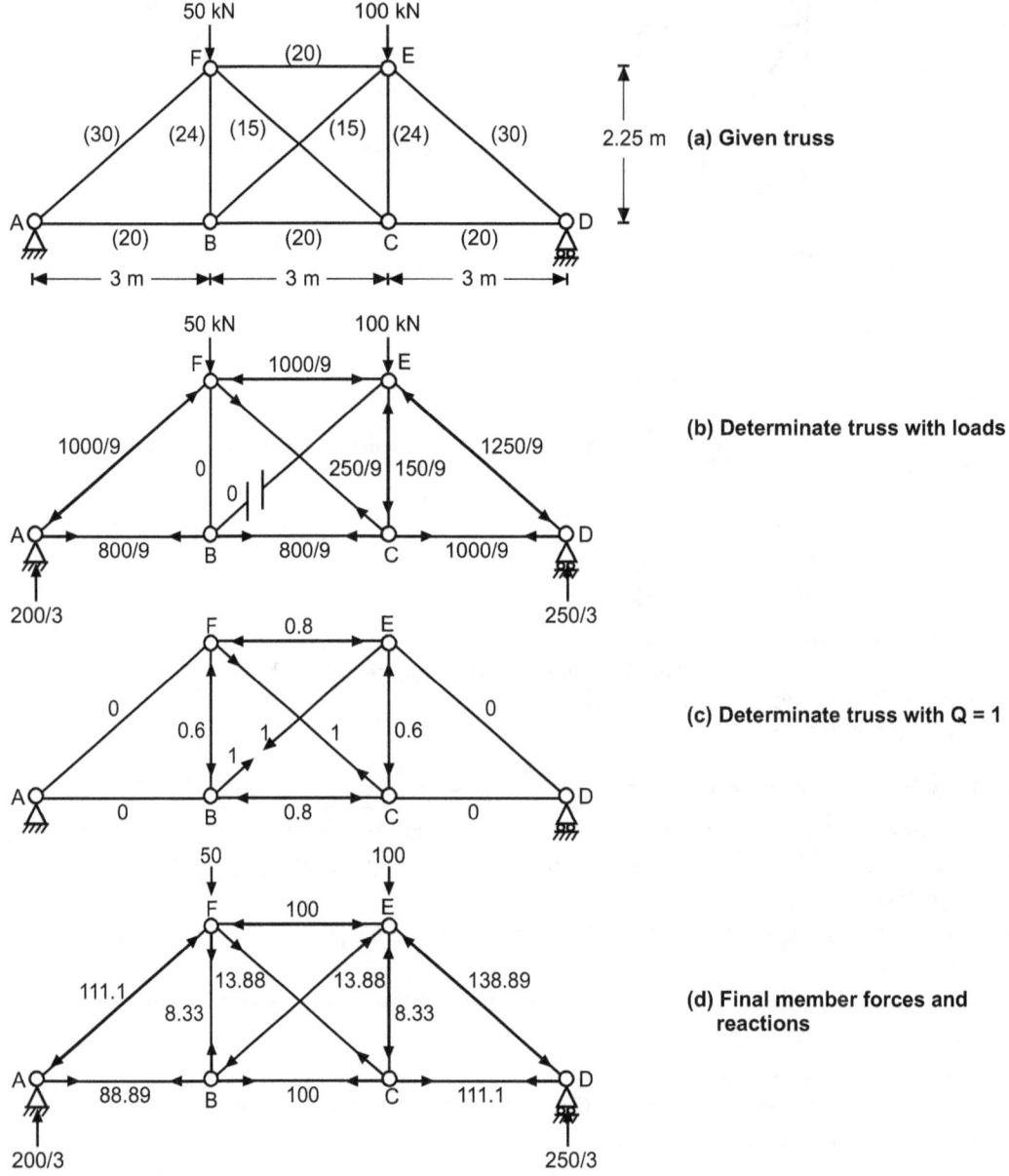

Fig. 5.11 : Illustrative Example 5.8

Procedure :

Step I : Degree of static indeterminacy (D_{si}) :

(a) Degree of external indeterminacy = $(D_{si})_e$ = r – 3 = 3 – 3 = 0

(b) Degree of internal indeterminacy = $(D_{si})_i$ = m − (2j − 3) = 10 − (2 × 6 − 3) = 1

Total degree of static indeterminacy = D_{si} = $(D_{si})_e$ + $(D_{si})_i$ = 0 + 1 = 1

Step II : Selection of redundant force (Q) :

Let,   Q = Force in member BE (Tensile)

Step III : Basic determinate truss : Member BE is cut and determinate truss is obtained as shown in Fig. 5.11 (b).

Step IV : Superposition : The given indeterminate truss is considered as superposition of (a) basic determinate truss with given loads [Fig. 5.11 (b)] and (b) unknown redundant force 'Q' times the basic determinate truss with unit positive redundant force. [Fig. 5.11 (c)].

Step V : P-analysis of basic determinate truss due to applied loads : Considering static equilibrium of truss all the reaction components (R_p) are found out as shown in Fig. 5.11 (b). Also the forces (P) in all the members of truss are found out and are shown in Fig. 5.11 (b).

Step VI : K-analysis of basic determinate truss : Unit positive force corresponding to 'Q' is applied as shown in Fig. 5.11 (c).

Forces (K) in all the members of truss are found out and are shown in Fig. 5.11 (c). Reaction components (R_k) are zero for this analysis.

Step VII : Table for numerical computation :

Sr. No.	Member	Length (mm)	Area (mm²)	P (kN)	K	$\frac{PKL}{A}$	$\frac{K^2L}{A}$	Q (kN)	QK (kN)	$P_f = P + QK$ (kN)
1.	AB	3000	2000	800/9	0	0	0		0	88.89
2.	BC	3000	2000	800/9	−0.8	−106.67	0.96		11.1	100
3.	CD	3000	2000	1000/9	0	0	0		0	111.1
4.	EF	3000	2000	−1000/9	−0.8	133.33	0.96		11.1	−100
5.	BF	2250	2400	0	−0.6	0	0.34	−13.88	8.33	8.33
6.	CE	2250	2400	−150/9	−0.6	9.375	0.34		8.33	−8.33
7.	AF	3750	3000	−1000/9	0	0	0		0	−111.1
8.	DE	3750	3000	−1250/9	0	0	0		0	−138.89
9.	CF	3750	1500	250/9	1	69.44	2.5		−13.88	13.88
10.	BE	3750	1500	0	1	0	2.5		−13.88	−13.88
					Σ =	105.475	7.6			

Step VIII : Calculation of redundant force :

$$Q = -\left[\dfrac{\sum_{i=1}^{n}\left(\dfrac{PKL}{EA}\right)_i}{\sum_{i=1}^{n}\left(\dfrac{K^2 L}{EA}\right)_i}\right] = -\left[\dfrac{\sum\left(\dfrac{PKL}{A}\right)}{\sum\left(\dfrac{K^2 L}{A}\right)}\right] = -\left(\dfrac{105.475}{7.6}\right)$$

$$= -13.88 \text{ kN} = 13.88 \text{ kN (Compressive)}$$

Step IX : Final forces in all the members of truss (P_f) :

Using the equation,

$$P_f = P + QK$$

final forces in all the members of truss are computed and are as tabulated above and shown in Fig. 5.11 (d).

Step X : Final reaction components at supports (R) :

Using the equation,

$$Q = R_p + Q \cdot R_k$$

final reaction components at supports are computed and are as shown in Fig. 5.11 (d).

5.2.6 Indeterminate Trusses with Lack of Fit

The trusses are fabricated with the specific amount of tolerance in the length of members so that the members fit perfectly. But there may be errors in the fabrication, the length of a member of a truss may be slightly more or less than that required for the perfect assembly of members to form the truss. This is called the lack of fit due to the fabrication error.

The fabrication of a determinate truss with lack of fit can be accommodate this error and adjust itself without stressing. Whereas in an internally indeterminate truss, a member having fabrication error does not fit in well and the truss does not adjust the discrepancy. The member is to be forced for the right fit and the forces are developed in the members of the truss due to this lack of fit, before the external loading. Therefore, it is necessary to analyse indeterminate trusses for the effect of lack of fit independently. The forces in the members of the truss due to (i) lack of fit and (ii) external loads are then superposed to get the final forces.

Analysis of indeterminate trusses having lack of fit is effectively done by the force method with the following additional concepts :

- The member which has lack of fit should be selected as the redundant member.
- The known lack of fit of the redundant member is denoted by D_{QF}.

- The sign convention for D_{QF} is important which is as follows :

  D_{QF} is positive if the member is too long.

  D_{QF} is negative if the member is too short.

- The equation of the force method is used in the following form

$$D_Q = D_{QF} + F \cdot Q$$

$$0 = D_{QF} + \Sigma \left(\frac{K^2 L}{EA}\right) \cdot Q$$

$$\therefore Q = -\left[\frac{D_{QF}}{\sum_{i=1}^{n}\left(\frac{K^2 L}{EA}\right)_i}\right] \qquad \ldots (5.9)$$

Following Examples illustrate the procedure. Note that the numerical values of member properties and material properties are required.

Example 5.9 : *Analyse the truss supported as shown in Fig. 5.12 (a), if member AB is short by 5 mm. Take E = 200 GPa. Cross-sectional area of each member in cm² is indicated in brackets.*

Solution : Data :

(1) Truss is supported as shown in Fig. 5.12 (a).

(2) E = 200 GPa.

Objects :

(1) Redundant force,

(2) Forces in all the members of truss and

(3) Reactions at supports.

Concepts and Equations :

(1) Analysis of determinate truss,

(2) Compatibility condition and

(3) $Q = -\left[\dfrac{D_{QF}}{\sum_{i=1}^{n}\left(\frac{K^2 L}{EA}\right)_i}\right]$

Procedure :

Step I : Degree of static indeterminacy (D_{si}) :

(a) Degree of external indeterminacy = $(D_{si})_e$ = r − 3 = 4 − 3 = 1
(b) Degree of internal indeterminacy = $(D_{si})_i$ = m − (2j − 3) = 6 − (2 × 4 − 3) = 1

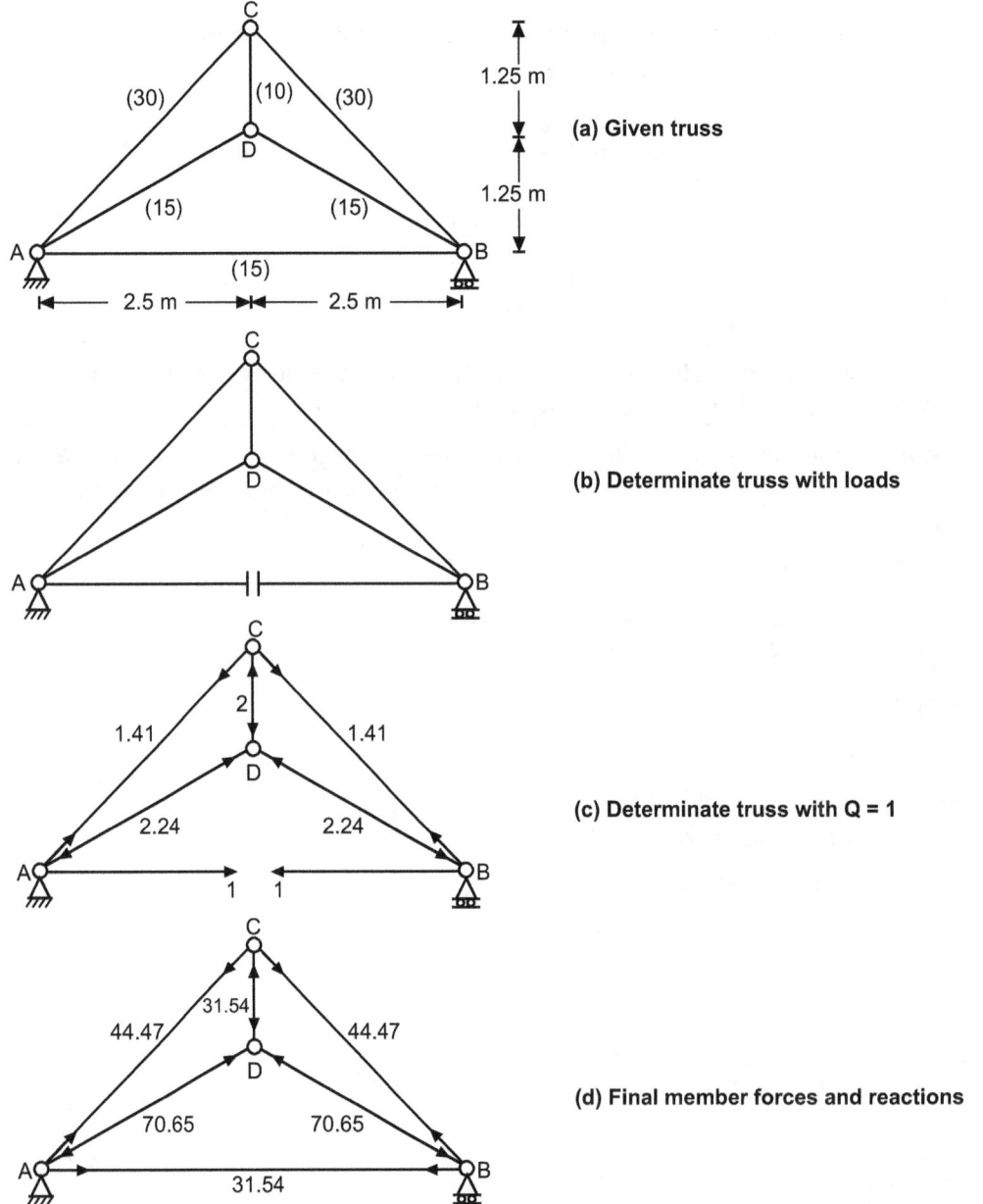

Fig. 5.12 : Illustrative Example 5.9

Step II : Selection of redundant force (Q) :

Let,   Q = Force in member AB (Tensile)

Step III : Basic determinate truss :

Member AB is cut and determinate truss is obtained as shown in Fig. 5.12 (b).

Step IV : K-analysis of basic determinate truss :

Unit positive force corresponding to 'Q' is applied as shown in Fig. 5.12 (c). Reaction components (R_k) are zero for this analysis. Forces (K) in all the members of truss are found out and are shown in Fig. 5.12 (c).

Step V : Table for numerical computation :

Sr. No.	Member	Length (mm)	Area (mm²)	K	$\dfrac{K^2 L}{A}$	Q (kN)	$P_f = QK$ (kN)
1.	AD	2795	1500	− 2.24	9.35		− 70.65
2.	BD	2795	1500	− 2.24	9.35		− 70.65
3.	AC	3535	3000	1.41	2.34	31.54	44.47
4.	BC	3535	3000	1.41	2.34		44.47
5.	CD	1250	1000	− 2	5.00		− 63.08
6.	AB	5000	1500	1	3.33		31.54
				Σ =	31.71		

Step VI : Calculation of redundant force :

$$Q = -\left[\dfrac{D_{QF}}{\sum_{i=1}^{n} \left(\dfrac{K^2 L}{EA}\right)_i}\right]$$

$$= -\left(\dfrac{-5}{\dfrac{31.71}{200}}\right)$$

= 31.54 kN (Tensile)

Step VII : Final forces in all the members of truss (P_f) :

Using the equation,

$$P_f = QK$$

final forces in all the members of truss are computed and are as tabulated above and shown in Fig. 5.12 (d).

Step VIII : Final reaction components at supports (R) : Reaction components at supports are zero.

Example 5.10 : *Analyse the truss supported as shown in Fig. 5.13 (a), if member AC is long by 7 mm. Take E = 200 GPa and cross-sectional area of each member = 350 mm².*

Solution : Data :
(1) Truss is supported and loaded as shown in Fig. 5.13 (a).
(2) E = 200 GPa.

Objects :
(1) Redundant force
(2) Forces in all the members of truss and
(3) Reactions at supports.

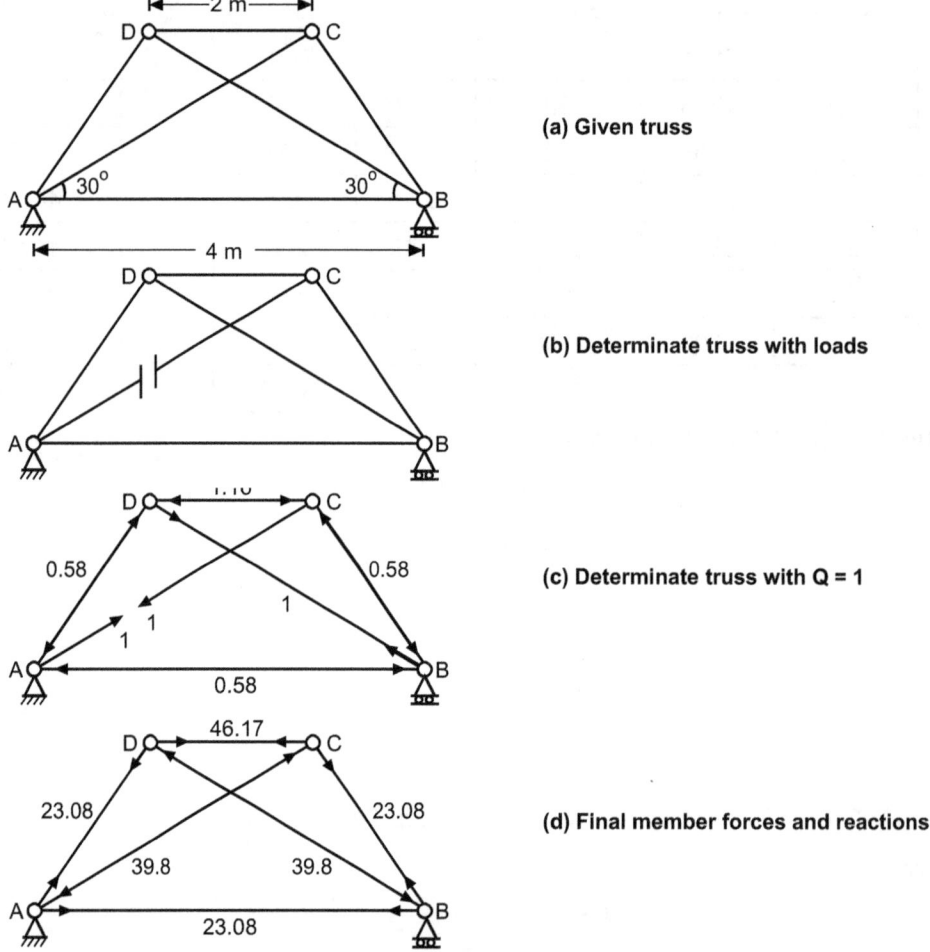

(a) Given truss

(b) Determinate truss with loads

(c) Determinate truss with Q = 1

(d) Final member forces and reactions

Fig. 5.13 : Illustrative Example 5.10

Concepts and Equations :
(1) Analysis of determinate truss,
(2) Compatibility condition and
(3) $Q = -\left[\dfrac{D_{QF}}{\sum_{i=1}^{n}\left(\dfrac{K^2 L}{EA}\right)_i}\right]$

Procedure :
Step I : Degree of static indeterminacy (D_{si}) :
(a) Degree of external indeterminacy = $(D_{si})_e$ = r − 3 = 4 − 3 = 1
(b) Degree of internal indeterminacy = $(D_{si})_i$ = m − (2j − 3) = 6 − (2 × 4 − 3) = 1

Step II : Selection of redundant force (Q) :
Let, Q = Force in member AC (Tensile)

Step III : Basic determinate truss :
Member AC is cut and determinate truss is obtained as shown in Fig. 5.13 (b).

Step IV : K-analysis of basic determinate truss : Unit positive force corresponding to 'Q' is applied as shown in Fig. 5.13 (c). Reaction components (R_k) are zero for this analysis. Forces (K) in all the members of truss are found out and are shown in Fig. 5.13 (c).

Step V : Table for numerical computation :

Sr. No.	Member	Length (m)	K	K² L	Q (kN)	P_f = KQ (kN)
1.	AB	4	− 0.58	1.345		23.08
2.	BC	2	− 0.58	0.673		23.08
3.	CD	2	− 1.16	2.691	− 39.80	46.17
4.	DA	2	− 0.58	0.673		23.08
5.	BD	3.464	1	3.464		− 39.80
6.	AC	3.464	1	3.464		− 39.80
			Σ =	12.31		

Step VI : Calculation of redundant force :

$$Q = -\left[\dfrac{D_{QF}}{\sum_{i=1}^{n}\left(\dfrac{K^2 L}{EA}\right)_i}\right] = -\left[\dfrac{7}{12.31 \times \dfrac{1000}{200} \times 350}\right]$$

= − 39.80 kN = 39.80 kN (Compressive)

Step VII : Final forces in all the members of truss (P_f) :
Using the equation
$$P_f = QK$$
final forces in all the members of truss are computed and are as tabulated above and shown in Fig. 5.13 (d).

Step VIII : Final reaction components at supports (R) :
Reaction components at supports are zero.

5.2.7 Temperature Effects in Indeterminate Trusses

The rise in temperature causes the increase in length of a member and the fall in temperature causes the decrease in length of a member if the member is free to expand or contract. This is called free thermal change in the length and given by (αtL) where α is the coefficient of linear expansion of the material, t is the change in temperature and L is the length of the member. If the free thermal expansion or contraction is prevented, then the stresses are developed. This is in general the effect of temperature.

In this context the following hints will be useful to consider the effects of temperature in trusses.

- In a statically determinate structure no internal forces are developed due to temperature changes as the thermal expansions or contractions are not prevented.
- Due to uniform temperature variation in an externally determinate structure, no internal forces are induced.
- Due to non-uniform temperature changes in an externally determinate structure, the internal forces are developed.
- In an externally indeterminate structure there are always temperature effects irrespective of uniform or non-uniform temperature variations.

The forces in members of a truss due to temperature effects are obtained by the force method with the following techniques and for the following common situations.

(A) Externally and Internally Indeterminate Truss :

Subjected to the temperature change in a particular member :

- The temperature-affected member is selected as the redundant member.
- The force in the redundant member is Q.
- Free thermal change in the redundant member is calculated as (αtL) and denoted by D_{Qt}.
- D_{Qt} is positive if expansion i.e. rise in temperature and D_{Qt} is negative if contraction i.e. fall in temperature.
- The usual procedure of the force method is used to find Q and the member forces.
- The basic equation is modified as

$$D_Q = D_{Qt} + F \cdot Q$$

$$\therefore \quad 0 = (\alpha tL) + \sum \left(\frac{K^2 L}{EA}\right) \cdot Q$$

$$\therefore \quad Q = -\left[\frac{\alpha tL}{\sum \left(\frac{K^2 L}{EA}\right)}\right] \qquad \ldots (5.10)$$

(B) Externally Indeterminate Truss Subjected to the Uniform Temperature Change :

- The reaction component in the direction of axis of member connecting two supports is selected as the redundant force Q.
- Free thermal expansion / contraction in the complete length of the member connecting the supports is calculated as (αtL) and denoted by D_{Qt}.
- It is to be noted that this D_{Qt} corresponds to Q.

$$Q = -\left[\frac{(\alpha tL)}{\sum_{i=1}^{n}\left(\frac{K^2 L}{EA}\right)_i}\right]$$

Following illustrative examples will clarify the procedure in detail.

Example 5.11 : Analyse the truss supported as shown in Fig. 5.14 (a), if member AD is subjected to temperature drop of 30°C. Take E = 200 GPa and coefficient of thermal expansion = α = 1.1×10^{-5} /°C, cross-sectional area of each member in cm² is indicated in brackets.

Solution : Data :
(1) Truss is supported and loaded as shown in Fig. 5.14 (a).
(2) E = 200 GPa.
(3) α = 1.1×10^{-5} /°C.

Objects :
(1) Redundant force
(2) Forces in all the members of truss and
(3) Reactions of supports :

Concepts and Equations :
(1) Analysis of determinate truss,
(2) Compatibility condition and
(3) $Q = -\left[\dfrac{D_{Qt}}{\sum_{i=1}^{n}\left(\dfrac{K^2 L}{EA}\right)_i}\right]$

Procedure :
Step I : Degree of static indeterminacy (D_{si}) :
(a) Degree of external indeterminacy $(D_{si})_e$ = r − 3 = 4 − 3 = 1
(b) Degree of internal indeterminacy $(D_{si})_i$ = m − (2j − 3) = 6 − (2 × 4 − 3) = 1

Step II : Selection of redundant force (Q) :
Let,   Q = Force in member AD (Tensile)
Step III : Basic determinate truss :
Member AD is cut and determinate truss is obtained as shown in Fig. 5.14 (b).

Step IV : K-Analysis of Basic Determinate Truss : Unit positive force corresponding to 'Q' is applied as shown in Fig. 5.14 (c). Reaction components (R_k) are zero for this analysis, forces (K) in all the members of truss are found out and are shown in Fig. 5.14 (c).

Step V : Table for numerical computations :

Sr. No.	Member	Length (mm)	Area (mm²)	K	$\dfrac{K^2 L}{A}$	Q (kN)	$P_f = QK$ (kN)
1.	AB	4000	2000	1.33	3.56		11.84
2.	BC	3000	1500	1	2		8.90
3.	CD	4000	2000	1.33	3.56	8.90	11.84
4.	AC	5000	2500	− 1.67	5.56		− 14.86
5.	BD	5000	2500	− 1.67	5.56		− 14.86
6.	AD	3000	1500	1	2		8.90
				Σ =	22.24		

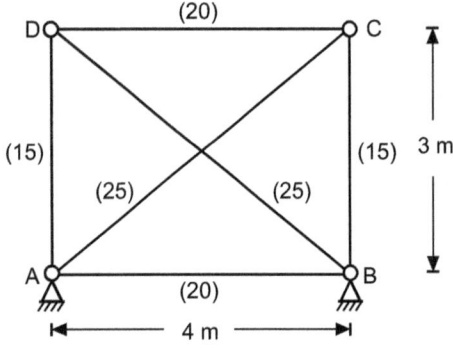

(a) Given truss

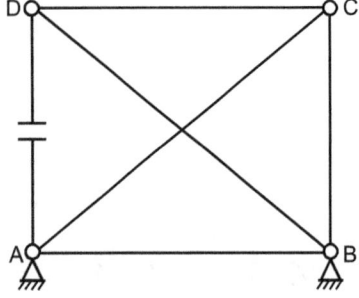

(b) Determinate truss with loads

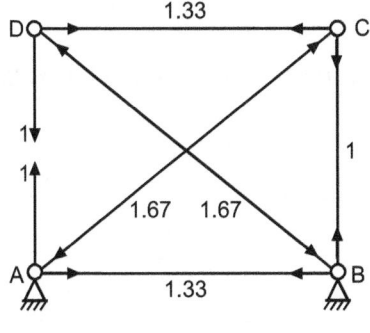

(c) Determinate truss with Q = 1

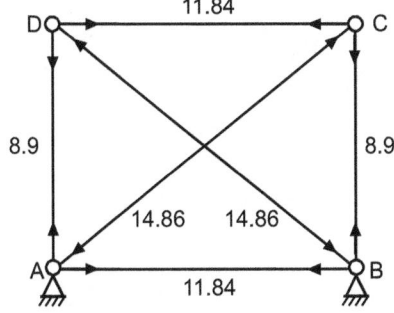

(d) Final member forces and reactions

Fig. 5.14 : Illustrative Example 5.11

Step VI : Calculation of redundant force :

$$Q = -\left[\frac{D_{Qt}}{\sum_{i=1}^{n}\left(\frac{K^2L}{EA}\right)_i}\right] = -\left[\frac{\alpha tL}{\sum K^2L/EA}\right]$$

$$= -\left[\frac{-1.1 \times 10^{-5} \times 30 \times 3000}{22.24/200}\right] = 8.90 \text{ kN (Tensile)}$$

Step VII : Final forces in all the members of truss (P_f) :

Using the equation

$$P_f = QK$$

final forces in all the members of truss are computed and are as tabulated above and shown in Fig. 5.14 (d).

Step VIII : Final reaction components at supports (R) : Reaction components at supports are zero.

Example 5.12 : *Analyse the truss supported as shown in Fig. 5.15 (a), if the member AC is subjected to temperature rise of 20°C. Take E = 200 GPa and coefficient of thermal expansion = α = 1.2 ×10⁻⁵/°C, cross-sectional area of each member in cm² is indicated in brackets.*

Solution : Data :

(1) Truss is supported and loaded as shown in Fig. 5.15 (a).

(2) E = 200 GPa,

(3) $\alpha = 1.2 \times 10^{-5}$/ °C.

Objects :

(1) Redundant force,

(2) Forces in all the members of truss and

(3) Reactions at supports.

Concepts and Equations :

(1) Analysis of determinate truss,

(2) Compatibility condition and

(3) $Q = -\left[\dfrac{D_{Qt}}{\sum\limits_{i=1}^{n} \left(\dfrac{K^2 L}{EA} \right)_i} \right]$

Procedure :

Step I : Degree of static indeterminacy (D_{si}) :

(a) Degree of external indeterminacy = $(D_{si})_e$ = r − 3 = 4 − 3 = 1

(b) Degree of internal indeterminacy = $(D_{si})_i$ = m − (2j − 3) = 6 − (2 × 4 − 3) = 1

Step II : Selection of redundant force (Q) :

Let,   Q = Force in member AC (Tensile)

Step III : Basic determinate truss : Member AC is cut and determinate truss is obtained as shown in Fig. 5.15 (b).

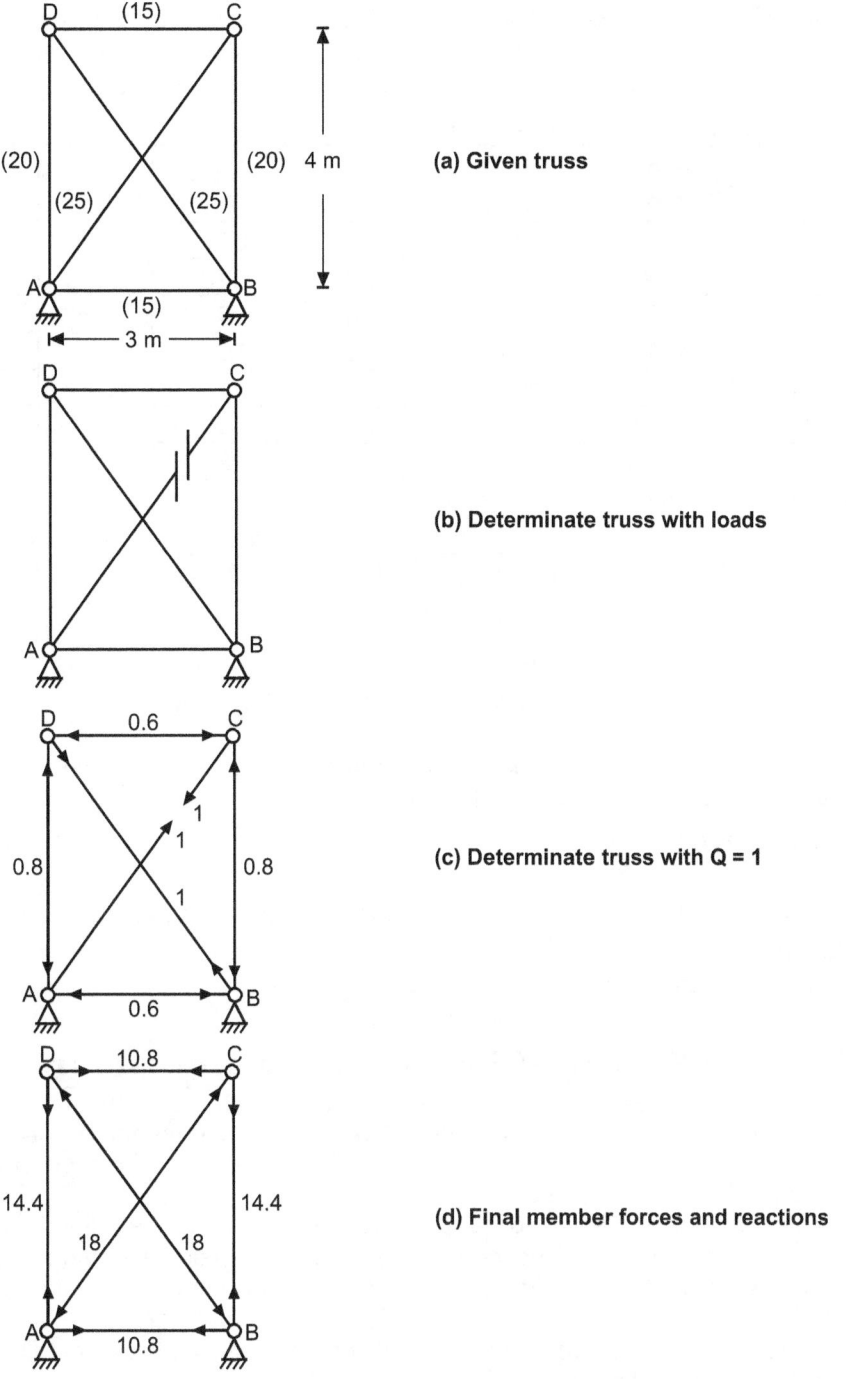

Fig. 5.15 : Illustrative Example 5.12

Step IV : K-Analysis of Basic Determinate Truss : Unit positive force corresponding to 'Q' is applied as shown in Fig. 5.15 (c). Reaction components (R_k) are zero for this analysis. Force (K) in all the members of truss are found out and are shown in Fig. 5.15 (c).

Step V : Table for numerical computation :

Sr. No.	Member	Length (mm)	Area (mm²)	K	$\frac{K^2L}{A}$	Q (kN)	$P_f = QK$ (kN)
1.	AB	3000	1500	– 0.6	0.72		10.8
2.	BC	4000	2000	– 0.8	1.28		14.4
3.	CD	3000	1500	– 0.6	0.72	– 18	10.8
4.	DA	4000	2000	– 0.8	1.28		14.4
5.	BD	5000	2500	1	2		– 18
6.	AC	5000	2500	1	2		– 18
					Σ = 8		

Step VI : Calculation of redundant force :

$$Q = -\left[\frac{D_{Qt}}{\sum_{i=1}^{n}\left(\frac{K^2L}{EA}\right)_i}\right] = -\left[\frac{\alpha t L}{\Sigma K^2L/EA}\right]$$

$$= -\left[\frac{1.2 \times 10^{-5} \times 20 \times 3000}{8/200}\right] = -18 \text{ kN}$$

$$= 18 \text{ kN (Compressive)}$$

Step VII : Final forces in all the members of truss (P_f) :

Using the equation,

$$P_f = QK$$

final forces in all the members of truss are computed and are as tabulated above and shown in Fig. 5.15 (d).

Step VIII : Final reaction components at supports (R) :

Reaction components at supports are zero.

5.2.8 Effects of Yielding of Support in Indeterminate Trusses

The yielding of the support of externally indeterminate truss induces the internal forces in the members of truss. The conventional procedure of the force method is used to analyse the externally indeterminate trusses for the effect of the yielding of the support employing the following particular techniques :
- Force corresponding to yielding of support must be selected as the redundant.
- Basic determinate truss is obtained by removing the constraint corresponding to yielding of support. The redundant force is the reaction component corresponding to the yielding.
- The geometrical condition of deformation at the yielding support is that D_Q should be equal to the amount of yielding.

- The basic equation of the force method in the following form is applied to determine the redundant force i.e. the reaction component due to the effect of yielding of support only.

$$D_Q = F \cdot Q$$

∴ $$D_Q = \Sigma \left(\frac{K^2 L}{EA}\right) \cdot Q$$

∴ $$Q = \left[\frac{D_Q}{\sum_{i=1}^{n} \left(\frac{K^2 L}{EA}\right)_i}\right] \qquad \ldots (5.11)$$

where D_Q is the known amount of the yielding of the support i.e. known translation. Generally it is the settlement of support.

- D_Q is considered a positive or negative according to the co-ordinate system i.e. positive in the positive direction of the co-ordinate axes and negative in the negative direction of the co-ordinate axes.

The following example illustrates the procedure for this case.

Example 5.13 : *Analyse the truss supported as shown in Fig. 5.16 (a), if support B sinks by 3 mm. Take E = 210 GPa and cross-sectional area of each member = 400 mm².*

Solution : Data :
(1) Truss is supported and loaded as shown in Fig. 5.16 (a).
(2) E = 210 GPa.

Objects :
(1) Redundant force, (2) Forces in all the members of truss and
(3) Reactions at supports.

Concepts and Equations :
(1) Analysis of determinate truss, (2) Compatibility condition and

(3) $$Q = \left[\frac{D_Q}{\sum_{i=1}^{n} \left(\frac{K^2 L}{EA}\right)_i}\right]$$

Procedure :

Step I : Degree of static indeterminacy (D_{si}) :
(a) Degree of external indeterminacy = $(D_{si})_e$ = r − 3 = 4 − 3 = 1
(b) Degree of internal indeterminacy = $(D_{si})_i$ = m − (2j − 3) = 9 − (2 × 6 − 3) = 0
Total degree of static indeterminacy = D_{si} = $(D_{si})_e$ + $(D_{si})_i$ = 1 + 0 = 1

Step II : Selection of redundant force (Q) :
Let, $Q = V_B$ (↑)

Step III : Basic Determinate Truss : Roller support at B is removed and determinate truss is obtained as shown in Fig. 5.16 (b).

Step IV : K-analysis of basic determinate truss : Unit positive force corresponding to 'Q' is applied as shown in Fig. 5.16 (c). Reaction components (R_k) and forces (K) in all the members of truss are found out and are shown in Fig. 5.16 (c).

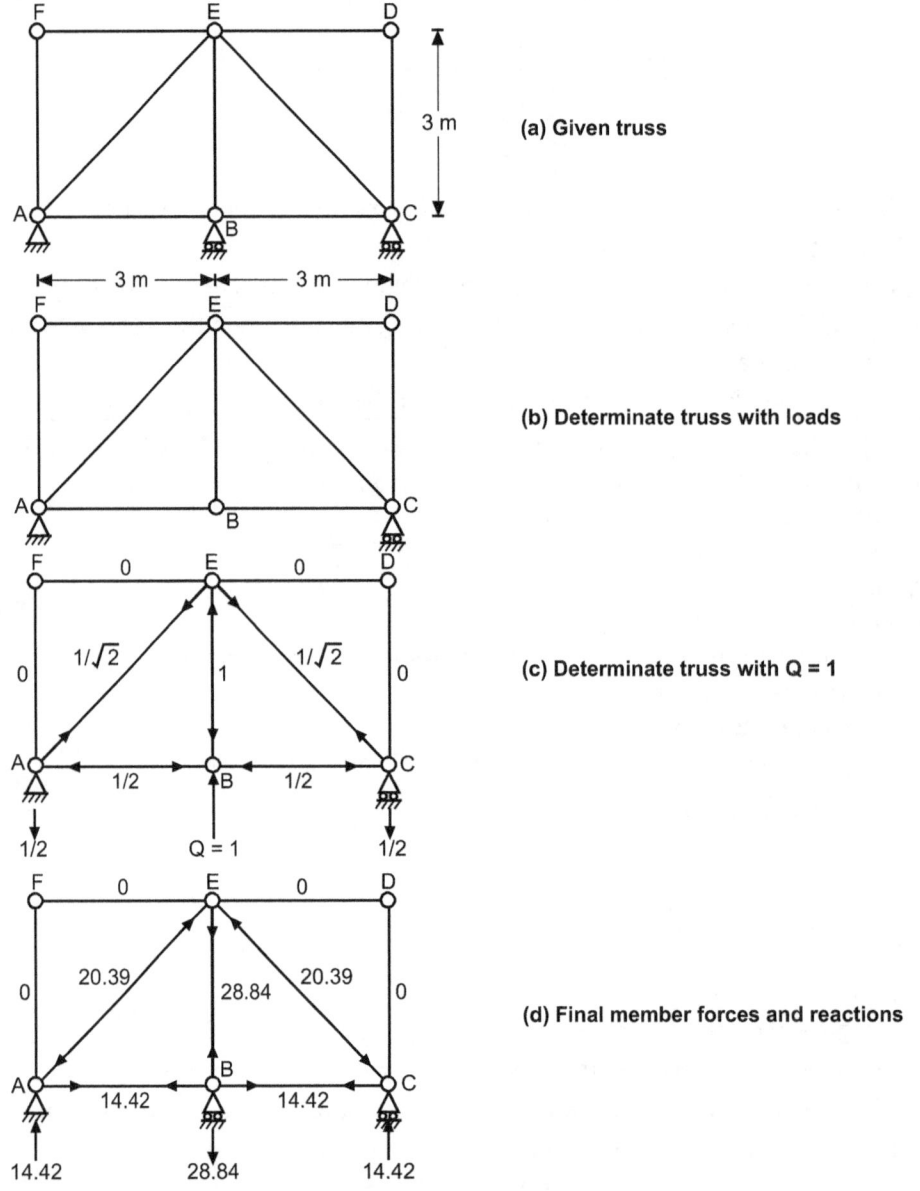

Fig. 5.16 : Illustrative Example 5.13

Step V : Table for numerical computation :

Sr. No.	Member	Length (m)	K	K²L	Q (kN)	P_f = KQ (kN)
1.	AB	3	–1/2	0.75		14.42
2.	BC	3	–1/2	0.75		14.42
3.	CD	3	0	0		0
4.	DE	3	0	0		0
5.	EF	3	0	0	–28.84	0
6.	FA	3	0	0		0
7.	EB	3	–1	3		28.84
8.	AE	3√2	1/√2	3/√2		–20.39
9.	CE	3√2	1/√2	3/√2		–20.39
				Σ = 8.74		

Step VI : Calculation of redundant force :

$$Q = \left[\dfrac{D_Q}{\sum\limits_{i=1}^{n}\left(\dfrac{K^2L}{EA}\right)_i}\right]$$

$$= \left[\dfrac{-3}{8.74 \times 1000/(210 \times 400)}\right] = -28.84 \text{ kN}$$

Step VII : Final forces in all the members of truss (P_f) :

Using the equation

$$P_f = QK$$

final forces in all the members of truss are computed and are as tabulated above and shown in Fig. 5.16 (d).

Step VIII : Final reaction components at supports (R) :

Using the equation

$$R = Q \cdot R_k$$

final reaction components at supports are computed and are as shown in Fig. 5.16 (d).

Example 5.14 : Analyse the truss supported and loaded as shown in Fig. 5.17 (a). If support B sinks by 3 mm. Take E = 210 GPa and cross-sectional area of each member = 400 mm².

Solution : Data :
(1) Truss is supported and loaded as shown in Fig. 5.17 (a).
(2) E = 210 GPa

Objects :
(1) Redundant force,
(2) Forces in all the members of truss and
(3) Reactions at supports.

Concepts and Equations :
(1) Principle of superposition, (2) Analysis of determinate truss,
(3) Compatibility condition and (4) $D_Q = D_{QL} + FQ$

Procedure :

Step I : Degree of static indeterminacy (D_{si}) :
(a) Degree of external indeterminacy = $(D_{si})_e = r - 3 = 4 - 3 = 1$
(b) Degree of internal indeterminacy = $(D_{si})_i = m - (2j - 3) = 9 - (2 \times 6 - 3) = 0$
   Total degree of static indeterminacy = $(D_{si})_e + (D_{si})_i = 1 + 0 = 1$

Step II : Selection of redundant force (Q) :
Let, $Q = V_B$ (↑)

Step III : Basic Determinate Truss :
Roller support at B is removed and determinate truss is obtained as shown in Fig. 5.17 (b).

Step IV : Superposition : The given indeterminate truss is considered as superposition of (a) basic determinate truss with given loads [Fig. 5.17 (b)] and (b) unknown redundant force 'Q' times the basic determinate truss with unit positive redundant force (Fig. 5.17 (c)).

Step V : P-analysis of basic determinate truss due to applied loads : Considering static equilibrium of truss all the reaction components (R_p) are found out as shown in Fig. 5.17 (b). Also the forces (P) in all the members of truss are found out and are shown in Fig. 5.17 (b).

Step VI : K-analysis of basic determinate truss : Unit positive force corresponding to 'Q' is applied as shown in Fig. 5.17 (c). All the reaction components (R_k) and forces (K) in all the members of truss are found out and are shown in Fig. 5.17 (c).

Step VII : Table for numerical computation :

Sr. No.	Member	Length (m)	P (kN)	K	PKL	K^2L	Q (kN)	QK (kN)	P_f = P + QK (kN)
1.	AB	3	47.5	$-1/2$	-71.25	0.75		-11.93	35.57
2.	BC	3	47.5	$-1/2$	-71.25	0.75		-11.93	35.57
3.	CD	3	0	0	0	0		0	0
4.	DE	3	0	0	0	0	23.85	0	0
5.	EF	3	-20	0	0	0		0	-20
6.	FA	3	0	0	0	0		0	0
7.	EB	3	0	-1	0	3		-23.85	-23.85
8.	AE	$3\sqrt{2}$	$-27.5\sqrt{2}$	$1/\sqrt{2}$	$-82.5\sqrt{2}$	$3/\sqrt{2}$		16.86	-22.03
9.	CE	$3\sqrt{2}$	$-47.5\sqrt{2}$	$1/\sqrt{2}$	$-142.5\sqrt{2}$	$3/\sqrt{2}$		16.86	-50.32
				Σ =	-460.69	8.74			

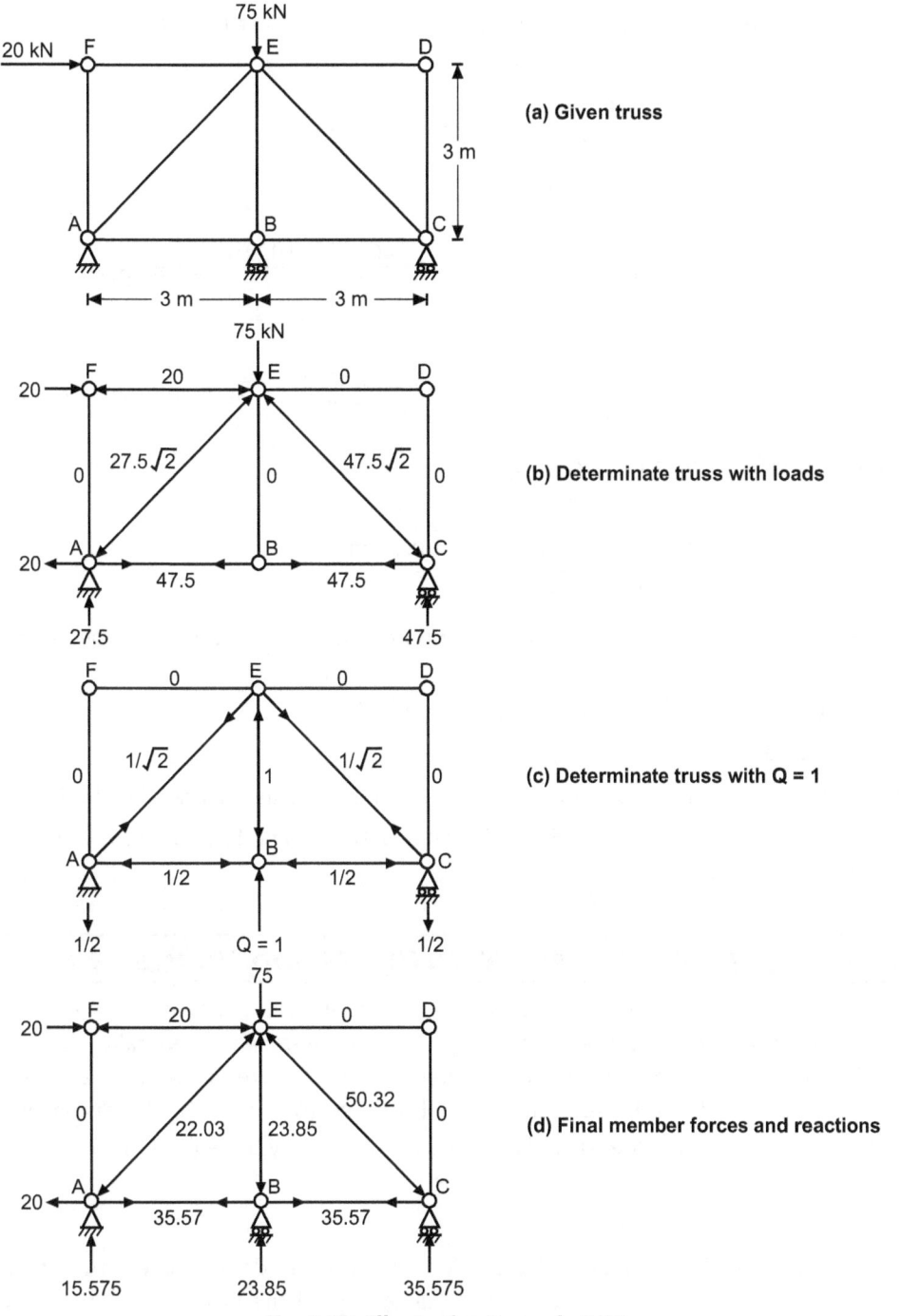

Fig. 5.17 : Illustrative Example 5.14

Step VIII : Physical requirement of displacement (D_Q) : Vertical translation at B in the given structure = 3 mm (↓) ∴ D_Q = − 3 mm.

Step IX : Calculation of redundant force :

$$D_Q = D_{QL} + FQ$$

where, $\quad D_Q = -3$ mm

$$D_{QL} = \sum_{i=1}^{n} \left(\frac{PKL}{EA}\right)_i = \frac{-460.69 \times 1000}{210 \times 400} = -5.48 \text{ mm}$$

$$F = \sum_{i=1}^{n} \left(\frac{K^2 L}{EA}\right)_i = \frac{8.74 \times 1000}{210 \times 400} = 0.104 \text{ mm/kN}$$

Substituting in above equation, we get,

$$Q = 23.85 \text{ kN} (\uparrow)$$

Step X : Final forces in all the members of truss (P_f) :

Using the equation, $\quad P_f = P + QK$

final forces in all the members of truss are computed and are as tabulated above and shown in Fig. 5.17 (d).

Step XI : Final reaction components at supports (R) :

Using the equation, $\quad R = R_p + Q \cdot R_k$

final reaction components at supports are computed and are as shown in Fig. 5.17 (d).

Note : Similar results of above Example can also be obtained by superposition of results of Examples 5.1 and 5.13.

5.3 FLEXIBILITY METHOD APPLIED TO BEAMS AND FRAMES

The method, illustrated for simple problem, is extended to beams and frames in general using matrix formulation. The beams and single storeyed frames are generally indeterminate externally. Displacement analysis of basic determinate structure is the main concern. Unit load method is used to find displacements and forming {D_{QL}} and [F]. The displacement at co-ordinate i in a structure due to applied loads is obtained by the equation

$$D_{QLi} = \int \frac{M \cdot m_i \cdot dx}{EI} \qquad \ldots (5.12 \text{ a})$$

where M is the bending moment at a section of the basic determinate structure due to applied loads, m_i is the bending moment at the section of the basic determinate structure due to unit positive force at co-ordinate i.

Integration is to be performed over the entire structure with due care of limits and validity of BM equation and origin. The displacement at co-ordinate i due to the unit force at co-ordinate i is the direct flexibility coefficient and given by the equation

$$F_{ii} = \int \frac{m_i \, m_i \, dx}{EI} = \int \frac{(m_i)^2 \, dx}{EI} \qquad \ldots (5.12\ b)$$

The displacement at co-ordinate i, as the effect, due to the unit force at co-ordinate j, as the cause, is the indirect or cross flexibility coefficient and given by equation

$$F_{ij} = \int \frac{m_i \, m_j \, dx}{EI} \qquad \ldots (5.12\ c)$$

$$F_{ij} = F_{ji} \text{ by reciprocal theorem.}$$

The remaining procedure is same. The complete method is illustrated with the examples having 1 to 3 unknown redundant forces.

Example 5.15 : *Analyse the beam shown in Fig. 5.18 (a) by force method. Take EI = constant.*

Solution : Data : The beam is supported and loaded as shown in Fig. 5.18 (a). The data includes the following information :

1. Structural configuration : Type and arrangement of members, joints and supports, dimensions.
2. Cross-sectional properties of members : moment of inertia about bending axis.
3. Material properties of members.
4. Applied loads : Member loads, joint loads - magnitude, direction, position.
5. Type of structure : beam.

Objects :

1. Unknown redundant forces as the initial target.
2. Analysis.

Assumptions :

1. Linear Elastic Analysis.
2. Axial deformations are neglected in beams.

Concepts and Equations :

1. Statically determinate structure (Released structure)
2. Displacement analysis of determinate structure.
3. Superposition equations or compatibility of displacements.

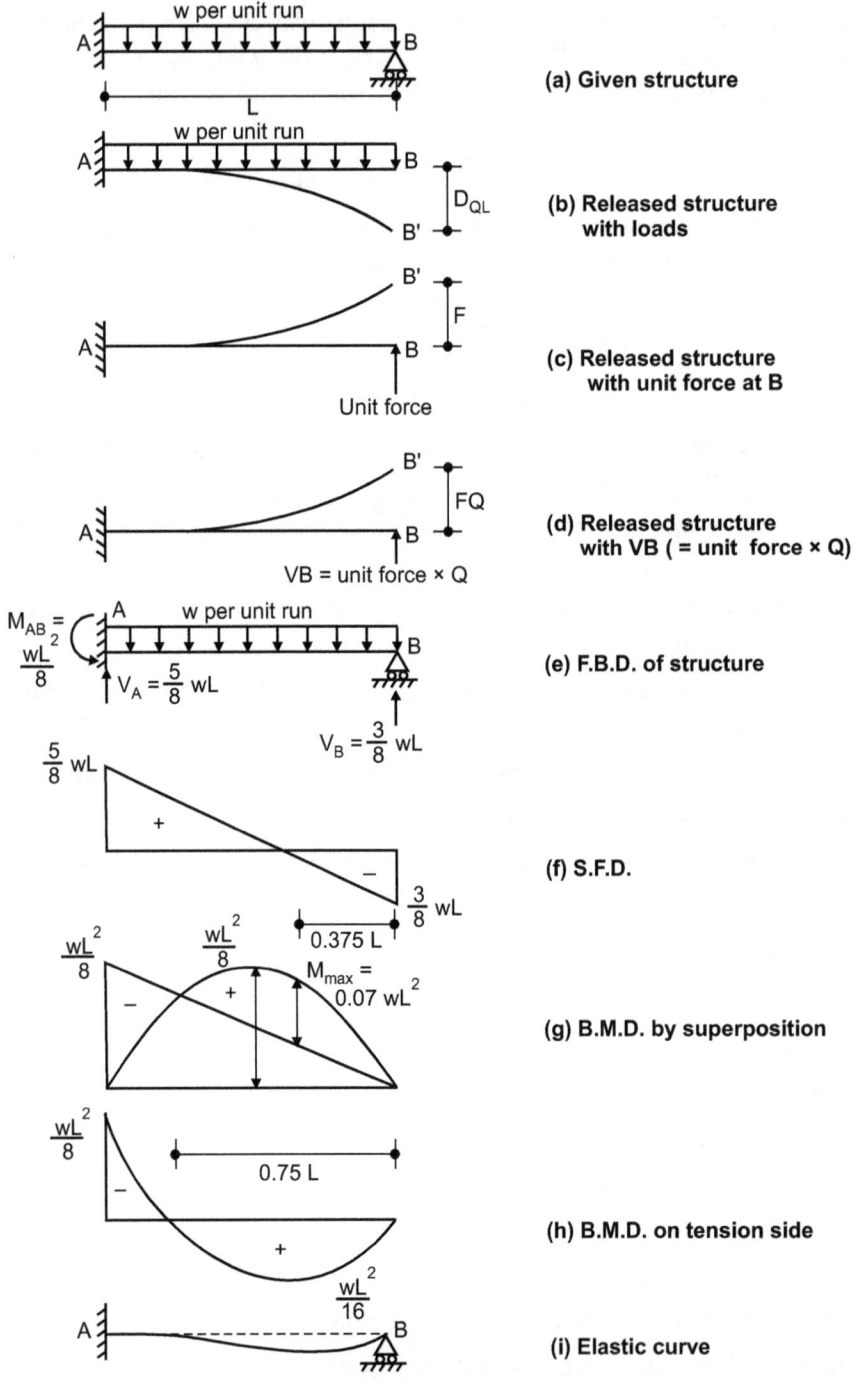

Fig. 5.18 : For Illustrative Example 5.15

Procedure :

Step I : The degree of static indeterminacy (D_{si})

(a) External indeterminacy : Total number of reaction components = 3 i.e. V_A, M_A, V_B.

Equations of equilibrium = 2 i.e. $\sum V = 0$, $\sum M = 0$.

∴ Degree of external static indeterminacy $(D_{si})_e$ = 3 – 2 = 1.

(b) Internal indeterminacy - once reactions are known the internal forces i.e. SF and BM can be obtained statically.

∴ Degree of internal static indeterminacy = $(D_{si})_i$ = 0.

(c) Total degree of static indeterminacy = (D_{si}) = $(D_{si})_e$ + $(D_{si})_i$ = 1.

Step II : Selection of unknown redundant force denoted by Q.

∴ $Q = V_B(\uparrow)$ i.e. vertical reaction at B.

Step III : Released Structure : The roller support at B is removed and statically determinate structure is obtained. Thus, the given indeterminate beam is considered as equivalent to the superposition of :

(a) Released structure under given loads, and

(b) Released structure under unit force at B and then under V_B as shown in Fig. 5.18 (b), Fig. 5.18 (c) and Fig. 5.18 (d).

Step IV : Displacement analysis of the released structure.

(a) Vertical translation i.e. deflection at B due to given loading is calculated. For this problem, the standard result is used to obtain the deflection at B. This is denoted by D_{QL}.

∴ $$Q_{QL} = -\frac{wL^4}{8 EI} \text{ (downward)}$$

(b) Deflection at B due to unit force at B is the flexibility denoted by F.

∴ $$F = \frac{L^3}{3 EI}$$

(c) Deflection at B due to the redundant force V_B. This is denoted by D_{QQ} and expressed in terms of F.

∴ $$D_{QQ} = FQ$$

∴ $$D_{QQ} = +\left(\frac{L^3}{3 EI}\right) V_B \text{ (upward)}$$

Step V : The physical requirement of displacement :

In the given structure, the deflection at B must be zero because of support condition. This displacement is denoted by D_Q.

$$\therefore \quad D_Q = 0$$

Step VI : Superposition equation of compatibility of displacements :

$$\therefore \quad D_Q = D_{QL} + D_{QQ} = D_{QL} + FQ$$

$$\therefore \quad 0 = \frac{wL^4}{8EI} + \frac{V_B L^3}{3EI}$$

Step VII : Solution of equation for unknown redundant force

$$\therefore \quad V_B = +\frac{3}{8}(wL)$$

The positive result of V_B indicates that the direction of V_B corresponds to the direction of unit force.

Step VIII : Other reaction components.

For FBD of structure, the equations of equilibrium, $\sum M_A = 0$ and $\sum V = 0$, are applied and the results are obtained.

$$M_A = +\frac{wL^2}{8} \text{ and } V_A = \frac{5}{8}wL$$

FBD of structure is shown in Fig. 5.18 (e).

Step IX : Shear Force and Bending Moment Diagrams :

(a) SFD is as shown in Fig. 5.18 (f).

(b) BMD is drawn by superposition technique. It is shown in Fig. 5.18 (g). BMD can also be drawn on tensile side as shown in Fig. 5.18 (h), however this requires additional ordinates to compute.

Step X : Elastic Curve :

As per support conditions and nature of BMD, the deflected shape of the beam i.e. elastic curve is drawn qualitatively as shown in Fig. 5.18 (i).

Alternate Solution to the Simple Problem of Force Method

The choice of the redundant force is not unique, therefore, the solution is altered accordingly, however the procedure remains the same. For the problem in hand if the moment reaction at the support A is selected as the redundant force, the procedure of the solution proceeds through the following important steps :

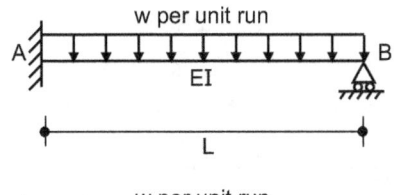

(a) Given structure

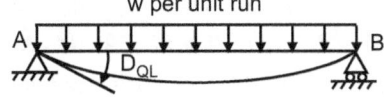

(b) Released structure with loads

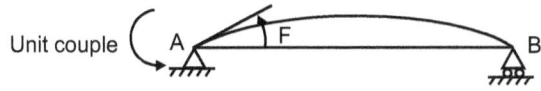

(c) Released structure with unit couple at A

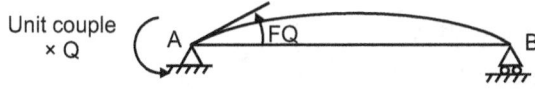

(d) Released structure with M_{AB} (= unit force × Q)

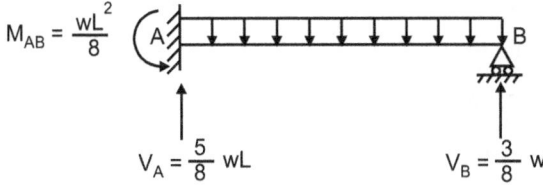

(e) F.B.D. of structure

Fig. 5.19 : Alternate solution to Example 5.15

Step I : $D_{si} = 1$.

Step II : $Q = M_{AB}$ (↺)

Step III : Released structure – As shown in Fig. 5.19 (b), 5.19 (c) and 5.19 (d).

Step IV : $D_{QL} = -\dfrac{wL^3}{24\,EI}$.

$F = \dfrac{L^3}{3\,EI}$

Step V : $D_Q = \theta_A = 0$.

Step VI : ∴ $D_Q = D_{QL} + F \cdot Q$ i.e. $0 = -\dfrac{wL^3}{24\,EI} + \left(\dfrac{L^3}{3\,EI}\right)Q$

Step VII : $Q = M_{AB} = \dfrac{wL^2}{8}$ (↺)

Step VIII : Other reaction components : As shown in Fig. 5.19 (e).

Step IX : Shear force and bending moment diagrams :

SFD is as shown in Fig. 5.19 (f). BMD by superposition and on tension side are as shown in Fig. 5.19 (g) and 5.19 (h) respectively.

Step X : **Elastic curve :** As shown in Fig. 5.19 (i).

Example 5.16 *: Analyse the beam shown in Fig. 5.20 (a) by flexibility method. Take EI = constant. The stiffness coefficient of spring at B is as shown in figure.*

Solution : (1) Data : The beam is supported and loaded as shown in Fig. 5.20 (a).

(2) $K_B = (EI/2)$ kN/m.

Object : Structural analysis.

Concepts and Equations :

(1) Statically determinate structure (released structure).

(2) Displacement analysis of released structure.

(3) Superposition equations of compatibility of displacements.

Procedure :

Step I : The degree of static indeterminacy (D_{si}) :

(a) Degree of external static indeterminacy = $(D_{si})_e = 1$.

(b) Degree of internal static indeterminacy = $(D_{si})_i = 0$.

(c) Total degree of static indeterminacy = $D_{si} = (D_{si})_e + (D_{si})_i = 1 + 0 = 1$.

Step II : Selection of unknown redundant force (Q) :

Let, $Q_1 = V_B (\uparrow)$

Step III : Released Structure : Elastic support at B is removed and basic released structure is as shown in Fig. 5.20 (b). Also released structure subjected to unit value of Q_1 is shown in Fig. 5.20 (c).

Step IV : Displacement analysis of released structure :

(a) Displacements in the released structure subjected to loads corresponding to redundant actions :

$$D_{QL1} = -\frac{wL^4}{8\,EI} = -\frac{10 \times 3^4}{8\,EI} = -\frac{101.25}{EI}$$

(b) Displacements in the released structure subjected to unit value of Q_1 corresponding to redundant actions :

$$F_{11} = \frac{(Q_1)L^3}{3\,EI} = \frac{3^3}{3\,EI} = \frac{9}{EI}$$

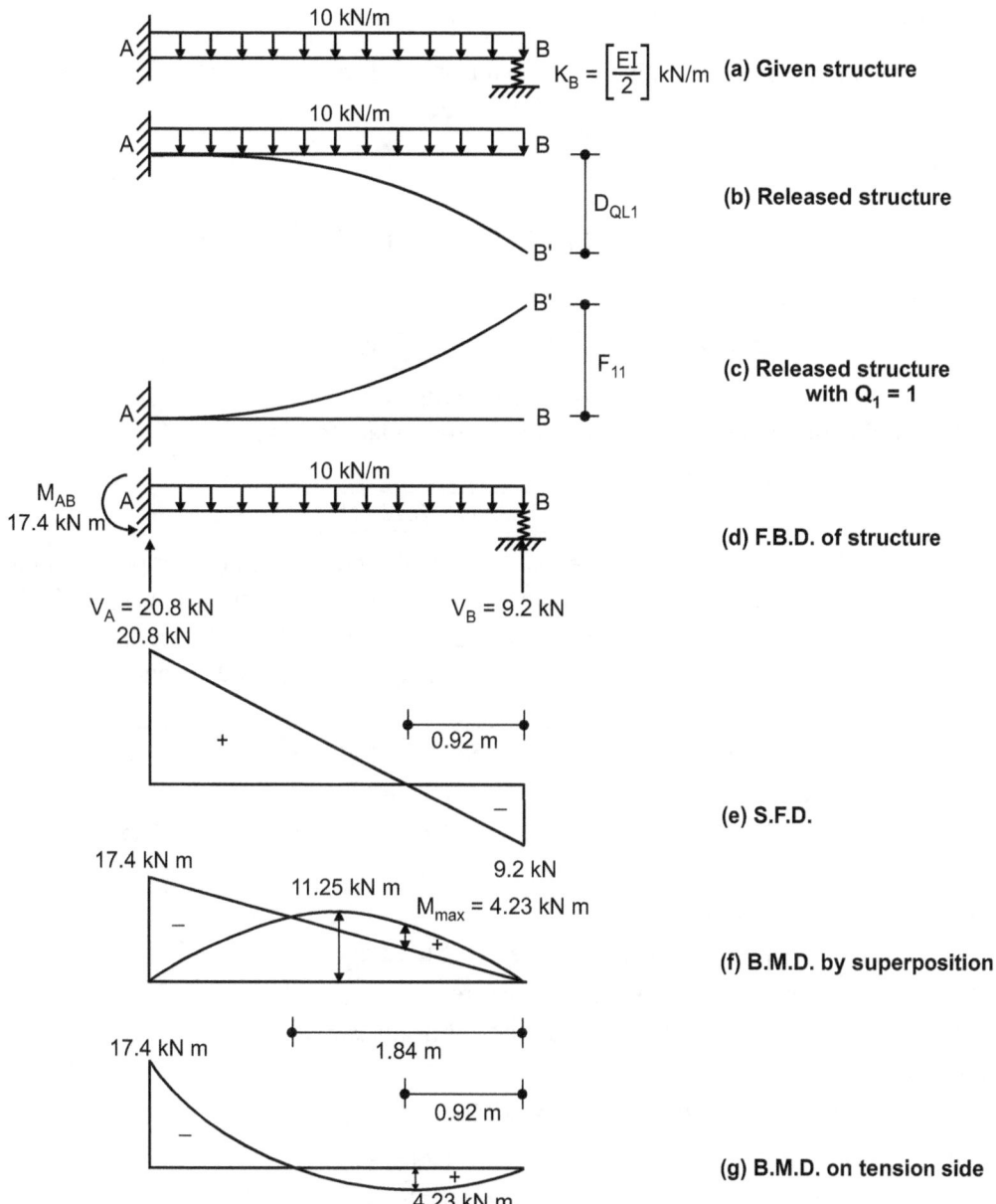

Fig. 5.20 : For Illustrative Example 5.16

Step V : The physical requirement of displacements : The flexibility coefficient of spring at $B = F_B = \dfrac{1}{K_B} = \dfrac{2}{EI}$ m/kN.

∴ Vertical translation at $B = D_{Q1} = \left(\dfrac{2}{EI}\right) Q_1 (\downarrow) = -\left(\dfrac{2}{EI}\right) Q_1$

Step VI : Superposition equation of compatibility of displacements :

$$\{D_Q\} = \{D_{QL}\} + [F] \cdot \{Q\}$$

where $[F] = \left[\dfrac{9}{EI}\right]$

Also, $\{D_{QL}\} = \dfrac{1}{EI}\{-101.25\}$ and $\{D_Q\} = \dfrac{1}{EI}\{-2 Q_1\}$

Substituting, we get,

$$\dfrac{1}{EI}\{-2 Q_1\} = \dfrac{1}{EI}\{-101.25\} + \dfrac{1}{EI}[9] \cdot \{Q_1\}$$

i.e. $-2 Q_1 = -101.25 + 9(Q_1)$ ... (A)

Step VII : Solution of equations for unknown redundant forces :
Solving equation (A), we get

$$\boxed{Q_1 = V_B = 9.20 \text{ kN} = 9.20 \text{ kN} (\uparrow)}$$

Step VIII : Other reaction components : Considering equilibrium of complete structure, other reaction components are found out and FBD of structure is as shown in Fig. 5.20 (d).

Step IX : Shear force and bending moment diagrams : SFD is as shown in Fig. 5.20 (e). BMD by superposition and on tension side is as shown in Fig. 5.20 (f) and Fig. 5.20 (g) respectively.

Example 5.17 : *Analyse the beam shown in Fig. 5.21 (a) by flexibility method. Take EI = constant.*

Solution : Data : The beam is supported and loaded as shown in Fig. 5.21 (a).

Object : Structural analysis.

Concepts and Equations :

(1) Statically determinate structure (Released structure).
(2) Displacement analysis of released structure.
(3) Superposition equations of compatibility of displacements.

Procedure :

Step I : The degree of static indeterminacy (D_{si}) :

(a) Degree of external static indeterminacy = $(D_{si})_e = 1$.
(b) Degree of internal static indeterminacy = $(D_{si})_i = 0$.
(c) Total degree of static indeterminacy = $D_{si} = (D_{si})_e + (D_{si})_i = 1 + 0 = 1$.

Step II : Selection of unknown redundant forces (Q) :
Let, $Q_1 = V_B (\uparrow)$

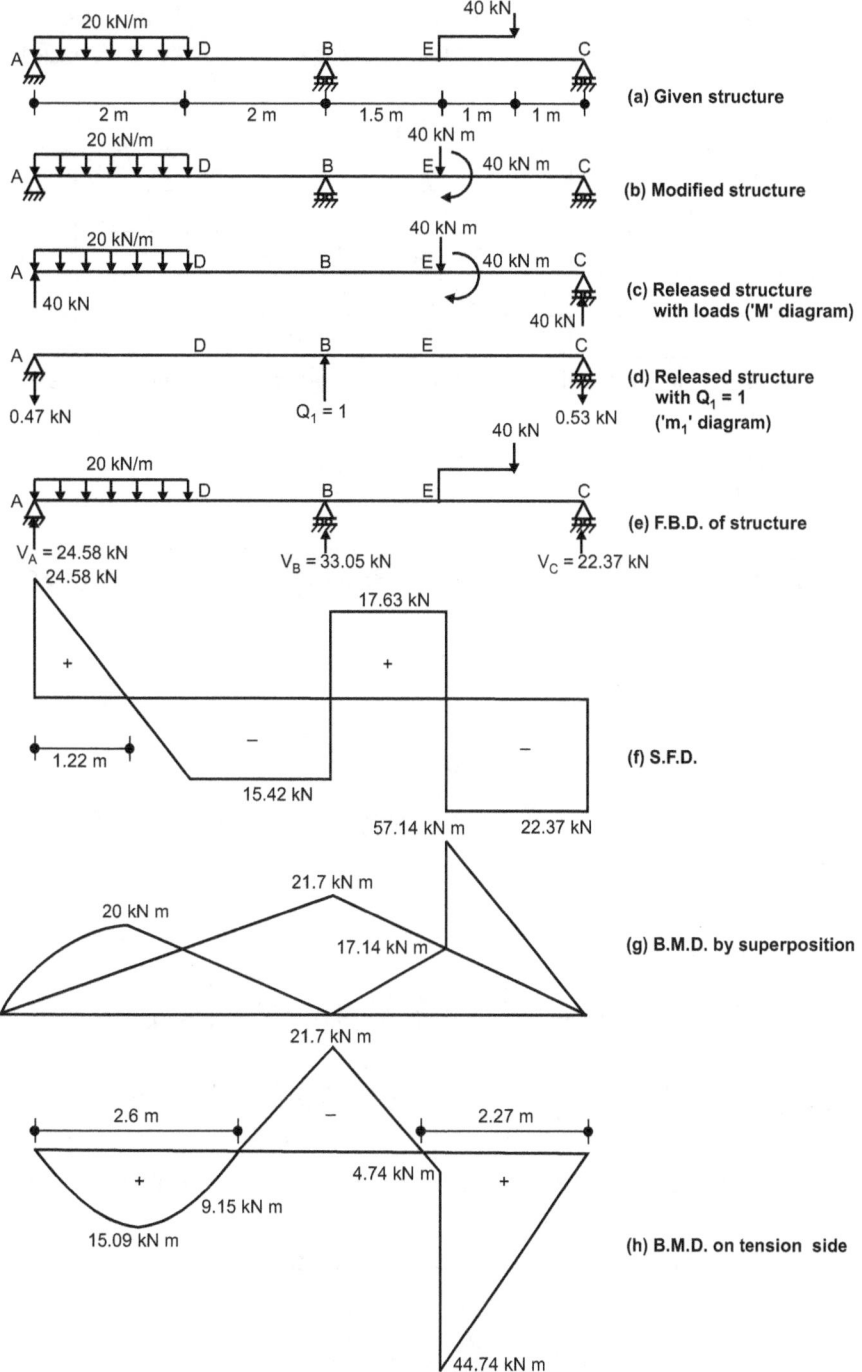

Fig. 5.21 : For Illustrative Example 5.17

Step III : Released structure : Roller support at B is removed and basic released structure is as shown in Fig. 5.21 (c). Also released structure subjected to unit value of Q_1 is shown in Fig. 5.21 (d).

Step IV : Displacement analysis of released structure :

Zone	Origin	Limits	M	m_1
CE	C	0 – 2	40x	– 0.533 (x)
EB	C	2 – 3.5	40x – 40 – 40 (x – 2) = 40	– 0.533 (x)
AD	A	0 – 2	40x – 20x²/2 = 40x – 10x²	– 0.467 (x)
DB	A	2 – 4	40x – 20 × 2 (x – 1) = 40x – 40 (x – 1) = 40	– 0.467 (x)

(a) Displacement in the released structure subjected to loads corresponding to redundant actions :

$$D_{QL1} = \int_0^L \frac{Mm_1 \cdot dx}{EI}$$

$$= \int_0^2 (40x)(-0.533x) \cdot \frac{dx}{EI} + \int_2^{3.5} (40)(-0.533x) \cdot \frac{dx}{EI} + \int_0^2 (40x - 10x^2)(-0.467x) \cdot \frac{dx}{EI}$$

$$+ \int_2^4 (40)(-0.467x) \frac{dx}{EI}$$

$$= -(56.85 + 87.94 + 31.13 = 112.08)/EI = \frac{-288}{EI}$$

(b) Displacement in the released structure subjected to unit value of Q_1 corresponding to redundant actions :

$$F_{11} = \int_0^1 \frac{m_1 \cdot m_1 \cdot dx}{EI}$$

$$= \int_0^2 (-0.533x)^2 \cdot \frac{dx}{EI} + \int_2^{3.5} (-0.533x)^2 \cdot \frac{dx}{EI} + \int_0^2 (-0.477x)^2 \cdot \frac{dx}{EI} + \int_2^4 (-0.467x)^2 \cdot \frac{dx}{EI}$$

$$= \int_0^{3.5} (-0.533x)^2 \cdot \frac{dx}{EI} + \int_0^4 (-0.467x)^2 \cdot \frac{dx}{EI} = \frac{(4.060 + 4.65)}{EI} = \frac{8.71}{EI}$$

Step V : The physical requirement of displacements : The vertical translation at B must be zero i.e. $D_{Q1} = 0$

Step VI : Superposition equation of compatibility of displacements :

$$\{D_Q\} = \{D_{QL}\} + [F] \cdot \{Q\}$$

i.e. $$0 = -\frac{288}{EI} + \left(\frac{8.71}{EI}\right)(Q_1) \quad \ldots (A)$$

Step VII : Solution of equations for unknown redundant forces : Solving equation (A), we get,

$$\boxed{Q_1 = V_B = 33.06 \text{ kN } (\uparrow)}$$

Step VIII : Other reaction components : Considering equilibrium of complete structure, other unknown reaction components are found out and FBD of structure is as shown in Fig. 5.21 (e).

Step IX : Shear force and bending moment diagrams : SFD is as shown in Fig. 5.21 (f). BMD by superposition and on tension side are as shown in Fig. 5.21 (g) and (h).

Example 5.18 : *Analyse the beam shown in Fig. 5.22 (a) by flexibility method. Take EI = constant.*

Solution : Data : The beam is supported and loaded as shown in Fig. 5.22 (a).

Object : Structural analysis.

Concepts and Equations :

(1) Statically determinate structure (Released structure).
(2) Displacement analysis of released structure.
(3) Superposition equations of compatibility of displacements.

Procedure :

Step I : The degree of static indeterminacy (D_{si}) :

(a) Degree of external static indeterminacy = $(D_{si})_e$ = 2.
(b) Degree of internal static indeterminacy = $(D_{si})_i$ = 0.
(c) Total degree of static indeterminacy = $D_{si} = (D_{si})_e + (D_{si})_i = 2 + 0 = 2$.

Step II : Selection of unknown redundant forces (Q) :

Let,
$$Q_1 = V_B (\uparrow) \text{ and}$$
$$Q_2 = V_C (\uparrow)$$

Step III : Released Structure : Roller supports at B and C are removed and the basic released structure is as shown in Fig. 5.22 (b). Also released structure subjected to the unit values of Q_1 and Q_2 is shown in Fig. 5.22 (c).

Step IV : Displacement analysis of released structure and Fig. 5.22 (d) respectively.

Zone	Origin	Limits	M	m_1	m_2
DC	D	0 – 2	$-10x^2/2 = -5x^2$	0	0
CB	D	2 – 6	$-10x^2/2 = -5x^2$	0	(x – 2)
BA	D	6 – 11	$-10 \times 6 \times (x-3) - 6(x-6)^2/2$ $= -60(x-3) - 3(x-6)^2$	(x – 6)	(x – 2)

(a) Displacements in the released structure subjected to loads corresponding to redundant actions :

$$D_{QL1} = \int_0^L \frac{Mm_1 \cdot dx}{EI}$$

$$= \int_0^2 (-5x^2)(0)\frac{dx}{EI} + \int_2^6 (-5x^2)(0)\frac{dx}{EI} + \int_6^{11} [-60(x-3) - 3(x-6)^2](x-6)\frac{dx}{EI}$$

$$= \frac{(0 + 0 - 5218.75)}{EI} = -\frac{5218.75}{EI}$$

$$D_{QL2} = \int_0^L \frac{Mm_2 \cdot dx}{EI}$$

$$= \int_0^2 (-5x^2)(0)\frac{dx}{EI} + \int_2^6 (-5x^2)(x-2)\cdot\frac{dx}{EI} + \int_6^{11} [-60(x-3) - 3(x-6)^2](x-2)\frac{dx}{EI}$$

$$= \frac{(0.906.67 - 12318.75)}{EI} = -\frac{13225.42}{EI}$$

(b) Displacements in the released structure subjected to unit values of Q_1 and Q_2 corresponding to redundant actions :

$$F_{11} = \int_0^L \frac{m_1 \cdot m_1 \cdot dx}{EI}$$

$$= \int_0^2 (0)\cdot\frac{dx}{EI} + \int_2^6 (0)\cdot\frac{dx}{EI} + \int_6^{11} (x-6)^2\cdot\frac{dx}{EI} = \frac{(0 + 0 + 41.67)}{EI} = \frac{41.67}{EI}$$

$$F_{21} = F_{12} = \int_0^L \frac{m_1 \cdot m_2 \cdot dx}{EI} = \int_0^2 (0)\frac{dx}{EI} + \int_2^6 (0) + (x-2)\frac{dx}{EI} + \int_6^{11}(x-6)(x-2)\frac{dx}{EI}$$

$$= \frac{(0 + 0 + 91.67)}{EI} = \frac{91.67}{EI}$$

$$F_{22} = \int_0^L \frac{m_2 \cdot m_2 \cdot dx}{EI} = \int_0^2 (0)\cdot\frac{dx}{EI} + \int_2^6 (x-2)^2\cdot\frac{dx}{EI} + \int_6^{11}(x-2)^2\cdot\frac{dx}{EI}$$

$$= \int_2^{11} (x-2)^2\cdot\frac{dx}{EI} = \frac{243}{EI}$$

Step V : The physical requirement of displacements : The vertical translations at B and C must be zero. i.e. $D_{Q1} = D_{Q2} = 0$

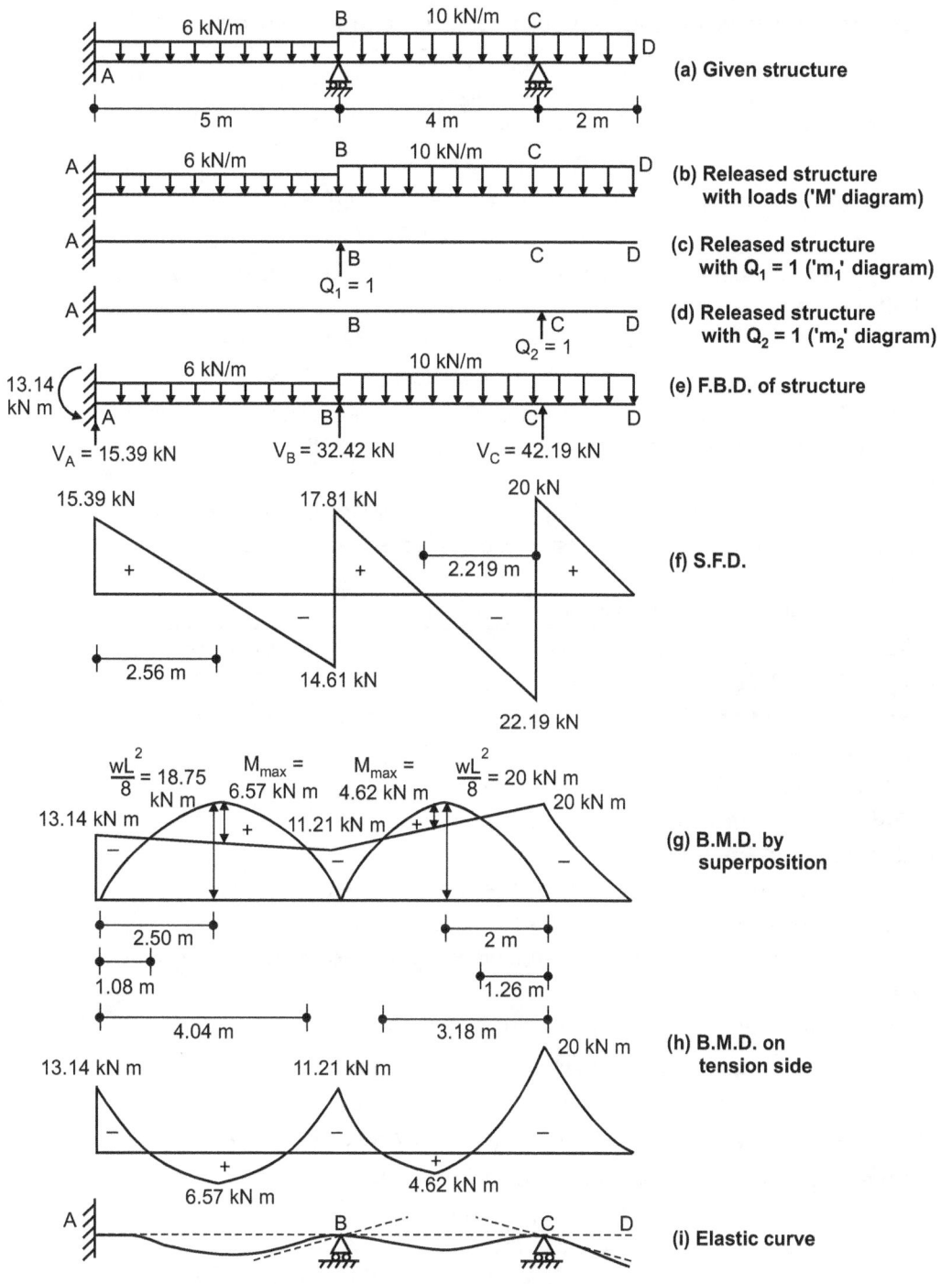

Fig. 5.22 : For Illustrative Example 5.18

Step VI : Superposition equation of compatibility of displacements :

$$\{D_Q\} = \{D_{QL}\} + [F]\{Q\}$$

i.e.
$$\begin{Bmatrix}0\\0\end{Bmatrix} = \frac{1}{EI}\begin{Bmatrix}-5218.75\\-13225.42\end{Bmatrix} + \frac{1}{EI}\begin{bmatrix}41.67 & 91.67\\91.67 & 243\end{bmatrix}\cdot\begin{Bmatrix}Q_1\\Q_2\end{Bmatrix}$$

i.e.
$$0 = -5218.75 + 41.67(Q_1) + 91.67(Q_2) \quad ...(A)$$
$$0 = -13225.42 + 91.67(Q_1) + 243(Q_2) \quad ...(B)$$

Step VII : Solution of equations for unknown redundant forces : Solving equations (A) and (B), we get,

$$Q_1 = V_B = 32.42 \text{ kN} = 32.42 \text{ kN } (\uparrow)$$
$$Q_2 = V_C = 4.2.19 \text{ kN} = 42.19 \text{ kN } (\uparrow)$$

Step VIII : Other reaction components : Considering equilibrium of complete structure, other unknown reaction components are found out and FBD of structure is as shown in Fig. 5.22 (e).

Step IX : Shear force and bending moment diagrams : SFD is as shown in Fig. 5.22 (f). BMD by superposition and on tension side is as shown in Fig. 5.22 (g) and 5.22 (h) respectively.

Step X : Elastic Curve : As shown in Fig. 5.22 (i).

Example 5.19 : *Analyse the beam shown in Fig. 5.23 (a) by flexibility method; if support B sinks by 25 mm. Take EI = 3800 kN-m².*

Solution : (1) **Data :** The beam is supported and loaded as shown in Fig. 5.23 (a),
(2) EI = 3800 kNm²
(3) AB = 25 mm ($\downarrow$).

Object : Structural analysis.

Concepts and Equations :
(1) Statically determinate structure (Released structure).
(2) Displacement analysis of released structure.
(3) Superposition equations of compatibility of displacements.

Procedure :

Step I : The degree of static indeterminacy (D_{si}) :
(a) Degree of external static indeterminacy = $(D_{si})_e = 2$.
(b) Degree of internal static indeterminacy = $(D_{si})_i = 2$.
(c) Total degree of static indeterminacy = $D_{si} = (D_{si})_e + (D_{si})_i = 2 + 0 = 2$.

Step II : Selection of unknown redundant forces (Q).
Let,
$$Q_1 = V_B (\uparrow) \text{ and}$$
$$Q_2 = V_C (\uparrow)$$

Step III : Released structure : Roller supports at B and C are removed and basic released structure is as shown in Fig. 5.23 (b). Also released structure subjected to unit values of Q_1 and Q_2 is shown in Fig. 5.23 (c) and Fig. 5.23 (d) respectively.

Step IV : Displacement analysis of released structure :

Zone	Origin	Limits	M	m_1	m_2
CD	C	0 – 4	0	0	x
DB	C	4 – 6	– 30 (x – 4)	0	x
BA	C	6 – 12	– 30 (x – 4) – 10 (x – 6)²/2 = – 5x² + 30x – 60	(x – 6)	x

(a) Displacements in the released structure subjected to loads corresponding to redundant actions :

$$D_{QL1} = \int_0^L \frac{M m_1 \cdot dx}{EI}$$

$$= \int_0^4 (0) \cdot \frac{dx}{EI} + \int_4^6 -30(x-4)(0) \cdot \frac{dx}{EI} + \int_6^{12} (-5x^2 + 30x - 60)(x-6) \cdot \frac{dx}{EI}$$

$$= \frac{(0 + 0 - 4860)}{EI} = -\frac{4860}{EI}$$

$$D_{QL2} = \int_0^L \frac{M m_2 \cdot dx}{EI}$$

$$= \int_0^4 (0) \cdot (x) \cdot \frac{dx}{EI} + \int_4^6 -30(x-4)(x) \cdot \frac{dx}{EI} + \int_6^{12} (-5x^2 + 30x - 60)(x) \cdot \frac{dx}{EI}$$

(d) Displacements in the released structure subjected to unit values of Q_1 and Q_2 corresponding to redundant actions.

$$F_{11} = \int_0^L \frac{m_1 \cdot m_1 \cdot dx}{EI}$$

$$= \int_0^4 (0) \cdot \frac{dx}{EI} + \int_4^6 (0) \cdot \frac{dx}{EI} + \int_6^{12} (x-6)^2 \cdot \frac{dx}{EI}$$

$$= \frac{(0 + 0 + 72)}{EI} = \frac{72}{EI}$$

$$F_{21} = F_{12} \int_0^L \frac{m_1 \cdot m_2 \cdot dx}{EI}$$

$$= \int_0^4 (0)(x) \cdot \frac{dx}{EI} + \int_4^6 (0)(x) \cdot \frac{dx}{EI} + \int_6^{12} (x-6)(x) \cdot \frac{dx}{EI}$$

$$= \frac{0 + 0 + 180}{EI} = \frac{180}{EI}$$

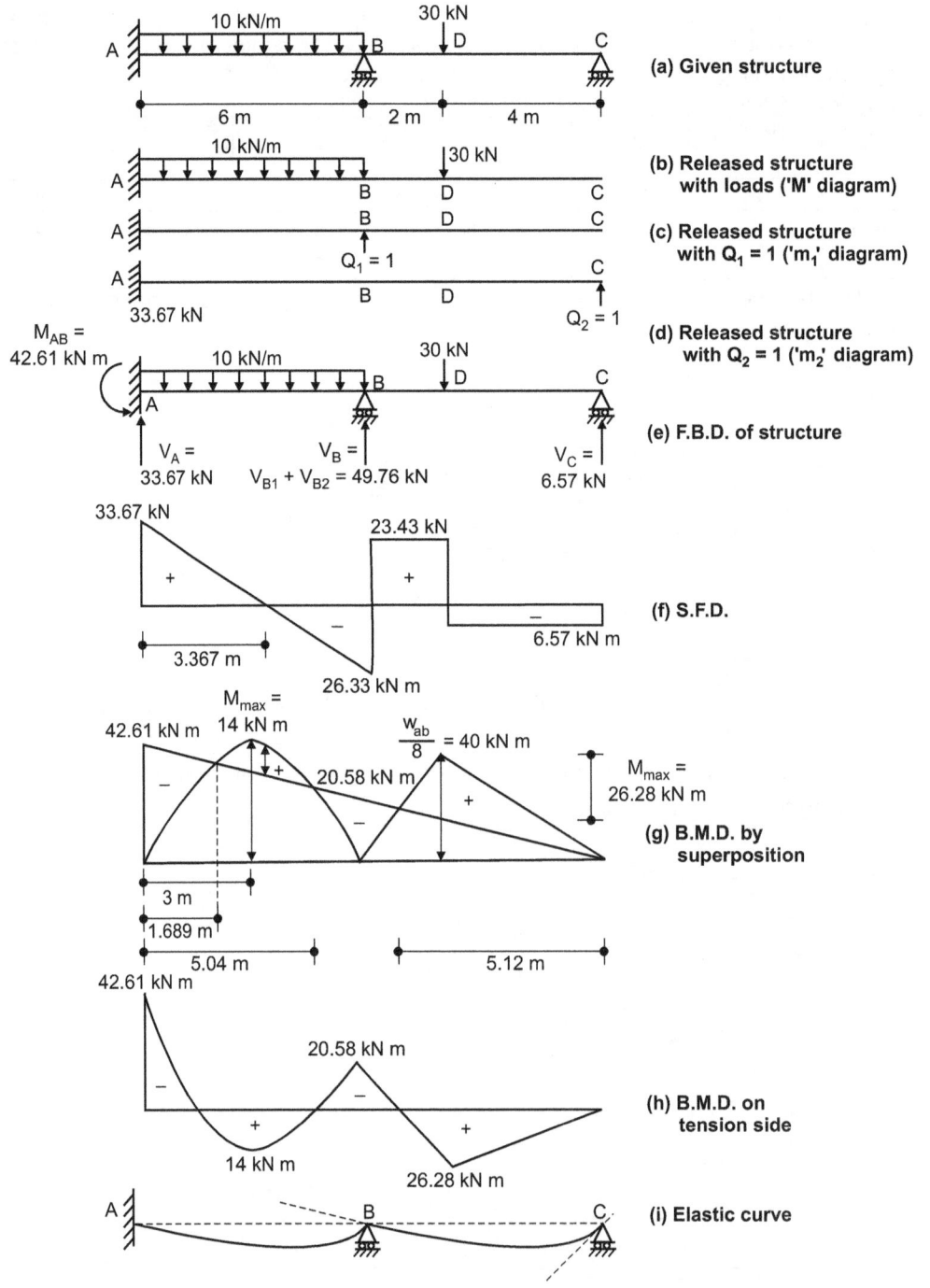

Fig. 5.23 : For Illustrative Example 5.19

$$F_{22} = \int_0^L \frac{m_2 \cdot m_2 \cdot dx}{EI}$$

$$= \int_0^4 (x)^2 \cdot \frac{dx}{EI} + \int_4^6 (x)^2 \cdot \frac{dx}{EI} + \int_6^{12} (x)^2 \cdot \frac{dx}{EI} = \int_0^{12} x^2 \cdot \frac{dx}{EI}$$

$$= \frac{576}{EI}$$

Step V : The physical requirement of displacements :

The vertical translation at B = 25 mm (↓) = – 0.025 m and the vertical translation at C = 0.

i.e. $D_{Q1} = -0.025$ m and $D_{Q2} = 0$

Step VI : Superposition equation of compatibility of displacements :

$$\{D_Q\} = \{D_{QL}\} + [F] \cdot \{Q\}$$

i.e. $$\begin{Bmatrix} -0.025 \\ 0 \end{Bmatrix} = \frac{1}{EI} \begin{Bmatrix} -4860 \\ -12740 \end{Bmatrix} + \frac{1}{EI} \begin{bmatrix} 72 & 180 \\ 180 & 576 \end{bmatrix} \begin{Bmatrix} Q_1 \\ Q_2 \end{Bmatrix}$$

i.e. $$EI \cdot \begin{Bmatrix} -0.025 \\ 0 \end{Bmatrix} = \begin{Bmatrix} -4860 \\ -12740 \end{Bmatrix} + \begin{bmatrix} 72 & 180 \\ 180 & 576 \end{bmatrix} \cdot \begin{Bmatrix} Q_1 \\ Q_2 \end{Bmatrix}$$

i.e. $$3800 \cdot \begin{Bmatrix} -0.025 \\ 0 \end{Bmatrix} = \begin{Bmatrix} -4860 \\ -12740 \end{Bmatrix} + \begin{bmatrix} 72 & 180 \\ 180 & 576 \end{bmatrix} \cdot \begin{Bmatrix} Q_1 \\ Q_2 \end{Bmatrix}$$

i.e. $-95 = -4860 + 72 (Q_1) + 180 (Q_2)$ ... (A)

$0 = -12740 + 180 (Q_1) + 576 (Q_2)$ ... (B)

Step VII : Solution of equations for unknown redundant forces. Solving equations (A) and (B), we get

$$\boxed{\begin{aligned} Q_1 &= V_B = 49.76 \text{ kN} = 49.76 \text{ kN (↑)} \\ Q_2 &= V_C = 6.57 \text{ kN} = 6.57 \text{ kN (↑)} \end{aligned}}$$

Step VIII : Other reaction components : Considering equilibrium of complete structure, other reaction components are found out and FBD of structure is as shown in Fig. 5.23 (e).

Step IX : Shear force and bending moment diagrams :

SFD is as shown in Fig. 5.23 (f).

BMD by superposition and on tension side is as shown in Fig. 5.23 (g) and Fig. 5.23 (h) respectively.

Step X : Elastic Curve : as shown in Fig. 5.23 (i).

Example 5.20 : Analyse the beam shown in Fig. 5.24 (a) by flexibility method. Take EI = constant. The stiffness coefficients of spring at B and C are as shown in figure.

Solution : (1) **Data :** The beam is supported and loaded as shown in Fig. 5.24 (a).

(2) $K_B = (EI)$ kN/m and $K_C = (EI/2)$ kN/m

Object : Structural analysis.

Concepts and Equations :

(1) Statically determinate structure (Released structure).

(2) Displacement analysis of released structure.

(3) Superposition equations of compatibility of displacements.

Procedure :

Step I : The degree of static indeterminacy (D_{si}) :

(a) Degree of external static indeterminacy = $(D_{si})_e = 2$.

(b) Degree of internal static indeterminacy = $(D_{si})_i = 0$.

(c) Total degree of static indeterminacy = $D_{si} = (D_{si})_e + (D_{si})_i = 2 + 0 = 2$.

Step II : Selection of unknown redundant forces (Q) :

Let, $Q_1 = V_B (\uparrow)$ and

$Q_2 = V_C (\uparrow)$

Step III : Released structure : Elastic supports at B and C are removed and basic released structure is as shown in Fig. 5.24 (b). Also released structure subjected to unit values of Q_1 and Q_2 is shown in Fig. 5.24 (c) and Fig. 5.24 (d) respectively.

Step IV : Displacement analysis of released structure : same as explained in example (5.19), step (iv).

Step V : The physical requirement of displacements :

Flexibility coefficient of spring at B = $F_B = \dfrac{1}{K_B} = \left(\dfrac{1}{EI}\right)$ m/kN

Flexibility coefficient of spring at C = $F_C = \dfrac{1}{K_C} = \left(\dfrac{2}{EI}\right)$ m/kN

The vertical translation at B = $\left(\dfrac{1}{EI}\right) Q_1 (\downarrow)$ $\therefore D_{Q_1} = -\dfrac{Q_1}{EI}$

The vertical translation at C = $\left(\dfrac{2}{EI}\right) Q_2 (\downarrow)$ $\therefore D_{Q_2} = -\left(\dfrac{2}{EI}\right) Q_2$

Step VI : Superposition equation of compatibility of displacements :

$$\{D_Q\} = \{D_{QL}\} + [F] \cdot \{Q\}$$

where,
$$[F] = \frac{1}{EI} \begin{bmatrix} 72 & 180 \\ 180 & 576 \end{bmatrix}$$ as developed in Example 5.19.

Also
$$\{D_{QL}\} = \frac{1}{EI} \begin{Bmatrix} -4860 \\ -12740 \end{Bmatrix} \text{ and } \{D_Q\} = \frac{1}{EI} \begin{Bmatrix} -Q_1 \\ -2Q_2 \end{Bmatrix}$$

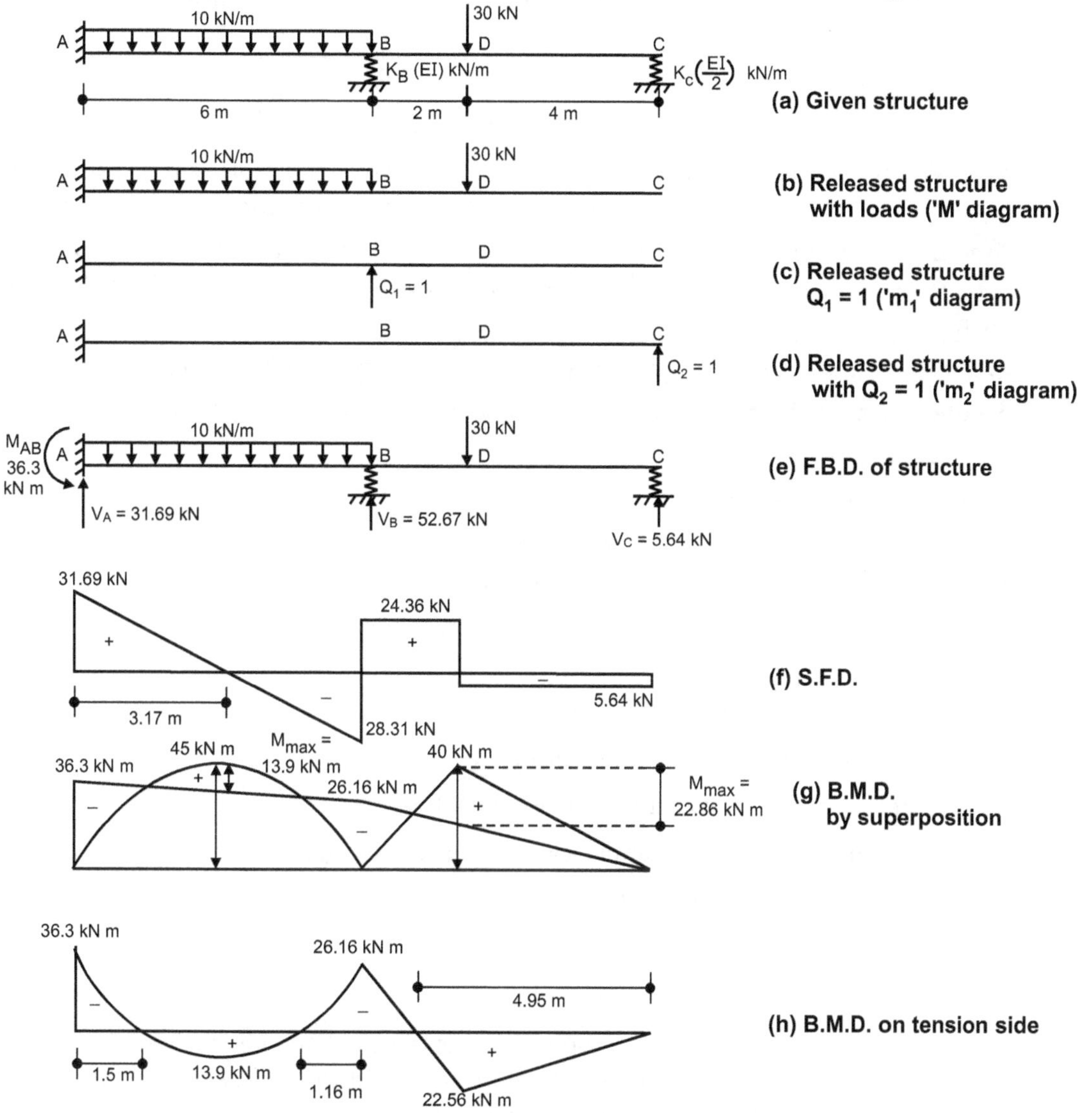

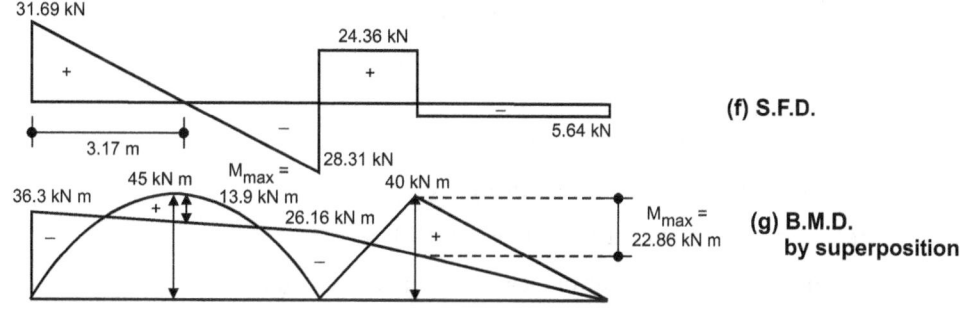

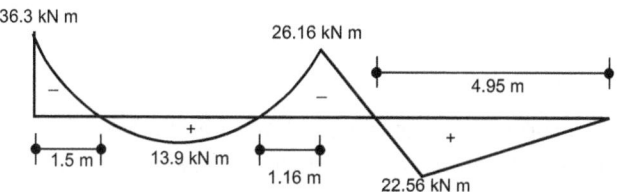

Fig. 5.24 : For Illustrative Example 5.20

Substituting, we get,

$$\frac{1}{EI}\begin{Bmatrix} -Q_1 \\ -2Q_2 \end{Bmatrix} = \frac{1}{EI}\begin{Bmatrix} -4860 \\ -12740 \end{Bmatrix} + \frac{1}{EI} \cdot \begin{bmatrix} 72 & 180 \\ 180 & 576 \end{bmatrix}\begin{Bmatrix} Q_1 \\ Q_2 \end{Bmatrix}$$

i.e.
$$-Q_1 = -4860 + 72(Q_1) + 180(Q_2) \qquad \ldots (A)$$
$$-2Q_2 = -12740 + 180(Q_1) + 576(Q_2) \qquad \ldots (B)$$

Step VII : Solution of equations for unknown redundant forces : Solving equations (A) and (B), we get,

$$\boxed{\begin{aligned} Q_1 &= V_B = 52.67 \text{ kN} = 52.67 \text{ kN} (\uparrow) \\ Q_2 &= V_C = 5.64 \text{ kN} = 5.64 \text{ kN} (\uparrow) \end{aligned}}$$

Step VIII : Other reaction components : Considering equilibrium of complete structure, other reaction components are found out and FBD of structure is as shown in Fig. 5.24 (e).

Step IX : Shear force and bending moment diagrams : SFD is as shown in Fig. 5.24 (f). BMD by superposition and on tension side is as shown in Fig. 5.24 (g) and Fig. 5.24 (h) respectively.

Example 5.21 : *Analyse the beam shown in Fig. 5.25 (a) by flexibility method.*

Solution : Data : The beam is supported and loaded as shown in Fig. 5.25 (a).

Object : Structural analysis.

Concepts and Equations :

(1) Statically determinate structure (Released structure).

(2) Displacement analysis of released structure.

(3) Superposition equations of compatibility of displacements.

Procedure :

Step I : The degree of static indeterminacy (D_{si}) :

(a) Degree of external static indeterminacy = $(D_{si})_e$ = 2.

(b) Degree of internal static indeterminacy = $(D_{si})_i$ = 2.

(c) Total degree of static indeterminacy = $D_{si} = (D_{si})_e + (D_{si})_i = 2 + 0 = 2$.

Step II : Selection of unknown redundant forces (Q) :

Let,
$$Q_1 = V_C (\uparrow)$$
$$Q_2 = M_{CB} (\circlearrowleft)$$

Step III : Released structure : Fixed support at C is removed and basic released structure is as shown in Fig. 5.25 (b). Also released structure subjected to unit values of Q_1 and Q_2 is shown in Fig. 5.25 (c) and Fig. 5.25 (d) respectively.

Step IV : Displacement analysis of released structure.

Zone	Origin	Limits	EI	M	m_1	m_2
CB	C	0 – 2	EI	0	x	1
BD	C	2 – 3	2 EI	0	x	1
DA	C	3 – 4	2 EI	$-100(x-3)$	x	1

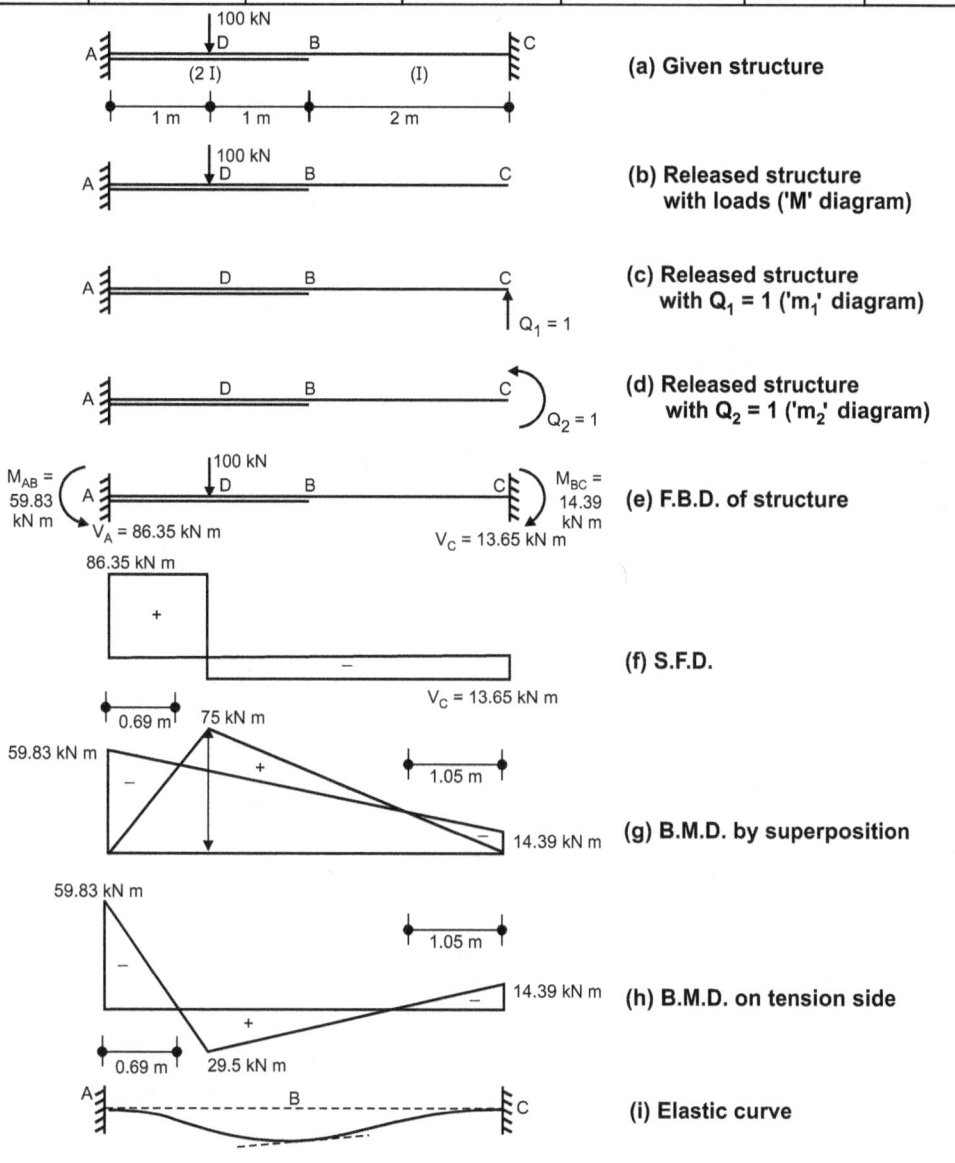

Fig. 5.25 : For Illustrative Example 5.21

(a) Displacements in the released structure subjected to loads corresponding to redundant actions :

$$D_{QL1} = \int_0^L \frac{Mm_1 \cdot dx}{EI}$$

$$= \int_0^2 (0) \cdot (x) \cdot \frac{dx}{EI} + \int_2^3 (0)(x) \cdot \frac{dx}{2EI} + \int_3^4 -100(x-3)(x) \cdot \frac{dx}{2EI}$$

$$= \frac{(0+0-91.67)}{EI} = \frac{-91.67}{EI}$$

$$D_{QL2} = \int_0^L \frac{Mm_2 \cdot dx}{EI}$$

$$= \int_0^2 (0)(1) \cdot \frac{dx}{EI} + \int_2^3 (0)(1) \frac{dx}{2EI} + \int_3^4 -100(x-3)(1) \cdot \frac{dx}{2EI}$$

$$= \frac{(0+0-25)}{EI} = -\frac{25}{EI}$$

(b) Displacements in the released structure subjected to unit values of Q_1 and Q_2 corresponding to redundant actions :

$$F_{11} = \int_0^L \frac{m_1 m_1 \cdot dx}{EI} = \int_0^2 (x)^2 \cdot \frac{dx}{EI} + \int_2^3 (x)^2 \cdot \frac{dx}{2EI} + \int_3^4 (x)^2 \cdot \frac{dx}{2EI}$$

$$= \int_0^2 (x)^2 \cdot \frac{dx}{EI} + \int_2^4 (x)^2 \cdot \frac{dx}{2EI} = \frac{(2.67+9.33)}{EI} = \frac{12}{EI}$$

$$F_{21} = F_{12} = \int_0^L \frac{m_1 \cdot m_2 \cdot dx}{EI}$$

$$= \int_0^2 (x)(1) \frac{dx}{EI} + \int_2^3 (x)(1) \cdot \frac{dx}{2EI} + \int_3^4 (x)(1) \cdot \frac{dx}{2EI}$$

$$= \int_0^2 x \cdot \frac{dx}{EI} + \int_2^4 x \cdot \frac{dx}{2EI} = \frac{(2+3)}{EI} = \frac{5}{EI}$$

$$F_{22} = \int_0^L \frac{m_2 \cdot m_2 \cdot dx}{EI} = \int_0^2 (1)^2 \cdot \frac{dx}{EI} + \int_2^3 (1)^2 \cdot \frac{dx}{2EI} + \int_3^4 (1)^2 \cdot \frac{dx}{2EI}$$

TOS – II (TE CIVIL SEM. VI NMU) FUNDAMENTAL CONCEPT OF FLEXIBILITY

$$= \int_0^2 (1) \cdot \frac{dx}{EI} + \int_2^4 (1) \cdot \frac{dx}{2EI} = \frac{(2+1)}{EI} = \frac{3}{EI}$$

Step V : The physical requirement of displacements : The vertical translation and rotation at C must be zero.

i.e. $\quad D_{Q1} = D_{Q2} = 0$

Step VI : Superposition equation of compatibility of displacements :

$$\{D_Q\} = \{D_{QL}\} + [F] \cdot \{Q\}$$

i.e. $\quad \begin{Bmatrix} 0 \\ 0 \end{Bmatrix} = \frac{1}{EI} \cdot \begin{Bmatrix} -91.67 \\ -25 \end{Bmatrix} + \frac{1}{EI} \begin{bmatrix} 12 & 5 \\ 5 & 3 \end{bmatrix} \begin{Bmatrix} Q_1 \\ Q_2 \end{Bmatrix}$

i.e. $\quad 0 = -91.67 + 12(Q_1) + 5(Q_2)$

$\quad 0 = -25 + 5(Q_1) + 3(Q_2)$

Step VII : Solution of equations for unknown redundant forces : Solving equations (A) and (B), we get

$\boxed{\begin{aligned} Q_1 &= V_B = 13.65 \text{ kN} = 13.65 \text{ kN} (\uparrow) \\ Q_2 &= M_{CB} = -14.385 \text{ kNm} = 14.39 \text{ kNm} \\ &(\circlearrowleft) \end{aligned}}$

Step VIII : Other reaction components : Considering equilibrium of complete structure, other reaction components are found out and FBD of structure is as shown in Fig. 5.25 (e).

Step IX : Shear force and bending moment diagrams : SFD is as shown in Fig. 5.25 (f). BMD by superposition and on tension side is as shown in Fig. 5.25 (g) and Fig. 5.25 (h) respectively.

Step X : Elastic Curve : As shown in Fig. 5.25 (i).

Example 5.22 : *Analyse the frame shown in Fig. 5.26 (a) by flexibility method. Take EI = constant.*

Solution : Data : The frame is supported and loaded as shown in Fig. 5.26 (a).

Object : Structural analysis.

Concepts and Equations :

(1) Statically determinate structure (Released structure).

(2) Displacement analysis of released structure.

(3) Superposition equations of compatibility of displacements.

Procedure :

Step I : The degree of static indeterminacy (D_{si})

(a) Degree of external static indeterminacy = $(D_{si})_e$ = 2

(b) Degree of internal static indeterminacy = $(D_{si})_i$ = 0

(c) Total degree of static indeterminacy = D_{si} = $(D_{si})_e + (D_{si})_i$ = 2 + 0 = 2.

Step II : Selection of unknown redundant forces (Q) :

Let, $\qquad Q_1 = V_C(\uparrow)$ and

$\qquad\qquad Q_2 = H_C(\rightarrow)$

Step III : Released structure : Hinged support at C is removed and the basic released structure is shown in Fig. 5.26 (b). Also released structure subjected to unit values of Q_1 and Q_2 is shown in Fig. 5.26 (c) and Fig. 5.26 (d) respectively.

Step IV : Displacement analysis of released structure :

Zone	Origin	Limits	M	m_1	m_2
CB	C	0 – 3	$-\dfrac{25x^2}{2}$	x	0
BD	B	0 – 2	– 112.5	3	– x
DA	B	2 – 4	– 112.5 – 50 (x – 2) = – 50x – 12.5	3	– x

(a) Displacements in the released structure subjected to loads corresponding to redundant actions :

$$D_{QL1} = \int_0^L \frac{M m_1 \cdot dx}{EI}$$

$$= \int_0^3 \left(-\frac{25x^2}{2}\right)(x) \cdot \frac{dx}{EI} + \int_0^2 (-112.5)(3) \cdot \frac{dx}{EI} + \int_2^4 (-50x - 12.5)(3) \cdot \frac{dx}{EI}$$

$$= \frac{(-253.125 - 675 - 975)}{EI} = \frac{(-1903.125)}{EI}$$

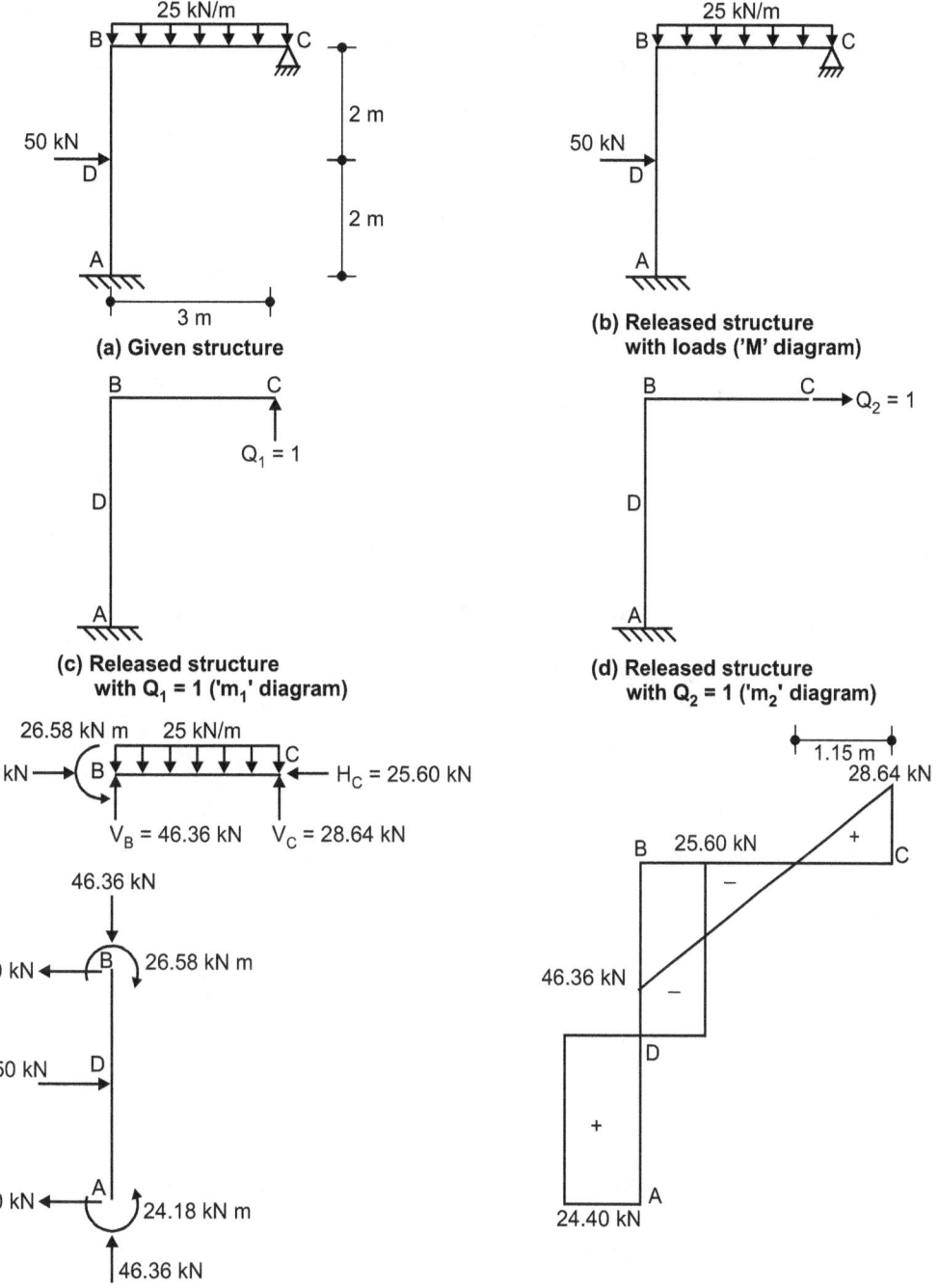

Fig. 5.26 : (Contd.)

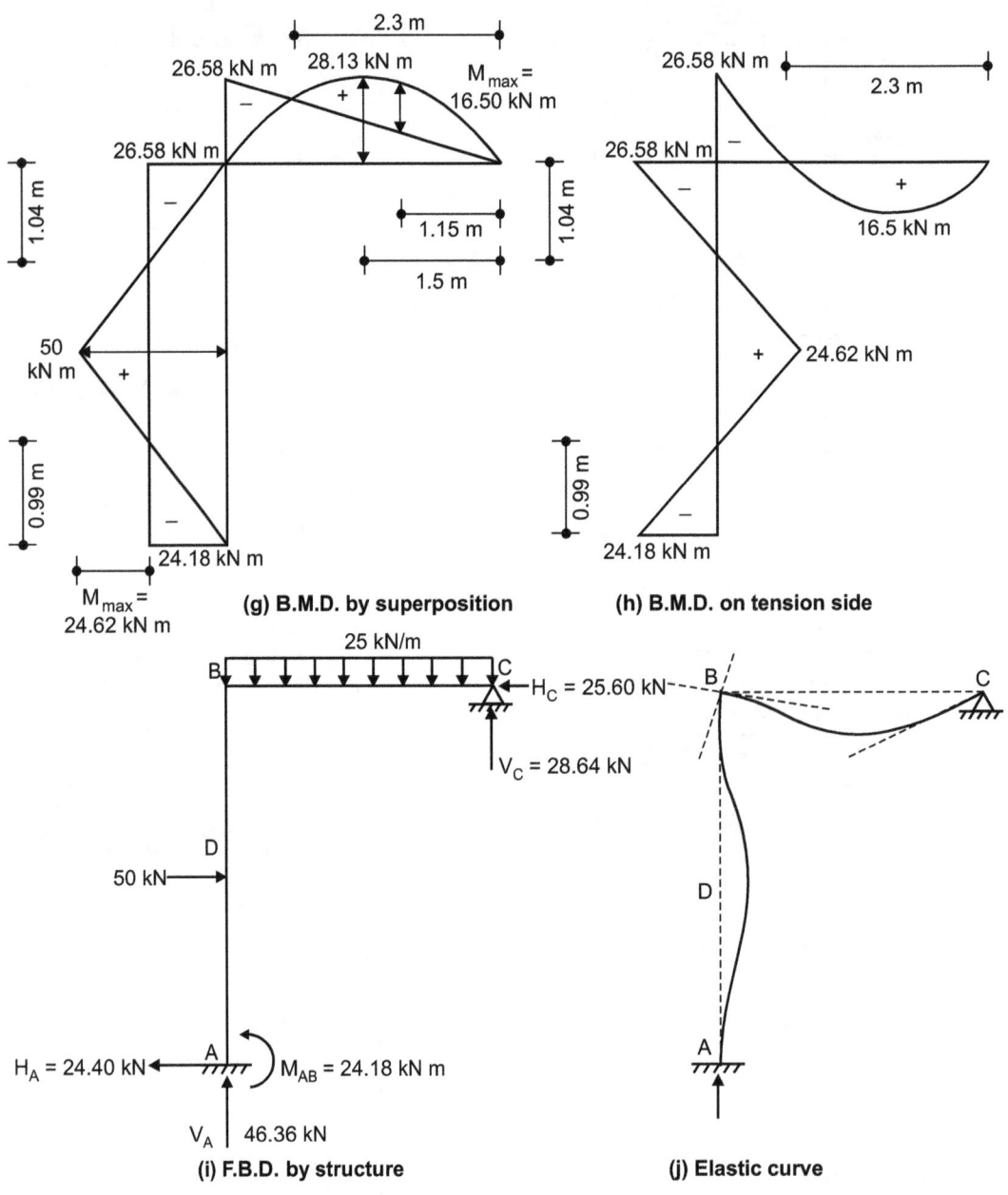

Fig. 5.26 : For Illustrative Example 5.22

$$D_{QL2} = \int_0^L \frac{M m_2 \cdot dx}{EI}$$

$$= \int_0^3 \left(-\frac{25x^2}{2}\right)(0)\frac{dx}{EI} + \int_0^2 (-112.5)(-x)\cdot\frac{dx}{EI} + \int_2^4 (-50x-12.5)(-x)\cdot\frac{dx}{EI}$$

$$= \frac{(0 + 225 + 1008.83)}{EI}$$

$$= \frac{1233.33}{EI}$$

(b) Displacements in the released structure subjected to unit values of Q_1 and Q_2 corresponding to redundant actions :

$$F_{11} = \int_0^L \frac{m_1 \cdot m_1 \cdot dx}{EI}$$

$$= \int_0^3 (x)^2 \cdot \frac{dx}{EI} + \int_0^2 (3)^2 \cdot \frac{dx}{EI} + \int_2^4 (3)^2 \cdot \frac{dx}{EI}$$

$$= \frac{(9 + 18 + 18)}{EI} = \frac{45}{EI}$$

$$F_{21} = F_{12} = \int_0^L \frac{m_1 \cdot m_2 \cdot dx}{EI}$$

$$= \int_0^3 (x)(0)\frac{dx}{EI} + \int_0^2 (3)(-x)\cdot\frac{dx}{EI} + \int_2^4 (3)(-x)\frac{dx}{EI}$$

$$= \int_0^4 (-3x)\frac{dx}{EI} = -\frac{24}{EI}$$

$$F_{22} = \int_0^L \frac{m_2 \cdot m_2 \cdot dx}{EI}$$

$$= \int_0^3 (0)\cdot\frac{dx}{EI} + \int_0^2 (-x)^2\cdot\frac{dx}{EI} + \int_2^4 (-x)^2\cdot\frac{dx}{EI} = \int_0^4 x^2\cdot\frac{dx}{EI} = \frac{21.33}{EI}$$

Step V : The physical requirement of displacements : The vertical and horizontal translation at C must be zero.

i.e. $\qquad D_{Q1} = D_{Q2} = 0$

Step VI : Superposition equation of compatibility of displacements :

i.e. $\qquad \{D_Q\} = \{D_{QL}\} + [F]\{Q\}$

i.e. $\qquad \begin{Bmatrix} 0 \\ 0 \end{Bmatrix} = \frac{1}{EI}\begin{Bmatrix} -1903.125 \\ 1233.33 \end{Bmatrix} + \frac{1}{EI}\begin{bmatrix} 45 & -24 \\ -24 & 21.33 \end{bmatrix}\begin{Bmatrix} Q_1 \\ Q_2 \end{Bmatrix}$

i.e. $\qquad 0 = -1903.125 + 45(Q_1) - 24(Q_2)$ ... (A)

$\qquad\qquad 0 = 1233.33 - 24(Q_1) + 21.33(Q_2)$ ... (B)

Step VII : Solution of equations for unknown redundant forces : Solving equations (A) and (B), we get

| Q_1 | = | V_C = 28.64 kN | = 28.64 kN (↑) |
| Q_2 | = | H_C = 25.60 kN | = 25.60 kN (←) |

Step VIII : Other reaction components : Considering equilibrium of each member and of complete structure, other reaction components are found out and FBD of members is as shown in Fig. 5.26 (e).

Step IX : Shear force and bending moment diagrams : SFD is as shown in Fig. 5.26 (f). BMD by superposition and on tension side is as shown in Fig. 5.26 (g) and Fig. 5.26 (h) respectively.

Step X : FBD of structure : as shown in Fig. 5.26 (i).

Step XI : Elastic Curve : as shown in Fig. 5.26 (j).

Example 5.23 : *Analyse the frame shown in Fig. 5.27 (a) by flexibility method.*

Solution : Data : The frame is supported and loaded as shown in Fig. 5.27 (a).

Object : Structural analysis.

Concepts and Equations : (1) Statically determinate structure (released structure).

(2) Displacement analysis of released structure.

(3) Superposition equations of compatibility of displacements.

Procedure :

Step I : The degree of static indeterminacy (D_{si}) :

(a) Degree of external static indeterminacy = $(D_{si})_e$ = 3

(b) Degree of internal static indeterminacy = $(D_{si})_i$ = 0

(c) Total degree of static indeterminacy = D_{si} = $(D_{si})_e$ + $(D_{si})_i$ = 3 + 0 = 3.

Step II : Selection of unknown redundant forces (Q) :
Let,
$$Q_1 = V_C (\uparrow)$$
$$Q_2 = H_C (\rightarrow) \text{ and}$$
$$Q_3 = M_{CB} (\circlearrowleft)$$

Step III : Released structure : Fixed support at C is removed and the basic released structure is shown in Fig. 5.27 (b). Also released structure subjected to unit values of Q_1, Q_2 and Q_3 is shown in Fig. 5.27 (c), Fig. 5.27 (d) and Fig. 5.27 (e) respectively.

Step IV : Displacement analysis of released structure :

Zone	Origin	Limits	EI	M	m_1	m_2	m_3
CB	C	0 – 3	EI	$-\dfrac{25x^2}{2}$	x	0	1
BD	B	0 – 2	2 EI	– 112.5	3	– x	1
DA	B	2 – 4	2 EI	– 112.5 – 50 (x – 2) = – 50x – 12.5	3	– x	1

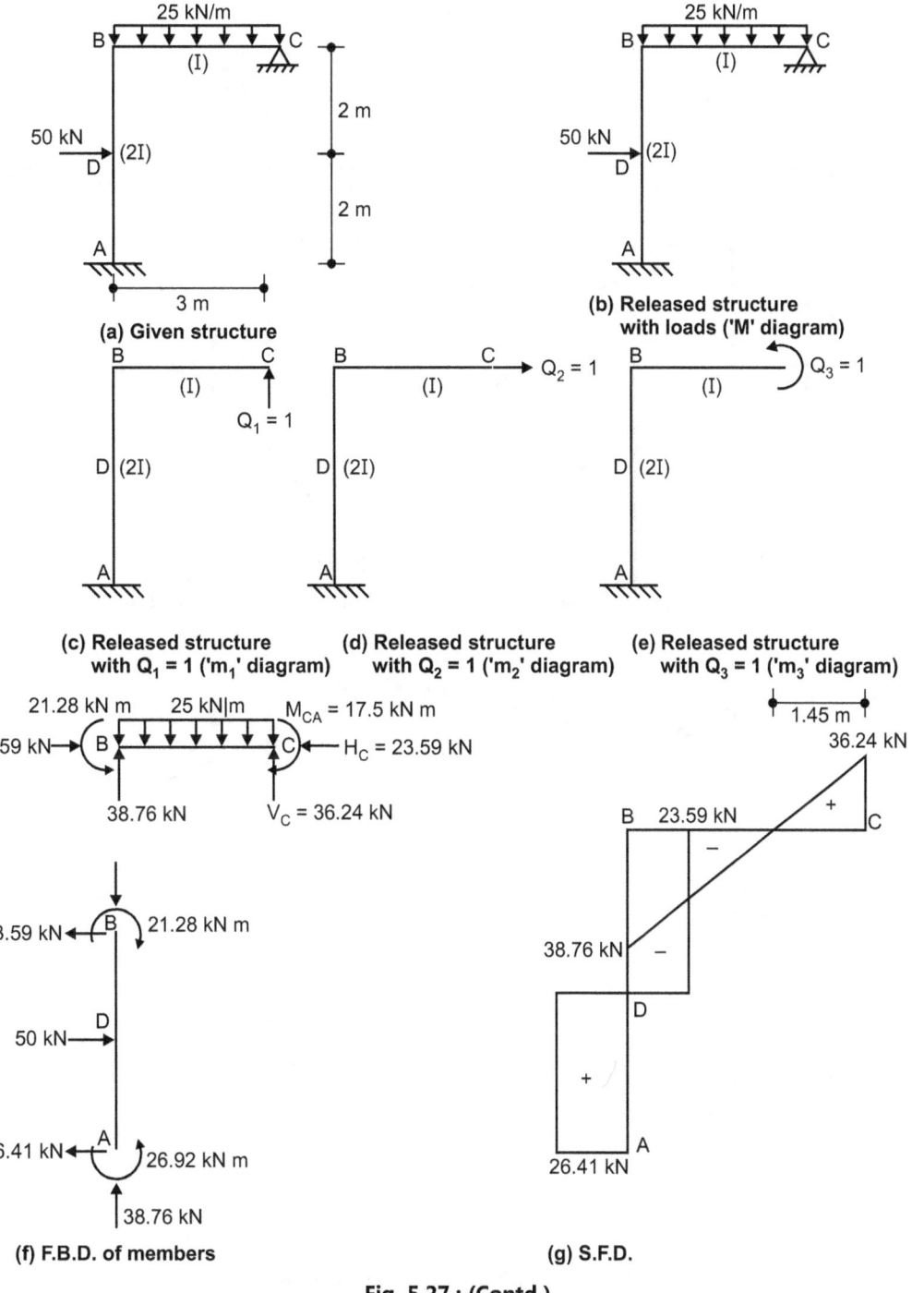

Fig. 5.27 : (Contd.)

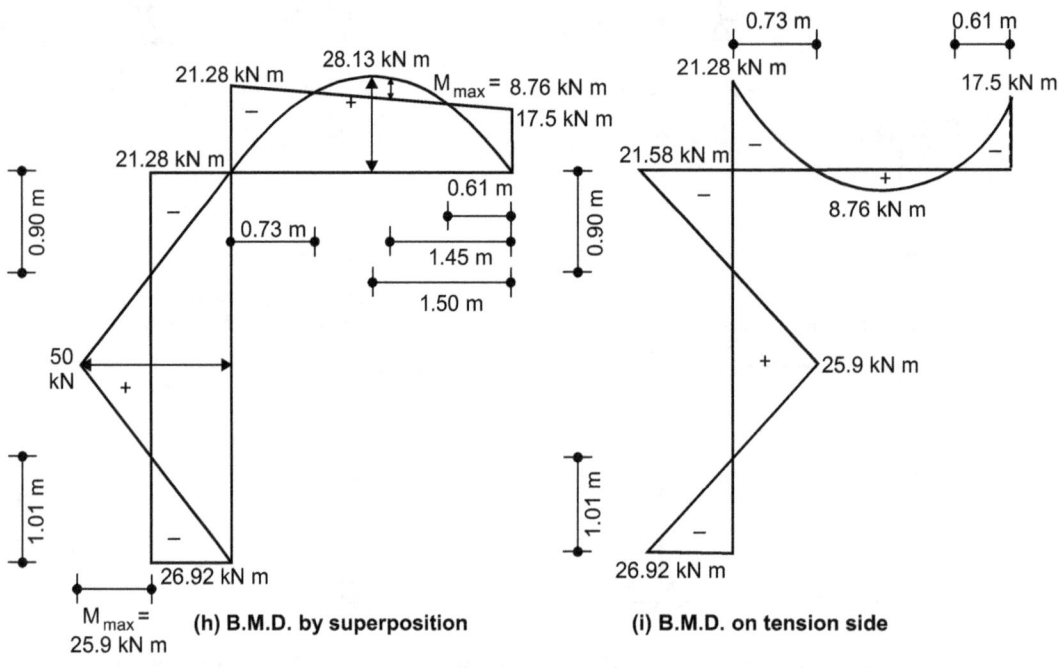

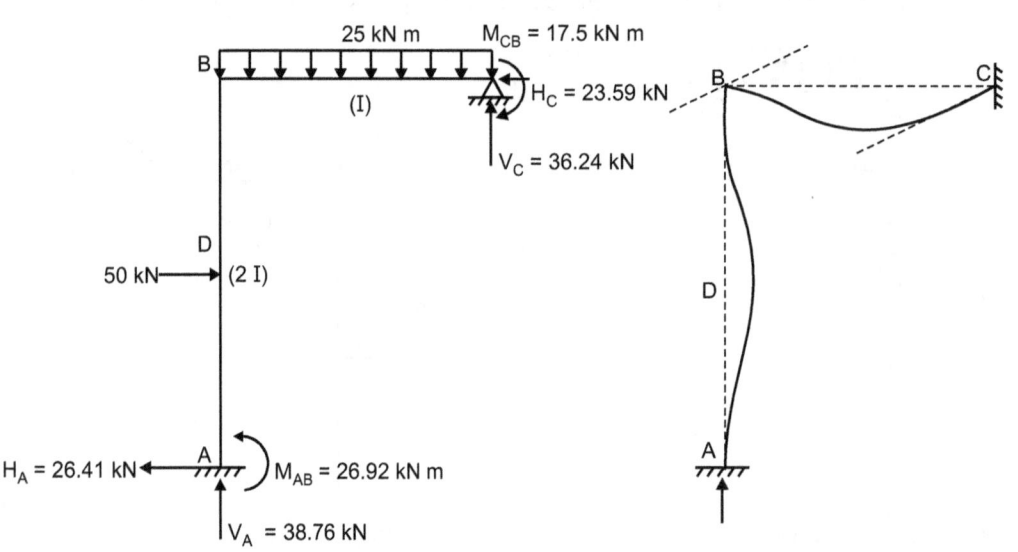

Fig. 5.27 : For Illustrative Example 5.23

(a) Displacements in the released structure subjected to loads corresponding to redundant actions :

$$D_{QL1} = \int_0^L \frac{M m_1 \cdot dx}{EI}$$

$$= \int_0^3 \left(-\frac{25x^2}{2}\right)(x) \cdot \frac{dx}{EI} + \int_0^2 (-112.5)(3) \cdot \frac{dx}{2EI} + \int_2^4 (-50x - 12.5)(3) \cdot \frac{dx}{2EI}$$

$$= \frac{(-253.125 - 337.5 - 487.5)}{EI} = \frac{-1078.125}{EI}$$

$$D_{QL2} = \int_0^L \frac{M m_2 \cdot dx}{EI}$$

$$= \int_0^3 \left(-\frac{25x^2}{2}\right)(0) \cdot \frac{dx}{EI} + \int_0^2 (-112.5)(-x) \cdot \frac{dx}{2EI} + \int_2^4 (-50x - 12.5)(-x) \cdot \frac{dx}{2EI}$$

$$= \frac{(0 + 112.5 + 504.165)}{EI} = \frac{616.665}{EI}$$

$$D_{QL3} = \int_0^L \frac{M m_3 \cdot dx}{EI}$$

$$= \int_0^3 \left(-\frac{25x^2}{2}\right)(1) \cdot \frac{dx}{EI} + \int_0^2 (-112.5)(1) \cdot \frac{dx}{2EI} + \int_2^4 (-50x - 12.5)(1) \cdot \frac{dx}{2EI}$$

$$= \frac{(-112.5 - 112.5 - 162.5)}{EI} = \frac{-387.5}{EI}$$

(b) Displacements in the released structure subjected to unit values of Q_1, Q_2 and Q_3 corresponding to redundant actions :

$$F_{11} = \int_0^L \frac{m_1 \cdot m_1 \cdot dx}{EI}$$

$$= \int_0^3 (x)^2 \cdot \frac{dx}{EI} + \int_0^2 (3)^2 \cdot \frac{dx}{2EI} + \int_2^4 (3)^2 \cdot \frac{dx}{2EI} = \frac{(9 + 9 + 9)}{EI} = \frac{27}{EI}$$

$$F_{21} = F_{12} = \int_0^L \frac{m_1 \cdot m_2 \cdot dx}{EI}$$

$$= \int_0^3 (x)(0) \cdot \frac{dx}{EI} + \int_0^2 (3)(-x) \frac{dx}{2EI} + \int_2^4 (3)(-x) \cdot \frac{dx}{2EI}$$

$$= \int_0^4 (3)(-x) \frac{dx}{2EI} = \frac{-12}{EI}$$

$$F_{31} = F_{13} = \int_0^L \frac{m_1 \cdot m_3 \cdot dx}{EI}$$

$$= \int_0^3 (x)(1) \cdot \frac{dx}{EI} + \int_0^2 (3)(1) \cdot \frac{dx}{2EI} + \int_2^4 (3)(1) \frac{dx}{2EI} = \frac{(4.5 + 3 + 3)}{EI} = \frac{10.5}{EI}$$

$$F_{22} = \int_0^L \frac{m_2 \cdot m_2 \cdot dx}{EI}$$

$$= \int_0^3 (0) \cdot \frac{dx}{EI} + \int_0^2 (-x)^2 \cdot \frac{dx}{2EI} + \int_2^4 (-x)^2 \cdot \frac{dx}{2EI}$$

$$= \int_0^4 x^2 \cdot \frac{dx}{2EI} = \frac{10.67}{EI}$$

$$F_{32} = F_{23} = \int_0^L \frac{m_2 \cdot m_3 \cdot dx}{EI}$$

$$= \int_0^3 (0)(1) \cdot \frac{dx}{EI} + \int_0^2 (-x)(1) \cdot \frac{dx}{2EI} + \int_2^4 (-x)(1) \cdot \frac{dx}{2EI}$$

$$= \int_0^4 (-x) \cdot \frac{dx}{2EI} = -\frac{4}{EI}$$

$$F_{33} = \int_0^L \frac{m_3 \cdot m_3 \cdot dx}{EI}$$

$$= \int_0^3 (1)^2 \cdot \frac{dx}{EI} + \int_0^2 (1)^2 \cdot \frac{dx}{2EI} + \int_2^4 (1)^2 \cdot \frac{dx}{2EI}$$

$$= \frac{(3 + 1 + 1)}{EI} = \frac{5}{EI}$$

Step V : The physical requirement of displacements : The vertical and horizontal translation at C must be zero. Also rotation at C must be zero.

i.e. $D_{Q1} = D_{Q2} = D_{Q3} = 0$

Step VI : Superposition equation of compatibility of displacements :

$$\{D_Q\} = \{D_{QL}\} + [F]\{Q\}$$

i.e. $\begin{Bmatrix} 0 \\ 0 \\ 0 \end{Bmatrix} = \frac{1}{EI} \begin{Bmatrix} -1078.125 \\ 616.665 \\ -387.5 \end{Bmatrix} + \frac{1}{EI} \begin{bmatrix} 27 & -12 & 10.5 \\ -12 & 10.67 & -4 \\ 10.5 & -4 & 5 \end{bmatrix} \begin{Bmatrix} Q_1 \\ Q_2 \\ Q_3 \end{Bmatrix}$

i.e. $0 = -1078.125 + 27(Q_1) - 12(Q_2) + 10.5(Q_3)$ ... (A)

$$0 = 616.665 - 12(Q_1) + 10.67(Q_2) - 4(Q_3) \quad ...(B)$$
$$0 = -387.50 + 10.5(Q_1) - 4(Q_2) + 5(Q_3) \quad ...(C)$$

Step VII : Solution of equations for unknown redundant forces : Solving equations (A), (B), and (C), we get,

$$Q_1 = V_C = 36.24 \text{ kN} = 36.24 \text{ kN} (\uparrow)$$
$$Q_2 = H_C = -23.59 \text{ kN} = 23.59 \text{ kN} (\leftarrow)$$
$$Q_3 = M_C = -17.5 \text{ kNm} = 17.5 \text{ kNm} (\circlearrowleft)$$

Step VIII : Other reaction components : Considering equilibrium of each member and of complete structure, other reaction components are found out and FBD of members is as shown in Fig. 5.27 (f).

Step IX : Shear force and bending moment diagrams : SFD is as shown in Fig. 5.27 (g). BMD by superposition and on tension side is as shown in Fig. 5.27 (h) and Fig. 5.27 (i) respectively.

Step X : FBD of structure : as shown in Fig. 5.27 (j).

Step XI : Elastic Curve : as shown in Fig. 5.27 (k).

Example 5.24 : *Analyse the frame shown in Fig. 5.28 (a) by flexibility method.*

Solution : Data : The frame is supported and loaded as shown in Fig. 5.28 (a).

Object : Structural analysis.

Concepts and Equations :

(1) Statically determinate structure (Released structure).

(2) Displacement analysis of released structure.

(3) Superposition equations of compatibility of displacements.

Procedure :

Step I : The degree of static indeterminacy (D_{si}) :

(a) Degree of external static indeterminacy = $(D_{si})_e$ = 2.

(b) Degree of internal static indeterminacy = $(D_{si})_i$ = 0.

(c) Total degree of static indeterminacy = $D_{si} = (D_{si})_e + (D_{si})_i = 2 + 0 = 2$.

Step II : Selection of unknown redundant forces (Q) :

Let, $Q_1 = V_D (\uparrow)$ and
$Q_2 = H_D (\rightarrow)$

Step III : Released structure : Hinged support at D is removed and the basic released structure is as shown in Fig. 5.28 (b). Also released structure subjected to unit values of Q_1 and Q_2 is shown in Fig. 5.28 (c) and Fig. 5.28 (d) respectively.

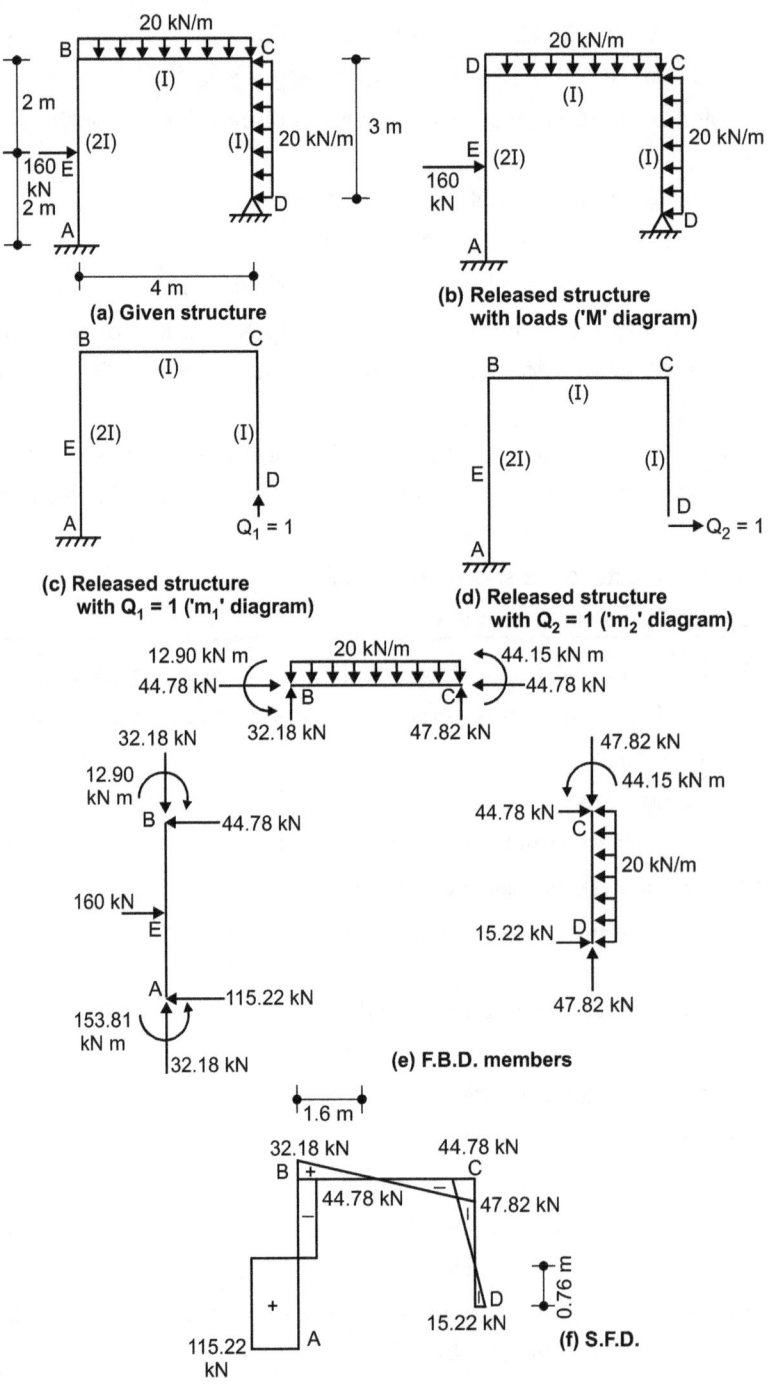

Fig. 5.28 : (Contd.)

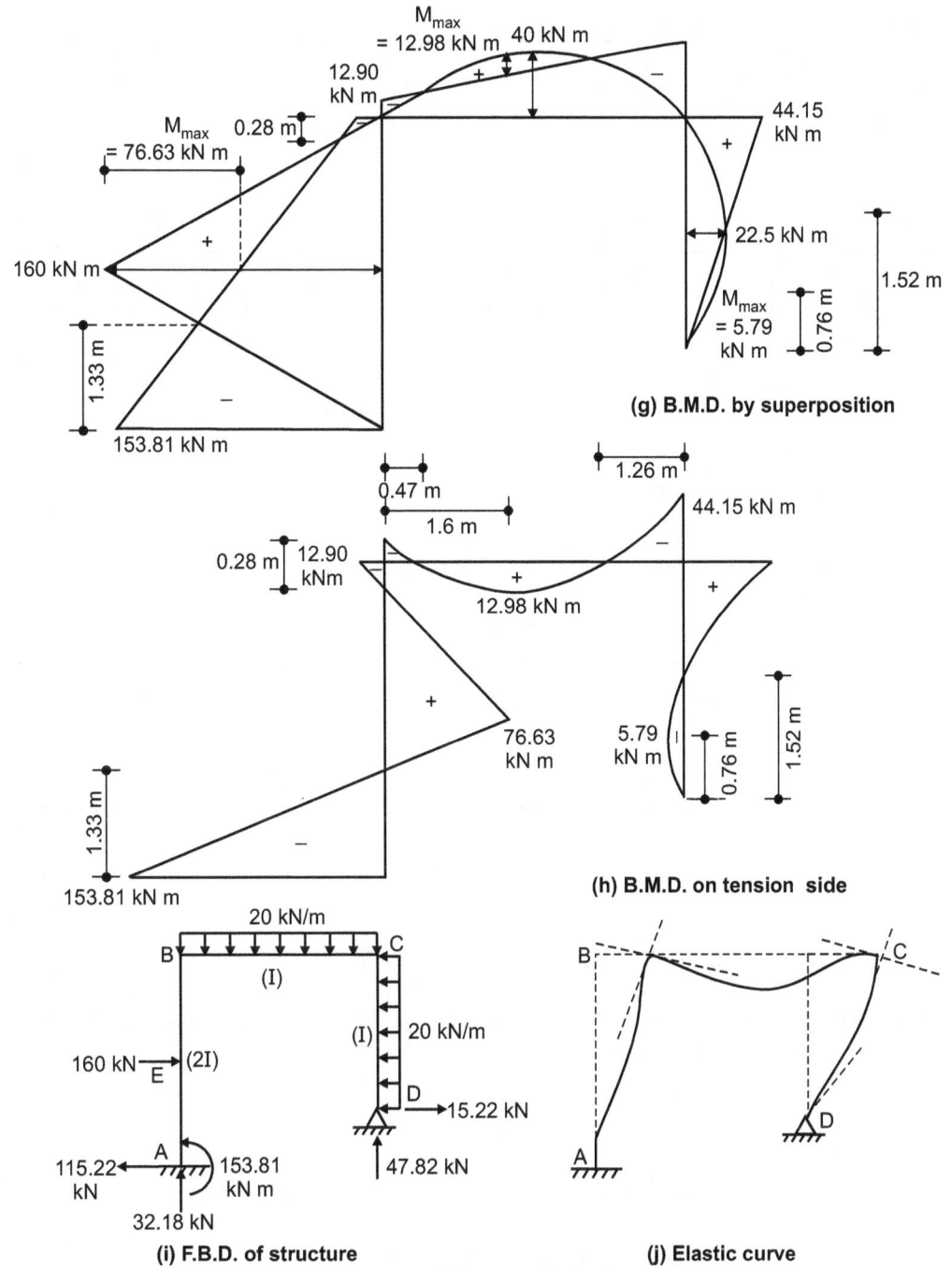

Fig. 5.28 : For Illustrative Example 5.24

Step IV : Displacement analysis of released structure :

Zone	Origin	Limits	EI	M	m_1	m_2
DC	D	0 – 3	EI	$-20\dfrac{x^2}{2}$	0	x
CB	C	0 – 4	EI	$-90 - \dfrac{20x^2}{2}$	x	3
BE	B	0 – 2	2 EI	$-250 + 60x$	4	3 – x
EA	B	2 – 4	2 EI	$-250 + 60 - 160(x-2) = 70 - 100(x)$	4	3 – x

(a) Displacements in the released structure subjected to loads corresponding to redundant actions :

$$D_{QL1} = \int_0^L \dfrac{M m_1 \cdot dx}{EI}$$

$$= \int_0^3 \left(\dfrac{20x^2}{2}\right)(0)\cdot \dfrac{dx}{EI} + \int_0^4 (-90 - 20x^2/2)(x)\cdot \dfrac{dx}{EI}$$

$$+ \int_0^2 (-250 + 60x)(4)\cdot \dfrac{dx}{2EI} + \int_2^4 (70 - 100x)(4)\cdot \dfrac{dx}{2EI}$$

$$= \dfrac{(0 - 1360 - 760 - 920)}{EI} = \dfrac{-3040}{EI}$$

$$D_{QL2} = \int_0^L \dfrac{M m_2 \cdot dx}{EI}$$

$$= \int_0^3 \left(\dfrac{20x^2}{2}\right)(-x)\cdot \dfrac{dx}{EI} + \int_0^4 (-90 - 20x^2/2)(3)\cdot \dfrac{dx}{EI} + \int_0^2 (-250 + 60x)(3-x)\cdot \dfrac{dx}{2EI}$$

$$+ \int_2^4 (70 - 100x)(3-x)\cdot \dfrac{dx}{2EI}$$

$$= \dfrac{(-202.5 - 1720 - 400 + 33.33)}{EI} = \dfrac{-2289.16}{EI}$$

(b) Displacements in the released structure subjected to unit values of Q_1 and Q_2 corresponding to redundant actions :

$$F_{11} = \int_0^L \dfrac{m_1 \cdot m_1 \cdot dx}{EI}$$

$$= \int_0^3 (0)\cdot \dfrac{dx}{EI} + \int_0^4 (x)^2 \cdot \dfrac{dx}{EI} + \int_0^2 (4)^2 \cdot \dfrac{dx}{2EI} + \int_2^4 (4)^2 \cdot \dfrac{dx}{2EI}$$

$$= \dfrac{(0 + 21.33 + 16 + 16)}{EI} = \dfrac{53.33}{EI}$$

$$F_{21} = F_{12} = \int_0^L \frac{m_1 \cdot m_2 \cdot dx}{EI}$$

$$= \int_0^3 (0)(-x)\frac{dx}{EI} + \int_0^4 (x)(3)\frac{dx}{EI} + \int_0^2 4(3-x)\frac{dx}{2EI} + \int_2^4 4(3-x)\frac{dx}{2EI}$$

$$= \frac{(0 + 24 + 8 + 0)}{EI} = \frac{32}{EI}$$

$$F_{22} = \int_0^L \frac{m_2 \cdot m_2 \cdot dx}{EI}$$

$$= \int_0^3 (-x)^2 \cdot \frac{dx}{EI} + \int_0^4 (3)^2 \cdot \frac{dx}{EI} + \int_0^2 (3-x)^2 \cdot \frac{dx}{2EI} + \int_2^4 (3-x)^2 \cdot \frac{dx}{2EI}$$

$$= \frac{(9 + 36 + 4.33 + 0.33)}{EI} = \frac{49.67}{EI}$$

Step V : The physical requirement of displacements :
The vertical and horizontal translation at D must be zero.
i.e. $\quad D_{Q1} = D_{Q2} = 0$

Step VI : Superposition equation of compatibility of displacements :

$$\{D_Q\} = \{D_{QL}\} + [F]\{Q\}$$

i.e. $\quad \begin{Bmatrix} 0 \\ 0 \end{Bmatrix} = \frac{1}{EI} \cdot \begin{Bmatrix} -3040 \\ -2289.16 \end{Bmatrix} + \frac{1}{EI} \begin{bmatrix} 53.33 & 32 \\ 32 & 49.67 \end{bmatrix} \begin{Bmatrix} Q_1 \\ Q_2 \end{Bmatrix}$

i.e. $\quad 0 = -3040 + 53.33(Q_1) + 32(Q_2)$ ... (A)
$\quad 0 = -2289.16 + 32(Q_1) + 49.67(Q_2)$ ... (B)
$\quad Q_2 = H_D = 15.22 \text{ kN} = 15.22 \text{ kN} (\rightarrow)$

Step VII : Solution of equations for unknown redundant forces. Solving equations (A) and (B), we get,

$$\boxed{\begin{aligned} Q_1 &= V_D = 47.82 \text{ kN} = 47.82 \text{ kN} (\uparrow) \\ Q_2 &= H_D = 15.22 \text{ kN} = 15.22 \text{ kN} (\rightarrow) \end{aligned}}$$

Step VIII : Other reaction components : Considering equilibrium of each member and of complete structure, other reaction components are found out and FBD of members is as shown in Fig. 5.28 (e).

Step IX : Shear force and bending moment diagrams : SFD is as shown in Fig. 5.28 (f). BMD by superposition and on tension side is as shown in Fig. 5.28 (g) and Fig. 5.28 (h) respectively.

Step X : FBD of structure : as shown in Fig. 5.28 (i).

Step XI : Elastic Curve : as shown in Fig. 5.28 (j).

TOS – II (TE CIVIL SEM. VI NMU) — FUNDAMENTAL CONCEPT OF FLEXIBILITY

Example 5.25 : *Analyse the frame shown in Fig. 5.29 (a) by flexibility method. Take EI = constant.*

Solution : Data : The frame is supported and loaded as shown in Fig. 5.29 (a).
Object : Structural analysis.
Concepts and Equations :
(1) Statically determinate structure (Released structure).
(2) Displacement analysis of released structure.
(3) Superposition equations of compatibility of displacements.

Procedure :

Step I : The degree of static indeterminacy (D_{si}) :
(a) Degree of external static indeterminacy = $(D_{si})_e$ = 3.
(b) Degree of internal static indeterminacy = $(D_{si})_i$ = 0.
(c) Total degree of static indeterminacy = D_{si} = $(D_{si})_e$ + $(D_{si})_i$ = 3 + 0 = 3.

Step II : Selection of unknown redundant forces (Q) :
Let,
Q_1 = $V_D (\uparrow)$
Q_2 = $H_D (\rightarrow)$ and
Q_3 = M_{DC}

Step III : Released structure : Fixed support at D is removed and the basic released structure is as shown in Fig. 5.29 (b). Also released structure subjected to unit values of Q_1, Q_2 and Q_3 is shown in Fig. 5.29 (c), Fig. 5.29 (d), and Fig. 5.29 (e) respectively.

Step IV : Displacement analysis of released structure :

Zone	Origin	Limits	M	m_1	m_2	m_3
DF	D	0 – 1	0	0	x	1
FC	D	1 – 3	40 (x – 1)	0	x	1
CE	C	0 – 1.5	– 80	x	3	1
EB	C	1.5 – 3	– 50 (x – 1.5) – 80	x	3	1
BA	B	0 – 4	$-25\dfrac{x^2}{2} - 155 + 40x$	3	3 – x	1

(a) Displacements in the released structure subjected to loads corresponding to redundant actions :

$$D_{QL1} = \int_0^L \frac{M m_1 \cdot dx}{EI}$$

$$= \int_0^1 (0) \cdot \frac{dx}{EI} + \int_1^3 40(x-1)(0) \cdot \frac{dx}{EI} + \int_0^{1.5} (-80)(x) \cdot \frac{dx}{EI} + \int_{1.5}^3 [-50(x-1.5) - 80](x) \cdot \frac{dx}{EI}$$

$$+ \int_0^4 \left(-25\frac{x^2}{2} - 155 + 40x\right)(3) \cdot \frac{dx}{EI}$$

$$= \frac{(0 + 9 - 90 - 410.625 - 1700)}{EI} = \frac{-2200.625}{EI}$$

Ch. 5 | 5.92

FUNDAMENTAL CONCEPT OF FLEXIBILITY

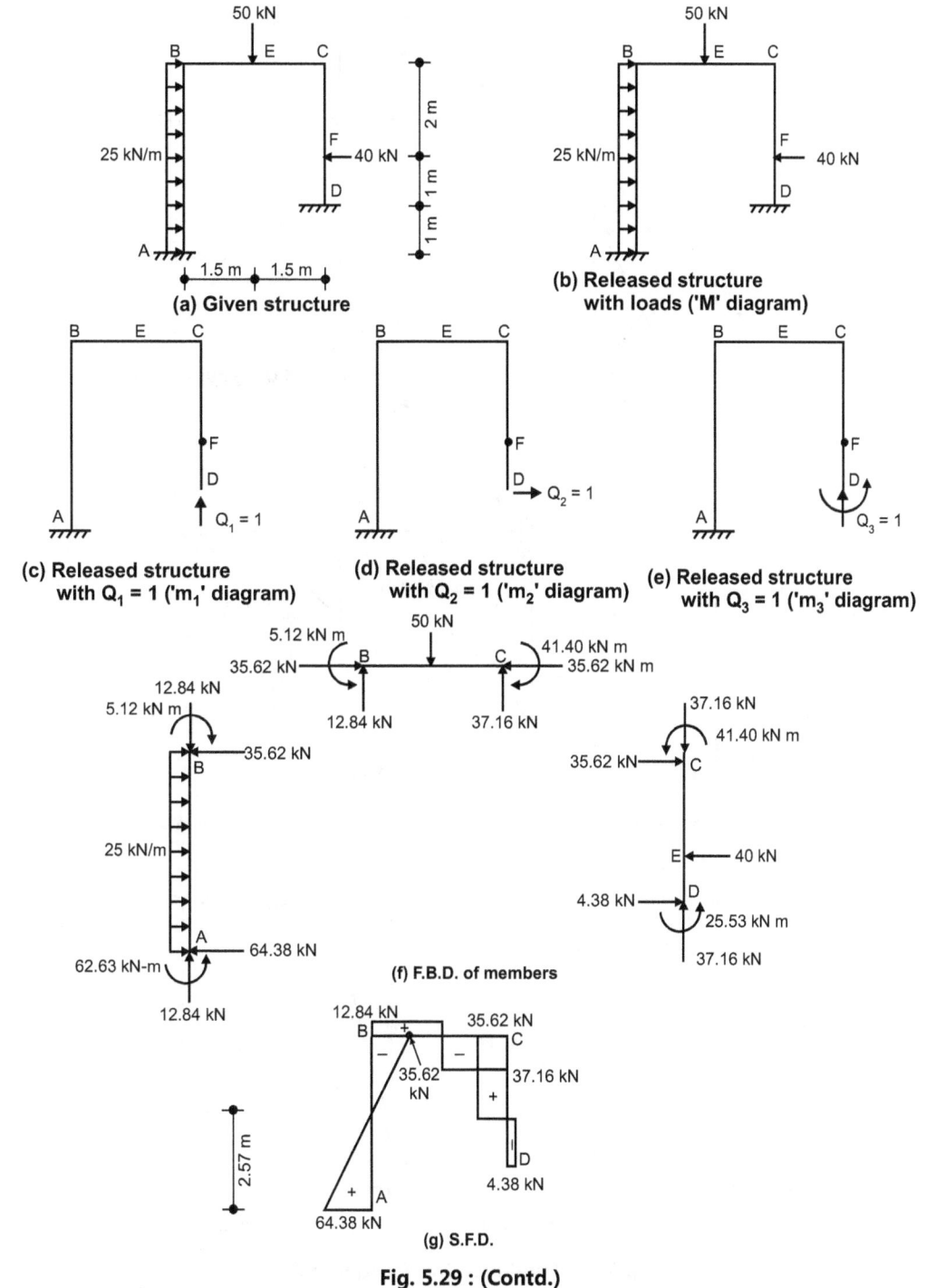

Fig. 5.29 : (Contd.)

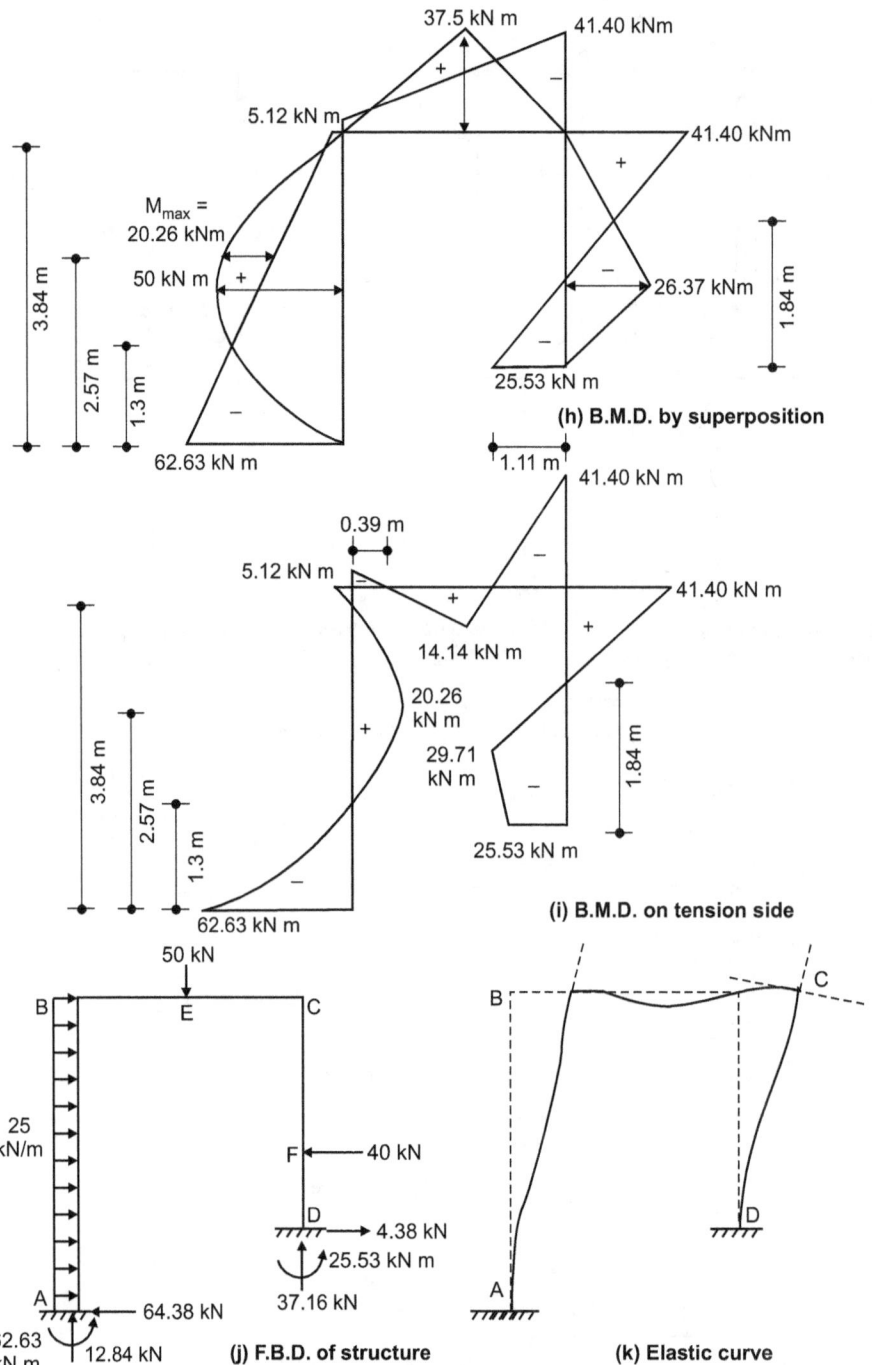

Fig. 5.29 : For Illustrative Example 5.25

FUNDAMENTAL CONCEPT OF FLEXIBILITY

$$D_{QL2} = \int_0^L \frac{Mm_2 \cdot dx}{EI}$$

$$= \int_0^1 (0)(-x) \cdot \frac{dx}{EI} + \int_1^3 40(x-1)(-x) \cdot \frac{dx}{EI} + \int_0^{1.5} (-80)(3) \frac{dx}{EI}$$

$$+ \int_{1.5}^3 [-50(x-1.5) - 80](3) \cdot \frac{dx}{EI} + \int_0^4 \left(-\frac{25x^2}{2} - 155 + 40x\right)(3-x) \frac{dx}{EI}$$

$$= \frac{(0 - 186.67 - 360 - 528.75 - 513.33)}{EI} = -\frac{1588.75}{EI}$$

$$D_{QL3} = \int_0^L \frac{Mm_3 \cdot dx}{EI}$$

$$= \int_0^1 (0)(-1) \cdot \frac{dx}{EI} + \int_1^3 40(x-1)(-1) \cdot \frac{dx}{EI} + \int_0^{1.5} (-80)(1) \cdot \frac{dx}{EI}$$

$$+ \int_{1.5}^3 [-50(x-1.5) - 80](1) \cdot \frac{dx}{EI} + \int_0^4 \left(-\frac{25x^2}{2} - 155 + 40x\right)(1) \cdot \frac{dx}{EI}$$

$$= \frac{(0 - 80 - 120 - 176.25 - 566.67)}{EI} = -\frac{942.92}{EI}$$

(b) Displacements in the released structure subjected to unit values of Q_1; Q_2 and Q_3 corresponding to redundant actions :

$$F_{11} = \int_0^L \frac{m_1 \cdot m_1 \cdot dx}{EI}$$

$$= \int_0^1 (0) \cdot \frac{dx}{EI} + \int_1^3 (0) \cdot \frac{dx}{EI} + \int_0^{1.5} (x)^2 \cdot \frac{dx}{EI} + \int_{1.5}^3 (x)^2 \cdot \frac{dx}{EI} + \int_0^4 (3)^2 \cdot \frac{dx}{EI}$$

$$= \frac{(0 + 0 + 1.125 + 7.875 + 36)}{EI} = \frac{45}{EI}$$

$$F_{21} = F_{12} = \int_0^L \frac{m_1 \cdot m_2 \cdot dx}{EI}$$

$$= \int_0^1 (0)(-x) \cdot \frac{dx}{EI} + \int_1^3 (0)(-x) \cdot \frac{dx}{EI} + \int_0^{1.5} (x)(3) \cdot \frac{dx}{EI} + \int_{1.5}^3 (x)(3) \cdot \frac{dx}{EI} + \int_0^4 (3)(3-x) \frac{dx}{EI}$$

$$= \frac{0 + 0 + 3.375 + 10.125 + 12}{EI} = \frac{25.5}{EI}$$

$$F_{31} = F_{13} = \int_0^L \frac{m_1 \cdot m_3 \cdot dx}{EI}$$

$$= \int_0^1 (0)(-1) \cdot \frac{dx}{EI} + \int_1^3 (0)(-1) \cdot \frac{dx}{EI} + \int_0^{1.5} (x)(1) \cdot \frac{dx}{EI} + \int_{1.5}^3 (x)(1) \cdot \frac{dx}{EI} + \int_0^4 (3)(1) \cdot \frac{dx}{EI}$$

$$= \frac{(0 + 0 + 1.125 + 3.375 + 12)}{EI} = \frac{16.5}{EI}$$

$$F_{22} = \int_0^L \frac{m_2 \cdot m_2 \cdot dx}{EI}$$

$$= \int_0^1 (-x)^2 \cdot \frac{dx}{EI} + \int_1^3 (-x)^2 \cdot \frac{dx}{EI} + \int_0^{1.5} (3)^2 \cdot \frac{dx}{EI} + \int_{1.5}^3 (3)^2 \cdot \frac{dx}{EI} + \int_0^4 (3-x)^2 \cdot \frac{dx}{EI}$$

$$= \frac{0.33 + 8.67 + 13.5 + 13.5 + 9.33}{EI} = \frac{45.33}{EI}$$

$$F_{32} = F_{23} = \int_0^L \frac{m_2 \cdot m_3 \cdot dx}{EI}$$

$$= \int_0^1 (-x)(-1) \cdot \frac{dx}{EI} + \int_1^3 (-x)(-1) \cdot \frac{dx}{EI} + \int_0^{1.5} (3)(1) \cdot \frac{dx}{EI}$$

$$+ \int_{1.5}^3 (3)(1) \cdot \frac{dx}{EI} + \int_0^4 (3-x)(1) \cdot \frac{dx}{EI}$$

$$= \frac{(0.5 + 4 + 4.5 + 4.5 + 4)}{EI} = \frac{17.5}{EI}$$

$$F_{33} = \int_0^L \frac{m_3 \cdot m_3 \cdot dx}{EI}$$

$$= \int_0^1 (-1)^2 \frac{dx}{EI} + \int_1^3 (-1)^2 \cdot \frac{dx}{EI} + \int_0^{1.5} (1)^2 \cdot \frac{dx}{EI} + \int_{1.5}^3 (1)^2 \cdot \frac{dx}{EI} + \int_0^4 (1)^2 \cdot \frac{dx}{EI}$$

$$= \frac{(1 + 2 + 1.5 + 1.5 + 4)}{EI} = \frac{10}{EI}$$

Step V : The physical requirement of displacements : The vertical and horizontal translation at D must be zero. Also rotation at D must be zero.

i.e. $D_{Q1} = D_{Q2} = D_{Q3} = 0$

Step VI : Superposition equation of compatibility of displacements :

$\{D_Q\} = \{D_{QL}\} + [F]\{Q\}$

i.e. $\begin{Bmatrix} 0 \\ 0 \\ 0 \end{Bmatrix} = \dfrac{1}{EI} \begin{Bmatrix} -2200.625 \\ -1588.75 \\ -942.91 \end{Bmatrix} + \dfrac{1}{EI} \begin{bmatrix} 45 & 25.5 & 16.5 \\ 25.5 & 45.33 & 17.5 \\ 16.5 & 17.5 & 10 \end{bmatrix} \begin{Bmatrix} Q_1 \\ Q_2 \\ Q_3 \end{Bmatrix}$

i.e.
$0 = -2200.625 + 45(Q_1) + 25.5(Q_2) + 16.5(Q_3)$ ... (A)
$0 = -1588.75 + 25.5(Q_1) + 45.33(Q_2) + 17.5(Q_3)$ ... (B)
$0 = -942.91 + 16.5(Q_1) + 17.5(Q_2) + 10(Q_3)$ ... (C)

Step VII : Solution of equations for unknown redundant forces : Solving equations (A), (B) and (C). we get,

$Q_1 = V_D = 37.16$ kN $= 37.16$ kN (↑)
$Q_2 = H_D = 4.38$ kN $= 4.38$ kN (→)
$Q_3 = M_{DC} = 25.33$ kNm $= 25.33$ kNm (↺)

Step VIII : Other reaction components : Considering equilibrium of each member and of complete structure, other reaction components are found out and FBD of members is as shown in Fig. 5.29 (f).

Step IX : Shear force and bending moment diagrams : SFD is as shown in Fig. 5.29 (g). BMD by superposition and on tension side is as shown in Fig. 5.29 (h) and Fig. 5.29 (i) respectively.

Step X : FBD of Structure : as shown in Fig. 5.29 (j).

Step XI : Elastic Curve : as shown in Fig. 5.29 (k).

Example 5.26 : *Analyse the portal frame as shown in Fig. 5.30 by flexibility method. EI = constant.*

Solution : Data : The frame is supported and loaded as shown in Fig. 5.30 (a).

Object : Structural analysis.

Concepts and Equations :

(1) Statically determinate structure (released structure).
(2) Displacement analysis of released structure.
(3) Superposition equations of compatability of displacements.

Procedure : Step I : The degree of static indeterminacy

(a) Degree of external static indeterminacy = $(D_{si})_e = 1$
(b) Degree of internal static indeterminacy = $(D_{si})_i = 0$
(c) Total degree of static indeterminacy = $(D_{si}) = (D_{si})_e + (D_{si})_i = 1 + 0 = 1$

Step II : Selection of unknown redundant forces (Q_1) :

Let, $\qquad Q = V_B$ (↑)

Step III : Released Structure : Roller support at B is removed and basic released structure is as shown in Fig. 5.30 (c). Also released structure is subjected to unit value of θ_1 is as shown in Fig. 5.30 (d).

Step IV : Displacement Analysis of Released Structure :

Zone	Origin	Limit	EI	M	m_1
CB	C	0 – 2.4	2EI	0	x
BA	B	0 – 4.8	EI	$-20x^2/2 = -10x^2$	2.4

(a) Displacement in the Released Structure Subjected to Loads Corresponding to Redundant Actions :

$$D_{QL1} = \int_0^L M m_1 \frac{dx}{EI}$$

$$= \int_0^{2.4} 0(x) \frac{dx}{2EI} + \int_0^{4.8} (-10x^2)(2.4) \frac{dx}{EI}$$

$$= -\frac{884.74}{EI}$$

(b) Displacement in the Released Structure Subjected to Unit Value of Q_1 Corresponding to Redundant Actions :

$$F_{11} = \int_0^L m_1 m_1 \frac{dx}{EI}$$

$$= \int_0^{2.4} x \cdot x \frac{dx}{2EI} + \int_0^{4.8} 2.4 \times 2.4 \frac{dx}{EI}$$

$$= \frac{2.30}{EI} + \frac{27.65}{EI} = \frac{29.95}{EI}$$

Step V : The physical requirement of displacements :

The vertical translation at must be zero i.e.

$$D_{Q1} = 0$$

Step VI : Superposition equation of compatibility of displacements :

$$\{D_Q\} = \{D_{QL}\} + [F]\{Q\}$$

$$0 = \frac{-884.74}{EI} + \left(\frac{29.95}{EI}\right) Q_1 \quad \ldots A$$

Step VII : Solution of equations for redundant forces :

Solving equation (A), we get,

$$Q_1 = 29.54 \text{ kN } (\uparrow)$$

Step VIII : Other Reaction Components : Consider equilibrium of complete structure, other unknown reaction components are found. FBD of structure is as shown in Fig. 5.30 (e).

Step IX : Shear Force and Bending Moment Diagrams : SFD is as shown in Fig. 5.30 (f), BMD by superposition and tension side as shown in Fig. 5.30 (g) and (h).

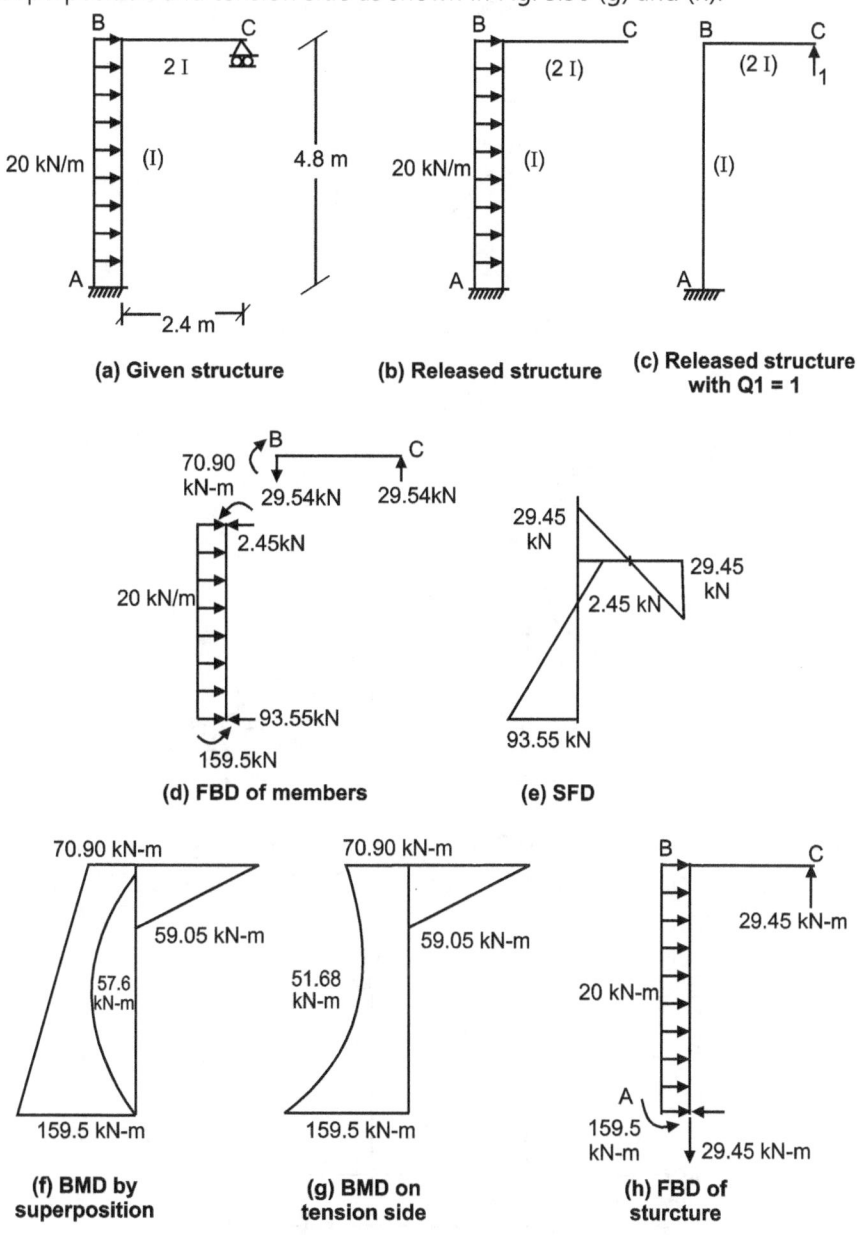

Fig. 5.30 : For Illustration – Example 5.26

EXERCISE

For pin jointed plane trusses in problems 1 to 17, find forces in all the members. Take E = constant. Figures in the bracket indicate cross-sectional areas of members in cm², wherever mentioned. Otherwise A shall be taken constant.

1.

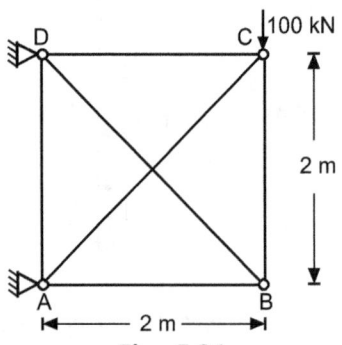

Fig. 5.31

(**Ans.** $F_{AB} = -54.84$ kN, $F_{BC} = -54.84$ kN, $F_{CD} = 45.16$ kN, $F_{AD} = 45.16$ kN, $F_{AC} = -63.87$ kN, $F_{DB} = 77.55$ kN)

2.

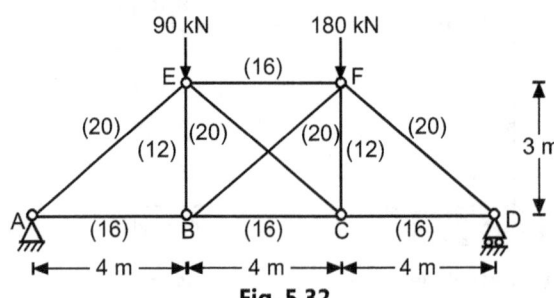

Fig. 5.32

(**Ans.** $F_{AE} = -200$ kN, $F_{AB} = 160$ kN, $F_{BC} = 175.65$ kN, $F_{BE} = 171.74$ kN, $F_{EF} = -184.35$ kN, $F_{EC} = 30.44$ kN, $F_{CF} = -18.26$ kN, $F_{DF} = -250$ kN, $F_{DC} = 200$ kN, $F_{BF} = -19.56$ kN)

3.

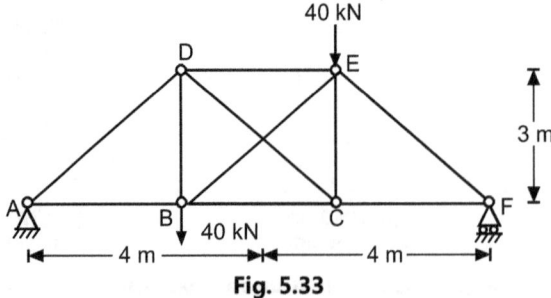

Fig. 5.33

(**Ans.** F_{AB} = 26.6 kN, F_{AD} = – 33.2 kN, F_{BD} = 31.2 kN, F_{DC} = – 18.7 kN, F_{BE} = 14.4 kN, F_{DE} = – 11.6 kN, F_{BC} = 15 kN, F_{EC} = – 48.8 kN)

4.

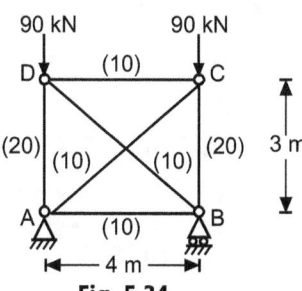

Fig. 5.34

(**Ans.** F_{AB} = 8 kN, F_{DC} = 8 kN, F_{AD} = – 84 kN, F_{BC} = – 84 kN, F_{AC} = – 10 kN, F_{BD} = – 10 kN)

5.

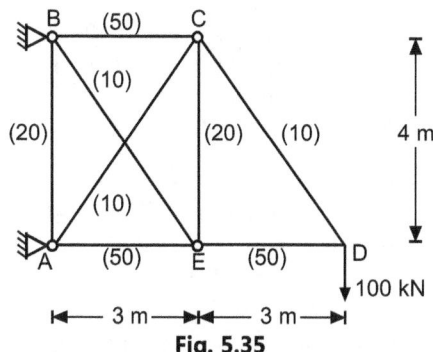

Fig. 5.35

(**Ans.** F_{AB} = – 40.14 kN, F_{AE} = – 105.11 kN, F_{BE} = 50.18 kN, F_{BC} = 119.89 kN, F_{CE} = – 40.14 kN, F_{DE} = – 75 kN, F_{DC} = 125 kN, F_{AC} = – 74.82 kN)

6.

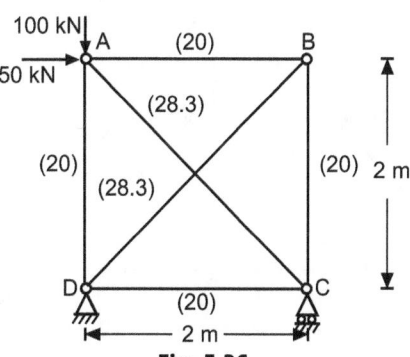

Fig. 5.36

(**Ans.** F_{AB} = – 12.5 kN, F_{BC} = 12.5 kN, F_{AC} = – 53 kN, F_{AD} = – 62.5 kN, F_{DC} = 37.5 kN, F_{DB} = 17.68 kN)

7.

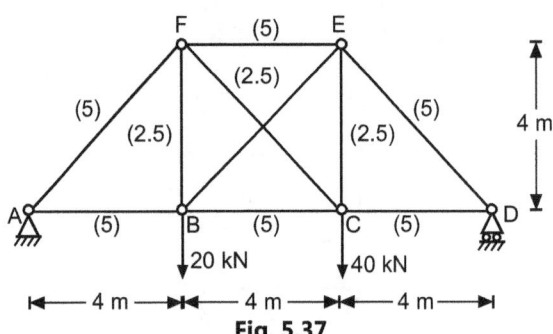

Fig. 5.37

(**Ans.** F_{AB} = 26.67 kN, F_{BC} = 23.06 kN, F_{CD} = 33.33 kN, F_{FE} = − 36.93 kN, F_{AF} = − 37.73 kN, F_{ED} = − 47.06 kN, F_{BF} = 23.06 kN, F_{CE} = 29.73 kN, F_{BE} = 5.08 kN, F_{CF} = 14.5 kN)

8.

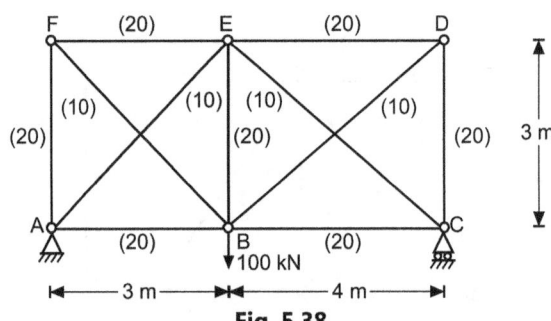

Fig. 5.38

(**Ans.** F_{AB} = 27.2 kN, F_{BC} = 27.2 kN, F_{FE} = − 29.95 kN, F_{ED} = − 30 kN, F_{AF} = 29.95 kN, F_{BE} = 47.55 kN, F_{CD} = − 22.5 kN, F_{AE} = − 38.5 kN, F_{FB} = − 42.3 kN, F_{BD} = − 37.55 kN, F_{EC} = − 33.9 kN)

9.

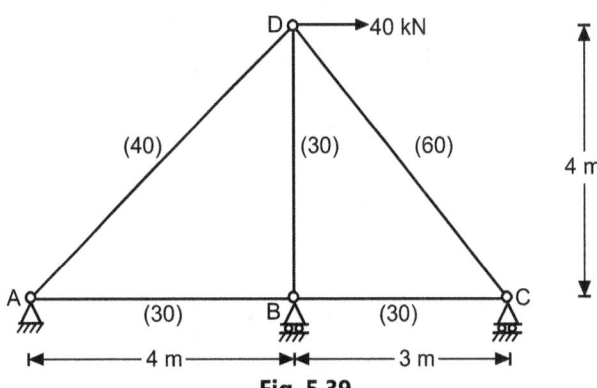

Fig. 5.39

(**Ans.** F_{AB} = 16.12 kN, F_{BC} = 16.12 kN, F_{AD} = 33.77 kN, F_{BD} = − 23.80 kN, F_{CD} = − 26.87 kN)

10.

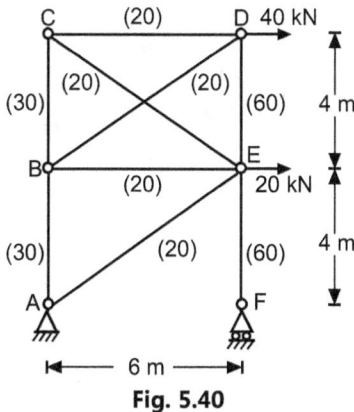

Fig. 5.40

(**Ans.** F_{AB} = 26.67 kN, F_{AE} = 72.11 kN, F_{EF} = – 72.11 kN, F_{BE} = – 40 kN, F_{BC} = 0, F_{BD} = 48.1 kN, F_{CE} = 0, F_{DE} = – 26.67 kN, F_{DC} = 0)

11.

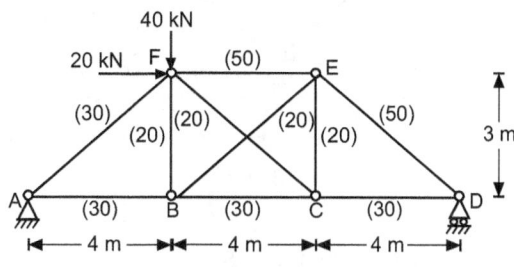

Fig. 5.41

(**Ans.** F_{AB} = 48.89 kN, F_{AF} = – 36.11, F_{BF} = – 10.43 kN, F_{FE} = – 38.35 kN, F_{FC} = – 13.18 kN, F_{BE} = 17.38 kN, F_{BC} = 35 kN, F_{DE} = – 30.55 kN, F_{CE} = 7.91 kN, F_{CD} = 24.44 kN)

12.

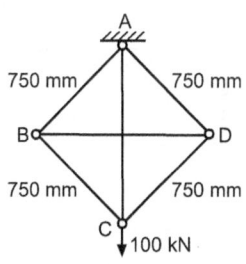

Fig. 5.42

(**Ans.** F_{AB} = 20.72 kN, F_{BC} = 20.72 kN, F_{CD} = 20.72 kN, F_{DA} = 20.72 kN, F_{BD} = – 29.3 kN, F_{AC} = 70.7 kN)

13.

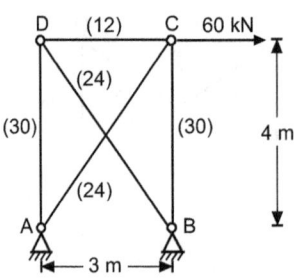

Fig. 5.43

(**Ans.** F_{AD} = 34.58 kN, F_{DC} = 26 kN, F_{CB} = – 45.42 kN, F_{AC} = 56.58 kN, F_{BD} = – 43.4 kN)

14.

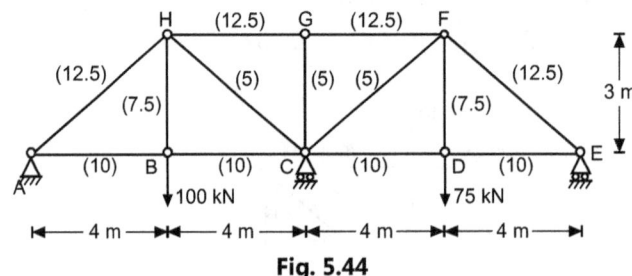

Fig. 5.44

(**Ans.** F_{AH} = – 85.75 kN, F_{HG} = – 3.92 kN, F_{GF} = – 3.92 kN, F_{FE} = – 64.91 kN, F_{AB} = 68.625 kN, F_{BC} = 68.625 kN, F_{CD} = 51.88 kN, F_{DE} = 51.88 kN, F_{BH} = 100 kN, F_{CH} = 80.75 kN, F_{CG} = 0, F_{CF} = 60.125 kN, F_{DF} = 75 kN)

15.

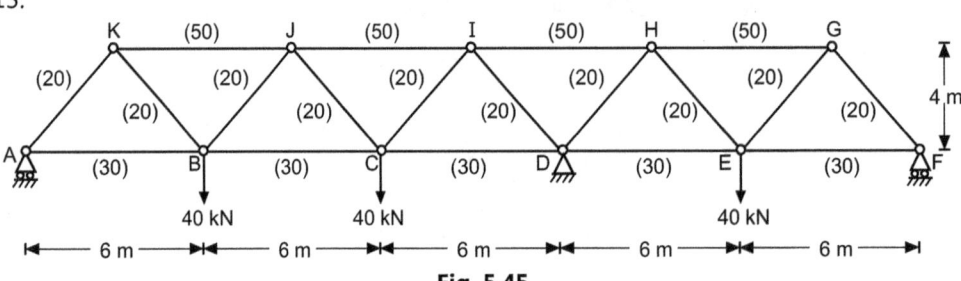

Fig. 5.45

(**Ans.** F_{AB} = 25.15 kN, F_{AK} = – 41.92 kN, F_{KB} = 41.92 kN, F_{KJ} = – 50.31 kN, F_{BC} = 45.46 kN, F_{BJ} = 8.1 kN, F_{CJ} = – 8.1 kN, F_{JI} = – 40.62 kN, F_{CD} = 5.77 kN, F_{CI} = 58.1 kN, F_{DI} = – 58.1 kN, F_{IH} = 29.1 kN, F_{DE} = – 6.81 kN, F_{DH} = – 37.11 kN, F_{EH} = 37.11 kN, F_{HG} = – 15.46 kN, F_{EF} = 7.73 kN, F_{EG} = 12.9 kN, F_{FG} = – 12.9 kN)

16.

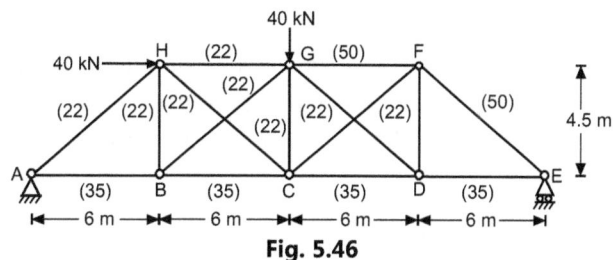

Fig. 5.46

(**Ans.** F_{AB} = 56.67 kN, F_{AH} = – 20.83 kN, F_{HB} = 10.17 kN, F_{HG} = – 59.78 kN, F_{HC} = 3.89 kN, F_{BG} = – 16.95 kN, F_{BC} = 70.22 kN, F_{GC} = – 17.22 kN, F_{DG} = – 21 kN, F_{GF} = – 56.53 kN, F_{CD} = 53.47 kN, F_{CF} = 24.83 kN, F_{DF} = 12.60 kN, F_{EF} = –45.83 kN, F_{DE} = 36.67 kN)

17.

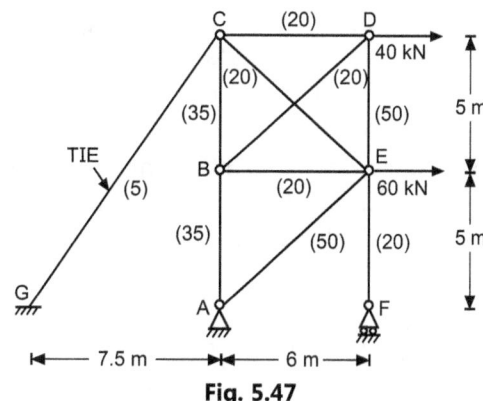

Fig. 5.47

(**Ans.** F_{AB} = 9.73 kN, F_{BC} = – 3.18 kN, F_{CD} = 24.50 kN, F_{CE} = – 17.72 kN, F_{BD} = 20.17 kN, F_{ED} = – 12.91 kN, F_{BE} = – 15.50 kN, F_{EF} = – 98.51 kN, F_{AE} = 115.99 kN, F_{GC} = 18.16 kN)

18. A pin jointed rectangular truss is as shown in Fig. 5.48. The member AD is last to be added and is short by 4 mm. Find the forces in all the members when it is forced into position. Take E = 200 GPa. Figures in the bracket indicate cross-sectional areas of members in cm².

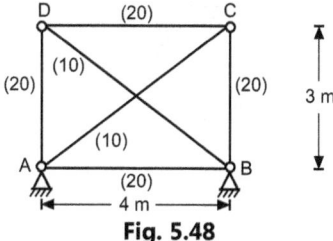

Fig. 5.48

(**Ans.** F_{AB} = 28.04 kN, F_{BC} = 21.08 kN, F_{CD} = 28.04 kN, F_{DA} = 21.08 kN, F_{DB} = – 35.2 kN, F_{AC} = – 35.2 kN)

19. A pin jointed truss is as shown in Fig. 5.49. The member EF is last to be added and is long by 2 mm. Find forces in all the members of truss when it is forced into position. Take E = 200 GPa. Figures in the bracket indicate cross-sectional areas of members in cm².

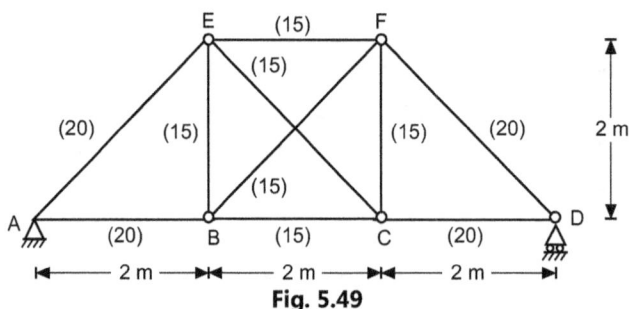

Fig. 5.49

(**Ans.** F_{AE} = 0, F_{AB} = 0, F_{BE} = – 31.1 kN, F_{EF} = – 31.3 kN, F_{EC} = 43.97 kN, F_{BF} = 43.97 kN, F_{BC} = – 31.1 kN, F_{CF} = – 31.1 kN, F_{FD} = 0, F_{CD} = 0)

20. A pin jointed truss is shown in Fig. 5.50. All members has cross-sectional area of 10 cm². If there is a rise of temperature of member BD by 30°C, determine forces due to change in temperature. Coefficient of linear expansion α = 12 × 10⁻⁶ per °C and E = 200 GPa.

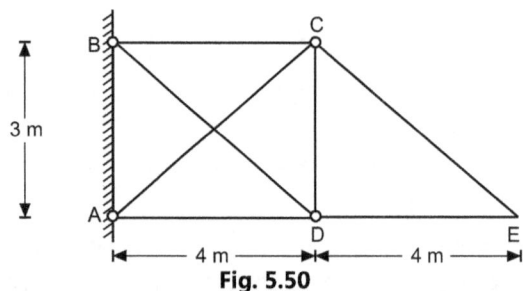

Fig. 5.50

(**Ans.** F_{BC} = 17.77 kN, F_{CD} = 13.33 kN, F_{AD} = 17.77 kN, F_{AC} = – 22.22 kN, F_{BD} = – 22.22 kN, F_{DE} = 0, F_{CE} = 0).

Chapter 6

FUNDAMENTAL CONCEPT OF STIFFNESS

6.1 DISPLACEMENT METHOD OR STIFFNESS METHOD

6.1.1 General

Displacement method, now-a-days has been an effective tool for structural analysis because of its specific and disciplined characteristics conducive to computer programming. Non-zero point displacements of a structure are considered as unknown. Therefore, the method is named as the displacement method.

The number of non-zero point displacements is also called as the degree of kinematic indeterminacy or degree of freedom of the structure. It is not necessary to identify the redundant in this method, therefore the method does not require the information of degree of static indeterminacy of the structure.

The method mainly consists of restraining, releasing and balancing the points of the structure. The logic of the displacement method is almost parallel to that of the force method and briefly described as follows :

- The unknown joint displacements of a structure are identified by which the compatibility is implied. All points are restrained i.e. locked and kinematically determinate structure is obtained. Kinematically determinate structure is also called as restrained structure.

- The forces of kinematically determinate structure at points of and corresponding to the unknown joint displacements, due to the given loads are found.

- The structure is released successively for the displacements corresponding to unknown. To do this, unit displacement, only one at a time is given to the kinematically indeterminate structure and forces due to this cause are obtained. The force required for unit displacement is termed as stiffness. The force due to unknown displacement is the product of the stiffness and the unknown displacement.

- The conditions of balancing the joints also called as the equilibrium equations also called as the superposition equations of forces are formulated in terms of unknown point displacements. There are always as many conditions of equilibrium as there are unknown displacements. The formulated equations are linear and algebraic.

- The solution of the equations gives the unknown joint displacements.

- Once the displacements are known the remaining analysis of the structure is completed by known force-displacement relations.

The fundamental principle of the method is the equilibrium requirements of the forces of the kinematically determinate structure at joints which are released for unknown displacements. Basic equilibrium requirements are as follows :

- If a joint is released for horizontal translation, then $\Sigma H = 0$.
- If a joint is released for vertical translation, then $\Sigma V = 0$.
- If a joint is released for rotation then $\Sigma M = 0$.

The displacement method begins with the compatibility and ends with the equilibrium of forces using the stiffness concept. The displacement method is also called as:

- Equilibrium method because the conditions of equilibrium are used to formulate the method, or
- Stiffness method because the force required for unit displacement termed as the stiffness is used to obtain the force in terms of unknown displacement.

6.1.2 Procedure of Displacement Method

The displacement method is mainly based on the force equations of equilibrium. It therefore involves the determination of the following forces of kinematically determinate structure corresponding to the unknown joint displacement, D :

- The force at D and corresponding to D due to given loads (L). This is denoted by A_{DL}.
- The force at D and corresponding to D due to unit displacement. This is called the stiffness and denoted by S.
- The force at D due to D. This is denoted by A_{DD} and given by

$$A_{DD} = S \cdot D \qquad \ldots (6.1)$$

- The known force at D and corresponding to D. This is denoted by A_D. With these forces the equilibrium of joint is formulated by the superposition principle.

$$\therefore \quad A_D = A_{DL} + A_{DD} \qquad \ldots (6.2)$$

$$\therefore \quad A_D = A_{DL} + S \cdot D$$

This is the basic equation of the displacement method. This equation is rearranged and shown as the fundamental equation of the stiffness.

$$\therefore \quad (A_D - A_{DL}) = S \cdot D$$

$$A = S \cdot D$$

The force at a point of kinematically determinate structure:

(1) Due to given loads is generally obtained from the standard results of fixed beam and

(2) Due to unit displacement is obtained from the standard results of stiffness, as given in Table 1.5.

The displacement method will be subsequently formulated in general as the stiffness matrix method. However the procedure of the displacement method is illustrated with the same simple problem of beam of the force method to pave the foundation of the stiffness matrix method, for multi-displacement and multi-force system i.e. structure. The problem of displacement method is illustrated by the following steps.

6.1.3 Simple Problem on Displacement Method

Example 6.1 : *Analyse the beam shown in Fig. 6.1 by displacement method. Take EI = Constant.*

Solution : Data : The beam is supported and loaded as shown in Fig. 6.1 (a). As the data is same as the problem of force method, only steps are listed.
1. Structural configuration
2. Cross-sectional properties of members
3. Material properties of members
4. Applied loads
5. Type of structure.

Objects :
1. Unknown joint displacements as the initial target
2. Analysis of structure.

Assumptions :
1. Linear Elastic Analysis
2. Axial deformations are neglected in beams

Concepts and Equations :
1. Kinematically determinate structure (Restrained structure).
2. Force analysis of restrained structure.
3. Superposition equations of equilibrium of forces.

Procedure :

Step I : The degree of kinematic indeterminacy i.e. Number of non-zero joint displacement or degree of freedom.

$$\therefore \qquad D_{ki} = 1$$

Step II : Unknown point displacement. It is denoted by D

$$\therefore \qquad D = \theta_B \text{ i.e. rotation at the joint B.}$$

Step III : The kinematically determinate structure: The joint B is locked and the restrained structure is obtained. Thus, the given beam is considered equivalent to the superposition of:

(a) Restrained beam under given loads as shown in Fig. 6.1 (b) and

(b) Restrained beam under unit rotation at B and then under θ_B, as shown in Fig. 6.1 (c) and Fig. 6.1 (d) respectively.

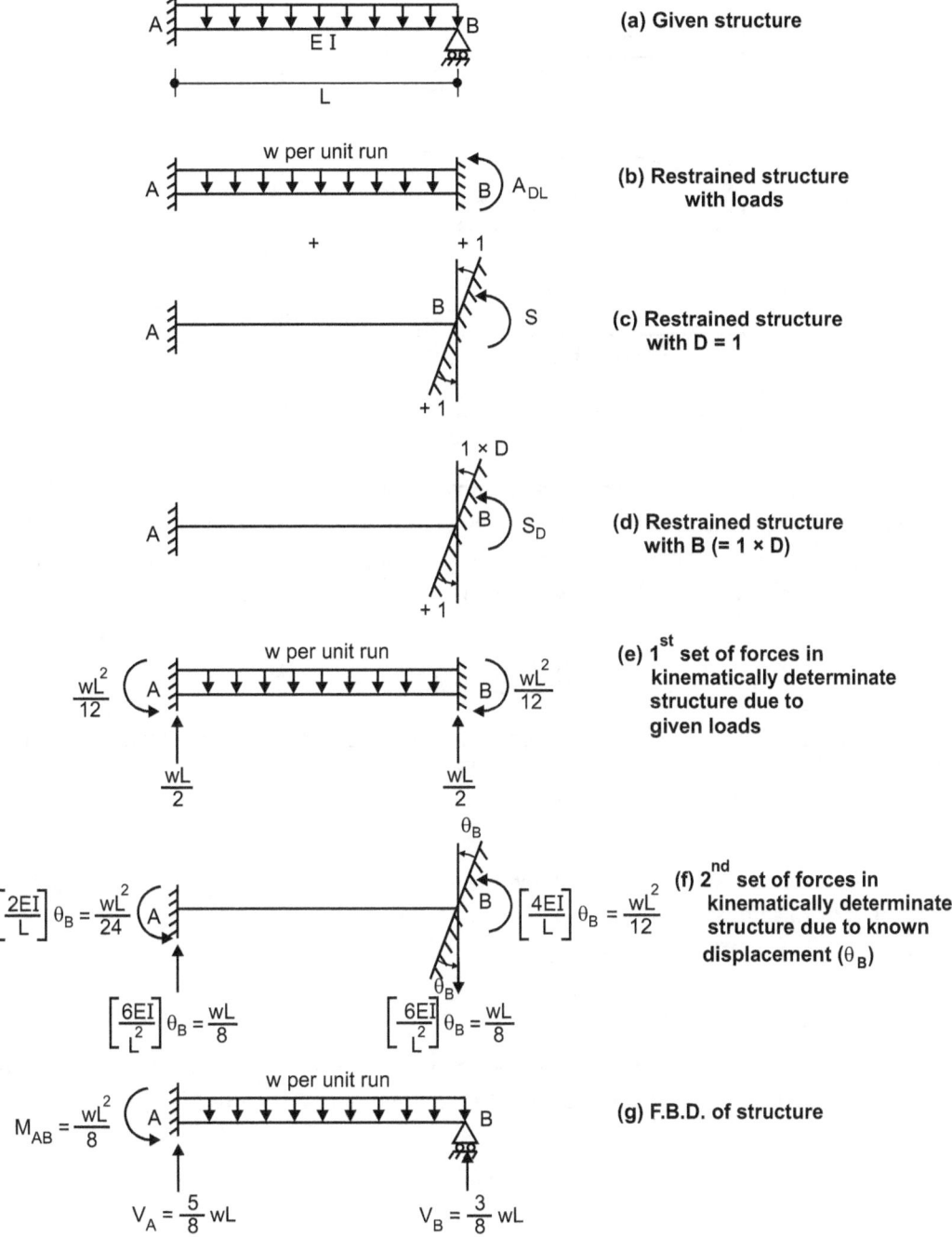

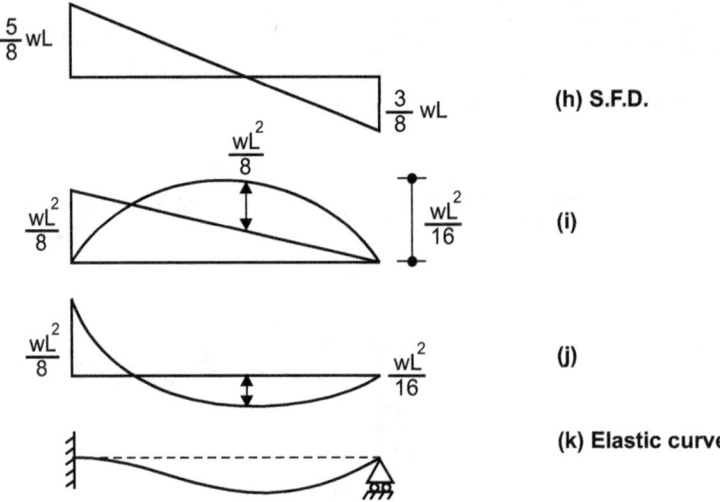

Fig. 6.1: Illustrative Example 6.1

Step IV : Force analysis of the kinematically determinate i.e. restrained structure.

(a) The member end moment at B due to given loading is calculated. For this problem the standard result of fixed beam with udl is used to obtain the moment at B. This is denoted by A_{DL}.

$$\therefore \quad A_{DL} = -\frac{wL^2}{12} \text{ (clockwise)}$$

(b) The moment at B required for unit rotation at B is the flexural rotational stiffness taken from the standard result. This is denoted by S.

$$\therefore \quad S = \frac{4EI}{L}$$

(c) The moment at B due to unknown rotation θ_B is denoted by A_{DD} and obtained in terms of θ_B from stiffness.

$$\therefore \quad A_{DD} = S \cdot D$$

$$\therefore \quad A_{DD} = \left(\frac{4EI}{L}\right) D$$

Step V : The equilibrium requirement of force. In the given structure there is no applied moment at B. This moment at B is known to be zero and denoted by A_D.

$$\therefore \quad A_D = 0$$

Step VI : Superposition equation of equilibrium of forces :

$$\therefore \quad A_D = A_{DL} + A_{DD}$$

$$\therefore \quad A_D = A_{DL} + S \cdot D$$

$$0 = -\frac{wL^2}{12} + \left(\frac{4EI}{L}\right)\theta_B$$

Step VII : Solution of equation for unknown displacement

$$\therefore \quad \theta_B = +\frac{wL^3}{48EI}$$

The positive result of θ_B indicates that the direction of θ_B corresponds to the direction of unit rotation.

Step VIII : Other forces: First set of other forces in the kinematically determinate structure due to given loads are obtained as shown in Fig. 6.1 (e).

Second set of other forces in the kinematically determinate structure due to now known θ_B are computed by the standard results of force-displacement relations of beam as shown in Fig. 6.1 (f).

The two sets of forces are superimposed and the analysis of beam is completed. The final results are as shown in Fig. 6.1 (g).

Step IX : SFD and BMD.

(a) SFD is same as shown in Fig. 6.1 (h).

(b) BMD drawn by two methods are same as shown in Fig. 6.1 (i) and Fig. 6.1 (j).

Step X : Elastic curve: Qualitative nature of the elastic curve is also same as shown in Fig. 6.1 (k).

6.2 STIFFNESS MATRIX

The action equations for the structure with 1, 2, ... n co-ordinates for actions $A_1, A_2 ... A_n$ producing displacements $D_1, D_2 ... D_n$ can be obtained similarly by using the principle of superposition, where n is the degree of kinematic indeterminacy.

If a unit positive displacement is given at co-ordinate i without any displacement at other co-ordinates, the forces required at co-ordinates 1, 2, ... n are represented by $S_{1i}, S_{2i}, ... S_{ii}, S_{ji}, S_{ni}$. S_{ij} is the force at co-ordinate i due to a unit positive displacement at co-ordinates j only. This is called stiffness coefficient. As per superposition principle, the total action at co-ordinate i due to displacements $D_1, D_2 ... D_n$ is given by

$$A_i = S_{i1} + S_{i2}D_2 + S_{ii}D_i + S_{ij}D_j + ... + S_{in}D_n$$

Therefore, action equations for a structure are :

$$A_1 = S_{11}D_1 + S_{12}D_2 + S_{1i}D_i + S_{1j}D_j + ... + S_{1n}D_n$$
$$A_2 = S_{21}D_1 + S_{22}D_2 + ... + S_{2i}D_i + S_{2j}D_j + ... + S_{2n}D_n$$
$$\vdots \quad \vdots \quad \quad \vdots \quad \quad \vdots$$
$$A_i = S_{i1}D_1 + S_{i2}D_2 + ... + D_{ii}D_i + S_{ij}D_j + ... + S_{in}D_n$$

$$A_j = S_{j1} D_1 + S_{j2} D_2 + \ldots + S_{ji} D_i + S_{jj} D_j + \ldots + D_{jn} D_n$$
$$\vdots \quad \vdots \quad \vdots \quad \vdots$$
$$A_n = S_{n1} D_1 + S_{n2} D_2 + \ldots + S_{ni} D_i + S_{ni} D_j + \ldots + S_{nn} D_n$$

The action displacement equations in matrix form are :

$$\begin{Bmatrix} A_1 \\ A_2 \\ \vdots \\ A_i \\ A_j \\ \vdots \\ A_n \end{Bmatrix} = \begin{bmatrix} S_{11} & S_{12} & \ldots & S_{1i} & S_{ij} & \ldots & S_{in} \\ S_{21} & S_{22} & \ldots & S_{2i} & S_{2j} & \ldots & S_{2n} \\ S_{i1} & S_{i2} & \ldots & S_{ii} & S_{ij} & \ldots & S_{in} \\ S_{j1} & S_{j2} & \ldots & S_{ji} & S_{jj} & \ldots & S_{jn} \\ S_{n1} & S_{n2} & \ldots & S_{ni} & S_{ni} & \ldots & S_{nn} \end{bmatrix} \begin{Bmatrix} D_1 \\ D_2 \\ \vdots \\ D_i \\ D_j \\ \vdots \\ D_n \end{Bmatrix} \quad \ldots (6.4)$$

i.e. $\{A\} = [S] \{D\}$
$n \times 1 = n \times n \quad n \times 1$

where, $\{A\}_{n \times 1}$ = A column matrix of order n × 1, known as action matrix

$[S]_{n \times n}$ = A square matrix of order n × n, known as stiffness matrix

$\{D\}_{n \times 1}$ = A column matrix of order n × 1, known as displacement matrix

In the concept of stiffness, cause is the unit positive displacement and the effect is the force. For S_{ij}, i stands for effect and j for cause. If j is kept same and i varies we get the effects i.e. forces at different coordinates as S_{1j}, S_{2j}, … S_{ij}, S_{jj}, S_{nj}. These are column coefficients of [S]. The column of [S] is generated by this technique i.e. keeping same cause the effects are obtained.

Each stiffness coefficient S_{ij} can be defined as the ith action due to a unit value of the jth 0 displacement assuming that the remaining displacements are zero. The jth column of the stiffness matrix are the forces at co-ordinates 1, 2, … n due to unit positive displacement at coordinate j. Hence in order to generate the jth column of the stiffness matrix, a unit displacement must be given at coordinate j without any displacement at other coordinates and the forces required at all the co-ordinates are determined. These forces are the elements of the jth column of the stiffness matrix. Hence in order to develop the stiffness matrix of a structure, unit positive displacement should be given successively at coordinates 1, 2 … n and forces at all the coordinates are calculated.

Properties of the stiffness matrix are :
- The stiffness matrix is a square matrix of order n × n where n is the number of coordinates for the problem, i.e. degree of kinematic indeterminacy.
- The stiffness matrix is a symmetrical matrix and hence $S_{ij} = S_{ji}$.

- Each stiffness coefficient S_{ij} represents a action caused by a unit positive displacement, while other displacements are zero.
- In general, S_{ij} is i^{th} action due to unit value of jth displacement.
- The coefficient S_{ij} is taken as positive when it is in positive direction of the ith coordinate.
- S_{ii} that appear on the principal diagonal of [S] are called direct coefficients and remaining coefficients are cross coefficients.
- For direct stiffness i = j.
- For indirect or cross stiffness i ≠ j.
- Direct stiffnesses are always positive.
- Cross stiffnesses may be positive or negative.
- For stable equilibrium structure, the stiffness matrix is non-singular i.e. | [S] | ≠ 0.
- If structure is unstable, the stiffness matrix does not exist or | [S]| = 0 i.e. singular.
- Stiffness matrix [S] of the given structure is invariant as it is the property of the structure.

If the flexibility and stiffness matrices have a common system of coordinates, the product of [F] and [S] is a unit matrix i.e. [F] [S] = [I]. For this condition the flexibility and stiffness matrices are reciprocal of each other or inverse of each other.

It is to be noted that the flexibility matrix [F] for a structure being analysed by the flexibility method is not the inverse of the stiffness matrix [S] for the same structure being analysed by the stiffness method. The reason is that different co-ordinate systems are used in the two methods.

6.3 PROCEDURE OF STIFFNESS MATRIX METHOD

The basic equation of the displacement method developed for one unknown is given a matrix form as $\{A_D\} = \{A_{DL}\} + [S]\{D\}$ for more number of unknowns. This is the governing matrix equation of the method. Using this equation the procedure of the stiffness method is outlined as follows :

- The degree of kinematic indeterminacy D_{ki} (= n, say) is determined.
- The independent joint displacements are identified.
- The coordinate numbering 1, 2 ... n is systematically assigned to unknown joint displacements. Thus $D_1, D_2 ... D_n$ are the displacements at coordinates 1, 2 ... n. This is the matrix $\{D\}_{n \times 1}$ of unknown displacements.
- The restrained structure i.e. kinematically determinate structure is obtained by restraining all joints i.e. preventing all the independent displacements.

- The restrained actions corresponding to coordinates 1, 2 ... n in the restrained structure due to applied member loads are calculated using fixed beam analysis. If number of members are meeting at a joint, the restrained actions for these members are cummulated. This is also termed as assembly of load vector. The assembled actions are $A_{DL1}, A_{DL2} ... A_{DLn}$. Thus the matrix $\{A_{DL}\}_{n \times 1}$ is formed.

- The restrained actions corresponding to coordinates 1, 2 . . . n in the restrained structure due to unit positive displacement imposed one at a time are calculated, memberwise and summed up for the members meeting at the joint. These are the stiffness coefficients generated columnwise. The technique is repeated and thus the stiffness matrix of a structure $[S]_{n \times n}$ is assembled.

- Given joint actions (forces and couples) corresponding to coordinates 1, 2 ... n form the matrix $\{A_D\}_{n \times 1}$.

- The action equations are formulated using superposition equations.

$$A_{D1} = A_{DL1} + S_{11} D_1 + S_{12} D_2 + ... + S_{1n} D_n$$
$$D_{D2} = A_{DL2} + S_{21} D_1 + S_{22} D_2 + ... + S_{2n} D_n$$
$$D_{Dn} = A_{DLn} + S_{n1} D_1 + S_{n2} D_2 + ... + S_{nn} D_n$$

i.e. in matrix form,

$$\{A_D\}_{n \times 1} = \{A_{DL}\}_{n \times 1} + [S]_{n \times n} \{D\}_{n \times 1}$$

- Equilibrium equations applicable to the joint actions corresponding to coordinates 1, 2 ... n are written. If there are no given joint loads at all coordinates then $\{A_D\}$ matrix will be null matrix. Otherwise as the case may be.

- Formulation of linear simultaneous equations for unknown joint displacements $\{D\}$ is ready at this stage.

- The joint displacements $D_1, D_2 ... D_n$ are obtained from solution of equations.

$$\{A_D\}_{n \times 1} = \{A_{DL}\}_{n \times 1} + [S]_{n \times n} \{D\}_{n \times 1}$$

- Knowing the displacements, all actions at member ends are obtained from cummulative effects of displacements according to the stiffness coefficients of member. In general the member end moments for member are obtained as :

$$M_{ij} = \left(\frac{4 EI}{L}\right) \theta_i + \left(\frac{2 EI}{L}\right) \theta_j \pm \left(\frac{6 EI}{L^2}\right) \Delta + M_{ij}^F$$

- Variations of actions along the member and structure are plotted as SFD and BMD.

- Deformed shape of a structure may be shown qualitatively from the information of joint displacements, compatibility and BMD. This is the elastic curve.

In short, the stiffness method involves the formation of following matrices.
(1) $\{A_D\}_{n \times 1}$
(2) $\{A_{DL}\}_{n \times 1}$
(3) $[S]_{n \times n}$
(4) $\{D\}_{n \times 1}$ – unknown joint displacement matrix to be obtained from basic equation of stiffness method

$$\{A_D\} = \{A_{DL}\} + [S]\{D\}$$

6.4 STIFFNESS COEFFICIENTS OF MEMBER

A stiffness matrix [S] of a structure is developed columnwise by considering the unit positive joint displacement, only one at a time, in the restrained structure. For the development of [S], the stiffness coefficients of the members meeting the joint, are required to be added and hence very important. Therefore it is the prerequisite of the stiffness method to know the standard results of stiffness coefficients of a member of a structure.

6.4.1 A Beam Member or Frame Member

In general, a prismatic member AB of length L and flexural rigidity EI as shown in Fig 6.2 (a) is considered having rigid joints at A and B. According to the possible joint displacements i.e. translations and rotations, the coordinate numbering is shown in Fig. 6.2 (b) to represent member end actions and joint displacements. The member is restrained and then released successively. The desired unit positive displacement, as the cause, is given, only one at a time, and corresponding member end actions, as the effects, are obtained. These effects are called the member stiffness coefficients and are developed as follows:

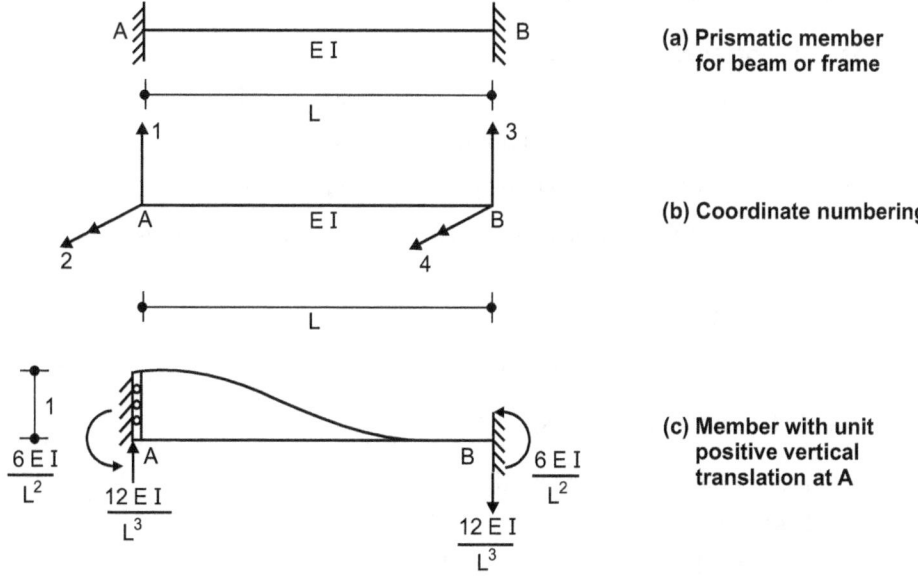

(a) Prismatic member for beam or frame

(b) Coordinate numbering

(c) Member with unit positive vertical translation at A

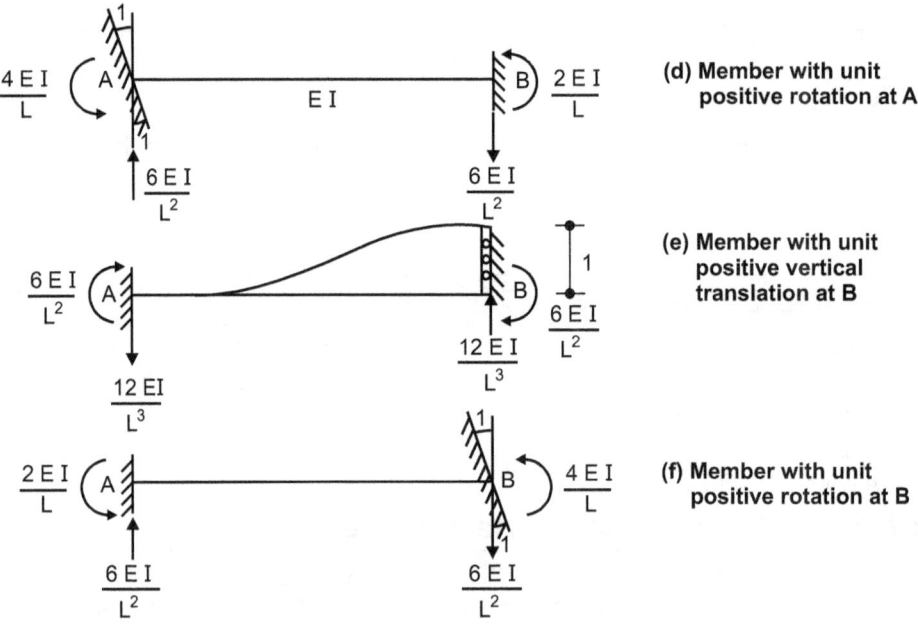

Fig. 6.2: Generation of stiffness for beam or frame

- **Cause :** Unit positive displacement i.e. transverse translation at coordinate 1 as shown in Fig. 6.2 (c).

Effects : Force at coordinate 1 = S_{11} = $\dfrac{12\,EI}{L^3}$

(from basic relation already derived)

  Moment at coordinate 2 (from equilibrium) = S_{21} = 6 EI/L^2

  Force at coordinate 3 (from equilibrium) = S_{31} = − 12 EI/L^3

  Moment at coordinate 4 (from equilibrium) = S_{41} = 6 EI/L^2

- **Cause :** Unit positive displacement i.e. rotation at co-ordinate 2 as shown in Fig. 6.2 (d).

  Effects : Force at coordinate 1 = S_{12} = 6 EI/L^2

       (from equilibrium)

  Moment at coordinate 2 = S_{22} = $\dfrac{4\,EI}{L}$

(from basic relation already derived)

  Force at coordinate 3 = S_{32} = − 6 EI/L^2

  Moment at coordinate 4 = S_{42} = 2 EI/L

- **Cause :** Unit positive displacement i.e. transverse translation at coordinate 3 as shown in Fig. 6.2 (e).

    Effects: This is the mirror image of case (i). Therefore

    Force at coordinate $1 = S_{13} = -12\ EI/L^3$

    Moment at coordinate $2 = S_{23} = -6\ EI/L^2$

    Force at coordinate $3 = S_{33} = 12\ EI/L^3$

    Moment at coordinate $4 = S_{43} = -6\ EI/L^2$

- **Cause :** Unit positive displacement i.e. rotation at coordinate 4 as shown in Fig. 6.2 (f).

    Effects : This is the mirror image of case (ii) therefore,

    Force at coordinate $1 = S_{14} = 6\ EI/L^2$

    Moment at coordinate $2 = S_{24} = 2\ EI/L$

    Force at coordinate $3 = S_{34} = -6\ EI/L^2$

    Moment at coordinate $4 = S_{44} = 4\ EI/L$

The stiffness coefficients thus obtained can be represented in the matrix form. This is the standard stiffness matrix of a beam member or a frame member with respect to the member coordinate and denoted by $[S_M]$. The size of the matrix is 4×4.

$$\therefore \quad [S_M]_{4 \times 4} = \begin{bmatrix} \dfrac{12\ EI}{L^3} & \dfrac{6\ EI}{L^2} & -\dfrac{12\ EI}{L^3} & \dfrac{6\ EI}{L^2} \\ \dfrac{6\ EI}{L^2} & \dfrac{4\ EI}{L} & -\dfrac{6\ EI}{L^2} & \dfrac{2\ EI}{L} \\ -\dfrac{12\ EI}{L^3} & -\dfrac{6\ EI}{L^2} & \dfrac{12\ EI}{L^3} & -\dfrac{6\ EI}{L^2} \\ \dfrac{6\ EI}{L^2} & \dfrac{2\ EI}{L} & -\dfrac{6\ EI}{L^2} & \dfrac{4\ EI}{L} \end{bmatrix}$$

It is to be noted that

1. Axial deformation is neglected.
2. $[S_m]$ is symmetrical.
3. Diagonal coefficients are direct stiffnesses.
4. Off-diagonal coefficients are indirect stiffnesses as side effects.
5. The determinant of $[S_m]$ is zero i.e. $|[S_M]| = 0$.
6. Thus $[S_M]$ is singular because all displacements are given and hence the member is not in stable equilibrium. This is not possible in case of the structure. The structure stiffness matrix should be non-singular as the structure is stable.

6.5 STIFFNESS METHOD APPLIED TO BEAMS AND FRAMES

Beams and frames mainly consist of rigid joints and bending members. The unknown joint displacements are rotations and or translations as per coordinate numbering to form the matrix $\{D\}_{n \times 1}$. The sizes of matrices is governed by 'n', the degree of kinematic indeterminacy. The given joint loads form the matrix $\{A\}_{n \times 1}$ directly. The analysis of fixed beam for the applied member loads will help in preparing the matrix $\{A_{DL}\}_{n \times 1}$. At a joint, if number of members are meeting then corresponding to the coordinate i, A_{DLi} is given by the equation

$$A_{DLi} = \sum_{\text{All members}} \text{Fixed end member actions at i}$$

The most critical part of the stiffness method is to generate stiffness matrix of a structure. $[S]_{n \times n}$. However it can be done very systematically as illustrated below.

Consider the frame shown in Fig. 6.3 (a).
- Unknown displacements
    (a) Rotations at B, C and D i.e. θ_B, θ_C and θ_D.
    (b) Horizontal translation at B i.e. $\Delta_B = \Delta_C = \Delta$.

    It may be noted specifically that $\Delta_B = \Delta_C$ as the axial deformations are neglected.
- Degree of kinematic indeterminacy

    n = 4
- Coordinate numbering

    Corresponding to unknown displacements it is shown in Fig. 6.3 (b). Again note that the coordinate number 4 is given to both Δ_B and Δ_C.
- The size of stiffness matrix

    $[S]_{4 \times 4}$
- Generation of [S]

    Note that [S] is independent of loading and it only requires the information of structural configuration, dimensions, cross-sectional properties and material properties.
- Restrain the structure. This is shown in Fig. 6.3 (c).
- Release the structure only for one displacement at a time.

    (a) Cause : Unit positive displacement at coordinate 1 i.e. $D_1 = \theta_B = +1$ as shown in Fig. 6.3 (c).

    (b) Effects : Member end actions in terms of stiffness coefficients for all members at all coordinates 1, 2, 3 and 4. Note that if the member does not deform there is no resistance to deformation and stiffness coefficients of the member will be zero. The effects are shown in Fig. 6.3 (d).

(c) Stiffness coefficients of column 1 of [S] :

$$S_{11} = \Sigma \text{ Stiffness coefficients at 1 of contributing members}$$
$$= \left(\frac{4\,EI}{L}\right)_{BA} + \left(\frac{4\,EI}{L}\right)_{BC} = \frac{4\,EI}{4} + \frac{4\,(2\,EI)}{6} = 2.33\,EI$$

$$S_{21} = \Sigma \text{ Stiffness coefficients at 2 members}$$
$$= \left(\frac{2\,EI}{L}\right)_{BC} = \frac{2\,(2\,EI)}{6} = 0.67\,EI$$

$$S_{31} = \Sigma \text{ Stiffness coefficients at 3 of members} = 0$$

$$S_{41} = \Sigma \text{ Stiffness coefficients at 4 of contributing member}$$
$$= \left(\frac{6\,EI}{L^2}\right)_{BA} = \frac{6\,EI}{4^2} = 0.375\,EI$$

Thus the coefficients of first column of [S] are obtained. The technique of columnwise generation of [S] is repeated for all coordinates, using the general concept.

$$S_{ij} = \Sigma \text{ Stiffness coefficients at i of contributing members}$$

where j is kept constant and i varies.

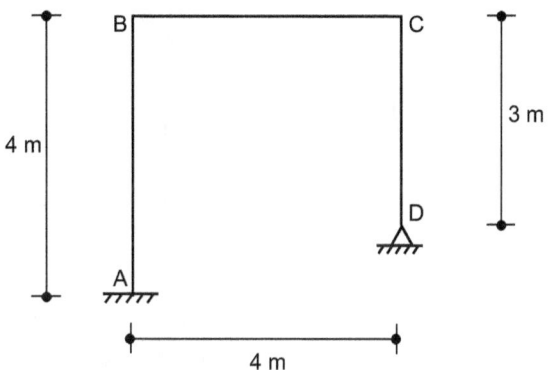

Fig. 6.3 (a) : Given structure

Fig. 6.3 (b) : Co-ordinate numbering for given structure

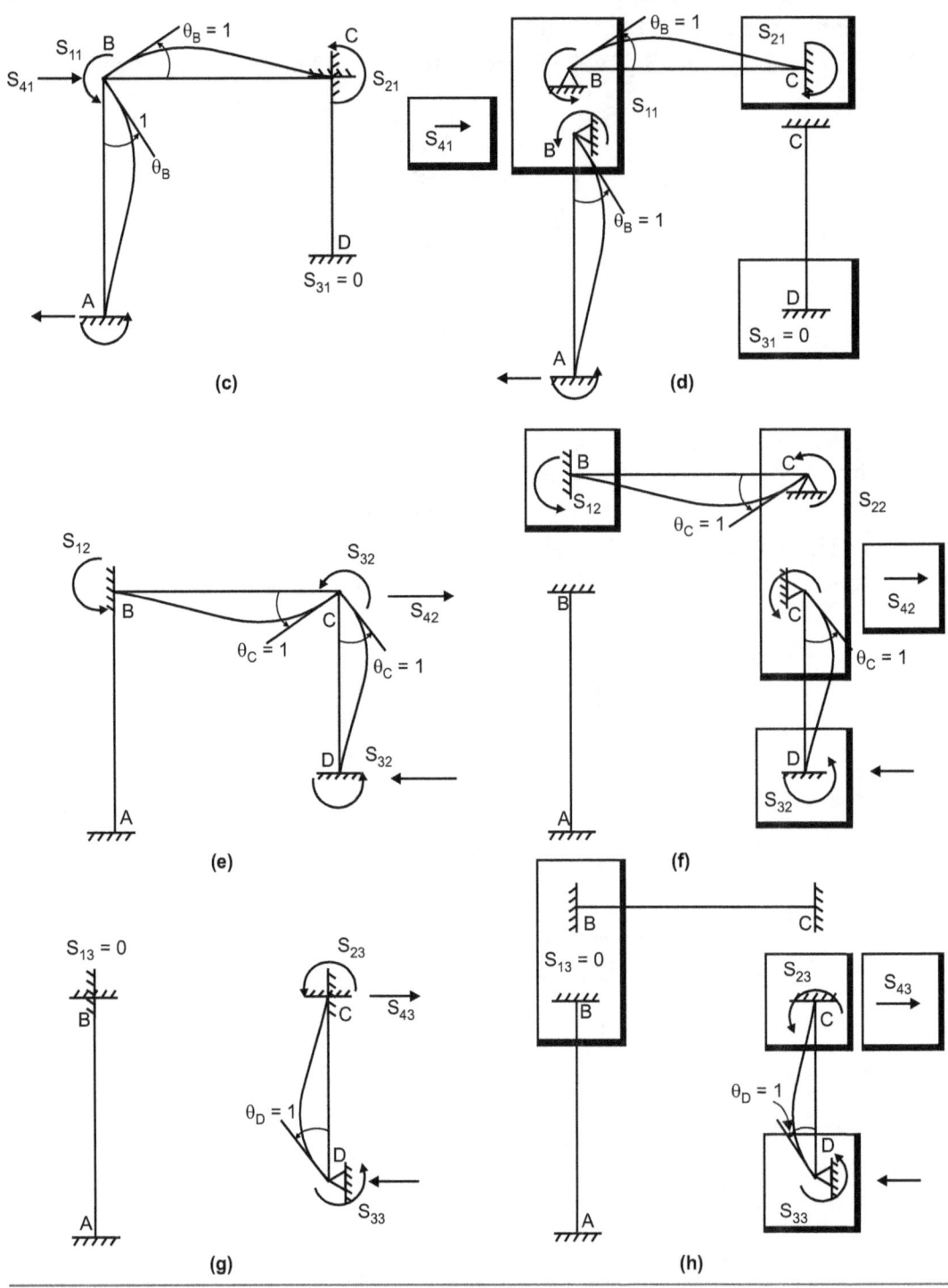

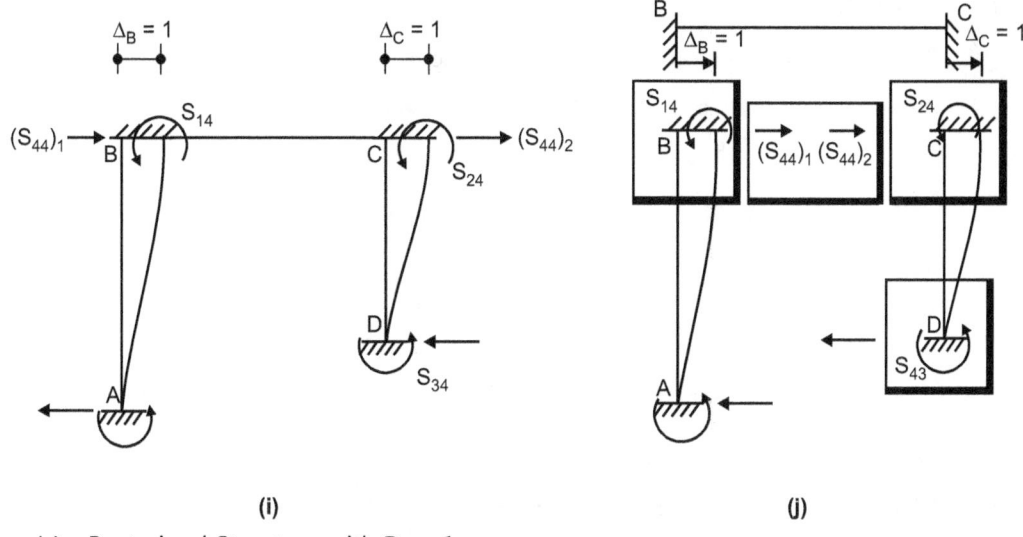

(i)   (j)

(c) Restrained Structure with $D_1 = 1$
(d) Effects of $D_1 = 1$ for Restrained Structure
(e) Restrained Structure with $D_2 = 1$
(f) Effects of $D_2 = 1$ for Restrained Structure
(g) Restrained Structure with $D_3 = 1$
(h) Effects of $D_3 = 1$ for Restrained Structure
(i) Restrained Structure with $D_4 = 1$
(j) Effects of $D_4 = 1$ for Restrained Structure

Fig. 6.3 : Generation of Stiffness Matrix of Structure

- (a) **Cause :** $D_2 = \theta_C = +1$ as shown in Fig. 6.3 (e).
  - (b) **Effects :** Member end actions as shown in Fig. 6.3 (f).
  - (c) Stiffness coefficients of column 2 of (S).

$$S_{12} = \left(\frac{2\,EI}{L}\right)_{BC} = \frac{2 \times 2\,EI}{6} = 0.67\,EI$$

$$S_{22} = \left(\frac{4\,EI}{L}\right)_{CB} + \left(\frac{4\,EI}{L}\right)_{CD} = \frac{4 \times 2\,EI}{4} = 2.33\,EI$$

$$S_{32} = \left(\frac{2\,EI}{L}\right)_{DC} = \frac{2\,EI}{4} = 0.5\,EI$$

$$S_{42} = \left(\frac{6\,EI}{42}\right)_{CD} = \frac{6\,EI}{42} = 0.375\,EI$$

- (a) **Cause** : $D_3 = \theta_D = +1$ as shown in Fig. 6.3 (g).
  - (b) **Effects** : Member end actions as shown in Fig. 6.3 (h).
  - (c) Stiffness coefficients of column 3 of [S].

$$S_{13} = 0$$

$$S_{23} = \left(\frac{2\,EI}{L}\right)_{CD} = \frac{2\,EI}{4} = 0.5\,EI$$

$$S_{33} = \left(\frac{4\,EI}{L}\right)_{CD} = \frac{4\,EI}{4} = EI$$

$$S_{43} = \left(\frac{6\,EI}{L^2}\right) = \frac{6\,EI}{4^2} = 0.375\,EI$$

- (a) **Cause** : $D_4 = \Delta = +1$ as shown in Fig. 6.3 (i).
  - (b) **Effects** : Member end actions as shown in Fig. 6.3 (j).
  - (c) Stiffness coefficients of column 4 of [S]

$$S_{14} = \left(\frac{6\,EI}{L^2}\right)_{BA} = \frac{6\,EI}{4^2} = 0.375\,EI$$

$$S_{24} = \left(\frac{6\,EI}{L^2}\right)_{CD} = \frac{6\,EI}{4^2} = 0.375\,EI$$

$$S_{34} = \left(\frac{6\,EI}{L^2}\right)_{DC} = \frac{6\,EI}{4^2} = 0.375\,EI$$

$$S_{44} = \left(\frac{12\,EI}{L^3}\right)_{BA} + \left(\frac{12\,EI}{L^3}\right)_{CD} = \frac{12\,EI}{4^3} + \frac{12\,EI}{4^3} = 0.375\,EI$$

This is to be noted that there is resistance i.e. stiffness contributions to A from members AB and CD. Therefore, transverse translation is resisted by the members perpendicular to the translation. For the rectangular frame this horizontal translation is called sway and sway is resisted by column members of the frame. Note that there is no effect of sway on beam as translation is along the member.

- Stiffness matrix of the structure

$$[S]_{4\times 4} = EI \begin{bmatrix} 2.33 & 0.67 & 0 & 0.375 \\ 0.67 & 2.33 & 0.5 & 0.375 \\ 0 & 0.5 & 1 & 0.375 \\ 0.375 & 0.375 & 0.375 & 0.375 \end{bmatrix}$$

Note that :
1. The matrix is square symmetrical.
2. The diagonal coefficients of [S] are positive and definite and dominant.
3. The matrix [S] is non-singular as the structure is stable i.e. | [S]| ≠ 0.
4. The stiffness matrix [S] of the structure for given data is invariant as it is the property of the structure.

The general procedure of the stiffness matrix method formulated earlier is applicable to the beams and frames and analysis can be completed. This is illustrated with the following examples. For problems of one unknown the matrix formulation is not necessary.

Example 6.2 : *Analyse the beam shown in Fig. 6.4 (a) by stiffness method. Take EI = constant. Stiffness coefficient of spring at B is as shown in the figure.*

Solution : (1) Data : The beam is supported and loaded as shown in Fig. 6.4 (a).

(2) Stiffness coefficient of spring at B = $\left(\dfrac{EI}{2}\right)$ kN/m.

Object : Structural analysis.

Concepts and Equations :

(1) Kinematically determinate structure (Restrained structure).

(2) Force analysis of restrained structure.

(3) Superposition equations of equilibrium of forces.

Procedure :

Step I : Degree of kinematic indeterminacy (D_{ki}):

Degree of kinematic indeterminacy = D_{ki} = 2.

Step II : Unknown joint displacements (D):

Let, $D_1 = \theta_B$ (↻) and $D_2 = \Delta_B$ (↑)

Step III : Restrained Structure: Joint B is locked and the restrained structure is as shown in Fig. 6.4 (b). Also restrained structure with unit values of D_1 and D_2 is shown in Fig. 6.4 (c) and 6.4 (d) respectively.

Step IV : Force analysis of restrained structure :

(a) Fixed end moments :

$$M_{BA}^F = -M_{BA}^F = \dfrac{wL^2}{12} = \dfrac{10 \times 3^2}{12} = 7.5 \text{ kNm}$$

(b) Forces in the restrained structure subjected to loads corresponding to unknown displacements :

$$A_{DL1} = M_{BA}^F = -7.5 \text{ kNm}$$

A_{DL2} = Vertical reaction component at B in the restrained structure subjected to loads = 15 kN.

(c) Forces in the restrained structure subjected to unit values of D_1 and D_2 corresponding to unknown displacements.

$$S_{11} = \left(\frac{4EI}{L}\right)_{AB} = \frac{4EI}{3}$$
$$= 1.33 \, EI$$

$$S_{12} = S_{21} = \left(-\frac{6EI}{L^2}\right) = \frac{-6EI}{3^2}$$
$$= -0.67 \, EI$$

$$S_{22} = \left(\frac{12EI}{L^3}\right)_{AB} = \frac{12EI}{3^3} = 0.44 \, EI$$

Step V : The equilibrium requirement of force :

There is no applied couple at B $\quad\therefore A_{D1} = 0$

There is no applied point load at B $\quad\therefore A_{D2} = 0$

Step VI : Superposition equation of equilibrium of forces :

$$\{A_D\} = \{A_{DL}\} + [S]\{D\}$$

i.e.
$$\begin{Bmatrix} 0 \\ 0 \end{Bmatrix} = \begin{Bmatrix} -7.5 \\ 15 \end{Bmatrix} + EI \begin{bmatrix} 1.33 & -0.67 \\ -0.67 & 0.44 \end{bmatrix} \begin{Bmatrix} D_1 \\ D_2 \end{Bmatrix}$$

* Because of the elastic support at B 'S_{22}' is to be modified as

$$S_{22} = \left(0.44 + \frac{1}{2}\right) EI = 0.94 \, EI$$

∴ Superposition equation of equilibrium of forces becomes,

$$\begin{Bmatrix} 0 \\ 0 \end{Bmatrix} = \begin{Bmatrix} -7.5 \\ 15 \end{Bmatrix} + EI \begin{bmatrix} 1.33 & -0.67 \\ -0.67 & 0.94 \end{bmatrix} \begin{Bmatrix} D_1 \\ D_2 \end{Bmatrix}$$

i.e.
$$0 = -7.5 + (1.33 \, EI) D_1 - (0.67 \, EI) D_2 \qquad \ldots (A)$$
$$0 = 15 - (0.67 \, EI) D_1 + (0.94 \, EI) D_2 \qquad \ldots (B)$$

Step VII : Solution of equations for unknown displacements: Solving equations (A) and (B), we get

$$D_1 = \frac{-3.7}{EI} = \frac{3.7}{EI} \, (\circlearrowleft)$$

$$D_2 = -\frac{18.54}{EI} = \frac{18.54}{EI} \, (\downarrow)$$

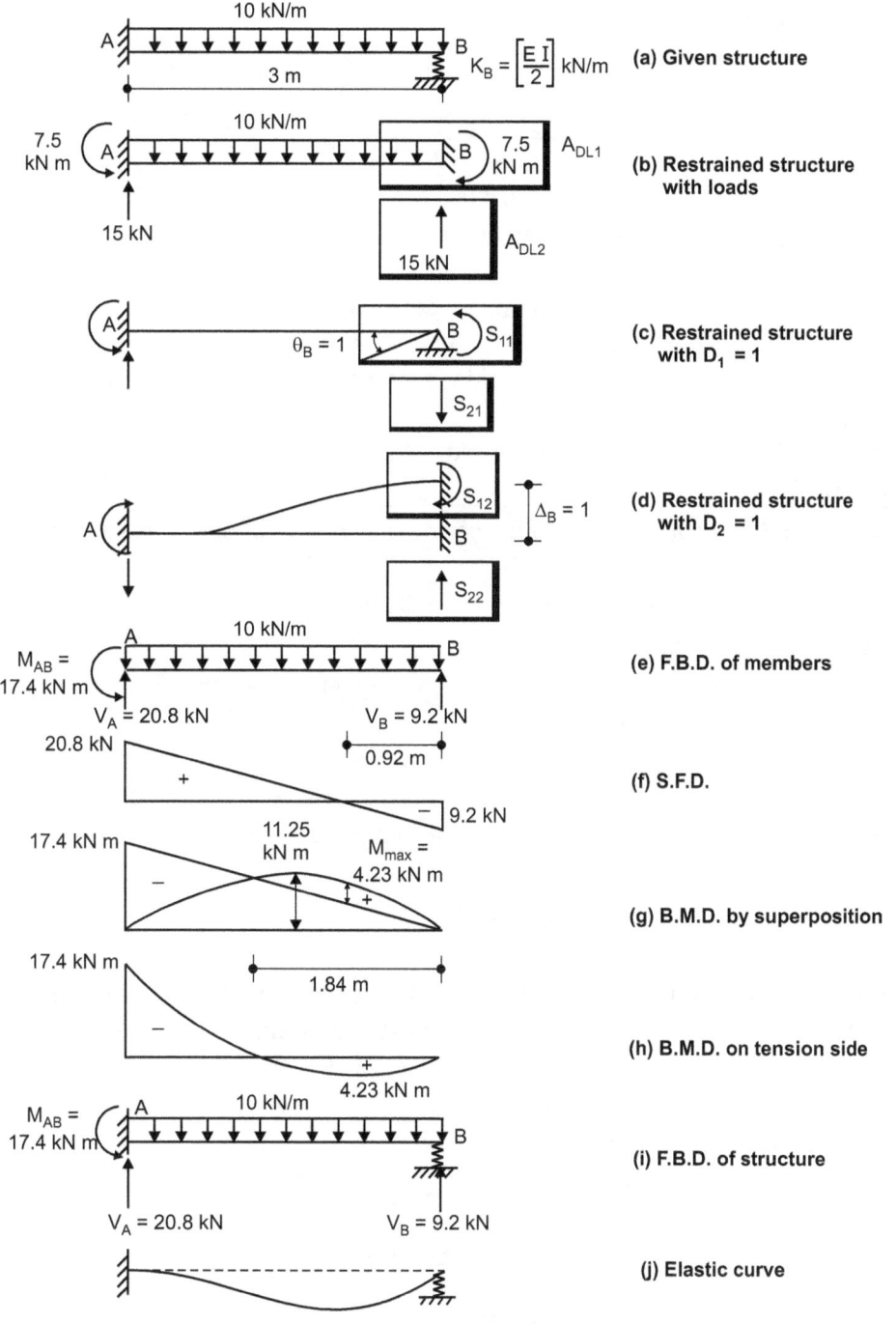

Fig. 6.4 : Illustrative Example 6.2

TOS – II (TE CIVIL SEM. VI NMU)   FUNDAMENTAL CONCEPT OF STIFFNESS

Step VIII : Other Forces :

$$M_{AB} = \frac{4EI}{3}(0) + \frac{2EI}{3}\left(-\frac{3.7}{EI}\right) + \frac{6EI}{3^2}\left(\frac{18.54}{EI}\right) + 7.5 = 17.4 \text{ kNm}$$

$$M_{BA} = \frac{4EI}{3}\left(-\frac{3.7}{EI}\right) + \frac{2EI}{3}(0) + \frac{6EI}{3^2}\left(\frac{18.54}{EI}\right) - 7.5 = 0$$

FBD of members is as shown in Fig. 6.4 (e).

Considering equilibrium of structure other reaction components are found out as shown in figure.

Step IX : Shear force and bending moment diagrams :

SFD is as shown in Fig. 6.4 (f).

BMD by superposition on tension side is as shown in Fig. 6.4 (g) and Fig. 6.4 (h) respectively.

Step X : FBD of structure : as shown in Fig. 6.4 (i).

Step XI : Elastic curve : as shown in Fig. 6.4 (j).

Example 6.3 : *Analyse the beam shown in Fig. 6.5 (a) by stiffness method. Take EI = Constant.*

Solution : Data : The beam is supported and loaded as shown in Fig. 6.5 (a).

Object : Structural Analysis.

Concepts and Equations : (1) Kinematically determinate structure (Restrained structure).

(2)   Force analysis of restrained structure.

(3)   Superposition equations of equilibrium of forces.

Procedure :

Step I : Degree of kinematic indeterminacy (D_{ki}) : Degree of kinematic indeterminacy = D_{ki} = 1.

Step II : Unknown joint displacements (D) :

Let, $D_1 = \theta_B$ (↻)

Step III : Restrained structure: The joint B is locked and the restrained structure is obtained as shown in Fig. 6.5 (b). Also restrained structure with unit value of D_1 is as shown in Fig. 6.5 (c).

Step IV : Force analysis of restrained structure :

(a)   Fixed End Moments:

$$M_{AB}^F = -M_{BA}^F = \frac{wL^2}{12} = \frac{15 \times 2^2}{12} = 5.0 \text{ kNm}$$

$$M_{BC}^F = \frac{Wab^2}{L^2} = \frac{30 \times 1 \times 2^2}{3^2} = 13.33 \text{ kNm}$$

$$M_{CB}^F = -\frac{Wba^2}{L^2} = -\frac{30 \times 2 \times 1^2}{3^2} = -6.67 \text{ kNm}$$

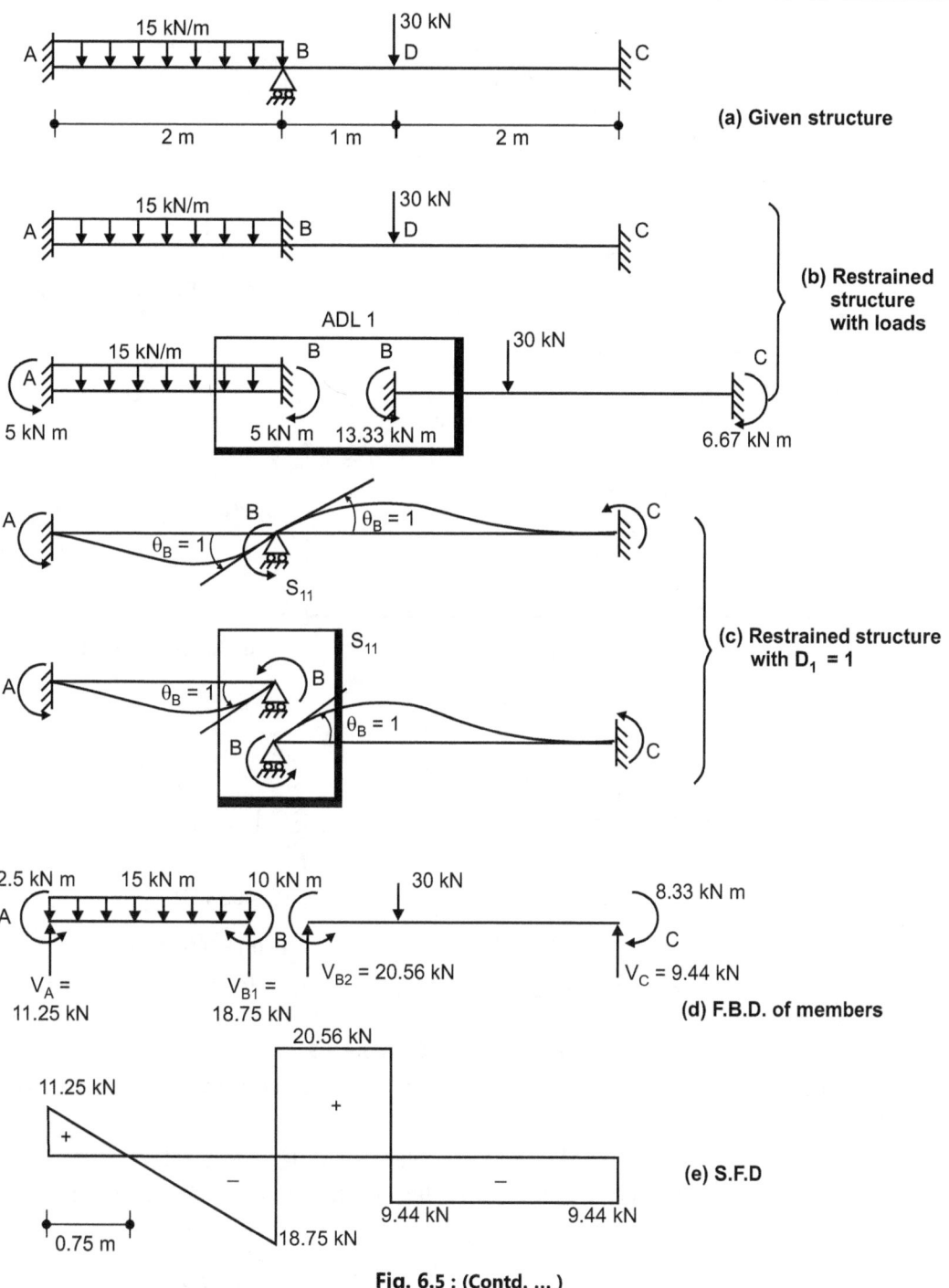

Fig. 6.5 : (Contd. ...)

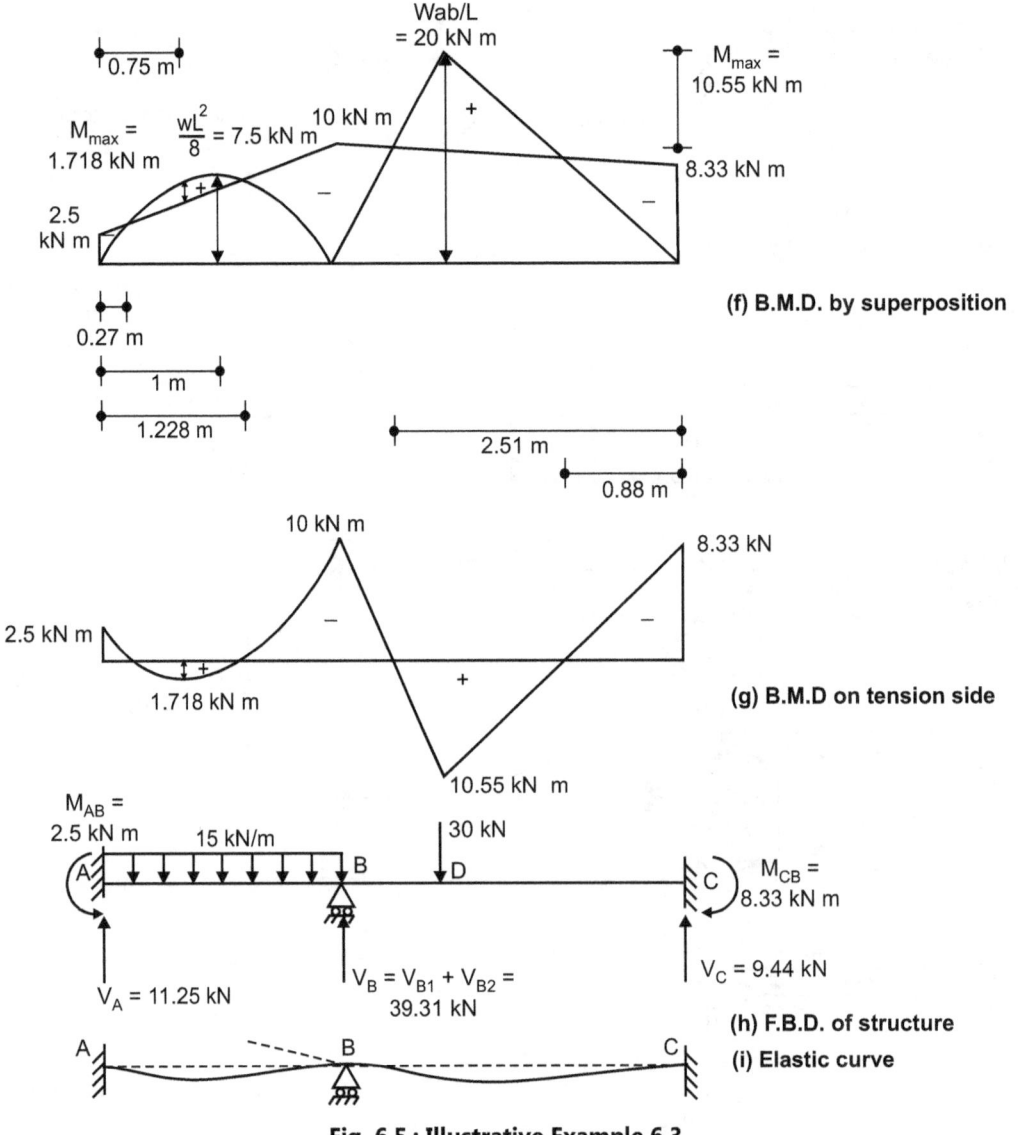

Fig. 6.5 : Illustrative Example 6.3

(b) Forces in the restrained structure subjected to loads corresponding to unknown displacements.

$$A_{DL1} = M_{BA}^F + M_{BC}^F = -5.0 + 13.33 = 8.33 \text{ kNm}$$

(c) Forces in the restrained structure subjected to unit values of D_1 corresponding to unknown displacement.

$$S_{11} = \left(\frac{4EI}{L}\right)_{BA} + \left(\frac{4EI}{L}\right)_{BC} = \frac{4EI}{2} + \frac{4EI}{3} = 3.33 \, EI$$

Step V : The equilibrium requirement of force :
There is no applied couple at B   ∴ $AD_1 = 0$
Step VI : Superposition equation of equilibrium of force :

$$\{A_D\} = \{A_{DL}\} + [S]\{D\}$$

i.e. $\{0\} = \{8.33\} + EI[3.33]\{D_1\}$ ... (A)

i.e. $0 = 8.33 + 3.33\, EI\,(D_1)$

Step VII : Solution of equations for unknown displacements: Solving equation (A), we get

$$\boxed{D_1 = \theta_B = \frac{-2.5}{EI} = \frac{2.5}{EI}\ (\circlearrowleft)}$$

Step VIII : Other Forces :

$$M_{AB} = \frac{4\,EI}{2}(0) + \frac{2\,EI}{2}\left(-\frac{2.5}{EI}\right) + 5.0$$
$$= 2.5 \text{ kNm}$$

$$M_{BA} = \frac{4\,EI}{2}\left(-\frac{2.5}{EI}\right) + \frac{2\,EI}{3}(0) + -5.0$$
$$= -10.0 \text{ kNm}$$

$$M_{BC} = \frac{4\,EI}{3}\left(\frac{-2.5}{EI}\right) + \frac{2\,EI}{3}(0) + 13.33$$
$$= 10.0 \text{ kNm}$$

$$M_{CB} = \frac{4\,EI}{3}(0) + \frac{2\,EI}{3}\left(\frac{-2.5}{EI}\right) - 6.67$$
$$= -8.33 \text{ kNm}$$

FBD of members is as shown in Fig. 6.5 (d).
Considering equilibrium of each member and of complete structure, all the reaction components are found out as shown in figure.

Step IX : Shear force and bending moment diagrams: SFD is shown in Fig. 6.5 (e).

BMD by superposition and on tension side is as shown in Fig. 6.5 (f) and Fig. 6.5 (g) respectively.

Step X : FBD of structure : as shown in Fig. 6.5 (h).

Step XI : Elastic curve : as shown in Fig. 6.5 (i).

Example 6.4 : *Analyse the beam shown in Fig. 6.6 (a) by stiffness method. Take EI = Constant.*

Solution: Data : The beam is supported and loaded as shown in Fig 6.6 (a).
Object : Structural analysis.
Concepts and Equations :
(1) Kinematically determinate structure (Restrained structure).
(2) Force analysis of restrained structure.
(3) Superposition equations of equilibrium of forces.

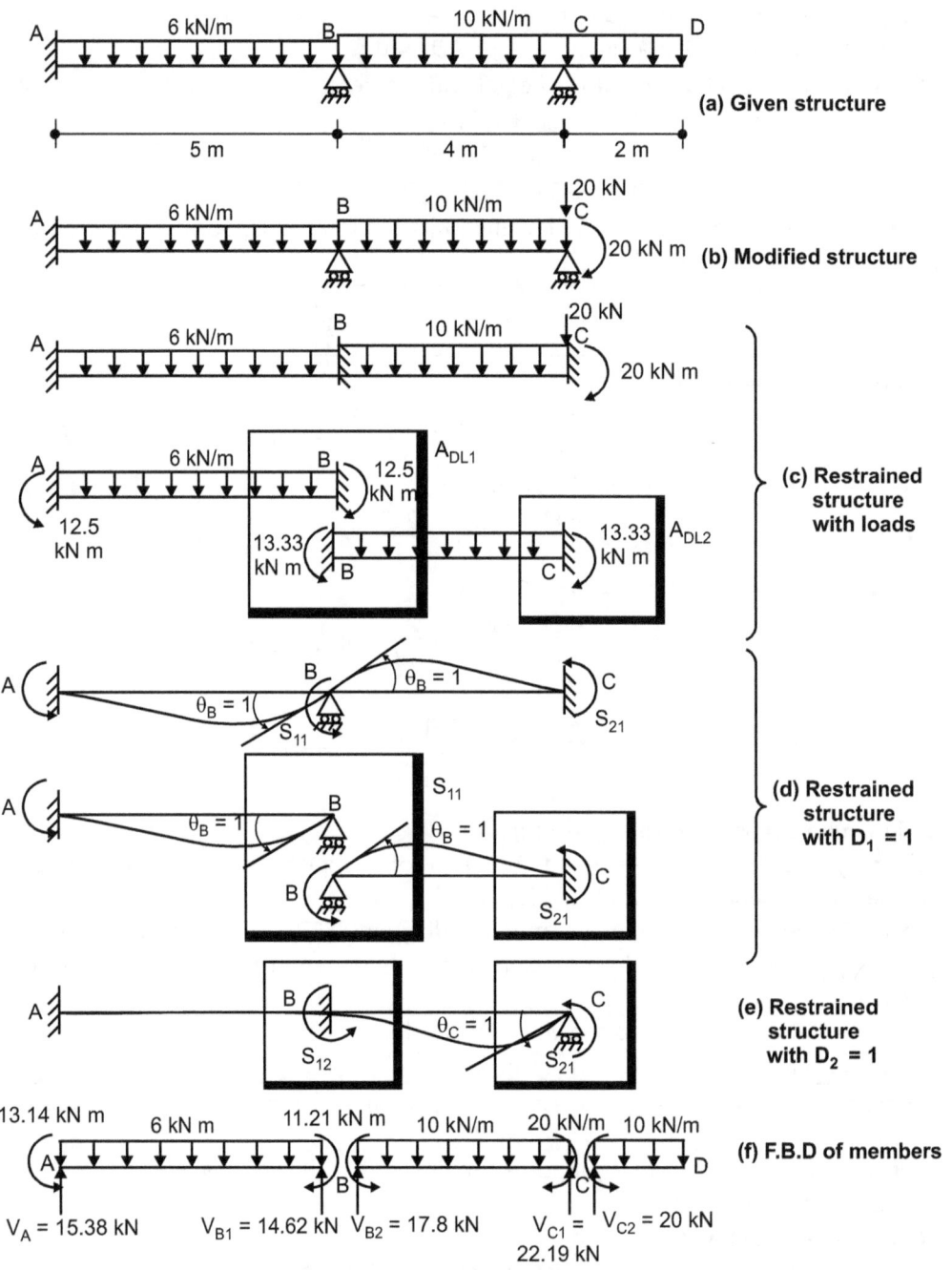

Fig. 6.6 : (Contd.)

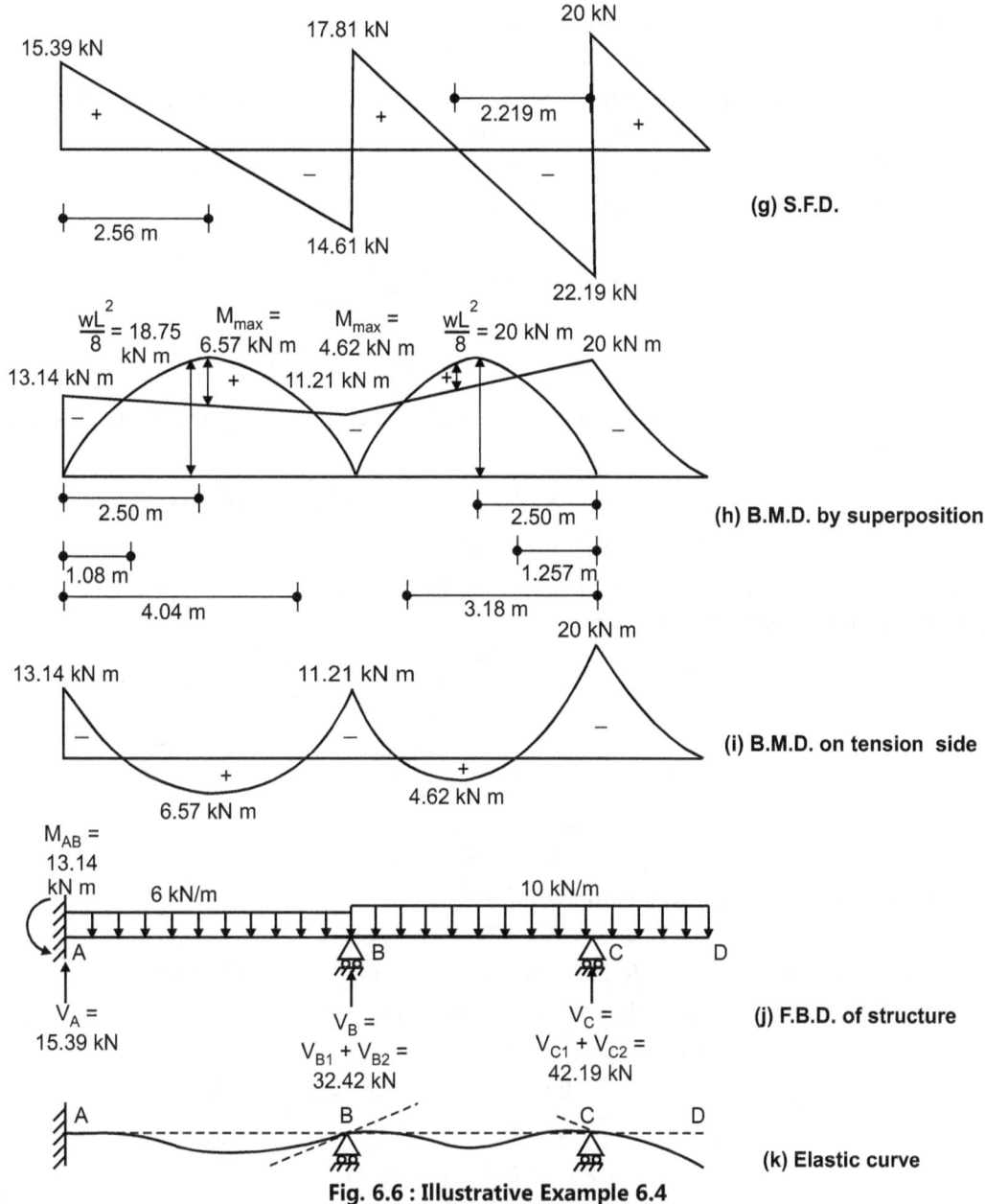

Fig. 6.6 : Illustrative Example 6.4

Procedure :

Step I : Degree of kinematic indeterminacy (D_{ki}) :

Degree of kinematic indeterminacy for given structure = D_{ki} = 4.

Degree of kinematic indeterminacy for modified structure = D_{ki} = 2.

Step II : Unknown joint displacements (D):
Let, $\quad D_1 = \theta_B \, (\circlearrowleft) \quad$ and $\quad D_2 = \theta_C \, (\circlearrowleft)$

Step III : Restrained Structure : The joints B and C are locked and the kinematically determinate i.e. restrained structure is obtained as shown in Fig. 6.6 (c). Also restrained structure with unit values of D_1 and D_2 is shown in Fig. 6.6 (d) and 6.6 (e) respectively.

Step IV : Force analysis of restrained structure :

(a) Fixed End Moments :

$$M_{AB}^F = -M_{BA}^F = \frac{wL^2}{12} = \frac{6 \times 5^2}{12} = 12.5 \text{ kNm}$$

$$M_{BC}^F = -M_{CB}^F = \frac{wL^2}{12} = \frac{10 \times 4^2}{12} = 13.33 \text{ kNm}$$

(b) Forces in the restrained structure subjected to loads corresponding to unknown displacements.

$$A_{DL1} = M_{BA}^F + M_{BC}^F = -12.5 + 13.33 = 0.83 \text{ kNm}$$

$$A_{DL2} = M_{CB}^F = -13.33 \text{ kNm}$$

(c) Forces in the restrained structure subjected to unit values of D_1 and D_2 corresponding to unknown displacements :

$$S_{11} = \left(\frac{4EI}{L}\right)_{BA} + \left(\frac{4EI}{L}\right)_{BC} = \frac{4EI}{4} + \frac{4EI}{4} = 1.8 \, EI$$

$$S_{21} = S_{12} = \left(\frac{2EI}{L}\right)_{BC} = \frac{2EI}{4} = 0.5 \, EI$$

$$S_{22} = \left(\frac{4EI}{L}\right)_{CB} = \frac{4EI}{4} = EI$$

Step V : The equilibrium requirement of forces :
There is no applied couple at B $\therefore A_{D1} = 0$.
Clockwise couple of magnitude 20 kNm is applied at C $\therefore A_{D2} = -20$ kNm.

Step VI : Superposition equation of equilibrium of forces :

$$\{A_D\} = \{A_{DL}\} + [S]\{D\}$$

i.e. $\quad \begin{Bmatrix} 0 \\ -20 \end{Bmatrix} = \begin{Bmatrix} 0.83 \\ -13.33 \end{Bmatrix} + EI \begin{bmatrix} 1.8 & 0.5 \\ 0.5 & 1.0 \end{bmatrix} \begin{Bmatrix} D_1 \\ D_2 \end{Bmatrix}$

$$0 = 0.83 + 1.8 \, EI \, (D_1) + 0.5 \, EI \, (D_2) \quad \ldots (A)$$

$$-20 = -13.33 + 0.5 \, EI \, (D_1) + 1.0 \, EI \, (D_2) \quad \ldots (B)$$

Step VII : Solution of equations for unknown displacements: Solving equations (A) and (B), we get

$$D_1 = \theta_B = \frac{1.61}{EI} = \frac{1.61}{EI} \; (\circlearrowleft)$$

$$D_2 = \theta_C = -\frac{7.47}{EI} = \frac{7.47}{EI} \; (\circlearrowright)$$

Step VIII : Other Forces :

$$M_{AB} = \frac{4EI}{5}(0) + \frac{2EI}{5}\left(\frac{1.61}{EI}\right) + 12.5 = 13.14 \text{ kNm}$$

$$M_{BA} = \frac{4EI}{5}\left(\frac{1.61}{EI}\right) + \frac{2EI}{5}(0) - 12.5 = -11.21 \text{ kNm}$$

$$M_{BC} = \frac{4EI}{4}\left(\frac{1.161}{EI}\right) + \frac{2EI}{4}\left(-\frac{7.47}{EI}\right) + 13.33 = 11.21 \text{ kNm}$$

$$M_{CB} = \frac{4EI}{4}\left(-\frac{7.47}{EI}\right) + \frac{2EI}{4}\left(\frac{1.61}{EI}\right) - 13.33 = -20 \text{ kNm}$$

$$M_{CD} = 20 \text{ kNm}$$

FBD of members is as shown in Fig. 6.6 (f).

Considering equilibrium of each member and of complete structure, all the reaction components are found out as shown in figure.

Step IX : Shear force and bending moment diagrams :

SFD is shown in Fig. 6.6 (g). BMD by superposition and on tension side is as shown in Fig. 6.6 (h) and 6.6 (i) respectively.

Step X : FBD of structure: as shown in Fig. 6.6 (j).

Step XI : Elastic curve: as shown in Fig. 6.6 (k).

Example 6.5 *: Analyse the beam shown in Fig. 6.7 (a) by stiffness method. Take EI = Constant.*

Solution : Data : The beam is supported and loaded as shown in Fig. 6.7 (a).

Object : Structural Analysis.

Concepts and Equations :

(1) Kinematically determinate structure (Restrained structure).
(2) Force analysis of restrained structure.
(3) Superposition equations of equilibrium of forces.

Procedure :

Step I : Degree of kinematic indeterminacy (D_{ki}) :

Degree of kinematic indeterminacy = D_{ki} = 3.

Step II : Unknown joint displacements (D):

Let, $D_1 = \theta_A$, $D_2 = \theta_B$ and $D_3 = \theta_C$

Step III : Restrained structure :

The joints A, B and C are locked and the restrained structure is obtained as shown in Fig. 6.7 (c). Also restrained structure with unit values of D_1, D_2 and D_3 is shown in Fig. 6.7 (d), Fig. 6.7 (e) and Fig. 6.7 (f) respectively.

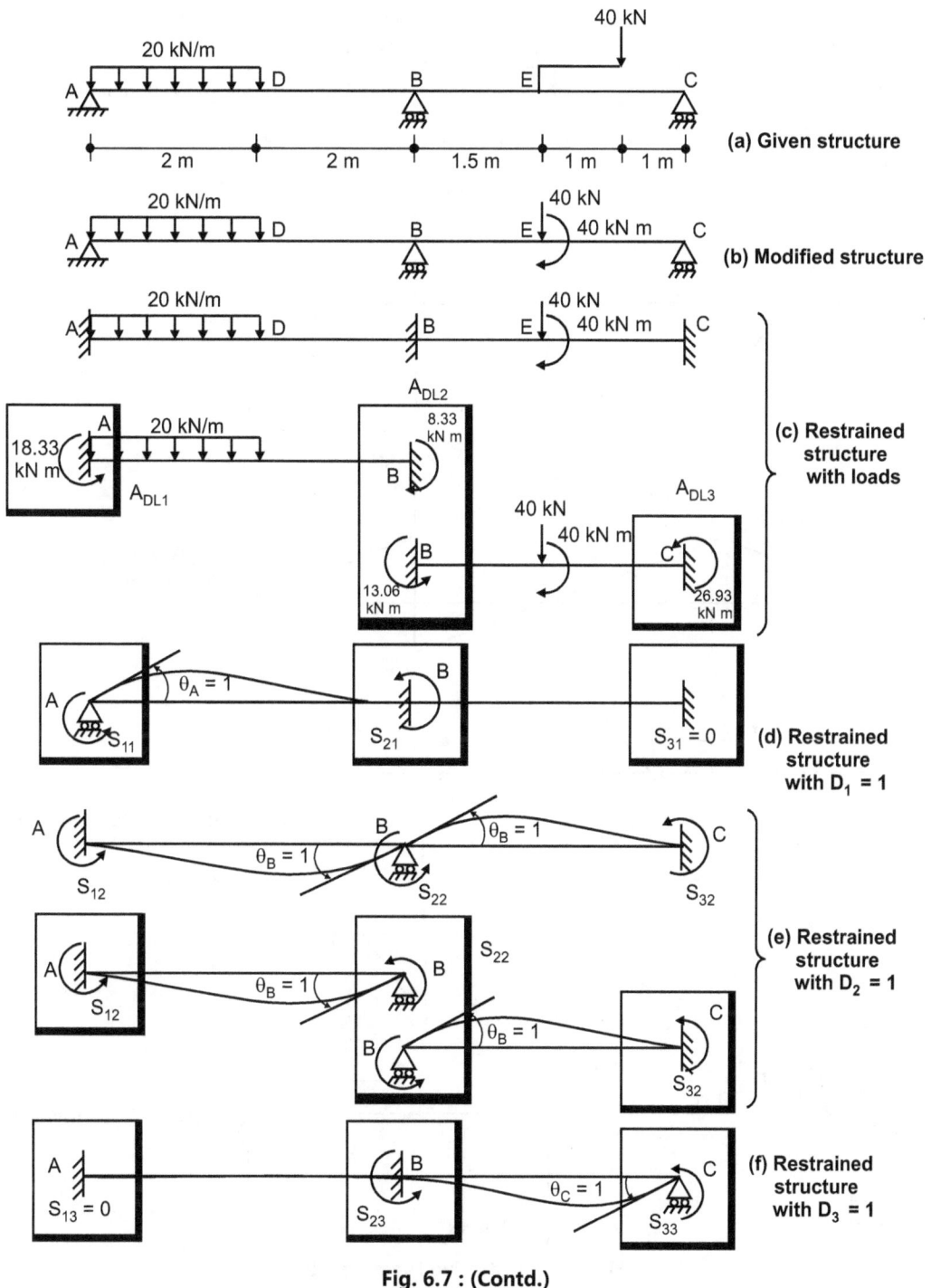

Fig. 6.7 : (Contd.)

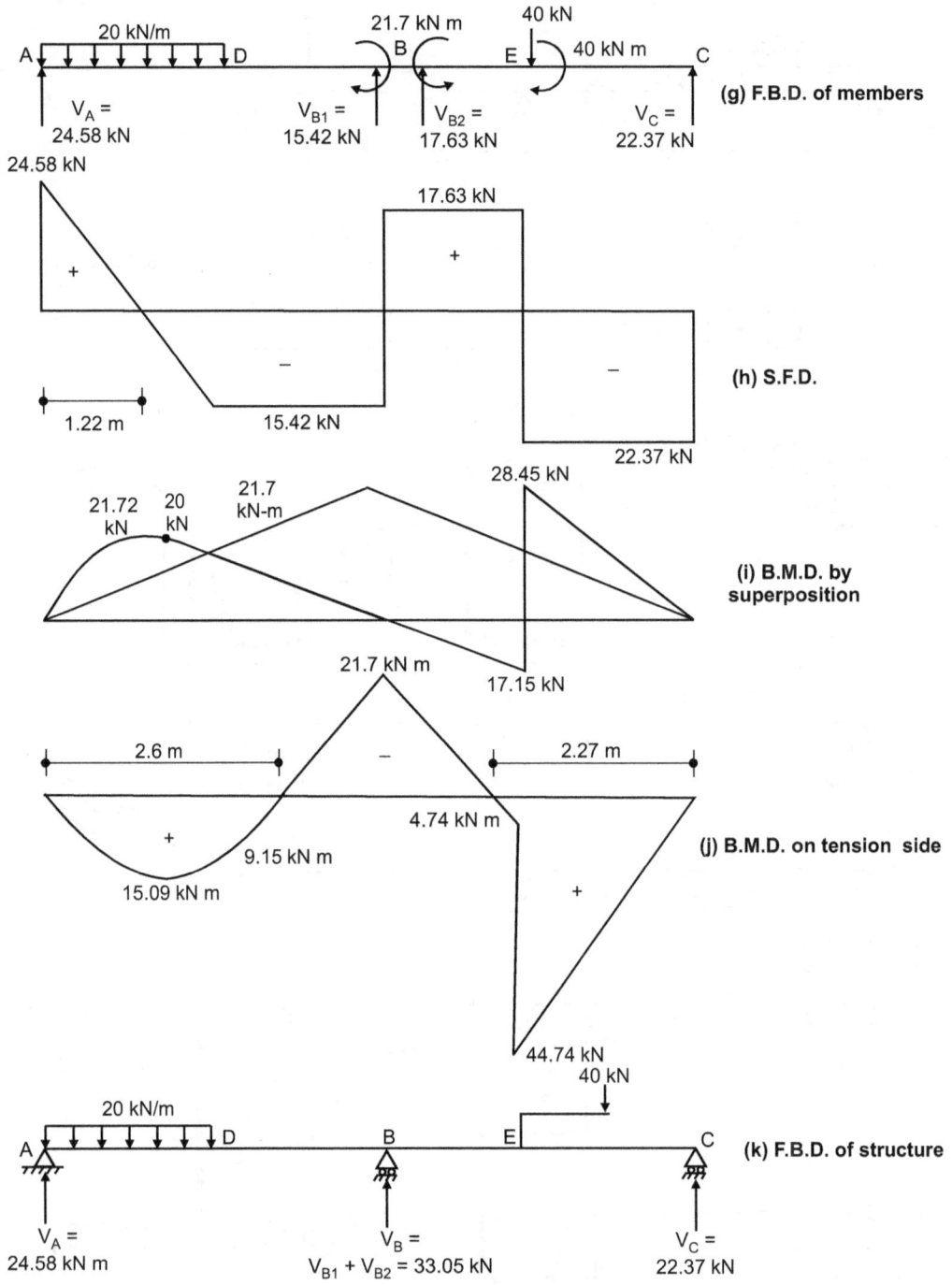

Fig. 6.7 : Illustrative Example 6.5

Step IV : Force analysis of restrained structure :

(a) Fixed End Moments :

$$M_{AB}^F = \frac{wa^2}{12 L^2}(6L^2 - 8aL + 3a^2) = \frac{20 \times 2^2}{12 \times 4^2}[6 \times 4^2 - 8 \times 2 \times 4 + 3 \times 2^2]$$

$$= 18.33 \text{ kNm}$$

$$M_{BA}^F = -\frac{wa^3}{12 L^2}(4L - 3a) = \frac{-20 \times 2^2}{12 \times 4^2}[4 \times 4 - 3 \times 2] = -8.33 \text{ kNm}$$

$$M_{BC}^F = \frac{Wab^2}{L^2} - \frac{Mb}{L^2}(2a - b) = \frac{40 \times 1.5 \times 2^2}{3.5^2} - \frac{40 \times 2 \times (2 \times 1.5 - 2)}{3.5^2}$$

$$= 13.06 \text{ kNm}$$

$$M_{CB}^F = -\frac{Wba^2}{L^2} - \frac{Ma}{L^2}(2b - a) = -\frac{40 \times 2 \times 1.5^2}{3.5^2} - \frac{40 \times 1.5(2 \times 2 - 1.5)}{3.5^2}$$

$$= -26.93 \text{ kNm}$$

(b) Forces in the restrained structure subjected to loads corresponding to unknown displacements.

$$A_{DL1} = M_{AB}^F = 18.33 \text{ kNm}$$

$$A_{DL2} = M_{BA}^F + M_{BC}^F = -8.33 + 13.06 = 3.73 \text{ kNm}$$

$$A_{DL3} = M_{CB}^F = -26.93 \text{ kNm}$$

(c) Forces in the restrained structure subjected to unit values of D_1, D_2 and D_3 corresponding to unknown displacements.

$$S_{11} = \left(\frac{4 EI}{L}\right)_{AB} = \frac{4 EI}{4} = 1 \text{ EI}$$

$$S_{12} = S_{21} = \left(\frac{2 EI}{L}\right)_{BA} = \frac{2 EI}{4} = 0.5 \text{ EI}$$

$$S_{22} = \left(\frac{5 EI}{L}\right)_{BA} + \left(\frac{4 EI}{L}\right)_{BC} = \frac{4 EI}{4} + \frac{4 EI}{3.5} = 2.14 \text{ EI}$$

$$S_{32} = S_{23} = \left(\frac{2 EI}{L}\right)_{CB} = \frac{2 EI}{3.5} = 0.57 \text{ EI}$$

$$S_{33} = \left(\frac{4 EI}{L}\right)_{CB} = \frac{4 EI}{3.5} = 2.14 \text{ EI}$$

$$S_{13} = S_{31} = 0$$

Step V : The equilibrium requirement of force :

There is no applied couple at A, B and C.

$$\therefore \quad A_{D1} = A_{D2} = A_{D3} = 0$$

Step VI : Superposition equation of equilibrium of forces:

$$\{A_D\} = \{A_{DL}\} + [S]\{D\}$$

i.e.
$$\begin{Bmatrix} 0 \\ 0 \\ 0 \end{Bmatrix} = \begin{Bmatrix} 18.33 \\ 4.73 \\ -26.93 \end{Bmatrix} + EI \begin{bmatrix} 1.0 & 0.5 & 0 \\ 0.5 & 2.14 & 0.57 \\ 0 & 0.57 & 2.14 \end{bmatrix} \begin{Bmatrix} D_1 \\ D_2 \\ D_3 \end{Bmatrix}$$

i.e.
$$0 = 18.33 + 1.0\, EI\,(D_1) + 0.5\, EI\,(D_2) + 0\, EI\,(D_3) \quad \ldots (A)$$
$$0 = 4.73 + 0.5\, EI\,(D_1) + 2.14\, EI\,(D_2) + 0.57\, EI\,(D_3) \quad \ldots (B)$$
$$0 = -256.93 + 0\, EI\,(D_1) + 0.57\, EI\,(D_2) + 2.14\, EI\,(D_3) \quad \ldots (C)$$

Step VII : Solution of equations for unknown displacements: Solving equations (A), (B) and (c) we get,

$$\boxed{\begin{aligned} D_1 &= \theta_A = \frac{-15.51}{EI} = \frac{15.51}{EI}\ (\circlearrowright) \\ D_2 &= \theta_B = \frac{-5.62}{EI} = \frac{5.62}{EI}\ (\circlearrowright) \\ D_3 &= \theta_C = \frac{26.38}{EI} = \frac{26.38}{EI}\ (\circlearrowleft) \end{aligned}}$$

Step VIII : Other Forces :

$$M_{AB} = \frac{4\,EI}{4}\left(\frac{-15.51}{EI}\right) + \frac{2\,EI}{4}\left(\frac{-5.62}{EI}\right) + 18.33 = 0\ \text{kNm}$$

$$M_{BA} = \frac{4\,EI}{4}\left(\frac{-5.62}{EI}\right) + \frac{2\,EI}{4}\left(\frac{-15.51}{EI}\right) + (-8.33) = -21.70\ \text{kNm}$$

$$M_{BC} = \frac{4\,EI}{3.5}\left(\frac{-5.62}{EI}\right) + \frac{2\,EI}{3.5} + \left(\frac{26.38}{EI}\right) + 13.06 = 21.70\ \text{kNm}$$

$$M_{CB} = \frac{4\,EI}{3.5}\left(\frac{26.38}{EI}\right) + \frac{2\,EI}{3.5}\left(\frac{-5.62}{EI}\right) + (-26.93) = 0\ \text{kNm}$$

FBD of members is as shown in Fig. 6.7 (g). Considering equilibrium of each member and of complete structure all the reaction components are found out as shown in figure.

Step IX : Shear force and bending moment diagrams : SFD is as shown in Fig. 6.7 (h).

BMD by superposition and on tension side is as shown in Fig. 6.7 (i) and 6.7 (j) respectively.

Step X : FBD of structure : as shown in Fig. 6.7 (k).

Example 6.6 : *Analyse the beam shown in Fig. 6.8 (a) by stiffness method. Support B sinks by 25 mm. Take EI = 3800 kNm².*

Solution : Data :
(1) The beam is supported and loaded as shown in Fig. 6.8 (a).
(2) $EI = 3800\ kNm^2$
(3) $\Delta_B = 25$ mm ($\downarrow$)
Object : Structural analysis.

Concepts and Equations :
(1) Kinematically determinate structure (Restrained structure).
(2) Force analysis of restrained structure.
(3) Superposition equations of equilibrium of forces.

Procedure :

Step I : Degree of kinematic indeterminacy (D_{ki}) :
Degree of kinematic indeterminacy = D_{ki} = 2.

Step II : Unknown joint displacements (D) :
Let, $D_1 = \theta_B$ and $D_2 = \theta_C$.

Step III : Restrained structure :

The joints B and C are locked and the restrained structure is obtained as shown in Fig. 6.8 (b). Also restrained structure with unit values of D_1 and D_2 is shown in Fig. 6.8 (c) and Fig. 6.8 (d) respectively.

Step IV : Force analysis of restrained structure :

(a) **Fixed End Moments :**

$$M^F_{AB} = \frac{wL^2}{12} + \frac{6\,EI}{L^2}(\Delta) = \frac{10 \times 6^2}{12} + \frac{6 \times 3800}{6^2}\left(\frac{25}{1000}\right) = 45.83 \text{ kNm}$$

$$M^F_{BA} = -\frac{wL^2}{12} + \frac{6\,EI}{L^2}(\Delta) = -\frac{10 \times 6^2}{12} + \frac{6 \times 3800}{6^2}\left(\frac{25}{10000}\right) = -14.16 \text{ kNm}$$

$$M^F_{BC} = \frac{Wab^2}{L^2} - \frac{6\,EI}{L^2}(\Delta) = \frac{30 \times 2 \times 4^2}{6^2} - \frac{6 \times 3800}{6^2}\left(\frac{25}{1000}\right) = 10.83 \text{ kNm}$$

$$M^F_{CB} = -\frac{Wba^2}{L^2} - \frac{6\,EI}{L^2}(\Delta) = -\frac{30 \times 4 \times 2^2}{6^2} - \frac{6 \times 3800}{6^2}\left(\frac{25}{1000}\right) = -29.16 \text{ kNm}$$

(b) Forces in the restrained structure subjected to loads corresponding to unknown displacements.

$$A_{DL1} = M^F_{BA} + M^F_{BC} = -14.16 + 10.83 = -3.33 \text{ kNm}$$

$$A_{DL2} = M^F_{CB} = -19.16 \text{ kNm}$$

(c) Forces in the restrained structure subjected to unit values of unit values of D_1 and D_2 corresponding to unknown displacements.

$$S_{11} = \left(\frac{4\,EI}{L}\right)_{BA} + \left(\frac{4\,EI}{L}\right)_{BC} = \frac{4\,EI}{6} + \frac{4\,EI}{6} = 1.33\,EI$$

$$S_{21} = S_{12} = \left(\frac{2\,EI}{L}\right)_{CB} = \frac{2\,EI}{6} = 0.33\,EI$$

$$S_{22} = \left(\frac{4\,EI}{L}\right)_{CB} = \frac{4\,EI}{6} = 0.66\,EI$$

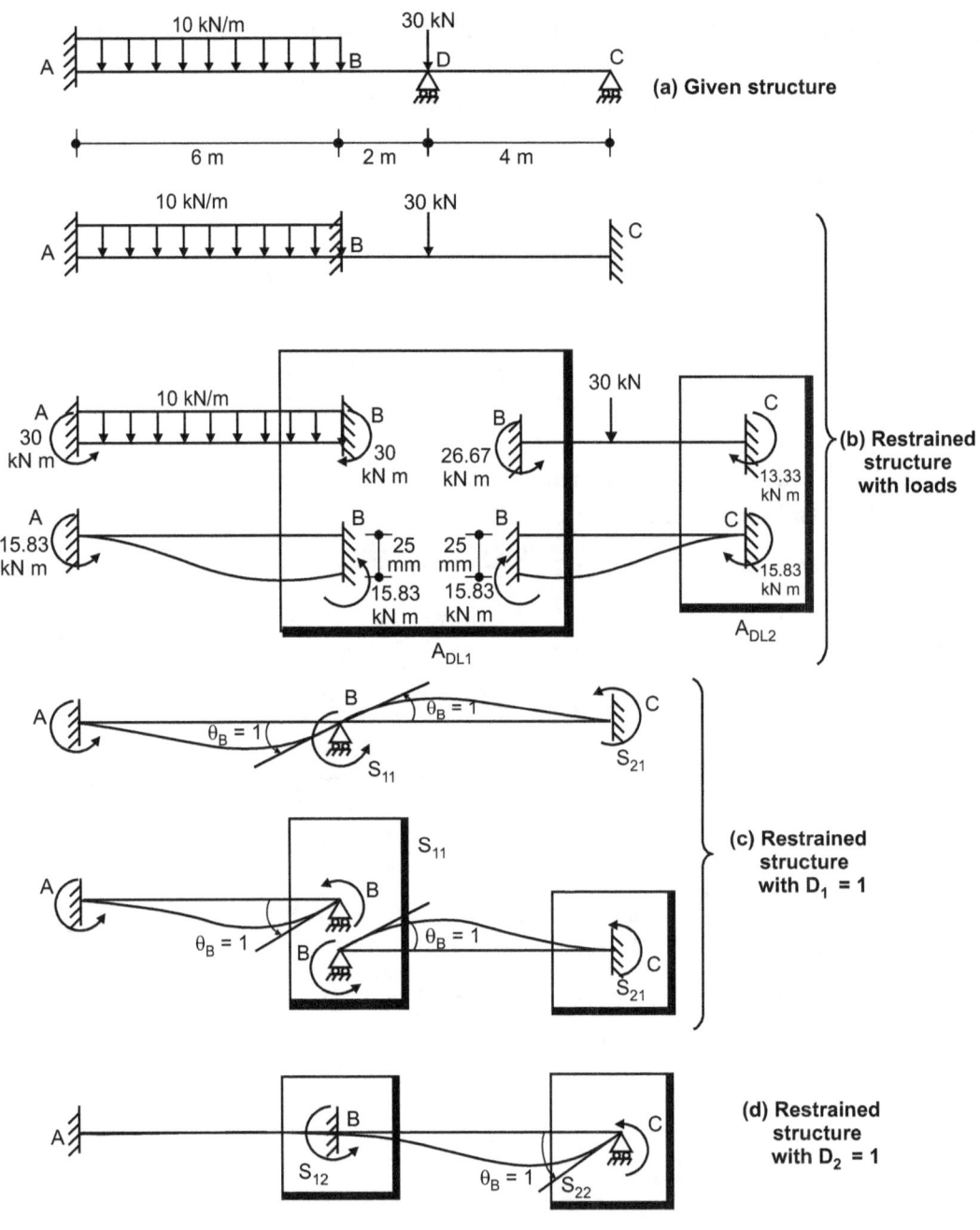

Fig. 6.8 : (Contd.)

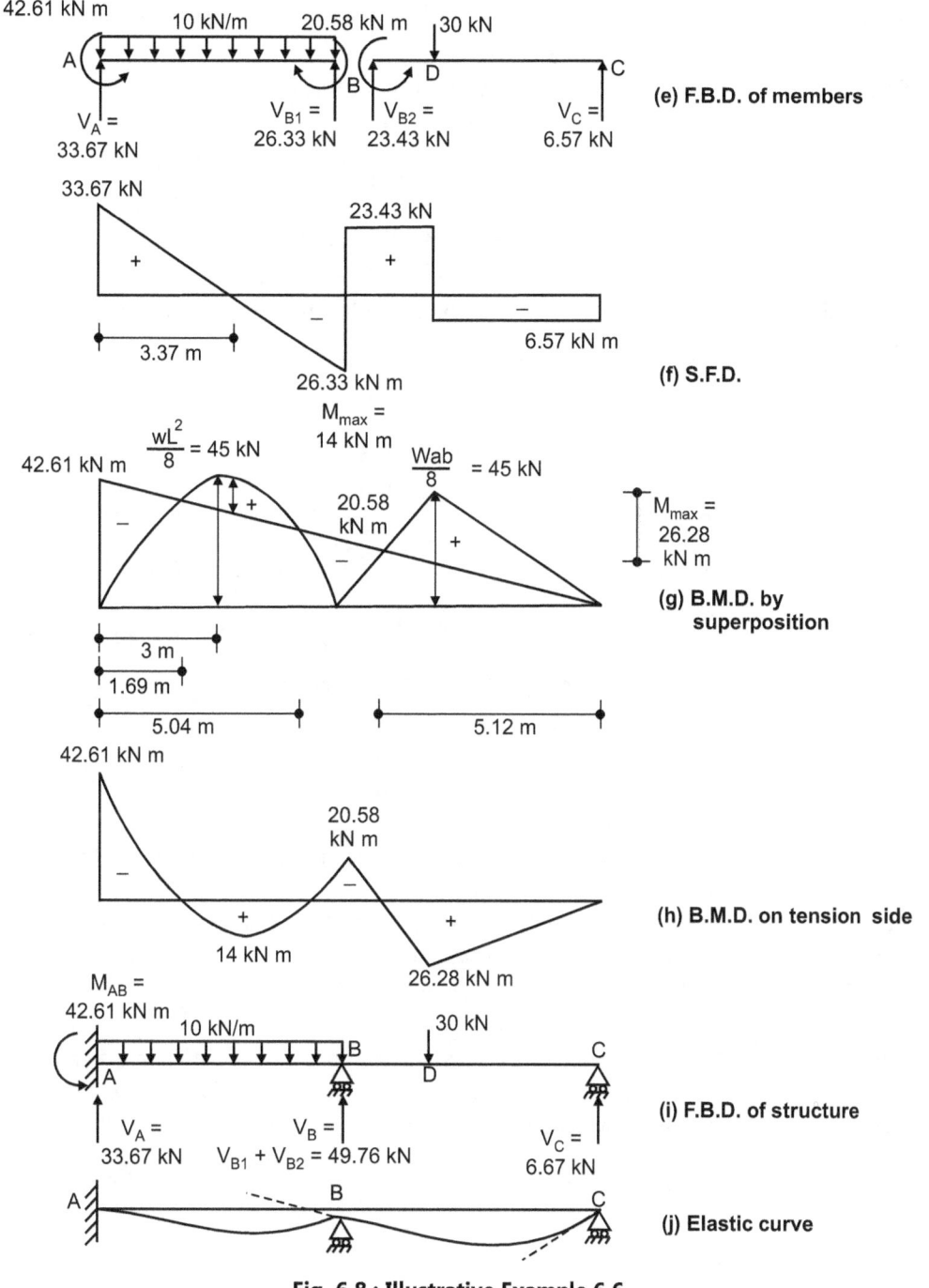

Fig. 6.8 : Illustrative Example 6.6

Step V : The equilibrium requirement of force : There is no applied couple at B and C.
$$\therefore \quad A_{D1} = A_{D2} = 0$$

Step VI : Superposition equations of equilibrium of forces :
$$\{AD\} = \{A_{DL}\} + [S]\{D\}$$

i.e.,
$$\begin{Bmatrix} 0 \\ 0 \end{Bmatrix} = \begin{Bmatrix} -3.33 \\ -29.16 \end{Bmatrix} + EI \begin{bmatrix} 1.33 & 0.33 \\ 0.33 & 0.66 \end{bmatrix} \begin{Bmatrix} D_1 \\ D_2 \end{Bmatrix}$$

i.e.,
$$0 = -3.33 + 1.33\, EI\,(D_1) + 0.33\, EI\,(D_2) \quad \ldots (A)$$
$$0 = -29.16 + 0.33\, EI\,(D_1) + 0.66\, EI\,(D_2) \quad \ldots (B)$$

Step VII : Solution of equations for unknown displacements: Solving equation (A) and (B) we get,

$$\boxed{\begin{aligned} D_1 &= \theta_B = \frac{-9.64}{EI} = \frac{9.64}{EI}\ (\circlearrowleft) \\ D_2 &= \theta_C = \frac{48.56}{EI} = \frac{48.56}{EI}\ (\circlearrowright) \end{aligned}}$$

Step VIII : Other forces :

$$M_{AB} = \frac{4\,EI}{6}(0) + \frac{2\,EI}{6}\left(\frac{-9.64}{EI}\right) + 45.83 = 42.61\ \text{kNm}$$

$$M_{BA} = \frac{4\,EI}{6}\left(\frac{-9.64}{EI}\right) + \frac{2\,EI}{6}(0) + (-14.16) = -20.58\ \text{kNm}$$

$$M_{BC} = \frac{4\,EI}{6}\left(\frac{-9.64}{EI}\right) + \frac{2\,EI}{6}\left(\frac{48.56}{EI}\right) + 10.83 = 20.58\ \text{kNm}$$

$$M_{CB} = \frac{4\,EI}{6}\left(\frac{48.56}{EI}\right) + \frac{2\,EI}{6}\left(\frac{-9.64}{EI}\right) + (-29.16) = 0\ \text{kNm}$$

FBD of members is as shown in Fig. 6.8 (e).
Considering equilibrium of each member and of complete structure all the reaction components are found out as shown in figure.

Step IX : Shear force and bending moment diagrams: SFD is shown in Fig. 6.8 (f).
BMD by superposition and on tension side is as shown in Fig. 6.8 (g) and 6.8 (h) respectively.

Step X : FBD of structure : as shown in Fig. 6.8 (i).

Step XI : Elastic curve : as shown in Fig. 6.8 (j).

Example 6.7 : *Analyse the beam shown in Fig. 6.9 (a) by stiffness method. Take EI = Constant. Stiffness coefficients of spring at B and C are as shown in the figure.*

Solution: (1) Data : The beam is supported and loaded as shown in Fig. 6.9 (a).

(2) $K_B = (EI)\ \text{kN/m}$ and $K_C = \left(\dfrac{EI}{2}\right)\ \text{kN/m}$.

Object : Structural analysis.

Concepts and Equations :

(1) Kinematically determinate structure (Restrained structure).

TOS – II (TE CIVIL SEM. VI NMU) FUNDAMENTAL CONCEPT OF STIFFNESS

(2) Force analysis of restrained structure.
(3) Superposition equations of equilibrium of forces.

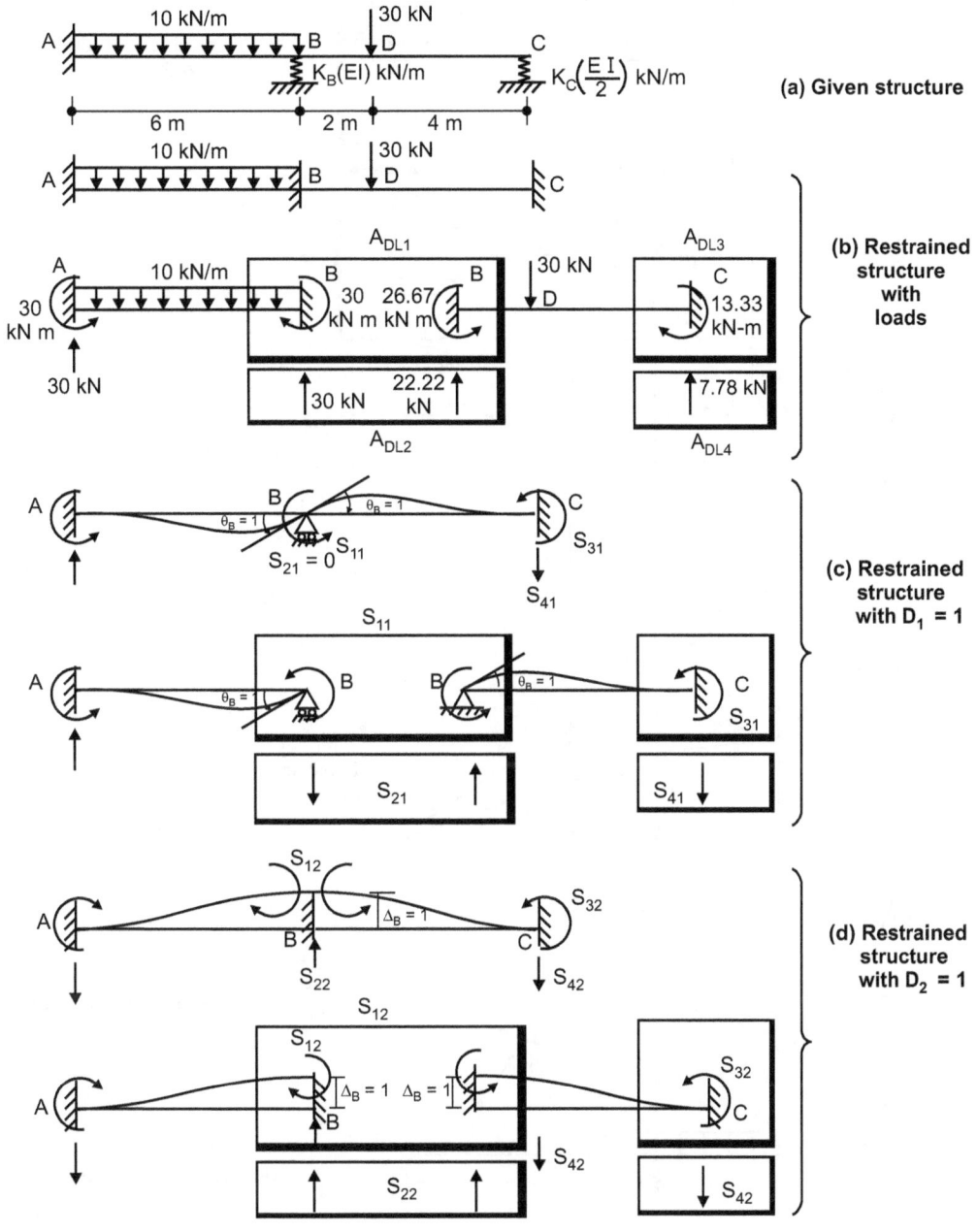

Fig. 6.9 : (Contd.)

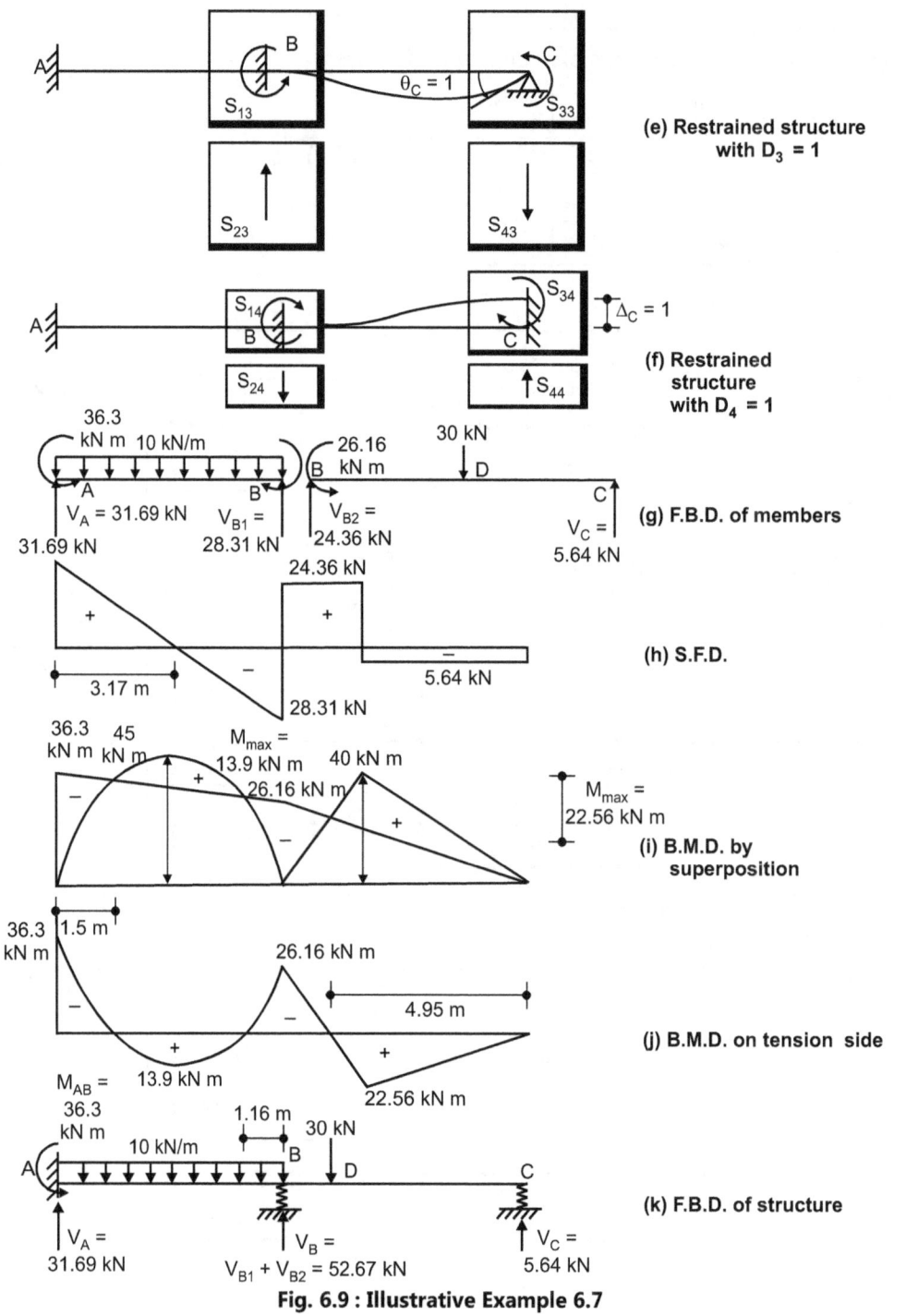

Fig. 6.9 : Illustrative Example 6.7

Procedure :

Step I : Degree of kinematic indeterminacy (D_{ki}):

Degree of kinematic indeterminacy = D_{ki} = 4.

Step II : Unknown joint displacements (D):

Let, $D_1 = \theta_B$ (↻), $D_2 = \Delta_B$ (↑), $D_3 = \theta_B$ (↻) and $D_4 = \Delta_C$ (↑)

Step III : Restrained structure: Joints B and C are locked and restrained structure is as shown in Fig. 6.9 (b). Also restrained structure with unit values of D_1, D_2, D_3 and D_4 is shown in Fig. 6.9 (c), Fig. 6.9 (d), Fig. 6.9 (e) and Fig. 6.9 (f) respectively.

Step IV : Force analysis of restrained structure :

(a) **Fixed End Moments :**

$$M^F_{AB} = -M^F_{BA} = \frac{wL^2}{12} = \frac{10 \times 6^2}{12} = 30 \text{ kNm}$$

$$M^F_{BC} = \frac{Wab^2}{L^2} = \frac{30 \times 2 \times 4^2}{6} = 26.67 \text{ kNm}$$

$$M^F_{CB} = -\frac{Wba^2}{L^2} = \frac{30 \times 4 \times 2^2}{6^2} = -13.33 \text{ kNm}$$

(b) Forces in the restrained structure subjected to loads corresponding to unknown displacements:

$A_{DL1} = M^F_{BA} + M^F_{BC} = -30 + 26.67 = -3.33$ kNm

A_{DL2} = Vertical reaction component at B in the restrained structure subjected to loads

= 30 + 22.22 = 52.22 kN

$A_{DL3} = M^F_{CB} = -13.33$ kNm

A_{DL4} = Vertical reaction component at C in the restrained structure subjected to loads

= 7.78 kN

(c) Forces in the restrained structure subjected to unit values of D_1, D_2, D_3 and D_4 corresponding to unknown displacements :

$$S_{11} = \left(\frac{4EI}{L}\right)_{BA} + \left(\frac{4EI}{L}\right)_{BC} = \frac{4EI}{6} + \frac{4EI}{6} = 1.33 \text{ EI}$$

$$S_{21} = S_{12} = -\left(\frac{6EI}{L^2}\right)_{BA} + \left(\frac{6EI}{L^2}\right)_{BC} = -\frac{6EI}{6^2} + \frac{6EI}{6^2} = 0$$

$$S_{31} = S_{13} = \left(\frac{2EI}{L}\right)_{BC} = \frac{2EI}{6} = -0.33 \text{ EI}$$

$$S_{41} = S_{14} = -\left(\frac{6EI}{L^2}\right)_{BC} = -\frac{6EI}{6^2} = -0.167\,EI$$

$$S_{22} = \left(\frac{12EI}{L^3}\right)_{BA} + \left(\frac{12EI}{L^3}\right)_{BC} = \frac{12EI}{6^3} + \frac{12EI}{6^3} = 0.11\,EI$$

$$S_{32} = S_{23} = \left(\frac{6EI}{L^2}\right)_{BC} = \frac{6EI}{6^2} = 0.167\,EI$$

$$S_{42} = S_{24} = -\left(\frac{12EI}{L^3}\right)_{BC} = -\frac{12EI}{6^3} = -0.055\,EI$$

$$S_{33} = \left(\frac{4EI}{L}\right)_{BC} = \frac{4EI}{6} = 0.67\,EI$$

$$S_{43} = S_{34} = -\left(\frac{6EI}{L^2}\right)_{BC} = -\frac{6EI}{6^2} = -0.167\,EI$$

$$S_{44} = \left(\frac{12EI}{L^3}\right)_{BC} = \frac{12EI}{6^3} = 0.055\,EI$$

Step V : The equilibrium requirements of forces.

There is no applied couple at B and C. $\therefore$ $A_{D1} = A_{D3} = 0$

There is no applied point load at B and C. $\therefore$ $A_{D2} = A_{D4} = 0$.

Step VI : Superposition equation of equilibrium of forces :

$$\{A_D\} = \{A_{DL}\} + [S]\{D\}$$

i.e.
$$\begin{Bmatrix} 0 \\ 0 \\ 0 \\ 0 \end{Bmatrix} = \begin{Bmatrix} -3.33 \\ 52.22 \\ -13.33 \\ 7.78 \end{Bmatrix} + EI \begin{bmatrix} 1.33 & 0 & 0.33 & -0.167 \\ 0 & 0.11 & 0.167 & -0.055 \\ 0.33 & 0.167 & 0.67 & -0.167 \\ -0.167 & -0.055 & -0.167 & 0.055 \end{bmatrix} \begin{Bmatrix} D_1 \\ D_2 \\ D_3 \\ D_4 \end{Bmatrix}$$

Because of the elastic supports at B and C, S_{22} and S_{44} are to be modified as :

$$S_{22} = (0.11 + 1)\,EI = 1.11\,EI$$

$$S_{44} = \left(0.055 + \frac{1}{2}\right)EI = 0.555\,EI$$

Superposition equation of equilibrium of forces becomes :

$$\begin{Bmatrix} 0 \\ 0 \\ 0 \\ 0 \end{Bmatrix} = \begin{Bmatrix} -3.33 \\ 52.22 \\ -13.33 \\ 7.78 \end{Bmatrix} + EI \begin{bmatrix} 1.33 & 0 & 0.33 & -0.167 \\ 0 & 0.11 & 0.167 & -0.055 \\ 0.33 & 0.167 & 0.67 & -0.167 \\ -0.167 & -0.055 & -0.167 & 0.055 \end{bmatrix} \begin{Bmatrix} D_1 \\ D_2 \\ D_3 \\ D_4 \end{Bmatrix}$$

i.e. $\quad 0 = -3.33 + (1.33\,EI)\,D_1 + (0)\,D_2 + (0.33\,EI)\,D_3 - (0.167\,EI)\,D_4$ ... (A)

$0 = 52.22 + (0) D_1 + (1.11\ EI) D_2 + (0.167\ EI) D_3\ (0.055\ EI) D_4$ ... (B)

$0 = -13.33 + (0.33\ EI) D_1 + (0.167\ EI) D_2 + (0.67\ EI) D_3 - (0.167\ EI) D_4$ ... (C)

$0 = 7.78 - (0.167\ EI) D_1 + (0.055\ EI) D_2 - (0.167\ EI) D_3 + (0.55\ EI) D_4$ ... (D)

Step VII : Solution of equations for unknown displacements :

Solving equations (A), (B), (C) and (D) we get,

$$D_1 = \theta_B = \frac{-7.23}{EI} = \frac{7.23}{EI}\ (\circlearrowleft)$$

$$D_2 = \Delta_B = \frac{-52.67}{EI} = \frac{52.67}{EI}\ (\downarrow)$$

$$D_3 = \theta_C = \frac{33.54}{EI} = \frac{33.54}{EI}\ (\circlearrowright)$$

$$D_4 = \Delta_C = \frac{-11.28}{EI} = \frac{11.28}{EI}\ (\downarrow)$$

Step VIII : Other forces :

$$M_{AB} = \frac{4\ EI}{6}(0) + \frac{2\ EI}{6}\left(-\frac{7.23}{EI}\right) + \frac{6\ EI}{6^2}\left(\frac{52.67}{EI}\right) + 30 = 36.3\ kNm$$

$$M_{BA} = \frac{4\ EI}{6}\left(-\frac{7.23}{EI}\right) + \frac{2\ EI}{6}(0) + \frac{6\ EI}{6^2}\left(\frac{52.67}{EI}\right) - 30 = -26.16\ kNm$$

$$M_{BC} = \frac{4\ EI}{6}\left(-\frac{7.23}{EI}\right) + \frac{2\ EI}{6}\left(\frac{33.54}{EI}\right) - \frac{6\ EI}{6^2}\left(\frac{52.67 - 11.28}{EI}\right) + 26.67$$

$$= 26.16\ kNm$$

$$M_{CB} = \frac{4\ EI}{6}\left(\frac{33.54}{EI}\right) + \frac{2\ EI}{6}\left(-\frac{7.23}{EI}\right) - \frac{6\ EI}{6^2}\left(\frac{52.67 - 11.28}{EI}\right) - 13.33 = 0$$

FBD of member is as shown in Fig. 6.9.(g). Considering equilibrium of each member and of complete structure other reaction components are found out as shown in figure.

Step IX : Shear force and bending moment diagrams: SFD is as shown in Fig. 6.9 (h). BMD by superposition and on tension side is as shown in Fig. 6.9 (i) and Fig. 6.9 (j) respectively.

Step X : FBD of structure: as shown in Fig. 6.9 (k).

Example 6.8 : *Analyse the beam shown in Fig. 6.10 (a) by stiffness method.*

Solution : Data : The beam is supported and loaded as shown in Fig. 6.10 (a).

Object : Structural analysis.

Concepts and Equations :

(1) Kinematically determinate structure (Restrained structure).

(2) Force analysis of restrained structure.

(3) Superposition equations of equilibrium of forces.

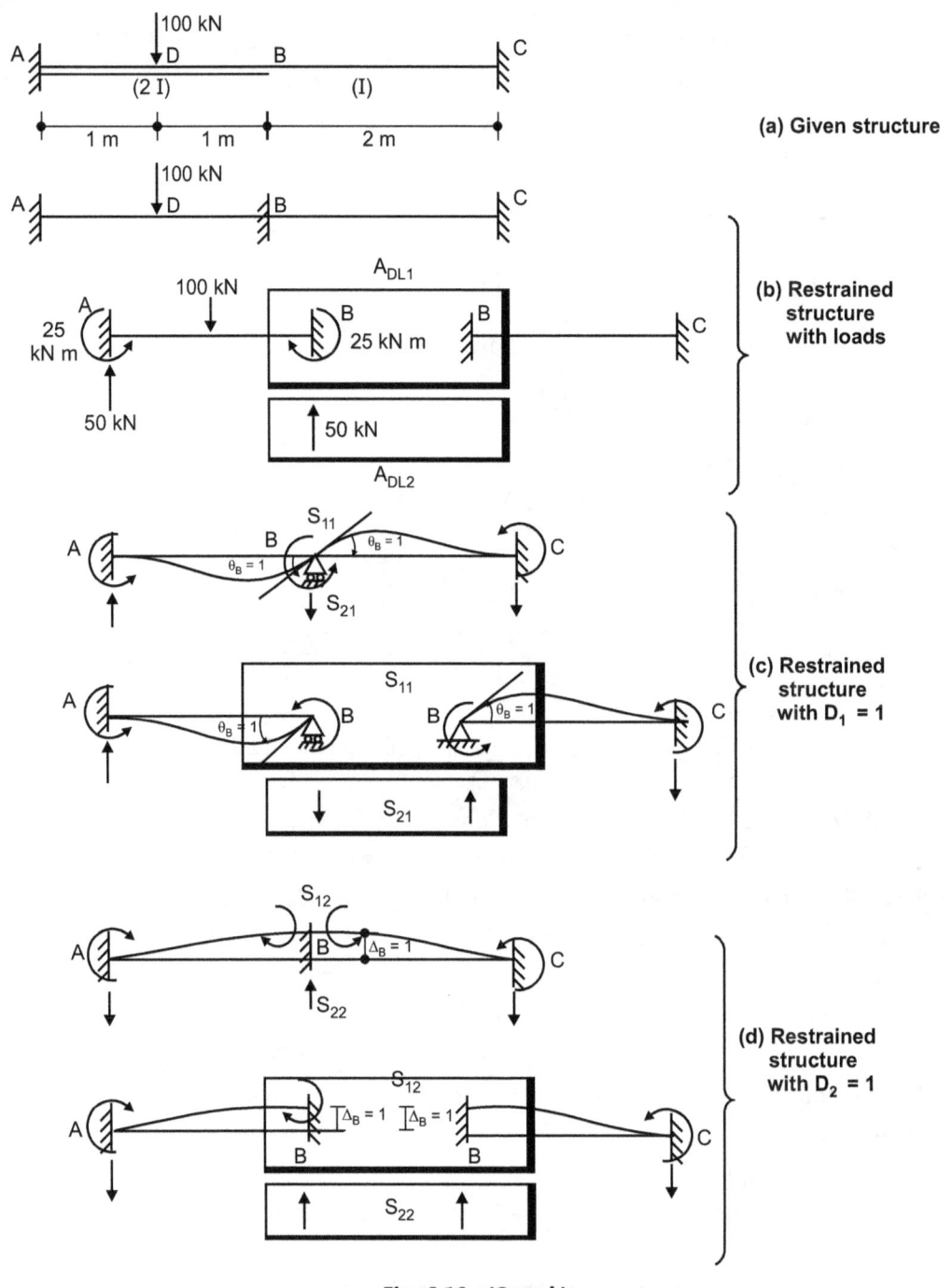

Fig. 6.10 : (Contd.)

FUNDAMENTAL CONCEPT OF STIFFNESS

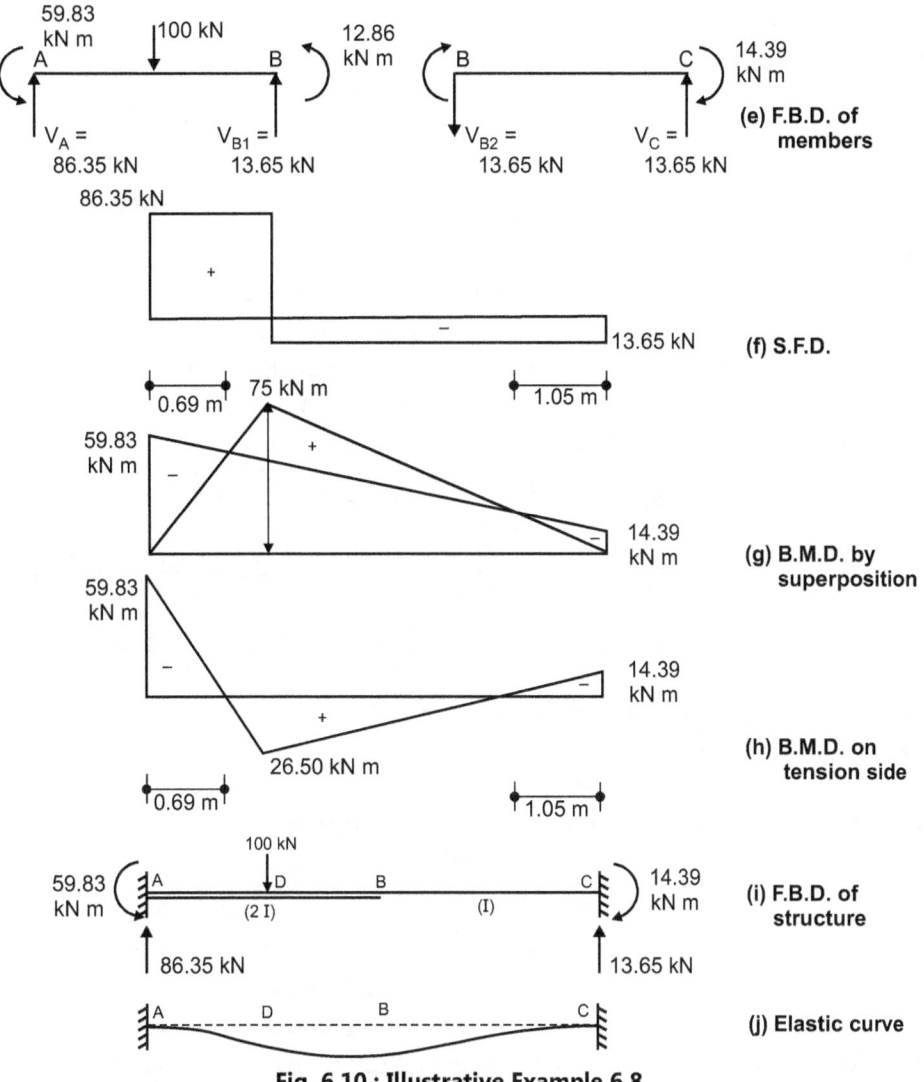

Fig. 6.10 : Illustrative Example 6.8

Procedure :

Step I : Degree of kinematic indeterminacy (D_{ki}):

Degree of kinematic indeterminacy = D_{ki} = 2.

Step II : Unknown joint displacements (D).

Let, $D_1 = \theta_B$ (↻) and $D_2 = \Delta_B$ (↑)

Step III : Restrained Structure :

The joint B is locked and the restrained structure is obtained as shown in Fig. 6.10 (b). Also restrained structure with unit values of D_1 and D_2 is shown in Fig. 6.10 (c) and Fig. 6.10 (d) respectively.

Step IV : Force analysis of restrained structure :
(a) Fixed end moments

$$M_{AB}^F = -M_{BA}^F = \frac{WL}{8} = \frac{100 \times 2}{8} = 25 \text{ kNm}$$

$$M_{BC}^F = M_{CB}^F = 0 \text{ kNm}$$

(b) Forces in the restrained structure subjected to loads corresponding to unknown displacements :

$$A_{DL1} = M_{BA}^F + M_{BC}^F = -25 + 0 = -25 \text{ kNm}$$

A_{DL2} = Vertical reaction component at B in the restrained structure subjected to loads = 50 kN

(c) Forces in the restrained structure subjected to unit values of D_1 and D_2 corresponding to unknown displacements.

$$S_{11} = \left(\frac{4EI}{L}\right)_{BA} + \left(\frac{4EI}{L}\right)_{BC} = \frac{4 \times 2EI}{2} + \frac{4EI}{2} = 6EI$$

$$S_{21} = S_{12} = -\left(\frac{6EI}{L^2}\right)_{BC} = \left(\frac{6EI}{L^2}\right)_{BC} = -\frac{6 \times 2EI}{2^2} + \frac{6EI}{2^2} = -1.5EI$$

$$S_{22} = \left(\frac{12EI}{L^3}\right)_{BA} + \left(\frac{12EI}{L^3}\right)_{BC} = \frac{12 \times 2EI}{2^2} + \frac{12EI}{2^3} = 4.5EI$$

Step V : The equilibrium requirement of force :
There is no applied couple at B.   ∴ $A_{D1} = 0$
There is no applied point load at B. ∴ $A_{D2} = 0$.

Step VI : Superposition equation of equilibrium of forces:

$$\{A_D\} = \{A_{DL}\} + [S]\{D\}$$

i.e.
$$\begin{Bmatrix} 0 \\ 0 \end{Bmatrix} = \begin{Bmatrix} -25 \\ 50 \end{Bmatrix} + EI \begin{bmatrix} 6 & -1.5 \\ -1.5 & 4.5 \end{bmatrix} \begin{Bmatrix} D_1 \\ D_2 \end{Bmatrix}$$

i.e.
$$0 = -25 + (6EI)D_1 - (1.5EI)D_2 \quad \ldots (A)$$
$$0 = 50 - (1.5EI)D_1 + (4.5EI)D_2 \quad \ldots (B)$$

Step VII : Solution of equations for unknown displacements : Solving equations (A) and (B), we get

$$D_1 = \theta_B = \frac{1.52}{EI} = \frac{1.52}{EI} \; (\circlearrowleft)$$

$$D_2 = \Delta_B = \frac{-10.60}{EI} = \frac{10.60}{EI} \; (\downarrow)$$

Step VIII : Other forces :

$$M_{AB} = \frac{4(2EI)}{2}(0) + \frac{2(2EI)}{2}\left(\frac{1.52}{EI}\right) + \left(\frac{6(2EI)}{2^2}\right)\left(\frac{10.60}{EI}\right) + 25$$

$$= 59.83 \text{ kNm}$$

TOS – II (TE CIVIL SEM. VI NMU) FUNDAMENTAL CONCEPT OF STIFFNESS

$$M_{BA} = \frac{4(2EI)}{2}\left(\frac{1.52}{EI}\right) + \frac{2(2EI)}{2}(0) + \frac{6(2EI)}{2^2}\left(\frac{10.60}{EI}\right) - 25$$
$$= 12.86 \text{ kNm}$$
$$M_{BC} = \frac{4EI}{2}\left(\frac{1.52}{EI}\right) + \frac{2EI}{2}(0) - \frac{6EI}{2^2}\left(\frac{10.60}{EI}\right) = -12.86 \text{ kNm}$$
$$M_{CB} = \frac{4EI}{2}(0) + \frac{2EI}{2}\left(\frac{1.52}{EI}\right) - \frac{6EI}{2^2}\left(\frac{10.60}{EI}\right) = -14.39 \text{ kNm}$$

FBD of members is as shown in Fig. 6.10 (e). Considering equilibrium of each member and of complete structure all the reaction components are found out as shown in figure.

Step IX : Shear force and bending moment diagrams: SFD is shown in Fig. 6.10 (f).

BMD by superposition and on tension side is as shown in Fig. 6.10 (g) and 6.10 (h) respectively.

Step X : FBD of structure: as shown in Fig. 6.10 (i).

Step XI : Elastic curve: as shown in Fig. 6.10 (j).

Example 6.9 : *Analyse the frame shown in Fig. 6.11 (a) by stiffness method. Take EI = Constant.*

Solution : Data : The frame is supported and loaded as shown in Fig. 6.11 (a).

Object : Structural analysis.

Concepts and Equations :

(1) Kinematically determinate structure (Restrained structure)
(2) Force analysis of restrained structure.
(3) Superposition equations of equilibrium of forces.

Procedure :

Step I : Degree of kinematic indeterminacy (D_{ki}) :

Degree of kinematic indeterminacy = D_{ki} = 2.

Step II : Unknown joint displacements (D) :

Let, $D_1 = \theta_B$ (↺) and $D_2 = \theta_C$ (↺)

Step III : Restrained structure:

The joints B and C are locked and the restrained structure is obtained as shown in Fig. 6.11 (b). Also restrained structure with unit values of D_1 and D_2 is shown in Fig. 6.11 (c) and 6.11 (d) respectively.

Step IV : Force analysis of restrained structure :

(a) **Fixed End Moments :**

$$M^F_{AB} = -M^F_{BA} = \frac{WL}{8} = \frac{50 \times 4}{8} = 25 \text{ kNm}$$

$$M^F_{BC} = -M^F_{CB} = \frac{wL^2}{12} = \frac{25 \times 3^2}{12} = 18.75 \text{ kNm}$$

Ch. 6 | 6.47

(b) Forces in the restrained structure subjected to loads corresponding to unknown displacements

$$A_{DL1} = M^F_{BA} + M^F_{BC} = -25 + 18.75 = -6.25 \text{ kNm}$$

$$A_{DL2} = M^F_{CB} = -18.75 \text{ kNm}$$

(c) Forces in the restrained structure subjected to unit values of D_1 and D_2 corresponding to unknown displacements.

$$S_{11} = \left(\frac{4EI}{L}\right)_{BA} + \left(\frac{4EI}{L}\right)_{BC} = \frac{4EI}{4} + \frac{4EI}{3} = 2.33 \text{ EI}$$

$$S_{21} = S_{12} = \left(\frac{2EI}{L}\right)_{CB} = \frac{2EI}{3} = 0.67 \text{ EI}$$

$$S_{22} = \left(\frac{4EI}{L}\right)_{CB} = \frac{4EI}{3} = 1.33 \text{ EI}$$

Step V : The equilibrium requirement of force :
There is no applied couple at B and C $\therefore A_{D1} = A_{D2} = 2$.

Step VI : Superposition equation of equilibrium of forces:

$$\{A_D\} = \{A_{DL}\} + [S]\{D\}$$

i.e. $\begin{Bmatrix} 0 \\ 0 \end{Bmatrix} = \begin{Bmatrix} -6.25 \\ -18.75 \end{Bmatrix} + EI \begin{bmatrix} 2.33 & 0.67 \\ 0.67 & 1.33 \end{bmatrix} \begin{Bmatrix} D_1 \\ D_2 \end{Bmatrix}$

i.e.
$$0 = -6.25 + 2.33 \text{ EI}(D_1) + 0.67 \text{ EI}(D_2) \qquad \ldots (A)$$
$$0 = -18.75 + 0.67 \text{ EI}(D_1) + 1.33 \text{ EI}(D_2) \qquad \ldots (B)$$

Step VII : Solution of equations for unknown displacements : Solving equations (A) and (B), we get

$$D_1 = \theta_B = -\frac{1.58}{EI} = \frac{1.58}{EI} \; (\circlearrowright)$$

$$D_2 = \theta_C = \frac{14.84}{EI} = \frac{14.84}{EI} \; (\circlearrowleft)$$

Step VIII : Other forces :

$$M_{AB} = \frac{4EI}{4}(0) + \frac{2EI}{4}\left(\frac{-1.58}{EI}\right) + 25 = 24.18 \text{ kNm}$$

$$M_{BA} = \frac{4EI}{4}\left(\frac{-1.58}{EI}\right) + \frac{2EI}{4}(0) - 25 = -26.58 \text{ kNm}$$

$$M_{BC} = \frac{4EI}{3}\left(\frac{-1.58}{EI}\right) + \frac{2EI}{3}\left(\frac{14.89}{EI}\right) + 18.75 = 26.58 \text{ kNm}$$

$$M_{CB} = \frac{4EI}{3}\left(\frac{14.84}{EI}\right) + \frac{2EI}{3}\left(\frac{-1.53}{EI}\right) - 18.75 = 0 \text{ kNm}$$

FBD of members is as shown in Fig. 6.11 (e).

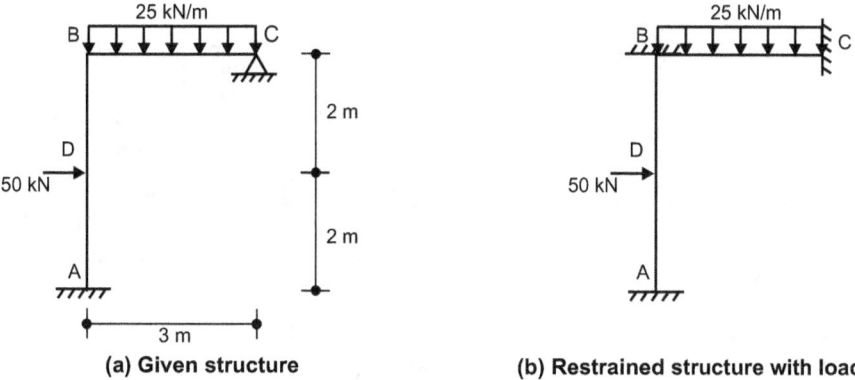

(a) Given structure

(b) Restrained structure with loads

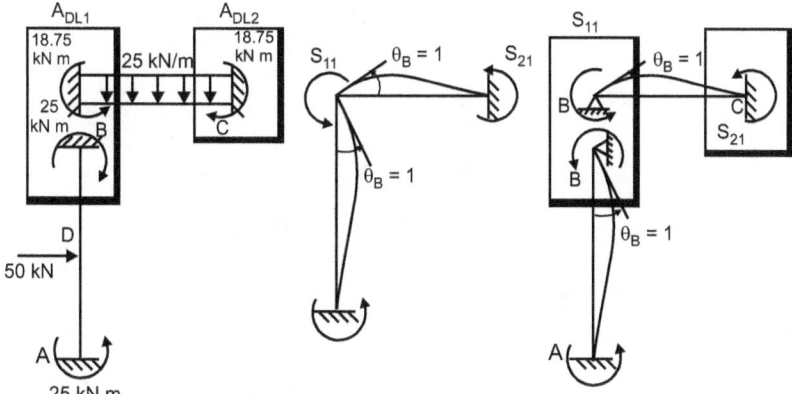

(c) Restrained structure with loads

(d) Restrained structure with $D_1 = 1$

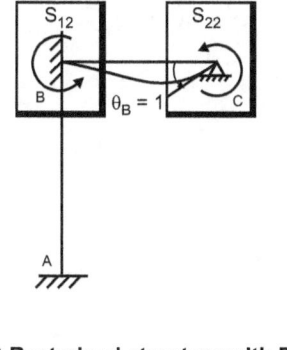

(e) Restrained structure with $D_2 = 1$

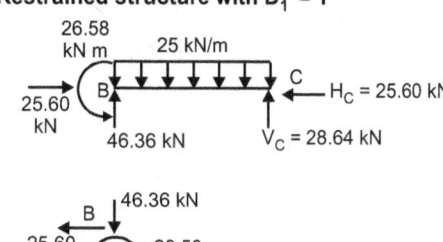

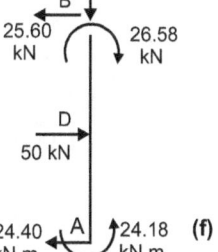

(f) F.B.D. of members

Fig. 6.11 : (Contd.)

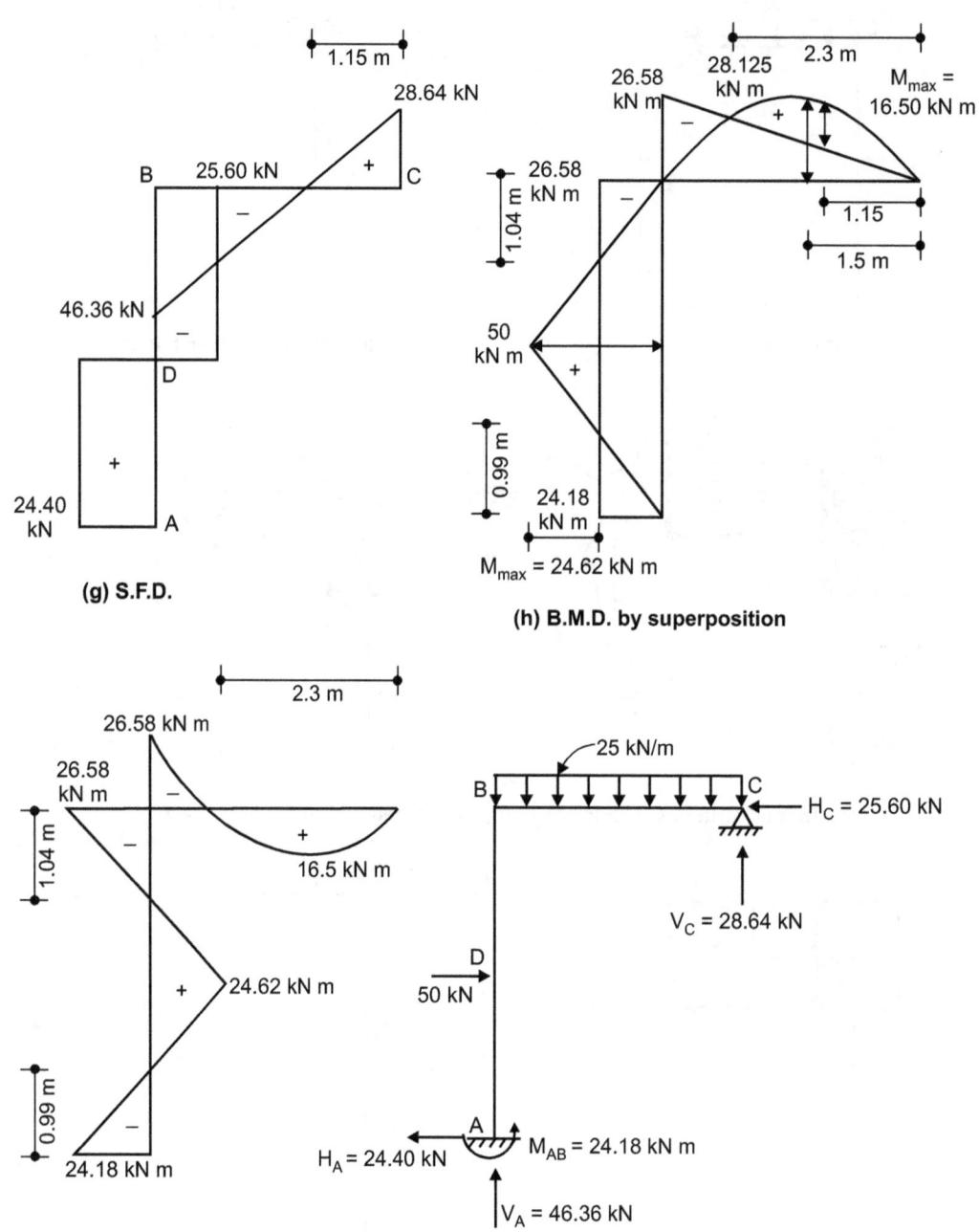

Fig. 6.11 : Illustrative Example 6.9

Considering equilibrium of each member and of complete structure, all the reaction components are found out as shown in figure.

Step IX : Shear force and bending moment diagrams: SFD is as shown in Fig. 6.11 (f).

BMD by superposition and on tension side is as shown in Fig. 6.11 (g) and 6.11 (h) respectively.

Step X : FBD of structure: as shown in Fig. 6.11 (i).

Example 6.10 : *Analyse the frame shown in Fig. 6.12 (a) by stiffness method.*

Solution : Data : The frame is supported and loaded as shown in Fig. 6.12 (a).

Object : Structural analysis.

Concepts and Equations :
(1) Kinematically determinate structure (Restrained structure).
(2) Force analysis of restrained structure.
(3) Superposition equations of equilibrium of forces.

Procedure :

Step I : Degree of kinematic indeterminacy (D_{ki}) :

Degree of kinematic indeterminacy = D_{ki} = 1.

Step II : Unknown joint displacements (D) :

Let, $\quad D_1 = \theta_B$ (↻)

Step III : Restrained structure:

The joint B is locked and the restrained structure is obtained as shown in Fig. 6.12 (b). Also restrained structure with unit value of D_1 is shown in Fig. 6.12 (c).

Step IV : Force analysis of restrained structure :

(a) Fixed end moments:

$$M_{AB}^F = -M_{BA}^F = \frac{WL}{8} = \frac{50 \times 4}{8} = 25 \text{ kNm}$$

$$M_{BC}^F = -M_{CB}^F = \frac{wL^2}{12} = \frac{25 \times 3^2}{12} = 18.75 \text{ kNm}$$

(b) Forces in the restrained structure subjected to loads corresponding to unknown displacements :

$$A_{DL1} = M_{BA}^F + M_{BC}^F = -25 + 18.75 = -6.25 \text{ kNm}$$

(c) Forces in the restrained structure subjected to unit values of D_1 corresponding to unknown displacement.

$$S_{11} = \left(\frac{4(2EI)}{L}\right)_{BA} + \left(\frac{4EI}{L}\right)_{BC} = \frac{8EI}{4} + \frac{4EI}{3} = 3.33 \text{ EI}$$

Step V : The equilibrium requirement of force: There is no applied couple at B

∴ $A_{D1} = 0$.

Step VI : Superposition equation of equilibrium of forces :

$$\{A_D\} = \{A_{DL}\} + [S]\{D\}$$

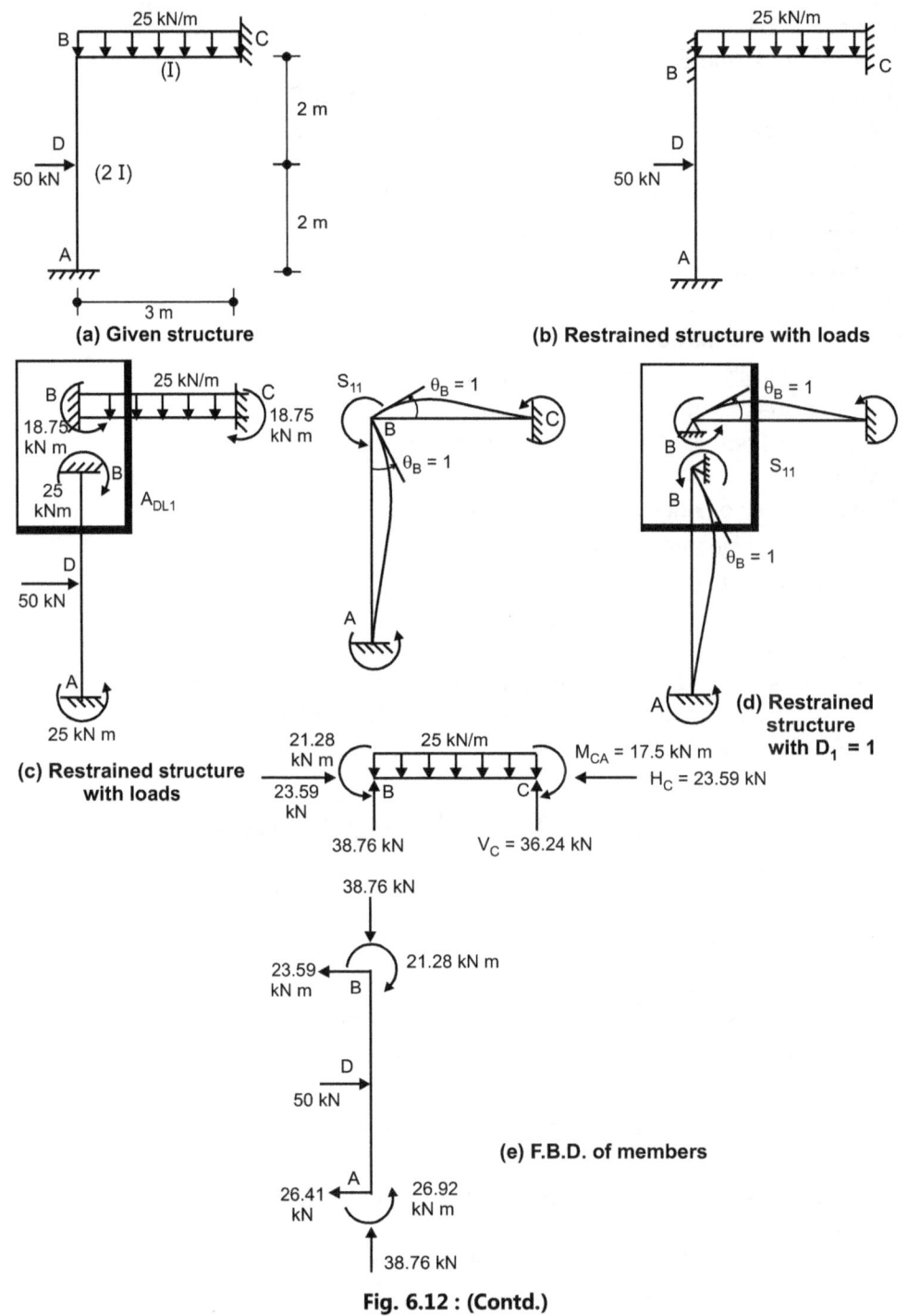

Fig. 6.12 : (Contd.)

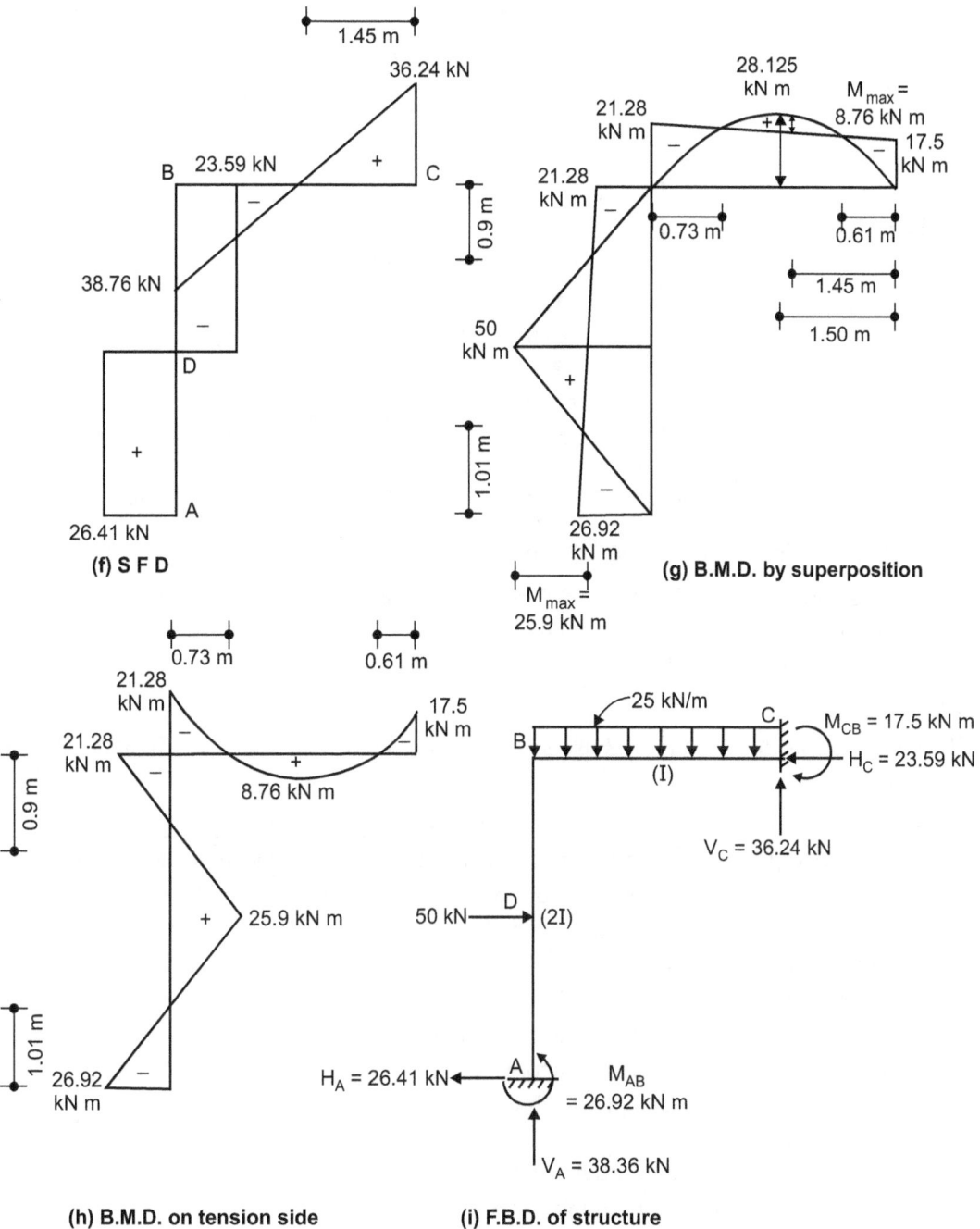

Fig. 6.12 : Illustrative Example 6.10

i.e. $\quad\quad\quad\quad \{0\} = \{-6.25\} + EI\,[3.33]\,[D_1]$

i.e. $\quad\quad\quad\quad 0 = -6.25 + 3.33\,EI\,(D_1)$ ... (A)

Step VII : Solution of equations for unknown displacements : solving equation (A) we get,

$$D_1 = \theta_B = \frac{1.87}{EI} = \frac{1.87}{EI}\,(\circlearrowleft)$$

Step VIII : Other forces:

$$M_{AB} = \frac{4\,(2\,EI)}{4}(0) + \frac{2\,(2\,EI)}{4}\left(\frac{1.87}{EI}\right) + 25 = 26.92\text{ kNm}$$

$$M_{BA} = \frac{4\,(2\,EI)}{4}\left(\frac{1.87}{EI}\right) + \frac{EI}{4}(0) - 25 = -21.28\text{ kNm}$$

$$M_{BC} = \frac{4\,EI}{3}\left(\frac{1.87}{EI}\right) + \frac{2\,EI}{3}(0) + 18.75 = 21.28\text{ kNm}$$

$$M_{CB} = \frac{4\,EI}{3}(0) + \frac{2\,EI}{3}\left(\frac{1.87}{EI}\right) - 18.75 = -17.50\text{ kNm}$$

FBD of members is as shown in Fig. 6.12 (d).

Considering equilibrium of each member and of complete structure all the reaction components are found out as shown in figure.

Step IX : Shear force and bending moment diagrams:

SFD is shown in Fig. 6.12 (e).

BMD by superposition and on tension side is as shown in Fig. 6.12 (f) and 6.12 (g) respectively.

Step X : FBD of structure: as shown in Fig. 6.12 (h).

Example 6.11 : *Analyse the frame shown in Fig. 6.13 (a) by stiffness method.*

Solution : (1) Data : The frame is supported and loaded as shown in Fig. 6.13 (a).

(2) Type of frame: sway frame.

Object : Structural analysis.

Concepts and Equations :

(1) Kinematically determinate structure (Restrained structure).
(2) Force analysis of restrained structure.
(3) Superposition equations of equilibrium of forces.

Procedure :

Step I : Degree of kinematic indeterminacy (D_{ki}) :

Degree of kinematic indeterminacy = D_{ki} = 4.

Step II : Unknown joint displacements (D) :

Let, $\quad D_1 = \theta_B\,(\circlearrowleft),\quad D_2 = \theta_C\,(\circlearrowleft),\quad D_3 = \theta_D\,(\circlearrowleft)$ and $D_4 = \Delta\,(\rightarrow)$

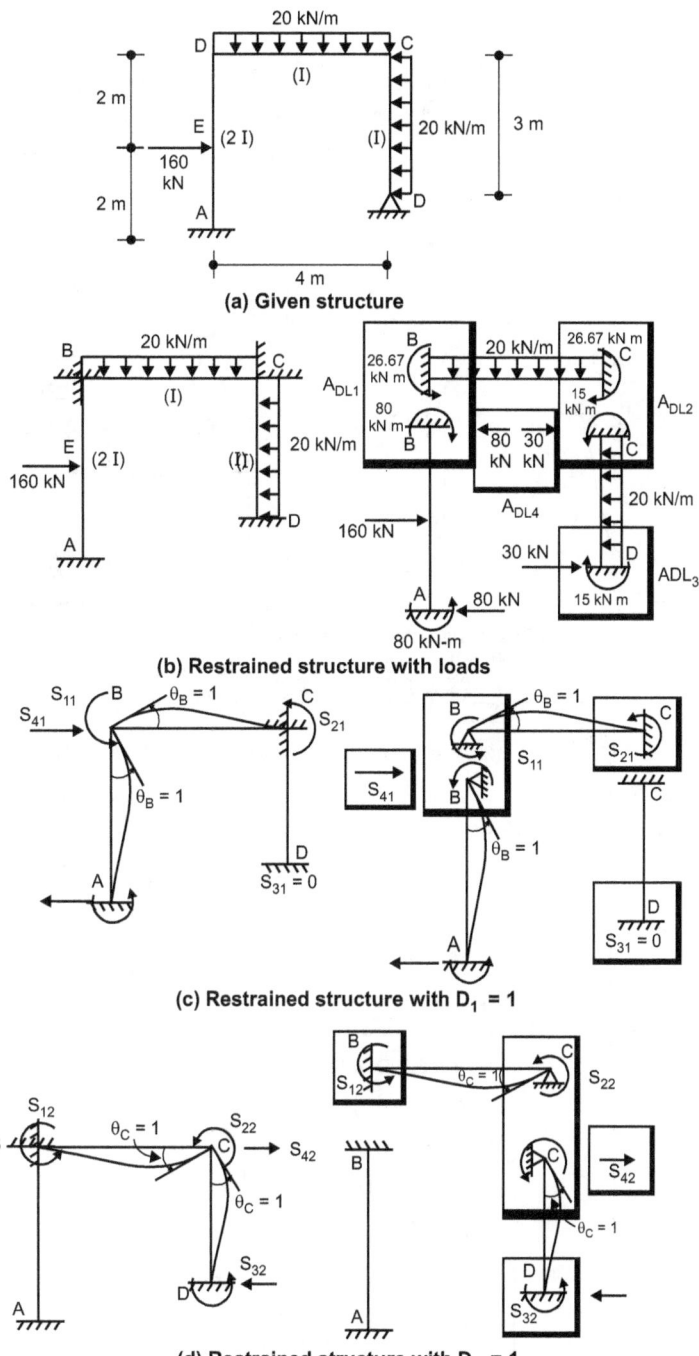

Fig. 6.13 : (Contd.)

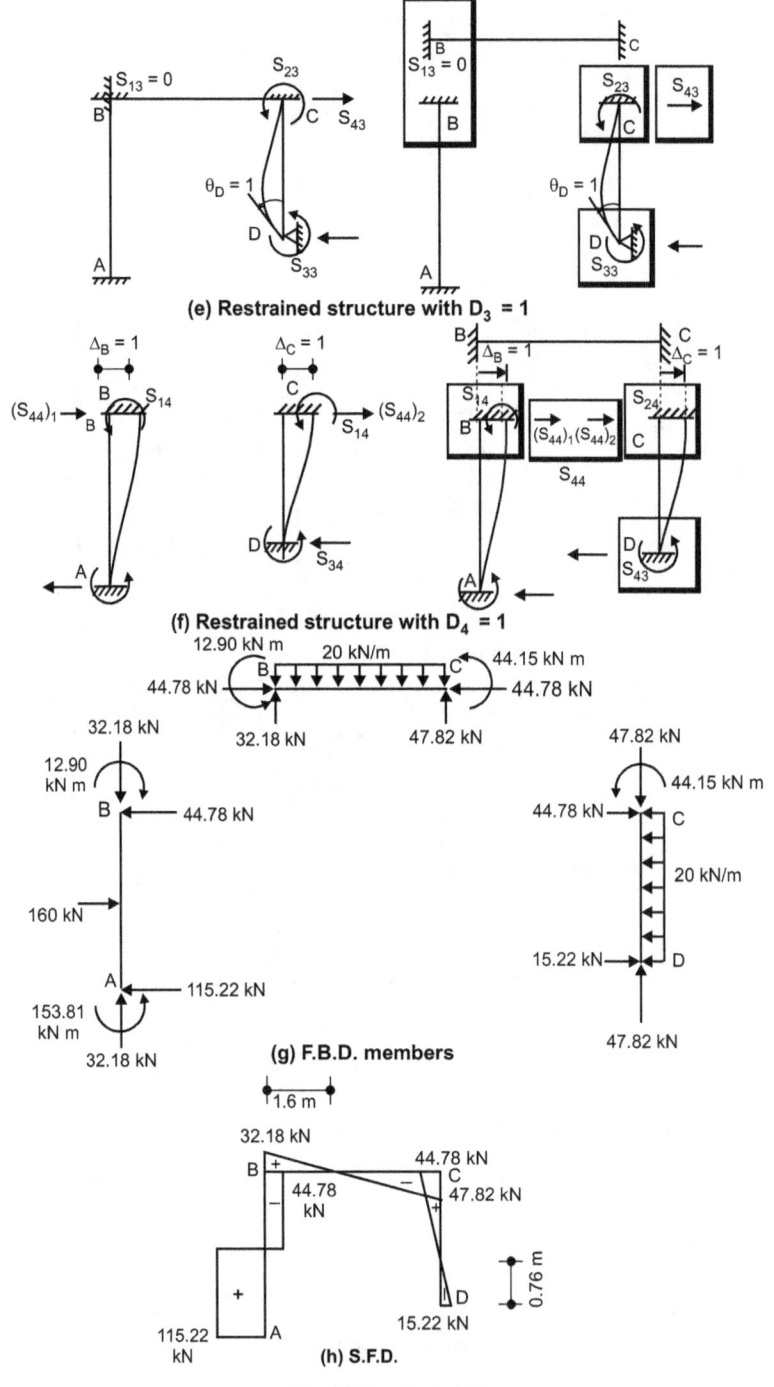

Fig. 6.13 : (Contd.)

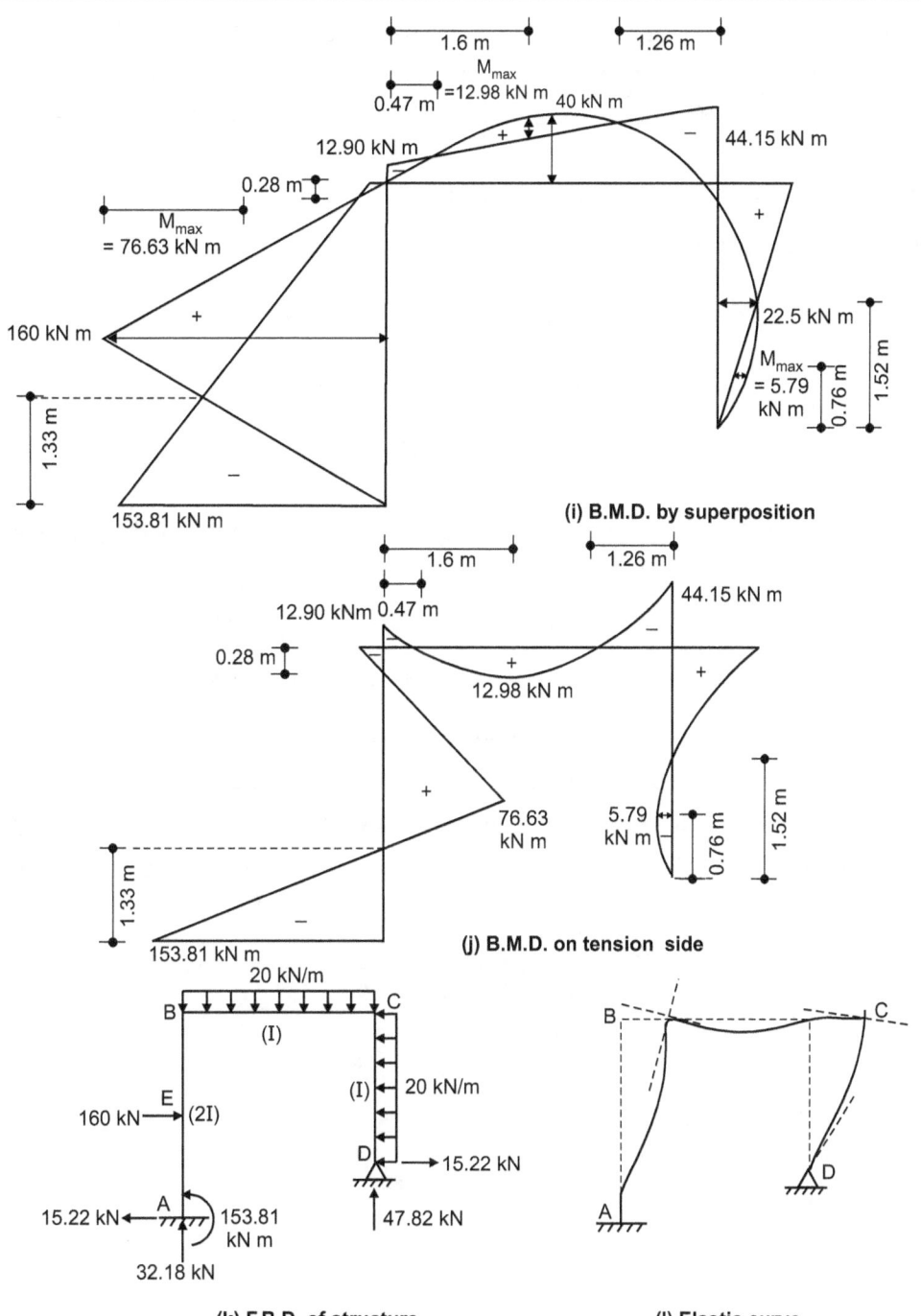

Fig. 6.13 : Illustrative Example 6.11

Step III : Restrained structure : The joints B, C and D are locked and the restrained structure is obtained as shown in Fig. 6.13 (b). Also restrained structure with unit values of D_1, D_2, D_3 and D_4 is shown in Fig. 6.13 (c), Fig. 6.13 (d), Fig. 6.13 (e), and Fig. 6.13 (f) respectively.

Step IV : Force analysis of restrained structure :

(a) **Fixed End Moments :**

$$M_{AB}^F = -M_{BA}^F = \frac{wL}{8} = \frac{160 \times 4}{8} = 80 \text{ kNm}$$

$$M_{BC}^F = -M_{CB}^F = \frac{wL^2}{12} = \frac{20 \times 4^2}{12} = 26.67 \text{ kNm}$$

$$M_{CD}^F = -M_{DC}^F = \frac{wL^2}{12} = \frac{20 \times 3^2}{12} = 15.0 \text{ kNm}$$

(b) Forces in the restrained structure subjected to loads corresponding to unknown displacements.

$$A_{DL1} = M_{BA}^F + M_{BC}^F = -80 + 26.57 = -53.33 \text{ kNm}$$

$$A_{DL2} = M_{CB}^F + M_{CD}^F = -26.67 + 15 = -11.67 \text{ kNm}$$

$$A_{DL3} = M_{DC}^F = -15 \text{ kNm}$$

A_{DL4} = Algebraic sum of horizontal reaction components at B and C in the restrained structure subjected to loads = $-80 + 30 = -50$ kN.

(c) Forces in the restrained structure subjected to unit values of D_1, D_2, D_3 and D_4 corresponding to unknown displacements.

$$S_{11} = \left(\frac{4(2EI)}{L}\right)_{BA} + \left(\frac{4EI}{L}\right)_{BC} = \frac{8EI}{4} + \frac{4EI}{4} = 3EI$$

$$S_{21} = S_{12} = \left(\frac{2EI}{L}\right)_{CB} = \frac{2EI}{4} = 0.5EI$$

$$S_{31} = S_{13} = 0$$

$$S_{41} = S_{14} = \left(\frac{6(2EI)}{L^2}\right)_{AB} = \frac{6(2EI)}{4^2} = 0.75EI$$

$$S_{22} = \left(\frac{4EI}{L}\right)_{CB} + \left(\frac{4(EI)}{L}\right)_{CD} = \frac{4EI}{4} + \frac{4EI}{3}$$

$$= 2.33EI$$

$$S_{32} = S_{23} = \left(\frac{2EI}{L}\right)_{DC} = \frac{2EI}{3} = 0.67\,EI$$

$$S_{42} = S_{24} + \left(\frac{6EI}{L^2}\right)_{CD} = \frac{6EI}{3^2} = 0.67\,EI$$

$$S_{33} = \left(\frac{4EI}{L}\right)_{DC} = \frac{4EI}{3} = 1.33\,EI$$

$$S_{43} = S_{34} = \left(\frac{6EI}{L^2}\right)_{CD} = \frac{6EI}{3^2} = 0.67\,EI$$

$$S_{44} = \left(\frac{12EI}{L^3}\right)_{AB} + \left(\frac{12EI}{L^3}\right)_{CD} = \frac{12(2EI)}{4^3} + \frac{12EI}{3^3} = 0.81\,EI$$

Step V : The equilibrium requirements of force :

There is no applied couple at B, C and D.   ∴ $A_{D1} = A_{D2} = A_{D3} = 0$

Also, there is no applied point load at B or C   ∴ $A_{D4} = 0$

Step VI : Superposition equation of equilibrium of forces:

$$\{A_D\} = \{A_{DL}\} + [S]\{D\}$$

i.e.
$$\begin{Bmatrix} 0 \\ 0 \\ 0 \\ 0 \end{Bmatrix} = \begin{Bmatrix} -53.33 \\ -11.67 \\ -15 \\ -50 \end{Bmatrix} + EI \begin{bmatrix} 3 & 0.5 & 0 & 0.75 \\ 0.5 & 2.33 & 0.67 & 0.67 \\ 0 & 0.67 & 1.33 & 0.67 \\ 0.75 & 0.67 & 0.67 & 0.81 \end{bmatrix} \begin{Bmatrix} D_1 \\ D_2 \\ D_3 \\ D_4 \end{Bmatrix}$$

i.e. $0 = -53.33 + (3\,EI)\,D_1 + (0.5\,EI)\,D_2 + (0)\,D_3 + (0.75\,EI)\,D_4$ ... (A)

$0 = -11.67 + (0.5\,EI)\,D_1 + (2.33\,EI)\,D_2 + (0.67\,EI)\,D_3 + (0.67\,EI)\,D_4$ ... (B)

$0 = -15 + (0)\,D_1 + (0.67\,EI)\,D_2 + (1.33\,EI)\,D_3 + (0.67\,EI)\,D_4$ ... (C)

$0 = -50 + (0.75\,EI)\,D_1 + (0.67\,EI)\,D_2 + (0.67\,EI)\,D_3 + (0.81\,EI)\,D_4$ ... (D)

Step VII : Solution of equations for unknown displacements: Solving equations (A), (B), (C) and (D), we get

$$D_1 = \theta_B = \frac{-6.70}{EI} = \frac{6.70}{EI}\ (\circlearrowleft)$$

$$D_2 = \theta_C = \frac{-14.128}{EI} = \frac{14.128}{EI}\ (\circlearrowleft)$$

$$D_3 = \theta_D = \frac{-35.37}{EI} = \frac{35.37}{EI} \; (\circlearrowleft)$$

$$D_4 = \Delta = \frac{107.35}{EI} = \frac{107.35}{EI} \; (\rightarrow)$$

Step VIII : Other forces :

$$M_{AB} = \frac{4\,(2\,EI)}{4}(0) + \frac{2\,(2\,EI)}{4}\left(\frac{-6.70}{EI}\right) + \frac{6\,(2\,EI)}{4^2}\left(\frac{+107.35}{EI}\right) + 80 = 153.81 \text{ kNm}$$

$$M_{BA} = \frac{4\,(2\,EI)}{4}\left(\frac{-6.70}{EI}\right) + \frac{2\,(2\,EI)}{4}(0) + \frac{6\,(2\,EI)}{4^2}\left(\frac{107.35}{EI}\right) - 80 = -12.90 \text{ kNm}$$

$$M_{BC} = \frac{4\,EI}{4}\left(\frac{-6.70}{EI}\right) + \frac{2\,EI}{4}\left(\frac{-14.128}{EI}\right) + 26.66 = 12.90 \text{ kNm}$$

$$M_{CB} = \frac{4\,EI}{4}\left(\frac{-14.128}{EI}\right) + \frac{2\,EI}{4}\left(\frac{-6.70}{EI}\right) - 26.66 = -44.14 \text{ kNm}$$

$$M_{CD} = \frac{4\,EI}{3}\left(\frac{-14.128}{EI}\right) + \frac{2\,EI}{3}\left(\frac{-35.37}{EI}\right) + \frac{6\,EI}{3^2}\left(\frac{107.35}{EI}\right) + 15 = 44.14 \text{ kNm}$$

$$M_{DC} = \frac{4\,EI}{3}\left(\frac{-35.37}{EI}\right) + \frac{2\,EI}{3}\left(\frac{-14.128}{EI}\right) + \frac{6\,EI}{3^2} - 15 = 0 \text{ kNm}$$

FBD of members is as shown in Fig. 6.13 (g).

Considering equilibrium of each member and of complete structure all the reaction components are found out as shown in figure.

Step IX : Shear force and bending moment diagrams: SFD is shown in Fig. 6.13 (h).

BMD by superposition and on tension side is as shown in Fig. 6.13 (i) and 6.13 (j) respectively.

Step X : FBD of structure: as shown in Fig. 6.13 (k).

Step XI : Elastic curve: as shown in Fig. 6.13 (l).

Example 6.12 : Analyse the frame shown in Fig. 6.14 (a) by stiffness method. Take EI = Constant.

Solution : Data : The frame is supported and loaded as shown in Fig. 6.14 (a).

Object : Structural analysis.

Concepts and Equations :

(1) Kinematically determinate structure (Restrained structure).

(2) Force analysis of restrained structure.

(3) Superposition equations of equilibrium of forces.

Procedure :

Step I : Degree of kinematic indeterminacy (D_{ki}):

Degree of kinematic indeterminacy = D_{ki} = 3.

Step II : Unknown joint displacements (D):

Let, $D_1 = \theta_B$ (↻), $D_2 = \theta_C$ (↻) and $D_3 = \Delta$ (→)

Step III : Restrained structure : The joints B and C are locked and the restrained structure is obtained as shown in Fig. 6.14 (b). Also restrained structure with unit values of D_1, D_2 and D_3 is shown in Fig. 6.14 (c), Fig. 6.14 (d) and Fig. 6.14 (e) respectively.

Step IV: Force analysis of restrained structure :

(a) **Fixed End Moments :**

$$M_{AB}^F = -M_{BA}^F = \frac{wL^2}{12} = \frac{25 \times 4^2}{12} = 33.33 \text{ kNm}$$

$$M_{BC}^F = -M_{CB}^F = \frac{wL}{8} = \frac{50 \times 3}{8} = 18.75 \text{ kNm}$$

$$M_{CD}^F = \frac{Wab^2}{L^2} = \frac{40 \times 2 \times 1^2}{3^2} = 8.88 \text{ kNm}$$

$$M_{DC}^F = -\frac{Wab^2}{L^2} = \frac{40 \times 1 \times 2^2}{3^2} = -17.77 \text{ kNm}$$

(b) Forces in the restrained structure subjected to loads corresponding to unknown displacements :

$$A_{DL1} = M_{BA}^F + M_{BC}^F = -33.33 + 18.75 = -14.58 \text{ kNm}$$

$$A_{DL2} = M_{CB}^F + M_{CD}^F = -18.75 + 8.88 = -9.87 \text{ kNm}$$

A_{DL3} = Algebraic sum of horizontal reaction component at B and C in the restrained structure subjected to loads = $-50 + 10.37 = -39.63$ kN

(c) Forces in the restrained structure subjected to unit values of D_1, D_2 and D_3 corresponding to unknown displacements.

$$S_{11} = \left(\frac{4EI}{L}\right)_{BA} + \left(\frac{4EI}{L}\right)_{BC} = \frac{4EI}{4} + \frac{4EI}{3} = 2.33 \text{ EI}$$

$$S_{21} = S_{12} = \left(\frac{2EI}{L}\right)_{CB} = \frac{2EI}{3} = 0.67\,EI$$

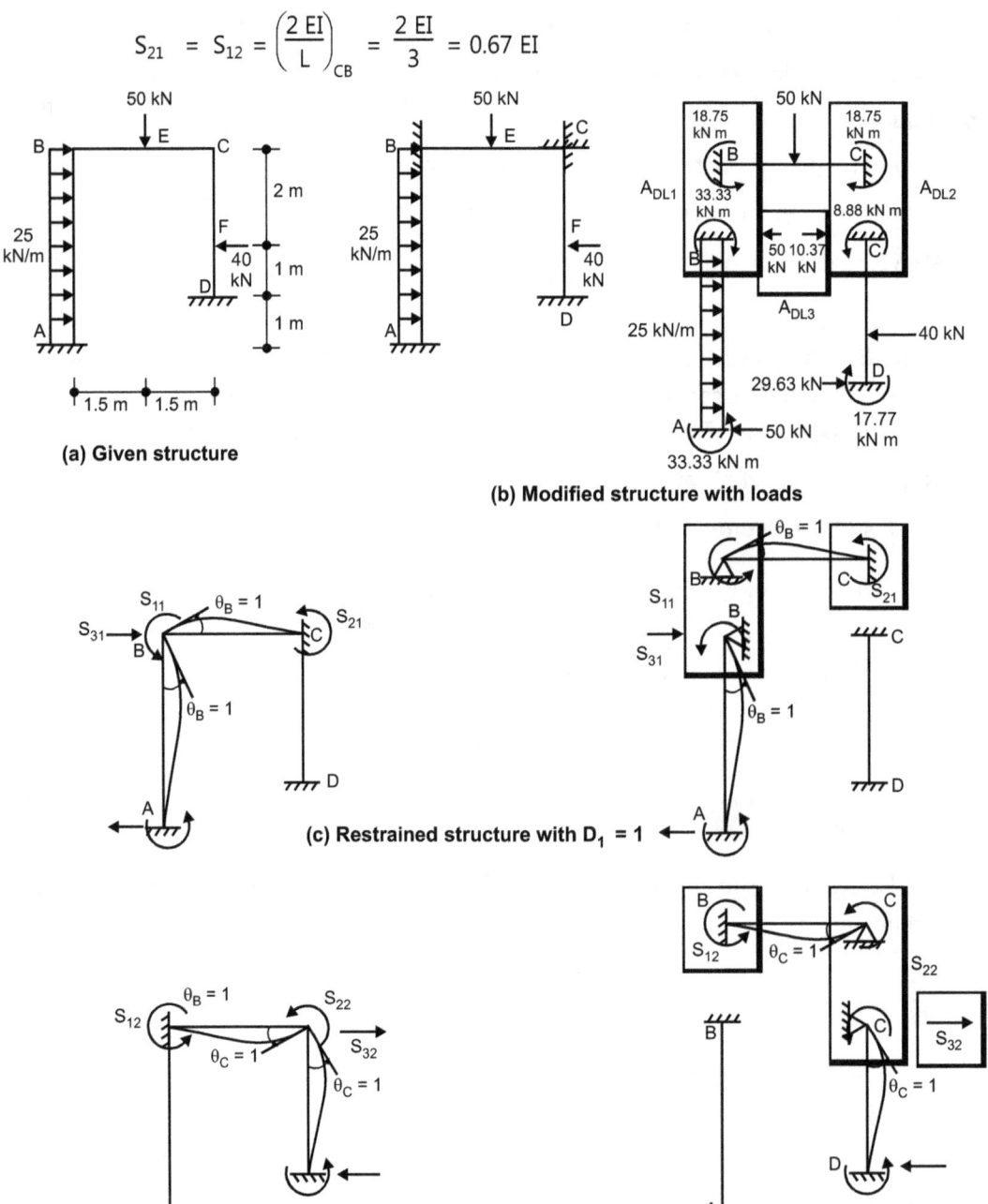

(a) Given structure

(b) Modified structure with loads

(c) Restrained structure with $D_1 = 1$

(d) Restrained structure with $D_2 = 1$

Fig. 6.14 : (Contd.)

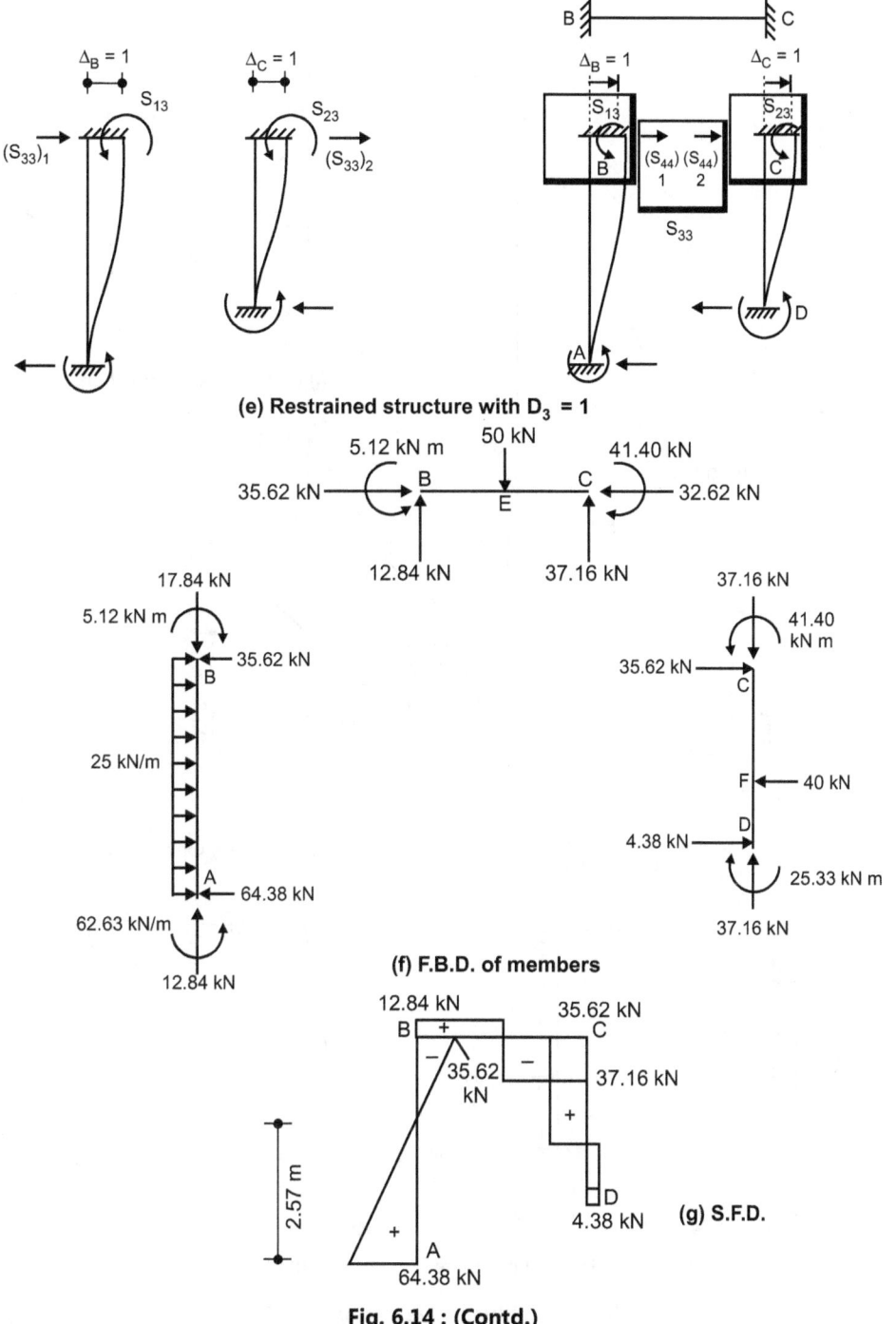

(e) Restrained structure with $D_3 = 1$

(f) F.B.D. of members

(g) S.F.D.

Fig. 6.14 : (Contd.)

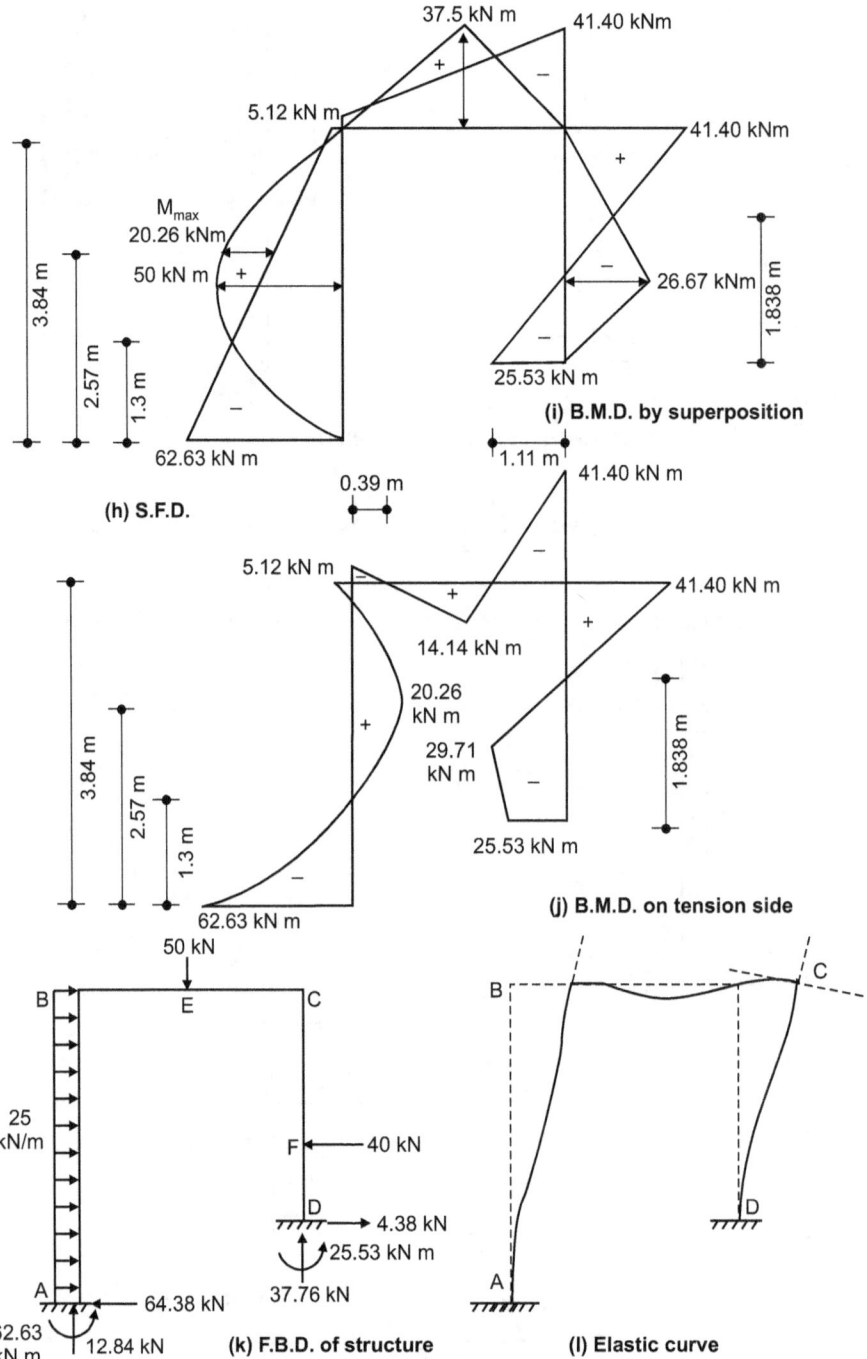

Fig. 6.14 : Illustrative Example 6.12

$$S_{31} = S_{13} = \left(\frac{6EI}{L^2}\right)_{AB} = \frac{6EI}{4^2} = 0.375\,EI$$

$$S_{22} = \left(\frac{4EI}{L}\right)_{CB} + \left(\frac{4EI}{L}\right)_{CD} = \frac{4EI}{3} + \frac{4EI}{3} = 2.67\,EI$$

$$S_{32} = S_{23} = \left(\frac{6EI}{L^2}\right)_{DC} = \frac{6EI}{3^2} = 0.67\,EI$$

$$S_{33} = \left(\frac{12EI}{L^3}\right)_{AB} + \left(\frac{12EI}{L^3}\right) = \frac{12EI}{4^3} + \frac{12EI}{3^3} = 0.63\,EI$$

Step V : The equilibrium requirements of force : There is no applied couple at B and C.

∴ $\quad A_{D1} = A_{D2} = 0$

Also, there is no applied point load at B or C ∴ $A_{D3} = 0$.

Step VI : Superposition equation of equilibrium of forces:

$$\{A_D\} = \{A_{DL}\} + [S]\{D\}$$

i.e.
$$\begin{Bmatrix} 0 \\ 0 \\ 0 \end{Bmatrix} = \begin{Bmatrix} -14.58 \\ -09.87 \\ -39.63 \end{Bmatrix} + EI \begin{bmatrix} 2.33 & 0.67 & 0.375 \\ 0.67 & 2.67 & 0.67 \\ 0.375 & 0.67 & 0.63 \end{bmatrix} \begin{Bmatrix} D_1 \\ D_2 \\ D_3 \end{Bmatrix}$$

i.e.
$0 = -14.58 + (2.33\,EI)\,D_1 + (0.67\,EI)\,D_2 + (0.375\,EI)\,D_3$ ... (A)

$0 = -9.87 + (0.67\,EI)\,D_1 + (2.67\,EI)\,D_2 + (0.67\,EI)\,D_3$ ... (B)

$0 = -39.63 + (0.375\,EI)\,D_1 + (0.67\,EI)\,D_2 + (0.63\,EI)\,D_3$ ...(C)

Step VII : Solution of equations for unknown displacements : Solving equations (A) and (B) and (C), we get

$$D_1 = \theta_B = \frac{-2.18}{EI} = \frac{2.18}{EI}\,(\circlearrowleft)$$

$$D_2 = \theta_C = \frac{-16.08}{EI} = \frac{16.08}{E}\,(\circlearrowleft)$$

$$D_3 = \Delta = \frac{81.04}{EI} = \frac{81.04}{EI}\,(\rightarrow)$$

Step VIII : Other forces :

$$M_{AB} = \frac{4EI}{4}(0) + \frac{2EI}{4}\left(\frac{-2.18}{EI}\right) + \frac{6EI}{4^2}\left(\frac{81.04}{EI}\right) + 33.33 = 62.63\,\text{kNm}$$

$$M_{BA} = \frac{4EI}{4}\left(\frac{-2.18}{EI}\right) + \frac{2EI}{4}(0) + \frac{6EI}{4^2}\left(\frac{81.04}{EI}\right) - 33.33 = -5.12\,\text{kNm}$$

$$M_{BC} = \frac{4EI}{3}\left(\frac{-2.18}{EI}\right) + \frac{2EI}{3}\left(\frac{-16.08}{EI}\right) + 18.75 = 5.12 \text{ kNm}$$

$$M_{CB} = \frac{4EI}{3}\left(\frac{-16.08}{E}\right) + \frac{2EI}{3}\left(-\frac{2.18}{EI}\right) - 18.75 = -41.40 \text{ kNm}$$

$$M_{CD} = \frac{4EI}{3}\left(-\frac{16.08}{EI}\right) + \frac{2EI}{3}(0) + \frac{6EI}{3^2}\left(\frac{81.04}{EI}\right) - 17.77 = 41.40 \text{ kNm}$$

$$M_{DC} = \frac{4EI}{3}(0) + \frac{2EI}{3}\left(\frac{-16.08}{EI}\right) + \frac{6EI}{3^2}\left(\frac{81.04}{EI}\right) + 8.88 = 25.53 \text{ kNm}$$

FBD of members is as shown in Fig. 6.14 (f). Considering equilibrium of each member and of complete structure all the reaction components are found out as shown in figure.

Step IX : Shear force and bending moment diagrams:

SFD is shown in Fig. 6.14 (g). BMD by superposition and on tension side is as shown in Fig. 6.14 (h) and (6.14) (i) respectively.

Step X : FBD of structure: as shown in Fig. 6.14 (j).

Step XI : Elastic curve: as shown in Fig. 6.14 (k).

Example 6.13 : *Analyse the portal frame as shown in Fig. 6.15 by stiffness method. Take EI = constant.*

Solution : Data : The frame is loaded and supported as shown in Fig. 6.15 (a)

Object: Structural analysis.

Concepts and Equations :

(1) Kinematically determinate structure. (Restrained structure).

(2) Force analysis of restrained structure.

(3) Superposition equations of equilibrium of forces.

Procedure: Step I : Degree of kinematic indeterminacy (D_{ki}) :

Degree of kinematic indeterminacy = D_{ki} = 2.

Step II : Unknown joint displacements (D) :

$D_1 = \theta_C$ (↺) and $D_2 = \theta_C$ (↺), $D_3 = \delta_C$ (→)

Step III : Restrained Structure : The joints B and C are locked and the restrained structure is obtained as shown in Fig. 6.15 (b). Also restrained structure with unit values of D_1, D_2 and D_3 is as shown in Fig. 6.15 (c), (d) respectively.

Step IV : Force analysis of restrained structure.

(a) Fixed End Moments :

$$M^F_{AB} = -M^F_{BA} = \frac{wL^2}{12} = \frac{20 \times 4.8^2}{12} = 38.4 \text{ kNm}$$

$$M^F_{BC} = -M^F_{CB} = 0$$

(b) Forces in the Restrained Structure Subjected to Loads Corresponding to Unknown Displacements :

$$A_{DL1} = M_{FBA} + M_{FBC} = -38.4 + 0$$
$$= -38.4 \text{ kN-m}$$

$$A_{DL2} = M_{FCB} = 0$$

A_{DL3} = Algebric sum of horizontal reaction components at B and C respectively in the restrained structure subjected to loads.

$$= -48 \text{ kN}$$

(c) Forces in the Restrained Structure Subjected to unit Values of D_1, D_2 and D_3 Corresponding to Unknown Displacements :

$$S_{11} = \left(\frac{4EI}{L}\right)_{BA} + \left(\frac{4(2EI)}{L}\right)_{BC} = \frac{4EI}{4.8} + \frac{8EI}{2.4}$$

$$= 0.83 \text{ EI} + 3.33 \text{ EI} = 4.16 \text{ EI}$$

$$S_{21} = S_{12} = \left(\frac{2(2EI)}{L}\right)_{CB} = \frac{4EI}{2.4} = 1.67 \text{ EI}$$

$$S_{31} = S_{13} = \left(\frac{6 EI}{L^2}\right)_{AB} = \frac{6EI}{(4.8)^2} = 0.26$$

$$S_{22} = \left(\frac{4(2EI)}{L}\right)_{CB} = \frac{8EI}{2.4} = 3.33 \text{ EI}$$

$$S_{23} = S_{32} = 0$$

$$S_{33} = \left(\frac{12(EI)}{L^3}\right)_{AB} = \frac{12EI}{(4.8)^3} = 0.11 \text{ EI}$$

Step V : The Equilibrium Requirement of Force :

There is no applied couple at B and C. $A_{D1} = A_{D2} = 0$, there is no applied point load at B.

$$\therefore \quad A_{D3} = 0$$

Step VI : Superposition Equation of Equilibrium of Forces :

$$\{A_D\} = \{A_{DL}\} + [S]\{D\}$$

$$\left\{\begin{array}{c}0\\0\\0\end{array}\right\} = \left\{\begin{array}{c}-38.4\\0\\-48\end{array}\right\} + EI\left[\begin{array}{ccc}4.16 & 1.67 & 0.26\\1.67 & 3.33 & 0\\0.26 & 0 & 0.11\end{array}\right]\left\{\begin{array}{c}D_1\\D_2\\D_3\end{array}\right\}$$

i.e.
$$0 = -38.4 + (4.16\,EI)\,D_1 + (1.67\,EI)\,D_2 + (0.26\,EI)\,D_3 \quad ...(A)$$
$$0 = 0 + (1.67\,EI)\,D_1 + (3.33\,EI)\,D_2 + (0\,EI)\,D_3 \quad ...(B)$$
$$0 = -48 + (0.26\,EI)\,D_1 + (0\,EI)\,D_2 + (0.11\,EI)\,D_3 \quad ...(C)$$

Step VII : Solution of Equations for Unknown Displacements : Solving equations (A), (B) and (C) we get,

$$D_1 = \theta_B = -\frac{28.35}{EI} = \frac{28.35}{EI} \;(\circlearrowleft)$$

$$D_2 = \theta_C = \frac{14.18}{EI} \;(\circlearrowleft)$$

$$D_3 = \delta_C = \frac{510.42}{EI} \;(\rightarrow)$$

Step VIII : Other Forces :

$$M_{AB} = \frac{4\,EI}{4.8}(0) + \frac{2EI}{4.8}\left(\frac{-28.61}{EI}\right) + \frac{6EI}{(4.8)^2}\left(\frac{510.42}{EI}\right) + 38.4$$
$$= 159.50 \text{ kN-m}$$

$$M_{BA} = \frac{4EI\,(-28.35)}{4.8\,EI} + \frac{2EI\,(0)}{4.8} + \frac{6EI}{(4.8)^2}\left(\frac{510.42}{EI}\right) - 38.4$$
$$= 709 \text{ kN-m}$$

$$M_{BC} = \frac{4\,(2EI)(-28.35)}{2.4\,EI} + \frac{2\,(2EI)}{2.4}\left(\frac{14.18}{EI}\right) = 0$$
$$= -70.90 \text{ kNm}$$

$$M_{CB} = \frac{2\,(2EI)}{2.4}\frac{(-28.35)}{EI} + \frac{4\,(2EI)}{2.4}\left(\frac{14.18}{EI}\right) = 0$$

FBD of members is an shown in Fig. 6.15.

Considering equilibrium of each member and of complete structure all the reaction components are found out as shown in Fig. 6.15.

Step IX : Shear force and bending moment diagrams.

SFD is as shown in Fig. 6.15 (g).

BMD by superposition and on tension side is as shown in Fig. 6.15 (h) and Fig. 6.15 (i) respectively.

Step X : FBD of structure is as shown in Fig. 6.15 (j).

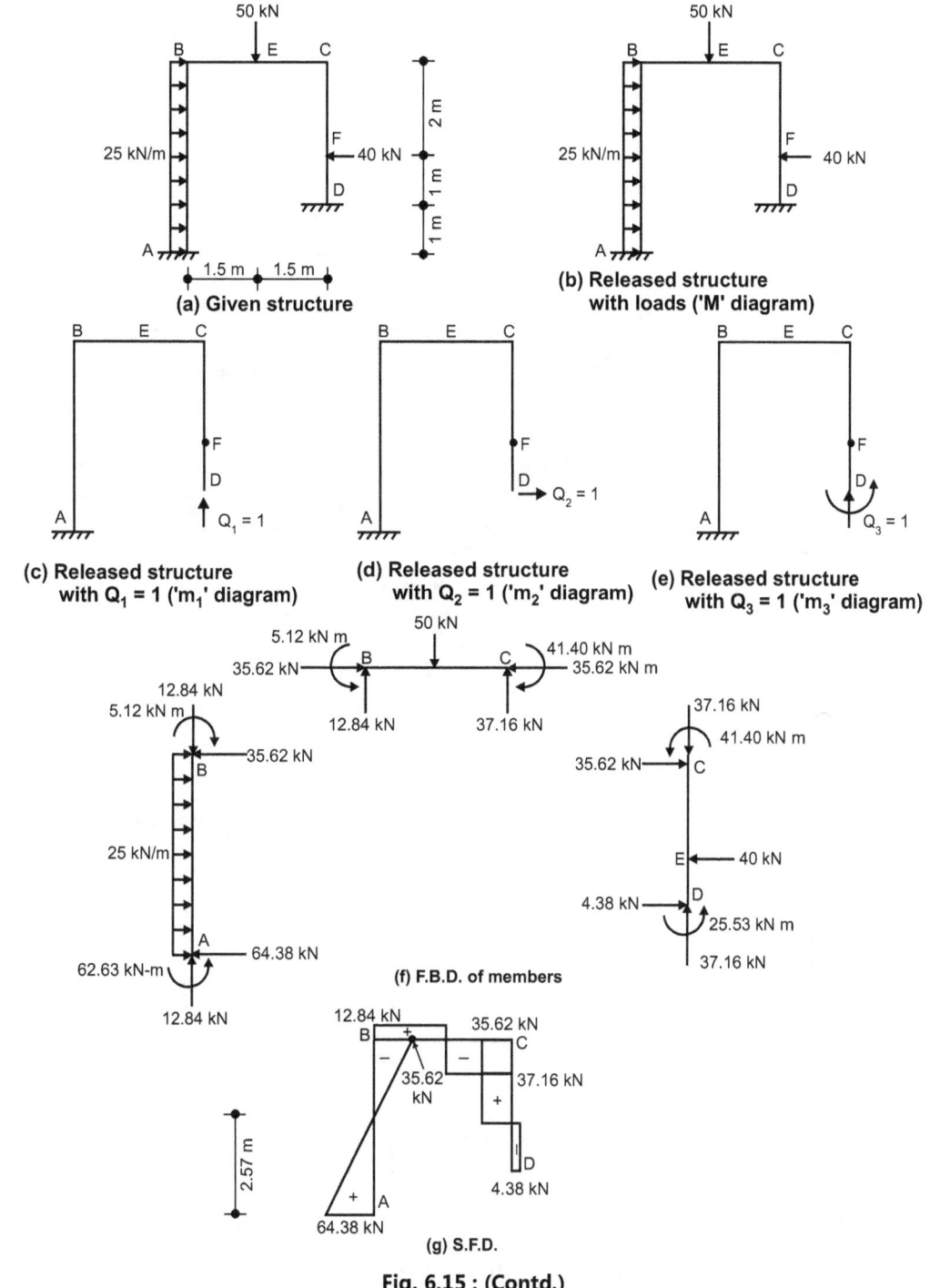

Fig. 6.15 : (Contd.)

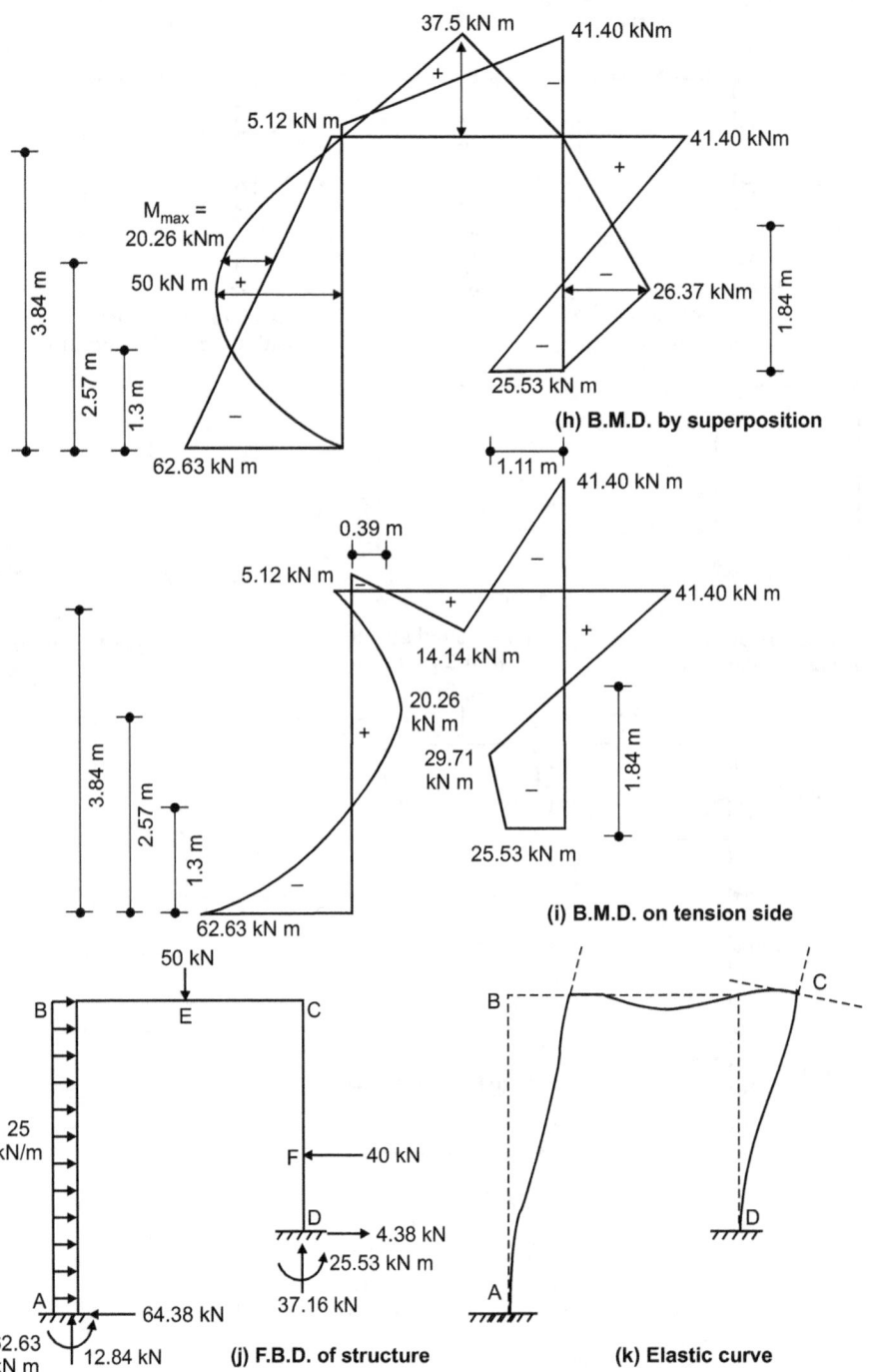

Fig. 6.15 : Illustrative Example 6.13

6.6 COMPARISON BETWEEN FLEXIBILITY AND STIFFNESS METHODS

The two methods of structural analysis show striking similarities with respect to the parallel steps in the procedure of solution of a problem. Yet there are also striking differences in the two approaches. The brief comparison between the two methods, given below, clarifies the logic and technique.

Table 6.1

	Flexibility Method		Stiffness Method
1.	Degree of static indeterminacy.	1.	Degree of kinematic indeterminacy.
2.	Unknown redundant forces {Q}.	2.	Unknown joint displacements {D}.
3.	Static admissibility.	3.	Kinematic admissibility.
4.	Equilibrium indirectly satisfied.	4.	Compatibility indirectly satisfied.
5.	Known joint displacement corresponding to $\{Q\} = \{D_Q\}$.	5.	Known joint forces corresponding to $D = \{A_D\}$.
6.	Statically determinate structure (SD) i.e. released structure.	6.	Kinematically determinate (KD) structure i.e. restrained structure.
7.	Displacement analysis of SD structure under given loads corresponding to $\{Q\} = \{D_{QL}\}$.	7.	Force analysis of KS structure under given loads corresponding to $\{D\} = \{A_{DL}\}$.
8.	Flexibility coefficient F_{ij} displacement at i due to unit force at j.	8.	Stiffness coefficients – S_{ij} force at i due to unit displacement at j.
9.	Flexibility matrix of the structure [F].	9.	Stiffness matrix of the structure [S].
10.	Superposition equations in terms of displacements as per compatibility conditions of joints.	10.	Superposition equations in terms of forces as per equilibrium conditions of joints.
11.	Linear simultaneous equations $\{D_Q\} = \{D_{QL}\} + [F]\{Q\}$.	11.	Linear simultaneous equations $\{A_D\} = \{A_{DL}\} + [S]\{Q\}$.
12.	Solution of equations for unknown redundant forces.	12.	Solution of equations for unknown joint displacement.
13.	Choice of {Q} is not unique.	13.	Choice of {D} is unique.
14.	Displacement analysis of SD structure is not simple with respect to $\{D_{QL}\}$ and [F].	14.	Force analysis of KD structure is simple with respect to $\{A_{DL}\}$ and [S].
15.	More physics.	15.	More mechanical.
16.	Not well disciplined.	16.	Very well disciplined.
17.	Not suitable to computer programming.	17.	Very much suitable to computer programming.
18.	Complex in case of analysis of continuum.	18.	Well extended to analysis of continuum.

EXERCISE

Analyse the following beams and frames using Flexibility matrix, Stiffness matrix, Slope Deflection, Moment distribution and Energy methods. Draw SFD, BMD and elastic curve.

1.

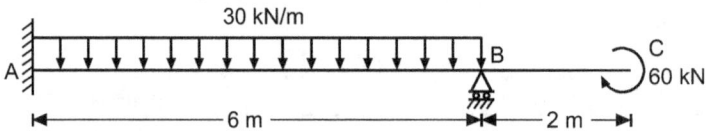

Fig. 6.16

(**Ans.** $M_A = -105$ kNm; $M_B = -60$ kNm)

2.

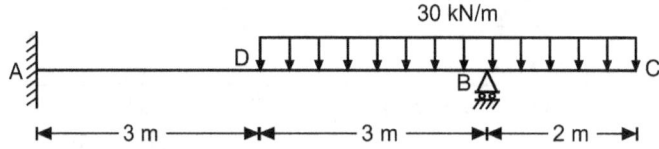

Fig. 6.17

(**Ans.** $M_A = -29.04$ kNm; $M_B = -60$ kNm)

3.

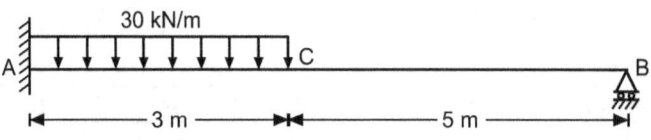

Fig. 6.18

(**Ans.** $M_A = -89.16$ kNm; $M_B = 0$)

4.

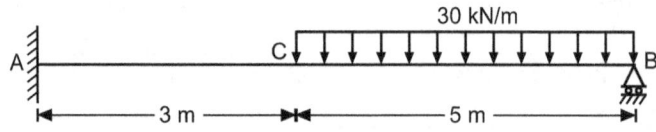

Fig. 6.19

(**Ans.** $M_A = -150.5$ kNm; $M_B = 0$)

5.

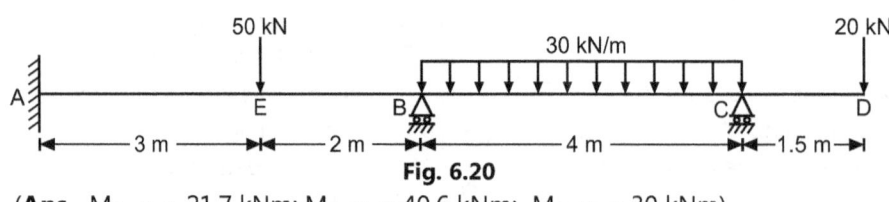

Fig. 6.20

(**Ans.** $M_A = -21.7$ kNm; $M_B = -40.6$ kNm; $M_C = -30$ kNm)

6.

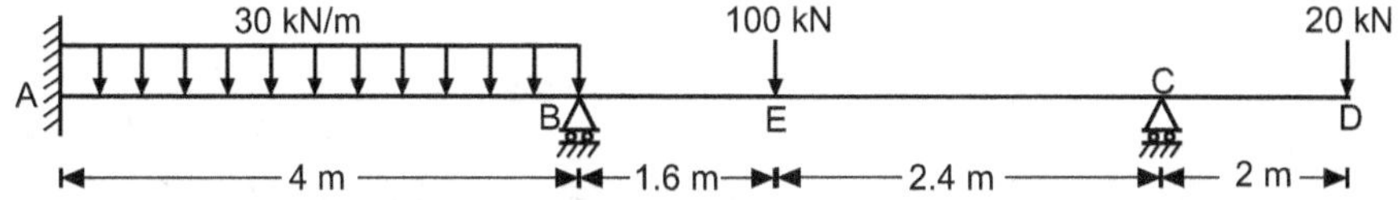

Fig. 6.21

(**Ans.** $M_A = -37.2$ kNm; $M_B = -49.6$ kNm; $M_C = -40$ kNm)

7.

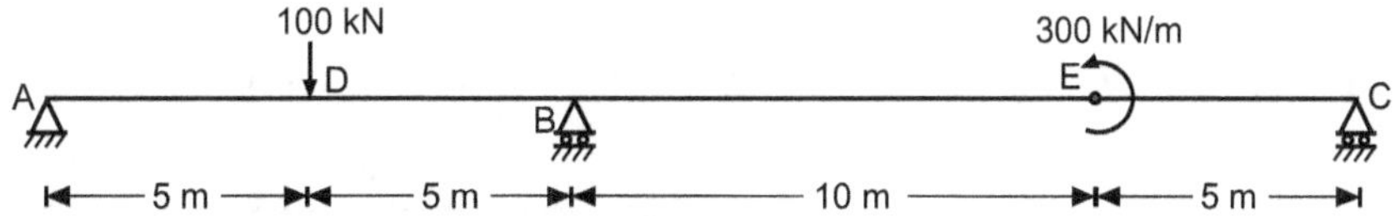

Fig. 6.22

(**Ans.** $M_A = M_C = 0$; $M_B = -135$ kNm)

8.

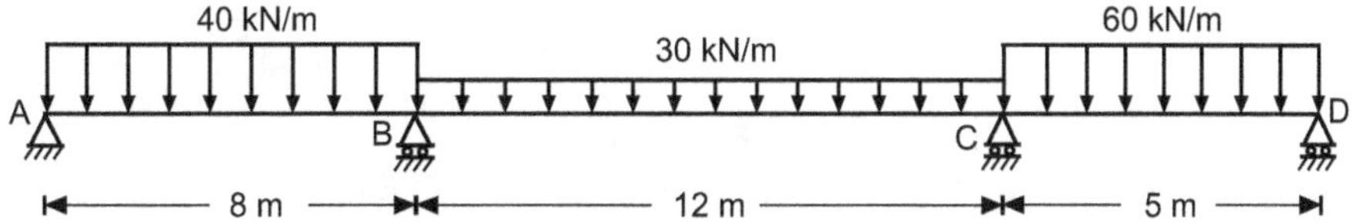

Fig. 6.23

(**Ans.** $M_A = M_D = 0$; $M_B = -359$ kNm; $M_C = -309.6$ kNm)

9.

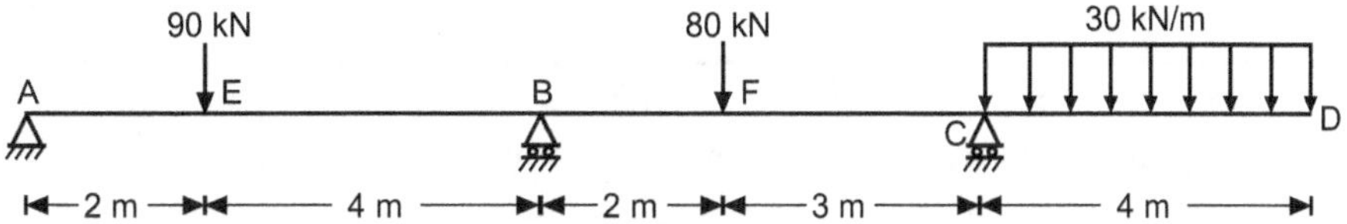

Fig. 6.24

(**Ans.** $M_A = M_D = 0$; $M_B = -68.4$ kNm; $M_C = -44.8$ kNm)

10.

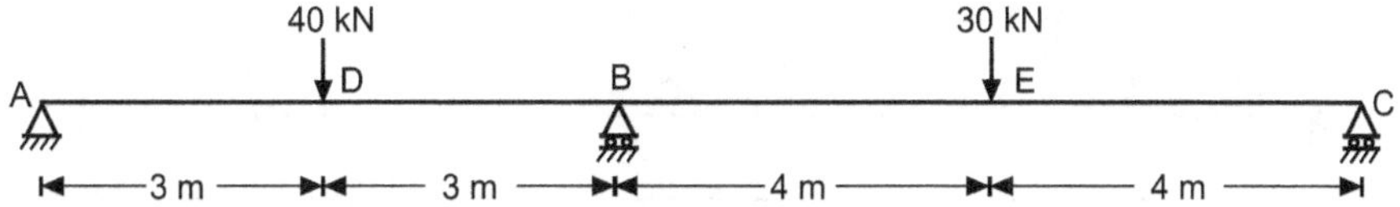

Fig. 6.25

(**Ans.** $M_A = M_C = 0$; $M_B = -45$ kNm)

11.

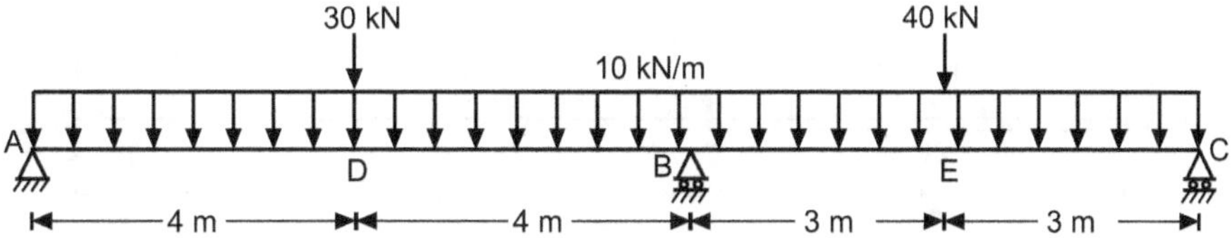

Fig. 6.26

(**Ans.** $M_A = M_C = 0$; $M_B = -110$ kNm)

12.

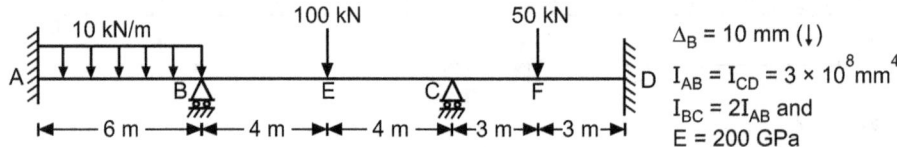

Fig. 6.27

(**Ans.** $M_A = -57.4$ kNm; $M_B = -25.7$ kNm, $M_C = -92$ kNm; $M_D = -20.7$ kNm)

13.

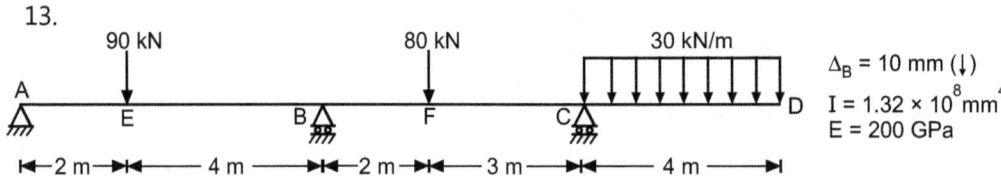

Fig. 6.28

(**Ans.** $M_A = M_D = 0$; $M_B = -35.87$ kNm, $M_C = -71.56$ kNm)

14.

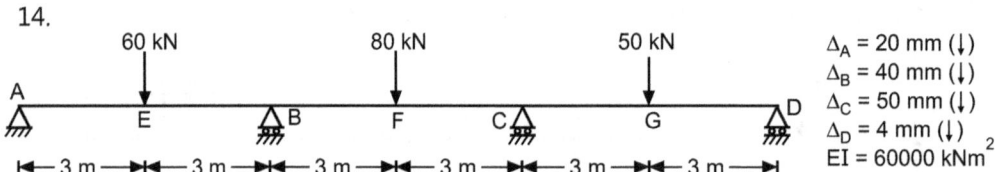

Fig. 6.29

(**Ans.** $M_A = M_D = 0$; $M_B = -68.5$ kNm, $M_C = 59$ kNm)

15.

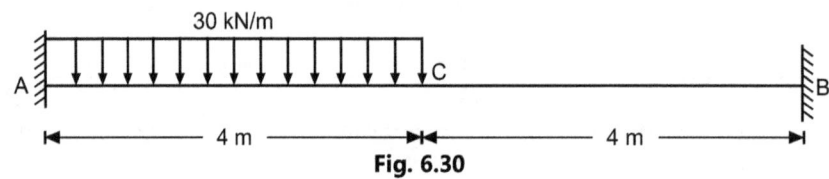

Fig. 6.30

(**Ans.** $M_A = -60$ kNm; $M_B = -180$ kNm; $M_C = 0$)

16.

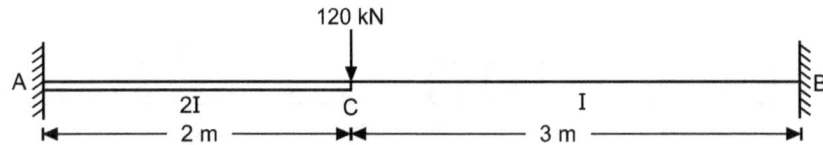

Fig. 6.31

(**Ans.** $M_A = -105.22$ kNm; $M_B = -47.45$ kNm)

17.

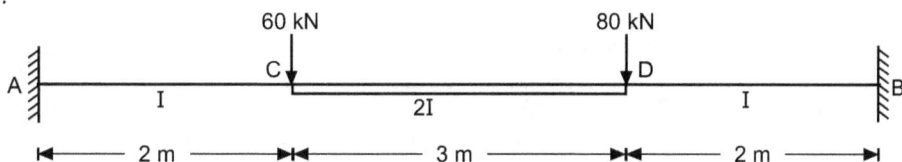

Fig. 6.32

(**Ans.** $M_A = -79.49$ kNm; $M_B = -98.68$ kNm)

18.

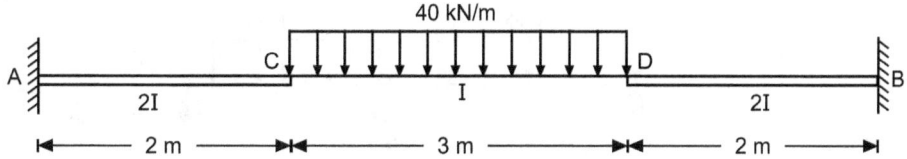

Fig. 6.33

(**Ans.** $M_A = M_B = -114$ kNm)

19.

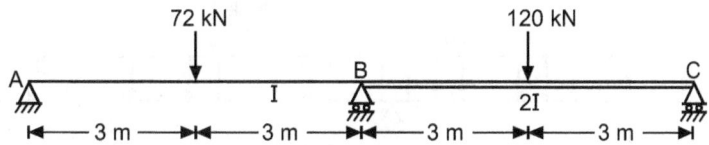

Fig. 6.34

(**Ans.** $M_B = -99$ kNm)

20.

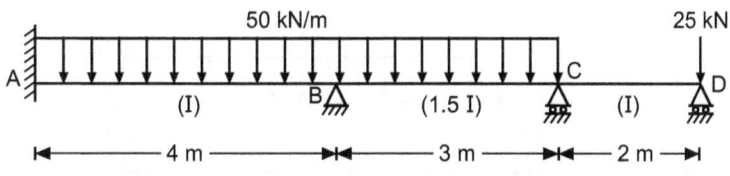

Fig. 6.35

(**Ans.** $M_A = -53.75$ kNm; $M_B = -52.5$ kNm; $M_C = -50$ kNm)

21.

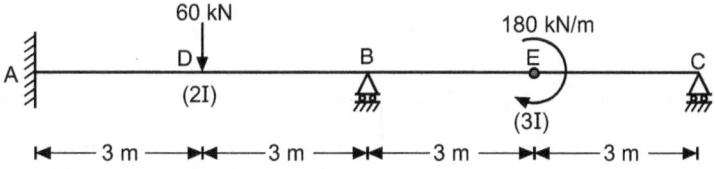

Fig. 6.36

(**Ans.** $M_A = -60.88$ kNm; $M_B = -13.24$ kNm; $M_C = 50$ kNm)

22.

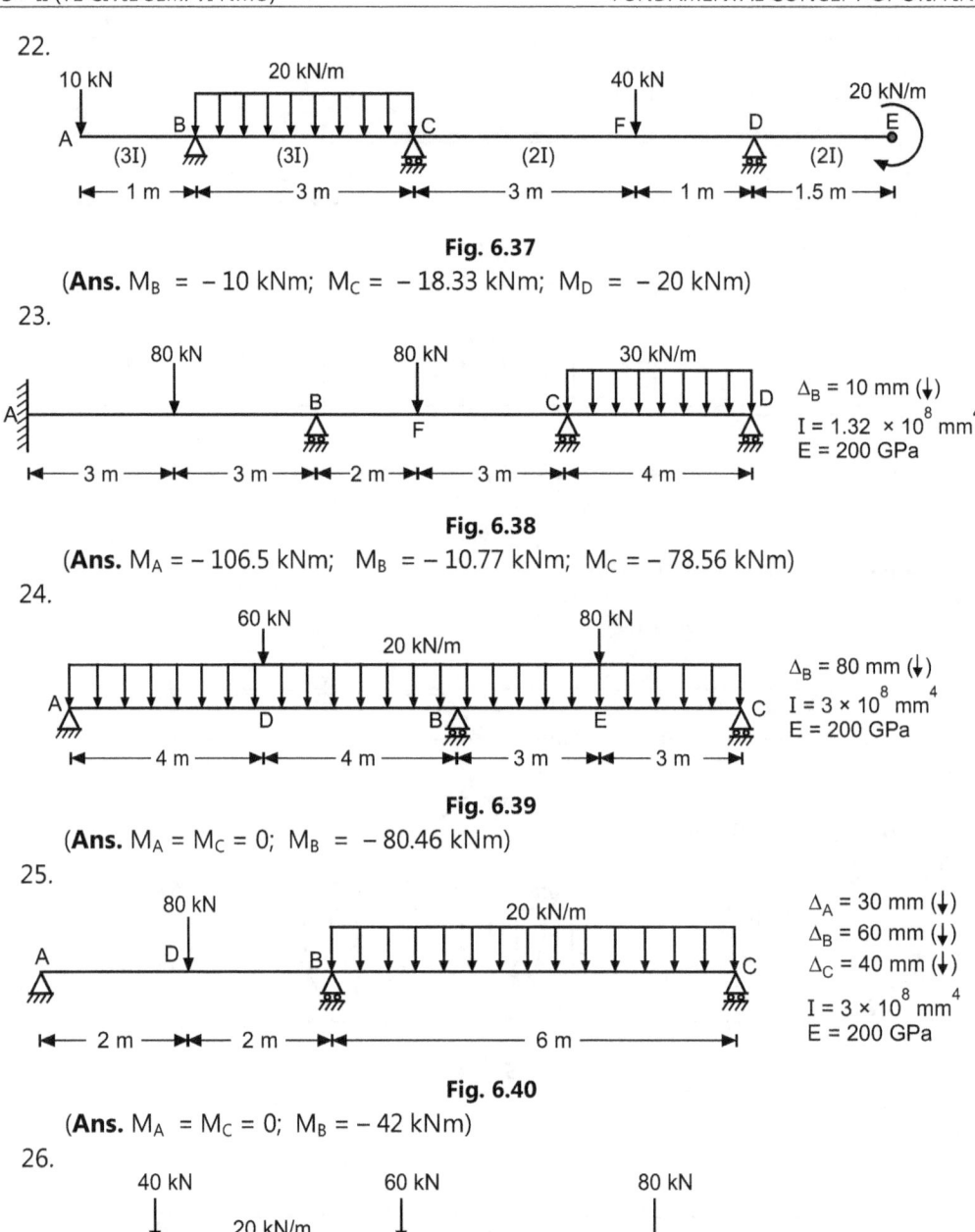

Fig. 6.37

(**Ans.** $M_B = -10$ kNm; $M_C = -18.33$ kNm; $M_D = -20$ kNm)

23.

Fig. 6.38

(**Ans.** $M_A = -106.5$ kNm; $M_B = -10.77$ kNm; $M_C = -78.56$ kNm)

24.

Fig. 6.39

(**Ans.** $M_A = M_C = 0$; $M_B = -80.46$ kNm)

25.

Fig. 6.40

(**Ans.** $M_A = M_C = 0$; $M_B = -42$ kNm)

26.

Fig. 6.41

(**Ans.** $M_A = M_D = 0$; $M_B = -203$ kNm; $M_C = +227$ kNm)

27.

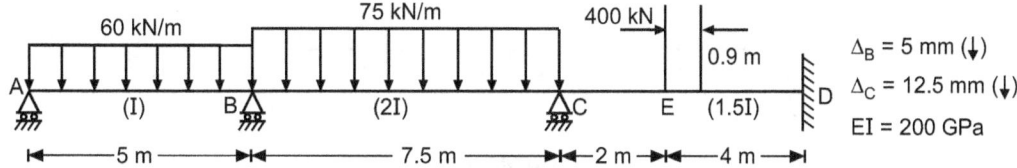

Fig. 6.42

(**Ans.** $M_A = 0$; $M_B = -226.1$ kNm; $M_C = -191.7$ kNm; $M_D = -42$ kNm)

28.

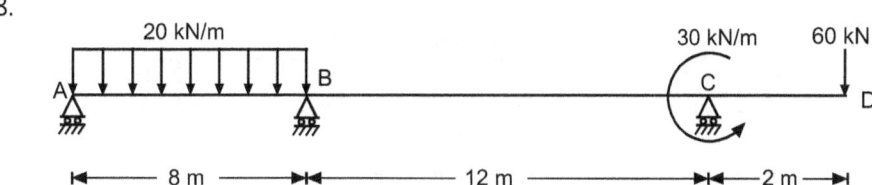

Fig. 6.43

(**Ans.** $M_A = -157$ kNm; $M_B = -5$ kNm; $M_{CD} = 120$ kNm; $M_{CB} = 90$ kNm)

29.

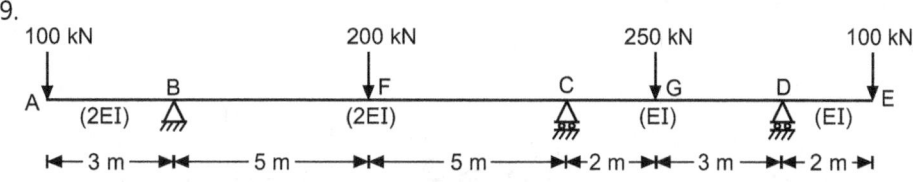

Fig. 6.44

(**Ans.** $M_B = -300$ kNm; $M_C = -182$ kNm; $M_D = -200$ kNm)

30.

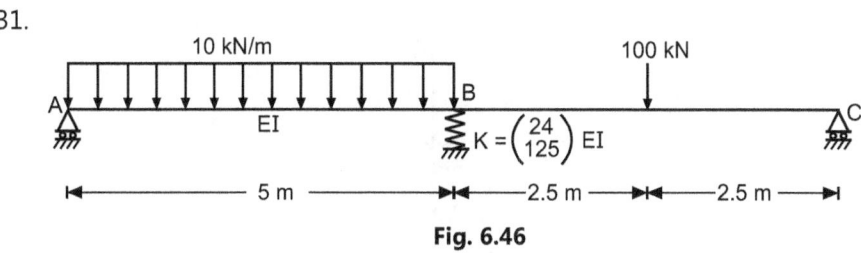

Fig. 6.45

(**Ans.** $M_A = -42.24$ kNm; $M_B = -78.05$ kNm)

31.

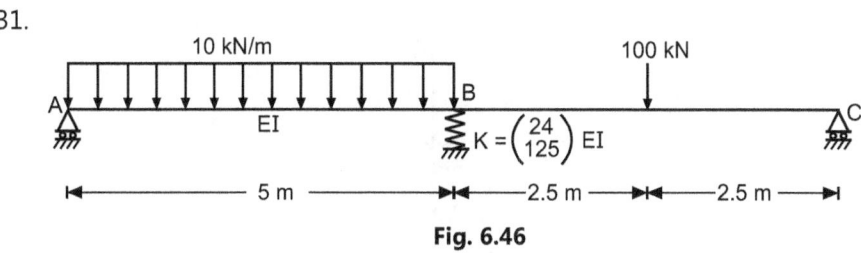

Fig. 6.46

(**Ans.** $M_B = -12.5$ kNm)

32.

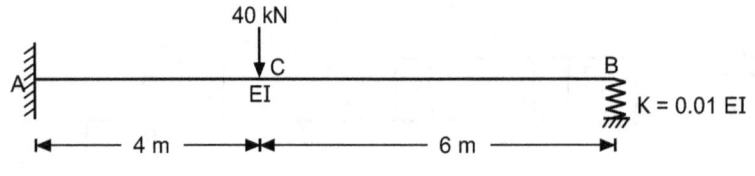

Fig. 6.47

(**Ans.** $M_A = -96$ kNm)

33.

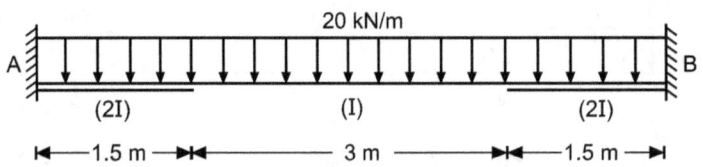

Fig. 6.48

(**Ans.** $M_A = M_B = -67.5$ kNm)

34.

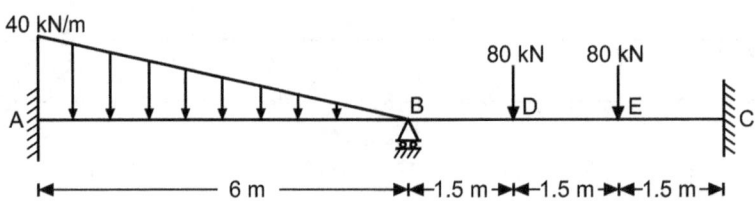

Fig. 6.49

(**Ans.** $M_A = -65.1$ kNm; $M_B = -61.7$ kNm; $M_C = -89.2$ kNm)

35.

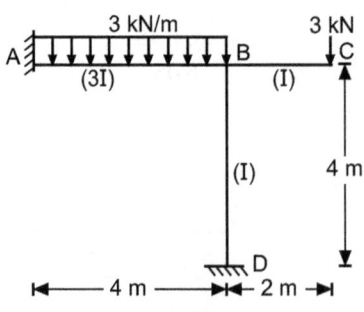

Fig. 6.50

(**Ans.** $M_{AB} = 3.25$ kNm; $M_{BA} = -5.5$ kNm; $M_{CD} = -0.5$ kNm; $M_{DB} = -0.2$ kNm)

36.

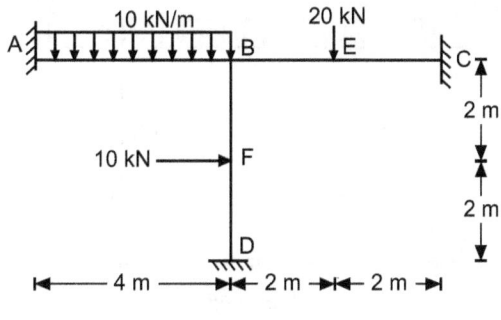

Fig. 6.51

(**Ans.** $M_{BC} = 47.5$ kNm; $M_{CB} = -8.75$ kNm; $M_{DB} = 23.75$ kNm; $M_{BD} = -32.5$ kNm)

37.

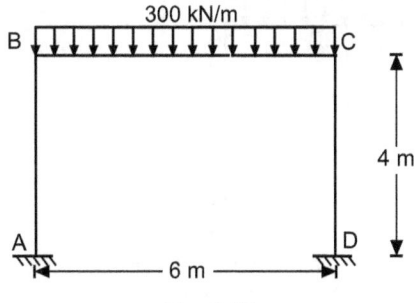

Fig. 6.52

(**Ans.** $M_{AB} = -M_{DC} = -336.9$ kNm; $M_{BA} = -M_{CD} = -673.8$ kNm;

$M_{BC} = -M_{CB} = 673.8$ kNm)

38.

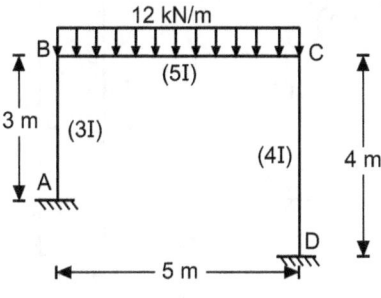

Fig. 6.53

(**Ans.** $M_{AB} = -5.97$ kNm; $M_{BA} = -15$ kNm; $M_{BC} = 15$ kNm;

$M_{CB} = -18$ kNm; $M_{CD} = 18$ kNm; $M_{DC} = 9.97$ kNm)

39.

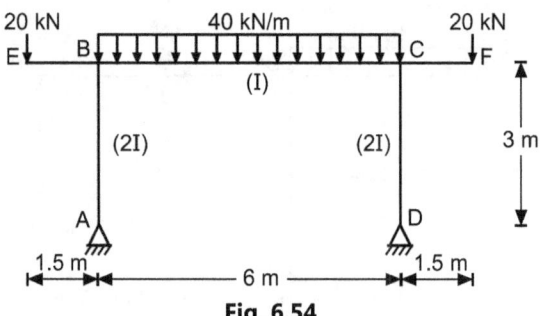

Fig. 6.54

(**Ans.** $M_{AB} = M_{DC} = 0$; $M_{BA} = -M_{CD} = -77$ kNm; $M_{BE} = -M_{CF} = -30$ kNm;
$M_{BC} = -M_{CB} = 107$ kNm)

40.

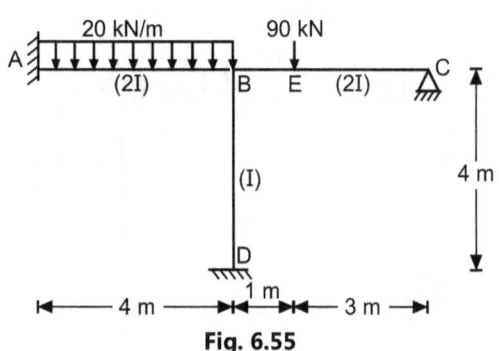

Fig. 6.55

(**Ans.** $M_{AB} = 22$ kNm; $M_{BA} = -36$ kNm; $M_{BD} = -4.67$ kNm;
$M_{BC} = 40.7$ kNm; $M_{CB} = 0$; $M_{DC} = -2.33$ kNm)

41.

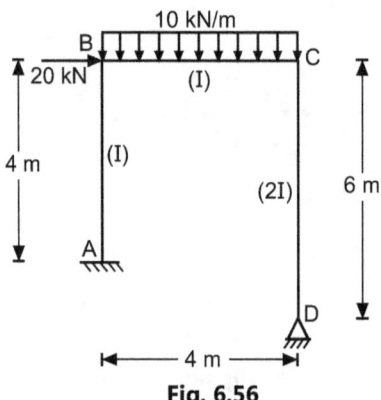

Fig. 6.56

(**Ans.** $M_{AB} = -4.16$ kNm; $M_{BA} = -8.75$ kNm; $M_{BC} = 8.75$ kNm; $M_{CB} = -8.75$ kNm;
$M_{CD} = 8.75$ kNm; $M_{DC} = 0$)

42.

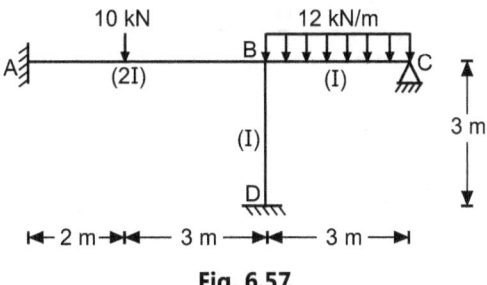

Fig. 6.57

(**Ans.** M_{AB} = 7.72 kNm; M_{BA} = –3.76 kNm; M_{BC} = 2.9 kNm; M_{CB} = 0; M_{BD} = 0.86 kNm; M_{DB} = 0.48 kNm)

43.

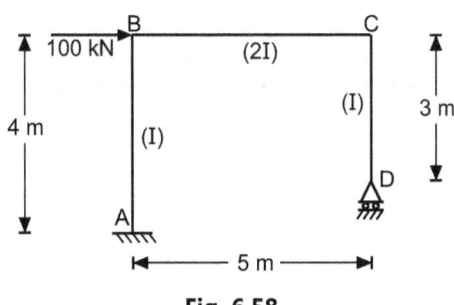

Fig. 6.58

(**Ans.** M_{AB} = 68.4 kNm; M_{BA} = 47.7 kNm; M_{BC} = – 47.7 kNm; M_{CB} = – 43.7 kNm; M_{CD} = 43.7 kNm; M_{DC} = 0)

44.

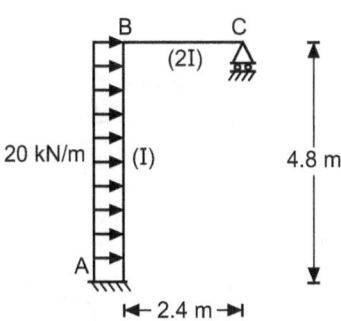

Fig. 6.59

(**Ans.** M_{AB} = 158.5; M_{BA} = – M_{BC} = 70 kNm)

45.

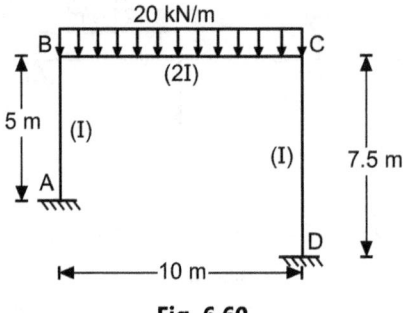

Fig. 6.60

(**Ans.** $M_{AB} = -21$ kNm; $M_{BA} = -M_{BC} = 91$ kNm; $M_{CB} = -M_{CD} = -106$ kN; $M_{DC} = 63.5$ kNm)

46.

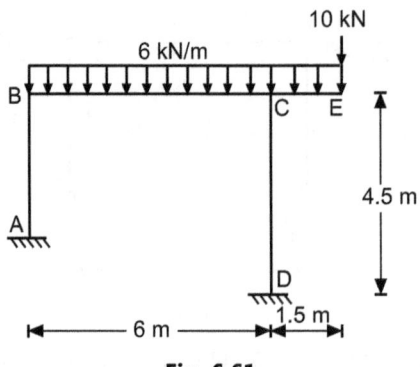

Fig. 6.61

(**Ans.** $M_{AB} = -0.62$ kNm; $M_{BA} = -M_{BC} = -7.14$ kNm; $M_{CB} = -24.94$ kNm;

$M_{CE} = 21.75$ kNm; $M_{CD} = 3.18$ kNm; $M_{DC} = 4.45$ kNm)

47.

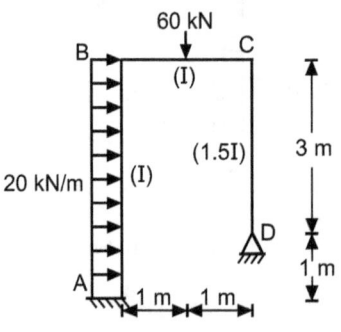

Fig. 6.62

(**Ans.** $M_{AB} = 75.2$ kNm; $M_{BA} = -M_{BC} = 17.1$ kNm; $M_{CB} = -M_{CD} = -50$ kNm; $M_{DC} = 0$)

48.

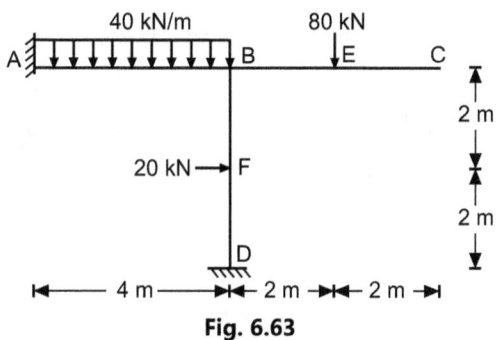

Fig. 6.63

(**Ans.** M_{AB} = 55.84 kNm; M_{BA} = –48.52 kNm;

M_{BC} = 63.66 kNm; M_{BD} = 15.12 kNm; M_{DB} = 22.44 kNm)

49.

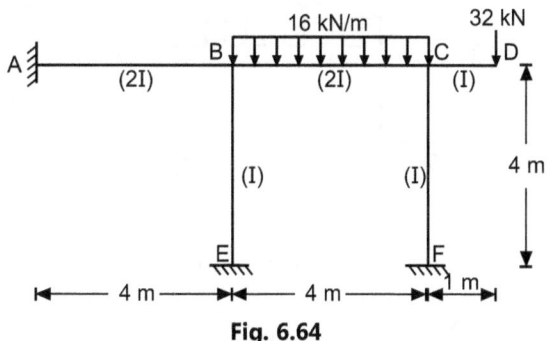

Fig. 6.64

(**Ans.** M_{AB} = – 3.8 kNm; M_{BA} = – 7.6 kNm; M_{BC} = 11.43 kNm; M_{CB} = – 29.72 kNm;

M_{CD} = 42 kNm; M_{BE} = – 3.8 kNm;

M_{EB} = – 1.9 kNm; M_{CF} = – 2.28 kNm; M_{FC} = – 1.14 kNm)

50.

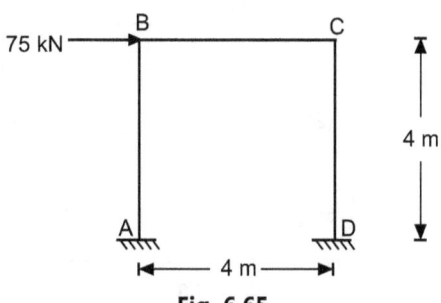

Fig. 6.65

(**Ans.** M_{AB} = 85.71 kNm; M_{BA} = –M_{BC} = 64.29 kNm; M_{CB} = – M_{CD} = – 64.29 kNm;

M_{DC} = 85.71 kNm)

51.

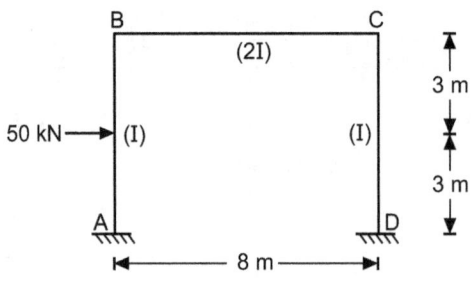

Fig. 6.66

(**Ans.** $M_{AB} = -123.72$ kNm; $B_{BA} = -M_{BC} = -42.527$ kNm; $M_{CB} = -M_{CD} = 58.675$ kNm; $M_{DC} = 75.275$ kNm)

52.

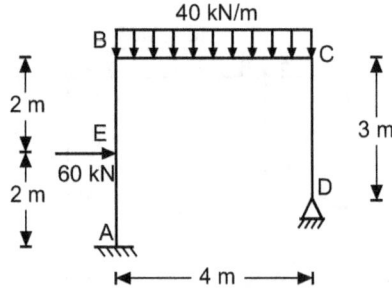

Fig. 6.67

(**Ans.** $M_{AB} = 60.50$ kNm; $M_{BA} = -M_{BC} = -19.70$ kNm; $M_{CB} = -M_{CD} = -59.40$ kNm; $M_{DC} = 0$)

53.

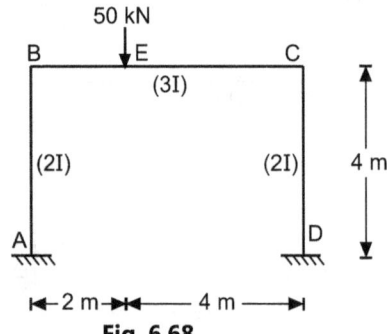

Fig. 6.68

(**Ans.** $M_{AB} = -9.52$ kNm; $M_{BA} = -M_{BC} = -23.82$ kNm; $M_{CB} = -M_{CD} = -20.63$ kNm; $M_{DC} = 12.71$ kNm)

54.

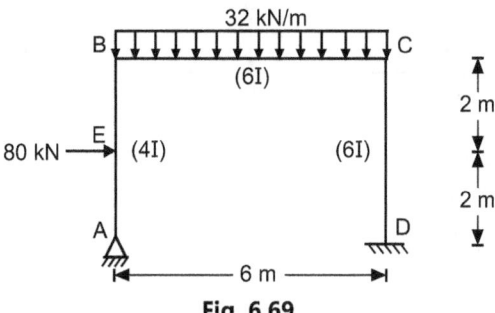

Fig. 6.69

(**Ans.** $M_{AB} = 0$; $M_{BA} = -M_{BC} = -50.92$ kNm; $M_{CB} = -M_{CD} = -108.64$ kNm; $M_{DC} = 102.14$ kNm)

55.

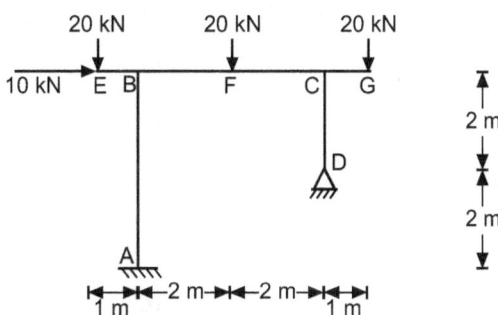

Fig. 6.70

(**Ans.** $M_{AB} = 14.92$ kNm; $M_{BA} = 15.87$ kNm; $M_{BE} = -20$ kNm; $M_{BC} = 4.13$ kNm; $M_{CB} = -24.60$ kNm; $M_{CA} = 20$ kNm; $M_{CD} = 4.60$ kNm)

56.

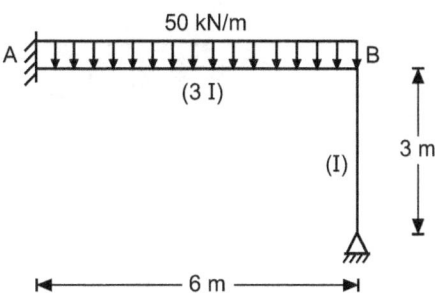

Fig. 6.71

(**Ans.** $M_{AB} = 200$ kNm; $M_{BA} = -50$ kNm; $M_{BC} = 50$ kNm; $M_{CB} = 0$)

57.

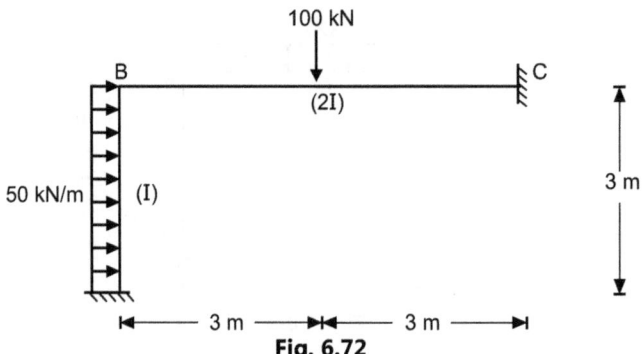

Fig. 6.72

(**Ans.** M_{AB} = 28.125 kNm; M_{BA} = −56.25 kNm; M_{BC} = 56.25 kNm; M_{CB} = −84.375 kNm)

58.

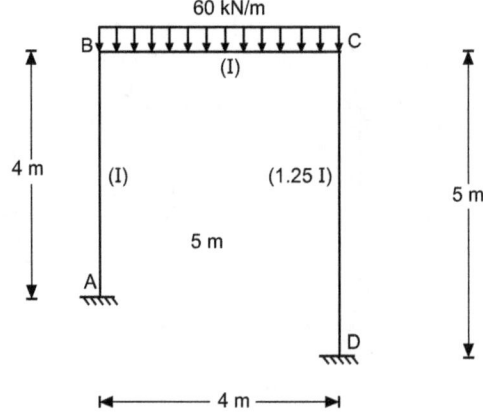

Fig. 6.73

(**Ans.** M_{AB} = 20.92 kNm; M_{BA} = − M_{BC} = − 49.2 kNm; M_{CD} = − M_{CB} = 56.8 kNm; M_{DC} = − 31.2 kNm)

UNIT - V

Chapter 7
PLASTIC THEORY

7.1 Primary Concepts of Plastic Collapse

Linear elastic analysis of structures have been discussed in earlier chapters to determine the stresses and deformations under working load. Plastic analysis will be introduced in this chapter to understand the behaviour of steel beams and frames in the plastic range. The aim of the plastic analysis is to assess the load at which a structure fails by the plastic collapse i.e. the development of excessive deflection. The basic concepts of plastic collapse are illustrated by the behaviour of a simply supported steel I-beam carrying a central concentrated load as shown in Fig. 7.1 (a). As the load increases, the central deflection also increases as shown in Fig. 7.1 (b).

Upto the load W_y, the beam is elastic and the extreme fibre stress reaches the yield stress σ_y. The stress distribution over the section at load position is shown in Fig. 7.1 (c). At the load W_y, the central deflection Δ increases very sharply for small increase in the load. As the load is increased further, the beam may fail catastrophically by buckling at the load W_{cr} as shown in Fig. 7.1 (b). But before the load W_{cr}, the collapse of the beam is considered at the load W_u due to excessive deflections.

Therefore, the behaviour of the beam is idealized by the indefinite deflection under the constant load W_u as represented by the dotted line in Fig. 7.1 (b). The idealized stress distribution over the cross-section of the beam at W_u is shown in Fig. 7.1 (c). The plastic hinge is said to be formed at the point C as shown in Fig. 7.1 (d) and the structure i.e. beam is transformed into a mechanism as shown in Fig. 7.1 (e). From the above illustration, the plastic behaviour is characterized by the following primary concepts:

- **Plasticity :** It is defined as the state of permanent deformation without fracture in a material, caused by the stresses which are greater than the yielding stresses. When all fibres of the beam section in compression and tension zones reach the yield stress σ_y of the material, the cross-section is said to be in fully plastic state as shown in Fig. 7.1 (c).

- **Plastic Hinge :** When the entire cross-section of the beam becomes fully plastic, an infinitely small increase in applied moment would cause large increase in curvature. This effect is known as the *plastic hinge*. The distinct feature of the plastic hinge is that it can undergo indefinite rotation at the constant moment. Plastic hinge is not a section but it is the zone of yielding near the section of full plasticity as shown in Fig. 7.1 (d). However, for the analysis, the plastic hinge is assumed at the section. Plastic hinge is different than a structural hinge. A structural hinge is physical arrangement of frictionless hinge which cannot resist moment. Plastic hinge is a virtual hinge due to effect of stresses, carrying constant moments on either side of the section. Therefore, it is considered as rusty hinge.

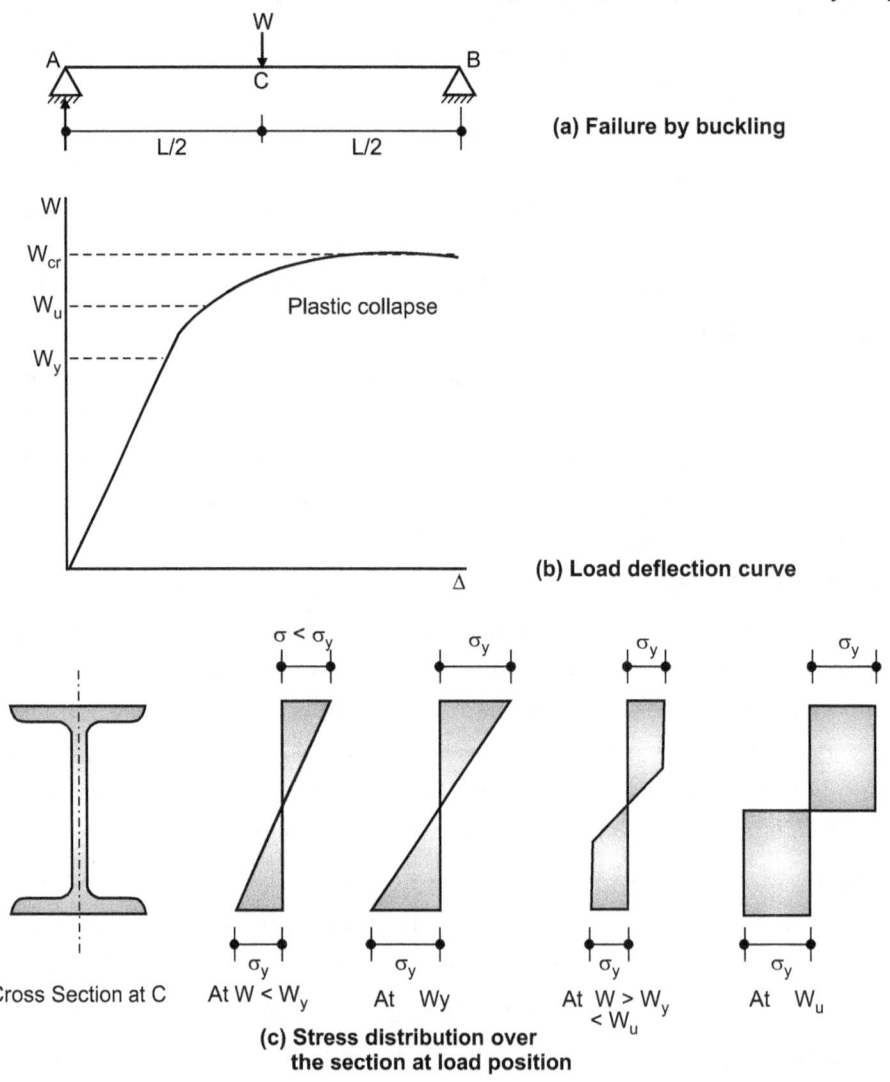

(a) Failure by buckling

(b) Load deflection curve

(c) Stress distribution over the section at load position

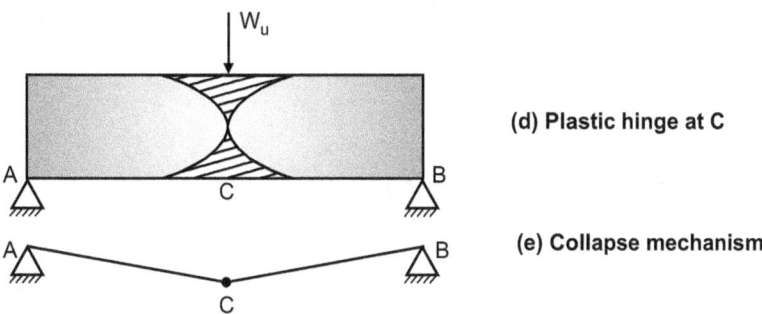

(d) Plastic hinge at C

(e) Collapse mechanism

Fig. 7.1 : Elastic - plastic behaviour of beam

$$M_p = \int_{Area} (\sigma_y \cdot dA)\, y$$

- **Plastic Moment :** The bending moment required to develop a plastic hinge is termed as the plastic moment and denoted by M_p. It is related to the yield stress of the material and the cross-section of the beam. Thus, it is the property of the section. Plastic moment is given by

- **Plastic Collapse :** It is a condition at which the indefinite deflection occurs at the constant load or a condition in which small increase in load will cause indefinite deformation. Plastic collapse is also termed as collapse mechanism.

- **Plastic Collapse Load :** The load at which plastic collapse occurs is the plastic collapse load.

It is also termed as the ultimate load and denoted by W_u.

- **Load Factor :** The ratio of the collapse load to the working load is called the load factor and it is denoted by λ.

With these primary concepts of plastic collapse, plastic theory is to be developed to analyze the beams and frames to predict the ultimate load.

7.2 Assumptions of Plastic Theory

Plastic analysis, mainly based on plastic theory of bending, is simplified on the following assumptions :

- The material is ductile and elastic plastic.
- The stress-strain relation is idealized as bilinear in tension as well as compression as shown in Fig. 7.2. The material follows Hooke's law upto the yield stress σ_y and then yields plastically at constant stress. This means that OA is a straight line having a

slope equal to the modulus of elasticity E and AB is horizontal extending without limit.

- Strain hardening is neglected.
- The deformations are small.
- Originally plane sections remain plane.
- There are no residual stresses.
- The beam is initially straight.
- The beam is bend by pure bending. The influence of axial force and shear force on the plastic moment is neglected.

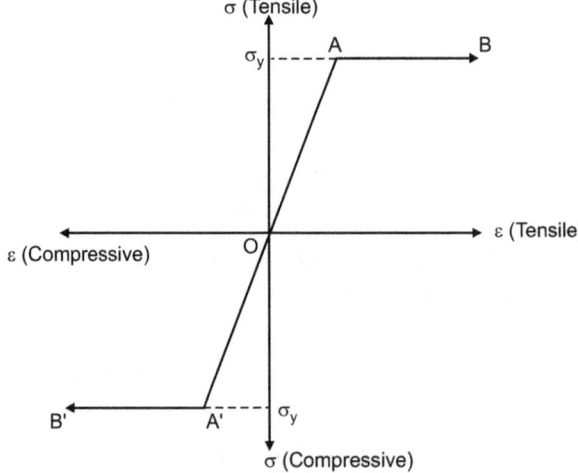

Fig. 7.2 : Idealized stress-strain curve

- The cross-section is symmetrical with respect to an axis which lies in the plane of bending.
- The loading is proportional.
- The cross-section has a maximum resisting moment equal to plastic moment.
- The spread of the plastic hinge is neglected and the plastic hinge forms at the critical section.
- Behaviour is elastic in between plastic hinges.
- Connections proportioned for full continuity transmit the plastic moment.
- No instability occurs prior to the attainment of the ultimate load.
- Sufficient number of plastic hinges are formed to transform a structure into a mechanism.

7.3 Elastic-Plastic Bending

The rectangular cross-section of breadth b and depth D is subjected to bending moment about an axis parallel to the breadth i.e. neutral axis, as shown in Fig. 7.3. The strain distributions and stress distributions are shown in Fig. 7.3 (a) to (c), as the applied moment is progressively increased. For both the elastic and elastic-plastic ranges, the relations between the extreme fibre stress, the bending moment and the curvature can be easily developed as given below.

It may be noted that the curvature ϕ is the rate of change of slope of the cross-section of the beam i.e. $\phi = \dfrac{d\theta}{ds}$. Following stages are important to investigate.

(i) When the entire section is elastic as shown in Fig. 7.3 (a), the bending stress is given by

$$\sigma = \frac{M}{I} \cdot y \qquad \ldots (7.1)$$

where I is the second moment of area about the neutral axis. The curvature is expressed by

$$\phi = \frac{\varepsilon}{y} = \frac{M}{EI}$$

(ii) When the extreme fibre stresses just equal to the yield stress, the elastic range ends and the bending moment is called the *yield moment*, M_y. Bending stress and yield moment and curvature are related by

$$\sigma_y = \frac{M_y}{I}(D/2)$$

$$\phi_y = \frac{2\varepsilon_y}{D} = \frac{M_y}{EI}$$

$$\therefore \quad M_y = \frac{\sigma_y I}{(D/2)}$$

$$= \sigma_y \left(\frac{bD^2}{6}\right) = \sigma_y Z_e \qquad \ldots (7.2)$$

where Z_e is the elastic section modulus.

(iii) As the moment is increased beyond M_y, the stress distribution may be partly elastic and partly plastic as shown in Fig. 7.3 (b). It may be noted that the maximum strains will exceed the yield strain ε_y but the maximum stresses remain constant at σ_y. It can be shown that bending moment is obtained by :

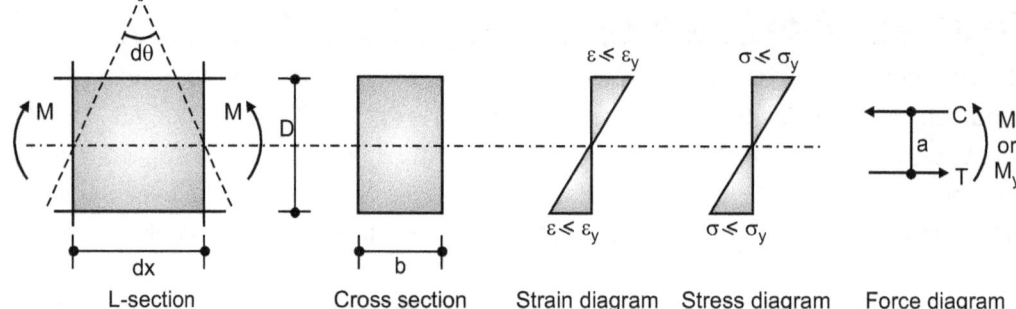

(a) **Elastic range**

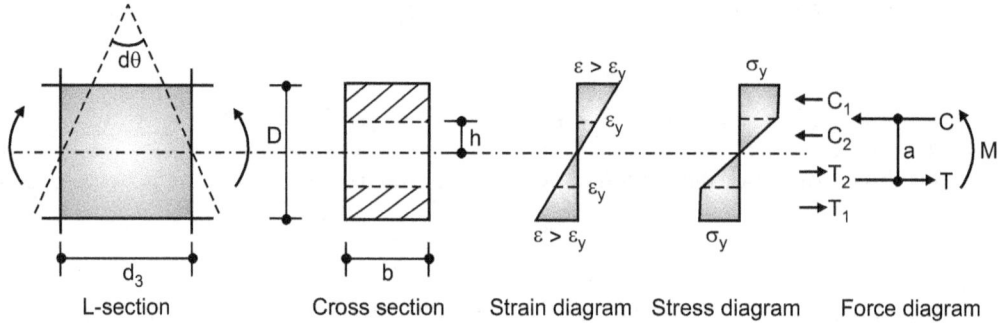

(b) **Plastic range**

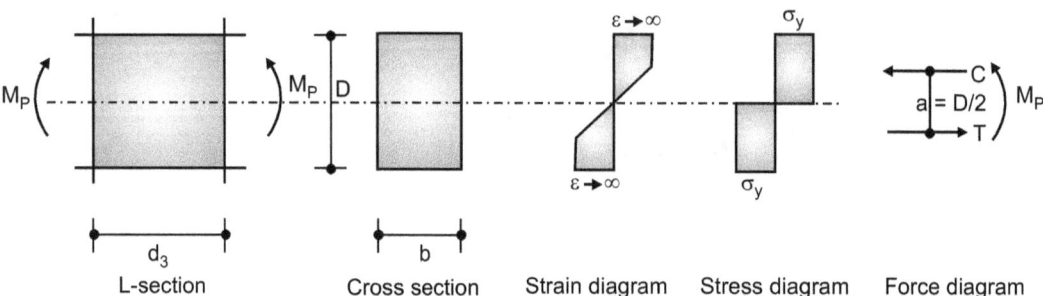

(c) **Fully plastic condition**

Fig. 7.3 : Elastic-plastic bending

$$M = \left(\frac{1}{2}\sigma_y \cdot b \cdot h\right)\left(\frac{4}{3}h\right) + \left[\sigma_y b\left(\frac{D}{2} - h\right)\right]\left(\frac{D}{2} + h\right)$$

$$= \sigma_y b \left[\frac{D^2}{4} - \frac{1}{3}h^2\right] \qquad \ldots (7.3)$$

The corresponding curvature is given by

$$\phi = \frac{\varepsilon_y}{h}$$

(iv) With further increase in M, more fibres become plastic until the whole cross-section is plastic as shown in Fig. 7.3 (c). The bending moment at full plasticity is called the plastic moment, M_p and expressed as :

$$M_p = (\sigma_y)\left(\frac{bD}{2}\right)\left(\frac{D}{2}\right) = (\sigma_y)\left(\frac{bD^2}{4}\right) = \sigma_y Z_p \qquad \ldots (7.4)$$

The quantity $\left(\frac{bD^2}{4}\right)$ is called plastic section modulus and denoted by Z_p.

From above discussions it is interesting to obtain the bending moment - curvature relation in non-dimensional form as follows :

$$\frac{M}{M_y} = \frac{\sigma_y b \left[\frac{D^2}{4} - \frac{1}{3}h^2\right]}{\sigma_y b \frac{D^2}{6}}$$

$$\therefore \quad \frac{M}{M_y} = \frac{\sigma_y b \frac{D^2}{4}}{\sigma_y b \frac{D^2}{6}} - \frac{\sigma_y bh^2/3}{\sigma_y bD^2/6}$$

$$\therefore \quad \frac{M}{M_y} = 1.5 - 2\frac{h^2}{D^2}$$

As $\quad \phi = \frac{\varepsilon_y}{h}$ and $\phi_y = \frac{2\varepsilon_y}{D}$

$$\therefore \quad \frac{M}{M_y} = 1.5 - 2\frac{(1\,\varepsilon_y/\phi)^2}{(2\,\varepsilon_y/\phi_y)^2}$$

$$\therefore \quad \frac{M}{M_y} = 1.5 - 0.5 \left(\frac{\phi_y}{\phi}\right)^2 \qquad \ldots (7.5)$$

The moment-curvature relation in non-dimensional form is shown in Fig. 7.4 which gives the following important conclusions.

M tends to a limiting value $1.5\,M_y$ as ϕ becomes very large. Therefore in the limit, when $M = 1.5\,M_y$, ϕ is infinite.

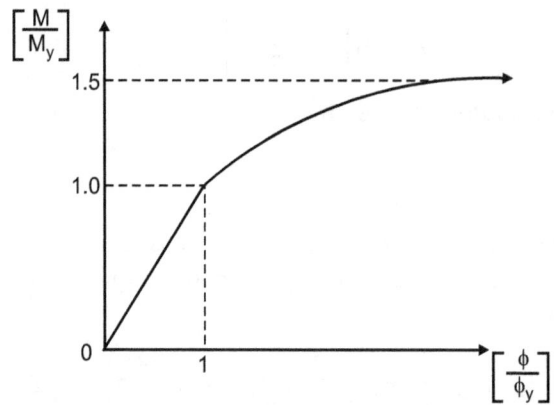

Fig. 7.4 : Non-dimensional moment-curvature relationship for rectangular section

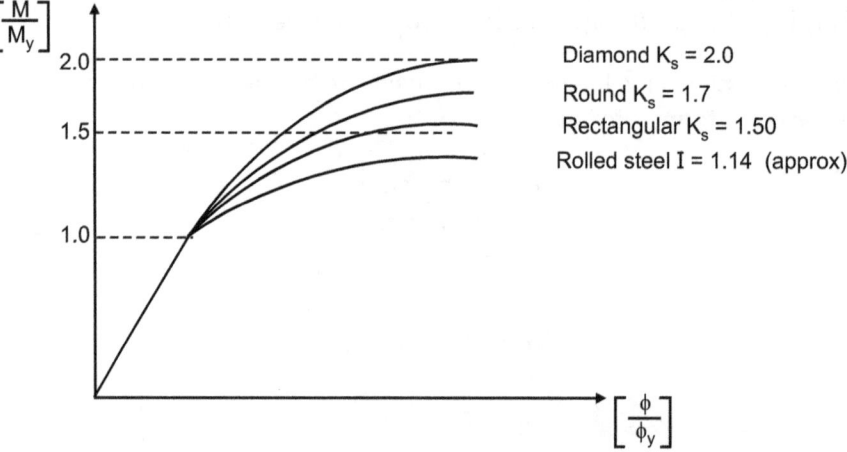

(a) Non-dimensional moment-curvature relationship for typical beam sections

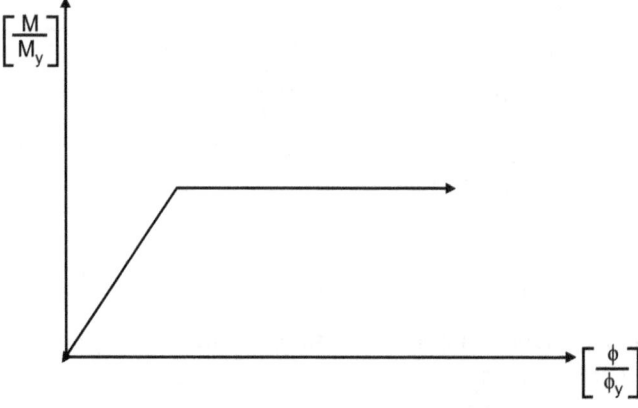

(b) Idealized non-dimensional moment-curvature relationship

Fig. 7.5 : Moment-curvature relationships

This limiting condition corresponds to the fully plastic state of the cross-section and the corresponding bending moment is the plastic moment M_p. Because of infinite curvature, this effect is considered as the formation of the plastic hinge at the section.

7.4 SHAPE FACTOR AND PLASTIC SECTION MODULUS

The ratio of the plastic moment M_p of a section to its yield moment M_y is called the *shape factor* and denoted by K_s.

The shape factor for a rectangular section is :

$$K_s = \frac{M_p}{M_y} = \frac{\sigma_y bD^2/4}{\sigma_y bD^2/6} = \frac{Z_p}{Z_e} = 1.5$$

The shape factor depends solely on the shape of the cross-section. For the given cross-section, the shape factor can be derived. Shape factors for various cross-sections are as follows :

    Diamond section   : 2.0
    Circular section   : 1.7
    Rectangular section : 1.5
    Rolled steel beam section : 1.15 (approximately)

At any stage of transverse loading on a beam, the equilibrium specifies that the resultant force on the cross-section must be zero i.e.

$$\int_{Area} (\sigma)(dA) = 0 \qquad \ldots (7.6)$$

Accordingly, in elastic bending, the neutral axis must pass through the centroid of the cross-section.

Under fully plastic condition, the above equilibrium equation becomes

$$\int_{Area} (\sigma_y)(dA) = 0 \qquad \ldots (7.7)$$

If σ_y is same for tension and compression, then

$$\int_{Area} (dA) = 0$$

Therefore in plastic bending, the neutral axis must divide the cross-section into two equal areas. For symmetrical section, plastic neutral axis coincides with the elastic neutral axis, passing through the centroid of the section.

For unsymmetrical section in plastic bending, the position of the neutral axis changes.
It means plastic neutral axis does not pass through the centroid but it divides the area into two equal parts as shown in Fig. 7.6 (a). If the yield stress is same in tension and compression, the position of the plastic neutral axis is determined from the condition.

$$A_c = A_t = \frac{A}{2}$$

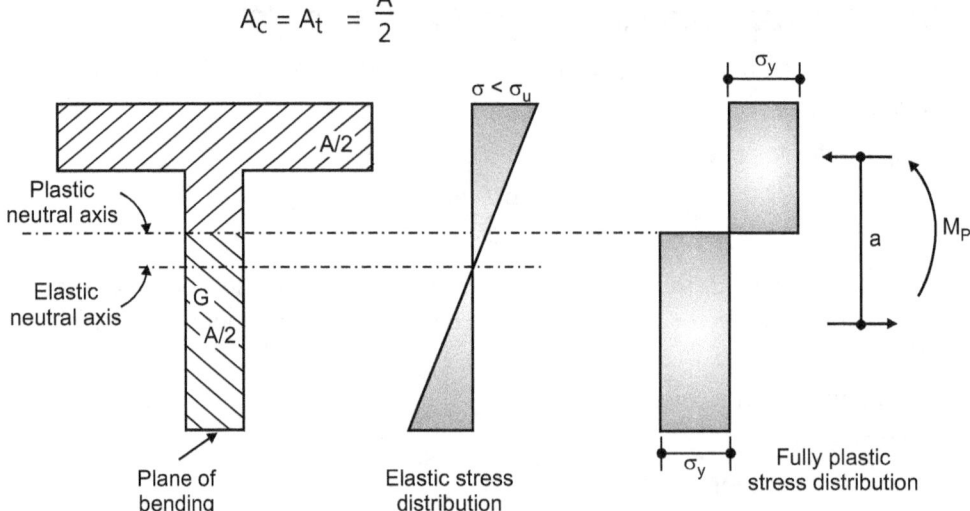

(a) Fully plastic stress distribution and moment for cross-section with $\sigma_{yc} = \sigma_{yt} = \sigma_y$

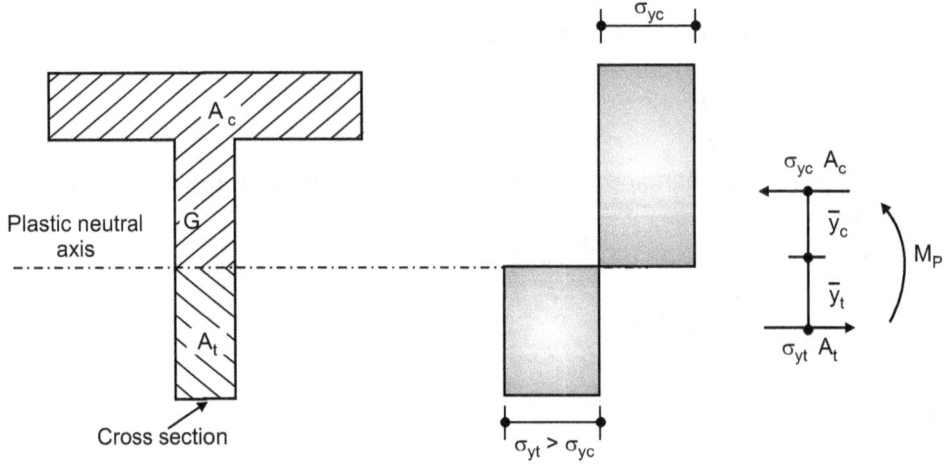

(b) Fully plastic stress distribution and moment for cross-section with $\sigma_{yt} > \sigma_{yc}$

Fig. 7.6

Where, A is the total area of cross-section of the beam.
A_c is the area of cross-section in compression.

A_t is the area of cross-section in tension.

And the plastic section modulus is computed from the equation

$$Z_p = \frac{A}{2} \cdot \bar{y}_c + \frac{A}{2} \cdot \bar{y}_t \qquad \ldots (7.8)$$

Where, $\bar{y}_c$ is the distance of the centroid of A_c from plastic neutral axis.

$\bar{y}_t$ is the distance of the centroid of A_t from plastic neutral axis.

Fig. 7.6 : Plastic moment for unsymmetrical beam section

The plastic moment of a section is the product of the yield stress and the plastic section modulus.

i.e.
$$M_p = \sigma_y \cdot Z_p = \sigma_y \cdot \frac{1}{2} A \cdot \bar{y}_c + \sigma_y \cdot \frac{1}{2} A \cdot \bar{y}_t \qquad \ldots (7.9)$$

It may be noted that if the yield stress is different in tension and compression, the plastic neutral axis will not divide the cross-section into two equal parts as shown in Fig. 7.6 (b). Therefore, the position of plastic neutral axis, in this case, is obtained from the equation

$$\sigma_{yc} \cdot A_c = \sigma_{yt} \cdot A_t \qquad \ldots (7.10)$$

And the plastic moment of the section is to be obtained carefully by taking moments of forces about the plastic neutral axis, as given by the equation

$$M_p = \sigma_{yc} \cdot A_c \cdot \bar{y}_c + \sigma_{yt} \cdot A_t \cdot \bar{y}_t \qquad \ldots (7.11)$$

The shape factor also measures the ratio of M_p to M_y, therefore, it is reflected in moment curvature curve in the form of transition from M_y to M_p, as shown in Fig. 7.5 (a) for different shapes.

If the shape factor is assumed as one then M_p is equal to M_y and the moment-curvature curve is idealized as bilinear as shown in Fig. 7.5 (b).

7.4.1 Plastic Analysis of Cross-Section

The procedure of plastic analysis of cross-section of a beam is formulated as below :

Data : (1) Cross-section : Shape and size. (2) Material : Yield stresses, σ_y.

Objects : (1) Shape factor : (2) Plastic moment.

Concepts and Equations : (1) Theory of plastic bending.

(2) $K_s = \frac{Z_p}{Z_e}$ or $K_s = \frac{M_p}{M_y}$ (3) $M_p = \sigma_y \cdot Z_p$ or $M_p = \sigma_{yc} A_c \bar{y}_c + \sigma_{yt} A_t \bar{y}_t$

Procedure :

(A) For symmetric sections having $\sigma_{yc} = \sigma_{yt}$

Step I : Locate elastic neutral axis.

Step II : Locate plastic neutral axis using $A_c = A_t$.

Step III : Find elastic section modulus (Z_e).

$$Z_e = \frac{I}{Y}$$

Step IV : Find plastic section modulus (Z_p).

$$Z_p = A_c \cdot \bar{y}_c + A_t \cdot \bar{y}_t$$

Step V : Find shape factor (K_s).

$$K_s = \frac{Z_p}{Z_e}$$

(B) (i) For symmetric sections having $\sigma_{yc} \neq \sigma_{yt}$

(ii) For unsymmetric sections having $\sigma_{yc} = \sigma_{yt}$ and

(iii) For unsymmetric sections having $\sigma_{yc} \neq \sigma_{yt}$

Step I : Locate elastic neutral axis.

Step II : Locate plastic neutral axis using $A_c = A_t$.

Step III : Find elastic section modulus (Z_e).

(a) Elastic section modulus with reference to compression side = $Z_{ec} = \dfrac{I}{y_c}$

(b) Elastic section modulus with reference to tension side = $Z_{et} = \dfrac{I}{y_t}$

Step IV : Find yield moment (M_y) :

(a) Yield moment with reference to compression side = $M_{yc} = \sigma_{yc} \cdot Z_{ec}$

(b) Yield moment with reference to tension side = $M_{yt} = \sigma_{yt} \cdot Z_{et}$.

∴ Yield moment = M_y

= Least of M_{yc} and M_{yt}

Step V : Find plastic moment (M_p):

$$M_p = \sigma_{yc}(A_c \cdot \bar{y}_c) + \sigma_{yt}(A_t \cdot \bar{y}_t)$$

Step VI : Find shape factor (K_s) :

$$K_s = \frac{M_p}{M_y}$$

SOLVED EXAMPLES

Example 7.1 : For the cross-section of a beam shown in Fig. 7.7 (a), find the shape factor.

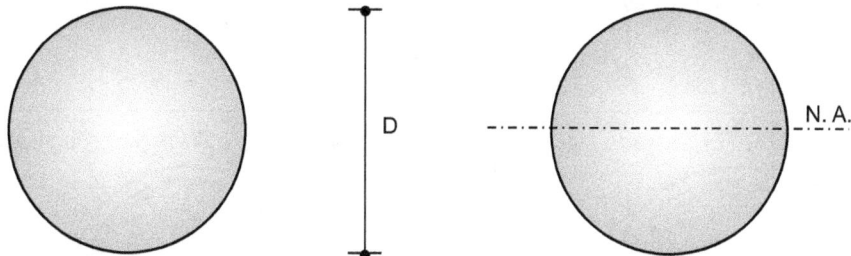

(a) Given cross-section of the beam   (b) Elastic and plastic neutral axis of cross-section

Fig. 7.7 : Illustrative Example 7.1

Solution : Data : Cross-section of the beam as shown in Fig. 7.7.

Object : Shape factor (K_s).

Concepts and Equations : (1) Theory of plastic bending. (2) $K_s = \dfrac{Z_p}{Z_e}$

Procedure :

Step I : Elastic neutral axis : Horizontal axis passing through the centroid of cross-section as shown in Fig. 7.7 (b).

Step II : Plastic neutral axis : Horizontal axis passing through the centroid of cross-section as shown in Fig. 7.7 (b).

Step III : Elastic section modulus (Z_e) :

$$I = \frac{\pi}{64}(D)^4$$

$$Z_e = \frac{I}{Y} = \frac{(\pi/64)D^4}{D/2} = \frac{\pi}{32}(D)^3$$

Step IV : Plastic section modulus (Z_p) :

Sr. No.	Area in compression	Distance of c.g. of 'A_c' from plastic neutral axis ($\bar{y}_c$)	$A_c \cdot \bar{y}_c$	Sr. No.	Area in tension (A_t)	Distance of c.g. of 'A_t' from plastic neutral axis ($\bar{y}_t$)	$A_t \cdot \bar{y}_t$
1.	$\dfrac{\pi}{8}(D)^2$	$\dfrac{4D}{6\pi}$	$\dfrac{D^3}{12}$	1.	$\dfrac{\pi}{8}(D)^2$	$\dfrac{4D}{6\pi}$	$\dfrac{D^3}{12}$

$$Z_p = A_c \cdot \bar{y}_c + A_t \cdot \bar{y}_t = \frac{D^3}{12} + \frac{D^3}{12} = \frac{D^3}{6}$$

Step V : Shape factor (K_s) :

$$K_s = \frac{Z_p}{Z_e} = \frac{D^3/6}{(\pi/32)\,D^3} = \frac{32}{6\pi} = 1.697$$

Example 7.2 : For the cross-section of a beam shown in Fig. 7.8 (a), find the shape factor.

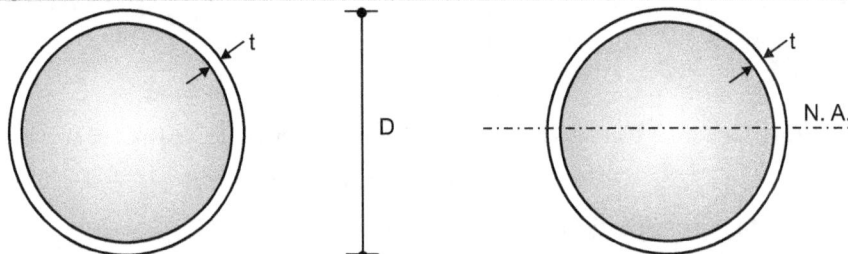

(a) Given cross-section of the beam   (b) Elastic and plastic neutral axis of cross-section

Fig. 7.8 : Illustrative Example 7.2

Solution : Data : Cross-section of the beam as shown in Fig. 7.8 (a).

Object : Shape factor (K_s).

Concepts and Equations :

(1) Theory of plastic bending.

(2) $K_s = \dfrac{Z_p}{Z_e}$.

Procedure :

Step I : Elastic neutral axis : Horizontal axis passing through the centroid of cross-section as shown in Fig. 7.8 (b).

Step II : Plastic neutral axis : Horizontal axis passing through the centroid of cross-section as shown in Fig. 7.8 (b).

Step III : Elastic section modulus (Z_e) :

$$I = \frac{\pi}{64}(D^4 - (D-2t)^4) = \frac{\pi}{64}(D^4 - (D^2 - 4tD + 4t^2)^2) = \frac{\pi D^3 t}{8}$$

($\because$ Neglecting terms of t^2 and t^3 as 't' is very small compared to 'D').

$$Z_e = \frac{I}{y} = \frac{\pi D^3 t/8}{D/2} = \frac{\pi D^2 t}{4}$$

Step IV : Plastic section modulus (Z_p) :

Using the result of Example 7.1.

$$Z_p = \frac{1}{6}(D^3 - (D-2t)^3) = \frac{1}{6}[D^3 - D^3 + 6D^2t + 12Dt^2 - 8t^3] = D^2t$$

(∵ Neglecting terms of $t^2 - 8t^3$)

Step V : Shape factor (K_s) :

$$K_s = \frac{Z_p}{Z_e} = \frac{D^2t}{\pi D^2 t/4} = 1.274$$

Example 7.3 : *For the cross-section of a beam shown in Fig. 7.9 (a), find the shape factor.*

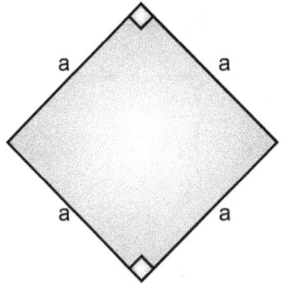   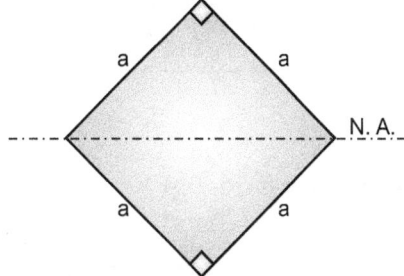

(a) Given cross-section of the beam   (b) Elastic and plastic neutral axis of cross-section

Fig. 7.9 : Illustrative Example 7.3

Solution : Data : Cross-section of the beam as shown in Fig. 7.9.

Object : Shape factor (K_s)

Concepts and Equations :

(1) Theory of plastic bending.

(2) $K_s = \dfrac{Z_p}{Z_e}$

Procedure :

Step I : Elastic neutral axis : Horizontal axis passing through the centroid of cross-section as shown in Fig. 7.9 (b).

Step II : Plastic neutral axis : Horizontal axis passing through the centroid of cross-section as shown in Fig. 7.9 (b).

Step III : Elastic section modulus (Z_e) :

$$I = 2\left[\frac{1}{12}(\sqrt{2}\,a)\left(\frac{1}{\sqrt{2}}\right)^3\right] = \frac{a^4}{12}$$

$$Z_e = \frac{I}{y} = \frac{a^4/12}{a/\sqrt{2}} = \frac{a^3}{6\sqrt{2}}$$

Step IV : Plastic section modulus (Z_p) :

Sr. No.	Area in compression (A_c) (mm²)	Distance of c.g. of 'A_c' from plastic neutral axis ($\bar{y}_c$) (mm)	$A_c \cdot \bar{y}_c$ (mm³)	Sr. No.	Area in tension (A_t) (mm²)	Distance of c.g. of 'A_t' from plastic neutral axis ($\bar{y}_t$) (mm)	$A_t \cdot \bar{y}_t$ (mm³)
1.	$\frac{1}{2}(\sqrt{2}\,a)\frac{a}{\sqrt{2}}$ $= \frac{a^2}{2}$	$\frac{1}{3}\left(\frac{a}{\sqrt{2}}\right)$ $= \frac{a}{3\sqrt{2}}$	$\frac{a^3}{6\sqrt{2}}$	1.	$\frac{1}{2}(\sqrt{2}\,a)\frac{a}{\sqrt{2}}$ $= \frac{a^2}{2}$	$\frac{1}{3}\left(\frac{a}{\sqrt{(2)}}\right)$ $= \frac{a}{3\sqrt{2}}$	$\frac{a^3}{6\sqrt{(2)}}$

$$Z_p = A_c \cdot \bar{y}_c + A_t \cdot \bar{y}_t = \frac{a^3}{6\sqrt{2}} + \frac{a^3}{6\sqrt{2}} = \frac{a^3}{3\sqrt{2}}$$

Step V : Shape factor (K_s) :

$$K_s = \frac{Z_p}{Z_c} = \frac{a^3/3\sqrt{2}}{a^3/6\sqrt{2}} = 2$$

Example 7.4 : *For the cross-section of a beam shown in Fig. 7.10 (a), find the shape factor.*

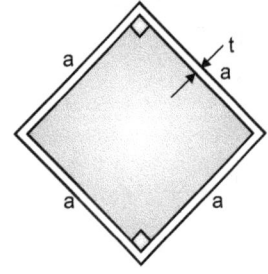 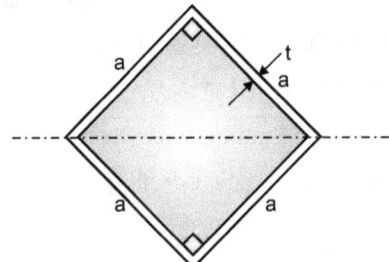

(a) Given cross-section of the beam (b) Elastic and plastic neutral axis of cross-section

Fig. 7.10 : Illustrative Example 7.4

Solution : Data : Cross-section of the beam as shown in Fig. 7.10.

Object : Shape factor (K_s).

Concepts and Equations : (1) Theory of plastic bending. (2) $K_s = \dfrac{Z_p}{Z_e}$

Procedure :

Step I : Elastic neutral axis: Horizontal axis passing through the centroid of cross-section as shown in Fig. 7.10 (b).

Step II : Plastic neutral axis : Horizontal axis passing through the centroid of cross-section as shown in Fig. 7.10 (b).

Step III : Elastic section modulus (Z_e) :

$$I = \frac{1}{12}(a^4 - (a-2t)^4) = \frac{2a^3 t}{3}$$

(∵ Neglecting terms of t^2 and t^3 as 't' is very small as compared to 'a')

$$Z_e = \frac{I}{y} = \frac{2a^3 t/3}{a/\sqrt{2}} = \frac{2\sqrt{2}\, a^2 t}{3}$$

Step IV : Plastic section modulus (Z_p) :

Using the result of example :

$$Z_p = \frac{1}{3\sqrt{2}}(a^3 - (a-2t)^3) = \frac{1}{3\sqrt{2}}[a^3 - (a^3 - 6a^2 t + 12at^2 - 8t^3)]$$

$$= \sqrt{2}\, a^2 t \qquad (\because \text{Neglecting terms of } t^2 \text{ and } t^3)$$

Step V : Shape factor (K_s) :

$$K_s = \frac{Z_p}{Z_e} = \frac{\sqrt{2}\, a^2 t}{2\sqrt{2}\, a^2 t/3} = \frac{3}{2} = 1.5$$

Example 7.5 : *For the cross-section of a beam shown in Fig. 7.11 (a), find the shape factor and plastic moment if permissible yield stress in compression and tension is 250 MPa.*

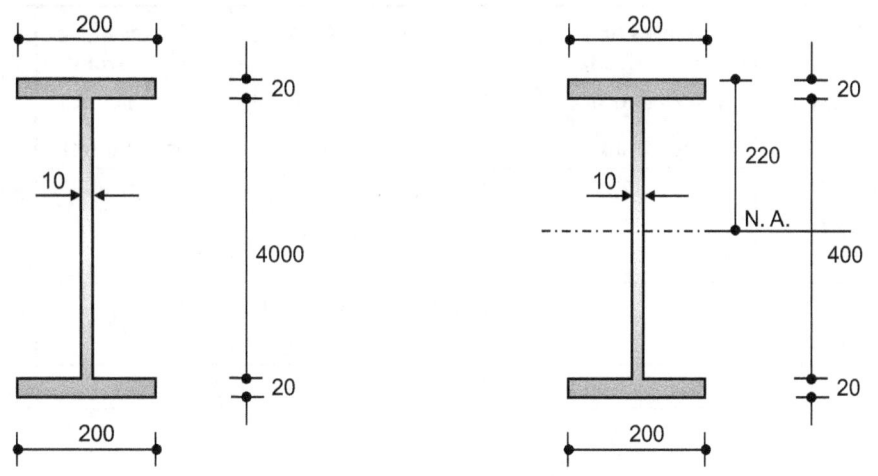

(a) Given cross-section of the beam (b) Elastic and plastic neutral axis of cross-section

Fig. 7.11 : Illustrative Example 7.5

Solution : Data : (1) Cross-section of the beam as shown in Fig. 7.11.

(2) Material yield stress: σ_y = 250 MPa.

Objects : (1) Shape factor (K_s).

(2) Plastic moment (M_p).

Concepts and Equations :

(1) Theory of plastic bending.

(2) $K_s = \dfrac{Z_p}{Z_e}$

(3) $M_p = \sigma_y \cdot Z_p$.

Procedure :

Step I : Elastic neutral axis : 220 mm from top (∵ By symmetry) as shown in Fig. 7.11 (b).

Step II : Plastic neutral axis : 220 mm from top (∵ By symmetry) as shown in Fig. 7.11 (b).

Step III : Elastic section modulus (Z_e) :

$$I = \dfrac{200 \times (440)^3}{12} - \dfrac{190 \times (400)^3}{12} = 406.4 \times 10^6 \text{ mm}^4$$

$$Z_e = \dfrac{I}{y} = \dfrac{406.4 \times 10^6}{220} = 1.847 \times 10^6 \text{ mm}^3$$

Step IV : Plastic section modulus (Z_p):

Sr. No.	Area in compression (A_c) (mm²)	Distances of c.g. of 'A_c' from plastic neutral axis ($\bar{y}_c$) (mm)	$A_c \cdot \bar{y}_c$ (mm³)	Sr. No.	Area in tension (A_t) (mm²)	Distances of c.g. of 'A_t' from plastic neutral axis ($\bar{y}_t$) (mm)	$A_t \cdot \bar{y}_t$ (mm³)
1.	200 × 20 = 4000	$200 + \dfrac{20}{2} = 210$	840000	1.	200 × 20 = 4000	$200 + \dfrac{20}{2} = 210$	840000
2.	200 × 10 = 2000	$\dfrac{200}{2} = 100$	200000	2.	200 × 10 = 2000	$\dfrac{200}{2} = 100$	200000
		Σ =	1040000			Σ =	1040000

$$Z_p = A_c \cdot \bar{y}_c + A_t \cdot \bar{y}_t$$
$$= 1040000 + 1040000 = 2.08 \times 10^6 \text{ mm}^3$$

Step V : Shape factor (K_s) :

$$K_s = \frac{Z_p}{Z_e} = \frac{2.08 \times 10^6}{1.847 \times 10^6} = 1.126$$

Step VI : Plastic moment (M_p) :

$$M_p = \sigma_y \cdot Z_p = (250 \times 2.08 \times 10^6) \times 10^{-6} = 520 \text{ kNm}$$

Example 7.6 : *Cross-section of the beam shown in Fig. 7.12 (a) is subjected to sagging bending moment. Find the shape factor if permissible yield stress in compression and tension is σ_y. Hence, assuming factor of safety = 1.7, find load factor.*

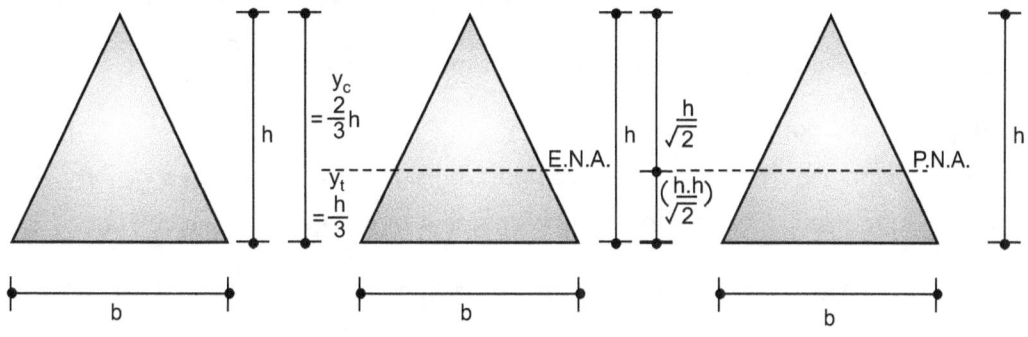

(a) Given cross-section of the beam

(b) Elastic neutral axis of the cross-section

(c) Plastic neutral axis of the cross-section

Fig. 7.12 : Illustrative Example 7.6

Solution : Data : (i) Cross-section of the beam as shown in Fig. 7.12 (a).

(ii) Material yield stresses : $\sigma_{yc} = \sigma_{yt} = \sigma_y$

Objects : (1) Plastic moment (M_p), (2) Shape factor (K_s).

Concepts and Equations :

(1) Theory of plastic bending; (2) Shape factor (K_s); (3) $K_s = \dfrac{M_p}{M_y}$

Procedure :

Step I : Elastic neutral axis : $2h/3$ from top.

∴ $y_c = \left(\dfrac{2}{3}\right)h$ and $y_t = h/3$ as shown in Fig. 7.12 (b).

Step II : Plastic neutral axis :

Width of triangle at a distance x_p from top = $b' = \left(\dfrac{b}{h}\right)x_p$

$$A_c = A_t$$

$$\therefore \quad \frac{1}{2}\left(\frac{b}{h}\right) x_p^2 = \frac{b + (b + h) x_p}{2} (h - x_p)$$

$$\therefore \quad 2x_p^2 = h^2 \text{ i.e. } x_p = \frac{h}{\sqrt{2}} \text{ from top.}$$

Step III : Elastic section modulus (Z_e) : $I = \frac{bh^3}{36}$

(a) Elastic section modulus with reference to compression side = $Z_{ec} = \frac{I}{y_c} = \frac{bh^3/36}{(2/3) h} = \frac{bh^2}{24}$

(b) Elastic section modulus with reference to tension side = $Z_{et} = \frac{I}{y_t} = \frac{bh^3/36}{h/3} = \frac{bh^2}{12}$

Step IV : Yield moment (M_y) :

(a) Yield moment with reference to compression side = $M_{yc} = \sigma_{yc} \cdot Z_{ec} = \sigma_y (bh^2/24)$

(b) Yield moment with reference to tension side = $M_{yt} = \sigma_{yt} \cdot Z_{et} = \sigma_y (bh^2/12)$

$$\therefore \quad \text{Yield moment} = M_y = \text{Least of } M_{yc} \text{ and } M_{yt} = \sigma_y \left(\frac{bh^2}{24}\right)$$

Step V : Plastic moment (M_p) :

Sr. No.	Area in compression (A_c) (mm²)	Distance of c.g. of 'A_c' from plastic neutral axis $(\bar{y}_c)$ (mm)	$A_c \cdot \bar{y}_c$ (mm³)	Sr. No.	Area in tension (A_t) (mm²)	Distance of c.g. of 'A_t' from plastic neutral axis $(\bar{y}_t)$ (mm)	$A_t \cdot \bar{y}_t$ (mm³)
1.	$\dfrac{bh}{4}$	$(1/3) h/\sqrt{2}$	$\dfrac{bh^2}{12\sqrt{2}}$	1.	$\dfrac{bh}{4}$	$\left(\dfrac{b' + 2b}{b' + b}\right) \times \left(\dfrac{h - h/\sqrt{2}}{3}\right)$ = 0.15 h	$(0.15) \times \dfrac{bh^2}{4}$

$$M_p = \sigma_{yc} (A_c \cdot \bar{y}_c) + \sigma_{yt} (A_t \cdot \bar{y}_t)$$

$$= \left[\sigma_y \left(\frac{bh^2}{12\sqrt{2}}\right) + \sigma_y \left(\frac{0.15\ bh^2}{4}\right)\right] = \sigma_y (0.096\ bh^2)$$

Step VI : Shape factor (K_s) : $K_s = \dfrac{M_p}{M_y} = \dfrac{\sigma_y (0.096\ bh^2)}{\sigma_y (bh^2/24)} = 2.31$

Step VII : Load factor :

Load factor = Factor of safety × Shape factor = $K_s \times K_s$ = 1.7 × 2.31 = 3.297

Example 7.7 : *Cross-section of the beam shown in Fig. 7.13 (a) is subjected to sagging bending moment. Find the shape factor if permissible yield stress in compression and tension is 230 MPa and 280 MPa respectively.*

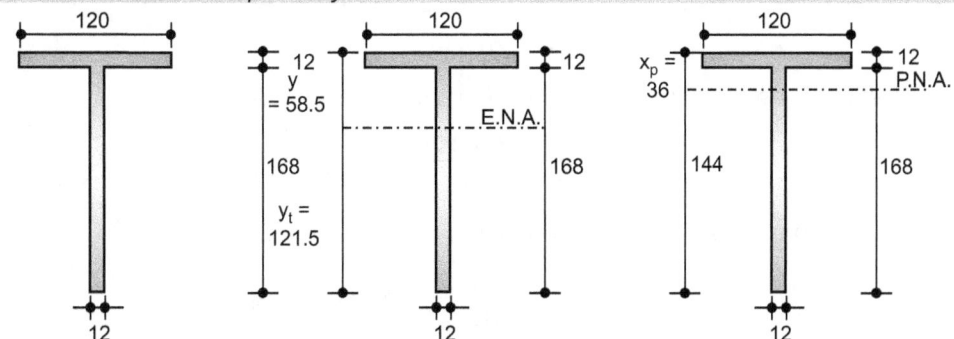

(a) Given cross-section of the beam
(b) Elastic neutral axis of the cross-section
(c) Plastic neutral axis of the cross-section

Fig. 7.13 : Illustrative Example 7.7

Solution : Data : (1) Cross-section of the beam: as shown in Fig. 7.13 (a).

(2) Material yield stresses: σ_{yc} = 230 MPa and σ_{yt} = 280 MPa.

Objects : (i) Plastic moment (M_p).

(ii) Shape factor (K_s).

Concepts and Equations :

(1) Theory of plastic bending

(2) $M_p = \sigma_{yc} (A_c \cdot \bar{y}_c) + \sigma_{yt} (A_t \cdot \bar{y}_t)$

(3) $K_s = \dfrac{M_p}{M_y}$

Procedure :

Step I : Elastic neutral axis :

$$x_e = \dfrac{120 \times 12 \times 6 + 168 \times 12 \times (12 + 168/2)}{120 \times 12 + 168 \times 12}$$

= 58.5 mm from top

∴ y_c = 58.5 m and y_t = 121 mm as shown in Fig. 7.13 (b).

Step II : Plastic neutral axis : Assuming that, plastic neutral axis lies in web :

$A_c = A_t$

$(120 \times 12) + (x_p - 12) \times 12 = (180 - x_p) \times 12$

∴ x_p = 36 mm from top (> 12 mm o.k.) as shown in Fig. 7.13 (c).

Step III : Elastic section modulus (Z_e) :

$$I = \frac{120 \times 12^3}{12} + (120 \times 12)(58.5 - 6)^2 + \frac{12 \times 168^3}{12} + (12 \times 168)(12 + 168/2 - 58.5)^2$$

$$= 11.56 \times 10^6 \text{ mm}^4$$

(a) Elastic section modulus with reference to compression side = Z_{ec}

$$= \frac{I}{y_c} = \frac{11.56 \times 10^6}{58.5} = 19.7 \times 10^4 \text{ mm}^3$$

(b) Elastic section modulus with reference to tension side = Z_{et}

$$= \frac{I}{y_t} = \frac{11.56 \times 10^6}{121.5} = 9.52 \times 10^4 \text{ mm}^3$$

Step IV : Yield moment (M_y) :

(a) Yield moment with reference to compression side = $M_{yc} = \sigma_{yc} \cdot Z_{ec}$

$$= (230 \times 19.7 \times 10^4) \, 10^{-6} = 45.31 \text{ kNm}$$

(b) Yield moment with reference to tension side = $M_{yt} = \sigma_{yt} \cdot Z_{et}$

$$= (280 \times 9.52 \times 10^5) \, 10^{-6} = 26.66 \text{ kNm}$$

$\therefore$ Yield moment = M_y = Least of M_{yc} and M_{yt} = 26.66 kNm

Step V : Plastic moment (M_p) :

Sr. No.	Area in compression (A_c) (mm²)	Distances of c.g. of 'A_c' from plastic neutral axis ($\bar{y}_c$) (mm)	$A_c \cdot \bar{y}_c$ (mm³)	Sr. No.	Area in tension (A_t) (mm²)	Distance of c.g. of 'A_t' from plastic neutral axis ($\bar{y}_t$) (mm)	$A_t \cdot \bar{y}_t$ (mm³)
1.	120×12 = 1440	$36 - \frac{12}{2} = 30$	43200	1.	144×12 = 1728	$\frac{144}{2} = 72$	124416
2.	$(36 - 12) \times 12$ = 288	$36 - \frac{12}{2} = 12$	3456			$\Sigma =$	124416
		$\Sigma =$	46656				

$$M_p = \sigma_{yc}(A_c \cdot \bar{y}_c) + \sigma_{yt}(A_t \cdot \bar{y}_t)$$
$$= (230 \times 46656 + 280 \times 124416) \times 10^{-6} \text{ kNm} = 45.567 \text{ kNm}$$

Step VI : Shape factor (K_s) :

$$K_s = \frac{M_p}{M_y} = \frac{45.567}{26.66} = 1.709$$

Example 7.8 : Cross-section of the beam shown in Fig. 7.14 (a) is subjected to sagging bending moment. Find the shape factor if permissible yield stress in compression and tension is 200 MPa and 250 MPa respectively.

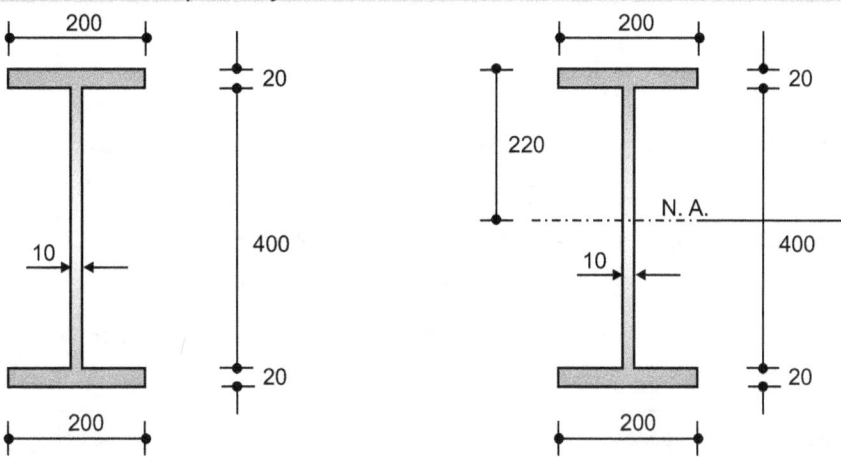

(a) Given cross-section of the beam (b) Elastic and plastic neutral axis of cross-section

Fig. 7.14 : Illustrative Example 7.8

Solution : Data : (1) Cross-section of the beam : as shown in Fig. 7.14 (a).

(2) Material yield stresses : σ_{yc} = 200 MPa and σ_{yt} = 250 MPa

Objects : (1) Plastic moment (M_p). (2) Shape factor (K_s).

Concepts and Equations :

(1) Theory of plastic bending. (2) $M_p = \sigma_{yc} (A_c \cdot \bar{y}_c) + \sigma_{yt} (A_t \cdot \bar{y}_t)$. (3) $K_s = \dfrac{M_p}{M_y}$

Procedure :

Step I : Elastic neutral axis : 220 mm from top (∵ By symmetry) as shown in Fig. 7.14 (b).

Step II : Plastic neutral axis : 220 mm from top (∵ By symmetry) as shown in Fig. 7.14 (b).

Step III : Elastic section modulus (Z_e) :

$$I = \dfrac{200 \times (440)^3}{12} - \dfrac{190 \times (400)^3}{12}$$

$$= 406.4 \times 10^6 \text{ mm}^4$$

(a) Elastic section modulus with reference to compression side = Z_{ec}

$$= \dfrac{I}{y_c} = \dfrac{406.4 \times 10^6}{220} = 1.847 \times 10^6 \text{ mm}^3$$

(b) Elastic section modulus with reference to tension side = Z_{et}

$$= \frac{I}{y_t} = \frac{406.4 \times 10^6}{220}$$

$$= 1.847 \times 10^6 \text{ mm}^3$$

Step IV : Yield moment (M_y) :

(a) Yield moment with reference to compression side = $M_{yc} = \sigma_{yc} \cdot Z_{ec}$

$$= (200 \times 1.847 \times 10^6) \, 10^{-6} = 369.4 \text{ kNm}$$

(b) Yield moment with reference to tension side = $M_{yt} = \sigma_{yt} \cdot Z_{et}$

$$= (250 \times 1.847 \times 10^6) \, 10^{-6} = 461.75 \text{ kNm}$$

Yield moment = M_y = Least of M_{yc} and M_{yt} = 369.4 kNm

Step V : Plastic moment (M_p) :

Sr. No.	Area in compression (A_c) (mm²)	Distances of c.g. of 'A_c' from plastic neutral axis ($\bar{y}_c$) (mm)	$A_c \cdot \bar{y}_c$ (mm³)	Sr. No.	Area in tension (A_t) (mm²)	Distances of c.g. of 'A_t' from plastic neutral axis ($\bar{y}_t$) (mm)	$A_t \cdot \bar{y}_t$ (mm³)
1.	200 × 20 = 4000	$\frac{200 + 20}{2} = 210$	840000	1.	200 × 20 = 4000	$\frac{200 + 20}{2} = 210$	840000
2.	200 × 10 = 2000	$\frac{200}{2} = 100$	200000	2.	200 × 10 = 2000	$\frac{200}{2} = 100$	200000
		$\Sigma =$	1040000			$\Sigma =$	1040000

$$M_p = \sigma_{yc} (A_c \cdot \bar{y}_c) + \sigma_{yt} (A_t \cdot \bar{y}_t)$$
$$= (200 \times 1040000 + 250 \times 1040000) \times 10^{-6} \text{ kNm}$$
$$= 468 \text{ kNm}$$

Step VI : Shape factor (K_s) :

$$K_s = \frac{M_p}{M_y} = \frac{468}{369.4}$$

$$= 1.27$$

Example 7.9 : Cross-section of the beam shown in Fig. 7.15 (a) is subjected to sagging bending moment. Find the shape factor if permissible yield stress in compression and tension is 200 MPa and 240 MPa respectively.

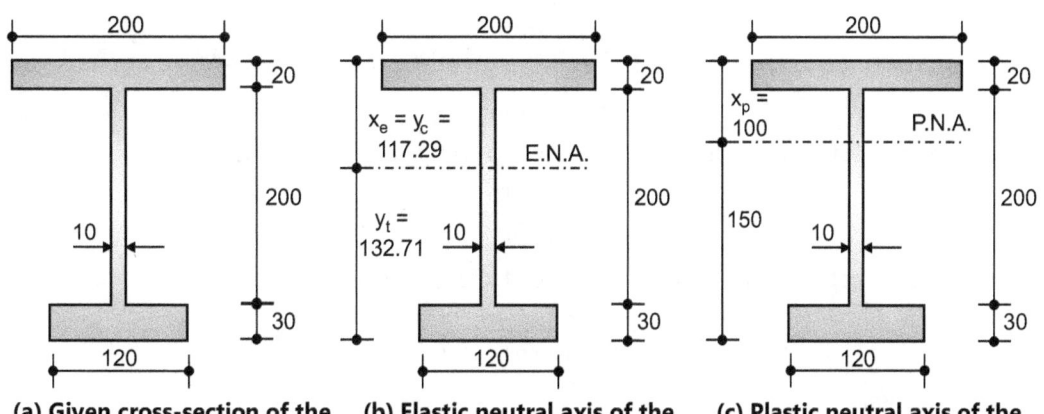

(a) Given cross-section of the beam (b) Elastic neutral axis of the cross-section (c) Plastic neutral axis of the cross-section

Fig. 7.15 : Illustrative Example 7.9

Solution : Data : (1) Cross-section of the beam : as shown in Fig. 7.15 (a).

(2) Material yield stresses : σ_{yc} = 200 MPa and σ_{yt} = 240 MPa

Objects : (1) Plastic moment (M_p).

(2) Shape factor (K_s).

Concepts and Equations :

(1) Theory of plastic bending

(2) $M_p = \sigma_{yc} (A_c \cdot \bar{y}_c) + \sigma_{yt} (A_t \cdot \bar{y}_t)$

(3) $K_s = \dfrac{M_p}{M_y}$

Procedure :

Step I : Elastic neutral axis :

$$x_e = \dfrac{200 \times 20 \times (20/2) + 200 \times 10 \times (20 + 200/2) + 120 \times 30 \times (220 + 30/2)}{200 \times 20 + 200 \times 10 + 120 \times 30}$$

= 117.29 mm from top

∴ y_c = 117.29 mm and y_t = 132.71 mm as shown in Fig. 7.15 (b).

Step II : Plastic neutral axis : Assuming that; plastic neutral axis lies in web.

$A_c = A_t$

$200 \times 20 + (x_p - 20) \times 10 = (220 - x_p) \times 10 + 120 \times 30$

∴ x_p = 100 mm from top (> 20 mm o.k.) as shown in Fig. 7.15 (c).

Step III : Elastic section modulus (Z_e) :

$$I = \dfrac{200 \times 20^3}{12} + (200 \times 20)(117.29 - 10)^2 + \dfrac{10 \times 200^3}{12} (120 - 117.29)^2$$

$$+ \frac{120 \times 30^3}{12} + (120 \times 30)(235 - 117.29)^2$$

$$= 1.03 \times 10^8 \text{ mm}^4$$

(a) Elastic section modulus with reference to compression side = Z_{ec}

$$= \frac{I}{y_c} = \frac{1.03 \times 10^8}{117.29} = 8.78 \times 10^5 \text{ mm}^3$$

(b) Elastic section modulus with reference to tension side = Z_{et}

$$= \frac{I}{y_t} = \frac{1.03 \times 10^8}{132.71} = 7.76 \times 10^5 \text{ mm}^3$$

Step IV : Yield moment (M_y) :

(a) Yield moment with reference to compression side = $M_{yc} = \sigma_{yc} \cdot Z_{ec}$

$$= (200 \times 8.78 \times 10^5) \times 10^{-6} = 175.6 \text{ kNm}$$

(b) Yield moment with reference to tension side = $M_{yt} = \sigma_{yt} \cdot Z_{et}$

$$= (240 \times 7.76 \times 10^5) \times 10^{-6} = 186.24 \text{ kNm}$$

∴ Yield moment = M_y = Least of M_{yc} and M_{yt} = 175.6 kNm

Step V : Plastic moment (M_p) :

Sr. No.	Area in compression (A_c) (mm²)	Distances of c.g. of 'A_c' from plastic neutral axis ($\bar{y}_c$) (mm)	$A_c \cdot \bar{y}_c$ (mm³)	Sr. No.	Area in tension (A_t) (mm²)	Distances of c.g. of 'A_t' from plastic neutral axis ($\bar{y}_t$) (mm)	$A_t \cdot \bar{y}_t$ (mm³)
1.	200 × 20 = 4000	$\frac{100 + 20}{2} = 210$	360000	1.	(150 − 30) × 10 = 1200	$\frac{(150 - 30)}{2} = 60$	72000
2.	(100 − 20) × 10 = 800	$\frac{(100 - 20)}{2} = 40$	32000	2.	120 × 30 = 3600	$150 - \frac{30}{2} = 135$	486000
	Σ =		392000		Σ =		558000

$$M_p = \sigma_{yc}(A_c \cdot \bar{y}_c) + \sigma_{yt}(A_t \cdot \bar{y}_t)$$
$$= (200 \times 392000 + 240 \times 558000) \times 10^{-6} \text{ kNm}$$
$$= 212.32 \text{ kNm}$$

Step VI : Shape factor (K_s) :

$$K_s = \frac{M_p}{M_y} = \frac{212.32}{175.6} = 1.209$$

Chapter 8
PLASTIC ANALYSIS

8.1 INTRODUCTION

The conversion of a structure into the collapse mechanism by the formation of plastic hinges is the key consideration of plastic analysis of structures. For the sake of simplicity it is assumed that a fully plastic hinge is formed at section as soon as the extreme fibre stress reaches the yield stress. In other words, the shape factor of the section is assumed as unity. Plastic hinge is capable of withstanding a constant bending moment equal to the plastic moment of the section, allowing continuous rotation. The load carrying capacity of a structure depends only on the value of the plastic moment and not on the complete moment-curvature relations. An idealized elastic-plastic moment-curvature relation, shown in Fig. 8.1 (a), taking the shape factor as unity, is further simplified to the rigid plastic relation shown in Fig. 8.1 (b). The rigid plastic behaviour neglects the elastic curvature being very small compared with the theoretically infinite curvature after plastic hinge formation.

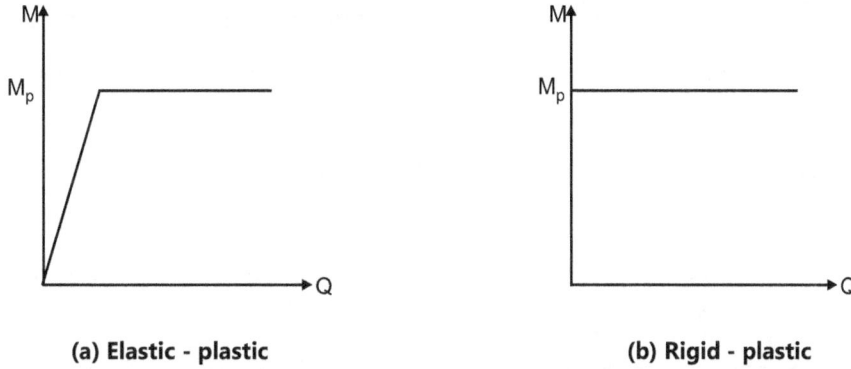

(a) Elastic - plastic   (b) Rigid - plastic

Fig. 8.1 : Plastic hinge hypothesis

When a statically indeterminate structure is subjected to steadily increasing loads, the formation of the first plastic hinge does not in general cause plastic collapse. Further increase of the loads can usually be carried and other plastic hinges form successively until finally there are sufficient number of plastic hinges to transform the structure into the mechanism. Further increase in load will cause indefinite deformation, thus the plastic collapse occurs. A mechanism specified by one displacement is called one degree of freedom (DOF). Mechanisms of one DOF are only considered in simple plastic analysis.

In plastic methods of structural analysis, no consideration is given to the sequence of formation of the plastic hinges which cause the collapse mechanism. Therefore, tracing of complete loading history is not required for the purposes of simple plastic analysis. Only the mechanism state of a structure is the main concern. The effects of axial forces and shear forces are neglected and local bucking, lateral bucking and shear failure are all prevented.

8.2 Types of Mechanisms

The possible hinge locations in a structure may be at the point of (i) fixed support, (ii) interior support, (iii) rigid joint, (iv) concentrated load, (v) internal point. The plastic hinge at end simple, hinged or roller support or at free end is not possible. The potential hinge locations are called *critical sections* or *cardinal sections*.

At a joint the critical section is considered in the weakest member. The bending moment diagram between two adjacent critical sections is straight lines, therefore plastic hinge cannot occur between critical sections in general.

Singe bay, single storey frame shown in Fig. 8.2 (a) is considered to illustrate the different types of mechanisms. Mechanisms are classified in different ways as given below :

- **Beam Mechanism** is shown in Fig. 8.2 (b). A beam mechanism, in general, requires three plastic hinges.

- **Sway Mechanism** is shown in Fig. 8.2 (c). A sway mechanism, in general, requires four plastic hinges.

- **Combined Mechanism** is shown in Fig. 8.2 (d) which is the combination of beam mechanism and sway mechanism.

- **Independent Mechanism :** A mechanism which cannot be obtained from linear combination of the others is called as *independent mechanism*. Any two of three mechanisms i.e. beam, sway and combined can be regarded as the independent mechanism. In general, there will be a number of independent mechanisms which is equal to the number of independent equations of equilibrium. If there are n possible plastic hinge positions and D_{si} is degree of redundancy there will be $(n - D_{si})$ independent mechanisms.

For the frame under consideration there are five critical sections as shown in Fig. 8.2 (a) and three redundancies. i.e. n = 5, D_{si} = 3. Therefore there will be two (5 − 3) independent mechanisms i.e. two out of beam, sway and combined mechanism.

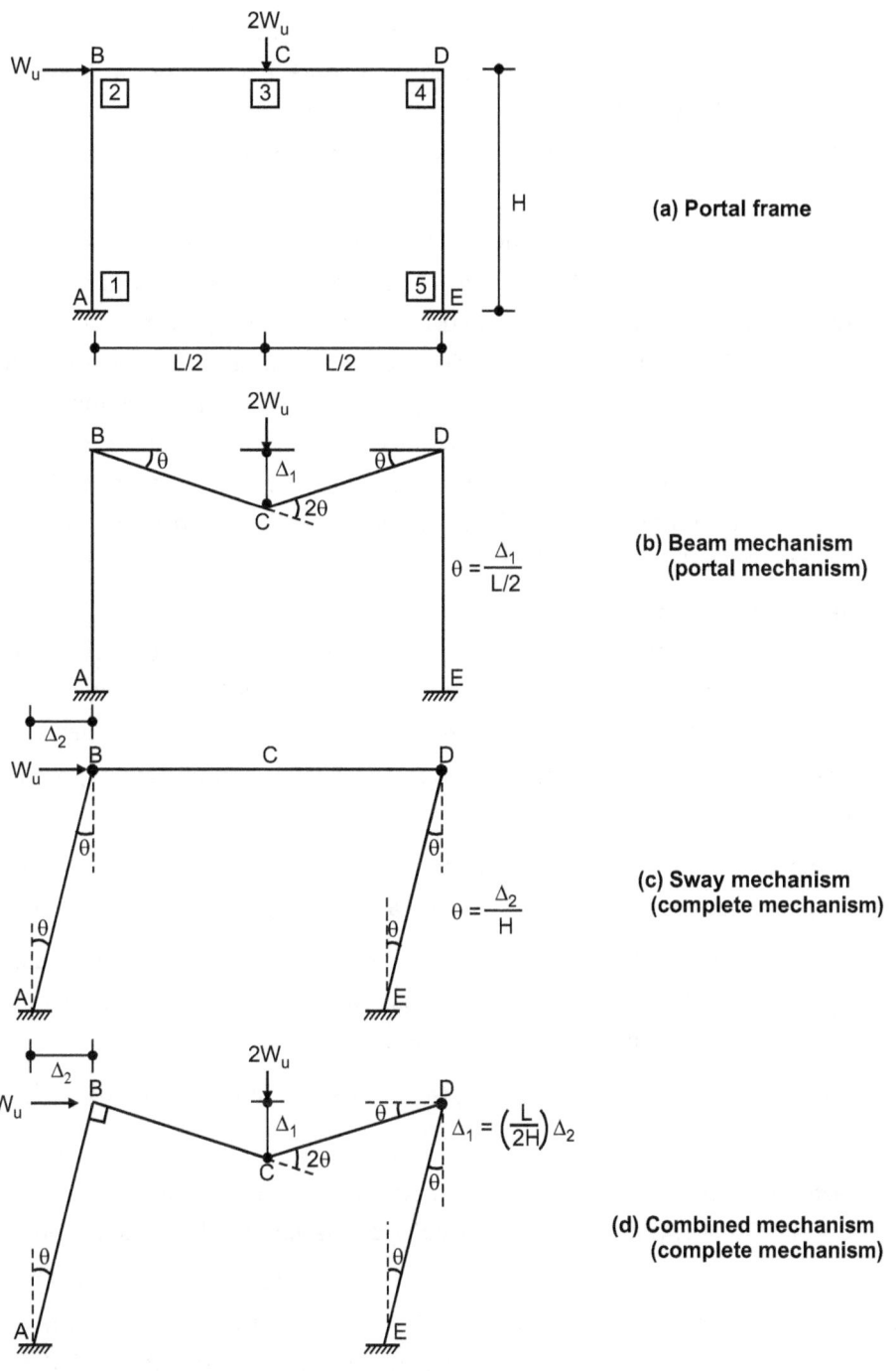

Fig. 8.2 : Types of mechanisms

- **Joint Mechanism :** A local rotation of the joint as a rigid body is known as joint mechanism or joint rotation. This is illustrated with respect to the portal frame shown in Fig. 8.3 (a) having different plastic moments for the beam and column sections. In such a case, the plastic hinges do not form at the joints but at the adjacent sections in the members.

Therefore, the number of critical sections n will be 7 as shown in Fig. 8.3 (a) and the number of independent mechanisms will be four i.e. 7 – 3 = 4. These mechanisms are beam sway, joint mechanisms of B and D. The combined mechanism is obtained from combination of these mechanisms. The beam mechanism with the plastic hinges in the beam is shown in Fig. 8.3 (b). The sway mechanism with the plastic hinges in the column is shown in Fig. 8.3 (c). The combination of beam and sway mechanisms is shown in Fig. 8.3 (d). The joint rotation at B as a rigid body cancels the two hinges at joint B and the combined mechanism shown in Fig. 8.3 (e) is obtained. The joint rotation at D is shown in Fig. 8.3 (f) and (g) resulting the corresponding mechanisms.

- **Complete Mechanism :** If the degree of redundancy of a structure is D_{si}, then formation of D_{si} number of plastic hinges will make the structure statically determinate and (D_{si} + 1) number of plastic hinges will convert the structure to a mechanism. This type of mechanism with (D_{si} + 1) hinges is termed as the complete collapse mechanism. The complete mechanism is statically determinate as the distribution of bending moments can be obtained by statics.

The sway mechanism and combined mechanism of the frame shown in Fig. 8.3 (c) and (d) contain four plastic hinges and hence considered as the complete collapse mechanisms.

In this context, it may be noted that a given statically determinate structure needs only one plastic hinge for the complete collapse mechanism and indeterminate structure needs more than one as per the degree of static indeterminacy.

When the collapse mechanism is not complete in this sense, it may be either partial or over complete.

- **Partial Collapse Mechanism :** A mechanism due to formation of number of plastic hinges less than (D_{si} + 1) is known as *partial collapse mechanism*. In this situation, there is a failure of part of the structure by the mechanism. Remaining part of the structure is intact. However, for the purpose of plastic analysis this is also considered as failure because of indefinite deflection of structure. A partial collapse mechanism is statically indeterminate. Beam mechanism of a portal frame, shown in Fig. 8.3 (b) is the partial collapse mechanism.

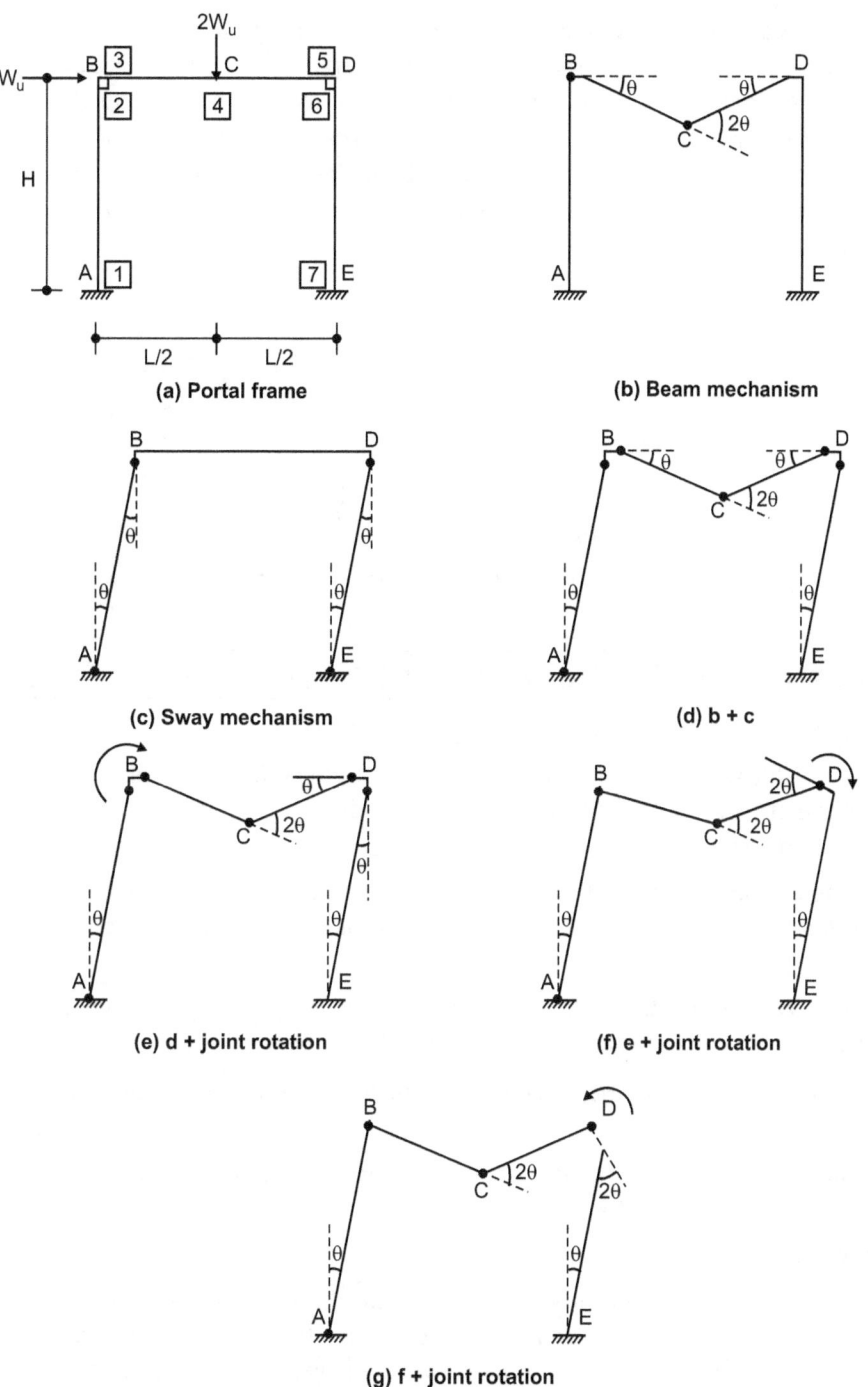

Fig. 8.3 : Types of mechanisms

- **Over Complete Mechanism :** The term over complete mechanism is used when there are two or more mechanisms. The over complete mechanism is specified by two degrees of freedom. The over complete mechanism involves more than (D_{si} + 1) plastic hinges. The over complete mechanism occurs at certain definite values of the ratios of the applied loads when the plastic moments of beam and columns are different. The over complete mechanism represented in Fig. 8.4 as an addition of sway mechanism and combined mechanism.

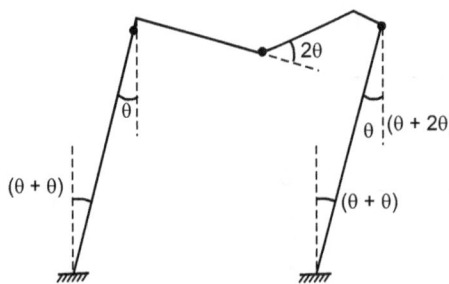

Fig. 8.4 : Over complete mechanism

8.3 FUNDAMENTAL THEOREMS OF PLASTIC ANALYSIS

A structure in its collapse state should satisfy three conditions :

- **The Mechanism Condition :** It means that the sufficient number of plastic hinges transform the structure into a mechanism. This condition is known as kinematical condition or kinematic admissibility.

- **The Equilibrium Condition :** It specifies that the bending moment distribution is in equilibrium with the collapse load. This condition is called as statical condition or static admissibility.

- **The Yield Condition :** It means that the bending moment nowhere exceeds the plastic moment M_p. This condition is termed as safe condition or safety.

These three conditions are necessary and sufficient for the determination of the true collapse load of a structure.

As per the master conditions of plastic collapse, following fundamental theorems are formulated to assess the collapse load.

- **Uniqueness Theorem :**

It states that if a bending moment distribution can be obtained which satisfies the three conditions of mechanism, equilibrium and yield, then the collapse load corresponding to such bending moment distribution will be the true collapse load. The uniqueness theorem does not mean that mechanism itself is unique.

- **Lower Bound Theorem :**

It states that if a bending moment distribution can be found which satisfies the conditions of equilibrium and yield then the corresponding load must be less than or equal to the true collapse load. As the mechanism condition is not satisfied, the structure will not collapse under the calculated load. The theorem is also known as *static theorem* since the equilibrium condition is fulfilled. The yield condition is ensured therefore the theorem is called as *safe theorem*. The theorem is not much useful and convenient for the plastic analysis of structures.

- **Upper Bound Theorem :**

It states that the collapse load obtained from any assumed mechanism for a given structure must be either greater than or equal to the true collapse load. It cannot be less than the true collapse load. As the mechanism is assumed, the mechanism condition is satisfied. Therefore, the theorem is also known as *kinematic theorem*. The equilibrium condition is satisfied but the yield condition is not satisfied and hence the theorem is called as *unsafe theorem*. This is also true in a design sense that the plastic moment M_p obtained from an assumed mechanism is smaller than that actually required. The theorem is useful and convenient to process the plastic analysis of structures.

The three theorems of plastic collapse are only valid for rigid - plastic structures.

The three theorems are consolidated in the following format :

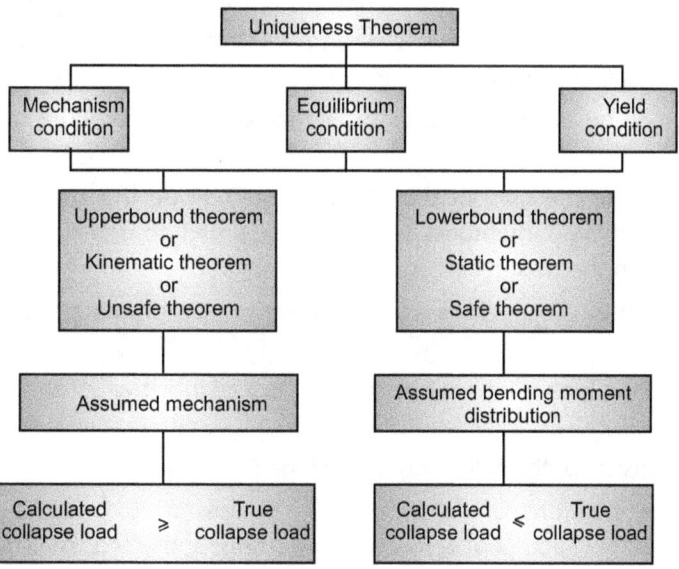

8.4 Plastic Analysis of Structures

8.4.1 General

The object of plastic analysis is to find the true collapse load of the given structure. There may be number of possible collapse mechanisms for the structure except the simple structure having only one mechanism. To arrive at the true collapse load, plastic analysis must satisfy the conditions of mechanisms, equilibrium and yield. It is difficult to include all three necessary and sufficient conditions in one operation. Therefore, two methods, based on the fundamental theorems of plastic collapse, are formulated as given below.

8.4.2 Mechanism Method

True collapse load of the given structure is obtained from collapse loads of different assumed mechanisms of the structure. The method involves the analysis of the mechanism. The kinematical theorem is the key of the method, therefore it is also known as kinematical method or upper bound method giving the upper values of collapse loads than the true collapse load.

The basic principle of the method is that during the plastic collapse the work done by the external loads is equal to the work absorbed in the plastic hinges. The mechanism is defined by the arbitrary displacement, other displacements are obtained from geometry. Therefore, this principle is expressed in a virtual work equation as

$$\Sigma (P \cdot \Delta) = \Sigma (M_p \cdot \theta) \qquad \ldots (8.1)$$

where the loads P and the plastic moments M_p are considered as the equivalent set of forces and the displacements of loads Δ and rotations of plastic moments θ are the compatible set of displacements.

The mechanism method is also called as work method or virtual work method. It may be noted that:

- at the collapse mechanism the plastic hinges divide the structure or part of the structure into several rigid members which are assumed to remain straight so that all rotations take place in the plastic hinges,
- the mechanism is specified by one common co-ordinate i.e. single degree of freedom,
- at each plastic hinge the work absorbed must be positive irrespective of the sign of the hinge rotation.

The method consists of the following main steps:

- Decide the locations of potential plastic hinges which may be supports, joints, concentrated load points, points of zero shear in portions subjected to distributed loading.
- Identify possible collapse mechanisms formed by the certain plastic hinges.

- Compute the collapse loads associated with each of these possible mechanisms by virtual work equation.
- The true collapse load will be the lowest of the collapse loads obtained in step IV.
- A statical check is necessary if there is uncertainty about the number of possible mechanisms.

The collapse bending moment diagram is drawn for the mechanism that gives the lowest collapse load.

If the bending moment ordinate nowhere exceeds the plastic moment M_p of that section, then the uniqueness theorem ensures that this mechanism will give the true collapse load.

- If bending moment somewhere is greater than M_p at that section then the yield condition is not satisfied and the correct mechanism is to be searched.

8.4.3 Equilibrium Method

The collapse load of a given structure is assessed by the assumed bending moment diagram satisfying the conditions of equilibrium and yield i.e. static theorem. Therefore, the method is also known as statical method or lower bound method giving lower values of loads than the collapse load. The general procedure of the method involves the following main steps :

- the redundant moments are selected,
- bending moment diagram is constructed by the superposition of the free moment diagram on to the redundant moment diagram in such a way that
- a mechanism is formed.
- the value of the collapse load is then calculated from statics.

The procedure of the equilibrium method is illustrated with respect to the following example of beam.

SOLVED EXAMPLE

Example 8.1 : *The beam is supported and loaded with ultimate loads as shown in Fig. 8.5 (a). Find the collapse load. The section of the beam is of constant M_p throughout and M_p = 32 kNm.*

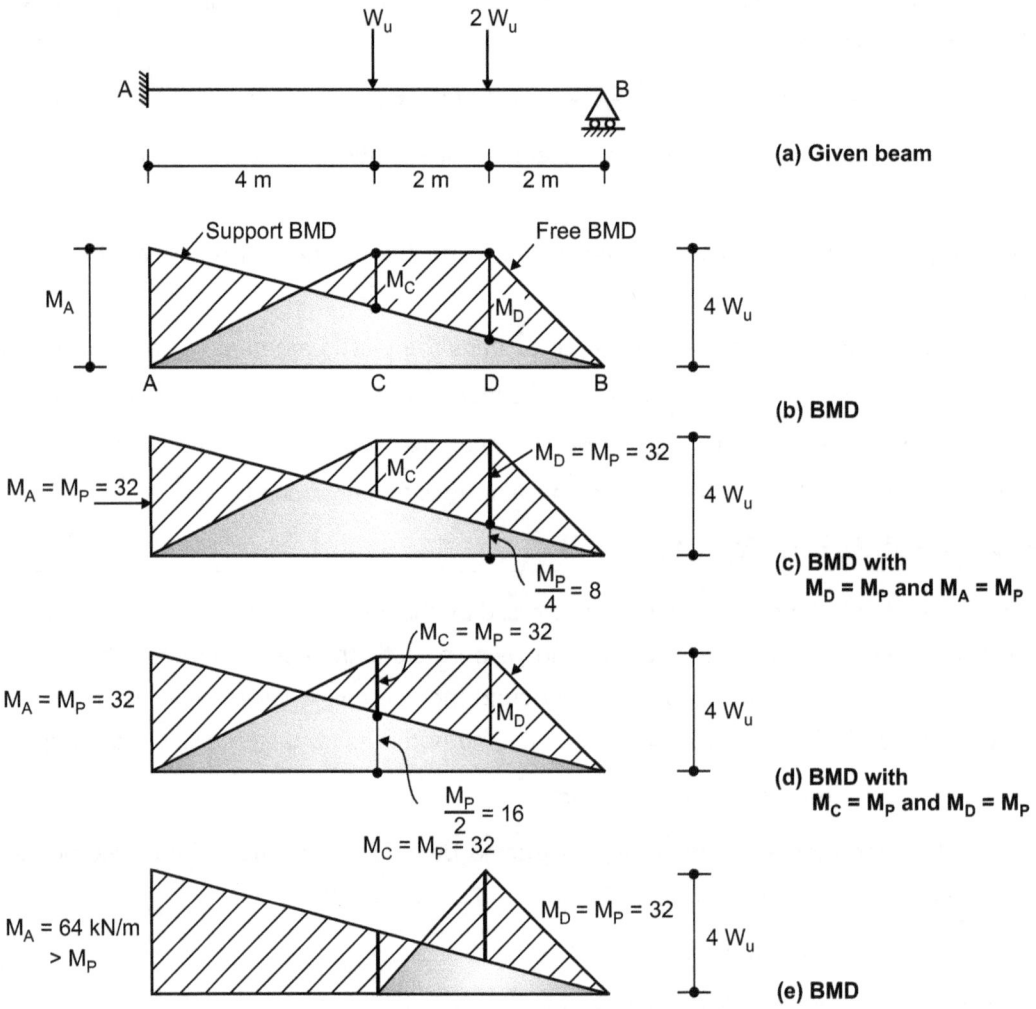

Fig. 8.5 : Equilibrium method (Illustrative Example 8.1)

Solution : Data :

(1) Structural configuration dimensions, support conditions.

(2) Loads - Magnitudes, directions and positions.

(3) Member properties : Uniform cross-section of the beam with plastic moment M_P = 32 kNm.

Object : Collapse load (or load factor).

Concepts and Equations :

(1) Equilibrium method.

(2) Bending moment and geometry of bending moment.

Procedure :

Step I : Free bending moment diagram is constructed as shown in Fig. 8.5 (b).

$$R_{Bf} = \frac{12W + 4W}{8} = 2W, \quad R_{Af} = W$$

$$M_{Bf} = 2W \times 2 = 4W, \quad M_{Cf} = 4W$$

Step II : Support bending moment diagram is superposed on free bending moment diagram as shown in Fig. 8.5 (b)

Step III : Two hinges are required for a mechanism.

Step IV : Three possible bending moment distributions for mechanism are considered as shown in Fig. 8.5 (c), (d) and (e).

Step V : Analysis of each possible bending moment distribution :

(i) Bending moment ordinates at A and C are equal to M_p as shown in Fig. 8.5 (c).

From geometry of BMD,

$$M_D = M_p = 32 = 4W_u - 8$$

$$\therefore \quad 4W_u = 40$$

$$\therefore \quad W_u = 10 \text{ kN}$$

(ii) Bending moment ordinates at C and A are equal to $M_p = 32$ kNm as shown in Fig. 8.5 (d).

$$M_C = M_p = 32 = 4W_u - 16$$

$$\therefore \quad 4W_u = 48$$

$$\therefore \quad W_u = 12 \text{ kN}$$

(iii) Bending moment ordinates at C and D are equal to $M_p = 32$ as shown in Fig. 8.5 (e).

This is not possible as M_D cannot be equal to M_p due to geometry of B.M.D. In fact, $M_D > M_C$. Also M_A is greater than M_p, therefore, this possibility is neglected.

Step VI : True Collapse Load : The possible bending moment distributions correspond to the possible mechanisms also.

True collapse load = Lower of 10 kN and 12 kN

$$\therefore \quad W_u = 10 \text{ kN}$$

8.5 APPLICATION OF PLASTIC ANALYSIS TO STEEL BEAMS

A statically determinate beam has an unique collapse mechanism and therefore very simple to analyze. A statically indeterminate beam e.g. fixed beam, continuous beam may fail by different possible beam mechanisms according to the data of structural configuration, support conditions, loading and plastic moment capacities. However, it is not a difficult task to identify the possible mechanisms in case of beam problems. Once the mechanisms are obtained the ultimate load can be obtained either by equilibrium method or mechanism method.

8.5.1 Equilibrium Method

In particular cases, the equilibrium method is suitable. The bending moment diagram is drawn by superposing the free bending moment diagram on the support (redundant) moment diagram. At the locations of plastic hinges of a mechanism the bending moment ordinates are considered as M_p of known values. And the ultimate or collapse load is found from the geometry of the bending moment diagram. If the bending moment anywhere in the beam exceeds M_p the corresponding mechanism and bending moment distribution are discarded and only the bending moment distribution satisfying the requirements of mechanism and yield are retained and accordingly the true collapse load will be the lowest of the collapse loads obtained. The equilibrium method, in general, is not convenient and therefore not recommended.

8.5.2 Mechanism Method

The possible mechanisms are identified and analyzed by work equation to obtain the collapse load of each mechanism. The true collapse load is the lowest of these values, if no mechanism is skipped and for each mechanism the conditions of equilibrium and yield are satisfied. The method is straight forward if all mechanisms are correctly identified which is possible in the normal situation of the beam problems. Therefore, mechanism method should be preferred.

Distributed Loads on a Beam :

Beams carrying the concentrated loads are comparatively simple to analyze as the potential plastic hinge locations are explicitly known at the load positions. If the beams are subjected to the distributed loads, the location of the plastic hinge is not known but can be obtained. Therefore, assuming the opposition of plastic hinge, by an unknown distance x the position of plastic hinge 'x' be obtained from the condition that moment is maximum or the shear force is zero at that point. Otherwise the collapse load of the mechanism is expressed in terms of x, using the work equation. As the lowest load is of concern, the concept of minima gives the value of x i.e. $\dfrac{dW_u}{dx} = 0$.

If M_p is of interest, M_p is expressed as the function of known ultimate load and unknown x, using work equation of the mechanism. And the position of the plastic hinge i.e. x is then obtained by $\dfrac{dM_p}{dx} = 0$. This additional consideration of location of the plastic hinge in the member under the distributed load will be clarified in the numerical examples.

The work done by the uniformly distributed ultimate load is calculated as the product of rate of loading and the area under the displacement diagram of the loaded part of the beam due to the mechanism. It may be noted again that in a mechanism the beam part remains straight in between the plastic hinges.

SOLVED EXAMPLES

Following Problems illustrate the application of plastic theory to analysis of beams :

Example 8.2 : *The beam is supported and loaded with ultimate load as shown in Fig. 8.6 (a). Find the collapse load and draw B.M.D. at collapse. The section of the beam is of constant M_p throughout.*

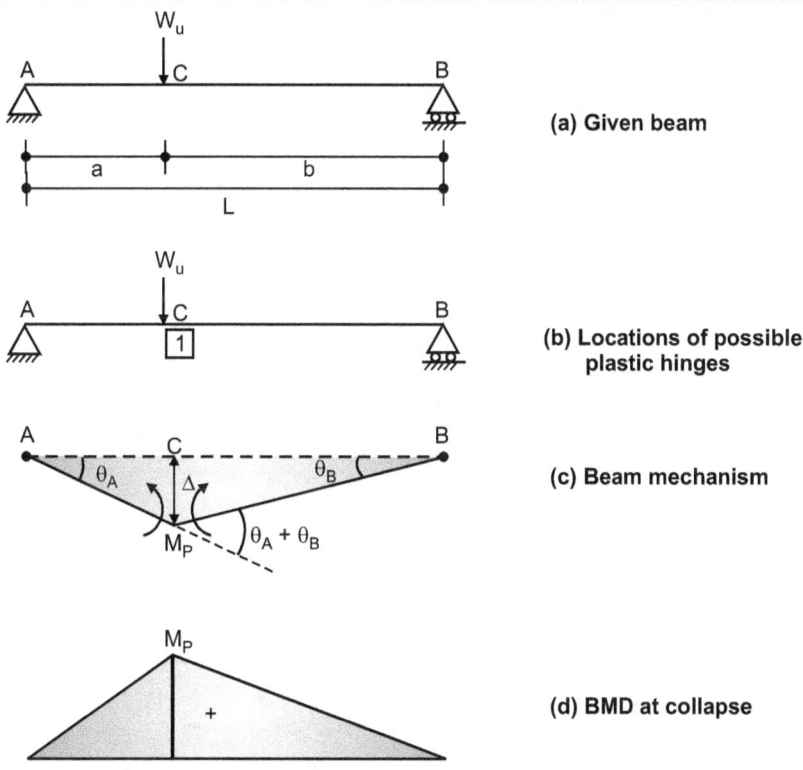

Fig. 8.6 : Illustrative Example 8.2

Solution :

Data : The beam is supported and loaded as shown in Fig. 8.6 (a).

Object : Collapse load.

Concepts and Equations :

(1) Mechanism method.

(2) Work equation : External work done (W_e) = Internal work done (W_i).

Procedure :

Step I : Degree of static indeterminacy = D_{si} = 0

Step II : Potential sections for plastic hinges : One location as shown in Fig. 8.6 (b).

Step III : Identification of possible collapse mechanism : Maximum plastic hinges for complete mechanism = D_{si} + 1 = 0 + 1 = 1.

Number of independent mechanisms = 1 − 0 = 1

Step IV : Analysis of possible mechanism :

Beam mechanism is as shown in Fig. 8.6 (c).

(a) Kinematics of the mechanism : The rotation of plastic hinge at C = $\theta_A + \theta_B$, where $\theta_A = \dfrac{\Delta}{a}$ and $\theta_B = \dfrac{\Delta}{b}$ as shown in Fig. 8.6 (c).

(b) Virtual work equation and collapse load :

$$W_e = W_i \text{ i.e. } W_u \cdot \Delta = M_p (\theta_A + \theta_B)$$

$$\therefore \quad W_u \cdot \Delta = M_p \left(\dfrac{\Delta}{a} + \dfrac{\Delta}{b} \right)$$

$$\therefore \quad \text{Collapse load} = W_u = \dfrac{M_p \cdot L}{ab}$$

Step V : B.M.D. at collapse as shown in Fig. 8.6 (d).

Note : If point load W_u is acting at centre, then collapse load is given by

$$W_u = \dfrac{4M_p}{L}$$

Example 8.3 : The beam is supported and loaded with ultimate load as shown in Fig. 8.7 (a). Find the collapse load and draw B.M.D. at collapse. The section of the beam is of constant M_p throughout.

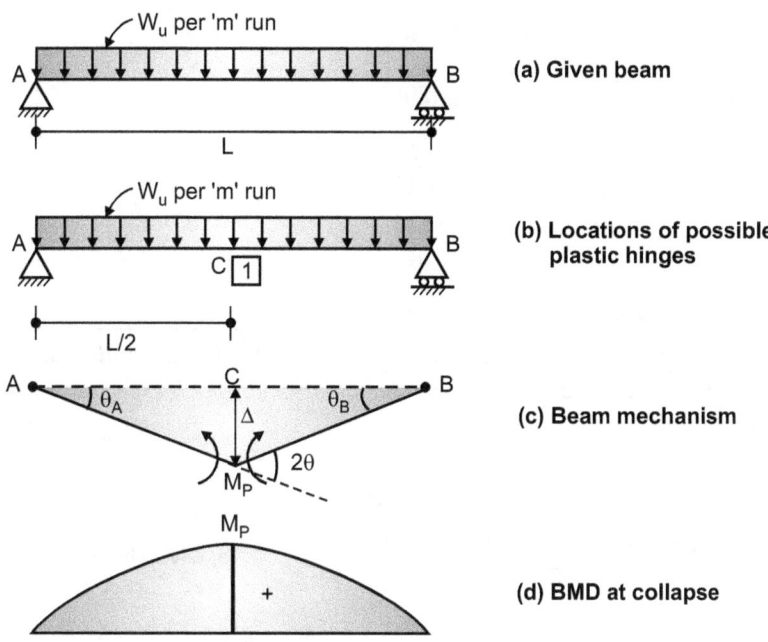

Fig. 8.7 : Illustrative Example 8.3

Solution :

Data : The beam is supported and loaded as shown in Fig. 8.7 (a).

Object : Collapse load.

Concepts and Equations :

(1) Mechanism method.

(2) Work equation : External work done (W_e) = Internal work done (W_i).

Procedure :

Step I : Degree of static indeterminacy = D_{si} = 0

Step II : Potential locations for plastic hinges : One location as shown in Fig. 8.7 (b).

Step III : Identification of possible collapse mechanisms : Maximum plastic hinges for complete mechanism = $D_{si} + 1 = 0 + 1 = 1$

Number of independent mechanisms = $1 - 0 = 1$

Step IV : Analysis of possible mechanism : Beam mechanism is as shown in Fig. 8.7 (c).

(a) Kinematics of the mechanism : The rotation of plastic hinge at C = 2θ.

where $\theta = \dfrac{\Delta}{L/2} = \dfrac{2\Delta}{L}$ as shown in Fig. 8.7 (c).

(b) Virtual work equation and collapse load :

$$W_e = W_i \text{ i.e. } W_u \left(\frac{1}{2} \times L \times \Delta\right) = M_p (2\theta)$$

$$\therefore \quad W_u \frac{1}{2} \cdot \Delta = M_p \cdot 2 \left(\frac{2\Delta}{L}\right)$$

$$\therefore \quad \text{Collapse load} = W_u = \frac{8M_p}{L}$$

Step V : B.M.D. at collapse as shown in Fig. 8.7 (d).

Example 8.4 : *The beam is supported and loaded with ultimate load as shown in Fig. 8.8 (a). Find the collapse load and draw B.M.D. at collapse. The section of the beam is of constant M_p throughout.*

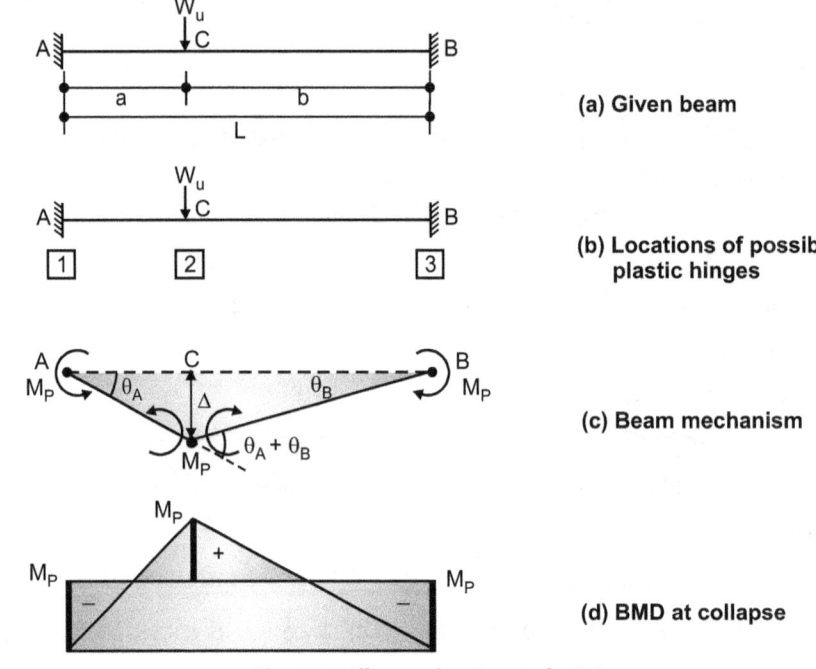

(a) Given beam

(b) Locations of possible plastic hinges

(c) Beam mechanism

(d) BMD at collapse

Fig. 8.8 : Illustrative Example 8.4

Solution :

Data : The beam is supported and loaded as shown in Fig. 8.8 (a).

Object : Collapse load.

Concepts and Equations :

(1) Mechanism method.

(2) Work equation : External work done (W_e) = Internal work done (W_i).

Procedure :

Step I : Degree of static indeterminacy = D_{si} = 2.

Step II : Potential locations for plastic hinges : Three locations as shown in Fig. 8.8 (b).

Step III : Identification of possible collapse mechanisms :

Maximum plastic hinges for complete mechanism = D_{si} + 1 = 2 + 1 = 3.

Number of independent mechanism = 3 – 2 = 1.

Step IV : Analysis of possible mechanism : Beam mechanism is as shown in Fig. 8.8 (c).

(a) Kinematics of the mechanism :

The rotation of plastic hinge at A = $\theta_A = \dfrac{\Delta}{a}$

The rotation of plastic hinge at B = $\theta_B = \dfrac{\Delta}{b}$

The rotation of plastic hinge at C = $\theta_A + \theta_B = \dfrac{\Delta}{a} + \dfrac{\Delta}{b}$ as shown in Fig. 8.8 (c).

(b) Virtual work equation and collapse load :

$W_e = W_i$ i.e. $\quad W_u \cdot \Delta = M_p(\theta_A) + M_p(\theta_A + \theta_B) + M_p(\theta_B)$

$\therefore \quad W_u \cdot \Delta = M_p\left(\dfrac{\Delta}{a}\right) + M_p\left(\dfrac{\Delta}{a} + \dfrac{\Delta}{b}\right) + M_p\left(\dfrac{\Delta}{b}\right)$

$\therefore \quad$ Collapse load $= W_u = \dfrac{2M_p \cdot L}{ab}$

Step V : B.M.D. at collapse load as shown in Fig. 8.8 (d).

Note : If point load W_u is acting at centre, then collapse load is given by,

$$W_u = \dfrac{8M_p}{L}$$

Example 8.5 : *The beam is supported and loaded with ultimate load as shown in Fig. 8.9 (a). Find the collapse load and draw B.M.D. at collapse. The section of the beam is of constant M_p throughout.*

Solution :

Data : The beam is supported and loaded as shown in Fig. 8.9 (a).

Object : Collapse load.

Concepts and Equations :

(1) Mechanism method.

(2) Work equation : External work done (W_e) = Internal work done (W_i).

Procedure :

Step I : Degree of static indeterminacy = D_{si} = 2

Step II : Potential locations for plastic hinges : Three locations as shown in Fig. 8.9 (b).

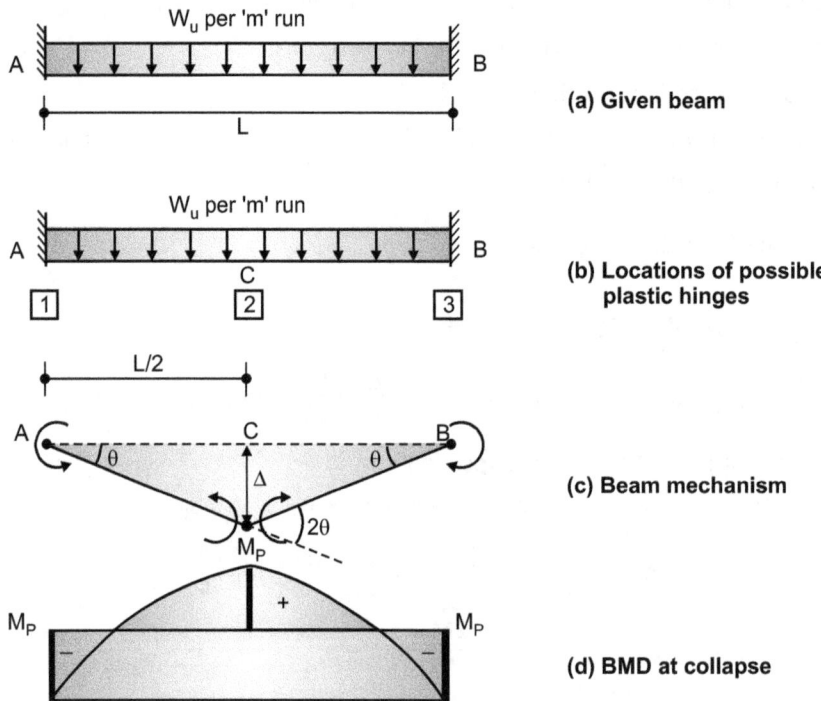

(a) Given beam

(b) Locations of possible plastic hinges

(c) Beam mechanism

(d) BMD at collapse

Fig. 8.9 : Illustrative Example 8.5

Step III : Identification of possible collapse mechanisms :

Maximum plastic hinges for complete mechanism = $D_{si} + 1 = 2 + 1 = 3$

Number of independent mechanism = 3 − 2 = 1

Step IV : Analysis of possible mechanism :

Beam mechanism is as shown in Fig. 8.9 (c).

(a) Kinematics of the mechanisms :

The rotation of plastic hinge at A = $\theta = \dfrac{\Delta}{L/2} = \dfrac{2\Delta}{L}$

The rotation of plastic hinge at B = $\theta = \dfrac{\Delta}{L/2} = \dfrac{2\Delta}{L}$

The rotation of plastic hinge at B = $2\theta = \dfrac{4\Delta}{L}$ as shown in Fig. 8.9 (c).

(b) Virtual work equation and collapse load :

$$W_e = W_i \text{ i.e. } W_u \left(\dfrac{1}{2} \cdot L \cdot \Delta\right) = M_p(\theta) + M_p(2\theta) + M_p(\theta)$$

∴ $\quad W_u \cdot \dfrac{L}{2} \cdot \Delta = M_p\left(\dfrac{2\Delta}{L}\right) + M_p\left(\dfrac{4\Delta}{L}\right) + M_p\left(\dfrac{2\Delta}{L}\right)$

∴ $\quad$ Collapse load $= W_u = \dfrac{16 M_p}{L^2}$

Step V : B.M.D. at collapse as shown in Fig. 8.9 (d).

Example 8.6 : *The beam is supported and loaded with ultimate load as shown in Fig. 8.10 (a). Find the collapse load and draw B.M.D. at collapse. The section of the beam is of constant M_p throughout.*

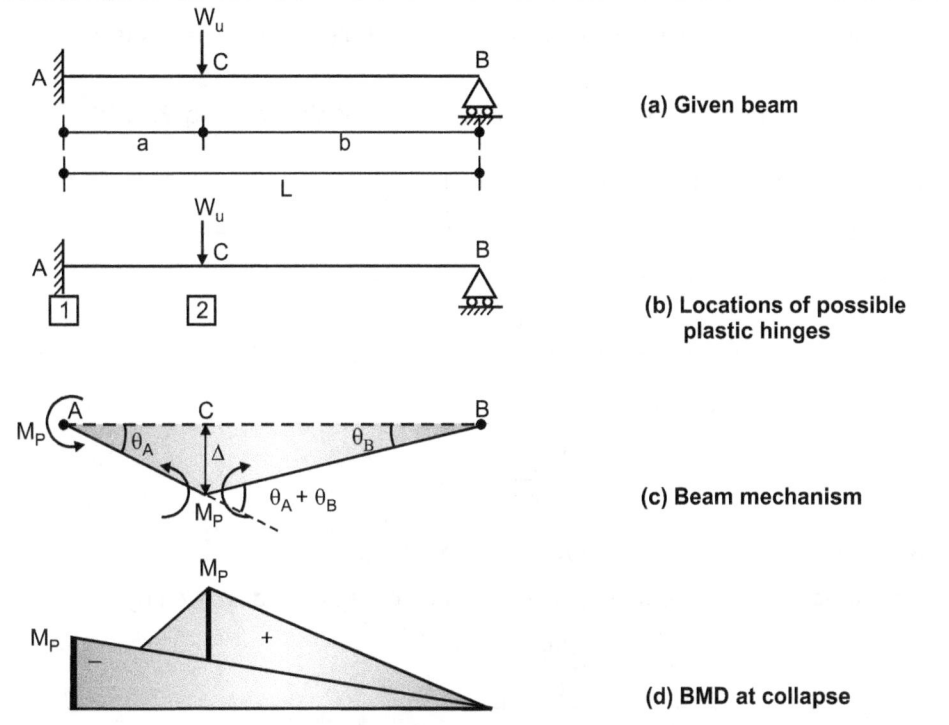

Fig. 8.10 : Illustrative Example 8.6

Solution : Data : The beam is supported and loaded as shown in Fig. 8.10 (a).

Object : Collapse load.

Concepts and Equations :

(1) Mechanism method.
(2) Work equation : External work done (W_e) = Internal work done (W_i).

Procedure :

Step I : Degree of static indeterminacy = D_{si} = 1.

Step II : Potential locations for plastic hinges : Two locations as shown in Fig. 8.10 (b).

Step III : Identification of possible collapse mechanisms :

Maximum plastic hinges for complete mechanism = D_{si} + 1 = 1 + 1 = 2.

Number of independent mechanism = 2 − 1 = 1.

Step IV : Analysis of possible mechanism :

Beam mechanism is as shown in Fig. 8.10 (c).

(a) Kinematics of the mechanism : The rotation of plastic hinge at A = $\theta_A = \dfrac{\Delta}{a}$.

The rotation of plastic hinge at C = $\theta_A + \theta_B = \dfrac{\Delta}{a} + \dfrac{\Delta}{b}$ as shown in Fig. 8.10 (c).

Note that the hinge at B is not a plastic hinge.

(b) Virtual work equation and collapse load :

$$W_e = W_i \text{ i.e. } W_u \Delta = M_p(\theta_A) + M_p(\theta_A + \theta_B)$$

$$\therefore \quad W_u \Delta = M_p\left(\dfrac{\Delta}{a}\right) + M_p\left(\dfrac{\Delta}{a} + \dfrac{\Delta}{b}\right)$$

$$\therefore \quad \text{Collapse load} = W_u = \dfrac{M_p(L + b)}{ab}$$

Step V : B.M.D. at collapse as shown in Fig. 8.10 (d).

Note : If point load W_u is acting at centre, then collapse load is given by

$$W_u = \dfrac{6M_p}{L}$$

Example 8.7 : *The beam is supported and loaded with ultimate load as shown in Fig. 8.11 (a). Find the collapse load and draw B.M.D. at collapse. The section of the beam is of constant M_p throughout.*

TOS – II (TE CIVIL SEM. VI NMU)   PLASTIC ANALYSIS

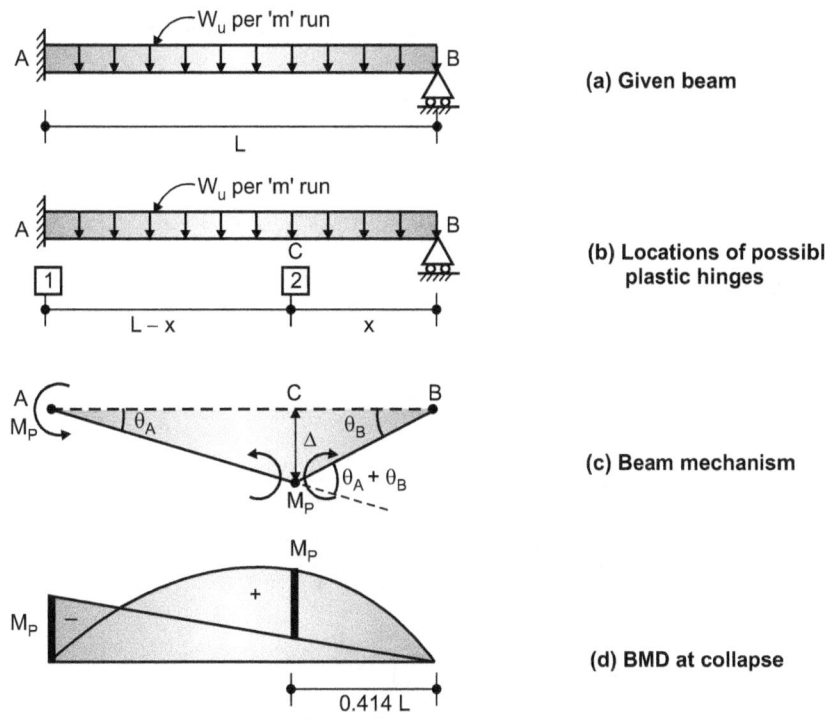

Fig. 8.11 : Illustrative Example 8.7

Solution :

Data : The beam is supported and loaded as shown in Fig. 8.11 (a).

Object : Collapse load.

Concepts and Equations :

(1) Mechanism method.

(2) Work equation : External work done (W_e) = Internal work done (W_i).

Procedure :

Step I : Degree of static indeterminacy = D_{si} = 1.

Step II : Potential locations for plastic hinges : Two locations as shown in Fig. 8.11 (b).

Let x be the distance from B where plastic hinge will be formed.

Step III : Identification of possible collapse mechanisms :

Maximum plastic hinges for complete mechanism = D_{si} + 1 = 1 + 1 = 2.

Number of independent mechanisms = 2 – 1 = 1.

Step IV : Analysis of possible mechanism : Beam mechanism is as shown in Fig. 8.11 (c).

(a) Kinematics of the mechanism : The rotation of plastic hinge at A is

$$\theta_A = \frac{\Delta}{L-x}$$

The rotation of plastic hinge at C is

$$\theta_A + \theta_B = \frac{\Delta}{L-x} + \frac{\Delta}{x} \text{ as shown in Fig. 8.11 (c).}$$

(b) Virtual work equation and collapse load :

$$W_e = W_i$$

$$\therefore \quad W_u \left(\frac{1}{2} L \cdot \Delta\right) = M_p (\theta_A) + M_p (\theta_A + \theta_B)$$

$$\therefore \quad W_u \cdot \frac{L}{2} \cdot \Delta = M_p \left(\frac{\Delta}{L-x}\right) + M_p \left(\frac{\Delta}{L-x} + \frac{\Delta}{x}\right)$$

$$\therefore \quad W_u \cdot \frac{L}{2} = M_p \left[\frac{1}{L-x} + \frac{1}{L-x} + \frac{1}{x}\right]$$

$$\therefore \quad W_u = \frac{2M_p}{L} \left[\frac{L+x}{x(L-x)}\right] \quad \ldots \text{(A)}$$

Theoretically, there are infinite mechanisms. The correct mechanism is the one which needs minimum load. Expression for W_u in terms of unknown distance x is formulated as above and now the load is minimized by differentiation.

∴ Differentiating equation (A) with respect to x and equating to zero,

$$\frac{dW_u}{dx} = \frac{d}{dx}\left[\frac{2M_p}{L}\left(\frac{L+x}{x(L-x)}\right)\right] = 0$$

$$\therefore \quad \frac{dW_u}{dx} = x^2 + 2xL - L^2 = 0 \quad \ldots \text{(B)}$$

Solving the quadratic equation (B), we get

$$x = 0.414 L$$

Substituting the value of x in equation (A), we get

$$W_u = \frac{2M_p}{L}\left[\frac{L + 0.414 L}{0.414 L (L - 0.414 L)}\right]$$

$$W_u = 11.656 \frac{M_p}{L^2}$$

Step V : B.M.D. at collapse : as shown in Fig. 8.11 (d).

Example 8.8 : The beam is supported and loaded with ultimate load as shown in Fig. 8.12 (a). Assuming beam of constant M_p throughout, compute the ultimate load for different values of 'a'.

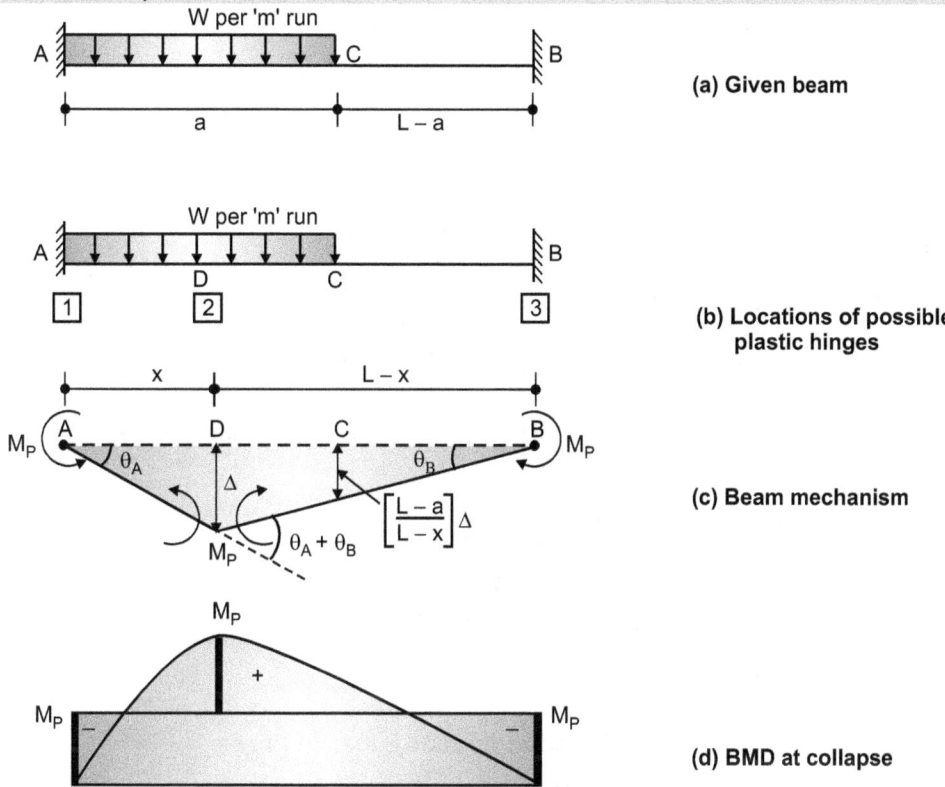

Fig. 8.12 : Illustrative Example 8.8

Solution :

Data : The beam is supported and loaded as shown in Fig. 8.12 (a).

Object : Collapse load.

Concepts and Equations :

(1) Mechanism method.

(2) Work equation : External work done (W_e) = Internal work done (W_i).

Procedure :

Step I : Degree of static indeterminacy = D_{si} = 2.

Step II : Potential locations for plastic hinges : Three locations as shown in Fig. 8.12 (b).

Step III : Identification of possible collapse mechanisms :

Maximum plastic hinges for complete mechanism = D_{si} + 1 = 2 + 1 = 3

Number of independent mechanism = 3 – 2 = 1

Step IV : Analysis of possible mechanisms :

Beam mechanism is as shown in Fig. 8.12 (c).

(a) Kinematics of the mechanism :

The rotation of plastic hinge at A = $\theta_A = \dfrac{\Delta}{x}$

The rotation of plastic hinge at B = $\theta_B = \dfrac{\Delta}{L-x}$

The rotation of plastic hinge at D = $\theta_A + \theta_B = \dfrac{\Delta}{x} + \dfrac{\Delta}{L-x}$

(b) Virtual work equation :

$W_e = W_i$ i.e. $W_u \left[\dfrac{1}{2} \times L \times \Delta - \dfrac{1}{2} \times (L-a) \times \left(\dfrac{L-a}{L-x}\right) \Delta \right] = M_p (\theta_A) + M_p (\theta_A + \theta_B) + M_p (\theta_B)$

$\therefore \quad \dfrac{W_u}{2} \cdot \Delta \left[L - \dfrac{(L-a)^2}{L-x} \right] = M_p \left(\dfrac{\Delta}{x}\right) + M_p \left(\dfrac{\Delta}{x} + \dfrac{\Delta}{L-x}\right) + M_p \left(\dfrac{\Delta}{L-x}\right)$

$\dfrac{W_u}{2} \left[L - \dfrac{(L-a)^2}{L-x} \right] = M_p \left(\dfrac{2L}{x(L-x)}\right)$

$W_u = \left[\dfrac{-4L}{a^2 x - 2aLx + Lx^2}\right] M_p$

For minimum value of W_u, $\dfrac{dw_u}{dx} = 0$

Differentiating equation (A) with respect to x and equating to zero;

$x = \dfrac{a(2L-a)}{2L}$, substituting in equation (A), we get

$W_u = \dfrac{16 M_p L^2}{a^2 (2L-a)^2}$

Step V : Different values of 'a' and corresponding collapse load : as given in Table 8.1.

Table 8.1

a	0.2 L	0.4 L	0.5 L	0.6 L	0.8 L	L
W_u	$123.45 \dfrac{M_p}{L^2}$	$39.06 \dfrac{M_p}{L^2}$	$28.44 \dfrac{M_p}{L^2}$	$22.675 \dfrac{M_p}{L^2}$	$17.36 \dfrac{M_p}{L^2}$	$16 \dfrac{M_p}{L^2}$

Step VI : B.M.D. at collapse : as shown in Fig. 8.12 (d).

Example 8.9 : *The beam is supported and loaded with ultimate loads as shown in Fig. 8.13 (a). Find the plastic moment and draw B.M.D. at collapse. Assume beam of constant M_p throughout.*

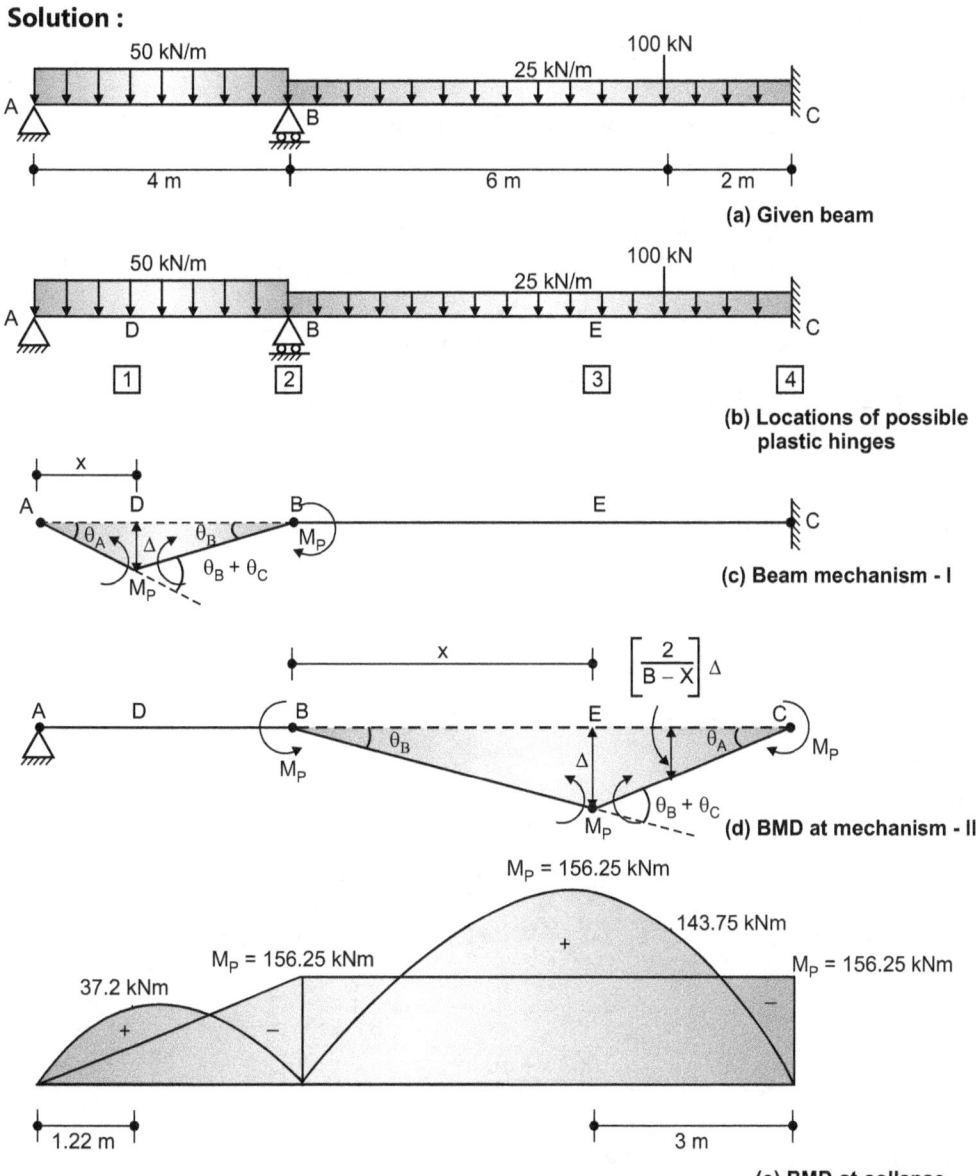

Fig. 8.13 : Illustrative Example 8.9

Data : The beam is supported and loaded as shown in Fig. 8.13 (a).
Object : Plastic moment.
Concepts and Equations :
(1) Mechanism method,
(2) Work equation : External work done (W_e) = Internal work done (W_i).

Procedure :
Step I : Degree of static indeterminacy = D_{si} = 2.
Step II : Potential locations for plastic hinges : Four locations as shown in Fig. 8.13 (b).
Step III : Identification of possible collapse mechanisms :
Maximum plastic hinges for complete mechanism = D_{si} = 1 + 2 = 3.
Number of independent mechanisms = 4 – 2 = 2.
Step IV : Analysis of possible mechanisms : Beam mechanism - I is as shown in Fig. 8.13 (c). This mechanism is similar to that of propped cantilever carrying u.d.l. throughout the span and having constant M_p.

∴ Using the result derived earlier in Example 8.16,
$$W_u = 11.656 \frac{M_p}{L^2} \text{ i.e. } M_p = \frac{W_u L^2}{11.656} = \frac{50 \times 4^2}{11.656} = 68.63 \text{ kNm}.$$
and x = 0.414 L = 0.414 × 4 = 1.656 m

Beam mechanism - II is as shown in Fig. 8.13 (d).
(a) Kinematics of the mechanism :

The rotation of plastic hinge at B = $\theta_B = \frac{\Delta}{x}$

The rotation of plastic hinge at C = $\theta_C = \frac{\Delta}{8-x}$

The rotation of plastic hinge at E = $\theta_B + \theta_C = \frac{\Delta}{x} + \frac{\Delta}{8-x}$

(b) Virtual work equation :
$$W_e = W_i \text{ i.e. } 25\left(\frac{1}{2} \times 8 \times \Delta\right) + 100\left(\frac{2}{8-x}\right)\Delta$$
$$= M_p(\theta_B) + M_p(\theta_B + \theta_C) + M_p(\theta_C)$$

∴ $$100 \Delta \left(\frac{200}{8-x}\right)\Delta = M_p\left(\frac{\Delta}{x}\right) + M_p\left(\frac{\Delta}{x} + \frac{\Delta}{8-x}\right) + M_p\left(\frac{\Delta}{8-x}\right)$$

∴ $$100 + \frac{200}{8-x} = M_p\left(\frac{1}{x} + \frac{1}{x} + \frac{1}{8-x} + \frac{1}{8-x}\right)$$

∴ $$M_p = \frac{1000 x - 100 x^2}{16}$$

For maximum value of M_p; $\frac{d}{dx}(M_p) = 0$

∴ Differentiating equation (A) with respect to x and equating to zero we get x = 5 m, substituting in equation (A).
$$M_p = 156.25 \text{ kNm}$$

∴ Plastic moment = M_p
= Greatest value of M_p obtained among all above mechanisms = 156.25 kNm

Step V : B.M.D. at collapse : as shown in Fig. 8.13 (e).

Example 8.10 : The beam is supported and loaded as shown in Fig. 8.14 (a). Find the plastic moment and draw B.M.D. at collapsed. Assume load factor = 1.8 and beam of constant M_p throughout.

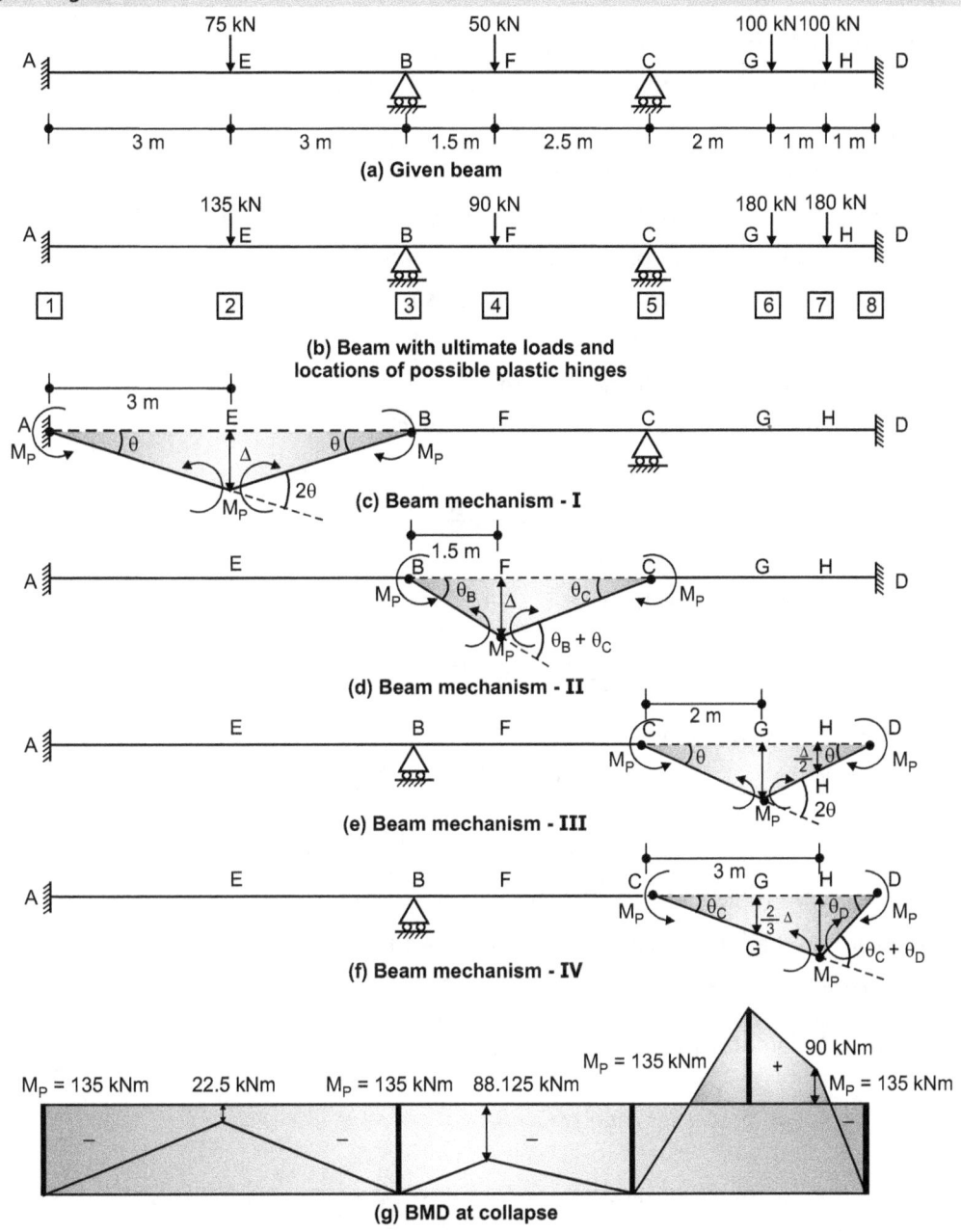

Fig. 8.14 : Illustrative Example 8.10

Solution :

Data : The beam is supported and loaded as shown in Fig. 8.14 (a).

Object : Plastic moment.

Concepts and Equations : (1) Mechanism method.

(2) Work equation : External work done (W_e) = Internal work done (W_i).

Procedure :

Step I : Degree of static indeterminacy = D_{si} = 4.

Step II : Potential locations for plastic hinges. Eight locations as shown in Fig. 8.14 (b).

Step III : Identification of possible collapse mechanisms :

Maximum plastic hinges for complete mechanism = D_{si} + 1 = 4 + 1 = 5.

Number of independent mechanisms = 8 – 4 = 4.

Step IV : Analysis of possible mechanisms :

(i) Beam mechanism : I is as shown in Fig. 8.14 (c).

(a) Kinematics of the mechanism :

The rotation of plastic hinge at A = $\theta = \dfrac{\Delta}{3}$

The rotation of plastic hinge at E = $2\theta = \dfrac{2\Delta}{3}$

The rotation of plastic hinge at B = $\theta = \dfrac{\Delta}{3}$

(b) Virtual work equation :

$W_e = W_i$ i.e. $\quad 135\,\Delta = M_p\,(\theta) + M_p\,(2\theta) + M_p\,(\theta)$

$\therefore \quad\quad 135\,\Delta = M_p\left(\dfrac{\Delta}{3}\right) + M_p\left(\dfrac{2\Delta}{3}\right) + M_p\left(\dfrac{\Delta}{3}\right)$

$\therefore \quad\quad M_p = 101.25$ kNm

(ii) Beam mechanism : II is as shown in Fig. 8.14 (d).

(a) Kinematics of the mechanism :

The rotation of plastic hinge at B = $\theta_B = \dfrac{\Delta}{1.5}$

The rotation of plastic hinge at C = $\theta_C = \dfrac{\Delta}{2.5}$

The rotation of plastic hinge at F = $\theta_B + \theta_C = \dfrac{\Delta}{1.5} + \dfrac{\Delta}{2.5}$

(b) Virtual work equation :

$W_e = W_i$ i.e. $\quad 90\Delta = M_p(\theta_B) + M_p(\theta_B + \theta_C) + M_p(\theta_C)$

$\therefore \quad 90\Delta = M_p\left(\dfrac{\Delta}{1.5}\right) + M_p\left(\dfrac{\Delta}{1.5} + \dfrac{\Delta}{2.5}\right) + M_p\left(\dfrac{\Delta}{2.5}\right)$

$\therefore \quad M_p = 42.1875$ kNm

(iii) Beam mechanism : III is as shown in Fig. 8.14 (e).

(a) Kinematics of the mechanism :

The rotation of plastic hinge at C = $\theta = \dfrac{\Delta}{2}$

The rotation of plastic hinge at G = $2\theta = \Delta$

The rotation of plastic hinge at D = $\theta = \dfrac{\Delta}{2}$

(b) Virtual work equation :

$W_e = W_i$ i.e. $180 \cdot \Delta + 180 \cdot \dfrac{\Delta}{2} = M_p(\theta) + M_p(2\theta) + M_p(\theta)$

$\therefore \quad 270\Delta = M_p\left(\dfrac{\Delta}{2}\right) + M_p(\Delta) + M_p\left(\dfrac{\Delta}{2}\right)$

$\therefore \quad M_p = 135$ kNm

(iv) Beam mechanism : IV is as shown in Fig. 8.14 (f).

(a) Kinematics of the mechanism :

The rotation of plastic hinge at C = $\theta_C = \dfrac{\Delta}{3}$

The rotation of plastic hinge at D = $\theta_D = \Delta$

The rotation of plastic hinge at H = $\theta_C + \theta_D = \dfrac{\Delta}{3} + \Delta$

(b) Virtual work equation :

$W_e = W_i$ i.e. $180 \cdot \Delta + 180 \times \dfrac{2}{3}\Delta = M_p(\theta_C) + M_p(\theta_C + \theta_D) + M_p(\theta_D)$

$\therefore \quad 300\Delta = M_p\left(\dfrac{\Delta}{3}\right) + M_p\left(\dfrac{\Delta}{3} + \Delta\right) + M_p(\Delta)$

$\therefore \quad M_p = 112.5$ kNm

Plastic moment = M_p

= Greatest value of M_p obtained among all above mechanisms

= 135 kNm

Step V : B.M.D. at collapse : as shown in Fig. 8.14 (g).

TOS – II (TE CIVIL SEM. VI NMU)   PLASTIC ANALYSIS

Example 8.11 : *The beam is supported and loaded with ultimate loads as shown in Fig. 8.15 (a). Find the plastic moment and draw B.M.D. at collapse. Assuming beam of constant M_p throughout.*

Solution : Data : The beam is supported and loaded as shown in Fig. 8.15 (a).

Object : Plastic moment.

Concepts and Equations :

(1) Mechanism method.

(2) Work equation : External work done (W_e) = Internal work done (W_i).

Procedure :

Step I : Degree of static indeterminacy = D_{si} = 2.

Step II : Potential locations for plastic hinges = Five locations as shown in Fig. 8.15 (b).

Step III : Identification of possible collapse mechanisms :

Maximum plastic hinges for complete mechanism = D_{si} + 1 = 2 + 1 = 3.

Number of independent mechanisms = 5 – 2 = 3.

Step IV : Analysis of possible mechanisms :

(i) Beam mechanism : I is as shown in Fig. 8.15 (c).

(a) Kinematics of the mechanism :

The rotation of plastic hinge at A = $\theta = \dfrac{\Delta}{2}$

The rotation of plastic hinge at E = $2\theta = \Delta$

The rotation of plastic hinge at B = $\theta = \dfrac{\Delta}{2}$

$\therefore \qquad 100\,\Delta = M_p\left(\dfrac{\Delta}{2}\right) + M_p\,(\Delta) + M_p\left(\dfrac{\Delta}{2}\right)$

$\therefore \qquad M_p = 50 \text{ kNm}$

(ii) Beam mechanism : II is as shown in Fig. 8.15 (d). Note that at C no plastic hinge is formed for this mechanism.

(a) Kinematics of the mechanism :

The rotation of plastic hinge at B = $\theta = \dfrac{\Delta}{2}$

The rotation of plastic hinge at F = $2\theta = \Delta$

The rotation of plastic hinge at C = $\theta = \dfrac{\Delta}{2}$

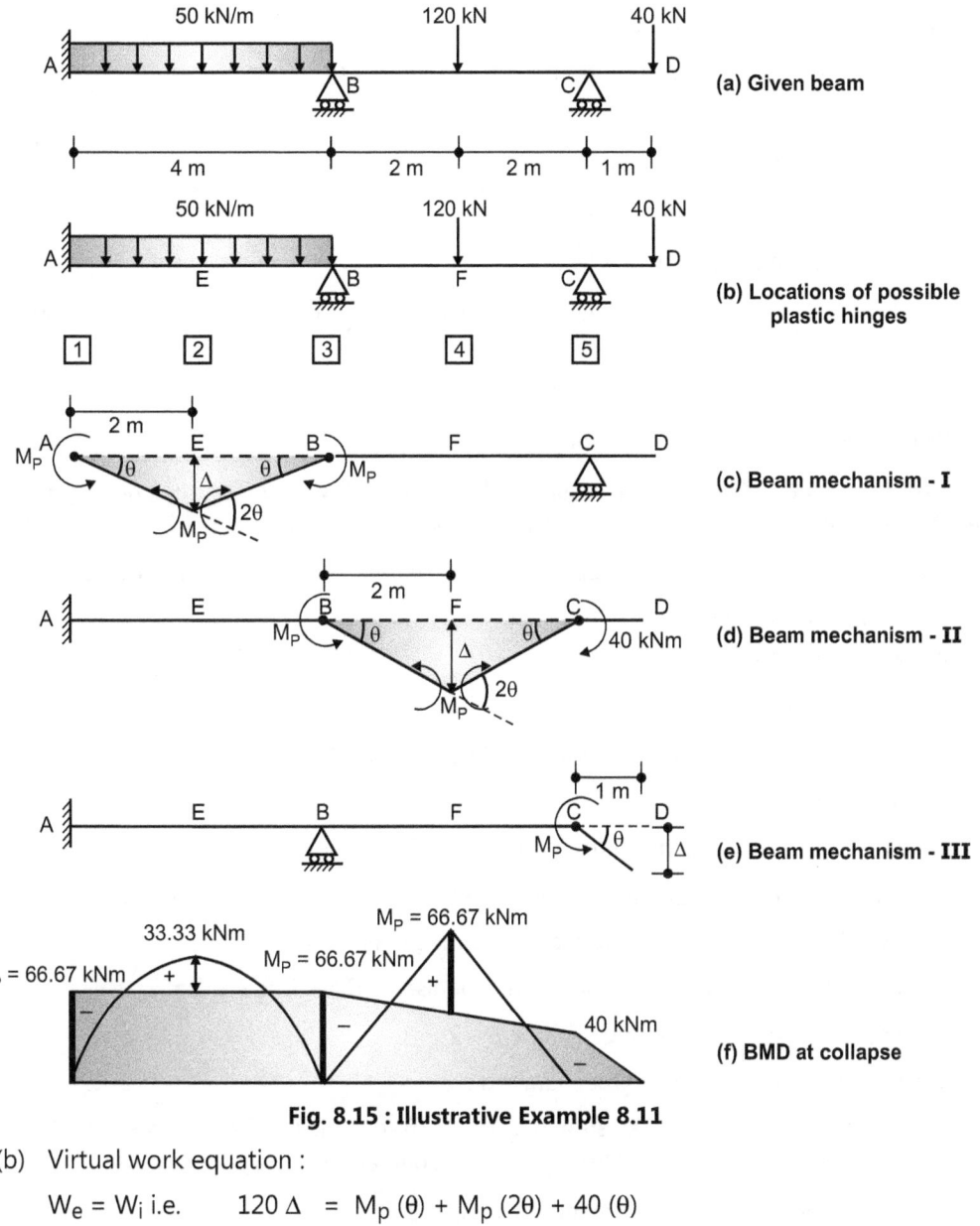

Fig. 8.15 : Illustrative Example 8.11

(b) Virtual work equation :

$W_e = W_i$ i.e. $\quad 120\,\Delta = M_p(\theta) + M_p(2\theta) + 40(\theta)$

$$= M_p\left(\frac{\Delta}{2}\right) + M_p(\Delta) + 40\left(\frac{\Delta}{2}\right)$$

∴ $\quad M_p = 66.67$ kNm

(iii) Beam mechanism : III is as shown in Fig. 8.15 (e).
(a) Kinematics of the mechanism :
The rotation of plastic hinge at C = θ = Δ
(b) Virtual work equation :
$W_e = W_i$ i.e. $40 \Delta = M_p (\theta) = M_p (\Delta)$

∴ $M_p = 40$ kNm

Plastic moment = M_p

= Greatest value of M_p obtained among all the above mechanisms

= 66.67 kNm

Step V : B.M.D. at collapse as shown in Fig. 8.15 (f).

Example 8.12 : *The beam is supported and loaded with ultimate loads as shown in Fig. 8.16 (a). Find the plastic moment and draw B.M.D. at collapse.*

Solution : Data : The beam is supported and loaded as shown in Fig. 8.16 (a).

Object : Plastic moment.

Concepts and Equations :

(1) Mechanism method.
(2) Work equation : External work done (W_e) = Internal work done (W_i).

Procedure :

Step I : Degree of static indeterminacy = D_{si} = 2

Step II : Potential locations for plastic hinges : Five locations as shown in Fig. 8.16 (b).

Step III : Identification of possible collapse mechanisms :

Maximum plastic hinges for complete mechanism = D_{si} + 1 = 2 + 1 = 3.

Number of independent mechanisms = 5 – 2 = 3.

Step IV : Analysis of possible mechanisms :

(i) Beam mechanism : I is as shown in Fig. 8.16 (c). This mechanism is similar to that of propped cantilever carrying u.d.l. throughout the span and having constant M_p.

∴ Using the result derived earlier in Example 8.7,

$$W_u = 11.656 \frac{M_p}{L^2} \text{ i.e. } M_p = \frac{W_u L^2}{11.656} = \frac{100 \times 4^2}{11.656} = 137.27 \text{ kNm}$$

and x = 0.414 L = 0.414 × 4 = 1.656 m

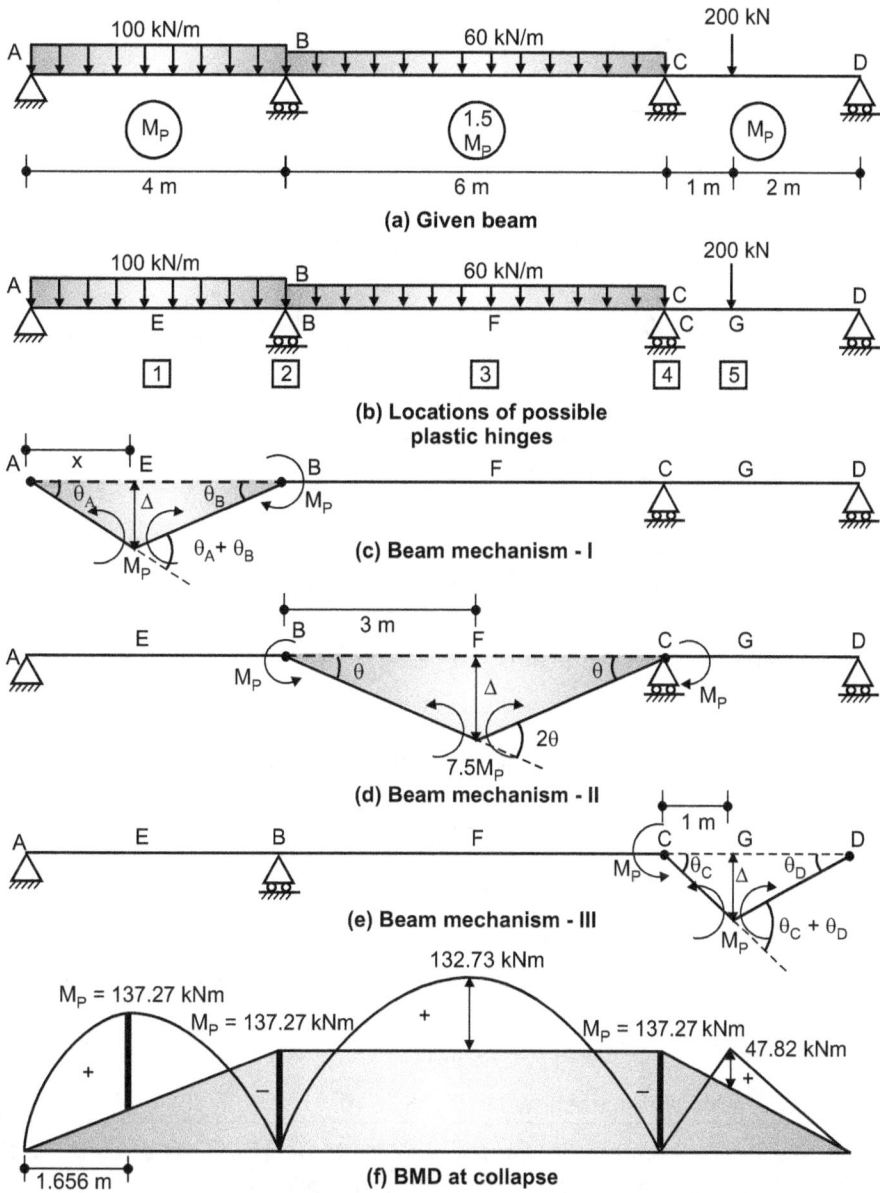

Fig. 8.16 : Illustrative Example 8.21

(ii) Beam mechanism : II is as shown in Fig. 8.16 (d).

(a) Kinematics of the mechanism :

The rotation of plastic hinge at B = $\theta = \dfrac{\Delta}{3}$

The rotation of plastic hinge at F = $2\theta = \dfrac{2}{3}\Delta$

The rotation of plastic hinge at C = $\theta = \dfrac{\Delta}{3}$

(b) Virtual work equation :

$W_e = W_i$ i.e. $60\left(\dfrac{1}{2} \times 6 \times \Delta\right) = M_p(\theta) + 1.5\,M_p(2\theta) + M_p(\theta)$

∴ $180\,\Delta = M_p\left(\dfrac{\Delta}{3}\right) + 1.5\,M_p\left(\dfrac{2}{3} \cdot \Delta\right) + M_p\left(\dfrac{\Delta}{3}\right)$

∴ $M_p = 108$ kNm

(iii) Beam mechanism : III is as shown in Fig. 8.16 (e).

(a) Kinematics of the mechanism :

The rotation of plastic hinge at C = $\theta_C = \Delta$

The rotation of plastic hinge at D = $\theta_D = \dfrac{\Delta}{2}$

The rotation of plastic hinge at G = $\theta_C + \theta_D = \Delta + \dfrac{\Delta}{2}$

(b) Virtual work equation :

$W_e = W_i$ i.e. $200\,\Delta = M_p(\theta_C) + M_p(\theta_C + \theta_D)$

∴ $200\,\Delta = M_p(\Delta) + M_p\left(\Delta + \dfrac{\Delta}{2}\right)$

∴ $M_p = 80$ kNm

Plastic moment = M_p

= Greatest value of M_p obtained among all the above mechanisms

= 137.27 kNm

Step V : B.M.D. at collapse : as shown in Fig. 8.16 (f).

Example 8.13 : *The beam is supported and loaded with ultimate loads as shown in Fig. 8.17 (a). Find the plastic moment and draw B.M.D. at collapse.*

Solution :

Data : The beam is supported and loaded as shown in Fig. 8.17 (a).

Object : Plastic moment.

Concepts and Equations :

(1) Mechanism method.

(2) Work equation : External work done (W_e) = Internal work done (W_i).

Procedure :

Step I : Degree of static indeterminacy = D_{si} = 2

Step II : Potential locations for plastic hinges : Five locations as shown in Fig. 8.17 (b).

Step III : Identification of possible collapse mechanisms :

Maximum plastic hinges for complete mechanism = D_{si} + 1 = 2 + 1 = 3.

Number of independent mechanisms = 5 – 2 = 3.

Step IV : Analysis of possible mechanisms :

(i) Beam mechanism : I is as shown in Fig. 8.17 (c).

This mechanism is similar to that of propped cantilever carrying u.d.l. throughout the span and having constant M_p.

∴ Using the result derived earlier in Example 8.7,

$$W_u = 11.656 \frac{M_p}{L^2} \text{ i.e. } M_p = \frac{W_u L^2}{11.656} = \frac{60 \times 3^2}{11.656} = 46.33 \text{ kNm}$$

and $\quad x = 0.414 L = 0.414 \times 3 = 1.242$ m

(ii) Beam mechanism : II is as shown in Fig. 8.17 (d). Here the moments are different at the ends, hence location of plastic hinge between B and C is not exactly known. Let plastic hinge be formed at a distance x from B.

(a) Kinematics of the mechanism :

The rotation of plastic hinge at B = $\theta_B = \dfrac{\Delta}{x}$

The rotation of plastic hinge at C = $\theta_C = \dfrac{\Delta}{4.5 - x}$

The rotation of plastic hinge at F = $\theta_F = \theta_B + \Delta_C = \dfrac{\Delta}{x} + \dfrac{\Delta}{4.5 - x}$

(b) Virtual work equation :

$$W_e = W_i \text{ i.e. } 90 \left(\frac{1}{2} \times 4.5 \times \Delta\right) = M_p (\theta_B) + 2M_p (\theta_B + \theta_C) + 2M_p (\theta_C)$$

∴ $\quad 202.5 \Delta = M_p \left(\dfrac{\Delta}{x}\right) + 2M_p \left(\dfrac{\Delta}{x} + \dfrac{\Delta}{4.5 - x}\right) + 2M_p \left(\dfrac{\Delta}{4.5 - x}\right)$

∴ $\quad 202.5 = \left[\dfrac{13.5 + x}{x (4.5 - x)}\right] M_p$

∴ $\quad M_p = 202.5 \left[\dfrac{x (4.5 - x)}{13.5 + x}\right]$ ... (A)

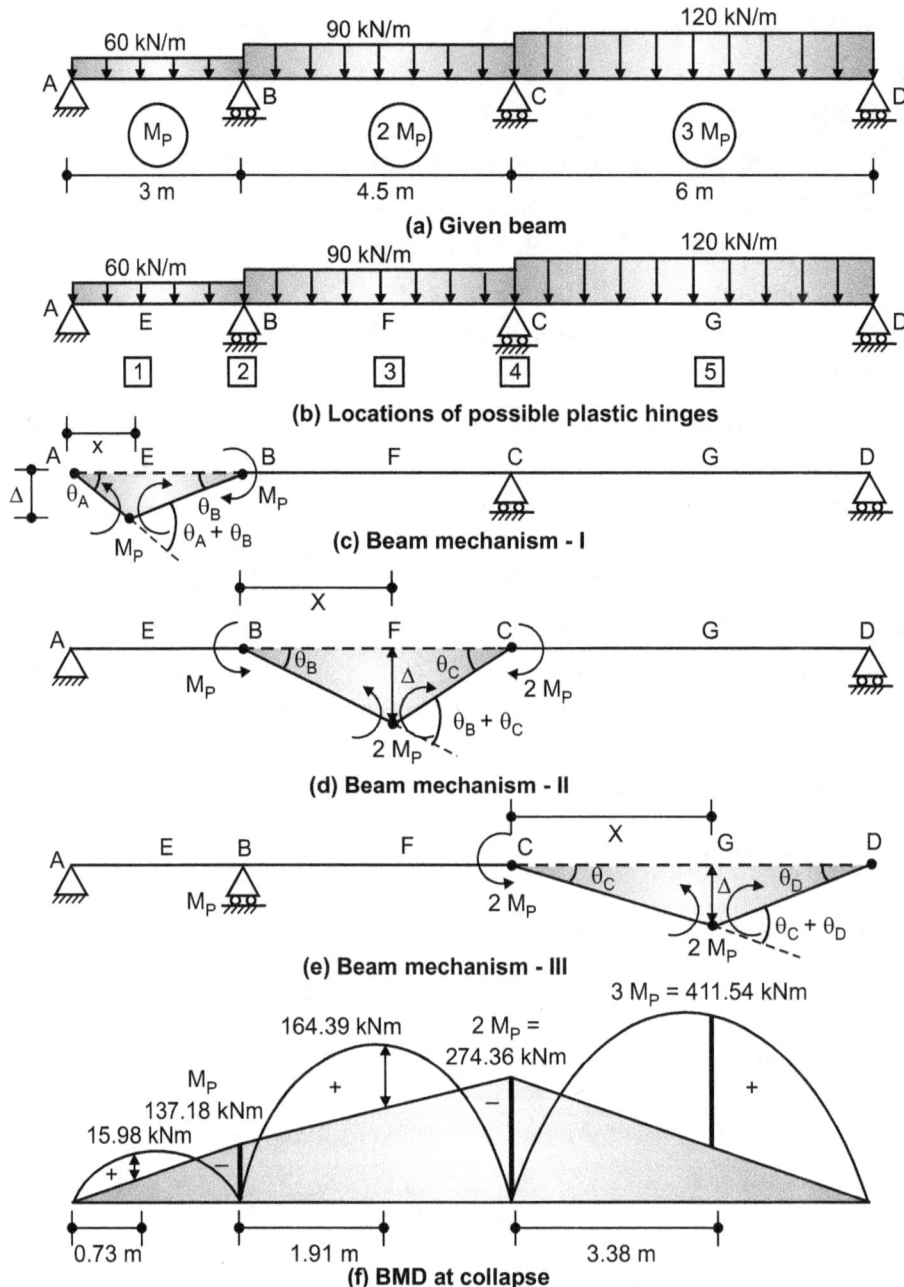

Fig. 8.17 : Illustrative Example 8.13

For maximum value of M_p, $\dfrac{dM_p}{dx} = 0$

∴ Differentiating equation (A) with respect to x and equating to zero, we get
$$x = 2.088$$
Substituting in equation (A), we get
$$M_p = 65.42 \text{ kNm}$$

(iii) Beam mechanism : III is as shown in Fig. 8.17 (e). Here the moments are different at the ends, hence location of plastic hinge between C and D is not exactly known. Let plastic hinge be formed at a distance x from C.

(a) Kinematics of the mechanism :

The rotation of plastic hinge at C = $\theta_C = \dfrac{\Delta}{x}$

The rotation of plastic hinge at D = $\theta_D = \dfrac{\Delta}{6-x}$

The rotation of plastic hinge at G = $\theta_C + \theta_D = \dfrac{\Delta}{x} + \dfrac{\Delta}{6-x}$

(b) Virtual work equation :

$$W_e = W_i \text{ i.e. } 120\left(\dfrac{1}{2} \times 6 \times \Delta\right) = 2M_p\,(\theta_C) + 3M_p\,(\theta_C + \theta_D)$$

∴ $$360\,\Delta = 2M_p\left(\dfrac{\Delta}{x}\right) + 3M_p\left(\dfrac{\Delta}{x} + \dfrac{\Delta}{6-x}\right)$$

∴ $$360 = \left[\dfrac{30 - 2x}{x\,(6-x)}\right] M_p$$

∴ $$M_p = 360\left[\dfrac{x\,(6-x)}{30 - 2x}\right] \quad \ldots \text{(B)}$$

For maximum value of M_p, $\dfrac{dM_p}{dx} = 0$

∴ Differentiating equation (B) with respect to x and equating to zero, we get
$$x = 3.28 \text{ m}$$

Substituting equation (B) with respect to x and equating, we get
$$M_p = 137.18 \text{ kNm}$$

Plastic moment = M_p
= Greatest value of M_p obtained among all the above mechanisms
= 137.18 kNm

Step V : B.M.D. at collapse : as shown in Fig. 8.17 (f).

8.6 APPLICATION OF PLASTIC ANALYSIS OF STEEL FRAMES

There may be number of possible mechanisms like beam, sway and combined, in rectangular frames as the frames are highly indeterminate. Therefore, plastic analysis of frames is more involved process. However, the present work is restricted to single bay single storey rectangular frames. Analysis of such frames is simpler and effectively carried out by the mechanism method after identifying all possible mechanisms correctly. The equilibrium method becomes complicated in case of frames and hence may not be used. Mechanism method is best suited for all types of loads including the distributed loads. The location of plastic hinge in a member subjected to uniform load is found by using the same concepts as explained previously. Work done by u.d.l. also needs attention.

Following problems illustrate the application of mechanism method to the analysis of frames.

SOLVED EXAMPLES

Example 8.14 : *The frame is supported and loaded with ultimate loads as shown in Fig. 8.18 (a). Find the plastic moment. The members of the frame are of constant M_p.*

Solution :

Data : The frame is supported and loaded as shown in Fig. 8.18 (a).

Object : Plastic moment.

Concepts and Equations :

(1) Mechanism method.

(2) Work equation : External work done (W_e) = Internal work done (W_i).

Step I : Degree of static indeterminacy = D_{si} = 3

Step II : Potential locations for plastic hinges : Five locations as shown in Fig. 8.18 (b).

Step III : Identification of possible collapse mechanism : Maximum plastic hinges for complete mechanism = $D_{si} + 1 = 3 + 1 = 4$

Number of independent mechanisms = 5 – 3 = 2

Combined mechanism is obtained from linear combination of beam and sway mechanism.

Step IV : Analysis of possible mechanisms :

(i) Beam mechanism is as shown in Fig. 8.18 (c).

(a) Kinematics of the mechanism :

The rotation of plastic hinges at B and D = $\theta = \dfrac{2\Delta'}{L}$

The rotation of plastic hinge at C = $2\theta = \dfrac{4\Delta}{L}$

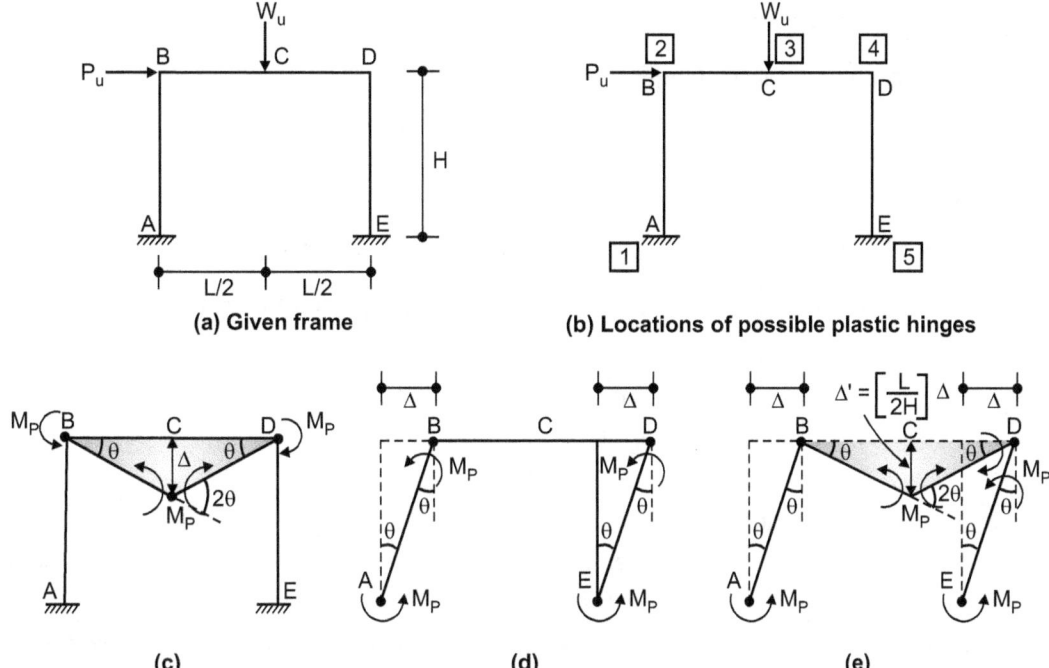

Fig. 8.18 : Illustrative Example 8.14

(b) Virtual work equation :

$W_e = W_i$ i.e. $\quad W_u \cdot \Delta' = M_p(\theta) + M_p(2\theta) + M_p(\theta)$

$\therefore \quad W_u \cdot \Delta' = M_p\left(\dfrac{2\Delta'}{L}\right) + M_p\left(\dfrac{4\Delta'}{L}\right) + M_p\left(\dfrac{2\Delta'}{L}\right)$

$\therefore \quad M_p = \dfrac{W_u L}{8}$

(ii) Sway mechanism is as shown in Fig. 8.18 (d).

(a) Kinematics of the mechanism :

The rotation of all plastic hinges = $\theta = \dfrac{\Delta}{H}$

(b) Virtual work equation :

$W_e = W_i$ i.e. $\quad P_u \cdot \Delta = M_p(\theta) + M_p(\theta) + M_p(\theta) + M_p(\theta)$

$\therefore \quad P_u \cdot \Delta = 4 M_p (\Delta/H)$

$\therefore \quad M_p = \dfrac{P_u \cdot H}{4}$

Combined mechanism is as shown in Fig. 8.18 (e).

(a) Kinematics of the mechanism :

The rotation of plastic hinges at A and E = $\theta = \dfrac{\Delta}{H}$

The rotation of plastic hinges at C and D = $2\theta = \dfrac{2\Delta}{H}$

(b) Virtual work equation :

$W_e = W_i$ i.e. $P_u \cdot \Delta + W_u \Delta' = M_p(\theta) + M_p(2\theta) + M_p(2\theta) + M_p(\theta)$

$\therefore \quad P_u \cdot \Delta + W_u \left(\dfrac{L}{2H}\right)\Delta = M_p\left(\dfrac{\Delta}{H}\right) + M_p\left(\dfrac{2\Delta}{H}\right) + M_p\left(\dfrac{2\Delta}{H}\right) + M_p\left(\dfrac{\Delta}{H}\right)$

$\therefore \quad P_u + \dfrac{W_u L}{2H} = \dfrac{6 M_p}{H}$

$\therefore \quad M_p = \dfrac{P_u \cdot H}{6} + \dfrac{W_u \cdot L}{12}$

$\therefore \quad$ Plastic moment $= M_p$
$\quad\quad\quad\quad\quad\quad\quad\quad\quad = $ Greatest value of M_p obtained among all the above mechanisms

Example 8.15 : *The frame is supported and loaded with ultimate loads as shown in Fig. 8.19 (a). Find the collapse load factor.*

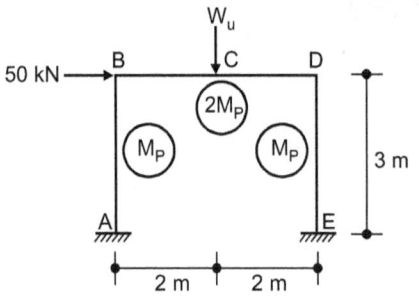
(a) Given frame

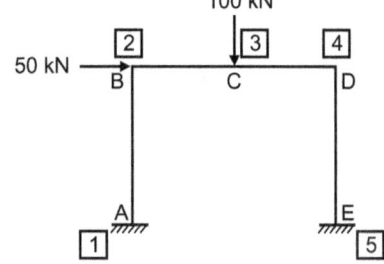
(b) Frame with ultimate loads and locations of possible plastic hinges

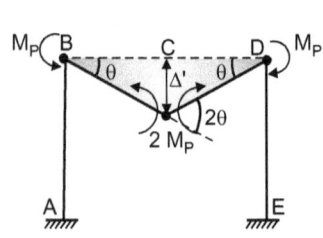
(c) Beam mechanism

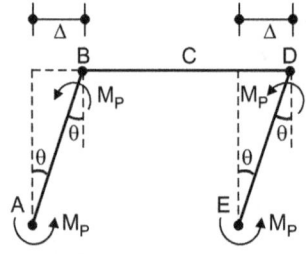
(d) Sway mechanism

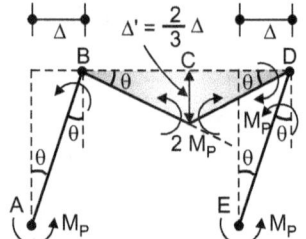
(e) Combined mechanism

Fig. 8.19 : Illustrative Example 8.15

TOS – II (TE CIVIL SEM. VI NMU)   PLASTIC ANALYSIS

Solution :
Data : The frame is supported and loaded as shown in Fig. 8.19 (a).
Object : Collapse load factor (λ).
Concepts and Equations :
(1) Mechanism method :
(2) Work equation : External work done (W_e) = Internal work done (W_i).
Procedure :
Step I : Degree of static indeterminacy = D_{si} = 3.
Step II : Potential locations for plastic hinges : Five locations as shown in Fig. 8.19 (b).
Step III : Identification of possible collapse mechanisms :
Maximum plastic hinges for complete mechanism = $D_{si} + 1 = 3 + 1 = 4$.
Number of independent mechanisms = 5 – 3 = 2.
Combined mechanism is obtained from linear combination of beam and sway mechanism.
Step IV : Analysis of possible mechanisms :
(i) Beam mechanism is as shown in Fig. 8.19 (c).
(a) Kinematics of the mechanisms :

    The rotation of plastic hinges at B and D = $\theta = \dfrac{\Delta'}{2}$

    The rotation of plastic hinge at C = $2\theta = \Delta'$

(b) Virtual work equation :
    $W_e = W_i$ i.e. $(100\,\lambda)\,\Delta' = M_p\,(\theta) + 2M_p\,(2\theta) + M_p\,(\theta)$

$\therefore$ $(100\,\lambda)\,\Delta' = M_p\left(\dfrac{\Delta}{2}\right) + 2M_p\,(\Delta') + M_p\left(\dfrac{\Delta'}{2}\right)$

$\therefore$ $\lambda = \dfrac{3M_p}{100}$

Sway mechanism is as shown in Fig. 8.19 (d).
(a) Kinematics of the mechanism :

    The rotation of all plastic hinges = $\theta = \dfrac{\Delta}{3}$

(b) Virtual work equation :
    $W_e = W_i$ i.e. $(50\,\lambda)\,\Delta = M_p\,(\theta) + M_p\,(\theta) + M_p\,(\theta) + M_p\,(\theta)$

$\therefore$ $(50\,\lambda)\,\Delta = 4M_p\left(\dfrac{\Delta}{3}\right)$ $\therefore \lambda = \dfrac{4M_p}{150}$

Combined mechanism is as shown in Fig. 8.19 (e).

(a) Kinematics of the mechanism : The rotation of plastic hinges at A and E = $\theta = \dfrac{\Delta}{3}$

    The rotation of plastic hinges at C and D = $2\theta = \dfrac{2\Delta}{3}$

(b) Virtual work equation :

$W_e = W_i$ i.e. $(50 \lambda) \Delta + (100 \lambda) \Delta' = M_p (\theta) + 2M_p (2\theta) + M_p (2\theta) + M_p (\theta)$

$\therefore (50 \lambda) \Delta + (100 \lambda) \dfrac{2}{3} \Delta = M_p \left(\dfrac{\Delta}{3}\right) + 2M_p \left(\dfrac{2\Delta}{3}\right) + M_p \left(\dfrac{2\Delta}{3}\right) + M_p \left(\dfrac{\Delta}{3}\right)$

$\left(\dfrac{350}{3}\right) \lambda = \dfrac{8 M_p}{3}$

$\therefore \lambda = \dfrac{8}{350} M_p$

$\therefore$ Collapse load factor = Smallest value of λ obtained among all above mechanisms

$\lambda = \dfrac{8}{350} M_p$

Example 8.16 : *The frame is supported and loaded with ultimate loads as shown in Fig. 8.20 (a). Find the plastic moment and draw B.M.D. at collapse.*

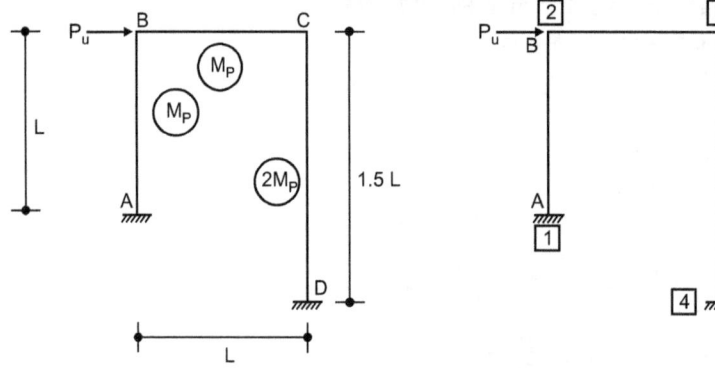

(a) Given beam (b) Locations of possible plastic hinges

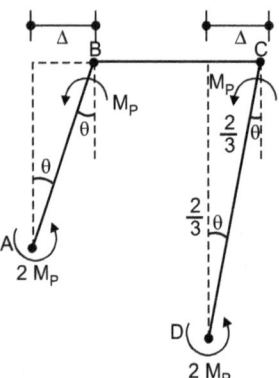

(c) Sway mechanism (d) BMD at collapse

Fig. 8.20 : Illustrative Example 8.16

Solution :
Data : The frame is supported and loaded as shown in Fig. 8.20 (a).
Object : Plastic moment.
Concepts and Equations :
(1) Mechanism method.
(2) Work equation : External work done (W_e) = Internal work done (W_i).

Procedure :
Step I : Degree of static indeterminacy = D_{si} = 3.
Step II : Potential locations for plastic hinges : Four locations as shown in Fig. 8.20 (b).
Step III : Identification of possible collapse mechanisms :
Maximum plastic hinges for complete mechanism = D_{si} + 1 = 3 + 1 = 4
Number of independent mechanism = 4 – 3 = 1
It should be noted that only sway mechanism is possible.
Step IV : Analysis of possible mechanisms :
Sway mechanism is as shown in Fig. 8.20 (c).
(a) Kinematics of the mechanism :

The rotation of plastic hinges at A and B = $\theta = \dfrac{\Delta}{L}$

The rotation of plastic hinges at C and D = $\dfrac{2}{3}\theta = \left(\dfrac{2}{3}\right)\dfrac{\Delta}{L}$

(b) Virtual work equation :

$W_e = W_i$ i.e. $\quad P_u \cdot \Delta = M_p(\theta) + M_p(\theta) + M_p\left(\dfrac{2}{3}\theta\right) + 2M_p\left(\dfrac{2}{3}\theta\right)$

$\therefore \quad P_u \cdot \Delta = M_p\left(\dfrac{\Delta}{L}\right) + M_p\left(\dfrac{\Delta}{L}\right) + M_p\left(\dfrac{2}{3}\right)\dfrac{\Delta}{L} + 2M_p\left(\dfrac{2}{3}\right)\dfrac{\Delta}{L}$

$\therefore \quad M_p = \dfrac{P_u \cdot L}{4}$

Step V : B.M.D. at collapse : as shown in Fig. 8.20 (d).

Example 8.17 : *The frame is supported and loaded with ultimate loads as shown in Fig. 8.21 (a). Find the plastic moment and draw B.M.D. at collapse.*

Solution :
Data : The frame is supported and loaded as shown in Fig. 8.21 (a).
Object : Plastic moment.
Concepts and Equations :
(1) Mechanism method.
(2) Work equation : External work done (W_e) = Internal work done (W_i).

Procedure :
Step I : Degree of static indeterminacy = D_{si} = 3.
Step II : Potential locations for plastic hinges : Five locations as shown in Fig. 8.21 (b).

Step III : Identification of possible collapse mechanisms :

Maximum plastic hinges for complete mechanism = $D_{si} + 1 = 3 + 1 = 4$

Number of independent mechanisms = 5 − 3 = 2.

Combined mechanism is obtained from linear combination of beam and sway mechanism.

Step IV : Analysis of possible mechanisms :

(i) Beam mechanism is as shown in Fig. 8.21 (c).

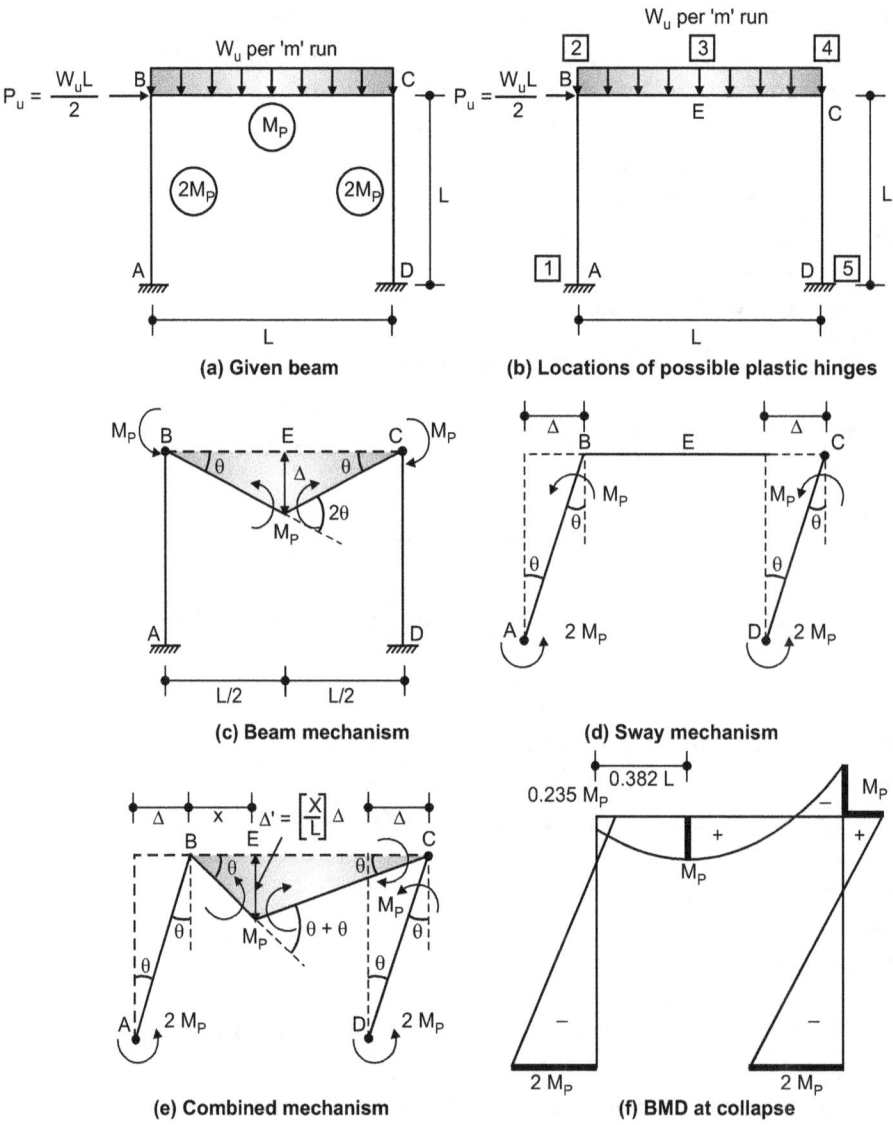

Fig. 8.21 : Illustrative Example 8.17

(a) Kinematics of the mechanism : The rotation of plastic hinges at B and C = $\theta = \dfrac{2\Delta'}{L}$

The rotation of plastic hinge at E = $2\theta = \dfrac{4\Delta'}{L}$

(b) Virtual work equation :

$W_e = W_i$ i.e. $W_u \left(\dfrac{1}{2} \times L \times \Delta'\right) = M_p(\theta) + M_p(2\theta) + M_p(\theta) + M_p(\theta)$

$\therefore \quad \dfrac{W_u L}{2} \cdot \Delta' = M_p\left(\dfrac{2\Delta'}{L}\right) + M_p\left(\dfrac{4\Delta'}{L}\right) + M_p\left(\dfrac{2\Delta'}{L}\right)$

$\therefore \quad M_p = \dfrac{W_u L^2}{16}$

(ii) Sway mechanism is as shown in Fig. 8.21 (d).

(a) Kinematics of the mechanism :

The rotation of all plastic hinges = $\theta = \dfrac{\Delta}{L}$

(b) Virtual work equation :

$W_e = W_i$ i.e. $\quad P_u \cdot \Delta = 2M_p(\theta) + M_p(\theta) + 2M_p(\theta) + M_p(\theta)$

$\therefore \quad \dfrac{W_u L}{2} \cdot \Delta = 6M_p\left(\dfrac{\Delta}{L}\right)$

$\therefore \quad M_p = \dfrac{W_u L^2}{12}$

(iii) Combined mechanism is as shown in Fig. 8.21 (e).

(a) Kinematics of the mechanism : The rotation of plastic hinges at A and D = $\theta = \dfrac{\Delta}{L}$

The rotation of plastic hinges at C and E = $\theta + \theta' = \dfrac{\Delta}{L} + \dfrac{x \cdot \Delta}{L(L-x)}$

(b) Virtual work equation :

$W_e = W_i$ i.e. $P_u \cdot \Delta + W_u\left(\dfrac{1}{2} \times L \times \Delta'\right) = 2M_p(\theta) + M_p(\theta + \theta') + M_p(\theta + \theta') + 2M_p(\theta)$

$\therefore \quad P_u \cdot \Delta + W_u \cdot \dfrac{1}{2} \cdot \left(\dfrac{x}{L}\right)\Delta = 2M_p\left(\dfrac{\Delta}{L}\right) + M_p\left(\dfrac{\Delta}{L} + \dfrac{x\Delta}{L(L-x)}\right) + M_p\left(\dfrac{\Delta}{L} + \dfrac{x\Delta}{L(L-x)}\right) + 2M_p\left(\dfrac{\Delta}{L}\right)$

$\therefore \quad \dfrac{W_u}{2}(L + x) = \left(\dfrac{6}{L} + \dfrac{2x}{L(L-x)}\right) M_p$

$\therefore \quad M_p = \dfrac{W_u}{4}\left(\dfrac{L^3 - x^2 L}{-2x + 3L}\right)$ ... (A)

For maximum value of M_p, $\dfrac{d}{dx}(M_p) = 0$

$\therefore$ Differentiating equation (A) with respect to x, we get

TOS – II (TE CIVIL SEM. VI NMU) — PLASTIC ANALYSIS

$$x = 0.382\ L$$

Substituting in equation (A), we get

$$M_p = \frac{W_u L^2}{10.47}$$

∴ Plastic moment $= M_p$
 = Greatest value of M_p obtained among all the above mechanisms

$$= \frac{W_u L^2}{10.47}$$

Step V : B.M.D. at collapse : as shown in Fig. 8.21 (f).

Example 8.18 : *The frame is supported and loaded with ultimate loads as shown in Fig. 8.22 (a). Find the plastic moment. The members of the frame are of constant M_p.*

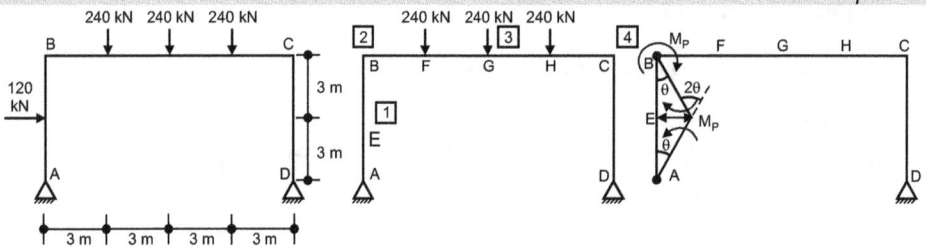

(a) Given beam   (b) Locations of possible plastic hinges   (c) Beam mechanism- I

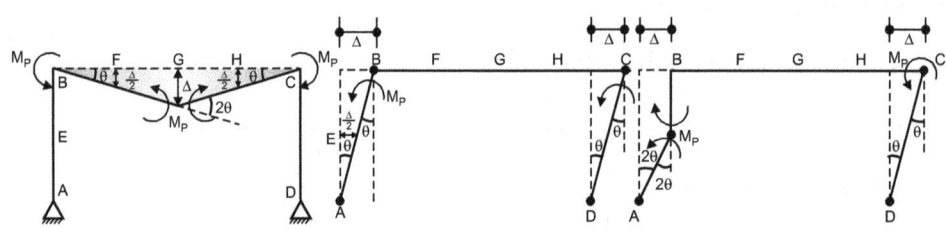

(d) Beam mechanism- II   (e) Sway mechanism   (f) Combined mechanism - I

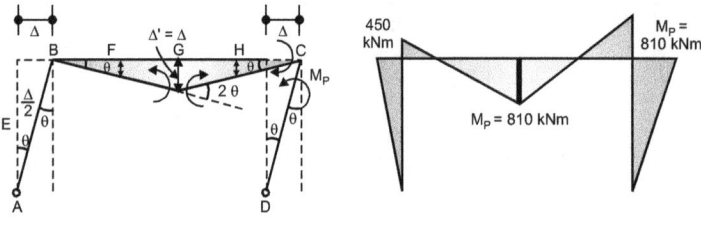

(g) Combined mechanism - II   (h) BMD of collapse

Fig. 8.22 : Illustrative Example 8.18

Solution :
Data : The frame is supported and loaded as shown in Fig. 8.22 (a).
Object : Plastic moment.
Concepts and Equations :
(1) Mechanism method.
(2) Work equation : External work done (W_e) = Internal work done (W_i)
Procedure :
Step I : Degree of static indeterminacy = D_{si} = 1.
Step II : Potential locations for plastic hinges : Four locations as shown in Fig. 8.22 (b).
Step III : Identification of possible collapse mechanisms :
Maximum plastic hinges for complete mechanism = D_{si} + 1 = 1 + 1 = 2.
Number of independent mechanisms = 4 – 1 = 3.
Two combined mechanisms are obtained from linear combination of beam and sway mechanism.
Step IV : Analysis of possible mechanisms :
(i) Beam mechanism : I is as shown in Fig. 8.22 (c).
(a) Kinematics of the mechanism :

The rotation of plastic hinge at B = $\theta = \dfrac{\Delta}{3}$

The rotation of plastic hinge at E = $2\theta = \dfrac{2\Delta}{3}$

(b) Virtual work equation :
$W_e = W_i$ i.e. $\quad 120\,\Delta = M_p\,(2\theta) + M_p\,(\theta)$

$\therefore \quad 120\,\Delta = M_p\left(\dfrac{2\Delta}{3}\right) + M_p\left(\dfrac{\Delta}{3}\right)$

$\therefore \quad M_p = 120\ \text{kNm}$

(ii) Beam mechanism : II is as shown in Fig. 8.22 (d).
(a) Kinematics of the mechanism :

The rotation of plastic hinges at B and C = $\theta = \dfrac{\Delta'}{6}$

The rotation of plastic hinge at G = $2\theta = \dfrac{\Delta'}{3}$

(b) Virtual work equation :
$W_e = W_i$ i.e. $240 \cdot \dfrac{\Delta'}{2} + 240 \cdot \Delta' + 240 \cdot \dfrac{\Delta'}{2} = M_p\,(\theta) + M_p\,(2\theta) + M_p\,(\theta)$

$\therefore \quad 480\,\Delta' = M_p\left(\dfrac{\Delta}{6}\right) + M_p\left(\dfrac{\Delta}{3}\right) + M_p\left(\dfrac{\Delta}{6}\right)$

$\therefore \quad M_p = 720\ \text{kNm}$

(iii) Sway mechanism is as shown in Fig. 8.22 (e).

(a) Kinematics of the mechanism : The rotation of all plastic hinges = $\theta = \dfrac{\Delta}{6}$

(b) Virtual work equation :

$W_e = W_i$ i.e. $\quad 120 \cdot \dfrac{\Delta}{2} = M_p (\theta) + M_p (\theta)$

$\therefore \quad 120 \cdot \dfrac{\Delta}{2} = 2M_p \left(\dfrac{\Delta}{6}\right)$

$\therefore \quad M_p = 180$ kNm

(iv) Combined mechanism : I is as shown in Fig. 8.22 (f).

(a) Kinematics of the mechanism :

The rotation of plastic hinges at A and E = $2\theta = \dfrac{\Delta}{3}$

The rotation of plastic hinge at C = $\theta = \dfrac{\Delta}{6}$

(b) Virtual work equation :

$W_e = W_i$ i.e. $\quad 120 \, \Delta = M_p (2\theta) + M_p (\theta)$

$\therefore \quad 120 \, \Delta = M_p \left(\dfrac{\Delta}{3}\right) + M_p \left(\dfrac{\Delta}{6}\right)$

$\therefore \quad M_p = 240$ kNm

(v) Combined mechanism : II is as shown in Fig. 8.22 (g).

(a) Kinematics of the mechanism :

The rotation of plastic hinges at G and C = $2\theta = 2\left(\dfrac{\Delta}{6}\right) = \dfrac{\Delta}{3}$

(b) Virtual work equation :

$W_e = W_i$ i.e. $120 \cdot \dfrac{\Delta}{2} + 240 \cdot \dfrac{\Delta}{2} + 240 \cdot \Delta + 240 \cdot \dfrac{\Delta}{2} = M_p (2\theta) + M_p (2\theta)$

$\therefore \quad 540 \cdot \Delta = 2M_p \left(\dfrac{\Delta}{3}\right)$

$\therefore \quad M_p = 810$ kNm

$\therefore \quad$ Plastic moment = M_p

= Greatest value of M_p obtained among all above mechanisms

= 810 kNm

Step V : B.M.D. at collapse : as shown in Fig. 8.22 (h).

8.7 STANDARD RESULTS OF PLASTIC ANALYSIS

Plastic analysis of simple structures like beams and portal frames, presented in the previous article are very much useful for further studies. Therefore, some of the results of standard cases are consolidated and given in Table 8.2 for direct applications to analysis and design problems of beams and frames.

Table 8.2

Sr. no.	Case	Sketch	Mechanism	Ultimate load W_u	Plastic moment M_p
1.	Fixed beam with central point load			$W_u = \dfrac{8M_p}{L}$	$M_p = \dfrac{W_u L}{8}$
2.	Fixed beam with off centre point load			$W_u = \dfrac{2LM_p}{ab}$	$M_p = \dfrac{W_u b}{2L}$
3.	Fixed beam with uniform load on the whole span			$w_u = \dfrac{16M_p}{L^2}$	$M_p = \dfrac{W_u L^2}{16}$
4.	Fixed beam with uniform load on the whole span			$w_u = \dfrac{16 M_p L^2}{a^2 (2L-a)^2}$	$M_p = \dfrac{W_u a^2 (2L-a)^2}{16 L^2}$
5.	Propped cantilever with central point load			$W_u = \dfrac{6M_p}{L}$	$M_p = \dfrac{W_u L}{6}$
6.	Propped cantilever with off centre point load			$W_u = \dfrac{M_p (L+b)}{ab}$	$M_p = \dfrac{W_u ab}{L+b}$
7.	Propped cantilever with uniform load on whole span			$W_u = \dfrac{11.67\, M_p}{L^2}$	$M_p = \dfrac{W_u L^2}{11.67}$
8.	Single bay single storey portal with central point load on beam and lateral point load		I, II, III	$W_u = \dfrac{8M_p}{L}$ $P_u = \dfrac{4M_p}{H}$	$M_p = \dfrac{W_u L}{8}$ $M_p = \dfrac{P_u H}{4}$ $M_p = \dfrac{P_u H}{6} + \dfrac{W_u L}{12}$

#	Description	Loading	Mechanism		
9.	Single bay single storey portal with uniform load on beam and lateral load (non-uniform section)	P_u, W_u/m, M_p, $2M_p$, $2M_p$, L, L	(i) Beam mechanism	$W_u = \dfrac{16 M_p}{L^2}$	$M_p = \dfrac{W_u L^2}{16}$
			(ii) Sway mechanism	$P_u = \dfrac{12 M_p}{L^2}$	$M_p = \dfrac{W_u L^2}{12}$
			(iii) Combined mechanism	$W_u = \dfrac{10.47 M_p}{L^2}$	$M_p = \dfrac{W_u L^2}{10.47}$
10.	Single bay single storey portal with hinged bases and with central point load on beam and colateral load (uniform section)	P_u, W_u, M_p, M_p, M_p, H, L/2, L/2	(i) Beam mechanism	$W_u = \dfrac{8 M_p}{L}$	$M_p = \dfrac{W_u L}{8}$
			(ii) Sway mechanism	$P_u = \dfrac{2 M_p}{H}$	$M_p = \dfrac{P_u H}{2}$
			(iii) Combined mechanism		$M_p = \dfrac{P_u H}{4} + \dfrac{W_u L}{8}$

8.8 Plastic Design of Steel Beams and Frames

There are two usual methods of structural design. The conventional method known as *working stress method* is based on the concept of allowable stress and elastic behaviour. The other method called as 'Ultimate strength method or *ultimate load method*, is based on the concept of inelastic or plastic behaviour and ultimate load. Ultimate strength method is more rational and is being accepted all over. With respect to steel structure this approach is known as *plastic design*. The plastic design procedure differs from the working stress method in three important aspects given below :

- Ultimate loads are used instead of working loads. In arriving at the ultimate loads, the dead and live loads are considered separately and each is increased by a different load factor suggested by the code, to account for the most severe loading combinations.
- Knowing the ultimate loads, the forces and moments in members are determined by plastic analysis, as a reverse procedure of obtaining the collapse or ultimate load.
- The members are so proportioned that their ultimate strength exceeds or at least equals, the forces and moments produced by ultimate loads.

- The members are checked for performance under working or service loads. This includes consideration of deflections, fatigue, dynamic response, buckling, local buckling, local yielding and other structural characteristics.

The concepts of plastic design of the members only for flexure are introduced here, although plastic design as a whole needs more explanation. It is interesting to note that plastic design allows to provide the plastic moment of members as we decide. In this context the basic principle of plastic design (ultimate load design) is that load distribution in statically indeterminate structure is based on the load carrying capacity of the members. This is *'the programmatic concept of structural action i.e. when one tells the structure what to do, it will try do it'*.

This concept is introduced and illustrated with the following simple examples of beam and portal.

SOLVED EXAMPLES

Example 8.19 : *Design the uniform section for the continuous beam supported and loaded as shown in Fig. 8.23 (a) if the load factor is 1.7 and yield stress of steel is 250 N/mm².*

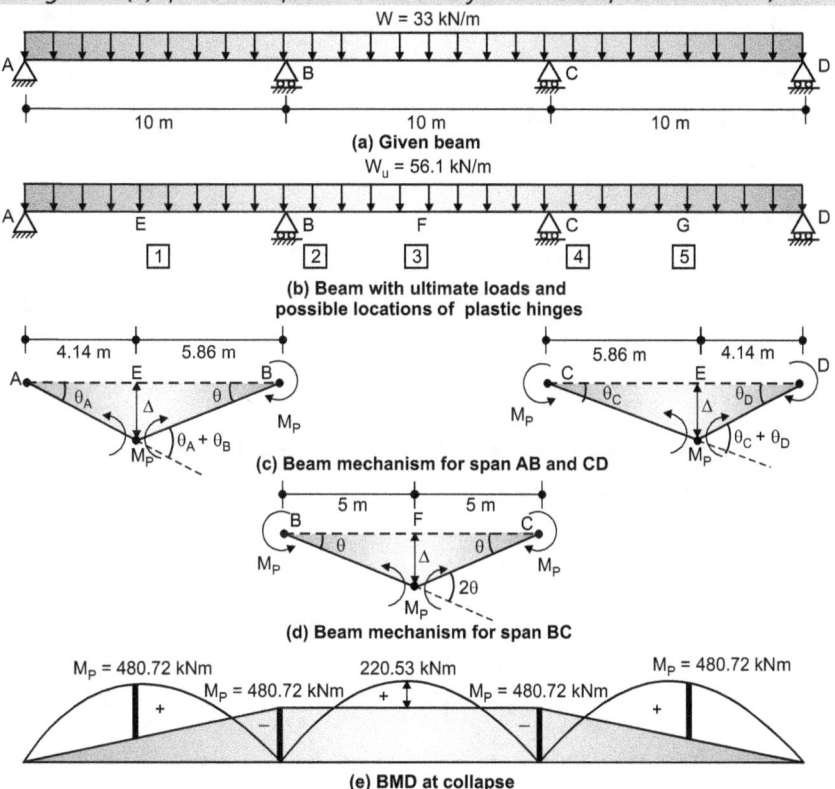

Fig. 8.23 : Illustrative Example 8.19

Solution : (1) Structural configuration : Dimensions, support conditions as shown in Fig. 8.23 (a). AB = BC = CD = L = 10 m.

(2) Loads : Uniformly distributed load of 33 kN/m on all spans as shown in Fig. 8.23 (a).

w = 33 kN/m

(3) Load factor = γ = 1.7

(4) Yield stress = σ_y = 250 N/mm^2

(5) Uniform section.

Object : Design of the beam section for flexure only.

Concepts and Equations :

(1) Plastic method : Mechanism method work equation of a mechanism.

$\Sigma W\Delta = \Sigma M\theta$ or standard results.

(2) Bending moment distribution - BMD.

(3) $Z_p = \dfrac{M_p}{\sigma_y}$

Procedure :

Step I : Ultimate load or collapse load.

$W_u = \gamma \times w = 1.7 \times 33 = 56.1$ kN/m

Step II : Plastic analysis :

(1) Degree of static indeterminacy = D_{si} = 2.

(2) Potential locations for plastic hinges : Five locations as shown in Fig. 8.23 (b).

(3) Maximum plastic hinges for complete mechanism = D_{si} + 1 = 2 + 1 = 3.

(4) Analysis of possible mechanisms :

(a) Beam mechanism for span AB and CD is as shown in Fig. 8.23 (c).

Using the standard result from Table 8.2,

$$M_p = \dfrac{W_u L^2}{11.67}$$

$$= \dfrac{56.1 \times 10^2}{11.67}$$

$$= 480.72 \text{ kNm}$$

Plastic hinge occurs at E and G i.e. 0.414 (L) = 0.414 × 10 = 4.14 m from A and D respectively.

(b) Beam mechanism for span BC is as shown in Fig. 8.23 (d).

Using the standard result from Table 8.2,

M_p = Greatest value of M_p obtained among all the above mechanisms

$$= 480.72 \text{ kNm}$$

Step III : Checking the yield condition :

BMD at collapse is as shown in Fig. 8.23 (e). It should be noted that no where BM exceeds

$$M_p = 480.72 \text{ kNm}$$

Step IV : Plastic section modulus required

$$Z_p = \frac{M_p}{\sigma_y}$$

$$= \frac{480.72 \times 10^6}{250}$$

$$= 1.922 \times 10^6 \text{ mm}^3$$

Step V : Elastic section modulus. Assuming shape factor 1.15 for I section,

$$K_s = \frac{Z_p}{Z_e}$$

$$\therefore \quad Z_e = \frac{Z_p}{K_s}$$

$$= \frac{1.922 \times 10^6}{1.15}$$

$$= 1.671 \times 10^6 \text{ mm}^3$$

Step VI : Selection of the section corresponding to Z_e, the rolled steel section is selected referring to the steel tables.

ISMB 500 @ 87.14 kg/m giving $Z_{xx} = 1810 \times 10^3 \text{ mm}^3$

It may be noted that as this design is not economical, it can be designed economically as illustrated in the next example.

Example 8.20 : *Design the economical section for the beam using the cover plates wherever necessary for the continuous beam supported and loaded as shown in Fig. 8.24 (a). Assume the load factor 1.7 and yield stress 250 N/mm².*

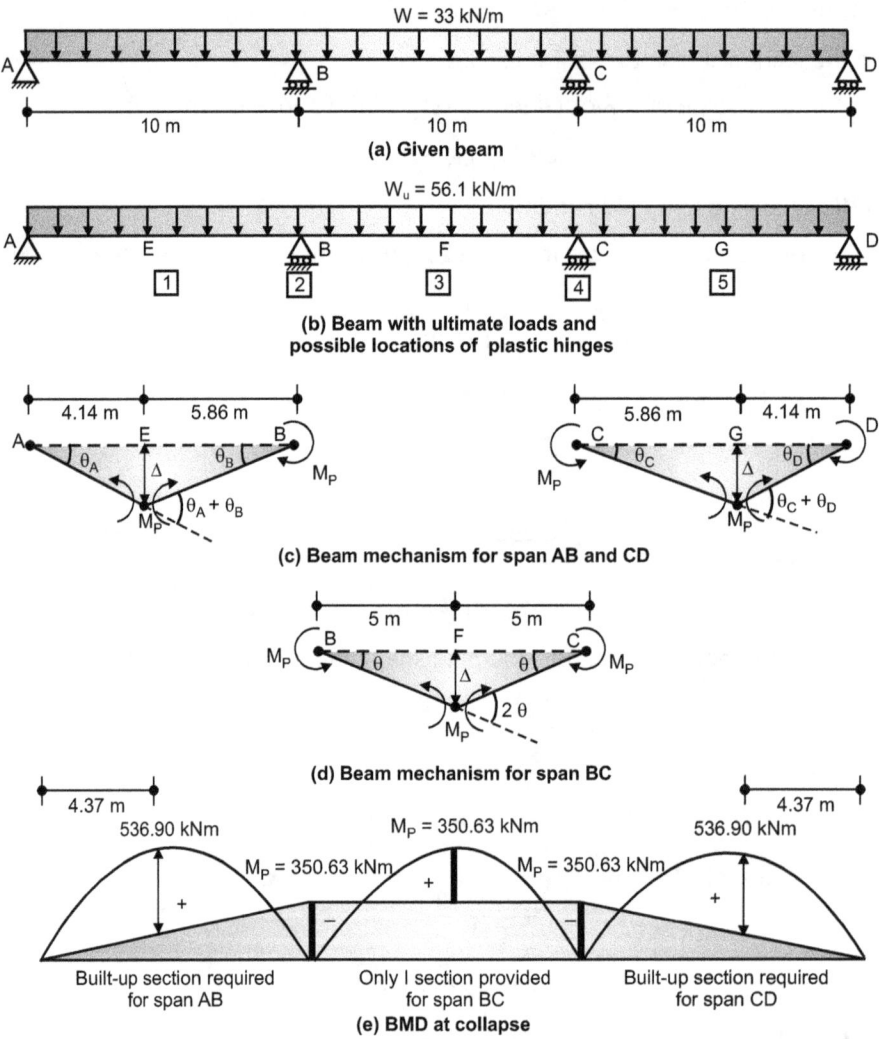

Fig. 8.24 : Illustrative Example 8.20

Solution : Data : (1) Structural configuration as shown in Fig. 8.24 (a).

$$AB = BC = CD = L = 10 \text{ m}$$

(2) Loads as shown in Fig. 8.24 (a).

$$w = 33 \text{ kN/m}$$

(3) Load factor $= \gamma = 1.7$

(4) Yield stress $= \sigma_y = 250 \text{ N/m}^2$

Object : Design of beam section with cover plates.

Concepts and Equations :
(1) Plastic method : Mechanism method.
(2) Work equation of a mechanism.
(3) $Z_p = \dfrac{M_p}{\sigma_y}$
(4) Bending moment distribution – B.M.D.

Procedure :

Step I : Ultimate load.
$$W_u = \gamma \cdot w = 1.7 \times 33 = 56.1 \text{ kN/m}$$

Step II : Plastic analysis :
(i) Degree of static indeterminacy = D_{si} = 2
(ii) Potential locations for plastic hinges : Five locations as shown in Fig. 8.24 (b).
(iii) Maximum plastic hinges for complete mechanism = $D_{si} + 1 = 2 + 1 = 3$.
(iv) Analysis of possible mechanisms :
(a) Beam mechanism for span AB and CD is as shown in Fig. 8.24 (c).
Using the standard result from Table 8.2,
$$M_p = \dfrac{W_u L^2}{11.67} = \dfrac{56.1 \times 10^2}{11.67} = 480.72 \text{ kNm}$$
Plastic hinge occurs at E and G i.e. 0.414 (L) = 0.414 × 10
$$= 4.14 \text{ m from A and D respectively}$$
(b) Beam mechanism for span BC is as shown in Fig. 8.24 (d).
Using the standard result from Table 8.2,
$$M_p = \dfrac{W_u L^2}{16} = \dfrac{56.1 \times 10^2}{16} = 350.63 \text{ kNm}$$
B.M.D. at collapse is as shown in Fig. 8.24 (e).
$$\text{Vertical reaction at A} = \dfrac{-350.63}{10} + \dfrac{56.1 \times 10}{2} = 245.44 \text{ kN } (\uparrow)$$
To locate point of zero SF in span AB, from A,
$$245.44 - 56.1 (x) = 0$$
∴ $\quad x = 4.37 \text{ m}$
∴ Maximum sagging moment for span AB
$$= 245.44 \times 4.37 - 56.1 \times \dfrac{(4.37)^2}{2}$$
$$= 536.90 \text{ kNm}$$
All above values are same for span CD by symmetry.

Step III : Minimum plastic moment required
M_p = 350.63 kNm as per the requirements of the central span BC

Step IV : Plastic section modulus
$$Z_p = \frac{M_p}{\sigma_y} = \frac{350.63 \times 10^6}{250} = 1.403 \times 10^6 \text{ mm}^2$$

Step V : Elastic section modulus :
Assuming $K_s = 1.15$
$$K_s = \frac{Z_p}{Z_e} \therefore Z_e = \frac{Z_p}{K_s} = \frac{1.403 \times 10^6}{1.15} = 1.220 \times 10^6 \text{ mm}^3$$

Step VI : Selection of section :
From steel table selecting the appropriate section.
ISLB 450 @ 65.26 kg/m giving
$$Z_{xx} = 1.223 \times 10^6 \text{ mm}^4$$

Step VII : Cover plates for end spans AB and CD.

(i) As the section ISLB is selected on the basis of the central span BC, it is not adequate for the end spans AB and CD.

(ii) M_p for end spans = 536.90 kNm

(iii) Z_p required for end spans = $\dfrac{M_p}{\sigma_y} = \dfrac{536.90 \times 10^6}{250} = 2.147 \times 10^6 \text{ mm}^3$

(iv) Z_e for end span = $\dfrac{Z_p}{K_s} = \dfrac{2.147 \times 10^6}{1.15} = 1.867 \times 10^6 \text{ mm}^3$

(v) Additional section modulus required and to be provided by cover plates
$$Z_{e\text{ plates}} = 1.867 \times 10^6 - 1.223 \times 10^6$$
$$= 0.643 \times 10^6 \text{ mm}^2$$

(vi) Area of cover plate one on either side (i.e. top or bottom) of the section
$$Z_{e\text{ plate}} = A_{plate} \times D$$
When D is taken as the depth of the I section provide
$$0.643 \times 10^6 = A_{plate} \times 450$$
$$\therefore A_{plate} = 1431 \text{ mm}^2$$

(vii) Size of the cover plate provided 180 mm × 8 mm one cover plate at top and bottom of ISLB 450.

$\therefore$ Area of plate provided = 180 × 8 = 1440 mm² > 1431 mm² ... O.K.

Step VII : Checking the section for the yield condition.

Accordingly the actual moment of inertia and modulus of section M_p can be calculated and BM distribution can be verified so that no where the bending moment exceeds M_p at that section at collapse at any of the possible mechanism.

Example 8.21 : *Design the uniform section of the beam and columns of the portal frame supported and loaded as shown in Fig. 8.25 (a). If the load factor is 2.0 and the yield stress of steel is 250 N/mm².*

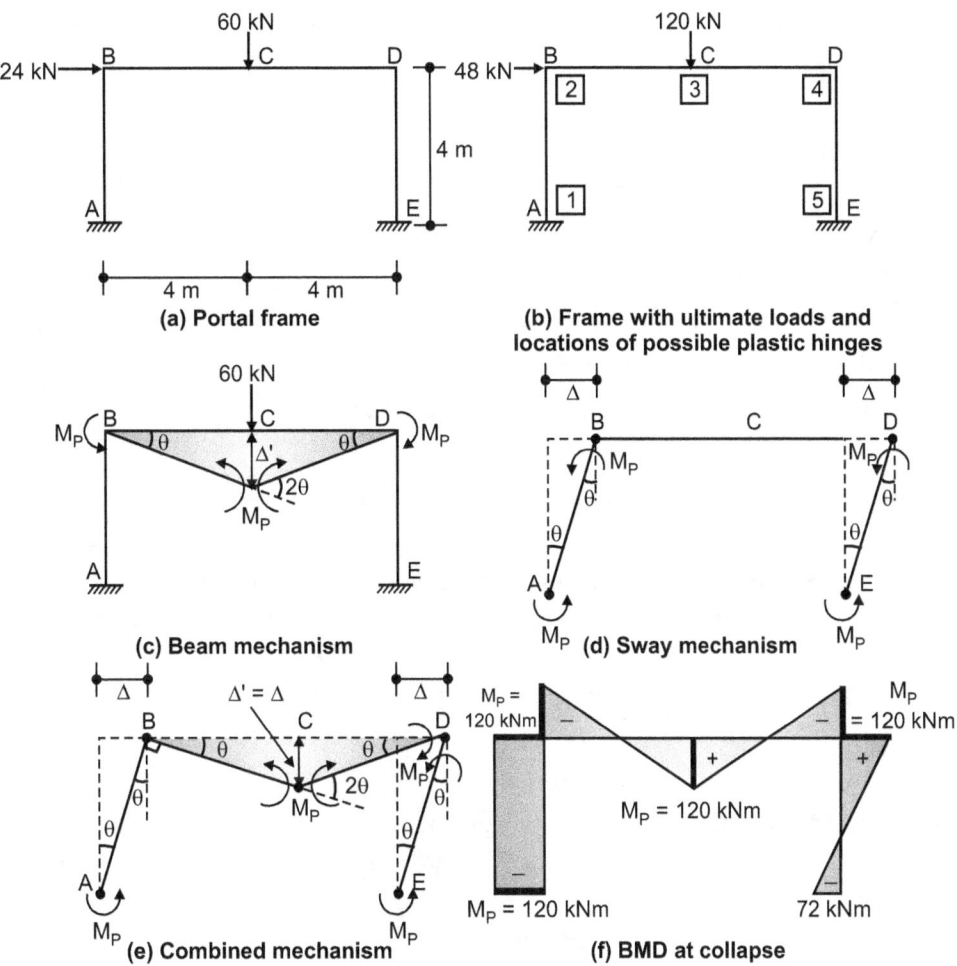

Fig. 8.25 : Illustrative Example 8.21

Solution : Data : (1) Structural configuration : Dimensions support conditions as shown in Fig. 8.25 (a), L = 8 m, H = 4 m.

(2) **Loads :** Magnitudes, directions and positions as shown in Fig. 8.25 (a) W = 60 kN, P = 24 kN

(3) Load factor = γ = 2.0

(4) Same section for beams and columns.

Object : Design of the section for flexure only.

Concepts and Equations :

(1) Plastic method : Mechanism method. (2) Work equation of a mechanism.

(3) $Z_p = \dfrac{M_p}{\sigma_y}$

Procedure : Step I : Ultimate load :

Beam load, W_u = 60 × 2 = 120 kN

Lateral load, P_u = 24 × 2 = 48 kN

Step II : Plastic analysis :

(i) Degree of static indeterminacy = D_{si} = 3.

(ii) Positions of plastic hinges as shown in Fig. 8.25 (b).

(iii) Maximum plastic hinges for complete mechanism.

$D_{si} + 1$ = 3 + 1 = 4

(iv) Minimum hinges for partial mechanism i.e. beam mechanism = 3.

(v) Possible mechanisms.

(a) Beam Mechanism for BD : Three plastic hinges at B, D and midspan of BD i.e. C as shown in Fig. 8.25 (*c). Either by work equation or by using the standard result of this case of mechanism :

$$M_p = \dfrac{W_u L}{8} = \dfrac{120 \times 8}{8}$$

= 120 kNm

(b) Sway Mechanism : Four plastic hinges at A, B, D and E as shown in Fig. 8.25 (d). Either by work equation or by using the standard result already derived for this case of mechanism :

$$M_p = \dfrac{P_u H}{4} = \dfrac{48 \times 4}{4}$$

= 48 kNm

(c) Combined Mechanism : Four plastic hinges at A, C, D and E as shown in Fig. 8.25 (e).

Either by work equation or by using the standard result already derived for this case of mechanism.

$$M_p = \frac{P_u H}{6} + \frac{W_u L}{12} = \frac{48 \times 4}{6} + \frac{120 \times 8}{12}$$

$$= 112 \text{ kNm}$$

Step III : Required plastic moment

$$M_p = \text{Largest of 120, 48 and 112}$$

$$= 120 \text{ kNm}$$

It represents that the beam mechanism governs the design and as the same uniform section is to be used the beam member dominates the design. The design is not economical for the column section.

Step IV : Checking the yield condition B.M.D. at collapse is as shown in Fig. 8.25 (f). No where the bending moment should exceed them M_p = 120 kNm at the collapse under the governing mechanism. Other mechanism will not be possible at the given ultimate load.

∴ $\quad M_p$ required = 120 kNm

Step V : Plastic section modulus required,

$$Z_p = \frac{M_p}{\sigma_y} = \frac{120 \times 10^6}{250}$$

$$= 0.48 \times 10^6 \text{ mm}^3$$

Step VI : Elastic section modulus :

$$Z_e = \frac{Z_p}{K_s}$$

$$= \frac{0.48 \times 10^6}{1.15}$$

Section VII : Selection of the section corresponding to Z_e, the rolled steel section is selected referring to the steel tables. ISMB 250 @ 57.37 kg/m giving Z_{xx} = 410 × 10³ mm³.

For economical design the different sections for columns and beams can be selected for which the proportion of M_p of columns and beams is to be decided and accordingly M_p required for columns and beams can be obtained from the plastic analysis. This is not illustrated here considering the limited scope of this topic in this subject of analysis.

EXERCISE

1. Explain and illustrate precisely the following :
(i) Linear elastic stress-strain curve for structural steels, (ii) Elastic-plastic stress-strain curve for structural steels, (iii) Rigid plastic stress-strain curve for structural steels, (iv) Moment curvature relation, (v) Plastic hinge, (vi) Shape factor, (vii) Plastic mount of resistance, (viii) Collapse mechanism, (ix) Load factor.

   State clearly (i) Upper-bound theorem and (ii) Lower-bound theorem.

   Illustrate the methods of plastic analysis with respect to a simple example.

2. Find the shape factor for the section shown in Fig. 8.26 to 8.29.

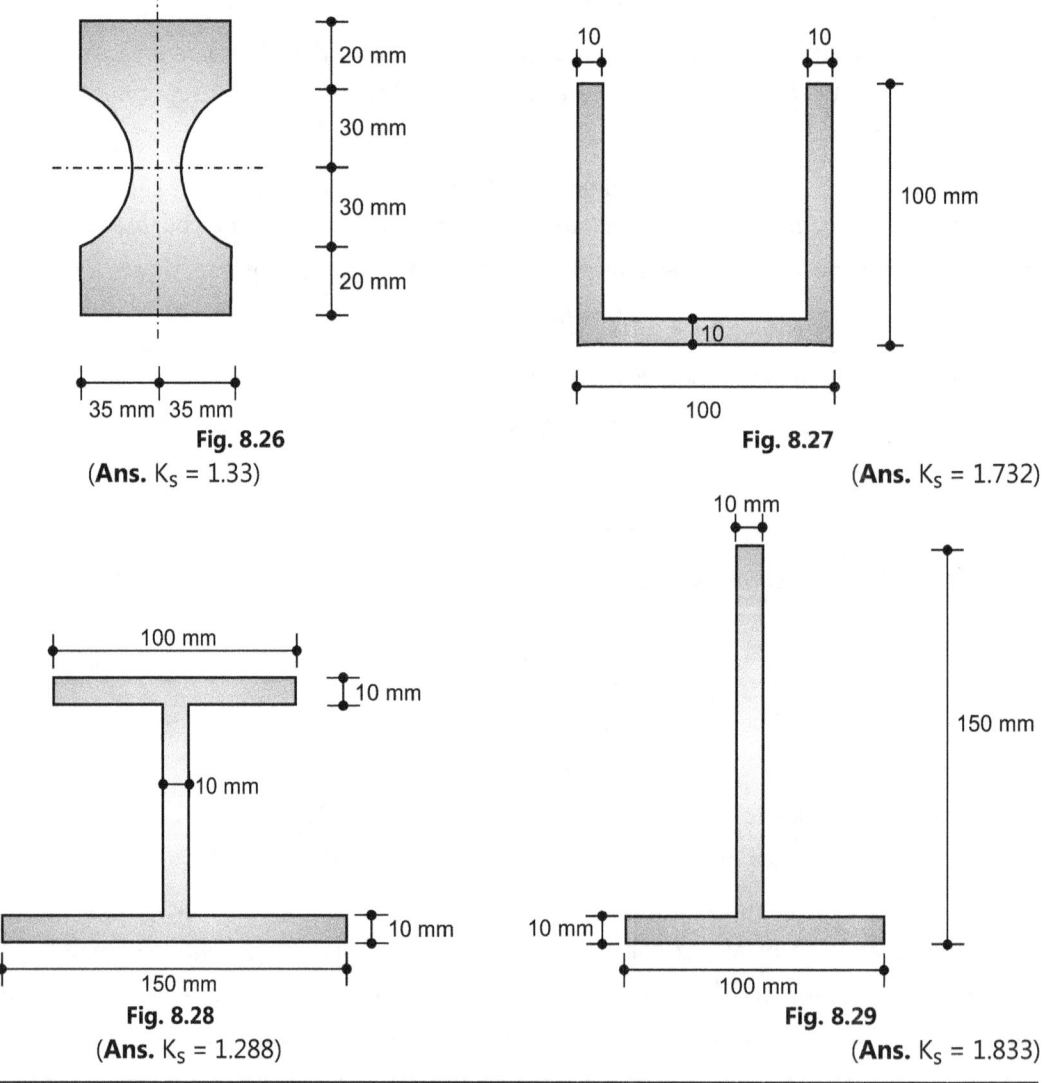

Fig. 8.26
(**Ans.** K_S = 1.33)

Fig. 8.27
(**Ans.** K_S = 1.732)

Fig. 8.28
(**Ans.** K_S = 1.288)

Fig. 8.29
(**Ans.** K_S = 1.833)

3. Determine the plastic section modulus of the section shown in Fig. 8.30.

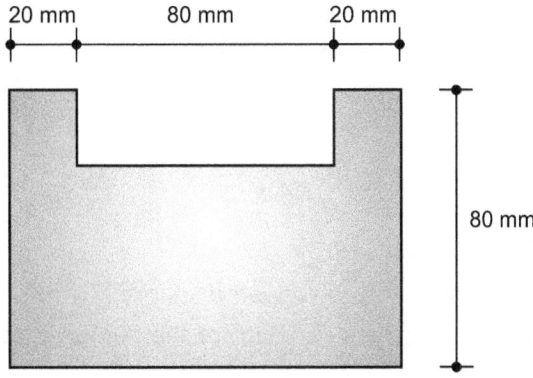

Fig. 8.30

(**Ans.** 10.2×10^4 mm³)

4. Show that the plastic moment capacity M_p of I-section shown in Fig. 8.31 is given by the expression

$$M_p = \frac{27.1 \, D^3}{800} \sigma_y f_y$$

where D is the overall depth of the beam and f_y is the field stress. Also calculate the shape factor.

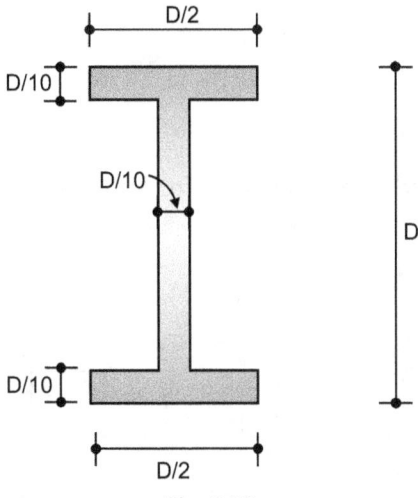

Fig. 8.31

5. A propped cantilever of span 5 m and of uniform plastic moment of resistance 150 kNm is subjected to a load 'W' as shown in Fig. 8.32. If the load W may be applied at any position within the span, determine the minimum value of W that will cause collapse.

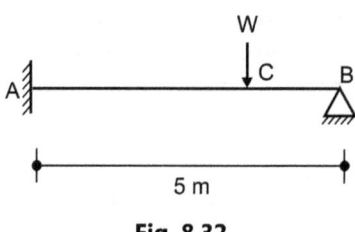

Fig. 8.32

(**Ans.** 174.85 m)

6. A fixed beam of 6 m span has to support a uniformly distributed load of 12 kNm on the left half span. If the plastic moment of the section is 100 kNm, determine the load factor.

(**Ans.** Load factor = 2).

7. A fixed beam AB of span 6 m and of uniform section is loaded as shown in Fig. 8.33. The load factor is 1.75 and shape factor is 1.15. The yield stress is 250 N/mm². Determine the sectional modulus of the beam. Also locate the positions of the plastic hinges.

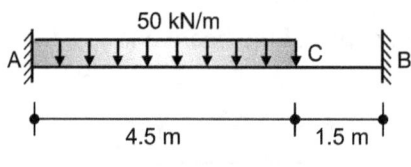

Fig. 8.33

(**Ans.** Z = 60.1 × 7 × 10³ mm³)

8. A fixed beam is loaded as shown in Fig. 8.34. Calculate the collapse load for the beam if the plastic moment of resistance of the uniform section of the beam is 30 kNm.

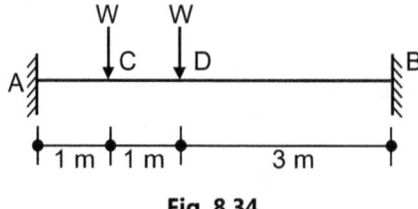

Fig. 8.34

(**Ans.** 40 kN)

9. A steel beam of uniform cross-section is to be designed for the ultimate loads as shown in Fig. 8.35. Estimate the plastic moment of resistance of the beam required.

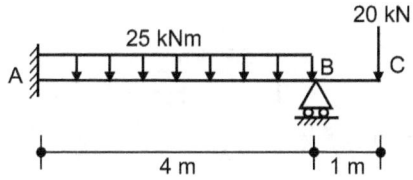

Fig. 8.35

(**Ans.** 26.67 kNm)

10. A beam ABC of uniform moment of resistance M_p is loaded with uniform load w/m throughout the length as shown in Fig. 8.36. Show that the ultimate load is given by the expression $W_u = \dfrac{15.42\, M_p}{L^2}$.

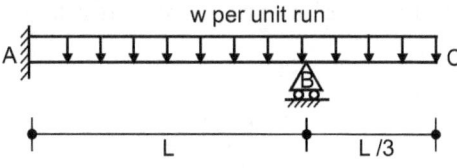

Fig. 8.36

11. A three span continuous beam ABCD is supported and loaded as shown in Fig. 8.37. The beam has uniform cross-section plastic moment of resistance of 80 kNm. Estimate the ultimate load and draw B.M.D. at the collapse.

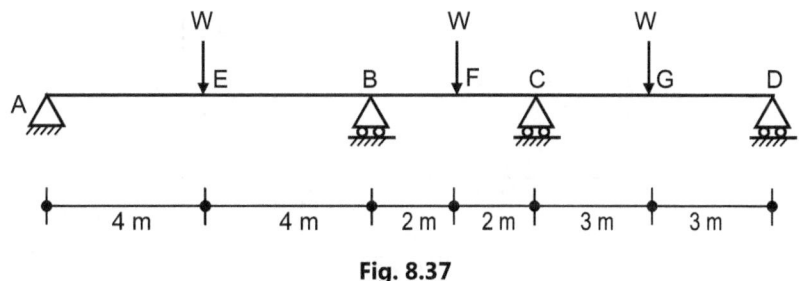

Fig. 8.37

(**Ans.** W_u = 60 kN)

12. The ultimate loads on each span of a continuous beam ABCD are shown in Fig. 8.38. Calculate the required values of plastic moments MP_1, MP_2, MP_3 of beam spans AB, BC, CD respectively, if MP_2 is greater uniform MP_1 and MP_3.

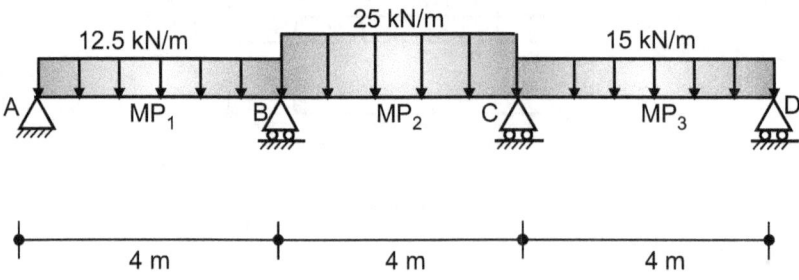

Fig. 8.38

(**Ans.** MP_1 = 171.48 kNm, MP_2 = 309 kNm, MP_3 = 205.8 kNm)

13. A portal frame shown in Fig. 8.39 carries the working loads as shown. The members of the frame are of uniform plastic moment of resistance of 100 kNm. Estimate the load factor.

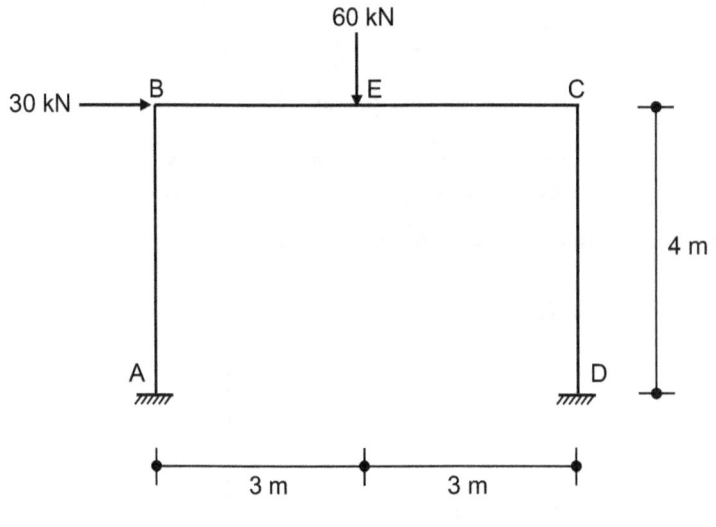

Fig. 8.39

(**Ans.** λ = 2.0)

14. A portal frame is supported and loaded as shown in Fig. 8.40. If the members of the frame have a constant plastic moment of resistance M_p, show that the collapse load for the frame is given by $W_u = \dfrac{2M_p L}{ab}$.

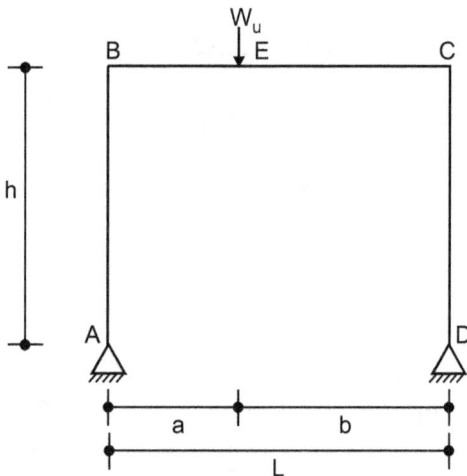

Fig. 8.40

15. A portal frame is supported and loaded as shown in Fig. 8.41. The plastic moment of resistance of the beam section is M_p and that of column sections is $2\,M_p$. Analyse the possible collapse mechanisms shown and determine the ultimate load for the frame.

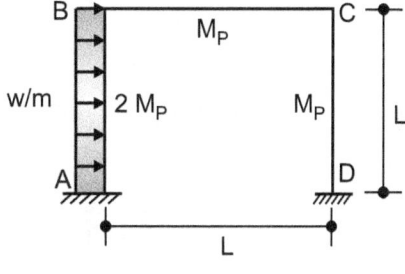

Fig. 8.41

$$\left(\textbf{Ans. } W_u = \frac{12\,M_p}{L^2}\right)$$

16. A portal frame is supported and loaded as shown in Fig. 8.42. The plastic moment of resistance of the section of the column AB and beam BC is 240 kNm, of the column CD is 120 kNm. Estimate the ultimate load for the frame.

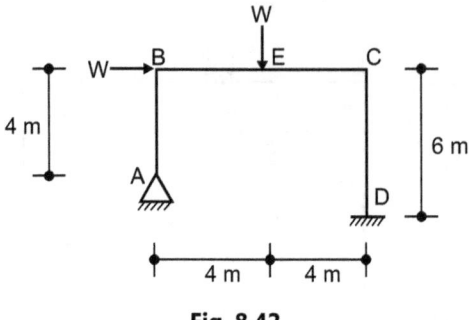

Fig. 8.42

(**Ans.** W_u = 95 kN)

17. A portal frame is supported and loaded as shown in Fig. 8.43. The members of the frame have uniform section of plastic moment of resistance of 100 kNm. Find the collapse load factor.

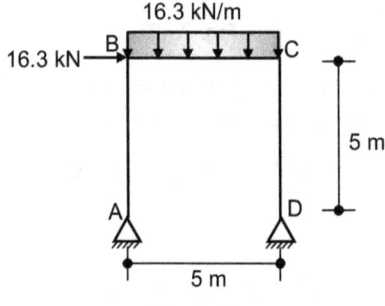

Fig. 8.43

www.ingramcontent.com/pod-product-compliance
Lightning Source LLC
Chambersburg PA
CBHW081753300426
44116CB00014B/2102